The Private Life of

MARIE ANTOINETTE

Portrait of Marie Antoinette by Madame Le Brun

The Private Life of
MARIE
ANTOINETTE

JEANNE LOUISE HENRIETTE CAMPAN

First published in English in 1883
This edition published 2008

The History Press Ltd
The Mill, Brimscombe Port
Stroud, Gloucestershire, GL5 2QG
www.thehistorypress.co.uk

British Library Cataloguing in Publication Data.
A catalogue record for this book is available from the British Library.

ISBN 978 1 84588 638 7

Printed in Great Britain

CONTENTS

LIST OF ILLUSTRATIONS

PREFACE BY THE AUTHOR

The shelves of our libraries bend under the weight of printed works relating to the last years of the eighteenth century. The great moral and political causes of our revolutions have already been ably traced by superior intellects. But posterity will look also for the secret springs by which those events were brought about. Memoirs, penned by ministers and favourites, will alone satisfy the inquisitiveness of our descendants, and even these only to a certain extent; for kings very seldom yield unbounded confidence.

Louis XVI possessed an immense crowd of confidants, advisers, and guides; he selected them even from among the factions which attacked him. Never, perhaps, did he make a full disclosure to any one of them, and certainly he spoke with sincerity to but very few. He invariably kept the reins of all secret intrigues in his own hand; and thence, doubtless, arose the want of co-operation and the weakness which were so conspicuous in his measures. From these causes considerable chasms will be found in the detailed history of the Revolution.

In order to become thoroughly acquainted with the latter years of the reign of Louis XV, memoirs written by the Duc de Choiseul, the Duc d'Aiguillon, the Maréchal de Richelieu,[1] and the Duc de La Vauguyon, should be before us. To give us a faithful portrait of the unfortunate reign of Louis XVI, the Maréchal du Muy, M. de Maurepas, M. de Vergennes, M. de Malesherbes, the Duc d'Orléans, M. de La Fayette, the Abbé de Vermond, the Abbé Montesguiou, Mirabeau, the Duchesse de Polignac, and the Duchesse de Luynes, should have noted faithfully in writing all the transactions in which they took decided parts. As to the secret history of affairs of a later period, it has been disseminated among a much greater number of persons; there are ministers who have published memoirs, but solely when they had their own measures to justify, and then they confined themselves to the vindication of their own characters, without which powerful motive they probably would have written nothing. In general, those nearest to the sovereign, either by birth or by office, have left no memoirs; and in absolute monarchies the mainsprings of great events will be found in particulars which the most exalted persons alone could know. Those who have had but little under their chargé find no subject in it for a book; and those who have long borne the burden of public business conceive themselves to be forbidden by duty, or by respect for authority, to disclose all they know. Others, again, preserve notes, with the intention of reducing them to order when they shall have reached the period of a happy leisure; vain illusion of the ambitious, which they cherish, for the most part, but as a veil to conceal from their sight the hateful image of their inevitable downfall! and when it does at length take place, despair or chagrin deprives them of fortitude to dwell upon the dazzling period which they never cease to regret.

Louis XVI meant to write his own memoirs: the manner in which his private papers were arranged indicated this design. The Queen also had the same intention; she long preserved a large correspondence, and a great number of minute reports, made in the spirit and upon the event of the moment. But after the 10th of June 1792 she was obliged to burn the larger portion of what she had so collected. Some parts of the correspondence preserved by the Queen were conveyed out of France.

Considering the rank and situations of the persons I have named as capable of elucidating by their writings the history of our political storms, it will not be imagined that I aim at placing myself on a level with them; but I have spent half my life either with the daughters of Louis XV, or with Marie Antoinette. I knew the characters of those Princesses; I became privy to some extraordinary facts, the publication of which may be interesting, and the truth of the details will form the merit of my work.

I was very young when I was placed about the Princesses, the daughters of Louis XV, in the capacity of reader. I was acquainted with the Court of Versailles before the time of the marriage of Louis XVI with the Archduchess Marie Antoinette.

My father, who was employed in the department of Foreign Affairs, enjoyed the reputation due to his talents, and to his useful labours. He had travelled much. Frenchmen, on their return home from foreign countries, bring with them a love for their own, increased in warmth; and no man was more penetrated with this feeling, which ought to be the first virtue of every placeman, than my father. Men of high title, academicians, and learned men, both natives and foreigners, sought my father's acquaintance; and were gratified by being admitted into his house.

Twenty years before the Revolution I often heard it remarked that the imposing character of the power of Louis XIV was no longer to be found in the Palace of Versailles; that the institutions of the ancient monarchy were rapidly sinking; and that the people, crushed beneath the weight of taxes, were miserable, though silent; but that they began to give ear to the bold speeches of the philosophers, who loudly proclaimed their sufferings, and their rights; and, in short, that the age would not pass away without the occurrence of some grand shock, which would unsettle France, and change the course of its progress.

Those who thus spoke were almost all partisans of M. Turgot's system of administration: they were Mirabeau, the father, Doctor Quesnay, Abbé Baudeau, and Abbé Nicole; *chargé d'affaires* to Leopold, Grand Duke of Tuscany, and as enthusiastic an admirer of the maxims of the innovators as his sovereign.

My father sincerely respected the purity of intention of these politicians. With them, he acknowledged many abuses in the Government; but he did not give these political sectarians credit for the talent necessary for conducting a judicious reform. He told them frankly that in the art of moving the great machine of Government, the wisest of them was inferior to a good magistrate; and that if ever the helm of affairs should be put into their hands they would be speedily checked in the execution of their schemes by the immeasurable difference existing between the most brilliant theories and the simplest practice of administration.

Destiny having formerly placed me near crowned heads, I now amuse my solitude when in retirement with collecting a variety of facts which may prove interesting to my family when I shall be no more. The idea of collecting all the interesting materials which my memory affords, occurred to me from reading the work entitled "Paris, Versailles, and the Provinces in the Eighteenth Century". That work, composed by a man accustomed to the best society, is full of piquant anecdotes, nearly all of which have been recognised as true by the contemporaries of the author. I have put together all that concerned the domestic life of an unfortunate Princess, whose reputation is not yet cleared of the stains it received from the attacks of calumny, and who justly merited a different lot in life, a different place in the opinion of mankind after her fall. These Memoirs, which were finished ten years since, have met with the approbation of some persons; and my son may, perhaps, think proper to print them after my decease.[2] I know not whether my Recollections will be thought worthy to see the light; but whilst I am occupied in writing them, my mind is diverted, I pass calmer hours, and I seem removed from the melancholy scenes by which I am now surrounded, so far as the sensibility of my heart will permit me to forget the present.

1. I heard the Maréchal de Richelieu desire M. Campan, who was librarian to the Queen, not to buy the Memoirs which would certainly be attributed to him after his death, declaring them false by anticipation; and adding, that he was ignorant of orthography, and had never amused himself with writing. Shortly after the death of the Maréchal, one Soulavie put forth Memoirs of the Maréchal de Richelieu.

2. When Madame Campan wrote these lines, she little thought that the death of her son would precede her own. See the Biographical Sketch of Madame Campan, p. 24.

BIOGRAPHICAL SKETCH OF MADAME CAMPAN

Prefatory memoir of Madame Campan

Jeanne Louise Henriette Genet was born at Paris, on the 6th of October 1752. M. Genet, her father, had obtained, through his own merit and the protection of the Duc de Choiseul, the place of first clerk in the office of the Minister for Foreign Affairs. Literature, which he had cultivated in his youth, was often the solace of his leisure hours.

Surrounded by a numerous family, he made the instruction of his children his chief recreation, and omitted nothing which was necessary to render them highly accomplished. The progress of the youthful Henriette in the study of music and of foreign languages was surprising; the celebrated Albaneze instructed her in singing, and Goldoni taught her Italian. Tasso, Milton, Dante, and even Shakespeare, soon became familiar to her. But her studies were particularly directed to the acquisition of a correct and elegant style of reading. From prose to verse, from an ode to an epistle, a comedy or a sermon, she was instructed to pass, with the requisite variations of modulation and delivery. Rochon de Chabannes, Duclos, Barthe, Marmontel, and Thomas, took pleasure in hearing her recite the finest scenes of Racine. Her memory and genius at the age of fourteen charmed them; they talked of her talents in society, and perhaps applauded them too highly. A young female is always sure to pay dearly for the celebrity she acquires: if she is beautiful, all the women become her rivals; if she has talents, there are many of the other sex weak enough to be jealous of them.

Mademoiselle Genet was spoken of at Court. Some ladies of high rank, who took an interest in the welfare of her family, obtained for her the place of reader to the Princesses. Her presentation, and the circumstances which preceded it, left a strong impression on her mind. "I was then fifteen;" she says, "my father felt some regret at yielding me up at so early an age to the jealousies of the Court. The day on which I first put on my court dress, and went to embrace him in his study, tears filled his eyes, and mingled with the expression of his pleasure. I possessed some agreeable talents, in addition to the instruction which it had been his delight to bestow on me. He enumerated all my little accomplishments, to convince me of the vexations they would not fail to draw upon me. 'The Princesses,' said he, 'will take pleasure in exercising your talents; the great have the art of applauding gracefully, and always to excess. Be not too much elated with these compliments, rather let them put you on your guard. Every time you receive such flattering marks of approbation, the number of your enemies will increase. I am warning you, my love, of the inevitable troubles attached to the course of life on which you are entering; and I protest to you even now, whilst you are thus transported with your good fortune, that could I have provided for you otherwise, I would never have abandoned my dear girl to the anxieties and dangers of a court.'"

Mademoiselle Genet, at fifteen, was naturally less of a philosopher than her father was at forty. Her eyes were dazzled by the splendour which glittered at Versailles. "The Queen, Maria Leczinska, the wife of Louis XV, died," she says, "just before I was presented at Court. The grand apartments hung with black, the great chairs of state, raised on several steps, and surmounted by a canopy adorned with plumes; the caparisoned horses, the immense retinue in court mourning, the enormous shoulder-knots, embroidered with gold and silver spangles, which decorated the coats of the pages and footmen—all this magnificence had such an effect on my senses that I could scarcely support myself when introduced to the Princesses. The first day of my reading in the inner apartment of Madame Victoire I found it impossible to pronounce more than two sentences; my heart palpitated, my voice faltered, and my sight failed. How well understood was the potent magic of the grandeur and dignity which ought to surround sovereigns! Marie Antoinette, dressed in white, with a plain straw hat, and a little switch in her hand, walking on foot, followed by a single servant, through the walks leading to the Petit Trianon, would never have thus disconcerted me; and I believe this extreme simplicity was the first and only real mistake of all those with which she is reproached."

When once her awe and confusion had subsided, Mademoiselle Genet was enabled to form a more accurate judgment of her situation. It was by no means attractive; the Court of the Princesses, far removed from the revels and licentious pleasures to which Louis XV was addicted, was grave, methodical, and dull. Madame Adelaide, the eldest of the Princesses, lived secluded in the interior of her apartments; Madame Sophie was haughty; Madame Louise a devotee. The gloomy pleasures of pride, and the exercises of scrupulous devotion have few charms for youth. Mademoiselle Genet, however, never quitted the Princesses' apartments; but she attached herself most particularly to Madame Victoire. This Princess had possessed beauty; her countenance bore an expression of benevolence, and her conversation was kind, free, and unaffected. The young reader excited in her that feeling which a woman in years, of an affectionate disposition, readily extends to young people who are growing up in her sight, and who already possess some useful talents. Whole days were passed in reading to the Princess, as she sat at work in her apartment. Mademoiselle Genet frequently saw there Louis XV, of whom she would often relate the following anecdote:—

One day, at the Château of Compiègne, the King came in whilst I was reading to Madame. I rose and went into another room. Alone, in an apartment from which there was no outlet, with no book but a Massillon, which I had been reading to the Princess; happy in all the lightness and gaiety of fifteen, I amused myself with turning swiftly round, with my court hoop, and suddenly kneeling down to see my rose-coloured silk petticoat swelled around me by the wind. In the midst of this grave employment enters his Majesty, followed by one of the Princesses. I attempt to rise; my feet stumble, and down I fall in the midst of my robes, puffed out by the wind. "*Daughter*," said Louis XV, laughing heartily, "*I advise you to send back to school a reader who makes cheeses.*"

The railleries of Louis XV were often much more cutting, as Mademoiselle Genet had experienced on another occasion, which, thirty years afterwards, she could not relate without an emotion of fear, which it seemed as if she had never overcome. "Louis XV," she said, "had the most imposing presence. His eyes remained fixed upon you all the time he was speaking; and, notwithstanding the beauty of his features, he inspired a sort of fear. I was very young, it is true, when he first spoke to me; you shall judge whether it was in a very gracious manner. I was fifteen. The King was going out to hunt, and a numerous retinue followed him. As he stopped opposite me he said, 'Mademoiselle Genet, I am assured you are very learned, and understand four or five foreign languages.' 'I know only two, Sire,' I answered, trembling. 'Which are they?' 'English and Italian.' 'Do you speak them fluently?' 'Yes Sire, very fluently.' 'That is quite enough to drive a husband mad.' After this pretty compliment the King went on; the retinue saluted me, laughing; and, for my part, I remained motionless with surprise and confusion for some moments on the spot where I stood."

It would have been well if Louis XV had never indulged in more cutting repartees. Kings have no right to be scoffers; raillery is a warfare that requires equal arms, for one does not banter to advantage with a wit who rules over 20 millions of subjects. Justice, however, demands the acknowledgment that although this monarch was often the aggressor, he endured the smartest retorts without losing his temper. Possibly the unexpected familiarity of attacks of this kind might be a pungent novelty to a King, so long wearied by the burthen of greatness. With an easy temper, a melancholy turn of mind, a satirical genius, this prince, majestic in his Court, irresolute in council, agreeable at an evening party, could no longer escape from ennui without the aid of intemperance or debauchery. A woman, whose youth and beauty were sullied by prostitution, astonished Versailles at this time by the disgraceful influence she had acquired. Madame du Barry was effecting the dismissal of the minister who had just negotiated the marriage of the Dauphin with the Archduchess Marie Antoinette of Austria. The intrigues of the favourite, the rivalry between the Ducs de Choiseul and d'Aiguillon, the disgrace of the one, and the shameful elevation of the other, occupied the last moments of the reign of Louis XV.

The Duc de Choiseul, fickle, haughty, and violent, but agreeable, brilliant, and generous, had an active mind, great talents, and vast ideas. By means of alterations which had become necessary in the army, new establishments in the navy, new institutions and alliances, he wished to raise France from the abasement into which she had sunk through a long course of reverses. He sought the support of public opinion, was a friend to parliaments, an enemy to the Jesuits, and wielded power with a light and easy hand. Resistance, provided it was open and honourable, did not exasperate him; he had faith in the nation when the Government endeavoured to render it happy at home, powerful and respected abroad. His pride, a natural failing, became a virtue when it taught him never to stoop to flatter shameful caprices. He was beloved whilst in power; sought, I had almost said flattered, when in exile; and he inspired courtiers with courage to remain faithful to the unfortunate, a virtue hitherto unknown to them.

D'Aiguillon, with considerable address, some boldness, and great perseverance, was obdurate, despotic, and tyrannical. He gained credit for talents because he possessed the spirit of intrigue; but the division of Poland, effected, as it were, in his sight, has for ever blasted his reputation both as a politician and as a man. As a subtle courtier, a bad man, and an unskilful minister, he became obnoxious to public hatred, which, though he defied it, overwhelmed him at last.

The Duc d'Aiguillon did not understand that force is one of the weakest springs of power, when it is not supported by the confidence created by extensive information, great services performed, and, above all, by striking successes. He was deceived by the example of his grandfather. Richelieu, while he oppressed the great, rendered essential services to France. The abasement of Austria; the humiliation of Spain; the violent restoration of order in the State; the honours paid to literature; the encouragement of commerce, redeemed in a great degree the tyrannical acts of which he is justly accused. He imparted to the measures of Government something of the loftiness of his own character. Undoubtedly, he was feared; but he was also admired.

Since the time of Louis XIII France and Austria had changed places; the one still rising, the other sinking. Under Louis XV the House of Bourbon reigned at Naples and Madrid as well as at Versailles. The triumphs of the arms of France or the wisdom of her treaties had successively acquired Alsace, Franche-Comté, Flanders, and Lorraine. The magnanimous Maria Theresa had just replaced a mutilated crown on her head; the pride of the heiress of Randolph of Hapsburg had stooped so low as to flatter the vanity of Jeanne Poisson, Marquise de Pompadour, by calling her her friend. A warlike power suddenly arising close to Austria, excited her jealousy, and occupied her attention and her forces. The Duc de Choiseul, being minister, was at liberty to direct his attention to a greater distance.

After the battle of Pultowa, Russia, long confined to the frozen regions of the north, began to be reckoned as one of the European powers. Four women, successively placed on the throne of the Czars, had completed the work of a great man. A persevering system of aggrandisement, and, what is more extraordinary, a system openly declared, was rapidly being carried into effect. Now that Russia has adopted only so much of the arts and civilisation of Europe as may increase her military power, without enervating her soldiers; now that that people, born on a barren soil, in a severe climate, has breathed the sweet pure air of our countries, if that powerful Colossus, which already presses upon the centre of Europe, should, with extended arms, succeed in reaching from the Baltic to the Mediterranean, what refuge, what rampart would remain for the independence of the threatened nations? They could find no security but in the coalition of the Southern States; which was precisely the object of the family compact, prudently conceived, and effected with address by the Duc de Choiseul, who thereby strengthened the alliance with Austria. Instead, therefore, of stigmatising the shallowness of the minister, it would be more just to pay honour to his foresight. Nevertheless, the alliance with Austria was the pretext for the attacks directed against him.

The Duc de Choiseul had the parliaments, the philosophers, and public opinion on his side. On that of the Duc d'Aiguillon were the devotees and Madame du Barry. The two factions disputed over the dying Louis XV, and disturbed the first years of Louis XVI; whilst the fatal influence which the anti-Austrian party exercised over the fate of the youthful Marie Antoinette will presently appear.

The idea of uniting the daughter of Maria Theresa with the grandson of Louis XV had been conceived by the Duc de Choiseul before his fall. By this marriage he cemented the alliance of the two States, and thought he was securing for himself the favour of a new reign. Thus was explained the sense of that distich, according to which Austria was to expect more from marriage than from war or treaties.[1]

Maria Theresa, happy, though afflicted, had no other uneasiness on her dear daughter's account than that which arose from their separation, and yet prophetic voices seemed already to threaten the future evils which awaited her.

Madame Campan often related an anecdote which she had heard from the governor of the children of Prince Kaunitz. There was at that time at Vienna a doctor named Gassner,[2] who had fled thither to seek an asylum against the persecutions of his sovereign, one of the ecclesiastical electors. Gassner, gifted with an extraordinary warmth of imagination, imagined that he received inspirations. The Empress protected him; saw him occasionally; rallied him on his visions, and, nevertheless, heard them with a sort of interest. "Tell me," said she to him one day, "whether my Antoinette will be happy." Gassner turned pale, and remained silent. Being still pressed by the Empress, and wishing to give a general kind of expression to the idea with which he seemed deeply occupied, "Madame," he replied, "there are crosses for all shoulders."

Goethe, who was then young, was completing his studies at Strasburg. In an isle in the middle of the Rhine a pavilion had been erected, intended to receive Marie Antoinette and her suite. "I was admitted into it," says Goethe in his Memoirs. "On my entrance I was struck with the subject depicted on the tapestry with which the principal pavilion was hung, in which were seen Jason, Creusa, and Medea—that is to say, a representation of the most fatal union commemorated in history. On the left of the throne the bride, surrounded by friends and distracted attendants, was struggling with a dreadful death. Jason, on the other side, was starting back, struck with horror at the sight of his murdered children, and the Fury was soaring into the air, in her chariot drawn by dragons. Superstition apart, this strange coincidence was really striking. The husband, the bride, and the children were victims in both cases; the fatal omen seemed accomplished in every point." Maria Theresa might have repeated the fine verses which the father of Creusa addresses to his expiring daughter, in the Medea of Corneille:—

This then, my child, the hymeneal day,
The royal union anxiously expected!
Stern fate extinguishes the bridal torch,
And for thy marriage-bed the tomb awaits there.

The occurrences at the Place Louis XV on the marriage festivities at Paris are generally known. The conflagration of the scaffolds intended for the fireworks, the want of foresight of the authorities, the avidity of robbers, the murderous career of the coaches, brought about and aggravated the disasters of that day; and the young Dauphiness, coming from Versailles, by the Cours la Reine, elated with joy, brilliantly decorated, and eager to witness the rejoicings of the whole people, fled, struck with consternation and drowned in tears, whilst the dreadful scene and the cries of the dying pursued her distracted imagination.

It is here that the Memoirs of Madame Campan[3] may truly be said to begin; the first chapter, descriptive of the Court of Louis XV, being only a lively introduction. During a period of twenty years, from the marriage festivities to the attack of the 10th of August, Madame Campan never quitted Marie Antoinette. On the Queen's side all was goodness and unreserved confidence; it will be seen whether Madame Campan did not return the favour of her patroness by gratitude, faith, and devotedness, proof against all calamity, and superior to all danger. In speaking of Marie Antoinette she has depicted the hatred of her enemies, the avidity of her flatterers, and the disinterestedness of the real friends whom she possessed, although seated on the throne. But as she generally confines herself to the domestic circle in which Marie Antoinette delighted, it is necessary to take a glance at the spirit of that period, and particularly at the manners of society.

I shall not recall the scandalous years of the regency, when the Court, escaping from the constraint of a long course of hypocrisy, combined the excesses of debauchery with the most audacious impiety. But it is necessary to notice particularly the reign of Louis XV, because the corruption of that reign may be divided into two distinct periods. Of the first of these Richelieu was the model and the hero. To love without pleasure; to yield without resistance; to part without regret; to call duty a weakness, honour a prejudice, delicacy affectation—such were the manners of the times; seduction had its code, and immorality was reduced to principles. Even these rapid successes soon tired those who obtained them; perhaps because the facility with which triumphs were gained diminished their value. Courtiers and rich financiers maintained, at enormous expense, beauties with whom they were not expected even to be acquainted; vice became a mere luxury of vanity; and the condition of a courtesan led rapidly to fortune and even to honour.

In the years preceding the accession of Louis XVI to the throne, and those immediately following, society presented a new spectacle. Manners were not improved, but altered. By a strange abuse, apologies were found for depravity, in the philosophical ideas which daily grew more fashionable. Partisans of these principles promulgated such noble maxims, and talked so well that they thought themselves not obliged to act with propriety. Men might be inconstant husbands, and women faithless wives, so that they spoke with respect, with enthusiasm, of the sacred duties of marriage. The love of virtue and of mankind was sufficient without practical morality. Women, surrounded by their lovers, discussed the means of regenerating social order. There was not a philosopher admitted into one of the fashionable circles who did not modestly compare himself to Socrates with Aspasia; and Diderot, the daring author of *Philosophical Thoughts*, and the licentious writer of *Bijoux Indiscrets*, though he aspired to the glory of Plato, did not blush to imitate Petronius.

The writings of the philosophers, ill understood at that period, but read with avidity, gave them a great influence over public opinion. The Court, long accustomed to the influence which wit, polished manners, and the habit of filling great offices secured to it, was astonished to see this new power springing up by its side. Instead of opposing, it flattered this competitor. At the tables and in the salons of the first nobles the distinctions of rank were boldly treated as prejudices. Principles of equality found partisans amongst the nobility, and it became almost an acknowledged truth that merit was superior to birth.

Thus, whilst the middle classes were rising, proud of their knowledge, their talents, their attainments, and the higher ranks met them half way, the Court was still a slave to the laws of etiquette. From the cradle to the grave, at table, at council, in the chase, in the army, even in their private apartments, princes in France were governed by ceremonial rules. The injudicious laws of etiquette pursued them to the mysteries of the nuptial bed. Judge how impatiently a young princess, lively, affectionate, and free, bred in the simplicity of the German courts, must have endured the tyrannical customs *which*, never suffering her for a single instant to be a wife, mother, or friend, reduced her to the dignified *ennui* of being always a queen. The respectable lady, who was placed near her as a vigilant minister of the laws of etiquette, instead of alleviating their weight, rendered their yoke intolerable to her. The evil was not, however, so serious when it only affected the attendants; because in these cases the Queen used merely to laugh at it. Let Madame Campan herself relate an anecdote on this subject in which she was concerned.

"Madame de Noailles," she says, in a manuscript fragment, "abounded in virtues; I cannot pretend to deny it. Her piety, charity, and irreproachable morals rendered her worthy of praise; but etiquette was to her a sort of atmosphere; at the slightest derangement of the consecrated order, one would have thought she would have been stifled, and that the principles of life would forsake her frame.

"One day, I unintentionally threw this poor lady into a terrible agony. The Queen was receiving I know not whom—some persons just presented, I believe; the lady of honour, the Queen's tire-woman, and the ladies of the bed-chamber, were behind the Queen. I was near the throne, with the two women on duty. All was right—at least I thought so. Suddenly I perceived the eyes of Madame de Noailles fixed on mine. She made a sign with her head, and then raised her eyebrows to the top of her forehead, lowered them, raised them again, then began to make little signs with her hand. From all this pantomime, I could easily perceive that something was not as it should be; and as I looked about on all sides to find out what it was, the agitation of the countess kept increasing. The Queen, who perceived all this, looked at me with a smile; I found means to approach her Majesty, who said to me in a whisper, 'Let down your lappets, or the countess will expire.' All this bustle arose from two unlucky pins which fastened up my lappets, whilst the etiquette of costume said, 'Lappets hanging down'."

This contempt of the silly vanities of etiquette became the pretext for the first reproaches levelled at the Queen. What misconduct might not be dreaded from a princess who could absolutely go out without a hoop! and who, in the salons of Trianon, instead of discussing the important rights to chairs and stools, good-naturedly invited everybody to be seated.[4] The anti-Austrian party, discontented and vindictive, became spies upon her conduct, exaggerated her slightest errors, and calumniated her most innocent proceedings. "What seems unaccountable at the first glance," says Montjoie, whose opinions must certainly be considered genuine, "and what overwhelms me with grief, is that the first attacks on the reputation of the Queen proceeded from the bosom of the Court. What interest could the courtiers have in seeking her destruction, which involved that of the King? Was it not drying up the source of all the advantages they enjoyed, or could hope for?"

A scandalous plot which was to compromise the most august name, and to dishonour that of a cardinal, was already in preparation. It was conceived by an intriguing female, its principal agent was a forger of writings, it was seconded by a courtesan, unravelled by a priest, and related by a Jesuit. As if the most singular coincidences were to appear in this famous suit, together with the most odious contrasts, the name of Valois now figured along with those of Rohan, Austria, and Bourbon. Whilst everything conspired to show the guilt of a libertine and credulous priest, a great lord, who with 800,000 livres per annum was nevertheless ruined, an ecclesiastical prince, at once the dupe of a swindler, a woman of intrigue, and a quack; yet it was the Queen whom his credulity injured, as much as did, perhaps, his guilty hopes; it was Marie Antoinette to whom suspicion was daringly attached. The Court, the clergy, and the parliaments leagued together to humble the throne, and the Queen who sat on it.

The issue of this famous suit is known. The cardinal was acquitted. Madame de Lamotte, condemned, exposed, and saved only by flight, hastened to publish a pamphlet of the most odious description against the Queen. From that period, so fatal to Marie Antoinette, until her death, attacks of this species were incessantly renewed against her. Party spirit lent force to them; the press and the arts lent themselves with equal subserviency to the fury of her enemies. Obscene prints, licentious verses, infamous libels, atrocious accusations—I have seen all, I have read all, and I wish I could add (like that unfortunate Princess, on one of the most honourable occasions of her life), I have forgotten all. The perusal of these monuments of implacable hatred leaves an impression of ineffable disgust, and of poignant distress at the idea of the woes accumulated by calumny on the head of the hapless Marie Antoinette.

When the terrible Danton exclaimed, "The kings of Europe menace us; it behoves us to defy them; let us throw down to them, as our gage, the head of a king!" These detestable words, followed by so cruel, so lamentable a result formed, however, a formidable stroke of policy. But the Queen! What horrible reasons of state could Danton, Collot d'Herbois, and Robespierre allege against her? Where did they find that those Greeks and Romans, whose military virtues our soldiers recalled, used to murder weak and defenceless beings? What savage greatness did they discover in stirring up a whole nation to avenge their quarrel on a woman? Rather what unprecedented cowardice! What remained of her former power? Had not the 10th of August torn the diadem from her brow? She was a captive, a widow, trembling for her children! In those judges, who at once outraged modesty and nature; in that people whose vilest scoffs pursued her to the scaffold, who could have recognised the generous people of France? No, of all the crimes which so shockingly disgraced the Revolution, none is more calculated to show to what a pitch the spirit of party, when it has fermented in the most corrupt hearts, can deprave the character of a nation.

The news of this dreadful event reached Madame Campan in an obscure retreat which she had chosen. She had not succeeded in her endeavours to share the Queen's captivity, and she expected every moment a similar fate. After escaping, almost miraculously, from the murderous fury of the Marseillais; after being repulsed by Pétion, when she implored the favour of being confined in the Temple; after being denounced and pursued by Robespierre, and entrusted, through the entire confidence of the King and

Queen, with papers of the utmost importance, Madame Campan went to conceal her charge and indulge her grief at Coubertin, in the valley of Chevreuse. Madame Auguié, her sister, had just committed suicide, at the very moment of her arrest.⁵ The scaffold awaited Madame Campan, when the 9th of Thermidor restored her to life; but did not restore to her the most constant object of her thoughts, her zeal, and her devotion.

A new career now opened to Madame Campan. The information and talents she possessed were about to become useful to her. At Coubertin, surrounded by her nieces, she was fond of directing their studies, as much to divert her mind for a time from her troubles as to form their disposition and judgment. This occupation caused her ideas to revert to the subject of education, and awakened once more the inclinations of her youth. At the age of twelve years Mademoiselle Genet could never meet a school of young ladies passing through the streets without feeling ambitious of the situation and authority of their mistress. Her abode at Court had diverted but not altered her inclinations. At a more advanced age, when able to enlarge her operations, she envied Madame de Maintenon, in the height of absolute power, not the success of her ambitious hypocrisy, not the mysterious honour of a royal and clandestine union, but the glory of having founded St Cyr.

Madame Campan had neither the treasures nor the authority of Louis XIV at her disposal for the realisation of her plans. "A month after the fall of Robespierre," she says, in a most interesting document, "I considered as to the means of providing for myself, for a mother seventy years of age, my sick husband, my child nine years old, and part of my ruined family. I now possessed nothing in the world but an assignat of five hundred francs. I had become responsible for my husband's debts, to the amount of thirty thousand francs. I chose St Germain to set up a boarding school, for that town did not remind me, as Versailles did, both of happy times and of the misfortunes of France. It was at some distance from Paris, where our dreadful disasters had occurred, and where people resided with whom I did not wish to be acquainted. I took with me a nun of l'Enfant-Jesus, to give an unquestionable pledge of my religious principles. The school of St Germain was the first in which the opening of an oratory was ventured on. The Directory was displeased at it, and ordered it to be immediately shut up. Not having the means of printing my prospectus, I wrote a hundred copies of it, and sent them to those persons of my acquaintance who had survived the dreadful commotions. At the year's end I had sixty pupils; soon afterwards a hundred. I bought furniture, and paid my debts."

The rapid success of the establishment at St Germain was undoubtedly owing to the talents, experience, and excellent principles of Madame Campan, seconded by public opinion. To cherish and show attention to any person who had been at Court, was to defy and humble the reigning power; and every one knows that people never deny themselves that pleasure in France. I was then very young, but I did not fail to observe that disposition in those about me. All property had changed hands; all ranks found themselves confusedly jumbled by the shock of the Revolution: society resembled a library, in which the books have been replaced at random, after tearing off the titles. The great lord dined at the table of the opulent contractor; and the witty and elegant marchioness was present at the ball by the side of the clumsy peasant lately grown rich.

In the absence of the ancient distinctions, elegant manners and polished language now formed an extraordinary kind of aristocracy. The house of St Germain, conducted by a lady who possessed the deportment and the habits of the best society, was not only a school of knowledge, but a school of the world.

"A friend of Madame de Beauharnais," continued Madame Campan, "brought me her daughter Hortense de Beauharnais, and her niece Emilie de Beauharnais. Six months afterwards she came to inform me of her marriage with a Corsican gentleman, who had been brought up in the military school, and was then a general. I was requested to communicate this information to her daughter, who long lamented her mother's change of name.

"I was also desired to watch over the education of little Eugéne de Beauharnais, who was placed at St Germain, in the same school with my son.

"A great intimacy sprang up between my nieces and these young people. Madame de Beauharnais set out for Italy, and left her children with me. On her return, after the conquests of Bonaparte, that general, much pleased with the improvement of his stepdaughter, invited me to dine at Malmaison, and attended two representations of Esther at my school."

Never had the establishment at St Germain been in a more flourishing condition than at this time (1802–3). What more could Madame Campan wish for? Her fortune was respectable; her occupation and duties agreeable to her taste. Absolute in her own house, she seemed also safe from the caprice of power. But the man who then disposed of the fate of France and Europe was soon to determine otherwise.

After the battle of Austerlitz the State undertook to bring up, at the public expense, the sisters, daughters or nieces of those who were decorated with the Cross of Honour. The children of the warriors killed or wounded in glorious battle were to find paternal care in the ancient abodes of the Montmorencys and the Condés. Accustomed to concentrate around him all superior talents, fearless himself of superiority, Napoleon sought for a person qualified by experience and abilities to conduct the institution of Écouen: he selected Madame Campan.

She was now to reap the fruits of ten years' experience at St Germain. The establishment of Écouen had to be created, and Madame Campan commenced this great undertaking. Count Lacepède, the pupil, friend, and rival of Buffon, then Grand Chancellor of the Légion of Honour, assisted her with his enlightened advice. Napoleon, who could descend with ease from the highest political subjects to the examination of the most minute details; and who was as much at home in inspecting a boarding school for young ladies as in reviewing the grenadiers of his guard; whom it was impossible to deceive, and who was not unwilling to find fault when he visited the establishment at Écouen, was forced to say, "It is all right."[6]

A second house was formed at St Denis, on the model of that of Écouen. Perhaps Madame Campan might have hoped for a title to which her long labours gave her a right; perhaps the superintendence of the two houses would have been but the fair recompense of her services; but her fortunate years had passed: her fate was now to depend on the most important events. Napoleon had accumulated such a mass of power as no one but himself in Europe could overturn. France, content with thirty years of victories, in vain asked for peace and repose. The army which had triumphed in the sands of Egypt, on the summits of the Alps, and in the marshes of Holland, was to perish amidst the snows of Russia. Nations combined against a single man. The territory of France was invaded. The orphans of Écouen, from the windows of the mansion which served as their asylum, saw in the distant plain the fires of the Russian bivouacs, and once more wept the deaths of their fathers. Paris capitulated. France hailed the return of the descendants of Henri IV; they reascended the throne so long filled by their ancestors, which the wisdom of an enlightened prince established on the empire of the laws.

This moment, which diffused joy amongst the faithful servants of the royal family, and brought them the rewards of their devotion, proved to Madame Campan a period of bitter vexation. The hatred of her enemies had revived. The suppression of the school at Écouen had deprived her of her position; the most absurd calumnies followed her into her retreat; her attachment to the Queen was suspected; she was accused not only of ingratitude but of perfidy. The object of such calumnies is Madame Campan, in whose favour Marie Antoinette wrote in 1792 a testamentary disposition, extremely honourable to the devotion of the subject and to the goodness of the sovereign. It is Madame Campan to whom Louis XVI in 1792 confided the most secret and dangerous papers; for whom Louis XVI, in the cell of the Feuillans, on the 10th of August 1792, cut off two locks of his hair, giving her one for herself, another for her sister, whilst the Queen, throwing her arms about their necks by turns, said to them: "Unhappy women, you are unfortunate only on my account: I am still more wretched than you." Slander has little effect on youth, but in the decline of life its darts are envenomed with a mortal poison. The wounds which Madame Campan had received were deep. Her sister, Madame Auguié, had destroyed herself; M. Rousseau, her brother-in-law, had perished a victim of the Reign of Terror. In 1813 a dreadful accident had deprived her of her niece, Madame de Broc, one of the most amiable and interesting beings that ever adorned the earth. Madame Campan seemed destined to behold those whom she loved go down to the grave before her. In the cemetery of Père la Chaise, amongst those ostentatious mausoleums, generally loaded with lying epitaphs, is a modest grave on which she has often been seen to weep. No marble decorates it; no inscription is read upon it; it is remarkable chiefly for its simplicity; the undulating turf giving the only clue to the secret of the tomb.

After so many troubles Madame Campan sought a peaceful retreat. Paris had become odious to her. She paid a visit to one of her most beloved pupils, Mademoiselle Crouzet, who had married a physician at Mantes, a man of talent, distinguished for his intelligence, frankness, and cordiality.[7] Mantes is a pleasant cheerful residence, and the idea of an abode there pleased her. A few intimate friends formed a pleasant society, and she enjoyed a little tranquillity after so many disturbances. The revival of her *Memoirs*, the arrangement of the interesting anecdotes of which her Recollections were to consist, alone diverted her mind from the one powerful sentiment which attached her to life. She lived only for her son. M. Campan deserved the tenderness of his mother. No sacrifice had been spared for his education. After having pursued that course of study, which, under the Imperial Government, produced men of such distinguished merit, he was waiting till time and circumstances should afford him an opportunity of

Portrait of Madame Campan

devoting his services to his country. Although the state of his health was far from good, it did not threaten any rapid or premature decay; he was, however, after a few days' illness, suddenly taken from his family. "I never witnessed so heartrending a scene," M. Maigne says, "as that which took place when Marshal Ney's lady, her niece, and Madame Pannelier, her sister, came to acquaint her with this misfortune. When they entered her apartment she was in bed. All three at once uttered a piercing cry. The two ladies threw themselves on their knees, and kissed her hands, which they bedewed with tears. Before they could speak to her she read in their faces that she no longer possessed a son. At that instant her large eyes, opening wildly, seemed to wander. Her face grew pale, her features changed, her lips lost their colour, she struggled to speak, but uttered only inarticulate sounds, accompanied by piercing cries. Her gestures were wild, her reason was suspended. Every part of her being was in agony. Her respiration scarcely sufficed for the efforts which this unhappy mother made to express her grief, and give vent to her sufferings. To this state of anguish and despair no calm succeeded, until her tears began to flow. Friendship and the tenderest cares succeeded for a moment in calming her grief, but not in diminishing its power. This violent crisis had disturbed her whole organisation. A cruel disorder, which required a still more cruel operation, soon manifested itself. The presence of her family, a tour which she made in Switzerland, a residence at the waters of Baden, and, above all, the sight, the tender and charming conversation of a person by whom she was affectionately beloved, occasionally diverted her mind, and in a slight degree relieved her suffering." She underwent a serious operation, performed with extraordinary promptitude and the most complete success. No unfavourable symptoms appeared; Madame Campan was thought to be restored to her friends: but the disorder was in the blood; it took another course; the chest became affected. "From that moment," says M. Maigne, who watched her malady with all the solicitude of friendship, "I could never look on Madame Campan as living; she herself felt that she belonged no more to this world."

"My friend," she said to her physician the day before her death, "I am attached to the simplicity of religion. I hate all that savours of fanaticism." When her codicil was presented for her signature, her hand trembled; "It would be a pity," she said, "to stop when so fairly on the road."

Her friends witnessed her decease on the 16th of March 1822. The cheerfulness she displayed throughout her malady had nothing affected in it. Her character was naturally powerful and elevated. At the approach of death she evinced the soul of a sage, without abandoning for an instant her feminine character.

One profound sentiment, her attachment to the Queen—one constant study, the education of youth, occupied her whole life. Napoleon once said to her, "The old systems of education were good for nothing; what do young women stand in need of, to be well brought up in France?"—"Of mothers," answered Madame Campan. "It is well said," replied Napoleon. "Well, Madame, let the French be indebted to you for bringing up mothers for their children."

Surrounded by pupils to whom her conversation was a delight, she talked to them of the duties of their sex, or of the most interesting facts in history. Sometimes her judicious and keen understanding would draw a salutary lesson from a little amusing story. In past events she often sought traits calculated to enlighten their minds and elevate their sentiments. I call on all the pupils of Écouen to bear witness how often she spoke to them of Louis IX, of Charles V, of Louis XII, of Henri IV, in particular, and of the virtues with which they and their successors had adorned the throne. When she came to the stormy period of the Revolution, she would explain to them the outrages committed against disarmed royalty, tell them of the descendants of kings living in a foreign land, of Louis XVI and his misfortunes, of the Queen and the afflictions she had been made to endure. These recitals affected their young hearts. When they heard her talk of the royal family of France, the daughters of Napoleon's warriors learned the respect that should be paid to calamity, and the gratitude due for benefits received.

Beyond the walls of the mansion of Écouen, in the village which surrounds it, Madame Campan had taken a small house where she loved to pass a few hours in solitary retirement. There, at liberty to abandon herself to the memory of the past, the superintendent of the Imperial establishment became, once more, for the moment, the first lady of the chamber to Marie Antoinette. To the few friends whom she admitted into this retreat she would show, with emotion, a plain muslin gown which the Queen had worn, and which was made from a part of Tippoo Saib's present. A cup, out of which Marie Antoinette had drunk; a writing stand, which she had long used, were, in her eyes, of inestimable value; and she has often been discovered sitting, in tears, before the picture which represented her royal mistress.

"Pardon me, august shade! unhappy Queen, pardon me," she says, in a fragment I have preserved in her handwriting; "thy portrait is near me whilst I am writing these words. My imagination, impressed with the remembrance of thy sorrows, every instant directs my eyes to those features which I wish to animate, and to read in them whether I am doing service to thy memory in writing this work. When I look at that noble head, which fell by the fury of barbarians, tears fill my eyes, and suspend my narration. Yes, I will speak the truth, by which thy shade can never be injured; truth must prove favourable to her whom falsehood so cruelly wronged."

F. Barrière

1. It is said that the Sultan, on receiving the decree of the Convention which ordained the abolition of royalty in France, could not help saying, "At least the Republic will not marry an archduchess."

2. Jean Joseph Gassner, born at Gratz, a pretender to miraculous powers.

3. The family of Campan, originally from the valley of Campan, in Berrie, had adopted the name of that place as their own surname. Their true name was Berthollet. Mademoiselle Genet had married M. Campan, whose father was Secretary of the Queen's Closet.

4. Even for the suppression of the most ridiculous customs the Queen was never forgiven. The respectable dowagers, who had passed their innocent youth in the Court of Louis XV, and under the regency, considered the abolition of the hoop as a violation of morals. Madame Campan herself mentions, almost with regret, that the great ruffs and fardingales worn in the Court of the last of the Valois, were not adopted without a motive; that those appendages, indifferent in appearance, actually had the effect of banishing every idea of gallantry.

   Although such a precaution may appear, at least, a little singular, in the dissolute Court of Henry III, I shall not pretend to deny the efficacy of the fardingale; I will only add a little anecdote quoted by Laplace.

   "M. de Fresne Forget, being one day in company with the Queen Marguerite, told her he was astonished how men and women with such great ruffs could eat soup without spoiling them; and still more how the ladies could be gallant with their great fardingales. The Queen made no answer at that time, but a few days after, having a very large ruff on, and some *bouilli* to eat, she ordered a very long spoon to be brought, and ate her *bouilli* with it, without soiling her ruff. Upon which, addressing herself to M. de Fresne, she said, laughing, 'There now, you see, with a little ingenuity one may manage anything.' 'Yes, faith, Madame,' said the good man, 'as far as regards the soup I am satisfied.'"—Vol. ii, p. 350, of *Laplace's Collection*.

5. Maternal affection prevailed over her religious sentiments; she wished to preserve the wreck of her fortune for her children. Had she deferred this fatal act for one day she would have been saved; the cart which conveyed Robespierre to execution stopped her funeral procession!

6. Napoleon had wished to be informed of every particular of the furniture, government, and order of the house, the instruction and education of the pupils. The internal regulations were submitted to him. One of the intended rules, drawn up by Madame Campan, proposed that the children should hear mass on Sundays and Thursdays. Napoleon himself wrote on the margin, *every day.*

7. M. Maigne, physician to the infirmaries at Mantes. Madame Campan found in him a friend and comforter, of whose merit and affection she knew the value.

NOTES OF CONVERSATIONS WITH MADAME CAMPAN, WITH OCCASIONAL ANECDOTES OF NAPOLEON

by M. Maigne

About the end of 1815 I saw Madame Campan for the first time. She then resided in Paris, in the Rue Saint Lazare.

The misfortunes with which she and her family were just then visited rendered her longer residence in the French capital so unpleasant that she resolved to retire into the country. Though this determination accorded with her slender fortune, she was unwilling to withdraw herself too far from the centre of public affairs. She wished still to be within the sphere of the political events of the day; and she was also anxious that her family and numerous friends might be enabled to visit her with facility. She therefore made choice of the little town of Mantes. Madame Maigne, whom she had educated, who had acted as her secretary at Écouen, and to whom she was tenderly attached, had resided at Mantes for the space of three years, a circumstance which materially influenced Madame Campan in giving the preference to that town, and I was sincerely glad of it. About the beginning of April 1816 she came to fix her abode among us.

From that period to the time when she was snatched from us I enjoyed the happiness of seeing her twice every day, and I always took leave of her with increased regret; such was the delight which her charming and varied conversation afforded me. Madame la Maréchale de Beauvau observed that no one knew better how to kill time than Madame Campan.

"At the time," Madame Campan told us, "when Mesmer made so much noise in Paris with his magnetism, M. Campan, my husband, was his partisan, like almost every person who moved in high life. To be magnetised was then a fashion; nay, it was more, it was absolutely a rage. In the drawing-rooms nothing was talked of but the brilliant discovery. There was to be no more dying; people's heads were turned, and their imaginations heated in the highest degree. To accomplish this object it was necessary to bewilder the understanding; and Mesmer, with his singular language, produced that effect. To put a stop to the fit of public insanity was the grand difficulty; and it was proposed to have the secret purchased by the Court. Mesmer fixed his claims at a very extravagant rate. However, he was offered 50,000 crowns. By a singular chance, I was one day led into the midst of the somnambulists. Such was the enthusiasm of the numerous spectators that in most of them I could observe a wild rolling of the eye, and a convulsed movement of the countenance. A stranger might have fancied himself amidst the unfortunate patients of Charenton. Surprised and shocked at seeing so many people almost in a state of delirium, I withdrew, full of reflections on the scene which I had just witnessed. It happened that about this time my husband was attacked with a pulmonary disorder, and he desired that he might be conveyed to Mesmer's house. Being introduced into the apartment occupied by M. Campan, I asked the worker of miracles what treatment he proposed to adopt; he very coolly replied, that to ensure a speedy and perfect cure it would be necessary to lay in the bed of the invalid, at his left side, one of three things—namely, a young woman of brown complexion, a black hen, or an empty bottle. 'Sir,' said I, 'if the choice be a matter of indifference, pray try the empty bottle.'

"M. Campan's side grew worse; he experienced a difficulty of breathing, and a pain in his chest. All the magnetic remedies that were employed produced no effect. Perceiving his failure, Mesmer took advantage of the periods of my absence to bleed and blister the patient. I was not informed of what had been done until after M. Campan's recovery. Mesmer was asked for a certificate to prove that the patient had been cured by means of magnetism only, and he gave it. Here was a trait of enthusiasm! Truth was no longer respected. When I next presented myself to the Queen, their Majesties asked what I thought of Mesmer's discovery. I informed them of what had taken place, earnestly expressing my indignation at the conduct of the barefaced quack. It was immediately determined to have nothing more to do with him."

The following anecdotes are put together without regard to order. It would, indeed, have been impossible to preserve any regular arrangement.

During the Consulate, Napoleon, one day after dinner, stood leaning against the drawing-room chimneypiece, in a very meditative attitude. A lady, one of his relatives, observing him, said, "You look like a conspirator." "True," he replied, "I am now conspiring against the monarchs of Europe. Time will show that a shrug of the shoulders is sufficient to overthrow a bad political system."

A lady asked Madame Campan, during her residence at Mantes, to recommend her to a good confessor. Madame Campan mentioned her own, who, she observed, was a man of intelligence and respectability. "But, madame," inquired the lady, "is he a reasonable man?"—"Oh, very much so," said Madame Campan, "he was one of the Court Abbés."—"Then he is just the man to suit me," said the lady.

At the time when Napoleon was commander-in-chief of the army of Italy, his sisters and younger brother, together with the children of Josephine, were at school at Saint Germain. During the summer they occasionally paid a visit to Paris, accompanied by Madame Voisin. One evening, to finish their holiday, they proposed going to the theatre, and being short of money, they were obliged to mount into the gallery.

Madame Campan, while she was at Mantes, frequently dwelt on the extraordinary occurrences brought about by chance. "I was," said she, "the instructress of a nest of kings and queens, without ever dreaming of such a thing; and, indeed, it was very fortunate for all parties that we did not know it. Their education was the same as that of my other pupils. There was no distinction observed among them. When they quitted me they were all possessed of an excellent stock of information, with the exception of one only, who, though gifted with a fine understanding, never evinced a willingness to learn. Had these young women been educated as queens, they would have been flattered instead of instructed. Being ignorant of their future destiny, they received the accomplishments of women of distinction, added to the more solid acquirements requisite to form good mistresses of families."

"At the period when the priests were again permitted to say mass during the Revolution, the churches were found to have been stripped of everything. I provided some fine lawn for the Church of Saint Germain. At the time of the confirmation, I directed those of my pupils who were most abundantly supplied with money, to purchase a sufficient quantity of lawn, cambric, lace, etc., to make surplices and albs. After the religious ceremony, they were left for the use of the church; and Saint Germain's was, at that period of my glory, one of the richest churches in France."[1]

In a conversation which Madame Campan had with Napoleon he said: "It is not the poor, but the rich, who require to be looked after in a State. It is the higher ranks who demand attention. If they were not reined in, they would pull down the sovereign in no time. I hold them with a firm hand, and keep them at a due distance, for they are full of ambition. They are pleasant companions, but they have keen appetites. The poor must be protected, or they would be devoured. The higher orders have every advantage in society. Their rank and wealth protect them but too well. The power of the throne is in the lower ranks, and all the dangers that threaten it proceed from the great."

"In 1801 M. Dubreuil, a physician, and Madame l'Hôpital, both inhabitants of St Germain, were arrested and conveyed to the Temple; the former for having felt the pulse of M. de Talon's child, and the latter for having been visited by M. Dubreuil. Though the last-mentioned individual lived perfectly retired, his presence nevertheless gave umbrage to the Government. The police, artful as it then was, could not find an excuse for putting him under arrest; but as the principal could not be got at, the accessories were taken in his stead.

"M. Dubreuil, on being conducted to prison, wrote to me, requesting that I would exert my influence in his behalf. He could not, he said, guess the cause of such a proceeding. I was much interested for M. Dubreuil, who was my physician and my friend; and I was the more astonished at his arrest as I well knew his quiet inoffensive habits and opinions. I immediately repaired to the Tuileries. As soon as the First Consul beheld me, he said, 'You have come to intercede for the inhabitants of St Germain. Your Madame de l'Hôpital is an intriguer.'—'I beg pardon, General, she might once, perhaps, have been reproached for a little levity; but surely that must be all over at the age of seventy-eight. An intriguer she cannot be; a little coquetry would perhaps be more to her taste, but she is blind. She receives company every evening, and through the fear of being thought impolite, she makes her courtesy even to the absent.'

"When Napoleon was informed of the real circumstances he grew angry, and said, in the presence of Josephine, 'A blind woman, seventy-eight years old, is always innocent of political offences. The minister has committed an act of cruelty, unworthy of my Government. Had Fouché been plotting with my enemies, he could not have done better. He must be mad. I cannot permit such proceedings to take place under the sanction of my authority. It is my wish that every act emanating from my power should be such as reason will approve. A Government should be actuated by exalted views and generous sentiments. The arbitrary act that has just been committed, is worthy only of a sovereign's mistress in a fit of passion. Matters must not go on in this way. The head of the State should never be biased by passion. History will record everything, and what will be said of such conduct as this? But what has the doctor done?'—'Why, General, he attended M. de Talon's child, and he has, for many years past, daily visited his fellow-prisoner in the Temple.' 'This business is almost incredible,' resumed Napoleon. 'A doctor may surely prescribe for my enemies as well as for my friends, without giving offence to the ministry. Medical professors are not, like the holders of Government places, required to embrace a particular set of opinions.

"'Abuses like this degrade, and compromise my authority. I must have some conversation with the minister, and the prisoners shall be liberated.' He rang the bell with violence, and sent for Fouché, who received a severe reprimand. However, the prisoners were not set at liberty until thirty hours after this conversation; such was the tardiness with which the minister went through the formalities necessary for procuring their release. One of Josephine's carriages was sent to convey them from the Temple; on hearing which, Madame de l'Hôpital exclaimed, 'Are these Madame Bonaparte's beautiful white horses?'—'It matters very little, Madame, whether they be white or black,' said M. Dubreuil peevishly, 'so that they draw us out of prison.'

During the hundred days Napoleon observed that nobility, inflated as it is with pride and ambition, is not a very manageable commodity. "In 1806, said he, "the Emperor Alexander thought me too happy in having none. The nobility was a trouble of my own creating, I should have made a nobleman of every individual paying fifty francs of taxes. This would have levelled a blow at the very roots of the old nobility, and the new nobles would have been less arrogant. My plans did not answer the ends I had in view. I wished for splendour, and I got nothing but vexation, through the avarice and ambition of those whom I elevated."

"The *counts* of his making," added Madame Campan, "were worth the *counting*,[2] they were the work of a master-hand."

Napoleon observed, that if he could fairly fight public opinion, he should not fear it. But as it could not be beaten down by his artillery, he found himself obliged to conciliate it by justice and equity, two powers by which it is always to be won. To pursue any other course is to endanger wealth and distinction. It is impossible to imprison public opinion: restraint serves only to irritate it. "Public opinion," added Madame Campan, "may be compared to an eel: the tighter one holds it, the sooner it escapes."

Napoleon likewise said:—"Revolutions are brought about only by injustice. Where would be the motive for them if governments were guided solely by the laws of equity? All revolutions, past and to come, must be attributed to injustice, and I defy the most artful politician to assign any other cause for them. In the object of the French Revolution there was nothing to condemn; all the mischief consisted in the excesses committed by misguided men. It is necessary to bear in mind these two facts, lest we should confound justice on the one hand, and iniquity on the other. What! must a man trace back his pedigree for fourteen centuries before he can be deemed worthy of respect? Before the Revolution it was necessary to be a nobleman to hold a commission in the army; and to be connected with a great family to obtain a bishopric. The Revolution was brought about by the nobility and the high clergy. That's a fact of which I am thoroughly convinced."

Madame Campan often told me she had heard from Napoleon that when he founded the convent of the Sisters of la Charité he was urgently solicited to permit perpetual vows. He, however, refused to do so, on the ground that tastes may change, and that he did not see the necessity of excluding from the world women who might some time or other return to it, and become useful members of society. "Nunneries," he added, "assail the very roots of population. It is impossible to calculate the loss which a nation sustains in having ten thousand women shut up in cloisters. War does but little mischief; for the number of males is at least one-twenty-fifth greater than that of females. Women may, if they please, be allowed to make perpetual vows at fifty years of age; for then their task is fulfilled."

"During the Directory the Government had ordered my chapel to be closed; and sometime after commissioners were sent to desire that the reading of the Scriptures should be suppressed in my school. I inquired what books were to be substituted in their stead. After some minutes' conversation, they observed: 'Citizeness, you are arguing after the old fashion; no reflections. The nation commands; we must have obedience, and no reasoning.'"

On the 19th of March 1815 a number of papers were left in the King's closet. Napoleon ordered them to be examined, and among them was found the letter written by Madame Campan to Louis XVIII, immediately after the first restoration. In this letter she enumerated the contents of the portfolio which Louis XVI had placed under her care. When Napoleon read this letter, he said, "Let it be sent to the office of Foreign Affairs, it is an historical document."

Napoleon, conversing one day with Madame Campan at the Tuileries, said, "I acknowledge no other titles than those which belong to personal merit; they who do not possess such distinctions are truly unfortunate. The men by whom I am surrounded have won their titles on the field of honour; they have given sufficient proofs of their merit; true nobility is in their mind, and nowhere else. I have espoused no party. Merit determines my choice. I am the patron of talent."

Madame Murat one day said to Madame Campan: "I am astonished that you are not more awed in our presence; you speak to us with as much familiarity as when we were your pupils!"—"The best thing you can do," replied Madame Campan, "is to forget your titles when you are with me; for I can never be afraid of queens whom I have held under the rod."

Talma and his brother-in-law dined with Madame Campan on their return from Rouen in 1821. She was delighted at the idea of seeing and conversing with so distinguished a man as Talma. Her countenance beamed with joy at the pleasure she anticipated. "I still retain," said she, "a taste for the truly beautiful. In spite of all my misfortunes my spirits will be revived and refreshed to-day. I require to be roused now and then from the dejection into which events have plunged me."

During dinner Madame Campan turned the conversation on the art of elocution; and Talma made some remarks on the subject which arrested the attention of all present. "Good delivery," he said, "is applicable to every class of composition. This art, notwithstanding the powerful effects it produces, is but too much neglected in France. It is indeed quite in its infancy with us. It forms no part of education, and is never thought of in our academies. Yet it presents so many advantages, that I cannot conceive how it should be lost sight of. What effect can even a clever speaker produce without good delivery? He merely fatigues his hearers. I could name several men of high merit in the legislature who are intolerable on account of their delivery; and similar examples may be found in the pulpit and at the bar. The sermons and speeches of some of our most celebrated preachers and advocates have occasionally dissatisfied me, owing to a want of just harmony between their mental and physical powers. When the mind of the speaker was deeply impressed with the truths he was expounding, he would betray no external signs of conviction; no change would be observable in his features, nor would his voice soften into the accents of persuasion. In Paris party spirit establishes the fame of public speakers; but people of judgment form their opinions differently from the loungers of the drawing-room.

"The difficulties which the actor has to surmount are greater than those which present themselves to the public orator. The latter has to express only his own ideas; when he speaks in public it is always in his own character. But the actor is obliged to model his mind, and even his body, according to the received notion of the character and manner of the individual he has to represent.

"How else would it be possible to portray vehement passions, enormous vices, and exalted virtues, or to develop the distinctive traits belonging to different characters? The actor is obliged, as it were, to seize the spirit of the individual he has to represent, in order that he may produce a living personification of one of whom no other trace remains on earth save a few lines recorded by the pen of history. This task, I may truly say, demands vast perseverance and study.

"Any dissonance between the thought, the look, and the gesture destroys the illusion, and defeats all chance of success. The countenance should be a mirror, reflecting distinctly all that passes in the mind; the voice, that powerful medium for the communication of impressions, should be clear, flexible, and sonorous, capable of expressing every feeling of the heart. The movements of the body should follow the same impulse; and the spectator should recognise, in the harmony of the representation, the perfect identity of the individual personified."

I was informed by Madame Campan that a female relative of the Empress Josephine received a letter from an uncle, residing at a distance from Paris, soliciting a place for one of his relations, with the remark that one was bound in *honour* and in affection *to remember one's family*. Madame Campan observed that Napoleon's heart was too full of family affection. He wished his relations to share the good fortune which he himself possessed; and this great ambition for his family gave umbrage to Europe. Had he been an only son, his affairs would probably have taken a different turn.

In 1814, when Masséna was presented at Court, or when he went to take leave of the King, on departing for his command at Marseilles, the great personages by whom his Majesty was surrounded cleared but very narrow space for him to pass through. He had no sooner delivered a few words than he found himself without the circle. Masséna was continually alluding to the clever way in which they cut him off, and separated him from the King. "When I was on the field of battle," said he "I did not employ so much dexterity in making my prisoners." "Courtiers," observed Madame Campan, "have a paramount interest in rendering the person of the sovereign inaccessible, so that every favour may fall upon themselves. They are a class of men who very well understand their own interests."

About the period of Madame Murat's marriage, and while she was yet at Saint Germain, Napoleon observed to Madame Campan: "I do not like those love matches between young people whose brains are excited by the flames of the imagination. I had other views for my sister. Who knows what high alliance I might have procured for her! She is thoughtless, and does not form a just notion of my situation. The time will come when, perhaps, sovereigns might dispute for her hand. She is about to marry a brave man; but in my situation that is not enough. Fate should be left to fulfil her decrees."

On one occasion Madame Campan related to me the following particulars:—"A few days after the battle of Paris the Emperor Alexander came to visit Écouen, and he did me the honour to breakfast with me. After showing him over the establishment I conducted him to the park, the most elevated point of which overlooked the plain of Saint Denis. 'Sire,' said I, 'from this point I saw the battle of Paris.' 'If,' replied the Emperor, 'that battle had lasted two hours longer we should not have had a single cartridge at our disposal. We feared that we had been betrayed; for on arriving so precipitately before Paris all our plans were laid, and we did not expect the firm resistance we experienced.' I next conducted the Emperor to the chapel, and showed him the seats occupied by *le connétable* (the constable) of Montmorency, and *la connétable* (the constable's lady), when they went to hear mass. 'Barbarians like us,' observed the Emperor, 'would say *la connétable and le connétable.*'

"The Emperor inquired into the most minute particulars respecting the establishment of Écouen, and I felt great pleasure in answering his questions. I recollect having dwelt on several points which appeared to me to be very important, and which were in their spirit hostile to aristocratic principles. For example, I informed his Majesty that the daughters of distinguished and wealthy individuals and those of the humble and obscure were indiscriminately confounded together in the establishment. 'If,' said I, 'I were to observe the least pretension on account of the rank or fortune of parents I should immediately put an end to it. The most perfect equality is preserved; distinction is awarded only to merit and industry. The pupils are obliged to cut out and make all their own clothes. They are taught to clean and mend lace; and two at a time, they by turns, three times a week, cook and distribute victuals to the poor of the village. The young girls who have been brought up at Écouen, or in my boarding-school at Saint Germain, are thoroughly acquainted with everything relating to household business, and they are grateful to me for having made that a part of their education. In my conversations with them I have

Écouen

always taught them that on domestic management depends the preservation or dissipation of their fortunes.'

"The postmaster of Écouen was in the courtyard at the moment when the Emperor, as he stepped into his carriage, told me he would send some sweetmeats for the pupils. I immediately communicated to them the intelligence, which was joyfully received; but the sweetmeats were looked for in vain. When Alexander set out for England he changed horses at Écouen, and the postmaster said to him: 'Sire, the pupils of Écouen are still expecting the sweetmeats which your Majesty promised them.' To which the Emperor replied that he had directed Saken to send them. The Cossacks had most likely devoured the sweetmeats, and the poor little girls, who had been so highly flattered by the promise, never tasted them."

"Prince Talleyrand, in a remarkable speech which he delivered in the Chamber of Deputies in 1821, expressed, in a single phrase, the whole spirit of policy. 'I know,' said he, 'where there is more wisdom than in Napoleon, or Voltaire, or in any minister, present or future: it is in public opinion.' I was struck with the justice of these few words. They told more than a whole treatise on the subject. What is the resting point of policy? Public opinion. Has it any other basis? Surely reason admits of no other. What should we think of the minister who follows any other guide? Silence may be commanded, it is true; but events will run counter to that command. Public opinion cannot be controlled. It must be followed, for it is always advancing. The brilliant light of the torch may be dimmed, but it cannot be extinguished. It is not to be found in the sneers of Court ladies, nor in the breviary of the Jesuits. Observe the conduct of a selfish politician, he seeks every opportunity to consult the favour of those in power. He is satisfied if he can give proofs of his devotedness; no matter on what conditions."

"I have been asked, by many persons, whether I have not been engaged in writing Memoirs on Napoleon and his Court.[3] My answer has been that this task is reserved for those who lived in his household, or who had frequent access to him; that I had undertaken to describe the private life of Marie Antoinette, and that I should do no more. I never made a single memorandum relative to the splendid and martial Court which Napoleon held at the Tuileries."

In the course of conversation with me, Madame Campan also made the following remarks:—"Napoleon's genius elevated him; but his temper proved his ruin. A restless, ambitious, reserved and hasty temper, united with Imperial power, was naturally calculated to give offence to those who approached him. Human vanity is a delicate string, which should be touched with the greatest caution. Napoleon conceived that his vast power exempted him from the forms which engage the love of subjects and call forth sentiments of attachment. He seemed to think that he was sufficient to himself, and the many imperfections which he observed in mankind rendered him somewhat misanthropic. This disposition caused him to feel the ingratitude of many persons, because he mortified their vanity; and the vanity of the great, when it is once wounded, never forgives. He knew how to govern his subjects, and Europe; but he could never govern himself; so true it is that all great men have a weak point. He was brave, generous, and magnanimous, and prized glory beyond all things; but, unfortunately, he could never conquer his passions. His luminous understanding had no influence on his temper. His genius gained him admirers; but his neglect of forms made him enemies. His admirers were far from his person, and his enemies were about him. A lady of the Imperial Court remarked that Napoleon was a piece of patchwork, made up of parts of a great and a common man. He wished that women should attend to their family affairs, and not interfere with politics. The influence of the mistresses of Louis XV alarmed him. He thought women might be commanded like an army. He little knew their restless, insinuating, inquisitive, and persevering spirit, and the direct influence they exercise over their husbands. He did not seem to understand women; they never relinquish their privileges."

As Madame Campan was returning from Switzerland she paid a visit to a duchess,[4] who had been educated at Saint Germain, and who addressed the following remarks to her:—"I never enjoyed so much happiness as since I have returned to my country residence. I have forgotten my title since I have retired hither, and I have not been the same creature that I was before. My head was full of chimerical fancies. The title of baron begins to disorder the mind; that of count produces a certain degree of imbecility; and a dukedom absolutely turns the brain. I know not what effect higher distinctions produce; but I suppose they complete the moral derangement. This progression is exact, and the result positive. All whom I have known to possess titles have experienced the same fate as myself. I pity them if they have not had courage to resume possession of their reason."

"These observations," said Madame Campan, "showed a justness of thinking which pleased me exceedingly. There appeared to me to be more philosophy in these few words than I have met with in the arguments of most of the men who profess themselves to be the disciples of Socrates. What is there in a title? It serves only to feed and inflate human vanity. This system of distinction, which is the original sin of politics; this food of vanity, so disgusting to the understanding, gives rise to pretensions of superiority over men who do not possess titles, or who only possess them in a lower degree. Can anything be more absurd and ridiculous than to suppose that the nicknames of baron, count, etc., afford grounds for assuming advantages over other men? This is madness, pure madness. On this subject Mirabeau said, 'Two things are necessary to make a citizen a nobleman: first, that he should declare himself to be so; and next, that those to whom he makes the declaration should be willing to believe him. Were it not for these two conditions, nobility would have no existence.' In the time of the Constituent Assembly this very just observation of Mirabeau's was repeated throughout Paris."

Madame Campan dined at the Tuileries in company with the Pope's Nuncio, at the period when the Concordat was in agitation. During dinner the First Consul astonished her by the able manner in which he conversed on the subject under discussion. She said he argued so logically that his talent quite amazed her.

"I formerly," said Madame Campan, "enjoyed a high degree of Court favour. When I was in childbed, previously to the birth of my poor Henry, four couriers were waiting at my house in Paris to convey intelligence of my delivery to Versailles. One was sent by Louis XVI, one by the Queen, one by Monsieur, now Louis XVIII, and one by the Princesses. Things have changed since then; such is the course of human affairs. I knew real happiness only at Saint Germain; and I have enjoyed tranquillity only since I have lived at Mantes.

"I have frequently heard the attendants of princely personages cry out to the people, '*Hats off!*' This is a piece of folly. These marks of courtesy should be inspired, not exacted. Confidence is not purchased—it is given; and, in like manner, respect should be given and not commanded. When people are happy they do spontaneously that which under other circumstances authority must compel. An experienced eye can judge with rapidity; it never takes a mistaken view of public opinion."

Molé, the actor, after paying a visit to the Duc de Fronsac on New-Year's Day, met Fleury on the staircase. The latter inquired whether he had been paying his court to Monseigneur, to which Molé replied, "Yes, certainly; it cost nothing. I always fancy I am on the stage when I lavish this kind of incense. It is a part to be played like any other."

Madame Campan related to me a fact so extraordinary that I cannot refrain from recording it here. The Marchioness de Forges, whose husband was grand falconer, resided at Versailles in the year 1775. The Marchioness was pregnant, and during childbirth some unpleasant intelligence was communicated to her. If I recollect rightly, she was informed that one of her houses had been burned down. The pains of childbirth immediately ceased, and the Marchioness continued pregnant for the space of twenty-five years. At the expiration of that period she died, and on her body being opened the child was found petrified.

The Abbé B—— one day told Madame Campan that during his residence in Italy he frequently saw in the public streets monks of various orders, mounted on chairs or planks of wood, preaching or holding conferences. When these conferences took place in the churches a Christ, as large as a child, whose head was made to move by means of a spring, was supported by one of the chorister boys, concealed within the pulpit. During these conferences the priests addressed the Christ, and inquired whether he would permit or forgive such or such things; and by help of the spring, which was moved by the boy, the Christ bowed in token of assent, or shook his head by way of disapproval, just as the priest thought proper to determine.

"When M. B—— told us this I said, 'Never repeat such a story again. I cannot conceive that the clergy would tolerate things of a nature calculated to turn into ridicule the most holy of all religions.' 'These facts,' replied the Abbé, 'are well known to travellers. At Naples they make St Januarius weep. I only relate what I saw.'"

"On the day after the publication of the ordinance for the expulsion of the Jesuits, M. Campan, my father-in-law, met Dr Quesnay in the grand gallery of Versailles, and said to him, 'Well, what think you of the Jesuits?' 'Hush! my friend,' answered M. Quesnay, 'we must not raise the cry of victory yet. Three days must elapse before a dead man be considered as really dead; these wicked rogues may come to life again.' Forty years afterwards the miracle dreaded by the doctor was fulfilled."

Napoleon used to say that sobriety and continence were indispensable qualities in a military man. Madame Campan quoted this observation, and added a remark made by her nephew, Marshal Ney, when in Spain, to another marshal, who had a mistress: "Such an *aide-de-camp* as you now possess will cost your army ten thousand men."[5]

A lady, connected with the establishment of Saint Denis, told Madame Campan that Napoleon visited it during the hundred days, and that the pupils were so delighted to see him that they crowded round him, endeavouring to touch his clothes, and evinced the most extravagant demonstrations of joy. The matron endeavoured to silence them; but Napoleon said, "Let them alone; let them alone. This may weaken the head, but it strengthens the heart."

One day during the Consulate Madame Campan dined at Malmaison, and after the coffee had been handed round several members of public bodies gathered about Napoleon, and tried to prevail on him to distrust the Jacobins, as being a very dangerous set of men. After hearing what they had to say, he replied, "It appears to me that you do not rightly know what a Jacobin is. He is merely an ambitious fellow, in search of a place. I shall therefore give places to the Jacobins, and make them hold their tongues."

"M. Brunier, the Court physician, was called to attend Madame B—— at Versailles. That distinguished lady was then far advanced in life, and in a bad state of health. After considering her case, the doctor jokingly said, 'What can I do, madame? when the oil is exhausted the lamp must die out.' 'A physician,' replied the lady, 'should at least have sufficient sense and humanity to speak less plainly. I do not want proverbs, but merely consolation, if there be no other remedy.'

"This same M. Brunier was physician to the children of the royal family; and during his visits to the palace, if the death of any of his patients happened to be alluded to, he never failed to say, 'Ah! there I lost one of my best friends.' 'Well,' said the Queen, 'if he loses all his patients, who are his friends, what will become of those who are not his friends?'"

"A petition was drawn up and addressed to the Queen by the people of a corporation in the neighbourhood of Paris, in which they prayed for the destruction of the game which destroyed their farming crops. I was myself the bearer of this petition to her Majesty, who said to me, 'I will undertake to have these good people relieved from so burthensome an annoyance.' She gave the document herself to M. de Vermond, in my presence, accompanying it with these words, '*I desire that immediate justice be done to this petition.*' An assurance was given that her order should be attended to. Six weeks afterwards a second petition was sent from the corporation; for the nuisance, after all, had not been abated. Thus are sovereigns deceived!

"I am persuaded," added Madame Campan, "that if the second petition had reached the Queen, M. de Vermond would have received a sharp reprimand. She was always so happy when it was in her power to do good."

"Previously to the 10th of August 1792 the Queen frequently kept me by her bedside, after she had retired, that we might talk over public events. Her Majesty, in taking a review of them, used to express a presentiment of their results. 'But, Madame,' said I, 'a door of escape from this perilous place is pointed out to you—do not, then, I beseech you, continue here.' 'History is busy with us,' replied the Queen, 'we neither can nor ought to accept the offers made to us. Were death itself the consequence, we cannot consent to be saved by the men who have possessed themselves of our authority.' 'Madame,' said I, 'history will take her own course; only save yourself and family in the first place.' The page of history was ever present to the mind of her Majesty; so true is it that misfortune is not to be fled from."

Madame Campan was very much affected whilst relating to me this conversation.

Madame Campan once observed: "A man should be in the world what a good book is in a library: an object always seen with interest and pleasure, and from whose acquaintance we never fail to gain something."

Madame Regnier, the wife of a law officer of Versailles, while talking in the presence of a numerous party assembled at her own house, dropped some remarks which were out of place, though not very important. Her husband reprimanded her before the whole company, saying, "Silence, madame; you are a fool." She lived twenty or thirty years after this, and never uttered a single word, even to her children. A pretended theft was committed in her presence, in the hope of taking her by surprise, but without effect; and nothing could induce her to speak. When her consent was requisite for the marriage of any of her children, she bowed her head, and signed the contract. Such an instance of resolute obstinacy was never known; her vanity never forgave the affront.

M. de Beaumont, chamberlain to the Empress Josephine, was one day at Malmaison, expressing his regret that M. D——, one of Napoleon's generals, who had recently been promoted, did not belong to a great family. "You mistake, sir," observed Madame Campan, "he is of very ancient descent; he is one of the nephews of Charlemagne. All the heroes of our army sprang from the elder branch of that sovereign's family, who never emigrated."

When Madame Campan related this circumstance to me, she added: "After the 30th of March 1814 some officers of the army of Condé presumed to say to certain French marshals that it was a pity they were not more nobly connected. In answer to this one of them said, 'True nobility, gentlemen, consists in giving proofs of it. The field of honour has witnessed ours; but where are we to look for yours? Your swords have rusted in their scabbards. Our laurels may well excite envy; we have earned them nobly, and we owe them solely to our valour. You have merely inherited a name. This is the distinction between us.'"[6]

Napoleon used to observe that if he had had two such field-marshals as Suchet in Spain he would have not only conquered but kept the Peninsula. Suchet's sound judgment, his governing yet conciliating spirit, his military tact, and his bravery, had procured him astonishing success. "It is to be regretted," added he, "that a sovereign cannot *improvise* men of his stamp."[7]

"In the summer of 1811 Napoleon, accompanied by Maria Louisa and several personages of distinction, visited the establishment at Écouen. After inspecting the chapel and the refectories Napoleon desired that the three principal pupils might be presented to him. 'Sire,' said I, 'I cannot select three; I must present six.' He turned on his heel and repaired to the platform, where, after seeing all the classes assembled, he repeated his demand. 'Sire,' said I, 'I beg leave to inform your Majesty that I should commit an injustice towards several other pupils who are as far advanced as those whom I might have the honour to present to you.'

"Berthier and others intimated to me, in a low tone of voice, that I should get into disgrace by my non-compliance. Napoleon looked over the whole of the house, entered into the most trivial details, and after addressing questions to several of the pupils: 'Well, madame,' said he, 'I am satisfied; show me your six best pupils.'" Madame Campan presented them to him; and as he stepped into his carriage, he desired that their names might be sent to Berthier. On addressing the list to the Prince de Neufchatel, Madame Campan added to it the names of four other pupils, and all the ten obtained a pension of 300 francs. During the three hours which this visit occupied the Empress did not utter a single word.

During the Consulate Napoleon one day said to Madame Campan, "If ever I establish a republic of women, I shall make you First Consul."

Josephine having been invited, during the Consulate, to dine with a rich army contractor, Napoleon said, "I do not object to your dining with bankers, they are merely dealers in money; but I will not have you visit contractors, for they are robbers of money."

Madame Campan has many times told me that Marshal Ney, just at the moment when the battle of the Moskowa was decided, sent to request of Napoleon the whole reserve of the guard. Napoleon inquired of the *aide-de-camp* whether the Russian guard had yet engaged; he was told that they had, and had been beaten by the troops of the line. "In that case," replied he, "it will be a finer thing to be able to say in the bulletin that the battle was gained without my reserve having been brought into action."

Marshal Ney had made this request with a view to cut off the retreat of the Russians; and had the reserve marched forward, it is probable that nearly the whole of their army would have been made prisoners, and that a treaty might have been arranged on the field of battle.

It was an oft-quoted saying of Napoleon's, that if you but scratched the skin of a Russian, you would instantly discern the barbarian.

"The talent of Madame de Staël," said Madame Campan, "gave her a masculine character. To silence her, it would have been necessary, as I told the Empress Josephine, to give her a Court dress with a long train; she would have sought no better. The man who persecuted her was at first her hero; her brilliant imagination exalted him into an idol. Napoleon feared her at home; but she did him a great deal more mischief abroad. Under his own wing he might have kept her in check; but when vexed and irritated she avenged herself with the bitterness that might be expected from a woman of superior talent wounded to the quick. A woman who can write manifestoes is worthy of consideration; indeed, policy renders it a duty to respect her. Napoleon one day interrupted Madame de Staël in the midst of a profound political argument to ask her whether she had nursed her children."

Napoleon was relating at the Tuileries, after his return from Austerlitz, that he could have made the two Emperors his prisoners in that battle. "Why did you not bring them with you?" said a princess to him, "we could have entertained them with the carnival." "In sooth," was the reply, "such prisoners are apt to create too much embarrassment."

He said on another occasion that his conscripts when they quitted their homes wore only the cloak of courage; but that after they had faced the enemy once or twice their hearts were filled with it.

"From the situation in which I am placed," said Napoleon to Madame Campan, "I very much pity all who are about me. Their characters are all known to me; and I could make a report of them just as you report the conduct of the scholars under your superintendence. Ambition is their ruling passion. All is right that promotes their advancement, but all is wrong that tends to their retrogression. Their pride is very elastic; their ingenuity enables them to lengthen or shorten it as circumstances require. But I keep them within due bounds. They look only to themselves, and they forget the nation, which is the first principle. What would they be without it? The favours of which I dispose belong to the people; but the men who are enjoying them would not scruple to show their ingratitude to the nation and to me if temptation should present itself."

"It must be confessed," said Madame Campan, "that he judged correctly."

Napoleon related that a few days before the battle of Austerlitz some agitation had prevailed, particularly in Paris. "The warmth of the Court party," said he, "had fallen to temperate; but on hearing of my success they rallied round me as if they had been charged by the Cossacks. This is the way of the world."

"If," said Napoleon, "I created so many princes and kings, it was that I might present to the world a specimen of my power. I should have acted very differently but for the reverses I experienced at Moscow. To have kept the English in subjection for three or four years would have sufficiently answered my views. I would have given liberty to all nations, and directed their views to elevated and noble principles. Honour should have been the basis of all. But fate thwarted my plans; this was the greatest calamity that could have befallen the nations of Europe."

The Empress Josephine, at the time of her divorce, requested permission to proceed to the United States. Napoleon informed her that he could not answer for her safety in crossing the sea. "Then your power finds an obstacle," said she, "would to Heaven there were seas to be crossed for the fulfilment of all your wishes! your glory would then beam for ever!"

End of memoir and conversations of Madame Campan

1. The paragraphs distinguished by inverted commas at the commencement of each one are to be understood as containing the exact words of Madame Campan.

2. "Les comtes de sa façon, ne se croyaient pas de contes pour rire. Il faut convenir qu'ils sont du fait d'un grand homme."

3. The reader is referred for one of the best books on this subject the *Memoirs of Madame Junot* (*Duchesse d'Abrantès*).

4. The Duchesse de St Leu, at Constance.

5. Vide *Memoirs of Madame Junot* (*Duchesse d'Abrantès*), edition 1883, vol. iii, p. 268, for a curious illustrative anecdote of the marshal in question.

6. When one of the princes of the smaller German States was showing Marshal Lannes, with a contemptuous superiority of manner but ill concealed, the portraits of his ancestors, and covertly alluding to the absence of Lannes's, that general turned the tables on him by haughtily remarking, "But I *am* an ancestor."

7. Apropos of the merits of his various generals, Napoleon said: "I give the preference to Suchet. Before his time Masséna was the first; but he may be considered as dead. Suchet, Clausel, and Gérard are now in my opinion the best French generals." Napoleon's words at St Helena, quoted in *Memoirs of Madame Junot (Duchesse d'Abrantès)*, edition 1883, vol. iii, p. 291.

NOTE

The following titles have the signification given below during the period covered by this work:—

MONSEIGNEUR The Dauphin.

MONSIEUR The eldest brother of the King, Comte de Provence, afterwards Louis XVIII.

MONSIEUR LE PRINCE The Prince de Condé, head of the House of Condé.

MONSIEUR LE DUC The Duc de Bourbon, the eldest son of the Prince de Condé, and the father of the Duc d'Enghien shot by Napoleon.

MONSIEUR LE GRAND The Grand Equerry under the *ancient régime*.

MONSIEUR LE PRÉMIER The First Equerry under the *ancient régime*.

ENFANS DE FRANCE The royal children.

MADAME}

MESDAMES} (Sisters or daughters of the King; or Princesses near the Throne; sometimes used also for the wife of Monsieur, the eldest brother of the King), the Princesses Adelaide, Victoire, Sophie, Louise, daughters of Louis XV, and aunts of Louis XVI.

MADAME ELIZABETH The Princess Elizabeth, sister of Louis XVI.

MADAME ROYALE The Princess Marie Thérèse, daughter of Louis XVI, afterwards Duchesse d'Angoulême.

MADEMOISELLE The daughter of Monsieur, the brother of the King.

INTRODUCTORY CHAPTER

Louis XV and his queen

The first event which made any impression on me in my earliest childhood was the attempt of Damiens to assassinate Louis XV. This occurrence struck me so forcibly that the most minute details relating to the confusion and grief which prevailed at Versailles on that day seem as completely present to my imagination as the most recent events. I had dined with my father and mother, in company with one of their friends. The drawing-room was lighted up with a number of candles, and four card-tables were already occupied, when a friend of the gentleman of the house came in, with a pale and terrified countenance, and said, in a voice scarcely audible, "I bring you terrible news. The King has been assassinated!" Two ladies in company instantly fainted; a brigadier of the Body Guards threw down his cards, and cried out, "I do not wonder at it; it is those rascally Jesuits."—"What are you saying, brother?" cried a lady, flying to him; "would you get yourself arrested?"—"Arrested! for what? for unmasking those wretches who want a bigot for a King?" My father came in; he recommended circumspection, saying that the blow was not mortal, and that all meetings ought to be suspended at so critical a moment. He had brought a chaise for my mother, who placed me on her knees. We lived in the Avenue de Paris, and throughout our drive I heard incessant cries and sobs from the footpaths. At last I saw a man arrested; he was an usher of the King's chamber, who had gone mad, and was crying out, "Yes, I know them; the wretches! the villains!" Our chaise was stopped by this bustle. My mother recognised the unfortunate man who had been seized; she gave his name to the trooper who had stopped him. The poor usher was therefore merely conducted to the *gens d'armes'* guard-room, which was then in the avenue. In times of public calamities, or national events, the slightest acts of imprudence may be fatal. When the people take part in an opinion or occurrence we ought to avoid coming in contact with them, and even alarming them. Informations are then no longer the result of careful investigation, and punishments cease to emanate from impartial justice. At the period of which I am speaking the love of the sovereign was a sort of religion, and this attempt against the life of Louis XV brought on a multitude of groundless arrests.[1] M. de la Serre, then Governor of the Invalides, his wife, his daughter, and some of his domestics, were taken up, because Mademoiselle de la Serre, who was that very day come from her convent to pass the holiday of the King's birthday with her family, said, in her father's drawing-room, on hearing this news from Versailles, "That is not to be wondered at; I have often heard Mother N—— say that it would certainly happen, because the King is not sufficiently attached to religion." Mother N——, the director, and several of the nuns of this convent, were interrogated by the lieutenant of police.

The public animosity against the Jesuits, kept up by the partisans of Port Royal and the adepts in the new philosophy, did not conceal the suspicions which they directed against the Jesuits; and although there was not the slightest proof against that Order, the attempt to assassinate the King was certainly made use of against it, a few years afterwards, by the party which effected the destruction of the Company of Jesus. The wretch Damiens avenged himself on various persons whom he had served in several provinces, by getting them arrested; and when they were confronted with him, he said to some of them, "It was out of revenge for your ill-treatment of me that I put you into this fright." To some women he said, "That he had amused himself in his prison with the thoughts of the terror they would feel.". This monster confessed that he had murdered the virtuous La Bourdonnaye, by giving him a *lavement* of aquafortis. He had also committed several other crimes. People are too careless about those whom they take into their service; such examples prove that too many precautions cannot be used in ascertaining the character of strangers before we admit them into our houses.

I have often heard M. de Landsmath, equerry and master of the hounds, who used to come frequently to my father's, say, that on the news of the attempt on the King's life he instantly repaired to his Majesty. I cannot repeat the coarse expressions he made use of to encourage his Majesty; but his account of the affair, long afterwards, amused the parties in which he was prevailed on to relate it, when all apprehensions respecting the consequences of the event had subsided. This M. de Landsmath was an old soldier, who had given proofs of extraordinary valour; nothing had been able to soften his manners or subdue his excessive bluntness to the respectful customs of the Court. The King was very fond of him. He possessed prodigious strength, and had often contended with Marshal Saxe, renowned for his great bodily power, in trying the strength of their respective wrists.[2] M. de Landsmath had a thundering voice. When he came into the King's apartment he found the Dauphin and Mesdames, his Majesty's daughters, there; the Princesses, in tears, surrounded the King's bed. "Send out all these weeping ladies, Sire," said the old equerry; "I want to speak to you alone." The King made a sign to the Princesses to withdraw. "Come," said Landsmath, "your wound is nothing; you had plenty of waistcoats and flannels on." Then uncovering his breast, "Look here," said he, showing four or five great scars, "these are something like wounds; I received them thirty years ago; now cough as loud as you can." The King did so. "'Tis nothing at all," said Landsmath; "you must laugh at it; we shall hunt a stag together in four days." "But suppose the blade was poisoned," said the King. "Old grandams' tales," replied Landsmath; "if it had been so, the waistcoats and flannels would have rubbed the poison off." The King was pacified, and passed a very good night.

This same M. de Landsmath, who by his peremptory and familiar language thus calmed the fears of Louis XV on the day of Damiens' horrible crime, was one of those people who, in the most haughty courts, often tell the truth bluntly. It is remarkable that there is a person of this description to be found in almost every court, who seems to supply the place of the ancient king's jester, and to claim the right of saying whatever he pleases. His Majesty one day asked M. de Landsmath how old he was? He was aged, and by no means fond of thinking of his age; he evaded the question. A fortnight after Louis XV took a paper out of his pocket and read aloud: "On such a day in the month of——one thousand six hundred and eighty——, was baptized by me, Rector of ——, the son of the high and mighty lord," etc. "What's that?" said Landsmath angrily; "has your Majesty been procuring the certificate of my baptism?" "There it is, you see, Landsmath," said the King. "Well, Sire, hide it as fast as you can; a prince entrusted with the happiness of twenty-five millions of people ought not wilfully to hurt the feelings of a single individual."

The King learned that Landsmath had lost his confessor, a missionary priest of the parish of Notre Dame. It was the custom of the Lazarists to expose their dead with the face uncovered. Louis XV wished to try his equerry's firmness. "You have lost your confessor, I hear," said the King.—"Yes, Sire."—"He will be exposed with his face bare?" "Such is the custom."—"I command you to go and see him."—"Sire, my confessor was my friend; it would be very painful to me."—"No matter; I command you."—"Are you really in earnest, Sire?"—"Quite so."—"It would be the first time in my life that I had disobeyed my sovereign's order. I will go." The next day the King at his *levée*, as soon as he perceived Landsmath, said, "Have you done as I desired you, Landsmath?" "Undoubtedly, Sire."—"Well, what did you see?"—"Faith, I saw that your Majesty and I are no great shakes!"[3]

At the death of Queen Maria Leczinska, M. Campan, who was afterwards secretary of the closet to Marie Antoinette, and at that time an officer of the chamber, having performed several confidential duties at the time of that Queen's decease, the King asked Madame Adelaide how he should reward him. She requested him to create an office in his household of master of the wardrobe, with a salary of 1,000 crowns for M. Campan. "I will do so," said the King; "it will be an honourable title; but tell Campan not to add a single crown to his expenses, for you will see they will never pay him."

The manner in which Mademoiselle de Romans, mistress to Louis XV and mother of the Abbé de Bourbon, was presented to him, deserves, I think, to be related. The King had gone, with a grand cavalcade, to Paris to hold a bed of justice. As he passed the terrace of the Tuileries he observed a chevalier de St Louis, dressed in a faded lutestring coat, and a woman of a pretty good figure, holding on the parapet of the terrace a young girl strikingly beautiful, much adorned, and dressed in a rose-coloured taffety frock.

The King's notice was involuntarily attracted by the marked manner in which he was pointed out to the girl. On returning to Versailles, he called Le Bel, the minister and confidant of his secret pleasures, and ordered him to seek in Paris a young female about twelve or thirteen years of age, describing her as I have just mentioned. Le Bel assured him he saw no probability of the success of such a commission. "Pardon me," said Louis XV, "this family must live in the neighbourhood of the Tuileries, on the side of the Faubourg St Honoré, or at the entrance of the Faubourg St Germain. These people certainly go on foot; they would not make the girl, of whom they seem so fond, cross all Paris. They are poor; the clothes of the child were so new that I have no doubt they were made for the very day I was to enter Paris. She will wear that dress all the summer; they will walk in the Tuileries on Sundays and holidays. Apply to the man who sells lemonade at the terrace of the Feuillans——children take refreshment there; you will discover her by these means."

Le Bel fulfilled his master's orders; and within a month discovered the dwelling of the girl; he found that Louis XV was not in the least mistaken with respect to the intentions which he supposed to exist. All conditions were easily agreed on; the King contributed, by considerable presents, to the education of Mademoiselle de Romans for the space of two years. She was kept totally ignorant of her future destiny; and when she had completed her fifteenth year she was taken to Versailles, on pretence of going to see the palace. Between four and five in the afternoon she was conducted into the mirror gallery. All the grand apartments were usually very solitary at that hour. Le Bel, who waited for them, opened the glass door which led from the gallery into the King's closet, and invited Mademoiselle de Romans to go in and examine its beauties. Encouraged by the sight of a man whom she knew, and excited by the curiosity so excusable at her age, she eagerly accepted the offer, but insisted on Le Bel's procuring the same pleasure for her parents. He assured her that it was impossible; that they were going to sit down in one of the windows of the gallery and wait for her, and that, when she had seen the inner apartments, he would bring her back to them. She consented; the glass door closed on her. Le Bel showed her the chamber, the Council-room, and talked with enthusiasm of the monarch who possessed the splendour with which she was surrounded; and at length conducted her to the private apartments, where Mademoiselle de Romans found the King himself, awaiting her arrival with all the impatience and all the desires of a prince who had been two years engaged in bringing about the moment of this interview.[4]

What painful reflections are excited by all this immorality! The art with which this intrigue had been carried on, and the genuine innocence of the youthful de Romans, were doubtless the motives of the King's particular attachment to this mistress. She was the only one who prevailed on him to allow her son to bear the name of Bourbon. At the moment of his birth she received a note in the King's handwriting, containing the following words: "The Rector of Chaillot, when he baptizes the child of Mademoiselle de Romans, will give him the following names: Louis N. de Bourbon." A few years afterwards the King, being dissatisfied at the consequence which Mademoiselle de Romans assumed on account of her good fortune in having given birth to an acknowledged son, and seeing, by the splendid way in which she was bringing him up, that she entertained the idea of causing him to be legitimatised, had him taken out of his mother's hands. This commission was executed with great severity. Louis XV had vowed never to legitimatise a natural child; the great number of princes of this description which Louis XIV had left was burdensome to the State, and made this determination of Louis XV truly laudable. The Abbé de Bourbon was very handsome, and exactly resembled his father; he was much beloved by the Princesses, the King's daughters; and his ecclesiastical prospects would have been advanced by Louis XV to the highest degree. A cardinal's hat was intended for him, as well as the Abbey of St Germain des Pres, and the Bishopric of Bayeux. Without being considered one of the Princes of the blood, he would have enjoyed a most happy lot. He died at Rome, of confluent smallpox, generally regretted; but the misfortunes with which his family have since been afflicted make us regard his death as a merciful dispensation of Providence. Mademoiselle de Romans married a gentleman named Cavanac; the King was displeased at it, and she was universally blamed for having in some degree abandoned by this alliance the plain title of mother of the Abbé de Bourbon.[5]

The monotonous habits of royal greatness too frequently inspire princes with the desire of procuring for themselves the enjoyments of private individuals; and then they vainly flatter themselves with the hope of remaining concealed in mysterious obscurity. They ought to be warned of these errors, and accustomed to support the tediousness of greatness, as well as to enjoy its extensive advantages, which they well know how to do. Louis XV, by his noble carriage, and the mild yet majestic expression of his features, was perfectly worthy to succeed to Louis the Great. But he too frequently indulged in secret pleasures, which at last were sure to become known. During several winters, he was passionately fond of *candles' end balls*, as he called those parties amongst the very lowest classes of society. He got intelligence of the *picnics* given by the tradesmen, milliners, and seamstresses of Versailles, whither he repaired in a black domino, and masked, accompanied by the Captain of his Guards, masked like himself. His great delight was to go *en brouette.*[6] Care was always taken to give notice to five or six officers of the King's or Queen's chamber to be there, in order that his Majesty might be surrounded by safe people, without perceiving it or finding it troublesome. Probably the Captain of the Guards also took other precautions of this description on his part. My father-in-law, when the King and he were both young, has often made one amongst the servants desired to attend masked at these parties, assembled in some garret, or parlour of a public-house. In those times, during the carnival, masked companies had a right to join the citizens' balls; it was sufficient that one of the party should unmask and name himself.

These secret excursions and his too habitual intercourse with ladies more distinguished for their personal charms than for the advantages of education, were no doubt the means by which the King acquired many vulgar expressions which otherwise would never have reached his ears.

Yet amidst the most shameful excesses the King sometimes resumed suddenly the dignity of his rank in a very noble manner. The familiar courtiers of Louis XV had one day abandoned themselves to the unrestrained gaiety of a supper, after returning from the chase. Each boasted of and described the beauty of his mistress. Some of them amused themselves with giving a particular account of their wives' personal defects. An imprudent word, addressed to Louis XV, and applicable only to the Queen, instantly dispelled all the mirth of the entertainment. The King assumed his regal air, and knocking with his knife on the table twice or thrice: "Gentlemen," said he, "here is the King!"

Three young men of the college of St Germain, who had just completed their course of studies, knowing no person about the Court, and having heard that strangers were always well treated there, resolved to dress themselves completely in the Armenian costume, and, thus clad, to present themselves to see the grand ceremony of the reception of several knights of the Order of the Holy Ghost. Their stratagem met with all the success with which they had flattered themselves. While the procession was passing through the long mirror gallery, the Swiss of the apartments placed them in the first row of spectators, recommending every one to pay all possible attention to the strangers. The latter, however, were imprudent enough to enter the *Œil de Bœuf* Chamber, where were Messieurs Cardonne and Ruffin, interpreters of Oriental languages, and the first clerk of the consuls' department, whose business it was to attend to everything which related to the natives of the East who were in France. The three scholars were immediately surrounded and questioned by these gentlemen, at first in modern Greek. Without being disconcerted, they made signs that they did not understand it. They were then addressed in Turkish and Arabic; at length one of the interpreters, losing all patience, exclaimed, "Gentlemen, you certainly must understand some of the languages in which you have been addressed. What country can you possibly come from then?" "From St Germain-en-Laye, sir," replied the boldest among them; "this is the first time you have put the question to us in French." They then confessed the motive of their disguise; the eldest of them was not more than eighteen years of age. Louis XV was informed of the affair. He laughed heartily, ordered them a few hours' confinement and a good admonition, after which they were to be set at liberty.

Louis XV liked to talk about death, though he was extremely apprehensive of it; but his excellent health and his royal dignity probably made him imagine himself invulnerable. He often said to people who had very bad colds, "You've a churchyard cough there." Hunting one day in the forest of Senard, in a year in which bread was extremely dear, he met a man on horseback carrying a coffin. "Whither are you carrying that coffin?" "To the village of ——," answered the peasant. "Is it for a man or a woman?"— "For a man." —"What did he die of?"—"Of hunger," bluntly replied the villager. The King spurred on his horse, and asked no more questions.

When I was young I often met with Madame de Marchais, the wife of the King's first *valet de chambre*, in company. She was a very well-informed woman, and had enjoyed the favour of Louis XV, being a relation of Madame de Pompadour. M. de Marchais was rich and much respected; he had served in the army, was a chevalier de St Louis, and, besides being principal *valet de chambre*, was Governor of the Louvre. Madame de Marchais was visited by the whole Court; the captains of the guards came there constantly, and many officers of the Body Guard. Eminent officers of every kind used to get introduced to her, as to Madame Geoffrin; she possessed some influence, particularly in soliciting votes for candidates for the academicians' chairs. I have seen all the celebrated men of the age at her house: La Harpe, Diderot, d'Alembert, Duclos, Thomas, etc. She was as remarkable for her wit and studious display as her husband for his good-nature and simplicity; he was fond of spoiling her most innocent schemes for obtaining admiration. No one could describe an academical speech, a sermon, or the subject of a new piece with so much precision and grace as Madame de Marchais. She had also the art of turning the conversation at pleasure upon any ancient or modern work; and her husband often delighted in saying to those who sat near him, "My wife read that this morning." Count Angiviller, charmed with the graces of her mind, paid assiduous court to her, and when she became the widow of M. de Marchais, married her. She was still living at Versailles in the early part of the reign of Napoleon, but never left her bed. She had retained her fondness for dress, and although unable to rise, always had her hair dressed as people used to wear it twenty years before that period. She disguised the ravages of time under a prodigious quantity of white and red paint, and seemed, by the feeble light which penetrated through her closed blinds and drawn curtains, nothing but a kind of doll, but a doll which spoke in a charming and most spirited manner. She had retained a very beautiful head of hair to an advanced age; it was said that the celebrated Count St Germain, who had appeared at the Court of Louis XV as one of the most famous alchemists of the day, had given her a liquor which preserved the hair, and prevented it from turning white through age.

Louis XV had, as is well known, adopted the whimsical system of separating Louis de Bourbon from the King of France. As a private individual he had his personal fortune, his own distinct financial interests. He used to deal as an individual in all the contracts and bargains he engaged in. He had bought a tolerably handsome house at the Parc-aux-Cerfs at Versailles, where he used to keep one of those obscure mistresses whom the indulgence or the policy of Madame de Pompadour tolerated, so long as she herself retained the title of his declared mistress.[7] After the King had relinquished this custom, he wished to sell the house. Sévin, first clerk of the War Office, offered to purchase it; the notary instructed to effect the sale informed the King of his proposals. The contract for the sale was made out between Louis de Bourbon and Pierre Sévin; and the King sent word to the purchaser to bring him the money himself in gold. The first clerk collected 40,000 francs in *louis d'or*, and being introduced by the notary of the King's private cabinet, delivered the purchase money of the house into his Majesty's own hands.[8]

Out of his private funds the King paid the household expenses of his mistresses, those of the education of his illegitimate daughters, who were brought up in convents at Paris, and their dowries when they married.

Those men who are most completely abandoned to dissolute manners are not, on that account, insensible to virtue in women. The Comtesse de Perigord was as beautiful as virtuous. During some excursions she made to Choisy, whither she had been invited, she perceived that the King took great notice of her. Her demeanour of chilling respect, her cautious perseverance in shunning all serious conversation with the monarch, were insufficient to extinguish this rising flame, and he at length addressed a letter to her, worded in the most passionate terms. This excellent woman instantly formed her resolution: honour forbade her returning the King's passion, whilst her profound respect for the sovereign made her unwilling to disturb his tranquillity. She therefore voluntarily banished herself to an estate she possessed, called Chalais, near Barbezieux, the mansion of which had been uninhabited nearly a century: the porter's lodge was the only place in a condition to receive her. From this seat she wrote to his Majesty, explaining her motives for leaving Court; and she remained there several years without visiting Paris. Louis XV was speedily attracted by other objects, and regained the composure to which Madame de Perigord had thought it her duty to sacrifice so much. Some years after, Mesdames' lady of honour died. Many great families solicited the place. The King, without answering any of their applications, wrote to the Comtesse de Perigord: "My daughters have just lost their lady of honour; this place, Madame, is your due, no less on account of your personal qualities, than of the illustrious name of your family."

Comte d'Halville, sprung from a very ancient Swiss house, commenced his career at Versailles in the humble rank of ensign in the regiment of Swiss guards. His name and distinguished ability gained him the patronage of some powerful friends, who, in order to support the honour of the ancient name he bore, by a handsome fortune, obtained for him in marriage the daughter of a very rich financier, named M. de la Garde. The offspring of this union was an only daughter, who married Count Esterhazy. Amongst the estates which belonged to Mademoiselle de la Garde was the Château des Trous, situate four leagues from Versailles, where the Count was visited by many people attached to the Court. A young ensign of the Body Guards, who had obtained that rank on account of his name, and of the favour which his family enjoyed, and possessed all the confidence which usually accompanies unmerited success, but of which the progress of time fortunately relieves young people, was one day taking upon him to give his opinion of the Swiss nobility, although he knew nothing of the great families of Switzerland. Without the least delicacy or consideration for the Count, his host, he asserted boldly that there were no ancient families in Switzerland. "Excuse me," said the Count very coolly, "there are several of great antiquity." "Can you name them, sir?" answered the youth. "Yes," said M. de Halville; "for instance, there is my house, and that of Hapsburg, which now reigns in Germany." "Of course you have your reasons for naming your own family first?" replied the impudent ensign. "Yes, sir," said M. de Halville sternly; "because the house of Hapsburg dates from the period when its founder was page to my ancestors. Read history, study the antiquities of nations and families; and in future be more circumspect in your assertions."

Weak as Louis XV was, the parliaments would never have obtained his consent to the convocation of the States-General. I heard an anecdote on this subject from two officers attached to that prince's household. It was at the period when the remonstrances of the parliaments, and the refusals to register the decrees for levying taxes, produced alarm with respect to the state of the finances. This became the subject of conversation one evening at the *coucher* of Louis XV. "You will see, Sire," said a courtier, whose office placed him in close communication with the King, "that all this will make it absolutely necessary to assemble the States-General." The King, roused by this speech from the habitual apathy of his character, seized the courtier by the arm, and said to him, in a passion, "Never repeat these words. I am not sanguinary; but had I a brother, and he were to dare to give me such advice, I would sacrifice him, within twenty-four hours, to the duration of the monarchy, and the tranquillity of the kingdom."

Several years prior to his death, the Dauphin, the father of Louis XVI, had confluent smallpox, which endangered his life; and after his convalescence, he was long troubled with a malignant ulcer under the nose. He was injudiciously advised to get rid of it by the use of extract of lead, which proved effectual; but from that time the Dauphin, who was corpulent, insensibly grew thin; and a short dry cough evinced that the humour, driven in, had fallen on the lungs. Some persons also suspected him of having taken acids in too great a quantity for the purpose of reducing his bulk. The state of his health was not, however, such as to excite alarm. At the camp at Compiègne, in July, 1764, the Dauphin reviewed the troops, and evinced much activity in the performance of his duties; it was even observed that he was seeking to gain the attachment of the army. He presented the Dauphiness to the soldiers, saying, with a simplicity which at that time made a great sensation, "Mes enfants, here is my wife." Returning late on horseback to Compiègne, he found he had taken a chill; the heat of the day had been excessive; the prince's clothes had been wet with perspiration. An illness followed, in which the prince began to spit blood. His principal physician wished to have him bled; the consulting physicians insisted on purgation, and their advice was followed. The pleurisy being ill-cured, assumed and retained all the symptoms of consumption; the Dauphin languished from that period until December 1765, and died at Fontainebleau, where the Court, on account of his condition, had prolonged its stay, which usually ended on the 2nd of November.

The Dauphiness, his widow, was excessively afflicted; but the immoderate despair which characterised her grief induced many to suspect that the loss of the Crown was an important part of the calamity she lamented. She long refused to eat enough to support life; she encouraged her tears to flow by placing portraits of the Dauphin in every retired part of her apartments. She had him represented pale, and ready to expire, in a picture placed at the foot of her bed, under draperies of gray cloth, with which the chambers of the Princesses were always hung in court mournings. Their grand cabinet was hung with black cloth, with an alcove, a canopy, and a throne, on which they received compliments of condolence after the first period of the deep mourning. The Dauphiness, some months before the end of her career, regretted her conduct in abridging it; but it was too late; the fatal blow had been struck. It may also be presumed that living with a consumptive man had contributed to her complaint. This princess had no opportunity of displaying her qualities; living in a court, in which she was eclipsed by the King and Queen, the only characteristics that could be remarked in her were her extreme attachment to her husband, and her great piety.

The Dauphin was little known, and his character has been much mistaken. He himself, as he confessed to his intimate friends, sought to disguise it. He one day asked one of his most familiar servants, "What do they say in Paris of that great fool of a Dauphin?" The person interrogated seeming confused, the Dauphin urged him to express himself sincerely, saying, "Speak freely; that is positively the idea which I wish people to form of me."

As he died of a disease which allows the last moment to be anticipated long beforehand, he wrote much, and transmitted his affections and his prejudices to his son by secret notes.[9] This was really what prevented the Queen from recalling M. de Choiseul at the death of Louis XV, and what promoted M. de Muy, the intimate friend of the Dauphin, to the place of Minister of War. The destruction of the Jesuits, effected by M. de Choiseul, had given the Dauphin's hatred of him that character of party spirit which induced him to transmit it to his son. Had he ascended the throne, he would have supported the Jesuits and priests in general, and kept down the philosophers. Maria Leczinska, the wife of Louis XV, placed her highest merit in abstaining from public affairs, and in the strict observance of her religious duties; never asking anything for herself, and sending all she possessed to the poor. Such a life ought to secure a person against future detraction, but has not preserved the memory of this princess from that venom which Soulavie makes the Duc de Choiseul deal around him indiscriminately.

Queen Maria Leczinska,[10] the wife of Louis XV, often spoke of the humble position in which she stood at the time when the policy of the Court of Versailles caused the marriage of the King with the young Infanta to be broken off, and raised a Polish princess, daughter of a dethroned monarch, to the rank of Queen of France. Before this unhoped-for event changed the destiny of this virtuous princess, there had been some idea of marrying her to the Duc d'Estrées; and, when the Duchess of that name came to pay her court to her at Versailles, she said to those who surrounded her, "I might have been in that lady's place myself, and curtseying to the Queen of France." She used to relate that the King, her father, informed her of her elevation in a manner which might have made too strong an impression on her mind; that he had taken care to avoid disturbing her tranquillity, to leave her in total ignorance of the first negotiations set on foot relative to her marriage; and that when all was definitively arranged, and the ambassador arrived, her father went to her apartment, placed an arm-chair for her, had her set in it, and addressed her thus: "Allow me, Madame, to enjoy a happiness which far outweighs all the misfortunes that I have suffered; I wish, to be the first to pay my respects to the Queen of France."

Maria Leczinska was not handsome; but she possessed much intelligence, an expressive countenance, and a simplicity of manners, set off by the gracefulness of the Polish lady. She loved the King, and found his early infidelities very grievous to endure. Nevertheless, the death of Madame de Châteauroux, whom she had known very young, and who had even been honoured by her kindness, made a painful impression on her. This good Queen continued to suffer from the bad effects of an early superstitious education. She was fearful of ghosts. The first night after she heard of this almost sudden death she could not sleep, and made one of her women sit up, who endeavoured to calm her restlessness by telling her stories, which she would in such cases call for, as children do with their nurses. On this night nothing could overcome her wakefulness; her lady-in-waiting, thinking that she was asleep, was leaving her bedside on tiptoe; the slightest noise on the floor roused the Queen, who cried, "Whither are you going? Stay; go on with your story." As it was past two in the morning, this woman, whose name was Boirot, and who was somewhat unceremonious, said, "What can be the matter with your Majesty to-night? Are you feverish? Shall I call up the physician?" "Oh no, no, my good Boirot, I am not ill; but that poor Madame de Châteauroux,—if she were to come again!" "Jesus, Madame," cried the woman, who had lost all patience, "if Madame de Châteauroux should come again, it certainly will not be your Majesty that she will look for." The Queen burst into a fit of laughter at this observation; her agitation subsided, and she soon fell asleep.

The nomination of Madame le Normand d'Etioles, Marquise de Pompadour, to the place of lady of the bed-chamber to the Queen, offended the dignity, as well as the sensibility, of this princess. Nevertheless, the respectful homage paid by the Marchioness, the interest which certain great personages, who were candidates for her favour, had in procuring her an indulgent reception from her Majesty, the respect of Maria Leczinska for the King's wishes, all conspired to secure her the Queen's favourable notice. Madame de Pompadour's brother received Letters of Nobility from his Majesty, and was appointed superintendent of the buildings and gardens. He often presented to her Majesty, through the medium of his sister, the rarest flowers, pine-apples, and early vegetables from the gardens of Trianon and Choisy. One day, when the Marchioness came into the Queen's apartments, carrying a large basket of flowers, which she held in her two beautiful arms, without gloves, as a mark of respect, the Queen loudly declared her admiration of her beauty; and seemed as if she wished to defend the King's choice, by praising her various charms in detail, in a manner that would have been as suitable to a production of the fine arts as to a living being. After applauding the complexion, eyes, and fine arms of the favourite, with that haughty condescension which renders approbation more offensive than flattering, the Queen at length requested her to sing, in the attitude in which she stood, being desirous of hearing the voice and musical talent by which the King's Court had been charmed in the performances of the private apartments, and thus combining the gratification of the ears with that of the eyes. The Marchioness, who still held her enormous basket, was perfectly sensible of something offensive in this request, and tried to excuse herself from singing. The Queen at last commanded her; she then exerted her fine voice in the solo of Armida—"At length he is in my power." The change in her Majesty's countenance was so obvious that the ladies present at this scene had the greatest difficulty to keep theirs.

The Queen received visitors with much grace and dignity; but it is very common with the great to reiterate the same questions; a sterility of ideas is very excusable on public occasions, when there is so little to say. The lady of an ambassador, however, made her Majesty feel that she did not choose to give way to her forgetfulness in matters concerning herself. This lady was *enceinte*, but nevertheless constantly appeared at the Queen's drawing-rooms, who never failed to ask her whether she was in the state alluded to, and, on receiving an answer in the affirmative, always inquired how many months of her time had elapsed. At length the lady, weary of the eternal repetition of the same question, and of the total forgetfulness which betrayed the insincerity of the Queen in pretending to take interest in her affairs, replied to the usual inquiry, "No, Madame." This answer instantly recalled to her Majesty's recollection those which the lady had so often given before. "How, madame," said she, "it appears to me that you have several times answered me that you were so; have you been brought to bed?"—"No, Madame; but I was apprehensive of fatiguing your Majesty by constantly repeating the same thing." From that time she was very coldly received by Maria Leczinska, and had her Majesty possessed more influence, the ambassador might have suffered for his wife's indiscretion. The Queen was affable and modest; but the more she was thankful in her heart to Heaven for having placed her on the first throne in Europe, the more unwilling she was to be reminded of her elevation. This sentiment induced her to insist on the observation of all the forms of respect due to royal birth; whereas in other princes the consciousness of that birth often induces them to disdain the ceremonies of etiquette, and to prefer habits of ease and simplicity. There was a striking contrast in this respect between Maria Leczinska and Marie Antoinette, as has been justly and generally observed. The latter unfortunate Queen, perhaps, carried her disregard of everything belonging to the strict forms of etiquette too far.[11] One day, when the Maréchale de Mouchy was teasing her with questions relative to the extent to which she would allow the ladies the option of taking off or wearing their cloaks, and of pinning up the lappets of their caps, or letting them hang down, the Queen replied to her, in my presence: "Arrange all those matters, madame, just as you please; but do not imagine that a Queen, born Archduchess of Austria, can attach that importance to them which might be felt by a Polish princess, who had become Queen of France."

The Polish princess, in truth, never forgave the slightest deviation from the respect due to her person, and to all belonging to her. The Duchesse de ———, a lady of her bed-chamber, who was of an imperious and irritable temper, often drew upon herself such petty slights as are constantly shown towards haughty and ill-natured people by the servants of princes, when they can justify those affronts by the plea of their duty, or of the customs of the Court. Etiquette, or indeed I might say a sense of propriety, prohibited all persons from laying things belonging to them on the seats of the Queen's chamber. At Versailles, one had to cross this chamber to reach the play-room. The Duchesse de——— laid her cloak on one of the folding-stools, which stood before the balustrade of the bed. The usher of the chamber, whose duty it was to attend to whatever occurred in this room whilst they were at play, saw this cloak, took it, and carried it into the footmen's ante-chamber. The Queen had a large favourite cat, which was constantly running about the apartments. This satin cloak, lined with fur, appeared very convenient to the cat, who took possession of it accordingly. Unfortunately, he left very unpleasant marks of his preference, which remained but too evident on the white satin of the pelisse, in spite of all the pains that were taken to efface them before it was given to the Duchess. She perceived them, took the cloak in her hand, and returned in a violent passion to the Queen's chamber, where her Majesty remained surrounded by almost all the Court. "Only see, Madame," said she, "the impertinence of *your people*, who have thrown my pelisse on a bench in the antechamber, where your Majesty's cat has served it in this manner!" The Queen, displeased at her complaints and familiar expressions, said to her, with the coldest look imaginable: "Know, madame, that it is you, and not I, who keep *people*. I have officers of my chamber who have purchased the honour of serving me, and are persons of good breeding and education; they know the dignity which ought to belong to a lady of the bedchamber; they are not ignorant that you, who have been chosen from amongst the first ladies of the kingdom, ought to be accompanied by a gentleman, or at least a *valet de chambre* as his substitute, to receive your cloak; and that had you observed the forms suitable to your rank, you would not have been exposed to the mortification of seeing your things thrown on the benches of the antechamber."

Queen Maria Leczinska possessed great talents. Her religious, noble, and resigned conduct, and the refinement and judiciousness of her understanding, sufficiently prove that her august father had promoted with the most tender care the development of all those excellent qualities with which Heaven had endowed her.

The virtues and information of the great are always evinced by their conduct; their accomplishments, coming within the scope of flattery, are difficult to be ascertained by any authentic proofs, and those who have lived near them may be excused for some degree of scepticism with regard to their attainments of this kind. If they draw or paint, there is always an able artist present, who, if he does not absolutely guide the pencil with his own hand, directs it by his advice; he sets the palette, and mixes the colours, on which the tones depend. If a princess attempt a piece of embroidery in colours, of that description which ranks amongst the productions of the arts, a skilful embroider-ess is employed to undo and repair whatever has been spoilt, and to cover the neglected tints with new threads. If the princess be a musician, there are no ears that will discover when she is out of tune; at least there is no tongue that will tell her so. This imperfec-tion in the accomplishments of the great is but a slight misfortune. It is sufficiently meritorious in them to engage in such pursuits, even with indifferent success, because this taste and the protection it extends produce abundance of talent on every side. The Queen delighted in the art of painting, and imagined she herself could draw and paint. She had a drawing-master, who passed all his time in her cabinet. She undertook to paint four large Chinese pictures, with which she wished to ornament her private draw-ing-room, which was richly furnished with rare porcelain and the finest marbles. This painter was entrusted with the landscape and background of the pictures; he drew the figures with a pencil, the faces and arms were also left by the Queen to his execution; she reserved to herself nothing but the draperies, and the least important accessories. The Queen every morning filled up the outline marked out for her, with a little red, blue, or green colour, which the master prepared on the palette, and even filled her brush with, constantly repeating, "Higher, up, Madame—lower down, Madame—a little to the right—more to the left." After an hour's work, the time for hearing mass, or some other family or pious duty, would interrupt her Majesty; and the painter, putting the shadows into the draperies she had painted, softening off the colour where she had laid too much, etc., finished the small figures. When the work was completed the private drawing-room was decorated with her Majesty's work; and the firm persuasion of this good Queen that she had painted it herself was so entire that she left this cabinet, with all its furniture and paintings, to the Comtesse de Noailles, her lady of honour. She added to the bequest: "The pictures in my cabinet being my own work, I hope the Comtesse de Noailles will preserve them for my sake." Madame de Noailles, afterwards Maréchale de Mouchy, had a new additional pavilion constructed in her hotel in the Faubourg St Germain, in order to form a suitable receptacle for the Queen's legacy; and had the following inscription placed over the door, in letters of gold: "The innocent falsehood of a good princess."

The Queen had selected as her intimate friends the Duc, the Duchesse, and the wor-thy Cardinal de Luynes. She called them her good folks. She often did the Duchess the honour to spend the evening and sup with her. The President Henault was the charm of this pious and virtuous society. This magistrate combined the weighty qualifications of his functions in society with the attainments of a man of letters and the polish of a courtier. The Queen one day surprised the Duchess writing to the President, who had just published his *Chronological Abridgment of the History of France*. She took the pen from Madame de Luynes, and wrote at the bottom of the letter this postscript: "I think that M. de Henault, who says a great deal in few words, cannot be very partial to the language of women, who use a vast number of words to say very little." Instead of sign-ing this, she added, "Guess who." The President answered this anonymous epistle by these ingenious lines:[12]

This sentence, written by a heav'nly hand,
Fills with perplexing doubts my conscious mind;
Presumptuous, if I dare to understand;
Ungrateful, if I fail the truth to find.

One evening the Queen, having entered the cabinet of the Duc de Luynes, took down several books successively, to read the titles. A translation of Ovid's *Art of Love* having fallen into her hands, she replaced it hastily, exclaiming, "Oh, fie!" "How, Madame," said the President, "is that the way in which your Majesty treats the art of pleasing?" "No, Monsieur Henault," answered the Queen, "I should esteem the art of pleasing; it is the art of seducing that I cast from me."

Madame de Civrac, daughter of the Duc d'Aumont, lady of honour to Mesdames, belonged to this intimate circle of the Queen's. Her virtues and amiable character procured her equal esteem and affection in that circle and in her family, from which a premature death removed her. The President Henault paid her a respectful homage, or rather delighted in being the medium of that which that distinguished society eagerly rendered to her talents, her virtues, and her sufferings. Some time before the death of Madame de Civrac she was ordered to try the mineral waters. She left Versailles much debilitated, and in very bad health. The wish to amuse her during a journey which removed her to a distance from all that was dear to her, inspired the President with the idea of an entertainment, which was given to her at every place she stopped to rest at. Her friends set out before her, in order to be a few posts in advance, and prepare their disguises. When she stopped at Berris, the interesting traveller found a group of lords dressed in the costume of ancient French knights, accompanied by the best musicians of the King's chapel. They sang to Madame de Civrac some stanzas composed by the President, the first of which began thus:[13]

> Can nought your cruel flight impede?
> Must distant climes your charms adore?
> Why thus to other conquests speed,
> And leave our hearts enslav'd before?

At Nemours the same persons, dressed as village swains and nymphs, presented her with a rural scene, in which they invited her to enjoy the simple pleasures of the country. Elsewhere they appeared as burgesses and their wives, with the Mayor and town-clerk, and these disguises, continually varied and enlivened by the amiable ingenuity of the President, followed Madame de Civrac as far as the watering-place to which she was going. I read about this ingenious and affecting entertainment when I was young; I know not whether the manuscript has been preserved by the heirs of the President Henault. The candour and religious simplicity of the good Cardinal formed a striking contrast to the gallant and agreeable character of the President, and people would sometimes divert themselves with his simplicity without forgetting the respect due to him.

One of these instances, however, produced such happy results as to justify the good Cardinal in a singular misapplication of his well-meant piety. Unwilling to forget the homilies which he had composed in his youth, and as jealous of his works as the Archbishop of Grenada, who discharged Gil Blas, the Cardinal used to rise at five in the morning, every Sunday, during the residence of the Court at Fontainebleau (which town was in his diocese), and go to officiate at the parish church, where, mounting the pulpit, he repeated one of his homilies, all of which had been composed to exhort people of rank and fashion to return to the primitive simplicity suitable to true Christians. A few hundred peasants, sitting in their sabots, surrounded by the baskets in which they had carried vegetables or fruit to market, listened to his Eminence without understanding a single word of what he was saying to them. Some people belonging to the Court, happening to go to mass previously to setting out for Paris, heard his Eminence exclaiming, with truly pastoral vehemence: "My dear brethren, why do you carry luxury even to the foot of the sanctuary? Wherefore are these velvet cushions, these bags covered with laces and fringe, carried before you into the temple of the Lord? Abandon these sumptuous and magnificent customs, which you ought to regard as a cumbrous appendage to your rank, and to put away from you when you enter the presence of your divine Saviour." The fashionable hearers of these homilies mentioned them at Court; every one wished to hear them: ladies of the highest rank would be awakened at break of day to hear the Cardinal say mass; and thus his Eminence became speedily surrounded by a congregation to which his homilies were perfectly adapted.

Maria Leczinska could never look with cordiality on the Princess of Saxony, who married the Dauphin; but the attention, respect, and cautious behaviour of the Dauphiness at length made her Majesty forget that the princess was the daughter of a King who wore her father's crown. Nevertheless, when the great entertain a deep resentment, some marks of it will occasionally be observed by those who constantly surround them; and although the Queen now saw in the Princess of Saxony only a wife beloved by her son, and the mother of the prince destined to succeed to the throne; she never could forget that Augustus wore the crown of Stanislaus. One day an officer of her chamber, having undertaken to ask a private audience of her for the Saxon minister, and the Queen being unwilling to grant it, he persisted in his request, and entered to add that he should not have presumed to ask this favour of the Queen had not the minister been the ambassador of a member of the family. "Say of an *enemy* of the family," replied the Queen angrily; "and let him come in."

The Queen was very partial to the Princesse de Tallard, governess of the children of France. This lady, having attained an advanced age, came to take leave of her Majesty, and to acquaint her with the resolution she had taken to quit the world, and to place an interval between her life and dissolution. The Queen expressed much regret, endeavoured to dissuade her from this scheme, and, much affected at the thoughts of the sacrifice on which the princess had determined, asked her whither she intended to retire. "To the *entresols* of my hotel, Madame," answered Madame de Tallard.

Comte de Tessé, father of the last count of that name, who left no children, was first equerry to Queen Maria Leczinska. She esteemed his virtues, but often diverted herself at the expense of his simplicity. One day, when the conversation turned on the noble military actions by which the French nobility was distinguished, the Queen said to the Count: "And your family, M. de Tessé, has been famous, too, in the field." "Ah! Madame, we have all been killed in our masters' service!" "How rejoiced I am," replied the Queen, "that you have revived to tell me of it." The son of this worthy M. de Tessé was married to the amiable and highly gifted daughter of the Duc d'Ayen, afterwards Maréchale de Noailles. He was excessively fond of his daughter-in-law, and never could speak of her without emotion. The Queen, to please him, often talked to him about the young countess, and one day asked him which of her good qualities seemed to him most conspicuous. "Her gentleness, Madame, her gentleness," said he, with tears in his eyes; "she is so mild, so soft—as soft as a good carriage." "Well," said her Majesty, "that's an excellent comparison for a first equerry."

In 1730 Queen Maria Leczinska going to mass met old Marshal Villars, leaning on a wooden crutch, not worth fifteen pence. She rallied him about it, and the Marshal told her that he had used it ever since he had received a wound which obliged him to add this article to the equipments of the army. Her Majesty, smiling, said she thought this crutch so unworthy of him that she hoped to induce him to give it up. On returning home she despatched M. Campan to Paris with orders to purchase at the celebrated Germain's the handsomest cane, with a gold enamelled crutch, that he could find, and carry it without delay to Marshal Villars' hotel, and present it to him from her. He was announced accordingly, and fulfilled his commission. The Marshal, in attending him to the door, requested him to express his gratitude to the Queen, and said, that he had nothing fit to offer to an officer who had the honour to belong to her Majesty; but he begged him to accept of his old stick, and that his grandchildren would probably some day be glad to possess the cane with which he had commanded at Marchiennes and Denain. The known character of Marshal Villars appears in this anecdote; but he was not mistaken with respect to the estimation in which his stick would be held. It was thenceforth kept with veneration by M. Campan's family. On the 10th of August 1792 a house which I occupied on the Carrousel, at the entrance of the court of the Tuileries, was pillaged and nearly burned down. The cane of Marshal Villars was thrown into the Carrousel as of no value, and picked up by my servant. Had its old master been living at that period we should not have witnessed such a deplorable day.

The Queen's father died in consequence of being severely burnt by his fireside. Like almost all old men, he disliked those attentions which imply the decay of the faculties, and had ordered a *valet de chambre*, who wished to remain near him, to withdraw into the adjoining room; a spark set fire to a taffety dressing-gown wadded with cotton, which his daughter had sent him. The poor old prince, who entertained hopes of recovering from the frightful state into which this accident reduced him, wished to inform the Queen of it himself, and wrote her a letter evincing the playfulness of his disposition, as well as the courage of his soul, in which he said: "What consoles me is the reflection that I am burning for you." To the last moment of her life Maria Leczinska never parted with this letter, and her women often surprised her kissing a paper, which they concluded to be this last farewell of Stanislaus.[14]

1. When the news of the attempt made against the King's life became publicly known the populace evinced the greatest rage and despair. They assembled under the windows of Madame (de Pompadour), uttering threatening cries. She began to dread the fate of Madame de Châteauroux. Her friends every moment came in to bring her intelligence. Many only came out of curiosity, to see how she behaved. She did nothing but weep and faint by turns. Dr Quesnay saw the King five or six times a day. "There is nothing to fear," said he; "if it were any other person he might go to a ball." I told Madame that the Keeper of the Seals had had an interview with the King, from which he had returned to his own residence, followed by a crowd of people. "*And that is a friend!*" said she, bursting into tears. The Abbé Berris said

this was not a time to form a precipitate judgment of him. Half an hour afterwards I returned into the drawing-room. The Keeper of the Seals came in. "*How is Madame de Pompadour?*" said he, with a cold and severe air. "*As you may easily imagine,*" I replied; and he entered her apartment, where he remained half an hour alone with her. At length she rang; I went in, followed by the Abbé Berris. "I must go, my dear Abbé," said she. She gave orders for all her domestics to be ready to set out. To several ladies, who came to condole with her, she compared the conduct of M. de Machault, the Keeper of the Seals, with that of the Duc de Richelieu at Metz. "He believes, or pretends to believe," said she, "that the priests will require me to be sent away with disgrace; but Quesnay and all the physicians say there is not the slightest danger."

Madame de Mirepoix came in, crying out, "What are all these trunks for, Madame? Your servants say you are leaving us."—"Alas! my dear friend, such is the will of the master; at least so says M. de Machault."—"And what is his advice?" "To set out immediately."—"He wishes to be master himself," said Madame de Mirepoix, "and he is betraying you. Whoever leaves the game, loses it."

M. de Maurigy afterwards told me that an appearance of an intended departure would be kept up to avoid irritating the enemies of Madame; that the little Maréchale (Madame de Mirepoix) had decided the matter; and that the Keeper of the Seals would be the sufferer. Quesnay came in, and, with his usual grimaces, related a fable of a fox, who, being at dinner with other animals, persuaded one of them that his enemies were seeking him, and having induced him to withdraw, devoured his share in his absence. I did not see Madame until much later, when she was going to bed. She was more calm; affairs were improving. Machault, that faithless friend, was dismissed. The King came as usual to Madame. A few days afterwards Madame paid a visit to M. d'Argenson. She returned much out of temper, and the King shortly afterwards arrived. I heard Madame sobbing. The Abbé Berris came to me, and desired me to carry her some Hoffman's drops. The King himself prepared the Pétion with some sugar, and presented it to her with the most gracious air. She smiled and kissed his hands. I withdrew, and the next day heard of the exile of M. d'Argenson. He was much to blame, and this was the greatest stretch of Madame's influence. The King was very much attached to M. d'Argenson, and the war by sea and land rendered it very impolitic to discard these two ministers.—*Journal of Madame de Hausset.*

2. One day when the King was hunting in the forest of St Germain, Landsmath, riding before him, wanted a cart, filled with the slime of a pond, that had just been cleansed, to draw up out of the way. The carter resisted, and even answered with impertinence. Landsmath, without dismounting, seized him by the breast of his coat, lifted him up, and threw him into his cart.—*Madame Campan.*

3. "The King often talked about death, burials, and cemeteries," says Madame de Hausset: "nobody could be more melancholy by nature. Madame de Pompadour has often told me that he felt a painful sensation whenever he was forced to laugh, and that he often requested her to put an end to a diverting story. He smiled, and that was all. He had, in general, the most gloomy ideas on all events. When a new minister came into office, the King would say, 'He spread out his goods, like the rest, and promised the finest things in the world, of which will ever happen. He does not know how the land lies: he will see.' When schemes for increasing the naval force were proposed to him, he used to say,

'I have heard it talked of continually for the last twenty years; France will never have a navy, I believe.' I had this from M. de Maurigy."

4. Among the young ladies of very tender age with whom the King amused himself during the influence of Madame de Pompadour, or afterwards, there was also a Mademoiselle de Tiercelin, whom his Majesty ordered to take the name of Bonneval the very day she was presented to him. The King was the first who perceived this child, when not above nine years old, in the care of a nurse, in the garden of the Tuileries, one day when he went in State to his "good city of Paris"; and having, in the evening, spoken of her beauty to Le Bel, the servant applied to M. de Sartine, who traced her out, and bought her of the nurse for a few *louis*. She was daughter of M. de Tiercelin, a man of quality, who could not patiently endure an affront of this nature. He was, however, compelled to be silent; he was told his child was lost; and that it would be best for him to submit to the sacrifice, unless he wished to lose his liberty also.

Mademoiselle de Tiercelin, now become Madame de Bonneval, was introduced under that name into the private apartments at Versailles, by the King's desire. She was naturally very wild, and did not like his Majesty. "You are an ugly man," said she, throwing the jewels and diamonds which the King had given her out of the window. The Duc de Choiseul had the weakness to be jealous of this child and her father, who were equally harmless. He was told that the King of Prussia, being tired of Madame de Pompadour, was secretly labouring to get Mademoiselle de Tiercelin declared the King's mistress; the King certainly doted on her. The minister was assured that M. de Tiercelin was engaged in most extensive operations for effecting the object of this foreign intrigue. The father and daughter were in consequence separately confined in the Bastille.—*Anecdotes of the Reign of Louis XV*, by Soulavie.

5. The following, written with extraordinary impartiality by M. de Lacretelle, leaves no possible doubt as to the origin and extent of these scandalous practices:

"Louis, satiated with the conquests which the Court offered him, was led by a depraved imagination to form an establishment for his pleasures, of such an infamous description that, after having depicted the debaucheries of the regency, it is difficult to find terms appropriate to an excess of this kind. Several elegant houses, built in an enclosure called the Parc-aux-Cerfs, were used for the reception of women, who there awaited the pleasure of their master. Hither were brought young girls, sold by their parents, and sometimes forced from them. They left this place loaded with gifts, but almost certain of never more beholding the King who had dishonoured them, even when they bore with them a pledge of his base passion. Hence corruption found its way into the most peaceful and obscure habitations. It was skilfully and patiently fostered by those who ministered to the debaucheries of Louis. Whole years were occupied in the seduction of girls not yet of marriageable age, and in undermining the principles of modesty and fidelity in young women. Some of these victims were so unhappy as to feel a true affection and sincere attachment to the King. For a few minutes he would seem moved by their fidelity; but he quickly repressed such feelings, and persuaded himself that it was all artifice, intended to govern him; and he himself became the informer against them to the Marchioness, who soon forced her rivals back into their original obscurity. Mademoiselle de Romans was the only one who procured her son to be acknowledged as the King's child. Madame de Pompadour succeeded in removing a rival who seemed to have made so profound an impression on the King's heart. Mademoiselle de Romans had her son taken from her; he was brought up by a peasant, and his mother durst not protest against this outrage, until after the King's death. Louis XVI restored her her son, and took him under his protection; he was afterwards known under the name of the Abbé de Bourbon."—*History of France*, by Lacretelle, vol. iii.

6. In a kind of sedan chair, running on two wheels, and drawn by a chairman.

7. Madame one day called me into her cabinet, where the King was walking up and down with a very serious air. "You must," said she, "go and pass a few days in the Avenue of St Cloud, at a house which will be pointed out to you, where you will find a young lady ready to lie in. Like one of the goddesses of the poets, you will preside at the birth. The object of your mission is that everything may take place according to the King's wishes, and secretly. You will be present at the christening, and give the names of the father and mother." The King began to laugh, and said, "*The father is a very worthy man.*" Madame added, "*Beloved by all the world, and adored by all who are acquainted with him.*" Madame went to a drawer, and took out a little casket, which she opened, and produced a diamond aigrette, saying to the King, "I had reasons for not getting a finer one." "It is too handsome as it is," said the King, embracing Madame; "how kind you are!" She shed tears of emotion, and placing her hand on the King's heart, said, "It is there that my wishes are centred." Tears now came into the King's eyes also, nor could I refrain from crying, though I scarcely knew why. The King then said to me, "Guimard will see you every day to advise and assist you, and at the critical moment you will send for him. But we have said nothing about the godfather and godmother. You are to announce them, as if they were coming, and an instant afterwards you will pretend to receive a letter informing you that they cannot come. You will then pretend not to know what to do, and Guimard will say, 'The best way is to have anybody you can get.' You will then take the servant of the house, and some pauper or chairman, and give them only twelve francs to avoid attracting notice."—"A *louis*," interrupted Madame, "that you may not make mischief in another way."

When the King was gone Madame said to me, "Well, what do you think of my part in this affair?" "It is that of a superior woman and an excellent friend," said I. "It is his heart that I wish to possess," answered she; "and none of these little uneducated girls will deprive me of that. I should not be so tranquil if some beautiful woman of the Court were to attempt the conquest." I asked Madame whether the young lady knew that the father of the child was the King. "I do not think so," said she; "but as he seemed to love this one it is thought that there has been too much readiness to let her know it. Were it not for that it was to have been insinuated to the world that the father was a Polish nobleman related to the Queen, and that he had apartments in the Château."

After receiving some additional instructions I went to the Avenue of St Cloud, where I found the Abbess and Guimard, a servant belonging to the Château, with a nurse and assistant, two old domestics, and a girl, half housemaid, half *femme de chambre*. The young lady was extremely pretty and elegantly dressed, but had nothing very striking in her appearance. I supped with her and the *gouvernante*, called Madame Bertrand. I gave the lady the aigrette, which delighted her wonderfully. The next day I had a private conversation with her, when she asked me, "How is the Count [meaning the King]? He will be very sorry that he cannot be with me; but he has been obliged to take a long journey." I assented. "He is a very handsome man," continued she, "and loves me with all his heart; he has promised me an annuity, but I love him disinterestedly, and if he would take me I would go to Poland with him." She afterwards talked of her parents. "My mother," said she, "kept a great druggist's shop, and my father belonged to the six companies, and everyone knows there is nothing better than that; he was twice very near being sheriff."

Six days afterwards she was delivered of a boy, but was told, according to my instructions, that it was a girl; and soon afterwards that it was dead, in order that no trace of its existence might remain for a certain period, after which it was to be restored to its mother. The King gave ten or twelve thousand francs a year to each of his natural children, and they inherited from one another. Seven or eight had already died. When I returned Madame asked me many questions. "The King," said she, "is disgusted with his princess, and I fancy he will set out for Poland in two days." "And what will become of the young lady?" said I. "She will be married to some country gentleman," said she, "and she will have a fortune of forty thousand crowns or so and a few diamonds." This little adventure, which thus placed me in the King's confidence, far from procuring me marks of his kindness, seemed to make him behave more coolly towards me, for he was ashamed that I should be acquainted with his low amours. He was also embarrassed about the services which Madame rendered him.—*Journal of Madame de Hausset.*

8. A different account of this transaction will, however, be found in a footnote a few pages further on.

9. The Dauphin had for several years superintended the education of his three children, the Duc de Berri, afterwards Louis XVI, the Comte de Provence, and the Comte d'Artois.

The deportment of the Duc de Berri was austere, serious, reserved, and often rough; he had no taste for play, exhibitions, or amusements; he was a youth of inviolable veracity, constantly employing himself in copying, and afterwards composing geographical maps, and in filing iron. His father had shown a predilection for him, which excited the jealousy of his brothers. Madame Adelaide, who tenderly loved him, used to say, in order to encourage him and overcome his timidity, "*Speak out freely, Berri; shout, scold, make an uproar, like your brother d'Artois; knock down my china and break it; make some noise in the world.*" The young Duc de Berri only became the more silent, and could not lay aside his natural character.—*Historical and Political Memoirs of the Reign of Louis XVI*, by Soulavie, vol. ii.

10. In some *Memoirs of the Reign of Maria Leczinska*, it is said that she was to have been married to the Duc de Bourbon. I know not whether this be certain, but I can affirm that she has often conversed with Madame Campan, my mother-in-law, on the project of her marriage with the Duc d'Estrées.—*Madame Campan.*

11. Marie Antoinette has been so often reproached for having derogated from the strictness of old customs, that it is extremely necessary to answer this accusation, once for all, by facts. No once was ever more jealously observant of the laws of etiquette than Louis XIV, in whose latter years the prudery of Madame Maintenon rather tended to increase than to weaken this inclination. Let those, therefore, who cannot excuse the slightest fraction of ceremony in Marie Antoinette compare her conduct with that of the Duchess of Burgundy.

"This princess," says the Duchesse d'Orléans, in her Memoirs, "was often entirely alone in her Château, unattended by any of her people; she would take the arm of one of the young ladies, and walk out without equerries, lady of honour, or tire-woman. At Marly and Versailles she went on foot without a corset; would go into the church, and sit down by the *femmes de chambre.* At Madame de Maintenon's no distinction of rank was observed, and the whole company seated themselves indiscriminately; she contrived this purposely, that her own rank might not be remarked. At Marly the Dauphiness walked in the garden all night, with the young people, until three or four in the morning. The King knew nothing of these nocturnal excursions." Whence, then, the blame so unjustly thrown on Marie Antoinette, whilst a profound silence is maintained respecting the imprudence, to say no worse, of the Duchess of Burgundy? It is because the excessive mildness of Louis XVI encouraged audacity and calumny amongst the courtiers, whilst under Louis XIV, on the contrary, the most prompt chastisement would have been the lot of any daring individual who had ventured to point his malignant slanders at a personage placed near the throne. The Duchesse d'Orléans makes this sufficiently evident. "Madame de Maintenon," she adds, "had prohibited the Duchesse du Lude from annoying the Duchess of Burgundy, that she might not put her in an ill-humour; because, when out of temper, the Dauphiness could not divert the King. She had also threatened with her eternal anger whomsoever should dare to accuse the Dauphiness to his Majesty."—*Note by the Editor.*

12. Ces mots tracés par une main divine,

    Ne peuvent me causer que trouble et qu'embarras.

    C'est trop oser, si mon cœur les devine;

    C'est être ingrat, s'il ne les devine pas.

13. Quoi! vous partez sans que rien vous arête!

    Vous allez plaire en de nouveaux climates!

    Pourquoi voler de conquete en conquête?

    Nos cœurs soumis ne suffisent-ils pas?

14. This anecdote does honour to the heart and filial piety of Maria Leczinska. That princess was equally gifted with wit and sensibility, if we may judge by many expressions which fell from her lips in conversation, and have been collected by the Abbé Proyart. Many of them are remarkable for the depth of thought they display, and frequently for an ingenious and lively turn of expression:—

We should not be great but for the little. We ought to be so only for their good.

To be vain of one's rank is to declare one's self beneath it.

A king who enforces respect to God has no occasion to command homage to be paid to himself.

The mercy of kings is to do justice; and the justice of queens is to exercise mercy.

Good kings are slaves, and their subjects are free.

Content seldom travels with fortune, but follows virtue even in adversity.

Solitude can be delightful only to the innocent.

To consider one's self great on account of rank and wealth is to imagine that the pedestal makes the hero.

Many princes when dying have lamented having made war; we hear of none who at that moment have regretted having loved peace.

Sensible people judge of a head by what it contains; frivolous women by what is on the outside of it.

Courtiers cry out to us, '*Give us without reckoning!*' and the people, '*Reckon what we give you!*'

I

Court of Louis XV—His character—The King's débotter—Characters of Mesdames—Retreat of Madame Louise to the Carmelites of Saint Denis— Madame du Barry—The Court divided between the party of the Duc de Choiseul and that of the Duc d'Aiguillon

I was fifteen years of age when I was appointed reader to Mesdames. I will begin by describing the Court at that period.

Maria Leczinska was just dead; the death of the Dauphin had preceded hers by three years; the Jesuits were suppressed, and piety was to be found at Court only in the apartments of Mesdames. The Duc de Choiseul ruled.

The King thought of nothing but the pleasures of the chase; it might have been imagined that the courtiers indulged themselves in making epigrams by hearing them say seriously on those days when the King did not hunt, *The King does nothing today.*

Little journeys were also affairs of great importance with the King. On the first day of the year he noted down in his almanac the days of departure for Compiègne, Fontainebleau, Choisy, etc. The weightiest matters, the most serious events, never deranged this distribution of his time.

Etiquette still existed at Court with all the forms it had acquired under Louis XIV; dignity alone was wanting. As to gaiety, there was none. Versailles was not the place at which to seek for assemblies where French spirit and grace were displayed. The focus of wit and intelligence was Paris.

Since the death of the Marquise de Pompadour, the King had had no titled mistress; he contented himself with his *seraglio* in the Parc-aux-Cerfs. It is well known that the monarch found the separation of Louis de Bourbon from the King of France the most animating feature of his royal existence. They would have it so; they thought it for the best, was his way of expressing himself when the measures of his ministers were unsuccessful. The King delighted to manage the most disgraceful points of his private expenses himself; he one day sold to a head clerk in the war department a house in which one of his mistresses had lodged; the contract ran in the name of Louis de Bourbon; and the purchaser himself took in a bag the price of the house in gold to the King in his private closet.[1]

Louis XV saw very little of his family; he came every morning by a private staircase into the apartment of Madame Adelaide.[2] He often brought and drank there coffee that he had made himself. Madame Adelaide pulled a bell which apprised Madame Victoire of the King's visit; Madame Victoire, on rising to go to her sister's apartment, rang for Madame Sophie, who in her turn rang for Madame Louise. The apartments of Mesdames were of very large dimensions. Madame Louise occupied the farthest room. This latter lady was deformed and very short; the poor Princess used to run with all her might to join the daily meeting, but, having a number of rooms to cross, she frequently; in spite of her haste, had only just time to embrace her father before he set out for the chase.

Every evening at six Mesdames interrupted my reading to them to accompany the Princes to Louis XV; this visit was called the King's *débotter*,[3] and was marked by a kind of etiquette. Mesdames put on an enormous hoop, which set out a petticoat ornamented with gold or embroidery; they fastened a long train round their waists, and concealed the undress of the rest of their clothing by a long cloak of black taffety which enveloped them up to the chin. The *chevaliers d'honneur*, the ladies-in-waiting, the pages, the equerries, and the ushers bearing large flambeaux, accompanied them to the King. In a moment the whole palace, generally so still, was in motion; the King kissed each Princess on the forehead, and the visit was so short that the reading which it interrupted was frequently resumed at the end of a quarter of an hour; Mesdames returned to their apartments, and untied the strings of their petticoats and trains; they resumed their tapestry and I my book.

During the summer season the King sometimes came to the residence of Mesdames before the hour of his *débotter*. One day he found me alone in Madame Victoire's closet, and asked me where Coche[4] was; I stared, and he repeated his question, but without being at all the more understood. When the King was gone I asked Madame of whom he spoke. She told me that it was herself, and very coolly explained to me, that being the fattest of his daughters, the King had given her the familiar name of *Coche*, that he called Madame Adelaide, *Loque*,[5] Madame Sophie, *Graille*,[6] and Madame Louise, *Chiffe*.[7] The people of the King's household observed that he knew a great number of such words; possibly he had amused himself with picking them out from dictionaries. If this style of speaking betrayed the habits and tastes of the King, his manner savoured nothing of such vulgarity; his walk was easy and noble, he had a dignified carriage of the head, and his aspect, without being severe, was imposing; he combined great politeness with a truly regal demeanour, and gracefully saluted the humblest female whom curiosity led into his path.

He was very expert in a number of trifling matters which never occupy attention but when there is a lack of something better to employ it; for instance, he would knock off the top of an egg-shell at a single stroke of his fork, he therefore always ate eggs when he dined in public, and the Parisians who came on Sundays to see the King dine, returned home less struck with his fine figure than with the dexterity with which he broke his eggs.

Repartees of Louis XV, which marked the keenness of his wit and the elevation of his sentiments, were quoted with pleasure in the assemblies of Versailles.

This Prince was still beloved; it was wished that a style of life suitable to his age and dignity should at length supersede the errors of the past, and justify the love of his subjects. It was painful to judge him harshly. If he had established avowed mistresses at Court, the uniform devotion of the Queen was blamed for it. Mesdames were reproached for not seeking to prevent the King's forming an intimacy with some new favourite. Madame Henriette, twin sister of the Duchess of Parma, was much regretted, for she had considerable influence over the King's mind, and it was remarked that if she had lived she would have been assiduous in finding him amusements in the bosom of his family, would have followed him in his short excursions, and would have done the honours of the *petits soupers* which he was so fond of giving in his private apartments.

Mesdames too much neglected the means of pleasing the King, but the cause of that was obvious in the little attention he had paid them in their youth.

In order to console the people under their sufferings, and to shut their eyes to the real depredations on the treasury, the ministers occasionally pressed the most extravagant measures of reform in the King's household, and even in his personal expenses.

Cardinal Fleury, who in truth had the merit of re-establishing the finances, carried this system of economy so far as to obtain from the King the suppression of the household of the four younger Princesses. They were brought up as mere boarders in a convent eighty leagues distant from the Court: Saint Cyr would have been more suitable for the reception of the King's daughters; but probably the Cardinal shared some of those prejudices which will always attach to even the most useful institutions; and which, since the death of Louis XIV, had been raised against the noble establishment of Madame de Maintenon. Madame Louise often assured me that at twelve years of age she was not mistress of the whole alphabet, and never learned to read fluently until after her return to Versailles.

Madame Victoire attributed certain paroxysms of terror, which she was never able to conquer, to the violent alarms she experienced at the Abbey of Fontevrault, whenever she was sent, by way of penance, to pray alone in the vault where the sisters were interred.

A gardener belonging to the Abbey died raving mad. His habitation, without the walls, was near a chapel of the Abbey, where Mesdames were taken to repeat the prayers for those in the agonies of death. Their prayers were more than once interrupted by the shrieks of the dying man.

The most absurd indulgences were mixed with these cruel practices. Madame Adelaide, the eldest of the Princesses, was haughty and passionate; the good sisters never failed to give way to her ridiculous fancies. The dancing-master, the only professor of graceful accomplishments who had followed Mesdames to Fontevrault, was teaching them a dance then much in fashion, which was called *the rose-coloured minuet*. Madame Adelaide insisted that it should be named *the blue minuet*. The teacher resisted her whim, and urged that he should be laughed at at Court if the Princess should talk of a blue minuet. The Princess refused to take her lesson, stamped, and repeated, "*Blue, blue.*" "*Rose, rose,*" said the master. The sisterhood assembled to decide the important case; the nuns cried "*Blue*" with the Princess; the minuet was re-christened, and she danced. Among women so little worthy of the office of instructress, there was, however, one sister who, by her judicious tenderness, and by the useful proofs which she gave of it to Mesdames, entitled herself to their attachment, and obtained their gratitude; this was Madame de Soulanges, whom they afterwards caused to be appointed Abbess of Royal-Lieu.[8] They also took upon themselves the promotion of this lady's nephews; those of the Mother MacCarthy, who had weakly indulged her charges, carried for a long time the musket of the King's Guard at the door of Mesdames without the latter thinking of advancing their fortune.

When Mesdames, still very young, returned to Court, they enjoyed the friendship of Monseigneur the Dauphin, and profited by his advice. They devoted themselves ardently to study, and gave up almost the whole of their time to it; they enabled themselves to write French correctly, and acquired a good knowledge of history. Italian, English, the higher branches of mathematics, turning and dialling, filled up in succession their leisure moments. Madame Adelaide, in particular, had a most insatiable desire to learn; she was taught to play upon all instruments, from the horn (will it be believed!) to the Jew's harp.

Madame Adelaide was graced for a short time with a charming figure; but never did beauty so quickly vanish. Madame Victoire was handsome and very graceful; her address, mien, and smile were in perfect accordance with the goodness of her heart. Madame Sophie was remarkably ugly; never did I behold a person with so unprepossessing an appearance; she walked with the greatest rapidity; and, in order to recognise the people who placed themselves along her path without looking at them, she acquired the habit of leering on one side, like a hare. This Princess was so exceedingly diffident that a person might be with her daily for years together without hearing her utter a single word. It was asserted, however, that she displayed talent, and even amiability, in the society of some favourite ladies. She taught herself a great deal, but she studied alone; the presence of a reader would have disconcerted her very much. There were, however, occasions on which the Princess, generally so intractable, became all at once affable and condescending, and manifested the most communicative good nature; this would happen during a storm; so great was her alarm on such an occasion that she then approached the most humble, and would ask them a thousand obliging questions; a flash of lightning made her squeeze their hands; a peal of thunder would drive her to embrace them, but with the return of the calm, the Princess resumed her stiffness, her reserve, and her repulsive air, and passed all by without taking the slightest notice of any one, until a fresh storm restored to her at once her dread and her affability.

Mesdames found in a beloved brother, whose rare attainments are known to all Frenchmen, a guide in everything wanting to their education. In their august mother, Maria Leczinska, they possessed the noblest example of every pious and social virtue; that Princess, by her eminent qualities and her modest dignity, veiled the failings of the King, and while she lived she preserved in the Court of Louis XV that decorous and dignified tone which alone secures the respect due to power. The Princesses, her daughters, were worthy of her; and if a few degraded beings did aim the shafts of calumny at them, these shafts dropped harmless, warded off by the elevation of their sentiments and the purity of their conduct.

If Mesdames had not tasked themselves with numerous occupations, they would have been much to be pitied. They loved walking, but could enjoy nothing beyond the public gardens of Versailles; they would have cultivated flowers, but could have no others than those in their windows.

The Marquise de Durfort, since Duchesse de Civrac,[9] afforded to Madame Victoire agreeable society. The Princess spent almost all her evenings with that lady, and ended by fancying herself domiciled with her.

Madame de Narbonne had, in a similar way, taken pains to make her intimate acquaintance pleasant to Madame Adelaide.

Madame Louise had for many years lived in great seclusion; I read to her five hours a day; my voice frequently betrayed the exhaustion of my lungs, the Princess would then prepare sugared water for me, place it by me, and apologise for making me read so long, on the score of having prescribed a course of reading for herself.

One evening, while I was reading, she was informed that M. Bertin, *ministre des parties casuelles*, desired to speak with her; she went out abruptly, returned, resumed her silks and embroidery, and made me resume my book; when I retired she commanded me to be in her closet the next morning at eleven o'clock. When I got there the Princess was gone out; I learned that she had gone at seven in the morning to the Convent of the Carmelites of Saint Denis, where she was desirous of taking the veil. I went to Madame Victoire; there I heard that the King alone had been acquainted with Madame Louise's project; that he had kept it faithfully secret, and that, having long previously opposed her wish, he had only on the preceding evening sent her his consent; that she had gone alone into the convent, where she was expected; and that a few minutes afterwards she had made her appearance at the grating, to show the Princesse de Guistel, who had accompanied her to the convent gate, and to her equerry, the King's order to leave her in the monastery.

Upon receiving the intelligence of her sister's departure, Madame Adelaide gave way to violent paroxysms of rage, and reproached the King bitterly for the secret, which he had thought it his duty to preserve. Madame Victoire missed the society of her favourite sister, but she only shed tears in silence. The first time I saw this excellent Princess after Madame Louise's departure, I threw myself at her feet, kissed her hand, and asked her, with all the confidence of youth, whether she would quit us as Madame Louise had done. She raised me, embraced me, and said, pointing to the lounge upon which she was extended, "Make yourself easy, my dear; I shall never have Louise's courage. I love the conveniences of life too well; *this lounge is my destruction.*" As soon as I obtained permission to do so, I went to Saint Denis to see my late mistress; she deigned to receive me with her face uncovered, in her private parlour; she told me she had just left the wash-house, and that it was her turn that day to attend to the linen. "I much abused your youthful lungs for two years before the execution of my project," added she, "I knew that here I could read none but books tending to our salvation, and I wished to review all the historians that had interested me."

She informed me that the King's consent for her to go to Saint Denis had been brought to her while I was reading; she prided herself, and with reason, upon having returned to her closet without the slightest mark of agitation, though she said she felt so keenly that she could scarcely regain her hair. She added that moralists were right when they said that happiness does not dwell in palaces; that she had proved it; and that, if I desired to be happy, she advised me to come and enjoy a retreat in which the liveliest imagination might find full exercise in the contemplation of a better world. I had no palace, no earthly grandeur to sacrifice to God; nothing but the bosom of a united family; and it is precisely there that the moralists whom she cited have placed true happiness. I replied that, in private life, the absence of a beloved and cherished daughter would be too cruelly felt by her family. The Princess said no more on the subject.[10]

The seclusion of Madame Louise was attributed to various motives; some were unkind enough to suppose it to have been occasioned by her mortification at being, in point of rank, the last of the Princesses. I think I penetrated the true cause.

Her soul was lofty; she loved everything sublime; often while I was reading she would interrupt me to exclaim, "That is beautiful! that is noble!" There was but one brilliant action that she could perform—to quit a palace for a cell, and rich garments for a stuff gown. She achieved it.

I saw Madame Louise two or three times more at the grating. I was informed of her death by Louis XVI. "My aunt Louise," said he to me, "your old mistress, is just dead at Saint Denis. I have this moment received intelligence of it. Her piety and resignation were admirable, and yet the delirium of my good aunt recalled to her recollection that she was a princess, for her last words were, '*To paradise, haste, haste, full speed.*' No doubt she thought she was again giving orders to her equerry."[11]

Madame Victoire, good, sweet-tempered, and affable, lived with the most amiable simplicity in a society wherein she was much caressed: she was adored by her household. Without quitting Versailles, without sacrificing her easy chair, she fulfilled the duties of religion with punctuality, gave to the poor all that she possessed, and strictly observed Lent and the fasts. The table of Mesdames acquired a reputation for dishes of abstinence, spread abroad by the assiduous parasites at that of their *maître d'hôtel*. Madame Victoire was not indifferent to good living, but she had the most religious scruples respecting dishes of which it was allowable to partake at penitential times. I saw her one day exceedingly tormented by her doubts about a water-fowl, which was often served up to her during Lent. The question to be determined was, whether it was *maigre* or *gras*. She consulted a bishop, who happened to be of the party: the prelate immediately assumed the grave attitude of a judge who is about to pronounce sentence. He answered the Princess that, in a similar case of doubt, it had been resolved that after dressing the bird it should be pricked over a very cold silver dish: if the gravy of the animal congealed within a quarter of an hour, the creature was to be accounted flesh; but if the gravy remained in an oily state, it might be eaten without scruple. Madame Victoire immediately made the experiment: the gravy did not congeal; and this was a source of great joy to the Princess, who was very partial to that sort of game. The abstinence which so much occupied the attention of Madame Victoire was so disagreeable to her, that she listened with impatience for the midnight hour of Holy Saturday being struck; and then she was immediately supplied with a good dish of fowl and rice, and sundry other succulent viands. She confessed with such amiable candour her taste for good cheer and the comforts of life, that it would have been necessary to be as severe in principle as insensible to the excellent qualities of the Princess, to consider it a crime in her.

Madame Adelaide had more mind than Madame Victoire; but she was altogether deficient in that kindness which alone creates affection for the great: abrupt manners, a harsh voice, and a short way of speaking, rendered her more than imposing. She carried the idea of the prerogative of rank to a high pitch. One of her chaplains was unlucky enough to say *Dominus vobiscum* with rather too easy an air: the Princess rated him soundly for it after mass, and told him to remember that he was not a bishop, and not again to think of officiating in the style of a prelate.

Mesdames lived quite separate from the King. Since the death of Madame de Pompadour he had lived alone. The enemies of the Duc de Choiseul did not know in what department, nor through what channel they could prepare and bring about the downfall of the man who stood in their way, The King was connected only with women of so low a class that they could not be made use of for any delicate intrigue; moreover the Parc-aux-Cerfs was a seraglio, the beauties of which were often replaced; it was desirable to give the King a mistress who could form a circle, and in whose draw-ing-room the long-standing attachment of the King for the Duc de Choiseul might be overcome. It is true that Madame du Barry was selected from a class sufficiently low. Her origin, her education, her habits, and everything about her bore a character of vulgarity and shamelessness; but by marrying her to a man whose pedigree dated from 1400, it was thought scandal would be avoided. The conqueror of Mahon conducted this coarse intrigue.[12] Such a mistress was judiciously selected for the diversion of the latter years of a man weary of grandeur, fatigued with pleasure, and cloyed with volup-tuousness. Neither the wit, the talents, the graces of the Marquise de Pompadour, her beauty, nor even her love for the King, would have had any further influence over that worn-out being.

He wanted a Roxalana of familiar gaiety, without any respect for the dignity of the sovereign. Madame du Barry one day so far forgot propriety as to desire to be present at a Council of State. The King was weak enough to consent to it. There she remained ridiculously perched upon the arm of his chair, playing all sorts of childish monkey tricks, calculated to please an old sultan.

Another time she snatched a packet of sealed letters from the King's hand. Among them she had observed one from Comte de Broglie. She told the King that she knew that rascal Broglie spoke ill of her to him, and that for once, at least, she would make sure he should read nothing respecting her. The King wanted to get the packet again; she resisted, and made him run two or three times round the table, which was in the middle of the Council chamber, and then, on passing the fireplace, she threw the let-ters into the grate, where they were consumed. The King became furious: he seized his audacious mistress by the arm, and put her out of the door without speaking to her. Madame du Barry thought herself utterly disgraced; she returned home, and remained two hours, alone, abandoned to the utmost distress. The King went to her: she threw herself at his feet, in tears, and he pardoned her.

Madame la Maréchale de Beauvau, the Duchesse de Choiseul, and the Duchesse de Grammont had renounced the honour of the King's intimate acquaintance rather than share it with Madame du Barry. But a few years after the death of Louis XV, Madame la Maréchale, being alone at the Val, a house belonging to M. de Beauvau, Mademoiselle de Dillon saw the Countess's calash take shelter in the forest of Saint Germain during a violent storm. She invited her in, and the Countess herself related these particulars, which I had from Madame de Beauvau.[13]

The Comte du Barry, surnamed *le roué* (the profligate), and Mademoiselle du Barry[14] advised, or rather prompted, Madame du Barry in furtherance of the plans of the party of the Maréchal de Richelieu and the Duc d'Aiguillon. Sometimes they even set her to act in such a way as to have a useful influence upon great political measures. Under pretence that the page who accompanied Charles I in his flight was a *du Barry* or *Barrymore*, they persuaded the Comtesse du Barry to buy in London that fine portrait which we now have in the Museum. She had the picture placed in her drawing-room, and when she saw the King hesitating upon the violent measure of breaking up his Parliament, and forming that which was called the Maupeou Parliament, she desired him to look at the portrait of a king who had given way to his Parliament.[15]

The men of ambition who were labouring to overthrow the Duc de Choiseul strengthened themselves by their concentration at the house of the favourite, and succeeded in their project. The bigots, who never forgave that minister the suppression of the Jesuits, and who had always been hostile to a treaty of alliance with Austria, influenced the minds of Mesdames. The Duc de La Vauguyon, the young Dauphin's governor, infected them with the same prejudices.

Such was the state of the public mind when the young Archduchess Marie Antoinette arrived at the Court of Versailles, just at the moment when the party which brought her there was about to be overthrown.

Madame Adelaide openly avowed her dislike to a princess of the House of Austria; and when M. Campan went to receive his orders, at the moment of setting off with the household of the Dauphiness, to go and receive the Archduchess upon the frontiers, she said she disapproved of the marriage of her nephew with an archduchess; and that, if she had the direction of the matter, she would not send for an Austrian.

1. Until recently little was known about the Parc-aux-Cerfs, and it was believed that a great number of girls had been maintained there at enormous expense. The investigations of M. J. A. Le Roi, Conservateur de la Bibliothèque de Versailles, given in his interesting work, *Curiosités Historiques sur Louis XIII, Louis XIV, Louis XV,* etc. (Paris, Plon, 1864), have cleared up the matter, the result he arrives at (see p. 229 of his work) is that the house in question was No. 4 Rue Saint Médéric in the quarter built on the site of the Parc-aux-Cerfs, or breeding-place for deer, of Louis XIII; in 1755 this house was very small, and placed in a lane which was not a thoroughfare, and with only one house near it, and that without windows in its direction; it belonged to Jean Michel Denis Crémer, a bourgeois of Paris, and on 25th November 1755 was bought by an usher of the Châtelet of Paris, François Vallet, who the same day declared before notaries that the purchase had really been made by the King—*Pour et au profit du Roi.* The house was held by the King from 1755 to 1771. It has since been enlarged, but at that time was very small, and could only have held one girl, the woman in charge of her, and a servant. Most of the girls only left it when about to be confined, and it sometimes stood vacant for five or six months. It may have been rented before the date of purchase, and other houses seem sometimes to have been used also; but in any case, it is evident that both the number of girls and the expense incurred have been absurdly exaggerated. The system flourished under Madame de Pompadour, but ceased as soon as Madame du Barry obtained full power over the King, and the house was then sold to M. J. B. Sévin for 16,000 livres, on 27th May 1771, —Louis not acting under the name of *Louis de Bourbon,* but as King: *Vente par le Roi, notre Sire.* Thus, in this case at least, Madame Campan is in error in saying that the King made the contract as Louis de Bourbon.

2. Louis XV seemed to feel for Madame Adelaide the tenderness he had had for the Duchess of Burgundy, his mother, who perished so suddenly under the eyes and almost in the arms of Louis XIV. The birth of Madame Adelaide, 23rd March 1732, was followed by that of Madame Victoire-Louise-Mare-Thérèse on the 11th May 1773. Louis had, besides, six daughters, Mesdames Sophie and Louise, who are mentioned in this chapter; the Princesses Marie and Felicité, who died young; Madame Henriette, died at Versailles in 1752, aged twenty-four; and finally, Madame the Duchess of Parma, who also died at the Court. See the *Life of Maria Leczinska* by the Abbé Proyart—*Note by the Editor*.

3. *Débotter*, meaning the time of unbooting.

4. Meaning an old sow, or a fat woman.

5. Rag

6. Scrap.

7. Bad silk or stuff.

8. This excellent woman fell a victim to the Revolutionary madness. She and her numerous sisters were led to the scaffold on the same day. While leaving the prison, they all chanted the *Veni Creator* upon the fatal car. When arrived at the place of punishment, they did not interrupt their strains. One head fell, and ceased to mix its voice with the celestial chorus—but the strain continued. The Abbess suffered last; and her single voice, with increased tone, still raised the devout versicle. It ceased suddenly—it was the silence of death!—*Madame Campan*.

9. Grandmother of two heroes of La Vendée, Lescure and La Roche-Jaquelin, by the marriage of her eldest daughter with M. d'Onissan; and of the unfortunate Labédoyère, by the marriage of her second daughter with M. de Chastellux.—*Madame Campan*.

10. *Les Souvenirs de Félicie* contain the account of a visit to Saint Denis made by Madame de Genlis:—"Madame Louise permitted questions, and answered them shortly but kindly. I wanted to know what in her new state she found the hardest to accustom herself to. 'You would never guess it,' answered she, smiling; 'it is to descend alone a back staircase. At first,' added she, 'it was to me the most fearful precipice. I was obliged to seat myself on the steps, and slide down in order to descend.' In fact, a Princess who had only descended the grand marble staircase of Versailles, leaning on the arm of her *chevalier d'honneur*, and surrounded by her pages, would tremble at finding herself left alone on a steep spiral staircase. She knew long before all the austerities of the religious life. For ten years she had secretly practised most of them in the Château of Versailles, but she had never thought of small staircases. This may well cause reflection on the education, ridiculous on so many accounts, that persons of this rank generally receive, who, always followed, helped, escorted, prompted, guarded from their childhood, are thus deprived of the greatest part of the faculties that nature has given them."

11. The retirement of Madame Louise, and her removal from Court, had only served to give her up entirely to the intrigues of the clergy. She received incessant visits from bishops, archbishops, and ambitious priests of every rank; she prevailed on the King, her father, to grant many ecclesiastical preferments, and probably looked forward to playing an important part when the King, weary of his licentious course of life, should begin to think of religion. This, perhaps, might have been the case had not a sudden and unexpected death put an end to his career. The project of Madame Louise fell to the ground in consequence of this event. She remained in her convent, from whence she continued to solicit favours, as I knew from the

complaints of the Queen, who often said to me, "Here is another letter from my aunt Louise. She is certainly the most intriguing little Carmelite in the kingdom." The Court went to visit her about three times a year, and I recollect that the Queen, intending to take her daughter there, ordered me to get a doll dressed like a Carmelite for her, that the young Princess might be accustomed, before she went into the convent, to the habit of her aunt the nun.—*Madame Campan.*

12. It appeared at this period as if every feeling of dignity was lost. "Few noblemen of the French Court," says a writer of the time, "preserved themselves from the general corruption. The Maréchal de Brissac was one of the latter. He was bantered on the strictness of his principles of honour and honesty; it was thought strange that he should be offended at being thought, like so many others, exposed to hymeneal disgrace. Louis XV, who was present, and laughed at his angry fit, said to him: 'Come, M. de Brissac, don't be angry; 'tis but a trifling evil; take courage.' 'Sire,' replied M. de Brissac, 'I possess all kinds of courage, except that which can brave shame.'"—*Note by the Editor.*

13. Chamfort gives a different version of Madame du Barry's visit to the Val.

   "Madame du Barry," says he, "being at Vincennes, was curious to see the Val. Madame de Beauvau was amused at the idea of going there and doing the honours. She talked of what had happened under Louis XV. Madame du Barry was complaining of various matters, which appeared to show that she was personally detested. 'By no means,' said Madame de Beauvau, 'we aimed at nothing but your place.' After this frank confession Madame du Barry was asked if Louis XV did not say a great deal against her (Madame de Beauvau) and Madame de Grammont. 'Oh! a great deal.'—'Well, and what of me, for instance?'—'Of you, madame? That you are haughty and intriguing, and that you lead your husband by the nose.' M. de Beauvau was present. The conversation was soon changed."—*Note by the Editor.*

14. The Comte Jean du Barry and Mademoiselle Claire du Barry, brother and sister-in law of Madame du Barry.

15. The *Memoirs of General Dumouriez*, vol. i, p. 142, contain some curious particulars about Madame du Barry; and novel details respecting her will be found at p. 243 of *Curiosités Historiques*, by J.A. Le Roi (Paris, Plon, 1864). His investigations lead to the result that her real name was Jeanne Bécu, born, 19th August 1743, at Vaucouleurs, the natural daughter of Anne Bécu, otherwise known as "Quantiny". Her mother afterwards married Nicolas Rancon. Comte Jean du Barry met her among the demi-monde, and succeeded, about 1767, and by the help of his friend Lebel, the *valet de chambre* of Louis XV, in introducing her to the King under the name of "Mademoiselle l'Ange". To be formally mistress a husband had to be found. The Comte Jean du Barry, already married himself, found no difficulty in getting his brother, Comte Guillaume, a poor officer of the marine troops, to accept the post of husband. In the marriage-contract, signed on 23rd July 1768, she was described as the daughter of Anne Bécu and of an imaginary first husband, "Sieur Jean-Jacques Gomard de VauBerriier", and three years were taken off her age. The marriage-contract was so drawn as to leave Madame du Barry entirely free from all control by her husband. The marriage was solemnised on 1st September 1768, after which the nominal husband returned to Toulouse. Madame du Barry in later years provided for him; and in 1772, tired of his applications, she obtained an act of separation from him. He married later Jeanne Madeleine Lemoine, and died in 1811. Madame du Barry took care of her mother, who figured as Madame de Montrable. In all she received from the King, Monsieur Le Roi calculates, about 12.5 million

of livres. On the death of Louis XV she had to retire first to the Abbey of Pont-aux-Dames, near Meaux, then she was allowed to go to her small house at Saint Vrain, near Arpajon, and finally, in 1775, to her Château at Louveciennes. Much to her credit be it said, she retained many of her friends, and was on the most intimate terms till his death with the Duc de Brissac (Louis-Hercule-Timoleon de Cossé-Brissac), who was killed at Versailles in the massacre of the prisoners in September 1792, leaving at his death a large legacy to her. Even the Emperor Joseph visited her. In 1791 many of her jewels were stolen and taken to England. This caused her to make several visits to that country, where she gained her suit. But these visits, though she took every precaution to legalise them, ruined her. Betrayed by her servants, among them by Zamor, the negro page, she was brought before the Revolutionary Tribunal, and was guillotined on 8th December 1793, in a frenzy of terror, calling for mercy and for delay up to the moment when her head fell.

II

Birth of Marie Antoinette attended by a memorable calamity—Maria Theresa's character—Education of the Archduchesses—Preceptors provided for Marie Antoinette by the Court of Vienna—Preceptor sent her by the Court of France—Abbé de Vermond—Change in the French Ministry— Cardinal de Rohan succeeds Baron de Breteuil as Ambassador at Vienna—Portrait of that Prelate

Marie-Antoinette-Josèphe-Jeanne de Lorraine, Archduchess of Austria, daughter of Francis of Lorraine and of Maria Theresa, was born on the 2nd of November 1755, the day of the earthquake at Lisbon; and this catastrophe, which appeared to stamp the era of her birth with a fatal mark, without forming a motive for superstitious fear with the Princess, nevertheless made an impression upon her mind. As the Empress already had a great number of daughters, she ardently desired to have another son, and playfully wagered against her wish with the Duc de Tarouka, who had insisted that she would give birth to an archduke. He lost by the birth of the Princess, and had executed in porcelain a figure with one knee bent on the earth, and presenting tablets, upon which the following verses by the celebrated Metastasio were engraved:—

> I lose by your fair daughter's birth
> Who prophesied a son
> But if she share her mother's worth,
> Why, all the world has won!'

The Queen was fond of talking of the first years of her youth. Her father, the Emperor Francis, had made a deep impression upon her heart; she lost him when she was scarcely seven years old. One of those circumstances which fix themselves strongly in the memories of children frequently recalled his last caresses to her. The Emperor was setting out for Innspruck; he had already left his palace, when he ordered a gentleman to fetch the Archduchess Marie Antoinette, and bring her to his carriage. When she came, he stretched out his arms to receive her, and said, after having pressed her to his bosom, "I wanted to embrace this child once more." The Emperor died suddenly during the journey, and never saw his beloved daughter again.

The Queen often spoke of her mother, and with profound respect, but she based all her schemes for the education of her children on the essentials which had been neglected in her own. Maria Theresa, who inspired awe by her great qualities, taught the Archduchesses to fear and respect rather than to love her; at least I observed this in the Queen's feelings towards her august mother. She therefore never desired to place between her own children and herself that distance which had existed in the Imperial family. She cited a fatal consequence of it, which had made such a powerful impression upon her that time had never been able to efface it.

The wife of the Emperor Joseph II was taken from him in a few days by an attack of smallpox of the worst kind. Her coffin had recently been deposited in the vault of the Imperial family. The Archduchess Josepha, who had been betrothed to the King of Naples, at the instant she was quitting Vienna received an order from the Empress not to set off without having offered up a prayer in the vault of her forefathers. The Archduchess, persuaded that she should take the disorder to which her sister-in-law had just fallen a victim, looked upon this order as her death-warrant. She loved the young Archduchess Marie Antoinette tenderly; she took her upon her knees, embraced her with tears, and told her she was about to leave her, not for Naples, but never to see her again; that she was going down then to the tomb of her ancestors, and that she should shortly go again there to remain. Her anticipation was realised; confluent smallpox carried her off in a very few days, and her youngest sister ascended the throne of Naples in her place.

The Empress was too much taken up with high political interests to have it in her power to devote herself to maternal attentions. The celebrated Wansvietten, her physician, went daily to visit the young Imperial family, and afterwards to Maria Theresa, and gave the most minute details respecting the health of the Archdukes and Archduchesses, whom she herself sometimes did not see for eight or ten days at a time. As soon as the arrival of a stranger of rank at Vienna was made known, the Empress brought her family about her, admitted them to her table, and by this concerted meeting induced a belief that she herself presided over the education of her children.

The chief governesses, being under no fear of inspection from Maria Theresa, aimed at making themselves beloved by their pupils by the common and blameable practice of indulgence, so fatal to the future progress and happiness of children. Marie Antoinette was the cause of her governess being dismissed, through a confession that all her copies, and all her letters, were invariably first traced out with pencil; the Comtesse de Brandès was appointed to succeed her, and fulfilled her duties with great exactness and talent. The Queen looked upon having been confided to her care so late as a misfortune, and always continued upon terms of friendship with that lady. The education of Marie Antoinette was certainly very much neglected.[2] The public prints, however, teemed with assertions of the superior talents of Maria Theresa's children. They often noticed the answers which the young Princesses gave in Latin to the harangues addressed to them; they uttered them, it is true, but without understanding them; they knew not a single word of that language.

Mention was one day made to the Queen of a drawing made by her, and presented by the Empress to M. Gérard, chief clerk of Foreign Affairs, on the occasion of his going to Vienna to draw up the articles for her marriage-contract. "I should blush," said she, "if that proof of the quackery of my education were shown to me. I do not believe that I ever put a pencil upon that drawing." However, what had been taught her she knew perfectly well. Her facility of learning was inconceivable, and if all her teachers had been as well informed and as faithful to their duty as the Abbé Metastasio, who taught her Italian, she would have attained as great a superiority in the other branches of her education. The Queen spoke that language with grace and ease, and translated the most difficult poets. She did not write French correctly, but she spoke it with the greatest fluency, and even affected to say that she had lost German. In fact she attempted in 1787 to learn her mother-tongue, and took lessons assiduously for six weeks; she was obliged to relinquish them, finding all the difficulties which a Frenchwoman, who should take up the study too late, would have to encounter. In the same manner she gave up English, which I had taught her for some time, and in which she had made rapid progress. Music was the accomplishment in which the Queen most delighted. She did not play well on any instrument, but she had become able to read at sight like a first-rate professor. She attained this degree of perfection in France, this branch of her education having been neglected at Vienna as much as the rest. A few days after her arrival at Versailles, she was introduced to her singing-master, La Garde, author of the opera of *Eglé*. She made a distant appointment with him, needing, as she said, rest after the fatigues of the journey and the numerous fêtes which had taken place at Versailles; but her motive was her desire to conceal how ignorant she was of the rudiments of music. She asked M. Campan whether his son, who was a good musician, could give her lessons secretly for three months. "The Dauphiness," added she, smiling, "must be careful of the reputation of the Archduchess." The lessons were given privately, and at the end of three months of constant application she sent for M. la Garde, and surprised him by her skill.

The desire to perfect Marie Antoinette in the study of the French language was probably the motive which determined Maria Theresa to provide for her as teachers two French actors; Aufresne, for pronunciation and declamation, and Sainville for taste in French singing; the latter had been an officer in France, and bore a bad character. The choice gave just umbrage to our Court. The Marquis de Durfort, at that time ambassador at Vienna, was ordered to make a representation to the Empress upon her selection. The two actors were dismissed, and the Princess required that an ecclesiastic should be sent to her. Several eminent ecclesiastics declined taking upon themselves so delicate an office; others who were pointed out by Maria Theresa (among the rest the Abbé Grisel) belonged to parties which sufficed to exclude them.

The Archbishop of Toulouse, since Archbishop of Sens,[3] one day went to the Duc de Choiseul at the moment when he was really embarrassed upon the subject of this nomination; he proposed to him the Abbé de Vermond, librarian of the College des Quatre Nations. The eulogistic manner in which he spoke of his *protégé* procured the appointment for the latter on that very day; and the gratitude of the Abbé de Vermond towards the prelate was very fatal to France, inasmuch as after seventeen years of persevering attempts to bring him into the ministry, he succeeded at last in getting him named Comptroller-General and President of the Council.

This Abbé de Vermond directed almost all the Queen's actions. He established his influence over her at an age when impressions are most durable and it was easy to see that he had taken pains only to render himself beloved by his pupil, and had troubled himself very little with the care of instructing her. He might have even been accused of having, by a sharp-sighted though culpable policy, purposely left her in ignorance. Marie Antoinette spoke the French language with much grace, but wrote it less perfectly. The Abbé de Vermond revised all the letters which she sent to Vienna. The insupportable folly with which he boasted of it displayed the character of a man more flattered at being admitted into her intimate secrets than anxious to fulfil worthily the high office of her preceptor.[4]

His pride received its birth at Vienna, where Maria Theresa, as much to give him authority with the Archduchess as to make herself acquainted with his character, permitted him to mix every evening with the private circle of her family, into which the future Dauphiness had been admitted for some time. Joseph II, the elder Archduchesses, and a few noblemen honoured by the confidence of Maria Theresa, composed the party; and reflections on the world, on courts, and the duties of princes, were the usual topics of conversation. The Abbé de Vermond, in relating these particulars, confessed the means which he had made use of to gain admission into this private circle. The Empress, meeting him at the Archduchess's, asked him if he had formed any connections in Vienna? "None, Madame," replied he; "the apartment of the Archduchess and the hotel of the ambassador of France are the only places which the man honoured with the care of the Princess's education should frequent." A month afterwards Maria Theresa, through a habit common enough among sovereigns, asked him the same question, and received precisely the same answer. The next day he received an order to join the Imperial family every evening.

It is extremely probable, from the constant and well-known intercourse between this man and Comte de Mercy, ambassador of the Empire during the whole reign of Louis XVI, that he was useful to the Court of Vienna,[5] and that he often caused the Queen to decide on measures, the consequences of which she did not consider. Born in a low class of citizens,[6] imbued with all the principles of the modern philosophy, and yet holding to the hierarchy of the Church more tenaciously than any other ecclesiastic; vain, talkative, and at the same time cunning and abrupt; very ugly and affecting singularity; treating the most exalted persons as his equals, sometimes even as his inferiors, the Abbé de Vermond received ministers and bishops when in his bath; but said at the same time that Cardinal Dubois was a fool; that a man such as he, having obtained power, ought to make cardinals, and refuse to be one himself.

Intoxicated with the reception he had met with at the Court of Vienna, and having till then seen nothing of grandeur, the Abbé de Vermond admired no other customs than those of the Imperial family; he ridiculed the etiquette of the House of Bourbon incessantly; the young Dauphiness was constantly incited by his sarcasms to get rid of it, and it was he who first induced her to suppress an infinity of practices of which he could discern neither the prudence nor the political aim. Such is the faithful portrait of that man whom the evil star of Marie Antoinette had reserved to guide her first steps upon a stage so conspicuous and so full of danger as that of the Court of Versailles.

It will be thought, perhaps, that I draw the character of the Abbé de Vermond too unfavourably; but how can I view with any complacency one who, after having arrogated to himself the office of confidant and sole counsellor of the Queen, guided her with so little prudence, and gave us the mortification of seeing that Princess blend, with qualities which charmed all that surrounded her, errors alike injurious to her glory and her happiness?

While M. de Choiseul, satisfied with the person whom M. de Brienne had presented, despatched him to Vienna with every eulogium calculated to inspire unbounded confidence, the Marquis de Durfort sent off a hairdresser and a few French fashions; and then it was thought sufficient pains had been taken to form the character of a Princess destined to share the throne of France.

It is universally known that the marriage of Monseigneur the Dauphin with the Archduchess was determined upon during the administration of the Duc de Choiseul. The Marquis de Durfort, who was to succeed the Baron de Breteuil in the embassy to Vienna, was appointed proxy for the marriage ceremony; but six months after the Dauphin's marriage the Duc de Choiseul was disgraced, and Madame de Marsan and Madame de Guéménée, who grew more powerful through the Duke's disgrace, conferred that embassy upon Prince Louis de Rohan, afterwards cardinal and grand almoner.

Hence it will be seen that the *Gazette de France* is a sufficient answer to those libellers, who dared to assert that the young Archduchess was acquainted with the Cardinal de Rohan before the period of her marriage. A worse selection in itself, or one more disagreeable to Maria Theresa, than that which sent to her in quality of ambassador a man so frivolous and so immoral as Prince Louis de Rohan could not have been made. He possessed but superficial knowledge upon any subject, and was totally ignorant of diplomatic affairs. His reputation had gone before him to Vienna, and his mission opened under the most unfavourable auspices. In want of money, and the House of Rohan being unable to make him any considerable advances, he obtained from his Court a patent which authorised him to borrow the sum of 600,000 livres upon his benefices, ran in debt above a million, and thought to dazzle the city and Court of Vienna by the most indecent and ill-judged extravagance. He formed a suite of eight or ten gentlemen of names sufficiently high-sounding; twelve pages equally well born, a crowd of officers and servants, a company of chamber musicians, etc. But this idle pomp did not last; embarrassment and distress soon showed themselves; his people, no longer receiving pay, in order to make money abused the privileges of ambassadors, and smuggled[7] with so much effrontery, that Maria Theresa, to put a stop to it without offending the Court of France, was compelled to suppress the privileges in this respect of all the diplomatic bodies, a step which rendered the person and conduct of Prince Louis odious in every foreign Court. He seldom obtained private audiences from the Empress, who did not esteem him, and who expressed herself without reserve upon his conduct both as a bishop and as an ambassador. He thought to obtain favour by assisting to effect the marriage of the Archduchess Elizabeth, the elder sister of Marie Antoinette, with Louis XV, an affair which was awkwardly undertaken, and of which Madame du Barry had no difficulty in causing the failure. I have deemed it my duty to omit no particular of the moral and political character of a man whose existence was subsequently so injurious to the reputation of Marie Antoinette.

1. Io perdei: l'augusta figlia
    A pagar m'a condannato;
    Ma s'è ver che a voi somiglia,
    Tutto il mondo ha guadagnato.

2. With the exception of the Italian language, all that related to *belles lettres*, and particularly to history, even that of her own country, was almost entirely unknown to her. This was soon found out at the Court of France, and thence arose the generally received opinion that she was deficient in sense. It will be seen, however, in the course of these memoirs, whether that opinion was well or ill-founded.—*Madame Campan.*

3. Étienne de Loménie, Comte de Brienne (1727–94), afterwards Archbishop of Toulouse and Archbishop of Sens.

4. The Abbé de Vermond encouraged the impatience of etiquette shown by Marie Antoinette while she was Dauphiness. When she became Queen he endeavoured openly to induce her to shake off the restraints she still respected. If he chanced to enter her apartment at the time she was preparing to go out, "For whom," he would say in a tone of raillery, "is this detachment of warriors which I found in the court? Is it some general going to inspect his army? Does all this military display become a young Queen adored by her subjects?" He would call to her mind the simplicity with which Maria Theresa lived; the visits she made without guards, or even attendants, to the Prince d'Esterhazy, to the Comte de Palfi, passing whole days far from the fatiguing ceremonies of the Court. The Abbé thus artfully flattered the inclinations of Marie Antoinette; and showed her how she might disguise, even from herself, her aversion from the ceremonies observed by the descendants of Louis XIV.—*Madame Campan.*

5. A person who had dined with the Abbé one day at the Comte de Mercy's said to that ambassador, "How can you bear that tiresome babbler?" "How can you ask it?" replied M. de Mercy; "you could answer the question yourself: it is because I want him."—*Madame Campan.*

6. The Abbé de Vermond was the son of a village surgeon, and brother of an *accoucheur*, who had acted in that capacity for the Queen: when he was with her Majesty, in speaking to his brother, he never addressed him otherwise than as *Monsieur l'Accoucheur.*—*Madame Campan.*

7. I have often heard the Queen say that, at Vienna, in the office of the secretary of the Prince de Rohan, there were sold in one year more silk stockings than at Lyons and Paris together. —*Madame Campan.*

III

Arrival of the Archduchess in France—Brilliant reception of
the Dauphiness at Versailles—She charms Louis XV—Madame
du Barry's jealousy—Court intrigues—The Dauphin—His
brothers and their wives

A superb pavilion had been prepared upon the frontiers near Kehl. It consisted of a vast saloon, connected with two apartments, one of which was assigned to the lords and ladies of the Court of Vienna, and the other to the suite of the Dauphiness, composed of the Comtesse de Noailles, her lady of honour; the Duchesse de Cossé, her *dame d'atours*; four ladies of the palace; the Comte de Saulx-Tavannes, *chevalier d'honneur*; the Comte de Tessé, first equerry; the Bishop of Chartres, first almoner; the officers of the Body Guard, and the equerries.

When the Dauphiness had been entirely undressed, in order that she might retain nothing belonging to a foreign court (an etiquette always observed on such an occasion), the doors were opened; the young Princess came forward, looking round for the Comtesse de Noailles; then, rushing into her arms, she implored her, with tears in her eyes, and with heartfelt sincerity, to direct her; to advise her, and to be in every respect her guide and support. It was impossible to refrain from admiring her airy walk; one smile alone was sufficient to win the heart.

While doing justice to the virtues of the Comtesse de Noailles, those sincerely attached to the Queen have always considered it as one of the earliest misfortunes of the latter—perhaps even the greatest that she could experience on her entrance into the world—not to have found, in the person naturally designed for her adviser, a woman indulgent, enlightened, and administering good counsel with that sweetness which disposes young persons to follow it. The Comtesse de Noailles had nothing agreeable in her appearance; her demeanour was stiff and her mien severe. She was perfect mistress of etiquette; but she wearied the young Princess with it, without making her sensible of its importance. So much ceremony was indeed oppressive; but it was adopted in order to present the young Princess to the French in such a manner as to command their respect, and guard her by an imposing barrier against the deadly shafts of calumny. It would have been proper to convince the Dauphiness that in France her dignity depended much upon customs by no means necessary at Vienna to secure the respect and love of the good and submissive Austrians for the Imperial family. The Dauphiness was thus perpetually tormented by the remonstrances of the Comtesse de Noailles; and at the same time caused by the Abbé de Vermond to ridicule both the lessons upon etiquette and her who gave them. She preferred raillery to argument, and nicknamed the Comtesse de Noailles, *Madame L'Etiquette*.[1]

The fêtes which were given at Versailles on the marriage of the Dauphin were very splendid. The Dauphiness arrived there at the hour for her toilette, after having slept at La Muette, where Louis XV had been to receive her; and where that Prince, blinded by a feeling unworthy of a sovereign and the father of a family, caused the young Princess, the royal family, and the ladies of the Court to sit down to supper with Madame du Barry.

The Dauphiness was hurt at this conduct; she spoke of it openly enough to those with whom she was intimate, but she knew how to conceal her dissatisfaction in public, and her behaviour showed no signs of it.[2]

She was received at Versailles in an apartment on the ground-floor, under that of the late Queen, which was not ready for her until six months after her marriage.

The Dauphiness, then fifteen years of age, beaming with freshness, appeared to all eyes more than beautiful. Her walk partook at once of the dignity of the Princesses of her house, and of the grace of the French; her eyes were mild, her smile amiable. When she went to chapel, as soon as she had taken the first few steps in the long gallery, she discerned, all the way to its extremity, those persons whom she ought to salute with the consideration due to their rank; those on whom she should bestow an inclination of the head; and lastly, those who were to be satisfied with a smile, calculated to console them for not being entitled to greater honours.

Louis XV was enchanted with the young Dauphiness; all his conversation was about her graces, her vivacity, and the aptness of her repartees. She was yet more successful with the royal family when they beheld her shorn of the splendour of the diamonds with which she had been adorned during the first days of her marriage. When clothed in a light dress of gauze or taffety she was compared to the Venus di Medicis, and the Atalanta of the Marly gardens. Poets sang her charms; painters attempted to copy her features. One artist's fancy led him to place the portrait of Marie Antoinette in the heart of a full-blown rose. His ingenious idea was rewarded by Louis XV.

The King continued to talk only of the Dauphiness; and Madame du Barry ill-naturedly endeavoured to damp his enthusiasm. Whenever Marie Antoinette was the topic, she pointed out the irregularity of her features, criticised the *bon-mots* quoted as hers, and rallied the King upon his prepossession in her favour. Madame du Barry was affronted at not receiving from the Dauphiness those attentions to which she thought herself entitled; she did not conceal her vexation from the King; she was afraid that the grace and cheerfulness of the young Princess would make the domestic circle of the royal family more agreeable to the old sovereign, and that he would escape her chains; at the same time, hatred to the Choiseul party contributed powerfully to excite the enmity of the favourite.

The fall of that minister took place in November 1770, six months after his long influence in the Council had brought about the alliance with the House of Austria, and the arrival of Marie Antoinette at the Court of France. The Princess, young, frank, volatile, and inexperienced, found herself without any other guide than the Abbé de Vermond, in a Court ruled by the enemy of the minister who had brought her there, and in the midst of people who hated Austria, and detested any alliance with the Imperial house.

The Duc d'Aiguillon, the Duc de la Vauguyon, the Maréchal de Richelieu, the Rohans, and other considerable families, who had made use of Madame du Barry to overthrow the Duke, could not flatter themselves, notwithstanding their powerful intrigues, with a hope of being able to break off an alliance solemnly announced, and involving such high political interests. They therefore changed their mode of attack, and it will be seen how the conduct of the Dauphin served as a basis for their hopes.

The Dauphiness continually gave proofs of both sense and feeling. Sometimes she even suffered herself to be carried away by those transports of compassionate kindness which are not to be controlled by the customs which rank establishes.

In consequence of the fire in the Place Louis XV, which occurred at the time of the nuptial entertainments, the Dauphin and Dauphiness sent their whole income for the year to the relief of the unfortunate families who lost their relatives on that disastrous day.

This was one of those ostentatious acts of generosity which are dictated by the policy of princes, at least as much as by their compassion; but the grief of Marie Antoinette was profound, and lasted several days; nothing could console her for the loss of so many innocent victims; she spoke of it, weeping, to her ladies, one of whom, thinking, no doubt, to divert her mind, told her that a great number of thieves had been found among the bodies, and that their pockets were filled with watches and other valuables: "They have at least been well punished," added the person who related these particulars. "Oh no, no, madame!" replied the Dauphiness; "they died by the side of honest people."

In passing through Rheims, on her way to Strasburg, she said, "That town is the one, in all France, which I hope not to see again for the longest possible time."³

The Dauphiness had brought from Vienna a considerable number of white diamonds; the King added to them the gift of the diamonds and pearls of the late Dauphiness, and also put into her hands a collar of pearls, of a single row, the smallest of which was as large as a filbert, and which had been brought into France by Anne of Austria, and appropriated by that Princess to the use of the Queens and Dauphinesses of France.⁴

The three Princesses, daughters of Louis XV, joined in making her magnificent presents. Madame Adelaide at the same time gave the young Princess a key to the private corridors of the Château, by means of which, without any suite, and without being perceived, she could get to the apartments of her aunts, and see them in private. The Dauphiness, on receiving the key, told them, with infinite grace, that if they had meant to make her appreciate the superb presents they were kind enough to bestow upon her, they should not at the same time have offered her one of such inestimable value; since to that key she should be indebted for an intimacy and advice unspeakably precious at her age. She did, indeed, make use of it very frequently; but Madame Victoire alone permitted her, so long as she continued Dauphiness, to visit her familiarly. Madame Adelaide could not overcome her prejudices against Austrian princesses, and was wearied with the somewhat petulant gaiety of the Dauphiness. Madame Victoire was concerned at this, feeling that their society and counsel would have been highly useful to a young person otherwise likely to meet with none but parasites. She endeavoured, therefore, to induce her to take pleasure in the society of the Marquise de Durfort, her lady of honour and favourite. Several agreeable entertainments took place at the house of this lady, but the Comtesse de Voailles and the Abbé de Vermond soon opposed these meetings.

A circumstance which happened in hunting, near the village of Acheres, in the forest of Fontainebleau, afforded the young Princess an opportunity of displaying her respect for old age, and her compassion for misfortune. A very old peasant was wounded by the stag; the Dauphiness jumped out of her calash, placed the peasant, with his wife and children in it, had the family taken back to their cottage, and bestowed upon them every attention and every necessary assistance. Her heart was always open to the feelings of compassion, and the recollection of her rank never restrained her sensibility. Several persons in her service entered her room one evening, expecting to find nobody there but the officer in waiting;⁵ they perceived the young Princess seated by the side of this man, who was advanced in years; she had placed near him a bowl full of water, was stanching the blood which issued from a wound he had received in his hand with her handkerchief which she had torn up to bind it, and was fulfilling towards him all the duties of a pious sister of charity. The old man, affected even to tears, out of respect allowed his august mistress to act as she thought proper. He had hurt himself in endeavouring to bring forward some rather heavy piece of furniture which the Princess had asked him for.

In the month of July 1770 an unfortunate occurrence that took place in a family which the Dauphiness honoured with her favour contributed again to show not only her sensibility but also the benevolence of her disposition. One of her women had a son who was an officer in the *gens d'armes* of the guard; this young man thought himself affronted by a clerk in the war department, and imprudently sent him a challenge; he killed his adversary in the forest of Compiègne. The family of the young man who was killed, being in possession of the challenge, demanded justice. The King, distressed on account of several duels which had recently taken place, had unfortunately declared that he would show no mercy on the first event of that kind which could be proved; the culprit was therefore arrested. His mother, in the deepest grief, hastened to throw herself at the feet of the Dauphiness, the Dauphin, and the young Princesses. After an hour's supplication they obtained from the King the favour so much desired. On the next day a lady of rank, while congratulating the Dauphiness, had the malice to add that the mother had neglected no means of success on the occasion, having solicited not only the royal family, but even Madame du Barry. The Dauphiness replied that the fact justified the favourable opinion she had formed of the worthy woman; that the heart of a mother should hesitate at nothing for the salvation of her son; and that in her place, if she had thought it would be serviceable, she would have thrown herself at the feet of Zamor.⁶

Some time after the marriage entertainments the Dauphiness made her entry into Paris, and was received with transports of joy. After dining in the King's apartment at the Tuileries, she was forced, by the reiterated shouts of the multitude, with which the garden was filled, to present herself upon the balcony fronting the principal walk. On seeing such a crowd of heads with their eyes fixed upon her, she exclaimed, "*Grand Dieu*! what a concourse!" "Madame," said the old Duc de Brissac, the Governor of Paris, "I may tell you, without fear of offending the Dauphin, that they are so many lovers."⁷ The Dauphin took no umbrage at either acclamations or marks of homage of which the Dauphiness was the object. The most mortifying indifference, a coldness which frequently degenerated into rudeness, were the sole feelings which the young

Prince then manifested towards her. Not all her charms could gain even upon his senses. This estrangement, which lasted a long time, was said to be the work of the Duc de la Vauguyon. The Dauphiness, in fact, had no sincere friends at Court except the Duc de Choiseul and his party. Will it be credited that the plans laid against Marie Antoinette went so far as divorce? I have been assured of it by persons holding high situations at Court, and many circumstances tend to confirm the opinion. On the journey to Fontainebleau, in the year of the marriage, the inspectors of public buildings were gained over to manage so that the apartment intended for the Dauphin, communicating with that of the Dauphiness, should not be finished, and a room at the extremity of the building was temporarily assigned to him. The Dauphiness, aware that this was the result of intrigue, had the courage to complain of it to Louis XV, who, after severe reprimands, gave orders so positive that within the week the apartment was ready. Every method was tried to continue and augment the indifference which the Dauphin long manifested towards his youthful spouse. She was deeply hurt at it, but she never suffered herself to utter the slightest complaint on the subject. Inattention to, even contempt for, the charms which she heard extolled on all sides, nothing induced her to break silence; and some tears, which would involuntarily burst from her eyes, were the sole symptoms of her inward sufferings, discoverable by those in her service.

Once only, when tired out with the misplaced remonstrances of an old lady attached to her person, who wished to dissuade her from riding on horseback, under the impression that it would prevent her producing heirs to the Crown, "Mademoiselle," said she, "in God's name, leave me in peace; be assured that I can put no heir in danger."

The Dauphiness found at the Court of Louis XV, besides the three Princesses, the King's daughters, the Princes also, brothers of the Dauphin, who were receiving their education, and Clotilde and Elizabeth, still in the care of Madame de Marsan, governess of the children of France. The elder of the two latter Princesses, in 1777, married the Prince of Piedmont, afterwards King of Sardinia. This Princess was in her infancy so extremely large that the people nicknamed her *gros Madame*.[8] The second Princess was the pious Elizabeth, the victim of her respect and tender attachment for the King, her brother, and whose exalted virtues have deserved a celestial crown.[9] She was still scarcely out of her leading-strings at the period of the Dauphin's marriage. The Dauphiness showed her marked preference. The governess, who sought to advance the Princess to whom Nature had been least favourable, was offended at the Dauphiness's partiality for Madame Elizabeth, and by her injudicious complaints weakened the friendship which yet subsisted between Madame Clotilde and Marie Antoinette. There even arose some degree of rivalry on the subject of education; and that which the Empress Maria Theresa bestowed on her daughters was talked of openly and unfavourably enough. The Abbé de Vermond thought himself affronted, took a part in the quarrel, and added his complaints and jokes to those of the Dauphiness on the criticisms of the governess; he even indulged himself in his turn in reflections on the tuition of Madame Clotilde. Everything becomes known at Court. Madame de Marsan was informed of all that had been said in the Dauphiness's circle, and was very angry with her on account of it.

From that moment a centre of intrigue or rather gossip against Marie Antoinette was established round Madame de Marsan's fireside; her most trifling actions were there construed ill; her gaiety, and the harmless amusements in which she sometimes indulged in her own apartments with the more youthful ladies of her train, and even with the women in her service, were stigmatised as criminal. Prince Louis de Rohan, sent ambassador to Vienna by this clique, was the echo there of these unmerited comments, and threw himself into a series of culpable accusations which he dignified with the name of zeal. He ceaselessly represented the young Dauphiness as alienating all hearts by levities unsuitable to the dignity of the French Court. The Princess frequently received from the Court of Vienna remonstrances, of the origin of which she could not long remain in ignorance. From this period must be dated that aversion which she never ceased to manifest for the Prince de Rohan.

About the same time the Dauphiness received information of a letter written by Prince Louis to the Duc d'Aiguillon, in which the ambassador expressed himself in very free language respecting the intentions of Maria Theresa with relation to the partition of Poland. This letter of Prince Louis had been read at the Comtesse du Barry's; the levity of the ambassador's correspondence wounded the feelings and the dignity of the Dauphiness at Versailles, while at Vienna the representations which he made to Maria Theresa against the young Princess terminated in rendering the motives of his incessant complaints suspected by the Empress.

Maria Theresa at length determined on sending her private secretary, Baron de Neni, to Versailles, with directions to observe the conduct of the Dauphiness with attention, and form a just estimate of the opinion of the Court and of Paris with regard to that Princess. The Baron de Neni, after having devoted sufficient time and intelligence to the subject, undeceived his sovereign as to the exaggerations of the French ambassador; and the Empress had no difficulty in detecting, among the calumnies which he had conveyed to her under the specious excuse of anxiety for her august daughter, proofs of the enmity of a party which had never approved of the alliance of the House of Bourbon with her own.[10]

At this period the Dauphiness, though unable to obtain any influence over the heart of her husband, dreading Louis XV, and justly mistrusting everything connected with Madame du Barry and the Duc d'Aiguillon, had not deserved the slightest reproach as to that sort of levity which hatred and her misfortunes afterwards construed into crime. The Empress, convinced of the innocence of Marie Antoinette, directed the Baron de Neni to solicit the recall of the Prince de Rohan, and to inform the Minister for Foreign Affairs of all the motives which made her require it; but the House of Rohan interposed between its *protégé* and the Austrian envoy, and an evasive answer merely was given.

It was not until two months after the death of Louis XV that the Court of Vienna obtained his recall. The avowed grounds for requiring it were, first, the public gallantries of Prince Louis with some ladies of the Court and others; secondly, his surliness and haughtiness towards other foreign ministers, which would have had more serious consequences, especially with the ministers of England and Denmark, if the Empress herself had not interfered; thirdly, his contempt for religion in a country where it was particularly necessary to show respect for it. He had been seen frequently to dress himself in clothes of different colours, assuming the hunting uniforms of various noblemen whom he visited, with so much audacity that one day in particular, during the Fête Dieu, he and all his legation, in green uniforms laced with gold, broke through a procession which impeded them, in order to make their way to a hunting party at the Prince de Paar's; and fourthly, the immense debts contracted by him and his people, which were tardily and only in part discharged.[II]

The succeeding marriages of the Comte de Provence and the Comte d'Artois with two daughters of the King of Sardinia, procured society for the Dauphiness more suitable to her age, and altered her mode of life.

A pair of tolerably fine eyes drew forth in favour of the Comtesse de Provence, upon her arrival at Versailles, the only praises which could reasonably be bestowed upon her.

The Comtesse d'Artois, though not deformed, was very small; she had a fine complexion; her face, tolerably pleasing, was not remarkable for anything except the extreme length of the nose. But being good and generous, she was beloved by those about her, and even possessed some influence so long as she was the only Princess who had produced heirs to the Crown.

From this time the closest intimacy subsisted between the three young families. They took their meals together, except on those days when they dined in public. This manner of living *en famille* continued until the Queen sometimes indulged herself in going to dine with the Duchesse de Polignac, when she was governess; but the evening meetings at supper were never interrupted; they took place at the house of the Comtesse de Provence. Madame Elizabeth made one of the party when she had finished her education, and sometimes Mesdames, the King's aunts, were invited. This custom, which had no precedent at Court, was the work of Marie Antoinette, and she maintained it with the utmost perseverance.

The Court of Versailles saw no change in point of etiquette during the reign of Louis XV. Play took place at the house of the Dauphiness, as being the first female of the State. It had, from the death of Queen Maria Leczinska to the marriage of the Dauphin, been held at the abode of Madame Adelaide. This removal, the result of an order of precedence not to be violated, was not the less displeasing to Madame Adelaide, who established a separate party for play in her apartments, and scarcely ever went to that which not only the Court in general, but also the royal family, were expected to attend. The full-dress visits to the King on his *débotter* were continued. High mass was attended daily. The airings of the Princesses were nothing more than rapid races in berlins, during which they were accompanied by Body Guards, equerries, and pages on horseback. They galloped for some leagues from Versailles. Calashes were used only in hunting.

The young Princesses were desirous to infuse animation into their circle of associates by something useful as well as pleasant. They adopted the plan of learning and performing all the best plays of the French theatre. The Dauphin was the only spectator. The three Princesses, the two brothers of the King, and Messieurs Campan, father and son were the sole performers, but they endeavoured to keep this amusement as secret as an affair of State; they dreaded the censure of Mesdames, and they had no doubt that Louis XV would forbid such pastimes if he knew of them. They selected a cabinet in the *entresol* which nobody had occasion to enter for their performance. A kind of proscenium, which could be taken down and shut up in a closet, formed the whole theatre. The Comte de Provence always knew his part with imperturbable accuracy; the Comte d'Artois knew his tolerably well, and recited elegantly; the Princesses acted badly. The Dauphiness acquitted herself in some characters with discrimination and feeling. The chief pleasure of this amusement consisted in all the costumes being elegant and accurate. The Dauphin entered into the spirit of these diversions, and laughed heartily at the comic characters as they came on the scene; from these amusements may be dated his discontinuance of the timid manner of his youth, and his taking pleasure in the society of the Dauphiness.

It was not till a long time afterwards that I learned these particulars, M. Campan having kept the secret; but an unforeseen event had well-nigh exposed the whole mystery. One day the Queen desired M. Campan to go down into her closet to fetch something that she had forgotten; he was dressed for the character of Crispin, and was rouged. A private staircase led direct to the *entresol* through the dressing-room. M. Campan fancied he heard some noise, and remained still, behind the door, which was shut. A servant belonging to the wardrobe, who was, in fact, on the staircase, had also heard some noise, and, either from fear or curiosity, he suddenly opened the door; the figure of Crispin frightened him so that he fell down backwards, shouting with all his might, "Help! help!" My father-in-law raised him up, made him recognise his voice, and laid upon him an injunction of silence as to what he had seen. He felt himself, however, bound to inform the Dauphiness of what had happened, and she was afraid that a similar occurrence might betray their amusements. They were therefore discontinued.

The Princess occupied her time in her own apartment in the study of music and the parts in plays which she had to learn; the latter exercise, at least, produced the beneficial effect of strengthening her memory and familiarising her with the French language.

The Abbé de Vermond visited her daily, but took care to avoid the imposing tone of a tutor; and would not, even as a reader, recommend the useful study of history. I believe he never read a single volume of history in his life to his august pupil; and, in truth, there never existed a Princess who manifested a more marked aversion for all serious studies.

While Louis XV reigned, the enemies of Marie Antoinette made no attempt to change public opinion with regard to her. She always was the object of the love of the French people in general, and particularly of the inhabitants of Paris; who went at every opportunity to Versailles, the majority of them attracted solely by the pleasure of seeing her. The courtiers did not fully enter into the popular enthusiasm which the Dauphiness had inspired; the disgrace of the Duc de Choiseul had removed her real support from her; and the party which had the ascendancy at Court since the exile of that minister was, politically, as much opposed to her family as to herself. The Dauphiness was therefore surrounded by enemies at Versailles.

Nevertheless everybody appeared outwardly desirous to please her; for the age of Louis XV, and the character of the Dauphin, sufficiently warned courtiers of the important part reserved for the Princess during the following reign, in case the Dauphin should become attached to her.

1. The Comtesse de Noailles, the Queen's lady of honour, possessed abundance of good qualities; piety, charity, and irreproachable morals rendered her worthy of reverence; but the Countess was also abundantly provided with all the obtrusiveness which a narrow mind could add even to the noblest qualifications. The Queen required a lady of honour who would explain to her the origin of forms, very inconvenient, it must be confessed, but invented as a fence against malevolence. The custom of having ladies and chevaliers of honour, and that of wearing hoops of three ells in circumference, were certainly invented to entrench young princesses so respectably, that the malicious gaiety of the French, their proneness to insinuations, and too often to calumny, should not by any possibility find an opportunity to attack them.— *Madame Campan.*

2. See the *Mémoires de Weber*, tome i. The memoirs of this writer, foster-brother of Marie Antoinette, generally complete what Madame Campan has said of this Princess. The two works are almost inseparable.—*Note by the Editor.*

3. The coronation of the French kings takes place in Rheims; so that when she should revisit that city, it would probably be in consequence of the death of Louis XV—*Note by the Editor.*

4. I mention this collar thus particularly because the Queen thought it her duty, notwithstanding this appropriation, to give it up to the commissaries of the National Assembly when they came to strip the King and Queen of the Crown diamonds.—*Madame Campan.*

5. The *valets de chambre* and the ushers were called *officiers de l'interieure.*—*Madame Campan.*

6. A little Indian who carried the Comtesse du Barry's train. Louis XV often amused himself with the little marmoset; having jestingly made him Governor of Louveciennes, he received an annual income of 3,000 francs.—*Madame Campan.*

7. John Paul Timoleon de Cossé, Duc de Brissac and Marshal of France. At the Court of Louis XV and XVI, he was a model of the virtue, gallantry, and courage of the ancient knights. The Comte de Charolais, finding him one day with his mistress, said to him abruptly, "Go out, sir." "Monseigneur," replied the Duc de Brissac, with emphasis, "your ancestors would have said, 'Come out.'" —*Note by the Editor.*

8. Madame Clotilde of France, a sister of the King, was extraordinarily fat for her height and age. One of her play-fellows, having been indiscreet enough even in her presence to make use of the nickname given to her, received a severe reprimand from the Comtesse de Marsan, who hinted to her that she would do well in not making her appearance again before the Princess. Madame Clotilde sent for her the next day: "My governess," said she, "has done her duty, and I will do mine; come and see us as usual, and think no more of a piece of inadvertence, which I myself have forgotten." This Princess, so heavy in body, possessed the most agreeable and playful wit. Her affability and grace rendered her dear to all who came near her. A certain poet, whose mind was solely occupied with the prodigious size of Madame Clotilde, when it was determined that she should marry the Prince of Piedmont, composed the following stanza. It must be remembered that two Princesses of Savoy had just married two French Princes:—

> Le bon Savoyard qui réclame
> Le prix de ses double présent,
> En échange reçoit Madame
> C'est le bien grassement.

Though we've only returned *one* princess for the *two,*
Who from Piedmont were sent us of late;
Yet surely no question of wrong can ensue,
Since the bargain's made up by her weight.
—*Note by the Editor.*

9. Elizabeth Philippine Marie Hélène of France, born at Versailles on the 3rd of May 1764; guillotined 1794. "Madame Elizabeth," says M. de la Salle, the author of a biographical article upon this interesting and unfortunate Princess, "had not, like Madame Clotilde, her august sister, received from nature that softness and flexibility of character which renders the practice of virtue easy; in more points than one she resembled the Duke of Burgundy, the pupil of Fénélon. Education and piety operated upon her as they did upon that Prince: precepts, and the examples which surrounded her, adorned her with all virtues, and left nothing of her original inclinations, but amiable sensibility, lively impressions, and a firmness which seemed formed to meet the dreadful trials for which Heaven reserved her."—*Note by the Editor.*

10. The Empress Maria Theresa knew very well which of the persons who composed the Court of Louis XV were favourable and which unfavourable to Marie Antoinette. It is said that at the moment of that Princess's departure for France, the Empress gave her the following note in her own handwriting:—

> *List of persons of my acquaintance*
> The Duc and Duchesse de Choiseul
> Comte de Broglie
> The Duc and Duchesse de Praslin
> Hautefort
> The Du Châtelets
> D'Estrée
> D'Aubeterre
> Comte de Broglie
> The brothers De Montazet
> M. d'Aumont
> M. Gérard
> M. Blondel
> La Beauvan, a nun
> Her companion
> The Durforts

To this last family you will take every opportunity of showing gratitude and attention.

The same to the Abbé de Vermond: I have the welfare of these persons at heart. My ambassador has orders to promote it. I shall be sorry to be the first to violate my own principle, which is to recommend nobody; but you and I owe too much to these persons not to seek all opportunities of being serviceable to them, if we can do it without too much *impegno.*

Consult with De Mercy. I recommend to you in general all the Lorraines in whatever you can do for them.

The Abbé Georgel, the clever Jesuit secretary of the French Embassy in Austria, obtained, by means of a mysterious unknown person, the most important secrets of the Court of Vienna.

"A masked man," says he in his memoirs, "one day placed in my hands two papers of secret instructions sent to Comte de Mercy, for him to give personally to the Queen. The first for the King's inspection; the second for the Queen alone. This last contained advice as to the method to be adopted for compensating for the King's inexperience, and for profiting by the facility of his character to influence the Government without appearing to interfere in it. The political lesson was given to Marie Antoinette with much art: she was led to feel that it was the surest way to render herself beloved by the French, whose happiness she might thereby secure; and at the same time cement the union of the two Houses of Austria and Bourbon."

What Georgel insinuates is obvious; but it must be remembered that he was one of Marie Antoinette's most implacable enemies.—*Note by the Editor.*

11. "On the departure of Prince Louis de Rohan for Compiègne," says the Abbé Georgel, "where the new King held his Court, I remained at Vienna, charged with the transaction of the affairs of France with the Austrian ministry. I consequently received instructions to continue the negotiations, as entrusted with the political correspondence with our ministry, and the King's ambassador at Constantinople. Upon his arrival, the Prince de Rohan heard of the complaints of Maria Theresa, and the steps already taken in her name by Marie Antoinette for his recall. He had an audience of the King; it was short, and far from satisfactory. Louis XVI listened to him a few minutes, and then abruptly said, 'I will soon let you know my pleasure.' He never could obtain an audience of the Queen, and, without deigning to receive him, she sent for the letter which her mother, the Empress Maria Theresa, had given him for her. His relations warned him that the prejudices of the King and Queen against him were very strong, and advised him not to make any attempts to return to Vienna, saying they would be quite thrown away, and would only give more publicity to his disgrace. Prince Louis remained in perplexity and suspense more than two months, and wrote a letter to the King, in which he described his situation in terms calculated to interest the monarch's feelings. His letter remained unanswered; but Louis XVI told the Comtesse de Marsan, a cousin of the ambassador, that the embassy to Vienna was intended for the Baron de Breteuil, a man preferred by the Empress and selected by the Queen."

IV

Death of Louis XV—Picture of the Court—Madame du Barry dismissed—Departure of the Court to Choisy—M. de Maurepas Minister—Influence of example upon the courtiers—Enthusiasm raised by the new reign—Mourning at La Muette—The Queen—The King and the Princes, his brothers, are inoculated—Stay at Marly—Calumnies against the Queen—Bœhmer, the jeweller—Mademoiselle Bertin—Changes of fashion—Simplicity of the Court of Vienna—Extreme temperance, decorum, and modesty of Marie Antoinette

About the beginning of May 1774 Louis XV, the strength of whose constitution had promised a long enough life, was attacked by confluent smallpox of the worst kind. Mesdames at this juncture inspired the Dauphiness with a feeling of respect and attachment, of which she gave them repeated proofs when she ascended the throne. In fact, nothing was more admirable nor more affecting than the courage with which they braved that most horrible disease: the air of the palace was infected; more than fifty persons took the smallpox, in consequence of having merely loitered in the galleries of Versailles; and ten died of it.

The end of the monarch was approaching. His reign, peaceful in general, had inherited strength from the power of his predecessor; on the other hand, his own weakness had been preparing misfortune for whoever should reign after him. The scene was about to change: hope, ambition, joy, grief; and all those feelings which variously affected the hearts of the courtiers, sought in vain to disguise themselves under a calm exterior. It was easy to detect the different motives which induced them every moment to repeat to every one the question: "How is the King?" At length, on the 10th of May 1774, the mortal career of Louis XV terminated.[1]

The Comtesse du Barry had, a few days previously, withdrawn to Ruelle, to the Duc d'Aiguillon's. Twelve or fifteen persons belonging to the Court thought it their duty to visit her there; their liveries were observed, and these visits were for a long time grounds for disfavour. More than six years after the King's death one of these persons being spoken of in the circle of the royal family, I heard it remarked, "That was one of the fifteen Ruelle carriages."

The whole Court went to the Château; the *Œil de Bœuf* was filled with courtiers, and the palace with the inquisitive. The Dauphin, had settled that he would depart with the royal family the moment the King should breathe his last sigh. But on such an occasion decency forbade that positive orders for departure should be passed from mouth

The death of Louis XV

to mouth. The heads of the stables, therefore, agreed with the people who were in the King's room, that the latter should place a lighted taper near a window, and that at the instant of the King's decease one of them should extinguish it.[2]

The taper was extinguished. On this signal the Body Guards, pages, and equerries mounted on horseback, and all was ready for setting off. The Dauphin was with the Dauphiness. They were expecting together the intelligence of the death of Louis XV. A dreadful noise, absolutely like thunder, was heard in the outer apartment; it was the crowd of courtiers who were deserting the dead sovereign's antechamber, to come and do homage to the new power of Louis XVI. This extraordinary tumult informed Marie Antoinette and her husband that they were called to the throne; and, by a spontaneous movement, which deeply affected those around them, they threw themselves on their knees; both, pouring forth a flood of tears, exclaimed: "O God! guide us, protect us, we are too young to reign."

The Comtesse de Noailles entered, and was the first to salute Marie Antoinette as Queen of France. She requested their Majesties to condescend to quit the inner apartments for the grand salon, to receive the Princes and all the great officers, who were desirous to do homage to their new sovereigns. Marie Antoinette received these first visits leaning upon her husband, with her handkerchief held to her eyes; the carriages drove up, the guards and equerries were on horseback. The Château was deserted— every one hastened to fly from contagion, which there was no longer any inducement to brave.

On leaving the chamber of Louis XV, the Duc de Villequier, first gentleman of the bed-chamber for the year, ordered M. Andouille, the King's chief surgeon, to open the body and embalm it. The chief surgeon would inevitably have died in consequence. "I am ready," replied Andouille; "but while I operate you shall hold the head; your office imposes this duty upon you." The Duke went off without saying a word, and the corpse was neither opened nor embalmed. A few under-servants and workmen continued with the pestiferous remains, and paid the last duty to their master; the surgeons directed that spirits of wine should be poured into the coffin.

The whole of the Court set off for Choisy at four o'clock; Mesdames the King's aunts in their private carriage, and the Princesses under tuition with the Comtesse de Marsan and the under-governesses. The King, the Queen, Monsieur, the King's brother, Madame, and the Comte and Comtesse d'Artois, went in the same carriage. The solemn scene that had just passed before their eyes—the multiplied ideas offered to their imaginations by that which was just opening, had naturally inclined them to grief and reflection; but, by the Queen's own confession, this inclination, little suited to their age, wholly left them before they had gone half their journey; a word, drolly mangled by the Comtesse d'Artois, occasioned a general burst of laughter—and from that moment they dried their tears. The communication between Choisy and Paris was incessant; never was a Court seen in greater agitation. What influence will the royal aunts have?— And the Queen?—What fate is reserved for the Comtesse du Barry?—Whom will the young King choose for his ministers?—All these questions were answered in a few days. It was determined that the King's youth required a confidential person near him; and that there should be a prime minister. All eyes were turned upon De Machault and De Maurepas, both of them much advanced in years. The first had retired to his estate near Paris; and the second to Pont Chartrain, to which place he had long been exiled. The letter recalling M. de Machault was written when Madame Adelaide obtained the preference of that important appointment for M. de Maurepas. The page to whose care the first letter had been actually consigned was recalled.[3]

The Duc d'Aiguillon had been too openly known as the private friend of the King's mistress; he was dismissed. M. de Vergennes, at that time ambassador of France at Stockholm, was appointed Minister for Foreign Affairs; Comte de Muy, the intimate friend of the Dauphin, the father of Louis XVI, obtained the war department. The Abbé Terray in vain said, and wrote, that he had boldly done all possible injury to the creditors of the State during the reign of the late King; that order was restored in the finances; that nothing but what was beneficial to all parties remained to be done; and that the new Court was about to enjoy the advantages of the regenerating part of his plan of finance; all these reasons, set forth in five or six memorials, which he sent in succession to the King and Queen, did not avail to keep him in office. His talents were admitted, but the odium which his operations had necessarily brought upon his character, combined with the immorality of his private life, forbade his further stay at Court; he was succeeded by M. de Clugny. De Maupeon, the Chancellor, was exiled; this caused universal joy. Lastly, the reassembling of the Parliaments produced the strongest sensation; Paris was in a delirium of joy, and not more than one person in a hundred foresaw that the spirit of the ancient magistracy would be still the same; and that in a short time it would make new attempts upon the royal authority. Madame du Barry had been exiled to Pont-aux-Dames. This was a measure rather of necessity than of severity; a short period of compulsory retreat was requisite in order completely to break off her connection with State affairs. The possession of Louveciennes and a considerable pension were continued to her.[4]

Everybody expected the recall of M. de Choiseul; the regret occasioned by his absence among the numerous friends whom he had left at Court, the attachment of the young Princess who was indebted to him for her elevation to the throne of France, and all concurring circumstances, seemed to foretell his return; the Queen earnestly entreated it of the King, but she met with an insurmountable and unforeseen obstacle. The King, it is said, had imbibed the strongest prejudices against that minister,[5] from secret memoranda penned by his father, and which had been committed to the care of the Duc de La Vauguyon, with an injunction to place them in his hands as soon as he should be old enough to study the art of reigning. It was by these memoranda that the esteem which he had conceived for the Maréchal de Muy was inspired, and we may add that Madame Adelaide, who at this early period powerfully influenced the decisions of the young monarch, confirmed the impressions they had made.

The Queen conversed with M. Campan on the regret she felt at having been unable to procure the recall of M. de Choiseul, and disclosed the cause of it to him. The Abbé de Vermond, who, down to the time of the death of Louis XV, had been on terms of the strictest friendship with M. Campan, called upon him on the second day after the arrival of the Court at Choisy, and, assuming a serious air, said, "Sir, the Queen was indiscreet enough yesterday to speak to you of a minister to whom she must of course be attached, and whom his friends ardently desire to have near her; you are aware that we must give up all expectation of seeing the Duke at Court; you know the reasons why; but you do not know that the young Queen, having mentioned the conversation in question to me, it was my duty, both as her preceptor and her friend, to remonstrate most sharply with her on her indiscretion in communicating to you those particulars of which you are in possession. I am now come to tell you that if you continue to avail yourself of the good nature of your mistress to initiate yourself in secrets of State, you will have me for your most inveterate enemy. The Queen should find here no other confidant than myself respecting things that ought to remain secret." M. Campan answered that he did not covet the important and dangerous character at the new Court which the Abbé wished to appropriate; and that he should confine himself to the duties of his office, being sufficiently satisfied with the continued kindness with which the Queen honoured him. Notwithstanding this, however, he informed the Queen, on the very same evening, of the injunction he had received. She owned that she had mentioned their conversation to the Abbé; that he had indeed seriously scolded her, in order to make her feel the necessity of being secret in concerns of State; and she added, "The Abbé cannot like you, my dear Campan; he did not expect that I should, on my arrival in France, find in my household a man who would suit me so exactly as you have done.[6] I know that he has taken umbrage at it; that is enough. I know, too, that you are incapable of attempting anything to injure him in my esteem; an attempt which would besides be vain, for I have been too long attached to him. As to yourself, be easy on the score of the Abbé's hostility, which shall not in any way hurt you. We run the risk of doing unjust actions, only when the persons about us possess the art of disguising those motives of jealousy or ambition by which they are prompted." The Abbé de Vermond having made himself master of the office of sole confidant to the Queen, was nevertheless agitated whenever he saw the young King; he could not be ignorant that the Abbé had been promoted by the Duc de Choiseul, and was believed to favour the Encyclopedists, against whom Louis XVI entertained a secret prejudice, although he suffered them to gain so great an ascendancy during his reign. The Abbé had, moreover, observed that the King had never, while Dauphin, addressed a single word to him; and that he very frequently only answered him with a shrug of the shoulders. He therefore determined on writing to Louis XVI, and intimating that he owed his situation at Court solely to the confidence with which the late King had honoured him; and that as habits contracted during the Queen's education placed him continually in the closest intimacy with her, he could not enjoy the honour of remaining near her Majesty without the King's consent. Louis XVI sent back his letter, after writing upon it these words: "I approve the Abbé de Vermond continuing in his office about the Queen."

At the period of his grandfather's death Louis XVI began to be exceedingly attached to the Queen. The first period of so deep a mourning not admitting of indulgence in the diversion of hunting, he proposed to her walks in the gardens of Choisy: they went out like husband and wife, the young King giving his arm to the Queen, and accompanied by a very small suite. The influence of this example had such an effect upon the courtiers that the next day several couples, who had long, and for good reasons, been disunited, were seen walking upon the terrace with the same apparent conjugal intimacy. Thus they spent whole hours, braving the intolerable wearisomeness of their protracted *tête-à-tête*, out of mere obsequious imitation.

The devotion of Mesdames to the King their father throughout his dreadful malady had produced that effect upon their health which was generally apprehended. On the fourth day after their arrival at Choisy they were attacked by pains in the head and chest, which left no doubt as to the danger of their situation. It became necessary instantly to send away the young royal family; and the Château de la Muette, in the Bois de Boulogne, was selected for their reception. Their arrival at that residence, which was very near Paris, drew so great a concourse of people into its neighbourhood, that even at daybreak the crowd had begun to assemble round the gates. Shouts of *Vive le Roi*!

were scarcely interrupted for a moment between six o'clock in the morning and sunset. The unpopularity the late King had drawn upon himself during his latter years, and the hopes to which a new reign gives birth, occasioned these transports of joy.

A fashionable jeweller made a fortune by the sale of mourning snuff-boxes, whereon the portrait of the young Queen, in a black frame of shagreen, gave rise to the pun: "*Consolation in chagrin*". All the fashions, and every article of dress, received names expressing the spirit of the moment. Symbols of abundance were everywhere represented, and the head-dresses of the ladies were surrounded by ears of wheat. Poets sang of the new monarch; all hearts, or rather all heads, in France were filled with enthusiasm. Never did the commencement of any reign excite more unanimous testimonials of love and attachment. It must be observed, however, that, amidst all this intoxication, the anti-Austrian party never lost sight of the young Queen, but kept on the watch, with the malicious desire to injure her through such errors as might arise from her youth and inexperience.

Their Majesties had to receive at La Muette the condolences of the ladies who had been presented at Court, who all felt themselves called on to pay homage to the new sovereigns. Old and young hastened to present themselves on the day of general reception; little black bonnets with great wings, shaking heads, low curtsies, keeping time with the motions of the head, made, it must be admitted, a few venerable dowagers appear somewhat ridiculous; but the Queen, who possessed a great deal of dignity, and a high respect for decorum, was not guilty of the grave fault of losing the state she was bound to preserve. An indiscreet piece of drollery of one of the ladies of the palace, however, procured her the imputation of doing so. The Marquise de Clermont-Tonnerre, whose office required that she should continue standing behind the Queen, fatigued by the length of the ceremony seated herself on the floor, concealed behind the fence formed by the hoops of the Queen and the ladies of the palace. Thus seated, and wishing to attract attention and to appear lively, she twitched the dresses of those ladies, and played a thousand other tricks. The contrast of these childish pranks with the solemnity which reigned over the rest of the Queen's chamber disconcerted her Majesty: she several times placed her fan before her face to hide an involuntary smile, and the severe old ladies pronounced that the young Queen had derided all those respectable persons who were pressing forward to pay their homage to her; that she liked none but the young; that she was deficient in decorum; and that not one of them would attend her Court again. The epithet *moqueuse* was applied to her; and there is no epithet less favourably received in the world.

The next day a very ill-natured song was circulated; the stamp of the party to which it was attributable might easily be seen upon it. I remember only the following chorus:—

> Little Queen, you must not be
> So saucy, with your twenty years;
> Your ill-used courtiers soon will see
> You pass, once more, the barriers.
> Fal lal lal, fal lal la.[7]

The errors of the great, or those which ill-nature chooses to impute to them, circulate in the world with the greatest rapidity, and become historical traditions, which every one delights to repeat. More than fifteen years after this occurrence I heard some old ladies in the most retired part of Auvergne relating all the particulars of the day of public condolence for the late King, on which, as they said, the Queen had laughed in the faces of the sexagenarian duchesses and princesses, who had thought it their duty to appear on the occasion.

The King and the Princes, his brothers, determined to avail themselves of the advantages held out by inoculation, as a safeguard against the illness under which their grandfather had just fallen; but the utility of this new discovery not being then generally acknowledged in France, many persons were greatly alarmed at the step; those who blamed it openly threw all the responsibility of it upon the Queen, who alone, they said, could have ventured to give such rash advice, inoculation being at this time established in the Northern Courts. The operation upon the King and his brothers, performed by Dr Jauberthou, was fortunately quite successful.

When the convalescence of the Princes was perfectly established, the excursions to Marly became cheerful enough. Parties on horseback and in calashes were formed continually. The Queen was desirous to afford herself one very innocent gratification; she had never seen the day break; and having now no other consent than that of the King to seek, she intimated her wish to him. He agreed that she should go, at three o'clock in the morning, to the eminences of the gardens of Marly; and, unfortunately, little disposed to partake in her amusements, he himself went to bed. Foreseeing some inconveniences possible in this nocturnal party, the Queen determined on having a number of people with her; and even ordered her women to accompany her. All precautions were ineffectual to prevent the effects of calumny, which thenceforward sought to diminish the general attachment that she had inspired. A few days afterwards, the most wicked libel that appeared during the earlier years of her reign was circulated in Paris. The blackest colours were employed to paint an enjoyment so harmless that there is scarcely a young woman living in the country who has not endeavoured to procure it for herself. The verses which appeared on this occasion were entitled "Sunrise".[8]

The Duc d'Orléans, then Duc de Chartres, was among those who accompanied the young Queen in her nocturnal ramble: he appeared very attentive to her at this epoch; but it was the only moment of his life in which there was any advance towards intimacy between the Queen and himself. The King disliked the character of the Duc de Chartres, and the Queen always excluded him from her private society. It is therefore without the slightest foundation that some writers have attributed to feelings of jealousy or wounded self-love the hatred which he displayed towards the Queen during the latter years of their existence.

It was on this first journey to Marly that Bœhmer, the jeweller, appeared at Court; a man whose stupidity and avarice afterwards fatally affected the happiness and reputation of Marie Antoinette. This person had, at great expense, collected six pear-formed diamonds of a prodigious size; they were perfectly matched and of the finest water. The earrings which they composed had, before the death of Louis XV, been destined for the Comtesse du Barry.

Bœhmer, by the recommendation of several persons about the Court, came to offer these jewels to the Queen. He asked 400,000 francs for them. The young Princess could not withstand her wish to purchase them; and the King having just raised the Queen's income, which, under the former reign, had been but 200,000 livres, to 100,000 crowns a year, she wished to make the purchase out of her own purse, and not burthen the royal treasury with the payment. She proposed to Bœhmer to take off the two buttons which formed the tops of the clusters, as they could be replaced by two of her own diamonds. He consented, and then reduced the price of the earrings to 360,000 francs; the payment for which was to be made by instalments, and was discharged in the course of four or five years by the Queen's first *femme de chambre*, deputed to manage the funds of her privy purse. I have omitted no details as to the manner in which the Queen first became possessed of these jewels, deeming them very needful to place in its true light the too famous circumstance of the necklace, which happened near the end of the reign of Marie Antoinette.

It was likewise on this first journey to Marly that the Duchesse de Chartres, afterwards Duchesse d'Orléans, introduced into the Queen's household Mademoiselle Bertin, a milliner who became celebrated at that time for the total change she effected in the dress of the French ladies.

It may be said that the mere admission of a milliner into the house of the Queen was followed by evil consequences to her Majesty. The skill of the milliner, who was received into the household, in spite of the custom which kept persons of her description out of it, afforded her the opportunity of introducing some new fashion every day. Up to this time the Queen had shown very plain taste in dress; she now began to make it a principal occupation; and she was of course imitated by other women.

All wished instantly to have the same dress as the Queen, and to wear the feathers and flowers to which her beauty, then in its brilliancy, lent an indescribable charm. The expenditure of the younger ladies was necessarily much increased; mothers and husbands murmured at it; some few giddy women contracted debts; unpleasant domestic scenes occurred; in many families coldness or quarrels arose; and the general report was—that the Queen would be the ruin of all the French ladies.

Fashion continued its fluctuating progress; and head-dresses, with their superstructures of gauze, flowers, and feathers, became so lofty that the women could not find carriages high enough to admit them; and they were often seen either stooping, or holding their heads out of the windows. Others knelt down in order to manage these elevated objects of ridicule with less danger.[9] Innumerable caricatures, exhibited in all directions, and some of which artfully gave the features of the Queen, attacked the extravagance of fashion, but with very little effect. It changed only, as is always the case, through the influence of inconstancy and time.

The Queen's toilette was a masterpiece of etiquette; everything was done in a prescribed form. Both the *dame d'honneur* and the *dame d'atours* usually attended and officiated, assisted by the first *femme de chambre*, and two ordinary women.[10] The *dame d'atours* put on the petticoat, and handed the gown to the Queen. The *dame d'honneur* poured out the water for her hands and put on her linen. When a Princess of the royal family happened to be present while the Queen was dressing, the *dame d'honneur* yielded to her the latter act of office, but still did not yield it directly to the Princesses of the blood; in such a case the *dame d'honneur* was accustomed to present the linen to the first *femme de chambre*, who, in her turn, handed it to the Princess of the blood. Each of these ladies observed these rules scrupulously as affecting her rights. One winter's day it happened that the Queen, who was entirely undressed, was just going to put on her shift; I held it ready unfolded for her; the *dame d'honneur* came in, slipped off her gloves, and took it. A scratching was heard at the door; it was opened, and in came the Duchesse d'Orléans: her gloves were taken off; and she came forward to take the garment; but as it would have been wrong in the *dame d'honneur* to hand it to her she gave it to me, and I handed it to the Princess. More scratching: it was, Madame the Comtesse de Provence; the Duchesse d'Orléans handed her the linen. All this while the Queen kept her arms crossed upon her bosom, and appeared to feel cold; Madame observed her uncomfortable situation, and merely laying down her handkerchief without taking off her gloves, she put on the linen, and in doing so knocked the Queen's cap off. The Queen laughed to conceal her impatience, but not until she had muttered several times, "How disagreeable! how tiresome!"

All this etiquette, however inconvenient, was suitable to the royal dignity, which expects to find servants in all classes of persons, beginning even with the brothers and sisters of the monarch.

Speaking here of etiquette, I do not allude to majestic state, appointed for days of ceremony in all Courts. I mean those minute ceremonies that were pursued towards our Kings in their inmost privacies, in their hours of pleasure, in those of pain, and even during the most revolting of human infirmities.[11]

These servile rules were drawn up into a kind of code; they offered to a Richelieu, a La Rochefoucauld, and a Duras, in the exercise of their domestic functions, opportunities of intimacy useful to their interests; and their vanity was flattered by customs which converted the right to give a glass of water, to put on a dress, and to remove a basin, into honourable prerogatives.

Princes thus accustomed to be treated as divinities naturally ended by believing that they were of a distinct nature, of a purer essence than the rest of mankind.

This sort of etiquette, which led our Princes to be treated in private as idols, made them in public martyrs to decorum. Marie Antoinette found in the Château of Versailles a multitude of established customs which appeared to her insupportable.

The ladies-in-waiting, who were all obliged to be sworn, and to wear full Court dresses, were alone entitled to remain in the room, and to attend in conjunction with the *dame d'honneur*, and the tire-woman. The Queen abolished all this formality. When her head was dressed, she curtsied to all the ladies who were in her chamber, and, followed only by her own women, went into her closet, where Mademoiselle Bertin, who could not be admitted into the chamber, used to await her.[12] It was in this inner closet that she produced her new and numerous dresses. The Queen was also desirous of being served by the most fashionable hairdresser in Paris. Now the custom which forbade all persons in inferior offices, employed by royalty, to exert their talents for the public, was no doubt intended to cut off all communication between the privacy of princes and society at large; the latter being always extremely curious respecting the most trifling particulars relative to the private life of the former. The Queen, fearing that the taste of the hairdresser would suffer if he should discontinue the general practice of his art, ordered him to attend as usual certain ladies of the Court and of Paris; and this multiplied the opportunities of learning details respecting the household, and very often of misrepresenting them.

One of the customs most disagreeable to the Queen was that of dining every day in public. Maria Leczinska had always submitted to this wearisome practice; Marie Antoinette followed it as long as she was Dauphiness. The Dauphin dined with her, and each branch of the family had its public dinner daily. The ushers suffered all decently dressed people to enter: the sight was the delight of persons from the country. At the dinner-hour there were none to be met upon the stairs but honest folks, who, after having seen the Dauphiness take her soup, went to see the Princes eat their *bouilli*, and then ran themselves out of breath to behold Mesdames at their dessert.

Very ancient usage, too, required that the Queens of France should appear in public surrounded only by women; even at meal-times no persons of the other sex attended to serve at table; and although the King ate publicly with the Queen, yet he himself was served by women with everything which was presented to him directly at table. The *dame d'honneur*, kneeling, for her own accommodation, upon a low stool, with a napkin upon her arm, and four women in full dress, presented the plates to the King and Queen. The *dame d'honneur* handed them drink. This service had formerly been the right of the maids of honour. The Queen, upon her accession to the throne, abolished the usage altogether. She also freed herself from the necessity of being followed in the Palace of Versailles by two of her women in Court dresses, during those hours of the day when the ladies-in-waiting were not with her. From that time she was accompanied only by a single *valet de chambre* and two footmen. All the errors of Marie Antoinette were of the same description; a disposition gradually to substitute the simple customs of Vienna for those of Versailles was more injurious to her than she could possibly have imagined. The Queen frequently spoke to the Abbé de Vermond of the perpetually recurring annoyances from which she had to release herself; and I always observed that, after having listened to what she had to say on the subject, she indulged with great pleasure in philosophical reveries on simplicity beneath the diadem, and paternal confidence in devoted subjects. This romance of royalty, which it is not given to all sovereigns to realise, flattered the tender heart and youthful fancy of Marie Antoinette to a singular extent.

This unfortunate Princess, against whom the opinions of the French people were at length so much excited, possessed qualities which deserved to obtain the greatest popularity. None could doubt this who, like myself, had heard her with delight describe the patriarchal manners of the House of Lorraine. She was accustomed to say that, by transplanting their manners into Austria, the Princes of that House had laid the foundation of the unassailable popularity enjoyed by the Imperial family.[13] She frequently related to me the interesting manner in which the Dukes of Lorraine levied the taxes. "The sovereign Prince," said she, "went to church; after the sermon he rose, waved his hat in the air, to show that he was about to speak, and then mentioned the sum whereof he stood in need. Such was the zeal of the good Lorrainers that men have been known to take away linen or household utensils without the knowledge of their wives, and sell them to add the value to their contribution. It sometimes happened, too, that the Prince received more money than he had asked for, in which case he restored the surplus."

All who were acquainted with the Queen's private qualities knew that she equally deserved attachment and esteem. Kind and patient to excess in her relations with her household, she indulgently considered all around her, and interested herself in their fortunes and in their pleasures. She had, among her women, young girls from the Maison de Saint Cyr, all well born; the Queen forbade them the play when the performances were not suitable; sometimes, when old plays were to be represented, if she found she could not with certainty trust to her memory, she would take the trouble to read them in the morning, to enable her to decide whether the girls should or should not go to see them; rightly considering herself bound to watch over their morals and conduct.

The Queen possessed in a high degree two valuable qualities—temperance and modesty. Her customary dinner was a chicken, roasted or boiled, and she drank water only. She showed no particular partiality for anything but her coffee in the morning, and a sort of bread to which she had been accustomed in her infancy at Vienna.

Her modesty in every particular of her private toilet was extreme. She bathed in a long flannel gown, buttoned up to the neck; and, while her two bathing women assisted her out of the bath, she required one of them to hold a sheet before her, raised so that her attendants might not see her. And yet Soulavie has dared, in the first volume of a most scandalous work, to say that the Queen was frightfully immodest, and that she had even given admittance to a venerable ecclesiastic while in her bath. What punishment can be too great for libellers who dare to give such perfidious falsehoods the title of historical memoirs!

1. Christopher de Beaumont, Archbishop of Paris, the ardent apostle of frequent communion, arrived at Paris with the intention of soliciting, in public, the administration of the sacrament to the King; and secretly retarding it as much as possible. The ceremony could not take place without the *previous* and *public expulsion of the concubine*, according to the canons of the Church and the Jesuitical party, of which Christopher was the leader. This party, which had made use of Madame du Barry to suppress the Parliaments, to support the Duc d'Aiguillon, and ruin the Choiseul faction, could not willingly consent to disgrace her canonically. The Archbishop of Paris had always said openly that she had rendered signal services to religion. This Molinist party was joined by the Ducs de Richelieu, de Fronsac, d'Aiguillon, Bertin, Maupeou, and Terray. Madame du Barry being their support with the pusillanimous King, they were bound to defend her, and prevent degradation and such retaliation as the Duchesse de Chateauroux had meditated in a similar case in 1745. The opposite party sought, on the other hand, to accelerate a religious ceremony which was to annihilate a favourite who had driven their leader, the Duc de Choiseul, from Court. It was amusing to see the latter party, which was the scourge of religion in France, calling it in to their aid during the King's sickness, in order to revenge themselves on Madame du Barry; while the party of the Archbishop and the bigots, in their turn, combined to prevent Louis XV from receiving the sacrament.

At that time they were coolly jobbing and bargaining about the King's conscience and penitence, said the Cardinal de Luynes to me. There was consequently an absolute uproar at court. The question was, *whether the King should or should not receive the sacrament immediately.* "Must we," said the Maréchal de Richelieu, "must we suffer Madame du Barry to be sent away with ignominy, and can we forget her services and expose ourselves to her vengeance in case of her return? or rather, shall we await the extremity of the invalid to effect a mere separation and proceed without noise or exposure to a plain administration of the sacrament?" On the morning of the 1st of May the Archbishop of Paris presented himself to the sick monarch. He had scarcely reached the door of the King's antechamber when Maréchal de Richelieu went to meet him, and conjured him not to kill the King by a theological proposition,[a] which had killed so many sick persons. "But if you are curious to hear some elegant little sins," said he to the prelate, "place yourself there, monsieur, and I will confess such as you have not heard since you became Archbishop of Paris. If, however, you will absolutely confess the King, and repeat here the *rôle* of the Archbishop of Soissons, at Metz; if you will send away Madame du Barry with disgrace, you complete the triumph of the Duc de Choiseul, from whom Madame du Barry has contributed so much to deliver you, and you persecute your friend for the benefit of your foe. Yes, sir; so much is she your friend that she said to me yesterday: 'Let the Archbishop leave us alone; he shall have his cardinal's cap; I will answer for it.'" The Archbishop then went into the King's bed-chamber, and found there Madame Adelaide, the Duc d'Aumont, the Bishop of Senlis, and Richelieu, in whose presence he resolved not to say one word about confession for that day. This reticence so encouraged Louis XV that, on the Archbishop withdrawing, he had Madame du Barry called in, and kissed her beautiful hands again with his wonted affection. On the 2nd of May the King found himself a little better. Madame du Barry had brought him two confidential physicians, Lorry and Bordeu, who were enjoined to conceal the nature of his sickness from him in order to keep off the priests and save her from humiliating dismissal. The King's improvement allowed of Madame du Barry diverting him by her usual playfulness and conversation. But La Martiniere, who was of the Choiseul party, and to whom they durst not refuse his right of entry, did not conceal from the King either the nature or the danger of his sickness. The King then sent for Madame du Barry, and said to her: "My love, I have got the smallpox, and my illness is very dangerous on account of my age and other disorders. I ought not to forget that I am the *most Christian King and the eldest son of the Church.* I am sixty-four; the time is perhaps approaching when we must separate. I wish to prevent a scene like that of Metz." [When, in 1744, he had dismissed the Duchesse de Chateauroux.] "Apprise the Duc d'Aiguillon of what I say, that he may arrange with you if my sickness grows worse; so that we may part without any publicity." The Jansenists and the Duc de Choiseul's party publicly said that M. d'Aiguillon and the Archbishop had resolved to let the King die without receiving the sacrament, rather than disturb Madame du Barry. Annoyed by their remarks, Beaumont determined to go and reside at the Lazaristes, his house at Versailles, to avail himself of the King's last moments, and sacrifice Madame du Barry when the monarch's condition should become desperate. He arrived on the 3rd of May, but did not see the King. Under existing circumstances, his object was to humble the enemies of his party and to support the favourite who had assisted to overcome them.

A contrary zeal animated the Bishop of Carcassonne, who urged "that the King ought to receive the sacrament; and by expelling the concubine to give an example of repentance to

France and Christian Europe, which he had scandalised." "By what right," said Cardinal de la Roche-Aymon, a complaisant courtier with whom the Bishop was at daggers drawn, "do you instruct me?"—"There is my authority," replied the Bishop, holding up his pectoral cross. "Learn, Monseigneur, to respect it, and do not suffer your King to die without the sacraments of the Church, of which he is the eldest son." The Duc d'Aiguillon and the Archbishop, who witnessed the discussion, put an end to it by asking for the King's orders relative to Madame du Barry. "She must be taken quietly to your seat at Ruelle," said the King; "I shall be grateful for the care Madame d'Aiguillon may take of her."

Madame du Barry saw the King again for a moment on the evening of the 4th, and promised to return to Court upon his recovery. She was scarcely gone when the King asked for her. "*She is gone,*" was the answer. From that moment the disorder gained ground; he thought himself a dead man, without the possibility of recovery. The 5th and 6th passed without a word of confession, viaticum, or extreme unction. The Duc de Fronsac threatened to throw the curé of Versailles out of the window if he dared to mention them. But on the 7th, at three in the morning, the King *imperatively* called for the Abbé Maudoux.[b] Confession lasted seventeen minutes. The Ducs de la Vrilliere and d'Aiguillon wished to delay the viaticum; but La Martiniere said to the King: "Sire, I have seen your Majesty in very trying circumstances; but never admired you as I have done to-day. No doubt your Majesty will immediately finish what you have so well begun." The King had his confessor Maudoux called back: this was a poor priest who had been placed about him for some years before because he was old and blind. He gave him absolution.

The formal renunciation desired by the Choiseul party, in order to humble and annihilate Madame du Barry with solemnity was no more mentioned. The grand almoner, in concert with the Archbishop, composed this formula, pronounced in presence of the viaticum: "Although the King owes an account of his conduct to none but God, he declares his repentance at having scandalised his subjects, and is desirous to live solely for the maintenance of religion and the happiness of his people."

On the 8th and 9th the disorder grew worse; and the King beheld the whole surface of his body coining off piecemeal and corrupted. Deserted by his friends and by that crowd of courtiers which had so long cringed before him, his only consolation was the piety of his daughters … These notes relative to the last sickness of Louis XV were furnished to me by M. de la Borde, his first *valet de chambre*, who left some valuable memoirs of the Court of Louis XV, by the Abbé Dupinet, Canon of Notre Dame, who had them from the Archbishop of Paris; by the Cardinal de Luynes, Madame d'Aiguillon, the Duc de Fronsac, and Maréchal de Richelieu. I have had recourse to both parties for the account of the intrigues by which the expiring King was tormented.—*Historical and Political Memoirs,* by Soulavie, vol. i.

    a. The truth of these particulars is confirmed by Besenval's *Memoirs*, vol. i.—*Note by the Editor.*

    b. In Carlyle's *French Revolution* the confessor of Louis XV is called Moudou.

2. One grudges to interfere with the beautiful theatrical "candle" which Madame Campan (i. 79) has lit on this occasion; and blown out at the moment of death. What candles may be lit or blown out in so large an establishment as that of Versailles, no man at such distance would like to affirm; at the same time, as it was two o'clock on a May afternoon, and these royal stables must have been five or six hundred yards from the royal sickroom, the candle

does threaten to go out in spite of us. It remains burning indeed—in her fantasy: throwing light on much in those Mémoires of hers.—Carlyle's *French Revolution*, vol. i, p. 21.

3. This fact has been doubted, but I am able to assert that Louis XVI desired M. Campan to recall the page, whom he found ready to mount his horse, and whom he desired to come back again to return the letter to the King himself; and that the Queen said upon the subject to my father-in-law: "If the letter had gone, M. de Machault would have been Prime Minister, for the King would never have consented to write a second letter in contradiction of his first intention."[a]—*Madame Campan*.

    a. If we may credit a contemporary writer, the Abbé de Radonvilliers was not without influence in this last determination. Chamfort relates the following anecdote *à propos* of the nomination of the Comte de Maurepas:

"It is a well-known fact that the King's letter, sent to M. de Maurepas, was written for M. de Machault. When M. de Maurepas arrived, the King would do no more than chat with him. At the end of the conversation, M. de Maurepas said to him: 'I will detail my ideas to-morrow at the Council.' It is related, too, that at this conversation he said to the King, 'Your Majesty, then, makes me Prime Minister?' 'No,' replied the King, 'I have no such intention.' 'I understand,' said M. de Maurepas; 'your Majesty wishes I should teach you to do without one.'"—*Note by the Editor*.

4. The Comtesse du Barry never forgot the mild treatment she experienced from the Court of Louis XVI; during the most violent convulsions of the Revolution she signified to the Queen that there was not in all France a female more grieved at the sufferings of her sovereign than herself; that the honour she had for years enjoyed, of living near the throne, and the unbounded kindness of the King and Queen, had so sincerely attached her to the cause of royalty, that she entreated the Queen to honour her by disposing of all she possessed. Though they did not accept her offer, their Majesties were affected at her gratitude. The Comtesse du Barry was, as is well known, one of the victims of the Revolution. She betrayed the lowest degree of weakness, and the most ardent desire to live. She was the only woman who wept upon the scaffold and implored for mercy. Her beauty and tears made an impression on the populace, and the execution was hurried to a conclusion.—*Madame Campan*.

5. These prejudices did not arise from the pretended crime of which calumny had accused this minister, but principally from the suppression of the Jesuits, in which he had, in fact, taken an active part.—*Madame Campan*.

6. The day after the arrival of the Dauphiness at Versailles, the Comtesse de Noailles asked her what orders she had to give M. Moreau, her librarian. She replied that the only order she had for him was to give up the key of her library to M. Campan, whom she installed in his office; adding that he might retain the title which the King had conferred upon him, but that she did not accept his services. She had been so prejudiced against M. Moreau by the Abbé de Vermond that she added that she would speak to the King about the matter; that she knew M. Moreau to be a good deal too clever, and that she desired to have no people about her but those on whom she could rely.—*Madame Campan*.

7. Petite reine de vingt ans,
    Vous qui traitez si mal le gens,
    Vous repasserez la barrière,
    Laire, laire, laire, lanlaire, laire lanla.

8. It was thus, with libels and ill-natured ballads, that the enemies of Marie Antoinette hailed the first days of her reign. They exerted themselves in every way to render her unpopular. Their aim was, beyond all doubt, to have her sent back to Germany; and there was not a moment to be lost in its accomplishment. That the indifference of the King towards his amiable and beautiful wife had lasted so long was already a kind of prodigy; any day the seductive charms of Marie Antoinette might undo all their machinations.—*Madame Campan.*

9. If the use of these extravagant feathers and head-dresses had continued, say the memoirs of that period very seriously, it would have effected a revolution in architecture. It would have been found necessary to raise the doors and ceilings of the boxes at the theatres, and particularly the bodies of carriages. It was not without mortification that the King observed the Queen's adoption of this style of dress: she was never so lovely in his eyes as when unadorned by art. One day Carlin, performing at Court as harlequin, stuck in his hat, instead of the rabbit's tail, its prescribed ornament, a peacock's feather of excessive length. This new appendage, which repeatedly got entangled among the scenery, gave him an opportunity for a great deal of buffoonery. There was some inclination to punish him: but it was presumed that he had not assumed the feather without authority.—*Note by the Editor.*

10. The distinction between the honorary service and the ordinary service is easily drawn. "I have the right to do it," says honorary service haughtily. "You must do it," answers ordinary service sulkily. Between people who have the right to act and do not act, and people whose duty it is to act and who will not act, the great are likely to be very ill served. Madame Campan took pains to collect particulars relative to the ordinary service of the Queen of France. They will be found at the end of the work.—*Note by the Editor.*

11. See Wraxall's *Memoirs.*

12. Mademoiselle Bertin, it is said, upon the strength of the Queen's kindness, became ridiculously proud. A lady one day went to her to ask for some patterns of mourning for the Empress. Several were shown to her, all of which she rejected. Mademoiselle Bertin exclaimed in a tone made up of vexation and self-sufficiency, "Show her, then, some specimens of my last negotiations with her Majesty." However ridiculous the expression may sound, it was actually used as related.—*Note by the Editor.*

13. Before the time of Francis Stephen, the Imperial Court of Germany was the most magnificent of all Europe. Nowhere was etiquette observed more rigorously. Francis suffered it to continue in State ceremonies, but banished it from the privacy of the Court. The Empress-Queen readily acceded to this alteration, and they substituted for ancient formalities the ease and simplicity in which they had indulged at Luneville. Except on days of ceremony their table was frugal, and they received at it persons of merit of both sexes, without distinction of birth. In their amusements they discarded all restraint, and their dress in no way distinguished them from their companions. Their mode of reception was even more gracious to the humble than the great, the poor than the rich ... Marie Antoinette deceived herself in thinking that she too could indulge in such familiarity with impunity. She did not know the disposition of our nation, which, as La Bruyére says, requires seriousness and dignity in its masters; and by the time she had learnt that truth. the lesson came too late.—*History of Marie Antoinette de Lorraine, Queen of France*, by Montjoie.

V

Revision of the papers of Louis XV by Louis XVI—Man in the iron mask—The late King's interest in certain financial companies—Representation of Iphigenia in Aulis—The King gives Petit Trianon to the Queen—The Archduke Maximilian's journey to France—Questions of precedence—Misadventure of the Archduke—Accouchement of the Comtesse d'Artois—The poissardes cry out to the Queen to give heirs to the throne—Death of the Duc de la Vauguyon—Portrait of Louis XVI—Of the Comte de Provence—Of the Comte d'Artois, etc.

During the first few months of his reign Louis XVI dwelt at La Muette, Marly, and Compiègne. When settled at Versailles he occupied himself with a general revision of his grandfather's papers. He had promised the Queen to communicate to her all that he might discover relative to the history of the man with the iron mask, who, he thought, had become so inexhaustible a source of conjecture only in consequence of the interest which the pen of a celebrated writer had excited respecting the detention of a prisoner of State, who was merely a man of whimsical tastes and habits.

I was with the Queen when the King, having finished his researches, informed her that he had not found anything among the secret papers elucidating the existence of this prisoner; that he had conversed on the matter with M. de Maurepas, whose age made him contemporary with the epoch during which the story must have been known to the ministers; and that M. de Maurepas had assured him he was merely a prisoner of a very dangerous character, in consequence of his disposition for intrigue. He was a subject of the Duke of Mantua, and was enticed to the frontier, arrested there, and kept prisoner, first at Pignerol, and afterwards in the Bastille. This transfer took place in consequence of the appointment of the governor of the former place to the Government of the latter. It was for fear the prisoner should profit by the inexperience of a new governor that he was sent with the Governor of Pignerol to the Bastille.

Such was, in fact, the truth about the man on whom people have been pleased to fix an iron mask. And thus was it related in writing, and published by M.—— twenty years ago. He had searched the archives of the Foreign Office, and laid the real story before the public; but the public, prepossessed in favour of a marvellous version, would not acknowledge the authenticity of his account. Every man relied upon the authority of Voltaire; and it was believed that a natural or a twin brother of Louis XIV lived many years in prison with a mask over his face. The story of this mask, perhaps, had its origin in the old custom, among both men and women in Italy, of wearing a velvet mask

Compiègne

when they exposed themselves to the sun. It is possible that the Italian captive may have sometimes shown himself upon the terrace of his prison with his face thus covered. As to the silver plate which this celebrated prisoner is said to have thrown from his window, it is known that such a circumstance did happen, but it happened at Valzin, in the time of Cardinal Richelieu. This anecdote has been mixed up with the inventions respecting the Piedmontese prisoner.

It was also in this review of the papers of Louis XV by his grandson that he found some very curious particulars relative to his private treasury. Certain shares in various financial companies afforded him a revenue, and had at last produced him a capital of some amount, which he applied to his secret expenses. The King collected his vouchers of title to these shares, and made a present of them to M. Thierry de Ville d'Avray, his chief *valet de chambre*.

The Queen was desirous to secure the comfort of Mesdames, the daughters of Louis XV, who were held in the highest respect. About this period she contributed to furnish them with a revenue sufficient to provide them an easy pleasant existence. The King gave them the Château of Bellevue; and added to the produce of it, which was given up to them, the expenses of their table and equipage, and payment of all the charges of their household, the number of which was even increased. During the lifetime of Louis XV, who was a very selfish Prince, his daughters, although they had attained forty years of age, had no other place of residence than their apartments in the Château of Versailles; no other walks than such as they could take in the large park of that palace; and no other means of gratifying their taste for the cultivation of plants but by having boxes and vases, filled with them, in their balconies or their closets. They had, therefore, reason to be much pleased with the conduct of Marie Antoinette, who had the greatest influence in the King's kindness towards his aunts.

Paris did not cease, during the first years of the reign, to give proofs of joy whenever the Queen appeared at any of the plays of the capital. At the representation of *Iphigenia in Aulis*, the actor who sang the words, "*Let us sing, let us celebrate our Queen!*" which were repeated by the chorus, directed by a respectful movement the eyes of the whole Assembly upon her Majesty. Reiterated cries of *Bis*! and clapping of hands, were followed by such a burst of enthusiasm that many of the audience added their voices to those of the actors in order to celebrate, it might too truly be said, another Iphigenia. The Queen, deeply affected, covered her streaming eyes with her handkerchief; and this proof of sensibility raised the public enthusiasm to a still higher pitch.[1]

The King gave Marie Antoinette Petit Trianon.[2] Henceforward she amused herself with improving the gardens, without allowing any addition to the building, or any change in the furniture, which was very shabby; and remained, in 1789, in the same state as during the reign of Louis XV. Everything there, without exception, was preserved; and the Queen slept in a faded bed, which had been used by the Comtesse du Barry. The charge of extravagance, generally made against the Queen, is the most unaccountable of all the popular errors respecting her character. She had exactly the contrary failing; and I could prove that she often carried her economy to a degree of parsimony actually blameable, especially in a sovereign. She took a great liking for Trianon, and used to go there alone, followed by a valet; but she found attendants ready to receive her—a concierge, and his wife who served her as *femme de chambre*; women of the wardrobe, footmen, etc.

When she first took possession of Petit Trianon, it was reported that she had changed the name of the seat which the King had given her, and called it *Little Vienna*, or *Little Schœnbrunn*. A person who belonged to the Court, and was silly enough to give this report credit, wishing to visit Petit Trianon with a party, wrote to M. Campan, requesting the Queen's permission to do so. In his note he called Trianon *Little Vienna*. Similar requests were usually laid before the Queen just as they were made: she chose to give the permissions to see her gardens herself, liking to grant these little favours. When she came to the words I have quoted she was very much offended, and exclaimed, angrily, that there were too many fools ready to aid the malicious; that she had been told of the report circulated, which pretended that she thought of nothing but her own country, and that she kept an Austrian heart, while the interests of France alone ought to engage her. She refused the request so awkwardly made, and desired M. Campan to reply, that Trianon was not to be seen for some time; and that the Queen was astonished that any man in good society should believe she would do so ill-judged a thing as to change the French names of her palaces to foreign ones.

Before the Emperor Joseph II's first visit to France the Queen received a visit from the Archduke Maximilian in 1775. A stupid act of the ambassador, seconded on the part of the Queen by the Abbé de Vermond, gave rise at that period, to a discussion which offended the Princes of the blood and the chief nobility of the kingdom. Travelling incognito, the young Prince claimed that the first visit was not due from him to the Princes of the blood; and the Queen supported his pretension.

From the time of the regency, and on account of the residence of the family of Orléans in the bosom of the capital, Paris had preserved a remarkable degree of attachment and respect for that branch of the royal house; and although the Crown was becoming more and more remote from the Princes of the House of Orléans, they had the advantage (a great one with the Parisians) of being the descendants of Henri IV. An affront to that popular family was a serious ground of dislike to the Queen. It was at this period that the circles of the city, and even of the Court, expressed themselves bitterly about her levity, and her partiality for the House of Austria. The Prince for whom the Queen had embarked in an important family quarrel—and a quarrel involving national prerogatives—was, besides, little calculated to inspire interest. Still young, uninformed, and deficient in natural talent, he was always making blunders.

He went to the Jardin du Roi; M. de Buffon, who received him there, offered him a copy of his works; the Prince declined accepting the book, saying to M. de Buffon in the most polite manner possible, "I should be very sorry to deprive you of it."[3] It may be supposed that the Parisians were much entertained with this answer.

The Queen was exceedingly mortified at the mistakes made by her brother; but what hurt her most was being accused of preserving an Austrian Heart. Marie Antoinette had more than once to endure that imputation during the long course of her misfortunes. Habit did not stop the tears such injustice caused; but the first time she was suspected of not loving France, she gave way to her indignation. All that she could say on the subject was useless; by seconding the pretensions of the Archduke she had put arms into her enemies' hands; they were labouring to deprive her of the love of the people; and endeavoured, by all possible means, to spread a belief that the Queen sighed for Germany, and preferred that country to France.

Marie Antoinette had none but herself to rely on for preserving the fickle smiles of the Court and the public. The King, too indifferent to serve her as a guide, as yet had conceived no love for her, notwithstanding the intimacy that grew between them at Choisy.

In his closet Louis XVI was immersed in deep study. At the Council he was busied with the welfare of his people; hunting and mechanical occupations engrossed his leisure moments, and he never thought on the subject of an heir.

The coronation took place at Rheims, with all the accustomed pomp. At this period the people's love for Louis XVI burst forth in transports not to be mistaken for party demonstrations or idle curiosity. He replied to this enthusiasm by marks of confidence, worthy of a people happy in being governed by a good King; he took a pleasure in repeatedly walking without guards, in the midst of the crowd which pressed around him, and called down blessings on his head. I remarked the impression made at this time by an observation of Louis XVI. On the day of his coronation he put his hand up to his head, at the moment of the crown being placed upon it, and said, "It pinches me." Henry III had exclaimed, "It pricks me." Those who were near the King were struck with the similarity between these two exclamations, though not of a class likely to be blinded by the superstitious fears of ignorance.

While the Queen, neglected as she was, could not even hope for the happiness of being a mother, she had the mortification of seeing the Comtesse d'Artois give birth to the Duc d'Angoulême.

Custom required that the royal family and the whole Court should be present at the *accouchement* of the Princesses; the Queen was therefore obliged to stay a whole day in her sister-in-law's chamber. The moment the Comtesse d'Artois was informed a Prince was born, she put her hand to her forehead and exclaimed with energy, "My God, how happy I am!" The Queen felt very differently at this involuntary and natural exclamation. Nevertheless, her behaviour was perfect. She bestowed all possible marks of tenderness upon the young mother, and would not leave her until she was again put into bed; she afterwards passed along the staircase, and through the hall of the guards, with a calm demeanour, in the midst of an immense crowd. The *poissardes*, who had assumed a right of speaking to sovereigns in their own vulgar language, followed her to the very doors of her apartments, calling out to her, with gross expressions, that *she* ought to produce heirs. The Queen reached her inner room, hurried and agitated; she shut herself up to weep with me alone, not from jealousy of her sister-in-law's happiness—of that she was incapable —but from sorrow at her own situation.

Deprived of the happiness of giving an heir to the Crown, the Queen endeavoured to interest herself in the children of the people of her household. She had long been desirous to bring up one of them herself, and to make it the constant object of her care. A little village boy, four or five years old, full of health, with a pleasing countenance, remarkably large blue eyes, and fine light hair, got under the feet of the Queen's horses, when she was taking an airing in a calash, through the hamlet of Saint Michel, near Louveciennes. The coachman and postilions stopped the horses, and the child was rescued without the slightest injury. Its grandmother rushed out of the door of her cottage to take it; but the Queen, standing up in her calash and extending her arms, called out that the child was hers, and that destiny had given it to her, to console her, no doubt, until she should have the happiness of having one herself. "Is his mother alive?" asked the Queen. "No, Madame; my daughter died last winter, and left five small children upon my hands."—"I will take this one, and provide for all the rest; do you consent?"—"Ah, Madame, they are too fortunate," replied the cottager; "but Jacques is a bad boy. I hope he will stay with you!" The Queen, taking little Jacques upon her knee, said that she would make him used to her; and gave orders to proceed. It was necessary, however, to shorten the drive, so violently did Jacques scream, and kick the Queen and her ladies.

The arrival of her Majesty at her apartments at Versailles, holding the little rustic by the hand, astonished the whole household; he cried out with intolerable shrillness that he wanted his grandmother, his brother Louis, and his sister Marianne,—nothing could calm him. He was taken away by the wife of a servant, who was appointed to attend him as nurse. The other children were put to school. Little Jacques, whose family name was Armand, came back to the Queen two days afterwards; a white frock trimmed with lace, a rose-coloured sash with silver fringe, and a hat decorated with feathers, were now substituted for the woollen cap, the little red frock, and the wooden shoes. The child was really very beautiful. The Queen was enchanted with him; he was brought to her every morning at nine o'clock; he breakfasted and dined with her, and often even with the King. She liked to call him my child,[4] and lavished caresses upon him, still maintaining a deep silence respecting the regrets which constantly occupied her heart.

This child remained with the Queen until the time when Madame was old enough to come home to her august mother, who had particularly taken upon herself the care of her education.

The Queen talked incessantly of the qualities which she admired in Louis XVI, and gladly attributed to herself the slightest favourable change in his manner; perhaps she displayed too unreservedly the joy she felt, and the share she appropriated in the improvement.

One day Louis XVI saluted her ladies with more kindness than usual, and the Queen laughingly said to them, "Now confess, ladies, that for one so badly taught as a child, the King has saluted you with very good grace!"

The Queen hated M. de La Vauguyon; she accused him alone of those points in the habits, and even the sentiments, of the King which hurt her.

A former first woman of the bed-chamber to Queen Maria Leczinska had continued in office near the young Queen. She was one of those people who are fortunate enough to spend their lives in the service of kings without knowing anything of what is passing at court. She was a great devotee; the Abbé Grisel, an ex-Jesuit, was her director. Being rich from her savings, and an income of 50,000 livres, she kept a very good table; in her apartment, at the Grand Commun, the most distinguished persons who still adhered to the Order of Jesuits often assembled. The Duc de La Vauguyon was intimate with her; their chairs at the Église des Récollets were placed near each other; at high mass and at vespers they sang the *Gloria in Excelsis* and the *Magnificat* together; and the pious virgin, seeing in him only one of God's elect, little imagined him to be the declared enemy of a Princess whom she served and revered. On the day of his death she ran in tears to relate to the Queen the piety, humility, and repentance of the last moments of the Duc de La Vauguyon. He had called his people together, she said, to ask their pardon.—"For what?" replied the Queen sharply; "he has placed and pensioned off all his servants; it was of the King and his brothers that the holy man you bewail should have asked pardon; for having paid so little attention to the education of Princes on whom the fate and happiness of twenty-five millions of men depend. Luckily," added she, "the King and his brothers, still young, have incessantly laboured to repair the errors of their preceptor."[5]

The progress of time, and the confidence with which the King and the Princes his brothers were inspired by the change in their situation since the death of Louis XV, had developed their characters. I will endeavour to depict them.

The features of Louis XVI were noble enough, though somewhat melancholy in expression; his walk was heavy and unmajestic; his person greatly neglected; his hair, whatever might be the skill of his hairdresser, was soon in disorder. His voice, without being harsh, was not agreeable; if he grew animated in speaking he often got above his natural pitch, and became shrill. The Abbé de Radonvilliers, his preceptor, one of the forty of the French Academy, a learned and amiable man, had given him and Monsieur a taste for study. The King had continued to instruct himself; he knew the English language perfectly; I have often heard him translate some of the most difficult passages in Milton's poems. He was a skilful geographer, and was fond of drawing and colouring maps; he was well versed in history, but had not perhaps sufficiently studied the spirit of it. He appreciated dramatic beauties, and judged them accurately. At Choisy, one day, several ladies expressed their dissatisfaction because the French actors were going to perform one of Molière's pieces; the King inquired why they disapproved of the choice. One of them answered that everybody must admit that Molière had very bad taste; the King replied that many things might be found in Molière contrary to fashion, but that it appeared to him difficult to point out any in bad taste.[6] This Prince combined with his attainments the attributes of a good husband, a tender father, and an indulgent master.

Unfortunately he showed too much predilection for the mechanical arts; masonry and lock-making so delighted him that he admitted into his private apartment a common lock-smith with whom he made keys and locks; and his hands, blackened by that sort of work, were often, in my presence, the subject of remonstrances and even sharp reproaches from the Queen, who would have chosen other amusements for her husband.[7]

Austere and rigid with regard to himself alone, the King observed the laws of the Church with scrupulous exactness. He fasted and abstained throughout the whole of Lent. He thought it right that the Queen should not observe these customs with the same strictness. Though sincerely pious, the spirit of the age had disposed his mind to toleration. Modest and simple in his habits, Turgot, Malesherbes, and Necker judged that a Prince of such a character would willingly sacrifice the royal prerogative to the solid greatness of his people. His heart, in truth, disposed him towards reforms; but his prejudices and fears, and the clamours of pious and privileged persons, intimidated him, and made him abandon plans which his love for the people had suggested.

Monsieur[8] had more dignity of demeanour than the King; but his corpulence rendered his gait inelegant. He was fond of pageantry and magnificence. He cultivated the *belles-lettres*, and under assumed names often contributed verses to the *Mercury* and other papers.[9]

His wonderful memory was the handmaid of his wit, furnishing him with the happiest quotations. He knew by heart from the finest passages of the Latin classics to the Latin of all the prayers; from the works of Racine to the vaudeville of *Rose et Colas*.

The Comte d'Artois[10] had an agreeable countenance, was well made, skilful in bodily exercises, lively, impetuous, fond of pleasure, and very particular in his dress. Some happy observations made by him were repeated with approval; several of them gave a favourable idea of his heart.[11] The Parisians liked the open and frank character of this Prince, which they considered national, and showed real affection for him.

The dominion that the Queen gained over the King's mind, the charms of a society in which Monsieur displayed his wit, and to which the Comte d'Artois gave life by the vivacity of youth, gradually softened that ruggedness of manner in Louis XVI, which a better-conducted education might have prevented. Still this defect often showed itself, and, in spite of his extreme simplicity, the King inspired those who had occasion to speak to him with diffidence. Courtiers, submissive in the presence of their sovereign, are only the more ready to caricature him; with little good breeding, they called those answers they so much dreaded, *les coups de boutoir du Roi*.[12]

Methodical in all his habits, the King always went to bed at eleven precisely. One evening the Queen was going with her usual circle to a party, either at the Duc de Duras' or the Princesse de Guémenée's. The hand of the clock was slyly put forward to hasten the King's departure by a few minutes; he thought bed-time was come, retired, and found none of his attendants ready to wait on him. This joke became known in all the drawing-rooms of Versailles, and was disapproved of there. Kings have no privacy. Queens have no boudoirs. If those who are in immediate attendance upon sovereigns be not themselves disposed to transmit their private habits to posterity, the meanest valet will relate what he has seen or heard; his gossip circulates rapidly, and forms public opinion, which at length ascribes to the most august persons characters which, however often they may be false, are almost always indelible.

1. The theatre was a constant topic of conversation at Court. When the Queen had not been present, she never omitted asking, "Was it well attended?" I have heard more than one courteous Duke reply with a bow, "There was not even a cat." This did not mean that the theatre was empty. It was even possible that it might be full; but only with honest citizens and country gentry. The nobility affected to know only their own class.—*Madame Campan.*

2. The Château of Petit Trianon, which was built for Louis XV, was not remarkably handsome as a building. The luxuriance of the hothouses rendered the place agreeable to that Prince. He spent a few days there several times in the year. It was when he was setting off from Versailles for Petit Trianon that he was struck in the side by the knife of Damiens; and it was there that he was attacked by the smallpox, of which he died on the 10th of May 1774.—*Madame Campan.*

3. Joseph II, on his visit to France, also went to see M. de Buffon, and said to that celebrated man, "I am come to fetch the copy of your works, which my brother forgot."—*Note by the Editor.*

4. This little unfortunate was nearly twenty in 1792; the fury of the people and the fear of being thought a favourite of the Queen's had made him the most sanguinary terrorist of Versailles. He was killed at the battle of Jemmappes.—*Madame Campan.*

5. Grimm gives the following passage:—"The Duc de La Vauguyon having lately departed to render an account, at the tribunal of eternal justice, of the manner in which he has acquitted himself of the appalling and important duty of educating a Dauphin of France; and to receive the punishment due to the most criminal of undertakings, if it was not fulfilled to the satisfaction of the nation; a remarkable act of vanity, which excited equally the attention of the Court and the city, was witnessed on that occasion: this was the card of invitation to the funeral, sent round to every house according to custom. Every one has wished to preserve this card, on account of its singularity. I will transcribe it here from beginning to end, as it is already scarce, notwithstanding the profusion with which it was distributed:—

You are requested to attend the funeral procession, service, and interment of Monseigneur Antoine-Paul-Jacques de Quélen, head of the names and arms of the ancient lords-castellans of Quélen, in Upper Brittany, *juveigneur* of the Counts of Porhoët, appointed to the name and arms of Siear de Caulsade, Duc de La Vauguyon, peer of France, Prince of Carency, Comte de Quilen, and du Boulay, Marquis de Saint Megrin, de Callonges and d'Archiac, Vicomte de Calvzgnac, Baron of the ancient and honourable baronies of Tonneins, Grattelout, Villeton, la Gruère and Picornet, lord of Larnagol and Talcoimur, *vidame*, knight, and protector of Sarlac, his Baron of Guyenne, second Baron of Quercy, lieutenant-general of the king's armies, knight of his orders, *menin* of Monseigneur the late Dauphin, first gentleman of the bed-chamber of Monseigneur the Dauphin, grand master of his wardrobe, formerly governor of his person, and of that of Monseigneur the Comte de Provence, governor of the person of Monseigneur the Comte d'Artois, first gentleman of his chamber, grand master of his wardrobe, and superintendent of his household,—which will take place on Thursday the 6th of February 1772, at ten o'clock in the morning, at the royal and parochial church of Notre Dame de Versailles, where his body will be interred. DE PROFUNDIS."

The terms *juveigneur* and *menin* are now obsolete: *juveigneur* signified a feudal dependant, the Duc d'Orléans being *juveigneur* of the House of France; *menin* was the title given to the six gentlemen-in-waiting on the Dauphin, and was first used when the household of the son of Louis XIV was formed.

6. The King, having purchased the Château of Rambouillet from the Duc de Penthièvre, amused himself with embellishing it. I have seen a register entirely in his own handwriting, which proves that he possessed a great variety of information on the minutiae of various branches of knowledge. In his accounts he would not omit an outlay of twelve pence. His figures and letters, when he wished to write legibly, were small and very neat, but in general he wrote very ill. He was so sparing of paper that he divided a sheet into eight, six, or four pieces, according to the length of what he had to write. Towards the close of the page he compressed the letters, and avoided interlineations. The last words were close to the edge of the paper; he seemed to regret being obliged to begin another page. He was methodical and analytical; he divided what he wrote into chapters and sections. He had extracted from the works of Nicole and Fénélon, his favourite authors, three or four hundred concise and sententious phrases, these he had classed according to subject, and formed a work of them in the style of Montesquieu. To this treatise he had given the following general title: *Of Moderate Monarchy* (De la Monarchie temperée), with chapters entitled, "Of the Person of the Prince"; "Of the Authority of Bodies in the State"; "Of the Character of the Executive Functions of the Monarchy". Had he been able to carry into effect all the grand precepts he had observed in Fénélon, Louis XVI would have been an accomplished monarch, France a powerful kingdom. The King used to accept the speeches his ministers presented to him to deliver on important occasions; but he corrected and modified them; struck out some parts, and added others; and sometimes consulted the Queen on the subject. The phrase of the minister erased by the King was frequently unsuitable, and dictated by the minister's private feelings; but the King's was always the natural expression. He himself composed, three times or oftener, his famous answers to the Parliament which he banished. But in his letters he was negligent, and always incorrect. Simplicity was the characteristic of the King's style; the figurative style of M. Necker did not please him; the sarcasms of Maurepas were disagreeable to him. Unfortunate Prince! he would predict, in his observations, that if such a calamity should happen, the monarchy would be ruined; and the next day he would consent in Council to the very measure which he had condemned the day before, and which brought him nearer the brink of the precipice.—*Historical and Political Memoirs of the Reign of Louis XVI*, by Soulavie, vol. ii.

7. Louis XVI saw that the art of lock-making was capable of application to a higher study. He was an excellent geographer. The most valuable and complete instrument for the study of that science was begun by his orders and under his direction. It was an immense globe of

copper, which was long preserved, though unfinished, in the Mazarine library. Louis XVI invented and had executed under his own eyes the ingenious mechanism required for this globe.—*Note by the Editor.*

8. Afterwards Louis XVIII.

9. During his stay at Avignon, Monsieur lodged with the Duc de Crillon; he refused the town-guard which was offered him, saying, "A son of France, under the roof of a Crillon, needs no guard."—*Note by the Editor.*

10. Afterwards Charles X.

11. A selfish courtier was foolish enough to remark that the Abbé de Besplas had complained improperly of the manner in which prisoners were treated in gaols, since it might be considered a part of the punishment which their crimes deserved. The Prince interrupted him, indignantly exclaiming, "How can one tell that they are guilty? That is never known till the sentence is passed."—*Note by the Editor.*

12. The literal meaning of the phrase "*coup de boutoir*" is a poke from the snout of a boar.

ANNEX TO CHAPTER V

The following extracts from works relating to this period illustrate the importance then attached to etiquette and ceremonial, and show the character and habits of Louis XVI:—

MADEMOISELLE DE LORRAINE'S MINUET

A few days before the Dauphin's marriage it was reported that Mademoiselle de Lorraine, daughter of the Comtesse de Brionne, and sister of the Prince de Lambesc, *grand écuyer* of France, was to dance her minuet at the dress ball immediately after the Princes and Princesses of the blood; and that the King had granted her that distinction just after an audience which his Majesty had given to the Comte de Mercy, the ambassador of the Emperor and Empress. The intelligence about Mademoiselle de Lorraine's minuet caused the greatest excitement among the dukes and peers, who enlisted all the superior nobility of the kingdom in their cause. They set it down as an incontrovertible principle that there could not be any intermediate rank between the Princes of the blood and the superior nobility; and that, consequently, Mademoiselle de Lorraine could have no rank distinct from that of women of quality presented at Court. The Archbishop of Rheims, the first ecclesiastical peer, being unwell, they met at the house of the Bishop of Noyon, the second ecclesiastical peer, brother of the Maréchal de Broglie. They drew up a memorial to be presented to the King; the dukes and peers left intervals between their signatures that the superior nobility might sign without distinction of title or rank. The Bishop of Noyon presented this memorial to his Majesty.

The request was hardly known when the following parody on it was publicly circulated:—

Sire, the Great, one and all
See, with sorrow and pain,
A Princess of Lorraine
Take the lead at the ball.
If your Majesty mean
Such affronts to project,
Such marked disrespect,
They will quit the gay scene;
And leave fiddlers and all:
Then think what is said,
The agreement is made,
Signed Bishop of Noyon,
De Villette, Beaufremont, etc.

In fact, it was openly said that if the King's answer were unfavourable, all the women of quality would find themselves suddenly indisposed, and not one of them would dance at the ball. The parody is not without point in other respects. Independently of the absurdity of a prelate's presiding over deliberations on the subject of a minuet, the names of some ancient and illustrious houses are enclosed in it, between two grandees of the monarchy of very recent date. This may be taken for a joke, but it is a positive truth that the Marquis de Villette, the son of a treasurer of war extraordinary, who never distinguished himself further than by a few trifling compositions, was permitted to sign a petition, at the bottom of which we read the names of Beaufremont, Clermont, and Montmorency. No doubt his descendants will be grateful to him for this signature. They will say, "One of our ancestors signed the famous minuet petition on the marriage of the grandson of Louis XV in concert with all the peers, and all the superior nobility of the kingdom; so that our name was thenceforward classed among the most illustrious in the kingdom." They may also say, "In 1770, at the dress ball on the marriage of the Dauphin, a Villette disputed precedence with the Princes of the House of Lorraine." "It is the great Villette," one of his grandsons will add, "who published, at his own expense, an eulogium upon *Charles V* and one upon Henri IV which have not escaped the attacks of time either in the archives of literature or in those of our house." There are plenty of historical proofs which rest on no better foundation.—Grimm's *Correspondence*, tome vii, p. 143.

The following particulars are added by Soulavie:—"Maria Theresa knew the Court of Versailles well; and yet she so far erred as to demand diplomatically, through M. de Mercy, her ambassador, that Mademoiselle de Lorraine, her relation, and the Prince de Lambesc, should rank next after the Princes of the blood in the entertainments on the marriage of her daughter with the Dauphin. Louis XV, in order to gratify the Dauphiness, who desired it, and Maria Theresa, who demanded it, thought fit to make it an affair of state. He knew the jealousy of the grandees of his Court with regard to their rights of etiquette, and he desired them, by virtue of the submission and attachment which they owed him, and which they had manifested to him, as well as to his predecessors, not to contradict him on this occasion, intimating his desire to mark his gratitude to the Empress for the present she made to France of her daughter. The King did not calculate on the obstacles the dukes would throw in the way of this new assumption. The ladies of the Court, from whom Louis XV had a right to expect most deference, played an obstinate and haughty part, opposing an insurmountable resistance to the King's request. They were firm in their resolution of depriving themselves of the pleasure of the ball rather than suffer their right to dance first to be infringed upon. Among all these ladies, Madame de Bouillon distinguished herself most by the asperity of her observations. Louis XV showed himself so much offended at them that she came no more to Court. The Dauphiness, on her part, was so vexed that she procured one of the letters that Louis XV had written to the peers, and shut it up in her desk, saying, "*I will remember it.*" However, in order to put an end to the matter, Mademoiselle de Lorraine agreed to dance with the Duchesse de Duras, whose situation kept her at Court.—*Historical and Political Memoirs of the Reign of Louis XVI,* vol. i.

CORONATION OF LOUIS XVI

The dresses worn by the principal dignitaries at the consecration were interesting, on account both of their richness and their ancient form. The lay peers were clad in long vests of gold brocade; they had girdles of gold, silver, and violet-coloured silk mixed, and over the long vest a ducal mantle of violet cloth, lined and edged with ermine; the round collar was likewise of ermine; and every one wore a crown upon a cap of violet satin, and the collar of the Order of the Holy Ghost over the mantle. The captain of the hundred Swiss of the King's Guard was dressed in silver stuff, with an embroidered shoulder-belt of the same; a black mantle lined with cloth of silver, and, as well as his trunk hose, trimmed with lace, and a black cap surmounted with a plume of feathers. The grand master and the master of the ceremonies were dressed in silver stuff doublets, black velvet breeches intersected by bands, and cloaks of black velvet, trimmed with silver lace, with caps of black velvet surmounted with white feathers.

On Sunday the 11th of June, at six in the morning, the canons in their copes arrived in the choir. They were soon followed by the Archbishop Duc de Rheims, the cardinals and prelates invited, the ministers, the marshals of France, the counsellors of state, and the deputies of the various companies. About half-past six the lay peers arrived. Monsieur represented the Duke of Burgundy; M. le Comte d'Artois, the Duke of Normandy; and the Duc d'Orléans the Duke of Aquitaine. The remainder of the ancient peers of France, the Counts of Toulouse, Flanders, and Champagne, were represented by the Duc de Chartres, the Prince de Condé, and the Duc de Bourbon, who wore counts' coronets. The ecclesiastical peers continued hooded and mitred during the whole ceremony.

At seven, the Bishop Duc de Laon, and the Bishop Comte de Beauvais, set out to fetch the King. These two prelates, in their pontifical dresses, with reliquaries suspended from their necks, were preceded by all the canons of the church of Rheims, with whom were the musicians. The chanter and sub-chanter walked after the clergy and before the Marquis de Dreux, grand master of the ceremonies, who immediately preceded the bishops; they passed through a covered gallery, and came to the King's door, which, according to custom from time immemorial, they found shut. The chanter strikes upon it with his baton; and the great chamberlain, without opening, says to him, "*What is it you require?*"—"*We ask for the King,*" replies the principal ecclesiastical peer.—"*The King sleeps,*" returns the great chamberlain. Then the grand chanter strikes again, with the same result. At length the chanter, having struck a third time, and the great chamberlain answered "*The King sleeps,*" the ecclesiastical peer pronounces these words, "*We demand Louis XVI, whom God has given us for King;*" and immediately the chamber doors open. The grand master of the ceremonies leads the bishops to his Majesty, who is stretched upon a state bed: they salute him profoundly. The monarch is clothed in a long crimson gown, trimmed with gold galoon, and, as well as the shirt, open at those places where he is to be anointed. Above the gown he has a long robe of silver stuff, and upon his head a cap of black velvet, ornamented with a string of diamonds, a plume, and a white double aigrette. The ecclesiastical peer presents the holy water to the King, and repeats the following prayer:—"Almighty and everlasting God, who hast raised thy servant, Louis, to the regal dignity, grant him throughout his reign to seek the good of his subjects, and that he may never wander from the paths of truth and justice." This prayer ended, the two bishops take his Majesty, the one by the right arm, and the other by the left, and raising him from the bed, conduct him in procession to the church through the covered gallery, chanting appropriate prayers. The King having reached the church, the Holy Ampulla arrived at the principal door. It was brought from the Abbey of Saint Rémi by the grand prior, in a cover of cloth of gold, and mounted upon a white horse from the King's stable, covered with a housing of cloth of silver, richly embroidered, and led by the reins by two chief grooms of the stable. The grand prior was under a canopy of similar materials, carried by four barons, called *knights of the Holy Ampulla,* clad in white satin, with a mantle of black silk, and a white velvet scarf, trimmed with silver fringe; they wore the knight's cross, suspended round the neck by a black ribbon. At the four corners of the canopy, the peers named by the King as hostages of the Holy Ampulla were seen on horseback, each preceded by his esquire with a standard, bearing on one side the arms of France, and on the other those of the peer. They had solemnly sworn upon the Holy Gospels that no injury should be done to the Holy Ampulla, for the preservation of which they promised, if necessary, to risk their lives, and declared that they would become hostages until the return of the Holy Ampulla. The Holy Ampulla, which is so conspicuous an article in the consecration of our Kings, is a sort of small bottle filled, it is asserted, with a miraculous balm, brought by a dove to Saint Rémi, who died about the year 535. It never diminishes; it is treasured in the tomb of the ancient archbishop, whose body remains entire in a shrine of the Abbey bearing his name; and it is enclosed in a silver gilt reliquary, enriched with diamonds and gems of various colours.[1] The Archbishop of Rheims received the Holy Ampulla at the gate of the church; on placing it in his hands, the grand prior addressed these words to him: "To you, my lord, I entrust this precious treasure sent from Heaven to the great Saint Rémi, for the consecration of Clovis and the Kings his successors: but I request you, according to ancient custom, to bind yourself to restore it into my hands, after the consecration of our King Louis XVI." The Archbishop took the required oath in these terms: "I receive this Holy Ampulla with reverence, and promise you, upon the faith of a prelate, to restore it into your hands at the conclusion of the ceremony of the consecration." The Cardinal de la Roche-Aymon then took the marvellous phial, and deposited it upon the altar. A few minutes afterwards he approached the King, to whom he administered the oath, called *the protection oath*, for all the churches in subjection to the Crown: a promise which his Majesty made sitting and covered. "I promise," said the King, "to prevent the commission of rapine and injustice of every description by persons of all ranks. I swear to apply myself sincerely, and with all my might, to the extermination of heretics, condemned and pointed out by the Church, from all countries subject to my government." After this oath, two ecclesiastical peers present the King to the Assembly, and demand whether Louis XVI is approved of for the dignity of King of France. A respectful silence announced the general consent.

The Archbishop of Rheims presented the book of the Gospels to the King, placing his hands upon which, his Majesty took the oath to maintain and preserve the Orders of the Holy Ghost and Saint Louis, and always to wear the cross of the latter order attached to a flame-coloured silk ribbon; and to enforce the edict against duels, without any regard to the intercessions of any princes or potentates. The former part of this oath is of very little importance, and the second is broken every day.

When the King, for the second time, received the sword of Charlemagne, he deposited it in the hands of the Maréchal de Clermont Tonnerre, officiating as constable, who held it point upwards during the ceremony of the consecration and coronation, as well as during the royal banquet. While the King was receiving and returning the sword of Charlemagne, several prayers were said. When they were finished, the officiating prelate opened the Holy Ampulla, and let a small quantity of oil drop from it, and this he diluted with some consecrated oil, called holy cream. The King prostrated himself before the altar upon a large square of violet-coloured velvet, embroidered with golden fleurs-de-lis, the old Archbishop Duc de Rheims being also prostrated on his right hand, and remaining in that lowly posture until the conclusion of the litanies chanted by four bishops alternately with the choir. At the end of the litanies the Archbishop of Rheims placed himself in his chair, and the King, kneeling down before him, was anointed upon the crown of the head, the breast, between the two shoulders, upon the right shoulder, the left, upon the joint of the right arm, and upon that of the left arm; at the same time the prelate pronounced certain prayers, the substance of which was as follows: "May he humble the proud; may he be a lesson for the rich; may he be charitable towards the poor; and may he be a peacemaker among nations." A little further on these words occur among the prayers: "May he never abandon his rights over the kingdoms of the Saxons, Mercians, people of the north, and the Cimbri." An anonymous author says that by the word Cimbri is meant the kingdom of England, over which our Kings expressly reserve their indisputable rights, from the time of Louis VIII, upon whom it was conferred by the free election of the people who had driven out John Sans Terre. After the seven anointings, the Archbishop of Rheims, assisted by the Bishops of Laon and Beauvais, laced up with gold laces the openings of the King's shirt and gown, and he, rising, was invested by the great chamberlain with the tunic, dalmatic, and royal mantle, lined and edged with ermine: these vestments are of violet velvet, embroidered with gold and fleurs-de-lis, and represent the dresses of sub-deacon, deacon, and priest; symbols by which, no doubt, the clergy seek to prove their union with the royal power. The King placed himself upon his knees again before the officiating Archbishop, who made the eighth unction upon the palm of the right hand, and the ninth and last upon that of the left; he afterwards placed a ring upon the fourth finger of the right hand, as a type of unlimited power, and of the intimate union thenceforward to reign between the King and his people. The Archbishop then took the royal sceptre from the altar, and put it into the King's right hand, and afterwards the hand of justice, which he put into the left hand. The sceptre is of enamelled gold, ornamented with Oriental pearls; it may be about six feet in height. Upon it is represented, in relief, Charlemagne, with the globe in his hand, seated in a chair of state, ornamented with two lions and two eagles. The hand of justice is a staff of massive gold, only one foot and a half in length, adorned with rubies and pearls, and terminated by a hand formed of ivory, or rather of the horn of a rhinoceros; and it has, at regular distances, three circles of leaves sparkling with pearls, garnets, and other precious stones.

The Keeper of the Seals of France, officiating as Chancellor, then ascended the altar, and summoned the peers to the coronation in the following words:—"Monsieur, representing the Duke of Burgundy, come forward to this act," etc., etc. The peers having approached the King, the Archbishop of Rheims took from the altar the Crown of Charlemagne, which had been brought from Saint Denis, and placed it upon the King's head; immediately the ecclesiastical and lay peers raised their hands to support it there. In one of the prayers at this part of the ceremony an Oriental expression of great energy is made use of: "May the King have the strength of the rhinoceros; and may he, like a rushing wind, drive before him the nations of our enemies, even to the extremity of the earth." The crown of Charlemagne, which is preserved in the treasury of the Abbey of Saint Denis, is of gold, and enriched with rubies and sapphires; it is lined with a crimson satin cap, embroidered with gold, and surmounted by a golden fleur-de-lis, covered with thirty-six Oriental pearls.

After these ceremonies the Archbishop Duc de Rheims took the King by the right arm, and, followed by the peers and all the officers of the Crown, led him to the throne raised upon a platform, where he seated him, reciting the enthroning prayers. In the first of these it is said: "As you see the clergy nearer than the rest of the faithful to the holy altar, so ought you to take care and maintain it in the most honourable place." Then the prelate took off his mitre, made a profound bow to the King, and kissed him, saying, "*Vivat Rex in aeternum!*" The other ecclesiastical and lay peers also kissed the King, one after the other, and as soon as they returned to their places the gates of the church were opened; the people rushed in, and made the roofs resound with shouts of, "*Long live the King!*" which were re-echoed by the crowd of persons engaged in the ceremony, who filled the enclosure of the choir like an amphitheatre; an irresistible impulse gave rise to a clapping of hands, which became general; the grandees, the Court, the people, animated by the same enthusiasm, expressed it in the same manner.

The Queen, overcome with emotion, was obliged to withdraw for a short time. When she reappeared she received a similar homage to that just offered by the nation to the King.

While exclamations of joy resounded, the fowlers, according to a very ancient usage, set at liberty in the church numbers of birds, symbolising the monarch's regard for the people, and that men are never more truly free than under the reign of an enlightened, just, and beneficent Prince.—*Secret Correspondence of the Court of Louis XVI.*

PURSUITS OF THE KING

The only passion ever shown by Louis XVI was for hunting. He was so much occupied by it that when I went up into his private closets at Versailles, after the 10th of August, I saw upon the staircase six frames, in which were seen statements of all his hunts, when Dauphin and when King. In them was detailed the number, kind, and quality of the game he had killed at each hunting party during every month, every season, and every year of his reign.

The interior of his private apartments was thus arranged: a saloon, ornamented with gilded mouldings, displayed the engravings which had been dedicated to him; drawings of the canals he had dug, with the model of that of Burgundy; and the plan of the cones and works of Cherbourg. The upper hall contained his collection of geographical charts, spheres, globes, and also his geographical cabinet. There were to be seen drawings of maps which he had begun, and some that he had finished. He had a clever method of washing them in. His geographical memory was prodigious. Over the hall was the turning and joining room, furnished with ingenious instruments for working in wood. He inherited some from Louis XV, and he often busied himself, with Duret's assistance, in keeping them clean and bright. Above was the library of books published during his reign. The prayer books and manuscript books of Anne of Brittany, Francis I, the latter Valois, Louis XIV, Louis XV, and the Dauphin, formed the great hereditary library of the Château. Louis XVI placed separately, in two apartments communicating with each other, the works of his own time, including a complete collection of Didot's editions, in vellum, every volume enclosed in a morocco case. There were several English works, among the rest the debates of the British Parliament, in a great number of volumes in folio (this is the *Moniteur of England*, a complete collection of which is so valuable and so scarce). By the side of this collection was to be seen a manuscript history of all the schemes for a descent upon that island, particularly that of Comte de Broglie. One of the presses of this cabinet was full of pasteboard boxes, containing papers relative to the House of Austria, inscribed in the King's own hand: "*Secret papers of my family respecting the House of Austria; papers of my family respecting the Houses of Stuart and Hanover.*" In an adjoining press were kept papers relative to Russia. Satirical works against Catherine II and against Paul I were sold in France under the name of histories; Louis XVI collected and sealed up with his small seal the scandalous anecdotes against Catherine II, as well as the works of Rhulières, of which he had a copy, to be certain that, the secret life of that Princess, which attracted the curiosity of her contemporaries, should not be made public by his means.

Above the King's private library were a forge, two anvils, and a vast number of iron tools; various common locks, well made and perfect; some secret locks, and locks ornamented with gilt copper. It was there that the infamous Gamin, who afterwards accused the King of having tried to poison him, and was rewarded for his calumny with a pension of 12,000 livres, taught him the art of lock-making. This Gamin, who became our guide, by order of the department and municipality of Versailles, did not, however, denounce the King on the 10th December 1792. He had been made the confidant of that Prince in an immense number of important commissions; the King had sent him the *Red Book*, from Paris, in a parcel; and the part which was concealed during the Constituent Assembly, still remained so in 1793. Gamin hid it in a part of the Château, inaccessible to everybody, and took it from under the shelves of a secret press before our eyes. This is a convincing proof that Louis XVI hoped to return to his Château. When teaching Louis XVI his trade Gamin took upon himself the tone and authority of a master. "The King was good, forbearing, timid, inquisitive, and addicted to sleep," said Gamin to me; he was fond to excess of lock-making, and he concealed himself from the Queen and the Court to file and forge with me. In order to convey his anvil and my own backwards and forwards we were obliged to use a thousand stratagems, the history of which would never "end". Above the King's and Gamin's forges and anvils was an observatory, erected upon a platform covered with lead. There, seated on an armchair, and assisted by a telescope, the King observed all that was passing in the courtyards of Versailles, the avenue of Paris, and the neighbouring gardens. He had taken a liking to Duret, one of the indoor servants of the palace, who sharpened his tools, cleaned his anvils, pasted his maps, and adjusted eye-glasses to the King's sight, who was short-sighted. This good Duret, and indeed all the indoor servants, spoke of their master with regret and affection, and with tears in their eyes.

The King was born weak and delicate; but, from the age of twenty-four, he possessed a robust constitution, inherited from his mother, who was of the House of Saxe, celebrated for generations for its robustness. There were two men in Louis XVI, *the man of knowledge*, and *the man of will*. The King knew the history of his own family and of the first houses of France perfectly. He composed the instructions for M. de la Peyrouse's voyage round the world, which the minister thought were drawn up by several members of the Academy of Sciences. His memory retained an infinite number of names and situations. He remembered quantities and numbers wonderfully. One day an account was presented to him in which the minister had ranked among the expenses an item inserted in the account of the preceding year. "There is a double charge," said the King; "bring me last year's account, and I will show it you there." When the King was perfectly master of the details of any matter, and saw injustice, he was obdurate even to harshness. Then he would be obeyed instantly, in order to be sure that he was obeyed.

But in important affairs of State the *man of will* was not to be found. Louis XVI was upon the throne exactly what those weak temperaments whom nature has rendered incapable of an opinion are in society. In his pusillanimity, he gave his confidence to a minister; and although amidst various counsels he often knew which was the best, he never had the resolution to say, "*I prefer the opinion of such an one.*" Herein originated the misfortunes of the State.—*Historical and Political Memoirs of the Reign of Louis XVI, by Soulavie, vol. ii.*

1. This phial was afterwards broken to pieces upon the pavement of the Abbey by the conventionary Ruhl, deputed for that purpose; the shrine and reliquaries, broken by his direction, were sent to La Monnaie.—*Note by the Editor.*

VI

*Severe winter—The Princesse de Lamballe appointed superintendent of
the Household—The Comtesse Jules de Polignac appears at Court—M. de
Vaudreuil—Duc and Duchesse de Duras—Fashionable games*

The winter following the confinement of the Comtesse d'Artois was very severe; the
recollection of the pleasure which sleighing-parties had given the Queen in her childhood made her wish to introduce similar ones in France. This amusement had already
been known in that Court, as was proved by sleighs being found in the stables which
had been used by the Dauphin, the father of Louis XVI. Some were constructed for the
Queen in a more modern style. The Princes also ordered several; and in a few days there
was a tolerable number of these vehicles. They were driven by the Princes and noblemen
of the Court. The noise of the bells and balls with which the harness of the horses was
furnished, the elegance and whiteness of their plumes, the varied forms of the carriages,
the gold with which they were all ornamented, rendered these parties delightful to the
eye. The winter was very favourable to them, the snow remaining on the ground nearly
six weeks; the drives in the park afforded a pleasure shared by the spectators.[1] No one
imagined that any blame could attach to so innocent an amusement. But the party were
tempted to extend their drives as far as the Champs Elysées; a few sleighs even crossed
the boulevards; the ladies being masked, the Queen's enemies took the opportunity of
saying that she had traversed the streets of Paris in a sleigh.

This became a matter of moment. The public discovered in it a predilection for the
habits of Vienna; but all that Marie Antoinette did was criticised. Factions formed in
courts do not openly carry insignia, as do those generated by revolutionary convulsions.
They are not, however, on that account the less dangerous, and the Queen was never
without a party against her.

Sleigh-driving, savouring of the Northern courts, had no favour among the Parisians.
The Queen was informed of this; and although all the sleighs were preserved, and several subsequent winters lent themselves to the amusement, she would not resume it.

It was at the time of the sleighing-parties that the Queen became intimately
acquainted with the Princesse de Lamballe, who made her appearance in them, wrapped
in fur, with all the brilliancy and freshness of the age of twenty; the emblem of spring,
peeping from under sable and ermine. Her situation, moreover, rendered her peculiarly
interesting; married, when she was scarcely past childhood, to a young prince, who
ruined himself by the contagious example of the Duc d'Orléans, she had had nothing
to do from the time of her arrival in France but to weep. A widow at eighteen, and
childless, she lived with the Duc de Penthièvre as an adopted daughter. She had the

tenderest respect and attachment for that venerable Prince; but the Queen, though doing justice to his virtues, saw that the Duc de Penthièvre's way of life, whether at Paris or at his country-seat, could neither afford his young daughter-in-law the amusements suited to her time of life, nor insure her in the future an establishment such as she was deprived of by her widowhood. She determined, therefore, to establish her at Versailles; and for her sake revived the office of superintendent, which had been discontinued at Court since the death of Mademoiselle de Clermont. It is said that Maria Leczinska had decided that this place should continue vacant; the superintendent having so extensive a power in the houses of queens as to be frequently a restraint upon their inclinations. Differences which soon took place between Marie Antoinette and the Princesse de Lamballe respecting the official prerogatives of the latter, proved that the wife of Louis XV had acted judiciously in abolishing the office; but a kind of treaty made between the Queen and the Princess smoothed all difficulties. The blame for too strong an assertion of claims fell upon a secretary of the superintendent's, who had been her adviser; and everything was so arranged that a firm friendship existed between these two Princesses down to the disastrous period which terminated their career.

Notwithstanding the enthusiasm which the splendour, graces, and kindness of the Queen generally inspired, secret intrigues continued in operation against her. A short time after the accession of Louis XVI to the throne, the minister of the King's household was informed that a most offensive libel against the Queen was about to appear. The lieutenant of police deputed a man named Goupil, a police inspector, to trace this libel; he came soon after to say that he had found out the place where the work was being printed, and that it was at a country house near Yverdun. He had already got possession of two sheets, which contained the most atrocious calumnies, conveyed with a degree of art which might make them very dangerous to the Queen's reputation. Goupil said that he could obtain the rest, but that he should want a considerable sum for that purpose. Three thousand *louis* were given him, and very soon afterwards he brought the whole manuscript and all that had been printed to the lieutenant of police. He received 1,000 *louis* more as a reward for his address and zeal; and a much more important office was about to be given him, when another spy, envious of Goupil's good fortune, gave information that Goupil himself was the author of the libel; that, ten years before, he had been put into the Bicêtre for swindling; and that Madame Goupil had only been three years out of the Salpétrière, where she had been placed under another name. This Madame Goupil was very pretty and very intriguing; she had found means to form an intimacy with Cardinal de Rohan, whom she led, it is said, to hope for a reconciliation with the Queen. All this affair was hushed up; but it shows that it was the Queen's fate to be incessantly attacked by the meanest and most odious machinations.[2]

Another woman, named Cahouette de Villers, whose husband held an office in the Treasury, being very irregular in conduct, and of a scheming turn of mind, had a mania for appearing in the eyes of her friends at Paris a person in favour at Court, to which she was not entitled either by birth or office. During the latter years of the life of Louis XV she had made many dupes, and picked up considerable sums by passing herself off as the King's mistress. The fear of irritating Madame du Barry was, according to her, the only thing which prevented her enjoying that title openly: she came regularly to Versailles, kept herself concealed in a furnished lodging, and her dupes imagined she was secretly summoned to Court. This woman formed the scheme of getting admission, if possible, to the presence of the Queen, or at least causing it to be believed that she had done so. She adopted as her lover Gabriel de Saint Charles, superintendent of her Majesty's finances; an office, the privileges of which were confined to the right of entering the Queen's apartment on Sunday. Madame de Villers came every Saturday to Versailles with M. de Saint Charles, and lodged in his apartment; M. Campan was there several times; she painted tolerably well; she requested him to do her the favour to present to the Queen a portrait of her Majesty which she had just copied. M. Campan knew the woman's character, and refused her. A few days after, he saw on her Majesty's couch the portrait which he had declined to present to her; the Queen thought it badly painted, and gave orders that it should be carried back to the Princesse de Lamballe, who had sent it to her. The ill success of the portrait did not deter the manoeuvrer from following up her designs; she easily procured through M. de Saint Charles patents and orders signed by the Queen; she then set about imitating her writ letters, as if written by her Majesty, in the tenderest and most familiar style. For many months she showed them as great secrets to several of her particular friends. Afterwards, she made the Queen appear to write to her, to procure various fancy articles. Under the pretext of wishing to execute her Majesty's commissions accurately, she gave these letters to the tradesmen to read; and succeeded having it said, in many houses, that the Queen had a particular regard for her. She then enlarged her scheme, and represented the Queen as desiring her to borrow 200,000 francs which she had need of, but which she did not wish to ask of the King from his private funds. This letter being shown to M. Beranger, *fermier-général* of the finances, took effect; he thought himself fortunate in being able to render this assistance to his sovereign, and lost no time in sending the 200,000 francs to Madame de Villers. This first step was followed by some doubts, which he communicated to people better informed than himself of what was passing at Court; they added to his uneasiness; he then went to M. de Sartine, who unravelled the whole plot. The woman was sent to Saint Pelagie; and the unfortunate husband was ruined, by replacing the sum borrowed, and by paying for the jewels fraudulently purchased in the Queen's name; the forged letters were sent to her Majesty; I compared them in her presence with her own handwriting, and the only distinguishable difference was a little more regularity in the letters.

This trick, discovered and punished with prudence and without passion, produced no more sensation out of doors than that of the Inspector Goupil.

A year after the nomination of Madame de Lamballe[3] to the post of superintendent of the Queen's household, balls and quadrilles gave rise to the intimacy of her Majesty with the Comtesse Jules de Polignac. This lady really interested Marie Antoinette. She was not rich, and generally lived upon her estate at Daye. The Queen was astonished at not having seen her at Court earlier. The confession that her want of fortune had even prevented her appearance at the celebration of the marriages of the Princes added to the interest which she had inspired.

The Queen was full of sensibility, and took delight in counteracting the injustice of fortune. The Countess was induced to come to Court by her husband's sister, Madame Diana de Polignac, who had been appointed lady of honour to the Comtesse d'Artois. The Comtesse Jules was really fond of a tranquil life; the impression she made at Court affected her but little; she felt only the attachment manifested for her by the Queen. I had occasion to see her from the commencement of her favour at Court; she often passed whole hours with me, while waiting for the Queen. She conversed with me freely and ingenuously about the honour, and at the same time the danger, she saw in the kindness of which she was the object. The Queen sought for the sweets of friendship; but can this gratification, so rare in any rank, exist between a Queen and a subject—when they are surrounded, moreover, by snares laid by the artifice of courtiers? This pardonable error was fatal to the happiness of Marie Antoinette.

The retiring character of the Comtesse Jules, afterwards Duchesse de Polignac, cannot be spoken of too favourably; but if her heart was incapable of forming ambitious projects, her family and friends in her fortune beheld their own, and endeavoured to secure the favour of the Queen.[4]

The Comtesse Diana, sister of M. de Polignac, and the Baron de Besenval and M. de Vaudreuil, particular friends of the Polignac family, made use of means, the success of which was infallible. One of my friends (Comte de Moustier), who was in their secret, came to tell me that Madame de Polignac was about to quit Versailles suddenly; that she would take leave of the Queen only in writing; that the Comtesse Diana and M. de Vaudreuil had dictated her letter, and that the whole affair was arranged for the purpose of stimulating the attachment of Marie Antoinette. The next day, when I went up to the palace, I found the Queen with a letter in her hand, which she was reading with much emotion; it was the letter from the Comtesse Jules; the Queen showed it to me. The Countess expressed in it her grief at leaving a Princess who had loaded her with kindness. The narrowness of her fortune compelled her to do so; but she was much more strongly impelled by the fear that the Queen's friendship, after having raised up dangerous enemies against her, might abandon her to their hatred, and to the regret of having lost the august favour of which she was the object.

This step produced the full effect that had been expected from it. A young and sensitive Queen cannot long bear the idea of contradiction. She busied herself in settling the Comtesse Jules near her, by making such a provision for her as should place her beyond anxiety. Her character suited the Queen; she had merely natural talents, no pedantry, no affectation of knowledge. She was of middle size; her complexion very fair, her eyebrows and hair dark brown, her teeth superb, her smile enchanting, and her whole person graceful. She was seen almost always in a *demi-toilette*, remarkable only for neatness and good taste. I do not think I ever once saw diamonds about her, even at the climax of her fortune, when she had the rank of Duchess at Court; I have always believed that her sincere attachment for the Queen, as much as her love of simplicity, induced her to avoid everything that might cause her to be thought a wealthy favourite. She had not one of the failings which usually accompany that position. She loved the persons who shared the Queen's affections, and was entirely free from jealousy. Marie Antoinette flattered herself that the Comtesse Jules and the Princesse de Lamballe would be her especial friends; and that she should possess a society formed according to her own taste. "I will receive them in my closet, or at Trianon," said she: "I will enjoy the comforts of private life, which exist not for us, unless we have the good sense to secure them for ourselves." The happiness the Queen thought to secure was destined to turn to vexation. All those courtiers who were not admitted to this intimacy became so many jealous and vindictive enemies.

It was necessary to make a suitable provision for the Countess. The place of first equerry, in reversion after the Comte de Tessé, given to Comte Jules unknown to the titular holder, displeased the family of Noailles. This family had just sustained another mortification; the appointment of the Princesse de Lamballe having in some degree rendered necessary the resignation of the Comtesse de Noailles, whose husband was thereupon made a marshal of France. The Princesse de Lamballe, although she did not quarrel with the Queen, was alarmed at the establishment of the Comtesse Jules at Court, and did not form, as her Majesty had hoped, a part of that intimate society which was in turn composed of Mesdames Jules and Diana de Polignac, d'Andlau, and de Châlon; and Messieurs de Guignes, de Coigny, d'Adhémar, de Besenval, lieutenant-colonel of the Swiss, de Polignac, de Vaudreuil, and de Guiche; the Prince de Ligne and the Duke of Dorset, the English ambassador, were also admitted.

It was a long time before the Comtesse Jules maintained any great state at Court. The Queen contented herself with giving her very fine apartments at the top of the marble staircase. The salary of first equerry, the trifling emoluments derived from M. de Polignac's regiment, added to their slender patrimony, and perhaps some small pension, at that time formed the whole fortune of the favourite. I never saw the Queen make her a present of value; I was even astonished one day at hearing her Majesty mention, with pleasure, that the Countess had gained 10,000 francs in the lottery: she was in great want of it, added the Queen.

Thus the Polignacs were not settled at Court in any degree of splendour which could justify complaints from others, and the substantial favours bestowed upon that family were less envied than the intimacy between them and their *protégés* and the Queen. Those who had no hope of entering the circle of the Comtesse Jules were made jealous by the opportunities of advancement it afforded.

However, at the time I speak of, the society around the Comtesse Jules was fully engaged in gratifying the young Queen. Of this the Marquis de Vaudreuil was a conspicuous member; he was a brilliant man, the friend and protector of men of letters and celebrated artists.[5]

The Baron de Besenval added to the bluntness of the Swiss all the adroitness of a French courtier. His fifty years and grey hairs made him enjoy among women the confidence inspired by mature age, although he had not given up the thought of love affairs. He talked of his native mountains with enthusiasm. He would at any time sing the "ranz des vaches" with tears in his eyes, and was the best story-teller in the Comtesse Jules' circle. The last new song or *bon-mot* and the gossip of the day were the sole topics of conversation in the Queen's parties. Wit was banished from them. The Comtesse Diana, more inclined to literary pursuits than her sister-in-law, one day recommended her to read the *Iliad* and *Odyssey*. The latter replied, laughing, that she was perfectly acquainted with the Greek poet, and said to prove it:

Homère était aveugle et jouait du hautbois.[6]
Homer was blind and played on the hautboy.

The Queen found this sort of humour very much to her taste, and said that no pedant should ever be her friend.

Before the Queen fixed her assemblies at Madame de Polignac's, she occasionally passed the evening at the house of the Duc and Duchesse de Duras, where a brilliant party of young persons met together. They introduced a taste for trifling games, such as question and answer, *guerre panpan*, blindman's buff, and especially a game called *descampativos*. The people of Paris, always criticising, but always imitating the customs of the Court, were infected with the mania for these childish sports. Madame de Genlis, sketching the follies of the day in one of her plays, speaks of these famous *descampativos*; and also of the rage for making a friend, called the *inséparable*, until a whim or the slightest difference might occasion a total rupture.

1. Louis XVI, touched with the wretched condition of the poor of Versailles during the winter of 1776, had several cartloads of wood distributed among them. Seeing one day a file of those vehicles passing by, while several noblemen were preparing to be drawn swiftly over the ice, he uttered these memorable words: "Gentlemen, here are my sleighs!"—*Note by the Editor.*

2. Readers wishing for fuller details of Goupil's manœuvres and their detection may consult *La Bastille Dévoilée*. The account contained there is too long for quotation here.

3. Marie Thérèse de Savoie-Carignan, born 1748, killed September 1792. Married Louis de Bourbon-Penthièvre, Prince de Lamballe (who died about 1767), son of the Duc de Penthièvre.

4. The Comtesse, afterwards Duchesse de Polignac, *née* Polastron, married the Comte (in 1780 the Duc) Jules de Polignac, the father of the Prince de Polignac of Napoleon's and of Charles X's time. She emigrated in 1789, and died at Vienna in 1793.

5. M. de Vaudreuil was passionately fond of the arts and of literature: he preferred encouraging them as an amateur rather than as a patron. He gave a dinner every week to a party consisting only of literary men and artists. The evening was spent in a saloon furnished with musical instruments, pencils, colours, brushes, and pens; and every one composed, or painted, or wrote, according to his taste or genius. M. de Vaudreuil himself pursued several of the fine arts. His voice was very pleasing, and he was a good musician. These accomplishments made him sought after, from his earliest entrance into society. The first time he visited Madame la Maréchale de Luxembourg, that lady said to him after supper, "I am told, sir, that you sing very well. I should be delighted to hear you. But if you do oblige me so far, pray do not sing any fine piece; no *cantata,* but some street ballad—just a mere street song. I like a natural style—something lively—something cheerful." M. de Vaudreuil begged leave to sing a street ballad then much in vogue. He did not know that Madame la Maréchale de Luxembourg was, before her widowhood, Comtesse de Boufflers. He sang out with a full and sonorous voice the first line of the couplet, beginning, "When Boufflers was first seen at Court." The company immediately began coughing and sneezing. M. de Vaudreuil went on: "Venus' self shone less beauteous than she did." The noise and confusion increased. But after the third

line: "To please her all eagerly sought," M. de Vaudreuil, perceiving that all eyes were fixed upon him, paused. "Pray go on, sir," said Madame la Maréchale, singing the last line herself: "And too well in his turn each succeeded." M. de Besenval's remarks respecting Madame de Luxembourg render the anecdote plausible. But perhaps, in such a delicate dilemma, she may be considered as having given a proof of presence of mind rather than of impudence.

According to the version of the Marquis de Gouffier, who was present on this occasion, the conversation turned on Time's ravages on beauty, when M. de Vaudreuil said, turning towards Madame de Luxembourg, "As to you, Madame, he has spared you—we still see that beauty which turned all the heads at Court, and has been celebrated by our best poets." "Yes," said the old lady gaily, "I remember when I first came out, there were a few songs written in my praise; there was this, for instance," and she began singing:

> When Boufflers was first seen at Court,
> Venus' self shone less beauteous than she did.
> To please her all eagerly sought—

Here she stopped, and did not give the last line:

> And too well in his turn each succeeded.

"Go on, Madame la Maréchale," said De Vaudreuil. "Ah!' said she, smiling, "all that was so long ago that I remember no more of it."—*Note by the Editor.*

6. This lively repartee of the Duchesse de Polignac is a droll imitation of a line in the *Mercure Galant*. In the quarrel scene one of the lawyers says to his brother:

> *Ton-père* était aveugle et jouait du hautbois.
> Your father was blind and played on the hautboy.

It was impossible that the Duchesse de Polignac, with her wit and refined taste, should do otherwise than highly value learning; but the following anecdote conveys a poor idea of the education of some of the men admitted into her society:—

"In 1781 the Duchesse de Polignac was *enceinte*, and in order to be nearer at hand to pay her respects to the Queen, she requested Madame de Boufflers to let her her house, called d'Auteuil, and famous for its gardens *à l'Anglaise*. Madame de Boufflers, who was very fond of her country house, wished to refuse the Duchess without disobliging her, and replied in the following lines:

> Around you all are sedulous to please;
> Your tranquil days roll on in cloudless ease;
> Empire to you is but the source of joy,
> Or if some grief awhile the charm destroy,
> Attentive courtiers with assiduous art
> Banish the transient feeling from your heart.
> Far otherwise with me; if sorrows press,

Here, lonely, no one shares in my distress;
My only solace are these fragrant flowers,
Whose rich perfumes beguile my heavy hours.

"Madame de Polignac showed these lines, and her flatterers, thinking they were written by Madame de Boufflers, pronounced them good for nothing. Of course the decision of the Duchess's friends was carried to Madame la Maréchale. 'I am sorry, then,' said she, 'for poor Racine; for the lines are his.'"

The lines will be found in *Britannicus*, Act 2, Scene 3. They are addressed to Nero by Junia. Madame de Boufflers had merely made a slight alteration in the four last lines, where the name of Britannicus is introduced.—*Secret Correspondence of the Court: Reign of Louis XVI.*

VII

The Duc de Choiseul returns to Court—The Queen obtains a pension of 1,200 francs for Chamfort—She invites Gluck to France and patronises music—Encouragement given to the art of printing—Turgot—M. de Saint Germain—Amusements at Court—Particulars of the household—Masked balls at the opera—The Queen goes there in a fiacre; slanderous reports—The heron plume—The Duc de Lauzun—The Queen's attachment to the Princesse de Lamballe and the Duchesse de Polignac—Anecdote of the Abbé de Vermond

The Duc de Choiseul had reappeared at Court on the ceremony of the King's coronation.[1] The state of public feeling on the subject gave his friends hope of seeing him again in administration, or in the Council of State; but the opposite party was too firmly fixed at Versailles, and the young Queen's influence was outweighed, in the mind of the King, by long-standing prejudices; she therefore gave up for ever her attempt to reinstate the Duke. Thus this Princess, who has been described as so ambitious, and so strenuously supporting the interest of the House of Austria, failed twice in the only scheme which could forward the views constantly attributed to her; and spent the whole of her reign surrounded by enemies of herself and her house.

Marie Antoinette took little pains to promote literature and the fine arts. She had been annoyed in consequence of having ordered a performance of the *Connétable de Bourbon*, on the celebration of the marriage of Madame Clotilde with the Prince of Piedmont. The Court and the people of Paris censured as indecorous the naming characters in the piece after the reigning family, and that with which the new alliance was formed.[2] The reading of this piece by the Comte de Guibert in the Queen's closet had produced in her Majesty's circle that sort of enthusiasm which obscures the judgment. She promised herself she would have no more readings. Yet, at the request of M. de Cubières, the King's equerry, the Queen agreed to hear the reading of a comedy written by his brother. She collected her intimate circle, Messieurs de Coigny, de Vaudreuil, de Besenval, Mesdames de Polignac, de Châlon, etc., and to increase the number of judges, she admitted the two Parnys, the Chevalier de Bertin,[3] my father-in-law, and myself. Molé[4] read for the author. I never could satisfy myself by what magic the skilful reader gained our unanimous approbation of a ridiculous work. Surely the delightful voice of Molé, by awakening our recollection of the dramatic beauties of the French stage, prevented the wretched lines of Dorat Cubières from striking on our ears. I can assert that the exclamation *Charming! charming!* repeatedly interrupted the reader. The piece was admitted for performance at Fontainebleau; and for the first time the King had the curtain dropped before the end of the play. It was called the *Dramomane* or *Dramaturge.* All the characters died of poison in a pie. The Queen, highly disconcerted at having recommended this absurd production, announced that she would never hear another reading; and this time she kept her word.

The tragedy of *Mustapha* and *Zéangir,* by M. de Chamfort, was highly successful at the Court theatre at Fontainebleau. The Queen procured the author a pension of 1,200 francs, but his play failed on being performed at Paris.

The spirit of opposition which prevailed in that city delighted in reversing the verdicts of the Court. The Queen determined never again to give any marked countenance to new dramatic works. She reserved her patronage for musical composers, and in a few years their art arrived at a perfection it had never before attained in France.

It was solely to gratify the Queen that the manager of the opera brought the first company of comic actors to Paris. Gluck, Piccini, and Sacchini were attracted there in succession. These eminent composers were treated with great distinction at Court. Immediately on his arrival in France, Gluck was admitted to the Queen's toilette, and she talked to him all the time he remained with her. She asked him one day whether he had nearly brought his grand opera of *Armide* to a conclusion, and whether it pleased him. Gluck replied very coolly, in his German accent, "Madame, it will soon be finished, and really it will be *superb*." There was a great outcry against the confidence with which the composer had spoken of one of his own productions.[5] The Queen defended him warmly; she insisted that he could not be ignorant of the merit of his works; that he well knew they were generally admired, and that no doubt he was afraid lest a modesty, merely dictated by politeness, should look like affectation in him.

The Queen did not confine her admiration to the lofty style of the French and Italian operas; she greatly valued Grétry's music, so well adapted to the spirit and feeling of the words. A great deal of the poetry set to music by Grétry is by Marmontel. The day after the first performance of *Zemira and Azor*, Marmontel and Grétry were presented to the Queen as she was passing through the gallery of Fontainebleau to go to mass. The Queen congratulated Grétry on the success of the new opera, and told him that she had dreamed of the enchanting effect of the trio by Zemira's father and sisters behind the magic mirror. Grétry, in a transport of joy, took Marmontel in his arms, "Ah! my friend," cried he, "excellent music may be made of this." "And execrable words," coolly observed Marmontel, to whom her Majesty had not addressed a single compliment.[6]

The most indifferent artists were permitted to have the honour of painting the Queen. A full-length portrait representing her in all the pomp of royalty was exhibited in the gallery of Versailles. This picture, which was intended for the Court of Vienna, was executed by a man who does not deserve even to be named, and disgusted all people of taste. It seemed as if this art had, in France, retrograded several centuries.

The Queen had not that enlightened judgment, or even that mere taste, which enables Princes to foster and protect great talents. She confessed frankly that she saw no merit in any portrait beyond the likeness. When she went to the Louvre, she would run hastily over all the little "genre" pictures, and come out, as she acknowledged, without having once raised her eyes to the grand compositions.

There is no good portrait of the Queen, save that by Werthmüller, chief painter to the King of Sweden, which was sent to Stockholm; and that by Madame le Brun, which was saved from the revolutionary fury by the commissioners for the care of the furniture at Versailles.[7] The composition of the latter picture resembles that of Henrietta of France, the wife of the unfortunate Charles I, painted by Vandyke. Like Marie Antoinette, she is seated, surrounded by her children, and that resemblance adds to the melancholy interest raised by this beautiful production.

While admitting that the Queen gave no direct encouragement to any art but that of music, I should be wrong to pass over in silence the patronage conferred by her and the Princes, brothers of the King, on the art of printing.[8]

To Marie Antoinette we are indebted for a splendid quarto edition of the works of Metastasio; to Monsieur, the King's brother, for a quarto Tasso, embellished with engravings after Cochin; and to the Comte d'Artois, for a small collection of select works, which is considered one of the *chef d'oeuvres* of the press of the celebrated Didot.

In 1775, on the death of the Maréchal du Muy, the ascendancy obtained by the sect of innovators occasioned M. de Saint Germain to be recalled to Court and made Minister at War. His first care was the destruction of the King's military household establishment, an imposing and effectual rampart round the sovereign power.

When Chancellor Maupeou obtained from Louis XV the destruction of the Parliament and the exile of all the ancient magistrates, the Mousquetaires were charged with the execution of the commission for this purpose; and at the stroke of midnight, the Presidents and members were all arrested, each by two Mousquetaires. In the spring of 1775 a popular insurrection had taken place in consequence of the high price of bread. M. Turgot's new regulation, which permitted unlimited trade in corn, was either its cause or the pretext for it;[9] and the King's household troops again rendered the greatest services to public tranquillity.

I have never been able to discover the true cause of the support given to M. de Saint Germain's policy by the Queen, unless in the marked favour shown to the captains and officers of the Body Guards, who by this reduction became the only soldiers of their rank entrusted with the safety of the sovereign; or else in the Queen's strong prejudice against the Duc d'Aiguillon, then commander of the light horse. M. de Saint Germain, however, retained fifty *gens d'armes* and fifty light horse to form a royal escort on State occasions; but in 1787 the King reduced both these military bodies. The Queen then said with satisfaction that at last she should see no more red coats in the gallery of Versailles.[10]

From 1775 to 1781 were the gayest years of the Queen's life. In the little journeys to Choisy, performances frequently took place at the theatre twice in one day: grand opera and French or Italian comedy at the usual hour; and at eleven at night they returned to the theatre for parodies in which the best actors of the opera presented themselves in whimsical parts and costumes. The celebrated dancer Guimard always took the leading characters in the latter performance; she danced better than she acted; her extreme leanness, and her weak hoarse voice, added to the burlesque in the parodied characters of Ernelinde and Iphigenia.

The most magnificent fête ever given to the Queen was one prepared for her by Monsieur, the King's brother, at Brunoy. That Prince did me the honour to admit me, and I followed her Majesty into the gardens, where she found in the first copse knights in full armour asleep at the foot of trees, on which hung their spears and shields. The absence of the beauties who had incited the nephews of Charlemagne and the gallants of that period to lofty deeds was supposed to occasion this lethargic slumber. But when the Queen appeared at the entrance of the copse they were on foot in an instant, and melodious voices announced their eagerness to display their valour. They then hastened into a vast arena, magnificently decorated in the exact style of the ancient tournaments. Fifty dancers dressed as pages presented to the knights twenty-five superb black horses, and twenty-five of a dazzling whiteness, all most richly caparisoned. The party led by Augustus Vestris wore the Queen's colours. Picq, ballet-master at the Russian Court, commanded the opposing band. There was running at the negro's head, tilting, and, lastly, combats *à outrance*, perfectly well imitated. Although the spectators were aware that the Queen's colours could not but be victorious, they did not the less enjoy the apparent uncertainty.

Nearly all the agreeable women of Paris were ranged upon the steps which surrounded the area of the tourney. The Queen, surrounded by the royal family and the whole Court, was placed beneath an elevated canopy. A play, followed by a ballet-pantomime and a ball, terminated the fête. Fireworks and illuminations were not spared. Finally, from a prodigiously high scaffold, placed on a rising ground, the words *Vive Louis! Vive Marie Antoinette!* were shown in the air in the midst of a very dark but calm night.

Pleasure was the sole pursuit of every one of this young family, with the exception of the King. Their love of it was perpetually encouraged by a crowd of those officious people who, by anticipating the desires and even the passions of princes, find means of showing their zeal and hope to gain or maintain favour for themselves.

Who would have dared to check the amusements of a Queen, young, lively, and handsome? A mother or a husband alone would have had the right to do it; and the King threw no impediment in the way of Marie Antoinette's inclinations. His long indifference had been followed by admiration and love. He was a slave to all the wishes of the Queen, who, delighted with the happy change in the heart and habits of the King, did not sufficiently conceal the ascendancy she was gaining over him.

The King went to bed every night at eleven precisely; he was very methodical, and nothing was allowed to interfere with his rules. The noise which the Queen unavoidably made when she returned very late from the evenings which she spent with the Princesse de Guéménée, or the Duc de Duras, at last annoyed the King, and it was amicably agreed that the Queen should apprise him when she intended to sit up late. He then began to sleep in his own apartment, which had never before happened from the time of their marriage.

During the winter the Queen attended the opera balls with a single lady of the palace, and always found there Monsieur and the Comte d'Artois. Her people concealed their liveries under grey cloth greatcoats. She never thought she was recognised, while all the time she was known to the whole Assembly, from the first moment she entered the theatre; they pretended, however, not to recognise her, and some masquerade manœuvre was always adopted to give her the pleasure of fancying herself incognito.

Louis XVI determined once to accompany the Queen to a masked ball; it was agreed that the King should hold not only the *grand* but the *petit coucher*, as if actually going to bed. The Queen went to his apartment through the inner corridors of the palace, followed by one of her women with a black domino; she assisted him to put it on, and they went alone to the chapel court, where a carriage waited for them, with the Captain of the Guard of the quarter, and a lady of the palace. The King was but little amused, spoke only to two or three persons, who knew him immediately, and found nothing to admire at the masquerade but Punches and Harlequins, which served as a joke against him for the royal family, who often amused themselves with laughing at him about it.

An event, simple in itself, brought lamentable suspicions upon the Queen. She was going out one evening with the Duchesse de Luynes, lady of the palace, when her carriage broke down at the entrance into Paris; she was obliged to alight; the Duchess led her into a shop, while a footman called a *fiacre*. As they were masked, if they had but known how to keep silence, the event would never have been known; but to ride in a *fiacre* is so unusual an adventure for a Queen that she had hardly entered the opera-house when she could not help saying to some persons whom she met there: "That I should be in a *fiacre*! Is it not droll?"[11]

From that moment all Paris was informed of the adventure of the *fiacre*. It was said that everything connected with it was mysterious; that the Queen had kept an assignation in a private house with the Duc de Coigny. He was indeed very well received at Court, but equally so by the King and Queen. These accusations of gallantry once set afloat, there were no longer any bounds to the calumnies circulated at Paris. If, during the chase or at cards, the Queen spoke to Lord Edward Dillon, De Lambertye, or others, they were so many favoured lovers. The people of Paris did not know that none of those young persons were admitted into the Queen's private circle of friends; the Queen went about Paris in disguise, and had made use of a *fiacre;* and a single instance of levity gives room for the suspicion of others. Conscious of innocence, and well knowing that all about her must do justice to her private life, the Queen spoke of these reports with contempt, contenting herself with the supposition that some folly in the young men mentioned had given rise to them. She therefore left off speaking to them or even looking at them. Their vanity took alarm at this, and revenge induced them either to say, or to leave others to think, that they were unfortunate enough to please no longer. Other young coxcombs, placing themselves near the private box which the Queen occupied incognito when she attended the public theatre at Versailles, had the presumption to imagine that they were noticed by her; and I have known such notions entertained merely on account of the Queen's requesting one of those gentlemen to inquire behind the scenes whether it would be long before the commencement of the second piece.

The list of persons received into the Queen's closet which I gave in the preceding chapter was placed in the hands of the ushers of the chamber by the Princesse de Lamballe; and the persons there enumerated could only present themselves to enjoy the distinction on those days when the Queen chose to be with her intimates in a private manner; and this was only when she was slightly indisposed. People of the first rank at Court sometimes requested special audiences of her; the Queen then received them in a room within that called the closet of the women on duty, and these women announced them in her Majesty's apartment.

The Duc de Lauzun (since Duc de Biron),[12] who made himself conspicuous in the Revolution, among the associates of the Duc d'Orléans, has left behind him some manuscript memoirs, in which he insults Marie Antoinette. He relates one anecdote respecting a heron plume. The following is the true history of the matter.

The Duc de Lauzun had a good deal of wit, and chivalrous manners. The Queen was accustomed to see him at the King's suppers, and at the house of the Princesse de Guéménée, and always showed him attention. One day he made his appearance at Madame de Guéménée's in uniform, and with the most magnificent plume of white heron's feathers that it was possible to behold. The Queen admired the plume, and he offered it to her through the Princesse de Guéménée. As he had worn it the Queen had not imagined that he could think of giving it to her; much embarrassed with the present which she had, as it were, drawn upon herself, she did not like to refuse it, nor did she know whether she ought to make one in return; afraid, if she did give anything, of giving either too much or too little, she contented herself with once letting M. de Lauzun see her adorned with the plume. In his secret memoirs the Duke attaches an importance to his present, which proves him utterly unworthy of an honour accorded only to his name and rank.[13]

A short time afterwards he solicited an audience; the Queen granted it, as she would have done to any other courtier of equal rank. I was in the room adjoining that in which he was received; a few minutes after his arrival the Queen re-opened the door, and said aloud, and in an angry tone of voice, "Go, sir." M. de Lauzun bowed low, and withdrew. The Queen was much agitated. She said to me: "That man shall never again come within my doors." A few years before the Revolution of 1789 the Maréchal de Biron died. The Duc de Lauzun, heir to his name, aspired to the important post of colonel of the regiment of French guards. The Queen, however, procured it for the Duc du Châtelet. The Duc de Biron espoused the cause of the Duc d'Orléans, and became one of the most violent enemies of Marie Antoinette.

It is with reluctance that I enter minutely on a defence of the Queen against two infamous accusations with which libellers have dared to swell their envenomed volumes. I mean the unworthy suspicions of too strong an attachment for the Comte d'Artois, and of the motives for the tender friendship which subsisted between the Queen, the Princesse de Lamballe, and the Duchesse de Polignac. I do not believe that the Comte d'Artois was, during his own youth, and that of the Queen, so much smitten as has been said with the loveliness of his sister-in-law; I can affirm that I always saw that Prince maintain the most respectful demeanour towards the Queen; that she always spoke of his good-nature and cheerfulness with that freedom which attends only the purest sentiments; and that none of those about the Queen ever saw in the affection she manifested towards the Comte d'Artois more than that of a kind and tender sister for her youngest brother. As to the intimate connection between Marie Antoinette and the ladies I have named, it never had, nor could have, any other motive than the very innocent wish to secure herself two friends in the midst of a numerous Court; and notwithstanding this intimacy, that tone of respect observed by persons of the most exalted rank towards majesty never ceased to be maintained.[14]

The Queen, much occupied with the society of Madame de Polignac, and an unbroken series of amusements, found less time for the Abbé de Vermond; he therefore resolved to retire from Court. The world did him the honour to believe that he had hazarded remonstrances upon his august pupil's frivolous employment of her time, and that he considered himself, both as an ecclesiastic and as instructor, now out of place at Court. But the world was deceived: his dissatisfaction arose purely from the favour shown to the Comtesse Jules. After a fortnight's absence we saw him at Versailles again, resuming his usual functions.

The Queen could express herself with winning graciousness to persons who merited her praise. When M. Loustonneau was appointed to the reversion of the post of first surgeon to the King, he came to make his acknowledgments. He was much beloved by the poor, to whom he had chiefly devoted his talents, spending nearly 30,000 francs a year on indigent sufferers. The Queen replied to his thanks by saying: "You are satisfied, sir; but I am far from being so with the inhabitants of Versailles. On the news of your appointment the town should have been illuminated."—"How so, Madame?" asked the astonished surgeon, who was excessively modest. "Why," replied the Queen, "if the poor whom you have succoured for the past twenty years had each placed a single candle in their windows it would have been the most beautiful illumination ever witnessed."

The Queen did not limit her kindness to friendly words. There was frequently seen in the apartments of Versailles a veteran captain of the grenadiers of France, called the Chevalier d'Orville, who, for four years, had been soliciting from the Minister of War the post of major, or of King's lieutenant. He was known to be very poor; but he supported his lot without complaining of this vexatious delay in rewarding his honourable services. He regularly attended the Maréchal de Ségur, at the hour appointed for receiving the numerous solicitations in his department. One day the Maréchal said to him: "You are still at Versailles, M. d'Orville?"—"Sir," he replied, "you may observe that, by this board of the flooring where I regularly place myself; it is already worn down several lines by the weight of my body." The Queen frequently stood at the window of her bed-chamber to observe with her glass the people walking in the park. Sometimes she inquired the names of those who were unknown to her. One day she saw the Chevalier d'Orville passing, and asked me the name of that knight of Saint Louis, whom she had seen everywhere for a long time past. I knew who he was, and related his history. "That must be put an end to," said the Queen, with some vivacity. "Such an example of indifference is calculated to discourage our soldiers." Next day, in crossing the gallery to go to mass, the Queen perceived the Chevalier d'Orville; she went directly towards him. The poor man fell back in the recess of a window, looking to the right and left to discover the person whom the Queen was seeking, when she thus addressed him: "M. d'Orville, you have been several years at Versailles, soliciting a majority or a King's lieutenancy. You must have very powerless patrons."—"I have none, Madame," replied the Chevalier, in great confusion. "Well! I will take you under my protection. To-morrow at the same hour be here with a petition, and a memorial of your services." A fortnight after M. d'Orville was appointed King's lieutenant, either at La Rochelle or at Rochefort.[15]

1. After his disgrace under Louis XV in 1770.

2. The *Connétable de Bourbon* was not, it must be admitted, a fit piece for performance before all the French Princes. It would create some surprise if the whole Court should be found approving a composition in which the Constable above all things desires "the rare pleasure of humbling a king".—*Note by the Editor.*

3. The Chevalier de Parny was already known by his erotic poems, and the Chevalier de Bertin by some valued verses.—*Madame Campan.*

4. An actor who was during thirty years the delight of the Theatre Français. He preceded Fleury, and took the same line of character.—*Madame Campan.*

5. Gluck often had to deal with self-sufficiency equal to his own. He was very reluctant to introduce long ballets into *Ipheginia.* Vestris deeply regretted that the opera was not terminated by a piece they called a *chaconne,* in which he displayed all his power. He complained to Gluck about it. Gluck, who treated his art with all the dignity it merits, replied that in so interesting a subject dancing would be misplaced. Being pressed another time by Vestris on the same subject, "A chaconne! a chaconne!" roared out the enraged musician, "we must describe the Greeks; and had the Greeks chaconnes?"—"They had not?" returned the astonished dancer; "faith then, so much the worse for them!"—*Note by the Editor.*

6. "The Court," says Grimm, "almost invariably confers favour upon the authors of the pieces performed at Fontainebleau, and those pieces may be performed at Paris immediately after their performance at Court. To this advantage may be attributed the importance attached to the privilege of being first judged of upon a stage where the result is never considered definitive, for it is agreed that a final appeal lies to the public of Paris from the judgments pronounced by the courtly public. And yet the manner of judging adopted at Court is very different now that it is allowable to applaud there as at other theatres. Formerly it was usual to listen in profound silence, which, while manifesting much respect for the presence of their Majesties, left vast uncertainty as to the feelings of the audience. Since the Queen has permitted this point of etiquette to be abrogated, it seldom happens that Paris annuls the decisions of Fontainebleau."—*Note by the Editor.*

7. See frontispiece to this edition and p. 192. The English publishers are indebted to the courtesy of their colleagues Messrs. E. Plon et Cie for fine impressions of two portraits which add to the completeness and interest of the work, *viz.*, one by Werthmüller named above, and one by Madame Vigée le Brun, a different one from that mentioned in the text.

8. In 1790 the King gave a proof of his particular goodwill to the bookselling trade. A contemporary writer says:—

"A company consisting of the first Parisian booksellers, being on the eve of stopping payment, succeeded in laying before the King a statement of their distressed situation. The monarch was affected by it; he took from the civil list the sum of which the society stood in immediate need, and became security for the repayment of the remainder of the 1,200,000 livres, which they wanted to borrow. Louis XVI wrote the following letter to M. Necker, at that time his Minister of Finance:—

'The interest I take in the welfare of the associated libraries, and of the numerous workmen they employ, as well in Paris as in the country, and who would have been out of work without prompt assistance (the *caisse d'escompte,* and other capitalists, to whom they have made application, being unable to help them), has induced me to advance them, as a loan, out of the funds of my civil list, the 50,000 crowns which they wanted indispensably on the 31st of last month. The same motive leads me to secure, upon the same fund, such sums as they may be able to procure, in order, with the 50,000 crowns which I have advanced them, to make up the sum of 1,200,000 livres, to be repaid in ten years, including my advance; for the repayment of which I fix no particular time. Saint Cloud, the 4th August 1790, (Signed) LOUIS.'"—*Note by the Editor.*

9. Liberty and economy were M. Turgot's two principles. At Court he insisted chiefly on the application of the last. His numerous retrenchments offended the nobles and clergy. A female relative of the minister once asked a bishop whether it was not allowable to keep Easter and the Jubilee at the same time. "Well, madam," replied the prelate, "we live in economical times—I think it can be done." —*Note by the Editor.*

10. The Queen finally said to M. de Saint Germain, "What will you do with the forty-four *gens d'armes* and forty-four light horse that you keep up? Apparently they are to escort the King to the beds of justice." "No, Madame, they are to accompany him when *Te Deums* are sung." It must be understood that the Queen would have liked a total suppression, and that the King should have been guarded at Versailles as the Empress, her mother, and the Emperor are at Vienna; and that would lave been simple and right.—*Secret Correspondence of the Court: Reign of* Louis *XVI.*

11. An adventure which took place at the masked ball given by the Comte de Viry is whispered about. It was as follows: After the banquet the Queen withdrew with her suite, and returned shortly afterwards, masked, to the ball. At three o'clock in the morning she was walking with the Duchesse de La Vauguyon; the two masks were accosted by a young foreign nobleman, who was unmasked, and who conversed with them a long time, taking them for two women of quality with whom he was acquainted. The mistake gave rise to a singular conversation, which amused her Majesty the more inasmuch as the topics were light and agreeable, without being indiscreet. Two gentlemen in masks came up and joined the party; after laughing a good deal together they separated. The two ladies intimated a desire to withdraw; the German baron conducted them; a very plain carriage drew up; when they were about to enter it, Madame de La Vauguyon unmasked. Judge of the stranger's surprise when, on turning round, he recognised the other lady, who had likewise unmasked; respect and confusion succeeded to familiarity. The affability of the charming Princess, however, reassured the foreigner, who, besides, had the advantage of being known to her Majesty. The Queen recommended secrecy, and left him. He complied no doubt, but to little purpose, as two or three spectators were not equally discreet. Meeting the Queen a few days afterwards, she asked him if he had kept her secret, in a tone which showed that she did not consider it of the slightest importance.—*Secret Correspondence of the Court: Reign of Louis XVI.*

12. Armand Louis, Duc de Lauzun (1747–93), afterwards (1788) Duc de Biron; commanded the army of the Rhine 1792, and against the Vendeans in 1793 as General Biron, but was guillotined in 1793.

13. It is interesting to compare the Duc de Lauzun's version of this incident (not, however, to be found in the edition of his memoirs published since those of Madame Campan were compiled) with Madame Campan's narrative: "Madame de Guéménée," he says, "came up to me and asked in an undertone, laughing, 'Are you very much attached to a certain white heron plume which was in your helmet when you took leave? The Queen is dying for it: will you refuse it her?' I replied that I should not dare to offer it to her, but that I should be most happy if she would condescend to receive it from Madame de Guéménée. I sent to Paris for it, and Madame de Guéménée gave it to the Queen the next evening. She wore it on the following

day; and at dinner she asked me what I thought of her head-dress. I replied that I liked it very much. 'I never,' said she, with infinite affability, 'saw myself so becomingly dressed before.' It certainly would have been better if she had not said anything about it, for the Duc de Coigny took notice both of the feather and the phrase. He asked whence the plume came. The Queen said, with some embarrassment, that I had brought it to Madame de Guéménée from my travels, and that she had given it to her. The Duc de Coigny told Madame de Guéménée in the evening, with much asperity, that nothing could be more indecorous than the footing I was on with the Queen; that to act the lover thus publicly was a thing unheard of; and that it was incredible that she should look as if she approved of it. What he said was not well received, and he began to contrive means to get me out of the way."—*Note by the Editor.*

14. The following note was written by the Queen to the Duchesse de Polignac, in answer to a letter in which the latter, after an illness that had confined her a few days to Paris, told the Queen that she should soon have the honour of paying her respects to her:—"Doubtless it is I who am the more impatient to embrace you, for to-morrow I shall come and dine with you in Paris." This close friendship between a sovereign and a subject is almost unexampled; unprincipled people, therefore, attributed a criminal motive to it. When a scheme for dethroning the unfortunate Louis XVI was once determined on, it was thought proper to begin by degrading him, and the most efficacious way was to attack the morals of the Queen. It was also essential for the success of this infernal plot that the Duchesse de Polignac should be lowered in public opinion. For if the Duchess could be made to appear deserving of universal contempt, the opprobrium cast on her would stain her august friend also. Libels against Madame de Polignac, therefore, were not spared; but all intelligent persons who were well acquainted with the Duc and Duchesse de Polignac, were convinced that the authors of those libels were vile calumniators, hired by the enemies of the King and Queen. The Duchess was beloved by her household, and in the bosom of her family she led a very decorous and regular life. —*History of Marie Antoinette*, by Montjoie.

15. Louis XVI vied with his Queen in benevolent actions of this kind. An old officer had in vain solicited a pension during the administration of the Duc de Choiseul. He returned to the charge in the times of the Marquis de Montesnard and the Duc d'Aiguillon. He urged his claims to Comte du Muy, who made a note of them. Tired of so many fruitless efforts, he at last appeared at the King's supper, and having placed himself so as to be seen and heard, cried out at a moment when silence prevailed, "*Sire.*" The people near him said, "What are you about? This is not the way to speak to the King."—"I fear nothing," said he, and raising his voice, repeated, "*Sire.*" The King, much surprised, looked at him and said, "What do you want, sir?"—"Sire," answered he, "I am seventy years of age; I have served your Majesty more than fifty years, and I am dying for want."—"Have you a memorial?" replied the King. "Yes, Sire, I have."—"Give it to me;" and his Majesty took it without saying anything more. Next morning he was sent for by the King, who said, "Sir; I grant you an annuity of 1,500 livres out of my privy purse, and you may go and receive the first year's payment, which is now due" (*Secret Correspondence of the Court: Reign of Louis XVI*). The King preferred to spend money in charity rather than in luxury or magnificence. Once during his absence, M. d'Angivillers caused an unused room in the King's apartment to be repaired at a cost of 30,000 francs. On his return the King made Versailles resound with complaints against M. d'Angivillers: "With that sum I could have made thirty families happy," he said.—*Note by the Editor.*

VIII

Joseph II's visit to France—His reception at the opera—Fête given to him by the Queen at Trianon—The Queen enceinte—Voltaire's return to Paris—Duel between the Comte d'Artois and the Duc de Bourbon —Return of the Chevalier d'Éon to France—Particulars relative to his missions, and the causes of his disguise—Night promenades upon the terrace of Trianon—Couplets against the Queen—Indignation of Louis XVI—Birth of Madame

From the time of Louis XVI's accession to the throne, the Queen had been expecting a visit from her brother, the Emperor Joseph II. That Prince was the constant theme of her discourse. She boasted of his intelligence, his love of occupation, his military knowledge, and the perfect simplicity of his manners. Those about her Majesty ardently wished to see at Versailles a Prince so worthy of his rank. At length the coming of Joseph II, under the title of Count Falkenstein, was announced, and the very day on which he would be at Versailles was mentioned. The first embraces between the Queen and her august brother took place in the presence of all the Queen's household. The sight of their emotion was extremely affecting.

The Emperor was at first generally admired in France; learned men, well-informed officers, and celebrated artists appreciated the extent of his information. He made less impression at Court, and very little in the private circle of the King and Queen. His eccentric manners, his frankness, often degenerating into rudeness, and his evidently affected simplicity—all these characteristics caused him to be looked upon as a Prince rather singular than admirable. The Queen spoke to him about the apartment she had prepared for him in the Château; the Emperor answered that he would not accept it, and that while travelling he always lodged at a cabaret (that was his very expression); the Queen insisted, and assured him that he should be at perfect liberty, and placed out of the reach of noise. He replied that he knew the Château of Versailles was very large, and that so many scoundrels lived there that he could well find a place; but that his *valet de chambre* had made up his camp-bed in a lodging house, and there he would stay.

He dined with the King and Queen, and supped with the whole family. He appeared to take an interest in the young Princess Elizabeth, then just past childhood, and blooming in all the freshness of that age. An intended marriage between him and this young sister of the King was reported at the time, but I believe it had no foundation in truth.

The table was still served by females only, when the Queen dined in private with the King, the royal family, or crowned heads.[1] I was present at the Queen's dinner almost

Versailles

every day. The Emperor would talk much and fluently; he expressed himself in French with facility, and the singularity of his expressions added a zest to his conversation. I have often heard him say that he liked spectaculous objects, when he meant to express such things as formed a show, or a scene worthy of interest. He disguised none of his prejudices against the etiquette and customs of the Court of France; and even in the presence of the King made them the subject of his sarcasms.[2] The King smiled, but never made any answer; the Queen appeared pained. The Emperor frequently terminated his observations upon the objects in Paris which he had admired by reproaching the King for suffering himself to remain in ignorance of them. He could not conceive how such a wealth of pictures should remain shut up in the dust of immense stores;[3] and told him one day that but for the practice of placing some of them in the apartments of Versailles he would not know even the principal *chef d'oeuvres* that he possessed.[4] He also reproached him for not having visited the Hotel des Invalides nor the École Militaire; and even went so far as to tell him before us that he ought not only to know what Paris contained, but to travel in France, and reside a few days in each of his large towns.

At last the Queen was really hurt at the Emperor's indiscretion, and gave him a few lectures upon the freedom with which he allowed himself to lecture others. One day she was busied in signing warrants and orders for payment for her household, and was conversing with M. Augéard, her secretary for such matters, who presented the papers one after another to be signed, and replaced them in his portfolio. While this was going forward, the Emperor walked about the room; all at once he stood still, to reproach the Queen rather severely for signing all those papers without reading them, or, at least, without running her eye over them; and he spoke most judiciously to her upon the danger of signing her name inconsiderately. The Queen answered, that very wise principles might be very ill applied; that her secretary, who deserved her implicit confidence, was at that moment laying before her nothing but orders for payment of the quarter's expenses of her household, registered in the Chamber of Accounts; and that she ran no risk of incautiously giving her signature.

The Queen's toilette was likewise a never-failing subject for animadversion with the Emperor. He blamed her for having introduced too many new fashions; and teased her about her use of rouge. One day, while she was laying on more of it than usual, before going to the play, he pointed out a lady who was in the room, and who was, in truth, highly painted. "A little more under the eyes," said the Emperor to the Queen; "lay on the rouge like a fury, as that lady does." The Queen entreated her brother to refrain from his jokes, or at all events to address them, when they were so rude, to her alone.

The Queen had made an appointment to meet her brother at the Italian theatre; she changed her mind, and went to the French theatre, sending a page to the Italian theatre to request the Emperor to come to her there. He left his box, lighted by the comedian Clairval, and attended by M. de la Ferté, comptroller of the Queen's privy purse, who was much hurt at hearing his Imperial Majesty, after kindly expressing his regret at not being present during the Italian performance, say to Clairval, "Your young Queen is very giddy; but, luckily, you Frenchmen have no great objection to that."

I was with my father-in-law in one of the Queen's apartments when the Emperor came to wait for her there, and knowing that M. Campan was librarian, be conversed with him about such books as would of course be found in the Queen's library. After talking of our most celebrated authors, he casually said, "There are doubtless no works on finance or on administration here?"

These words were followed by his opinion on all that had been written on those topics, and the different systems of our two famous ministers, Sully and Colbert; on the errors which were daily committed in France, in points so essential to the prosperity of the empire; and on the reform he himself would make at Vienna; holding M. Campan by the button, he spent more than an hour talking vehemently, and without the slightest reserve, about the French Government. My father-in-law and myself maintained profound silence, as much from astonishment as from respect; and when we were alone we agreed not to speak of this interview.

The Emperor was fond of telling secret anecdotes of the Italian Courts that he had visited. The jealous quarrels between the King and Queen of Naples amused him highly; he described to the life the manner and speech of that sovereign, and the simplicity with which he used to go and solicit the first chamberlain to obtain permission to return to the nuptial bed, when the angry Queen had banished him from it. The time which he was made to wait for this reconciliation was calculated between the Queen and her chamberlain, and always proportioned to the gravity of the offence. He also related several very amusing stories relative to the Court of Parma, of which he spoke with no little contempt. If what this Prince said of those Courts, and even of Vienna, had been written down, the whole would have formed an interesting collection. The Emperor told the King that the Grand Duke of Tuscany and the King of Naples being together, the former said a great deal about the changes he had effected in his State. The Grand

Duke had issued a mass of new edicts, in order to carry the precepts of the economists into execution, and trusted that in so doing he was labouring for the welfare of his people. The King of Naples suffered him to go on speaking for a long time, and then merely asked how many Neapolitan families there were in Tuscany. The Duke soon reckoned them up, as they were but few. "Well, brother," replied the King of Naples, "I do not understand the indifference of your people towards your great reforms; for I have four times the number of Tuscan families settled in my States that you have of Neapolitan families in yours."

The Queen being at the opera with the Emperor, the latter did not wish to show himself; but she took him by the hand, and with a little gentle force drew him to the front of the box. This kind of presentation to the public was most warmly received. The performance was *Iphigenia in Aulis*, and for the second time the chorus, *Chantons, celebrons notre Reine!* was called for with universal plaudits.

A fête of a novel description was given at Petit Trianon. The art with which the English garden was not illuminated but lighted, produced a charming effect. Earthen lamps, concealed by boards painted green, threw light upon the beds of shrubs and flowers, and brought out their varied tints. Several hundred burning faggots in the moat behind the Temple of Love made a blaze of light, which rendered that spot the most brilliant in the garden. After all, this evening's entertainment had nothing remarkable about it but the good taste of the artists, yet it was much talked of. The situation did not allow the admission of a great part of the Court; those who were uninvited were dissatisfied; and the people, who never forgive any fêtes but those they share in, so exaggerated the cost of this little fête as to make it appear that the faggots burnt in the moat had required the destruction of a whole forest. The Queen being informed of these reports, was determined to know exactly how much wood had been consumed; and she found that 1,500 faggots had sufficed to keep up the fire until four o'clock in the morning.

After staying a few months the Emperor left France, promising his sister to come and see her again. All the officers of the Queen's chamber had many opportunities of serving him during his stay, and expected that he would make them presents before his departure. Their oath of office positively forbade them to receive a gift from any foreign Prince; they had therefore agreed to refuse the Emperor's presents at first, but to ask the time necessary for obtaining permission to accept them. The Emperor, probably informed of this custom, relieved the good people from their difficulty by setting off without making a single present.

About the latter end of 1777 the Queen, being alone in her closet, sent for my father-in-law and myself, and giving us her hand to kiss, told us that, looking upon us both as persons deeply interested in her happiness, she wished to receive our congratulations: that at length she was the Queen of France, and that she hoped soon to have children; that till now she had concealed her grief, but that she had shed many tears in secret.

Dating from this happy but long-delayed moment, the King's attachment to the Queen assumed every characteristic of love; the good Lassone, first physician to the King and Queen, frequently spoke to me of the uneasiness that the King's indifference, the cause of which he had been so long in overcoming, had given him, and appeared to me at that time to entertain no anxiety except of a very different description.

In the winter of 1778 the King's permission for the return of Voltaire, after an absence of twenty-seven years, was obtained. A few strict persons considered this concession on the part of the Court very injudicious. The Emperor, on leaving France, passed by the Château of Ferney without stopping there. He had advised the Queen not to suffer Voltaire to be presented to her. A lady belonging to the Court learned the Emperor's opinion on that point, and reproached him with his want of enthusiasm towards the greatest genius of the age. He replied that for the good of the people he should always endeavour to profit by the knowledge of the philosophers; but that his own business of sovereign would always prevent his ranking himself amongst that sect. The clergy also took steps to hinder Voltaire's appearance at Court. Paris, however, carried to the highest pitch the honours and enthusiasm shown to the great poet. It was very unwise to let Paris pronounce with such transport an opinion so opposite to that of the Court. This was pointed out to the Queen, and she was told that, without conferring on Voltaire the honour of a presentation, she might see him in the State apartments. She was not averse to following this advice, and appeared embarrassed solely about what she should say to him. She was recommended to talk about nothing but the *Henriade*, *Mérope*, and *Zaira*. The Queen replied that she would still consult a few other persons in whom she had great confidence. The next day she announced that it was irrevocably decided Voltaire should not see any member of the royal family—his writings being too antagonistic to religion and morals. "It is, however, strange," said the Queen, "that while we refuse to admit Voltaire into our presence as the leader of philosophical writers, the Maréchale de Mouchy should have presented to me some years ago Madame Geoffrin, who owed her celebrity to the title of foster-mother of the philosophers."

On the occasion of the duel of the Comte d'Artois with the Prince de Bourbon the Queen determined privately to see the Baron de Besenval, who was to be one of the witnesses, in order to communicate the King's intentions. I have read with infinite pain the manner in which that simple fact is perverted in M. de Besenval's Memoirs.[5] He is right in saying that M. Campan led him through the upper corridors of the Château, and introduced him into an apartment unknown to him; but the air of romance given to the interview is equally culpable and ridiculous. M. de Besenval says that he found himself, without knowing how he came there, in an apartment unadorned, but very conveniently furnished, of the existence of which he was till then utterly ignorant. He was astonished, he adds, not that the Queen should have so many facilities, but that she should have ventured to procure them. Ten printed sheets of the woman De Lamotte's libels contain nothing so injurious to the character of Marie Antoinette as these lines, written by a man whom she honoured by undeserved kindness. He could not have had any opportunity of knowing the existence of these apartments, which consisted of a very small antechamber, a bed-chamber, and a closet. Ever since the Queen had occupied her own apartment, these had been appropriated to her Majesty's lady of honour in cases of illness, and were actually so used when the Queen was confined. It was so important that it should not be known the Queen had spoken to the Baron before the duel that she had determined to go through her inner room into this little apartment, to which M. Campan was to conduct him. When men write of recent times they should be scrupulously exact, and not indulge in exaggerations or inventions.

The Baron de Besenval appears mightily surprised at the Queen's sudden coolness, and refers it to the fickleness of her disposition. I can explain the reason for the change by repeating what her Majesty said to me at the time; and I will not alter one of her expressions. Speaking of the strange presumption of men, and the reserve with which women ought always to treat them, the Queen added that age did not deprive them of the hope of pleasing, if they retained any agreeable qualities; that she had treated the Baron de Besenval as a brave Swiss, agreeable, polished, and witty, whose grey hairs had induced her to look upon him as a man whom she might see without harm; but that she had been much deceived. Her Majesty, after having enjoined me to the strictest secrecy, told me that, finding herself alone with the Baron, he began to address her with so much gallantry that she was thrown into the utmost astonishment, and that he was mad enough to fall upon his knees, and make her a declaration in form. The Queen added, that she said to him: "Rise, sir; the King shall be ignorant of an offence which would disgrace you for ever;" that the Baron grew pale and stammered apologies; that she left her closet without saying another word, and that since that time she hardly ever spoke to him. "It is delightful to have friends," said the Queen; "but in a situation like mine it is sometimes difficult for the friends of our friends to suit us."

In the beginning of the year 1778 Mademoiselle d'Éon obtained permission to return to France, on condition that she should appear there in female dress. The Comte de Vergennes entreated my father, M. Genet, chief clerk of Foreign Affairs, who had long known the Chevalier d'Éon, to receive that strange personage at his house, to guide and restrain, if possible, her ardent disposition. The Queen, on learning of her arrival at Versailles, sent a footman to desire my father to bring her into her presence; my father thought it his duty first to inform the minister of her Majesty's wish. The Comte de Vergennes expressed himself pleased with my father's prudence, and desired that he would accompany him to the Queen. The minister had a few minutes' audience; her Majesty came out of her closet with him, and condescended to express to my father the regret she felt at having troubled him to no purpose; and added, smiling, that a few words from M. de Vergennes had for ever cured her of her curiosity. The discovery in London of the true sex of this pretended woman makes it probable that the few words uttered by the minister contained a solution of the enigma.

The Chevalier d'Éon had been useful in Russia as a spy of Louis XV. While very young he had found means to introduce himself at the Court of the Empress Elizabeth, and served that sovereign in the capacity of reader. Resuming afterwards his military dress, he served with honour and was wounded. Appointed chief secretary of legation, and afterwards minister plenipotentiary at London, he unpardonably insulted Comte de Guerchy, the ambassador. The official order for the Chevalier's return to France was actually delivered to the King's Council; but Louis XV delayed the departure of the courier who was to be its bearer, and sent off another courier privately, who gave the Chevalier d'Éon a letter in his own writing, in which he said, "I know that you have served me as effectually in the dress of a woman as in that which you now wear. Resume it instantly; withdraw into the city; I warn you that the King yesterday signed an order for your return to France; you are not safe in your hotel, and you would here find too powerful enemies." I heard the Chevalier d'Éon repeat the contents of this letter, in which Louis

XV thus separated himself from the King of France, several times at my father's. The Chevalier, or rather the *Chevalière* d'Éon had preserved all the King's letters. Messieurs de Maurepas and de Vergennes wished to get them out of his hands, as they were afraid he would print them. This eccentric being had long solicited permission to return to France; but it was necessary to find a way of sparing the family he had offended the insult they would see in his return; he was therefore made to resume the costume of that sex to which in France everything is pardoned. The desire to see his native land once more determined him to submit to the condition, but he revenged himself by combining the long train of his gown and the three deep ruffles on his sleeves, with the attitude and conversation of a grenadier, which made him very disagreeable company.[6]

At last, the event so long desired by the Queen, and by all those who wished her well, took place; her Majesty became *enceinte*. The King was in ecstasies. Never was there a more united or happier couple. The disposition of Louis XVI entirely altered, and became prepossessing and conciliatory; and the Queen was amply compensated for the uneasiness which the King's indifference during the early part of their union had caused her.

The summer of 1778 was extremely hot. July and August passed, but the air was not cooled by a single storm. The Queen spent whole days in close rooms, and could not sleep until she had breathed the fresh night air, walking with the Princesses and her brothers upon the terrace under her apartments. These promenades at first gave rise to no remark; but it occurred to some of the party to enjoy the music of wind instruments during these fine summer nights. The musicians belonging to the chapel were ordered to perform pieces suited to instruments of that description, upon steps constructed in the middle of the garden. The Queen, seated on one of the terrace benches, enjoyed the effect of this music, surrounded by the whole of the royal family with the exception of the King, who joined them but twice, disliking to change his hour of going to bed.

Nothing could be more innocent than these parties; yet Paris, France, nay, all Europe, were soon canvassing them in a manner most disadvantageous to the reputation of Marie Antoinette. It is true that all the inhabitants of Versailles enjoyed these serenades, and that there was a crowd near the spot from eleven at night until two or three in the morning. The windows of the ground floor occupied by Monsieur and Madame[7] were kept open, and the terrace was perfectly well lighted by the numerous wax candles burning in the two apartments. Lamps were likewise placed in the garden; and the lights of the orchestra illuminated the rest of the place.

I do not know whether a few incautious females might not have ventured farther, and wandered to the bottom of the park; it may have been so; but the Queen, Madame, and the Comtesse d'Artois were always arm-in-arm, and never left the terrace. The Princesses were not remarkable when seated on the benches, being dressed in cambric muslin gowns, with large straw hats and muslin veils, a costume universally adopted by females at that time; but when standing up their different figures always distinguished them; and the persons present stood on one side to let them pass. It is true that when they seated themselves upon the benches private individuals would sometimes, to their great amusement, sit down by their side. A young clerk in the war department, either not knowing or pretending not to know the Queen, spoke to her of the beauty of the night, and the delightful effect of the music. The Queen, fancying she was not recognised, amused herself by keeping up the incognito, and they talked of several private families of Versailles, consisting of persons belonging to the King's household or her own. After a few minutes the Queen and Princesses rose to walk, and on leaving the bench curtsied to the clerk. The young man knowing, or having subsequently discovered, that he had been conversing with the Queen, boasted of it in his office. He was merely desired to hold his tongue; and so little attention did he excite that the Revolution found him still only a clerk. Another evening one of Monsieur's Body Guards seated himself near the Princesses, and, knowing them, left the place where he was sitting and placed himself before the Queen, to tell her that he was very fortunate in being able to seize an opportunity of imploring the kindness of his sovereign; that he was "soliciting at Court"—at the word *soliciting* the Queen and Princesses rose hastily and withdrew into Madame's apartment.[8] I was at the Queen's residence that day. She talked of this little occurrence all the time of her *coucher*; though she only complained that one of Monsieur's guards should have had the effrontery to speak to her. Her Majesty added that he ought to have respected her incognito; and that that was not the place where he should have ventured to make a request. Madame had recognised him, and talked of making a complaint to his captain; the Queen opposed it, attributing his error to his ignorance and provincial origin.

The most scandalous libels were based on these two insignificant occurrences, which I have related with scrupulous exactness. Nothing could be more false than those calumnies. It must be confessed, however, that such meetings were liable to ill consequences. I ventured to say as much to the Queen, and informed her that one evening, when her Majesty had beckoned to me to go and speak to her, I thought I recognised on the bench on which she was sitting two women deeply veiled, and keeping profound silence; that those women were the Comtesse du Barry and her sister-in-law; and that my suspicions were confirmed when, at a few paces from the seat, and nearer to her Majesty, I met a tall footman belonging to Madame du Barry, whom I had seen in her service all the time she resided at Court.

My advice was useless. Misled by the pleasure she found in these promenades, and secure in the consciousness of blameless conduct, the Queen would not see the lamentable results which must necessarily follow. This was very unfortunate; for, besides the mortifications they brought upon her, it is highly probable that they prompted the vile plot which gave rise to the Cardinal de Rohan's fatal error.

Having enjoyed these evening promenades about a month, the Queen ordered a private concert within the colonnade which contained the group of Pluto and Proserpine. Sentinels were placed at all the entrances, and ordered to admit within the colonnade only such persons as should produce tickets signed by my father-in-law. A fine concert was performed there by the musicians of the chapel and the female musicians belonging to the Queen's chamber. The Queen went with Mesdames de Polignac, de Châlon, and d'Andlau, and Messieurs de Polignac, de Coigny, de Besenval, and de Vaudreuil; there were also a few equerries present. Her Majesty gave me permission to attend the concert with some of my female relations. There was no music upon the terrace. The crowd of inquisitive people, whom the sentinels kept at a distance from the enclosure of the colonnade, went away highly discontented; the small number of persons admitted no doubt occasioned jealousy, and gave rise to offensive comments which were caught up by the public with avidity. I do not pretend to apologise for the kind of amusements with which the Queen indulged herself during this and the following summer; the consequences were so lamentable that the error was no doubt very great; but what I have said respecting the character of these promenades may be relied on as true.

When the season for evening walks was at an end, odious couplets were circulated in Paris; the Queen was treated in them in the most insulting manner; her situation ranked among her enemies persons attached to the only Prince who for several years had appeared likely to give heirs to the Crown. People uttered the most inconsiderate language; and those improper conversations took place in societies wherein the imminent danger of violating to so criminal an extent both truth and the respect due to sovereigns ought to have been better understood. A few days before the Queen's confinement a whole volume of manuscript songs concerning her and all the ladies about her remarkable for rank or station was thrown down in the *Œil de Bœuf*.[9] This manuscript was immediately put into the hands of the King, who was highly incensed at it, and said that he had himself been at those promenades; that he had seen nothing connected with them but what was perfectly harmless; that such songs would disturb the harmony of twenty families in the Court and city; that it was a capital crime to have made any against the Queen herself; and that he wished the author of the infamous libels to be discovered and punished. A fortnight afterwards it was known publicly that the verses were by M. Champcenetz de Riquebourg,[10] who was not even reprimanded.

I knew for a certainty that the King spoke to M. de Maurepas, before two of his most confidential servants, respecting the risk which he saw the Queen ran from these night walks upon the terrace of Versailles, which the public ventured to censure thus openly, and that the old minister had the cruelty to advise that she should be suffered to go on; she possessed talent; her friends were very ambitious, and longed to see her take a part in public affairs; and to let her acquire the reputation of levity would do no harm. M. de Vergennes was as hostile to the Queen's influence as M. de Maurepas. It may therefore be fairly presumed, since the Prime Minister durst point out to his King an advantage to be gained by the Queen's discrediting herself, that he and M. de Vergennes employed all means within the reach of powerful ministers in order to ruin her in the opinion of the public.[11]

The Queen's *accouchement* approached; *Te Deums* were sung and prayers offered up in all the cathedrals. On the 11th of December 1778 the royal family, the Princes of the blood, and the great officers of State, passed the night in the rooms adjoining the Queen's bed-chamber. Madame, the King's daughter, came into the world before midday on the 19th of December.[12] The etiquette of allowing all persons indiscriminately to enter at the moment of the delivery of a queen was observed with such exaggeration that when the *accoucheur* said aloud, *La Reine va s'accoucher*, the persons who poured into the chamber were so numerous that the rush nearly destroyed the Queen. During the night the King had taken the precaution to have the enormous tapestry screens which surrounded her Majesty's bed secured with cords; but for this they certainly would have been thrown down upon her. It was impossible to move about the chamber, which was filled with so motley a crowd that one might have fancied himself in some place of public amusement. Two Savoyards got upon the furniture for a better sight of the Queen, who was placed opposite the fireplace. The noise and the sex of the infant, with which the Queen was made acquainted by a signal previously agreed on, as it is said, with the Princesse de Lamballe, or some error of the *accoucheur*, brought on symptoms which threatened fatal consequences; the *accoucheur* exclaimed, "Give her air—warm water—she must be bled in the foot!" The windows were stopped up; the King opened them with a strength which his affection for the Queen gave him at the moment. They were of great height, and pasted over with strips of paper all round. The basin of hot water not being brought quickly enough, the *accoucheur* desired the chief surgeon to use his lancet without waiting for it. He did so; the blood streamed out freely, and the Queen opened her eyes. The Princesse de Lamballe was carried through the crowd in a state of insensibility. The *valets de chambre* and pages dragged out by the collar such inconsiderate persons as would not leave the room. This cruel custom was abolished ever afterwards. The Princes of the family, the Princes of the blood, the chancellor and the ministers are surely sufficient to attest the legitimacy of an hereditary Prince. The Queen was snatched from the very jaws of death; she was not conscious of having been bled, and on being replaced in bed, asked why she had a linen bandage upon her foot.

The delight which succeeded the moment of fear was equally lively and sincere. We were all embracing each other, and shedding tears of joy. The Comte d'Esterhazy and the Prince de Poix, to whom I was the first to announce that the Queen was restored to life, embraced me in the midst of the cabinet of the nobles. We little imagined, in our happiness at her escape from death, for how much more terrible a fate our beloved Princess was reserved.

1. The custom was, even supposing dinner to have commenced, if a Princess of the blood arrived, and she was asked to sit down at the Queen's table, the comptrollers and gentlemen-in-waiting came immediately to attend, and the Queen's women withdrew. These had succeeded the maids of honour in several parts of their service, and had preserved some of their privileges. One day the Duchesse d'Orléans arrived at Fontainebleau, at the Queen's dinner-hour. The Queen invited her to the table, and herself motioned to her women to leave the room, and let the men take their places. Her Majesty said she was resolved to continue a privilege which kept places of that description most honourable, and rendered them suitable for ladies of nobility without fortune. Madame de Misery, Baronne de Biache, the Queen's first lady of the chamber, to whom I was made reversioner, was a daughter of M. le Comte de Chemant, and her grandmother was a Montmorency. M. le Prince de Tingry, in the presence of the Queen, used to call her *cousin*. The ancient household of the Kings of France had prerogatives acknowledged in the State. Many of the offices were tenable only by those of noble blood, and were sold at from 40,000 to 300,000 francs. A collection of edicts of the Kings in favour of the prerogatives and right of precedence of the persons holding office in the royal household is still in existence.—*Madame Campan.*

2. Joseph II had a taste, or perhaps we may say a talent, for satire. A collection of his letters has been published, in which his bitter raillery spares neither the nobility nor the clergy, nor even his brother Kings.—*Note by the Editor.*

3. Shortly after the Emperor's departure, the Comte d'Angivillers laid before the King plans for the erection of the Museum, which was then begun.—*Madame Campan.*

4. The Emperor loudly censured the existing practice of allowing shopkeepers to erect shops near the outward walls of all the palaces, and even to establish something like a fair in the galleries of Versailles and Fontainebleau, and even upon the landings of the staircases.—*Madame Campan.*

5. See the *Mémoires de Baron de Besenval*, tome i, in the *Collection des Mémoires sur la Révolution.*

6. The account given by Madame Campan of the Chevalier is now known to be incorrect in many particulars. Enough details for most readers will be found in the Duc de Broglie's *Secret of the King*, vol. ii, chaps. vi and x, and at p. 89, vol. ii of that work, where the Duke refers to the letter of most dubious authenticity spoken of by Madame Campan. The following details will be sufficient for these memoirs:—The Chevalier Charles d'Éon de Beaumont (born 1728, died 1810) was an ex-captain of dragoons, employed in both the open and the secret diplomacy of Louis XV. When at the Embassy in London he quarrelled with the ambassador, his superior, the Comte de Guerchy (Marquis de Nangis); and used his possession of papers concerning the secret diplomacy to shield himself. It was when hiding in London, in 1765, on account of this business, that he seems first to have assumed woman's dress, which he retained apparently chiefly from love of notoriety. In 1775 a formal agreement with the French Court, made by the instrumentality of Beaumarchais, of all people in the world, permitted him to return to France, retaining the dress of a woman. He went back to France, but again came to England and died there. He had been a brave and distinguished officer, but his form and a certain coldness of temperament always remarked in him assisted him in his assumption of another sex. There appears to be no truth in the story of his proceedings at the Russian Court, and his appearing in female attire was a surprise to those who must have known of any earlier affair of the sort.

7. The wife of Monsieur, the Comte de Provence.

8. Soulavie has most criminally perverted these two facts.—*Madame Campan.*

9. A large room at Versailles lighted by a bull's-eye window, and used as a waiting-room.

10. The author of a great many songs, some of which are very well written. Lively and satirical by nature, he did not lose either his cheerfulness or his carelessness before the Revolutionary Tribunal. After hearing his own sentence read, he asked his judges if he might not be allowed to find a substitute.—*Madame Campan.*

11. Madame Campan's account of the conduct of the Comte de Maurepas is confirmed by a writer with whom she is very seldom in accordance. "It is known," says Soulavie, "that in 1774, 1775, and 1776, M. de Maurepas stirred up private quarrels between Louis XVI and his wife on pretence of the Queen's inconsiderate conduct. M. de Maurepas was fond of interfering in family disputes. The go-betweens whom he made use of raised the strongest prejudices against the Queen."—*Note by the Editor.*

12. Marie Thérèse Charlotte (1778–1851), Madame Royale; married in 1799 Louis, Duc d'Angoulême, eldest son of the Comte d'Artois.

ANNEX TO CHAPTER VIII

We are tempted to add some specimens of the Emperor Joseph's correspondence, which forcibly demonstrate the vigour, shrewdness, and originality of his mind, and complete the portrait left of him by Madame Campan. The wholesale, eccentric, and somewhat cruel ecclesiastical economies effected by Joseph II, which reduced the Papal power in his dominions, suppressed bishoprics and monasteries, prohibited pilgrimages and pillaged churches, drew from Pius VI many ineffectual remonstrances;[1] to one of these the Emperor made the following reply:—

To Pope Pius VI

MOST HOLY FATHER—The funds of the clergy of my dominions are not destined, as has been boldly said at Rome, to expire with my reign, but rather to become a relief to my people; and as their continuation, as well as the displeasure which has burst forth upon this subject, are within the jurisdiction of history, posterity will be masters of the matter without our co-operation; this, then, will be a monument of my time, and I hope not the only one.

I have suppressed the superfluous convents, and the still more superfluous societies; their revenues serve to support curates and to ameliorate the primary institutions; but amidst all the confidence in matters of account which I am obliged to place in persons employed by the State, the funds of the latter have with me absolutely nothing in common with those of the Church. An action should be judged of only by its intention, and the results of this action can only be appreciated by their success, which will not be known for some years.

I see, however, that logic is not the same at Rome as it is in my dominions, and hence arises this want of harmony between Italy and the empire.

If your Holiness had taken the charitable care to inform yourself, at the proper source, of what was passing in my territories, many things would not have happened; but there were people at Rome who, as it appears to me, would have darkness spread itself more and more over our poor globe.

You have now the brief account of the causes which have compelled my arrangements; I hope you will excuse the conciseness of my letter on consideration that I have neither the time nor the talent necessary for discussing so vast a theme in the manner used in a Roman museum.

I pray God still long to preserve you to His Church, and to send one of His angels before you to prepare for you the way to heaven.—Your most obedient son in Jesus Christ, JOSEPH.

VIENNA, *July* 1784.

Few sovereigns have given their reasons for refusing appointments with the fullness and point of the following letter:—

To a Lady

MADAM—I do not think that it is amongst the duties of a monarch to grant places to one of his subjects merely because he is a gentleman. That, however, is the inference from the request you have made to me. Your late husband was, you say, a distinguished general, a gentleman of good family, and thence you conclude that my kindness to your family can do no less than give a company of foot to your second son, lately returned from his travels.

Madam, a man may be the son of a general and yet have no talent for command. A man may be of a good family and yet possess no other merit than that which he owes to chance—the name of gentleman.

I know your son, and I know what makes the soldier; and this twofold knowledge convinces me that your son has not the disposition of a warrior, and that he is too full of his birth to leave the country a hope of his ever rendering it any important service.

What you are to be pitied for, Madam, is, that your son is not fit either for an officer, a statesman, or a priest; in a word, that he is nothing more than a gentleman in the most extended acceptation of the word.

You may be thankful to that destiny, which, in refusing talents to your son, has taken care to put him in possession of great wealth, which will sufficiently compensate him for other deficiencies, and enable him at the same time to dispense with any favour from me.

I hope you will be impartial enough to see the reasons which prompt me to refuse your request. It may be disagreeable to you, but I consider it necessary. Farewell, Madam.—Your sincere well-wisher, JOSEPH.

LACHSENBURG, *4th August* 1787.

The application of another anxious and somewhat covetous mother was answered with still more decision and irony:—

To a Lady

MADAM—You know my disposition; you are not ignorant that the society of the ladies is to me a mere recreation, and that I have never sacrificed my principles to the fair sex. I pay but little attention to recommendations, and I only take them into consideration when the person in whose behalf I may be solicited possesses real merit.

Two of your sons are already loaded with favours. The eldest, who is not yet twenty, is chief of a squadron in my army, and the younger has obtained a canonry at Cologne, from the Elector, my brother. What would you have more? Would you have the first a general and the second a bishop?

In France you may see colonels in leading strings, and in Spain the royal princes command armies even at eighteen; hence Prince Stahremberg forced them to retreat so often that they were never able all the rest of their lives to comprehend any other manœuvre.

It is necessary to be sincere at Court, and severe in the field, stoical without obduracy, magnanimous without weakness, and to gain the esteem of our enemies by the justice of our actions; and this, Madam, is what I aim at. JOSEPH.

VIENNA, *September* 1787.

(From the inedited Letters of Joseph II, published at Paris, by Persan, 1822.)

1. See Coxe's *House of Austria*, vol. iii, p. 490.

IX

*Public rejoicings—Death of Maria Theresa; the Queen's
affliction—Anecdotes of Maria Theresa—Birth of the
Dauphin—Bankruptcy of the Prince de Guéménée—The Duchesse
de Polignac is appointed governess of the Children of France—Jealousy
of the Court—Mode of life at Trianon—Presumption of the Duc de
Fronsac—American War—Franklin—M. de La Fayette—Order for
admitting none but gentlemen to the rank of officer—Spirit of
the Third Estate*

During the alarm for the life of the Queen, regret at not possessing an heir to the throne was not even thought of. The King himself was wholly occupied with the care of preserving an adored wife. The young Princess was presented to her mother. "Poor little one," said the Queen, "you were not wished for, but you are not on that account less dear to me. A son would have been rather the property of the State. You shall be mine; you shall have my undivided care, shall share all my happiness, and console me in all my troubles."

The King despatched a courier to Paris; and wrote letters himself to Vienna, by the Queen's bedside; and part of the rejoicings ordered took place in the capital.[1]

A great number of attendants watched near the Queen during the first nights of her confinement. This custom distressed her; she knew how to feel for others, and ordered large armchairs for her women, the backs of which were capable of being let down by springs, and which served perfectly well instead of beds.

M. de Lassone, the chief physician, the chief surgeon, the chief apothecary, the principal officers of the buttery, etc., were likewise nine nights without going to bed. The royal children were watched for a long time, and one of the women on duty remained, nightly, up and dressed, during the first three years from their birth.

The Queen made her entry into Paris for the churching. One hundred maidens were portioned and married at Notre Dame. There were few popular acclamations, but her Majesty was perfectly well received at the opera.[2]

A few days after the Queen's recovery from her confinement, the Curé of the Magdelaine de la Cité at Paris wrote to M. Campan and requested a private interview with him; it was to desire he would deliver into the hands of the Queen a little box containing her wedding ring, with this note written by the Curé: "I have received under the seal of confession the ring which I send to your Majesty; with an avowal that it was stolen from you in 1771, in order to be used in sorceries, to prevent you having any children." On seeing her ring again the Queen said that she had in fact lost it about seven years before, while washing her hands, and that she had resolved to use no endeavour to discover the superstitious woman who had done her the injury.

The Queen's attachment to the Comtesse Jules increased every day; she went frequently to her house at Paris, and even took up her own abode at the Château de la Muette to be nearer during her confinement.[3] She married Mademoiselle de Polignac, when scarcely thirteen years of age, to M. de Grammont, who, on account of this marriage, was made Duc de Guiche, and captain of the King's Guards, in reversion after the Duc de Villeroi. The Duchesse de Civrac, Madame Victoire's *dame d'honneur*, had been promised the place for the Duc de Lorges, her son. The number of discontented families at Court increased.

The title of favourite was too openly given to the Comtesse Jules by her friends. The lot of the favourite of a Queen is not, in France, a happy one; the favourites of Kings are treated, out of gallantry, with much greater indulgence.

A short time after the birth of Madame the Queen became again *enceinte*; she had mentioned it only to the King, to her physician, and to a few persons honoured with her intimate confidence, when having exerted her strength in pulling up one of the glasses of her carriage, she felt that she had hurt herself, and eight days afterwards she miscarried. The King spent the whole morning at her bedside, consoling her, and manifesting the tenderest concern for her. The Queen wept exceedingly; the King took her affectionately in his arms, and mingled his tears with hers. The King enjoined silence among the small number of persons who were informed of this unfortunate occurrence; and it remained generally unknown. These particulars furnish an accurate idea of the manner in which this august couple lived together.

The Empress Maria Theresa did not enjoy the happiness of seeing her daughter give an heir to the Crown of France. That illustrious Princess died at the close of 1780, after having proved by her example that, as in the instance of Queen Blanche, the talents of a sovereign might be blended with the virtues of a pious Princess. The King was deeply affected at the death of the Empress; and on the arrival of the courier from Vienna said that he could not bring himself to afflict the Queen by informing her of an event which grieved even him so much. His Majesty thought the Abbé de Vermond, who had possessed the confidence of Maria Theresa during his stay at Vienna, the most proper person to discharge this painful duty. He sent his first *valet de chambre*, M. de Chamilly, to the Abbé on the evening of the day he received the despatches from Vienna, to order him to come the next day to the Queen before her breakfast hour, to acquit himself discreetly of the afflicting commission with which he was charged, and to let his Majesty know the moment of his entering the Queen's chamber. It was the King's intention to be there precisely a quarter of an hour after him, and he was punctual to his time; he was announced; the Abbé came out; and his Majesty said to him, as he drew up at the door to let him pass, "*I thank you, Monsieur l'Abbé for the service you have just done me.*" This was the only time during nineteen years that the King spoke to him.

Within an hour after learning the event the Queen put on temporary mourning, while waiting until her Court mourning should be ready; she kept herself shut up in her closets for several days; went out only to mass; saw none but the royal family; and received none but the Princesse de Lamballe and the Duchesse de Polignac. She never ceased talking of the courage, the misfortunes, the successes, and the virtues of her mother. The shroud and dress in which Maria Theresa was to be buried, made entirely by her own hands, were found ready prepared in one of her closets. The Queen found no other comfort in her affliction than talking of her beloved mother; she was thoroughly versed in the various events which distinguished the Empress' reign, and in all the qualities which rendered her dear to her family and her people. She often regretted that the numerous duties of her august mother had prevented her from watching in person over the education of her daughters; and modestly said that she herself would have been more worthy if she had had the good fortune to receive lessons directly from a sovereign so enlightened, and so deserving of admiration.[4]

The Queen told me one day that her mother was left a widow at an age when her beauty was yet striking; that she was secretly informed of a plot laid by her three principal ministers to make themselves agreeable to her; of a compact made between them, that the losers should not feel any jealousy towards him who should be fortunate enough to gain his sovereign's heart; and that they had sworn that the successful one should be always the friend of the other two. The Empress being assured of this scheme, one day after the breaking up of the Council over which she had presided, turned the conversation upon the subject of female sovereigns, and the duties of their sex and rank; and then applying her general reflections to herself in particular, told them that she hoped to guard herself all her life against weaknesses of the heart; but that if ever an irresistible feeling should make her alter her resolution, it should be only in favour of a man proof against ambition, not engaged in State affairs, but attached only to a private life and its calm enjoyments—in a word, if her heart should betray her so far as to lead her to love a man invested with any important office, from the moment he should discover her sentiments he would forfeit his place and his influence with the public. This was sufficient; the three ministers, more ambitious than amorous, gave up their projects for ever.

On the 22nd of October 1781 the Queen gave birth to a Dauphin.[5] So deep a silence prevailed in the room that the Queen thought her child was a daughter; but after the Keeper of the Seals had declared the sex of the infant, the King went up to the Queen's bed, and said to her, "Madame, you have fulfilled my wishes and those of France: you are the mother of a Dauphin." The King's joy was boundless: tears streamed from his eyes; he gave his hand to every one present; and his happiness carried away his habitual reserve. Cheerful and affable, he was incessantly taking occasion to introduce the words, *my son*, or *the Dauphin*. As soon as the Queen was in bed, she would see the long-looked-for infant. The Princesse de Guéménée brought him to her. The Queen said there was no need for commending him to the Princess, but in order to enable her to attend to him more freely, she would herself share the care of the education of her daughter. When the Dauphin was settled in his apartment, he received the customary homages and visits. The Duc d'Angoulême,[6] meeting his father at the entrance of the Dauphin's apartment, said to him, "Oh, papa! how little my cousin is!" "The day will come when you will think him great enough, my dear," answered the Prince, almost involuntarily.

The birth of the Dauphin appeared to give joy to all classes. Men stopped one another in the streets, spoke without being acquainted, and those who were acquainted embraced each other. In the birth of a legitimate heir to the sovereign every man beholds a pledge of prosperity and tranquillity.[7]

The rejoicings were splendid and ingenious. The artificers and tradesmen of Paris spent considerable sums in order to go to Versailles in a body, with their various insignia. Almost every troop had music with it. When they arrived at the Court of the palace, they there arranged themselves so as to present a most interesting living picture. Chimney-sweepers quite as well dressed as those that appear upon the stage, carried an ornamented chimney, at the top of which was perched one of the smallest of their fraternity. The chairmen carried a sedan highly gilt, in which were to be seen a handsome nurse and a little Dauphin. The butchers made their appearance with their fat ox. Cooks, masons, blacksmiths, all trades were on the alert. The smiths hammered away upon an anvil, the shoemakers finished off a little pair of boots for the Dauphin, and the tailors a little suit of the uniform of his regiment. The King remained a long time upon a balcony to enjoy the sight. The whole Court was delighted with it. So general was the enthusiasm that (the police not having carefully examined the procession) the gravediggers had the imprudence to send their deputation also, with the emblematic devices of their ill-omened occupation. They were met by the Princess Sophie, the King's aunt, who was thrilled with horror at the sight, and entreated the King to have the audacious fellows driven out of the procession, which was then drawing up on the terrace.

The "dames de la halle" came to congratulate the Queen, and were received with the suitable ceremonies. Fifty of them appeared dressed in black silk gowns, the established full dress of their order, and almost all wore diamonds. The Princesse de Chimay went to the door of the Queen's bedroom to receive three of these ladies, who were led up to the Queen's bed. One of them addressed her Majesty in a speech written by M. de la Harpe. It was set down on the inside of a fan, to which the speaker repeatedly referred, but without any embarrassment. She was handsome, and had a remarkably fine voice. The Queen was affected by the address, and answered it with great affability; wishing a distinction to be made between these women and the *poissardes*, who always left a disagreeable impression on her mind. The King ordered a substantial repast for all these women. One of his Majesty's *maîtres d'hôtel*, wearing his hat, sat as President and did the honours of the table.[8] The public were admitted, and numbers of people had the curiosity to go.

The *poissardes'* songs were numerous, and some of them tolerably good. The King and Queen were much pleased with the following one, and sang it several times during the Queen's confinement:

Ne craignez pas, cher papa,
D'voir augmenter vot' famille
Le bon Dieu z'y pourvoira:
Fait's-en tant qu' Versaille en fourmille
'Y eût-il cent Bourbons cheu nous,
'Y a du pain, du laurier pour tous.

The Gardes-du-Corps obtained the King's permission to give the Queen a dress ball in the great hall of the opera at Versailles. Her Majesty opened the ball in a minuet with a private selected by the corps, to whom the King granted the bâton of an exempt. The fête was most splendid. All then was joy, happiness, and peace.[9]

The Dauphin was a year old when the Prince de Guéménée's bankruptcy compelled the Princess, his wife, who was governess to the Enfants de France, to resign her situation.

The Queen was at La Muette for the inoculation of her daughter. She sent for me, and condescended to say she wished to converse with me about a scheme which delighted her, but in the execution of which she foresaw some inconveniences. Her plan was to appoint the Duchesse de Polignac to the office lately held by the Princesse de Guéménée. She saw with extreme pleasure the facilities which this appointment would give her for superintending the education of her children, without running any risk of hurting the pride of the governess; and that it would bring together the objects of her warmest affections—her children and her friend. "The friends of the Duchesse de Polignac," continued the Queen, "will be gratified by the splendour and importance conferred by the employment. As to the Duchess, I know her; the place by no means suits her simple and quiet habits, nor the sort of indolence of her disposition. She will give me the greatest possible proof of her devotion if she yields to my wish." The Queen also spoke of the Princesse de Chimay and the Duchesse de Duras, whom the public pointed out as fit for the post; but she thought the Princesse de Chimay's piety too rigid; and as to the Duchesse de Duras, her wit and learning quite frightened her. What the Queen dreaded as the consequence of her selection of the Duchesse de Polignac was principally the jealousy of the courtiers; but she showed so lively a desire to see her scheme executed that I had no doubt she would soon set at nought all the obstacles she discovered. I was not mistaken: a few days afterwards the Duchess was appointed governess.

The Queen's object in sending for me was no doubt to furnish me with the means of explaining the feelings which induced her to prefer a governess disposed by friendship to suffer her to enjoy all the privileges of a mother. Her Majesty knew that I saw a great deal of company.

The Queen frequently dined with the Duchess after having been present at the King's private dinner. Sixty-one thousand francs were therefore added to the salary of the governess as a compensation for this increase of expense.

The Queen was tired of the excursions to Marly; and had no great difficulty in setting the King against them. He did not like the expense of them, for everybody was entertained there *gratis*. Louis XIV had established a kind of parade upon these excursions, differing from that of Versailles, but still more annoying. Card and supper parties occurred every day, and required much dress. On Sundays and holidays the fountains played, the people were admitted into the gardens, and there was as great a crowd as at the fêtes of Saint Cloud.

Every age has its peculiar colouring; Marly showed that of Louis XIV even more than Versailles. Everything in the former place appeared to have been produced by the magic power of a fairy's wand. Not the slightest trace of all this splendour remains; the revolutionary spoilers even tore up the pipes which served to supply the fountains. Perhaps a brief description of this palace and the usages established there by Louis XIV may be acceptable.

Marly

The very extensive gardens of Marly ascended almost imperceptibly to the pavilion of the sun, which was occupied only by the King and his family. The pavilions of the twelve zodiacal signs bounded the two sides of the lawn. They were connected by bowers impervious to the rays of the sun. The pavilions nearest to that of the sun were reserved for the Princes of the blood and the ministers; the rest were occupied by persons holding superior offices at Court, or invited to stay at Marly. Each pavilion was named after fresco paintings, which covered its walls, and which had been executed by the most celebrated artists of the age of Louis XIV. On a line with the upper pavilion there was on the left a chapel; on the right a pavilion called La Perspective, which concealed a long suite of offices, containing a hundred lodging-rooms intended for the persons belonging to the service of the Court, kitchens, and spacious dining-rooms, in which more than thirty tables were splendidly laid out.

During half Louis XV's reign the ladies still wore the *habit de cour de Marly*, so named by Louis XIV, and which differed little from that devised for Versailles. The French gown, gathered in the back, and with great hoops, replaced this dress, and continued to be worn till the end of the reign of Louis XVI. The diamonds, feathers, rouge, and embroidered stuffs, spangled with gold, effaced all trace of a rural residence; but the people loved to see the splendour of their sovereign and a brilliant Court glittering in the shades of the woods.

After dinner, and before the hour for cards, the Queen, the Princesses, and their ladies, paraded among the clumps of trees in little carriages, beneath canopies richly embroidered with gold, drawn by men in the King's livery. The trees planted by Louis XIV were of prodigious height, which, however, was surpassed in several of the groups by fountains of the clearest water; while, among others, cascades over white marble, the waters of which, met by the sunbeams, looked like draperies of silver gauze, formed a contrast to the solemn darkness of the groves.

In the evening nothing more was necessary for any well-dressed man to procure admission to the Queen's card-parties than to be named and presented, by some officer of the Court, to the gentleman usher of the card-room. This room, which was very large, and of octagonal shape, rose to the top of the Italian roof, and terminated in a cupola, furnished with balconies, in which females who had not been presented easily obtained leave to place themselves and enjoy the sight of the brilliant assemblage.

Though not of the number of persons belonging to the Court, gentlemen admitted into this salon might request one of the ladies seated with the Queen at lansquenet or faro to bet upon her cards with such gold or notes as they presented to her. Rich people and the gamblers of Paris did not miss one of the evenings at the Marly salon, and there were always considerable sums won and lost. Louis XVI hated high play, and very often showed displeasure when the loss of large sums was mentioned. The fashion of wearing a black coat without being in mourning had not then been introduced, and the King gave a few of his *coups de boutoir* to certain Chevaliers de Saint Louis, dressed in this manner, who came to venture two or three *louis*, in the hope that fortune would favour the handsome duchesses who deigned to place them on their cards.[10]

Singular contrasts are often seen amidst the grandeur of courts. In order to manage such high play at the Queen's faro table, it was necessary to have a banker provided with large sums of money and this necessity placed at the table, to which none but the highest titled persons were admitted in general, not only M. de Chalabre, who was its banker, but also a retired captain of foot, who officiated as his second. A word, trivial, but completely appropriate to express the manner in which the Court was attended there, was often heard. Gentlemen presented at Court, who had not been invited to stay at Marly, came there notwithstanding as they did to Versailles, and returned again to Paris; under such circumstances, it was said such a one had been to Marly only *en polisson*;[11] and it appeared odd to hear a captivating marquis, in answer to the inquiry whether he was of the royal party at Marly, say, "No, I am only here *en polisson*" meaning simply "I am here on the footing of all those whose nobility is of a later date than 1400." The Marly excursions were exceedingly expensive to the King. Besides the superior tables, those of the almoners, equerries, *maîtres d'hôtel*, etc. etc., were all supplied with such a degree of magnificence as to allow of inviting strangers to them; and almost all the visitors from Paris were boarded at the expense of the Court.

The personal frugality of the unfortunate Prince who sank beneath the weight of the national debts thus favoured the Queen's predilection for her Petit Trianon; and for five or six years preceding the Revolution the Court very seldom visited Marly.

The King, always attentive to the comfort of his family, gave Mesdames, his aunts, the use of the Château de Bellevue, and afterwards purchased the Princesse de Guéménée's house, at the entrance to Paris, for Madame Elizabeth.[12] The Comtesse de Provence bought a small house at Montreuil; Monsieur already had Brunoy; the Comtesse d'Artois built Bagatelle; Versailles became, in the estimation of all the royal family, the least agreeable of residences. They only fancied themselves at home in the plainest houses, surrounded by English gardens, where they better enjoyed the beauties of nature. The taste for cascades and statues was entirely past.

The Queen occasionally remained a whole month at Petit Trianon, and had established there all the ways of life in a château. She entered the sitting-room without driving the ladies from their pianoforte or embroidery. The gentlemen continued their billiards or backgammon without suffering her presence to interrupt them. There was but little room in the small Château of Trianon. Madame Elizabeth accompanied the Queen there, but the ladies of honour and ladies of the palace had no establishment at Trianon. When invited by the Queen, they came from Versailles to dinner. The King and Princes came regularly to sup. A white gown, a gauze kerchief, and a straw hat were the uniform dress of the Princesses.[13] Examining all the manufactories of the hamlet, seeing the cows milked, and fishing in the lake, delighted the Queen; and every year she showed increased aversion to the pompous excursions to Marly.

The idea of acting comedies, as was then done in almost all country houses, followed on the Queen's wish to live at Trianon without ceremony. It was agreed that no young man except the Comte d'Artois should be admitted into the company of performers, and that the audience should consist only of the King, Monsieur, and the Princesses, who did not play; but in order to stimulate the actors a little, the first boxes were to be occupied by the readers, the Queen's ladies, their sisters and daughters, making altogether about forty persons.

The Queen laughed heartily at the voice of M. d'Adhémar, formerly a very fine one, but latterly become rather tremulous. His shepherd's dress in Colin, in the *Devin du Village*, contrasted very ridiculously with his time of life, and the Queen said it would be difficult for malevolence itself to find anything to criticise in the choice of such a lover. The King was highly amused with these plays, and was present at every performance. Caillot, a celebrated actor, who had long quitted the stage, and Dazincourt, both of acknowledged good character, were selected to give lessons, the first in comic opera, of which the easier sorts were preferred, and the second in comedy. The office of hearer of rehearsals, prompter, and stage manager was given to my father-in-law. The Duc de Fronsac, first gentleman of the chamber, was much hurt at this. He thought himself called upon to make serious remonstrances upon the subject, and wrote to the Queen, who made him the following answer: "You cannot be first gentleman when we are the actors. Besides, I have already intimated to you my determination respecting Trianon. I hold no court there, I live like a private person, and M. Campan shall be always employed to execute orders relative to the private fêtes I choose to give there." This not putting a stop to the Duke's remonstrances, the King was obliged to interfere. The Duke continued obstinate, and insisted that he was entitled to manage the private amusements as much as those which were public. It became absolutely necessary to end the argument in a positive manner.

The diminutive Duc de Fronsac never failed, when he came to pay his respects to the Queen at her toilette, to turn the conversation upon Trianon, in order to make some ironical remarks on my father-in-law, of whom, from the time of his appointment, he always spoke as "my colleague Campan". The Queen would shrug her shoulders, and say, when he was gone, "It is quite shocking to find so little a man in the son of the Maréchal de Richelieu."

La Gageure Imprévue was one of the pieces performed at Trianon. The Queen played the part of Gotte; the Comtesse Diana that of Madame de Clainville; Madame Elizabeth the young woman, and the Comte d'Artois one of the men's characters. Colette, in the *Devin du Village*, was really very well played by the Queen. They performed also in the course of the following seasons, *Le Roi et le Fernier; Rose et Colas; le Sorcier: l'Anglais à Bourdeaux: On ne s'avise jamais de tout; le Barbier de Seville*, etc.[14]

So long as no strangers were admitted to these performances they were but little censured; but the praise obtained by the performers made them look for a larger circle of admirers. The Queen permitted the officers of the Body Guards and the equerries of the King and Princes to be present at the plays. Private boxes were provided for some of the people belonging to the Court; a few more ladies were invited; and claims arose on all sides for the favour of admission. The Queen refused to admit the officers of the Body Guards of the Princes, the officers of the King's *Cent Suisses*, and many other persons, who were highly mortified at the refusal.

The company, for a private company, was good enough, and the acting was applauded to the skies; nevertheless, as the audience withdrew, adverse criticisms were occasionally heard.

While delight at having given an heir to the throne of the Bourbons, and a succession of fêtes and amusements filled up the happy days of Marie Antoinette, the public was engrossed by the Anglo-American war. Two Kings, or rather their ministers, planted and propagated the love of liberty in the new world; the King of England, by shutting his ears and his heart against the continued and respectful representations of subjects at a distance from their native land, who had become numerous, rich, and powerful, through the resources of the soil they had fertilised; and the King of France, by giving support to this people in rebellion against their ancient sovereign. Many young soldiers, belonging to the first families of the country, followed La Fayette's example, and forsook luxury, amusement, and love to go and tender their aid to the revolted Americans. Beaumarchais, secretly seconded by Messieurs de Maurepas and de Vergennes, obtained permission to send out supplies of arms and clothing. Franklin appeared at Court in the dress of an American agriculturist. His unpowdered hair, his round hat, his brown cloth coat, formed a contrast to the laced and embroidered coats and the powder and perfume of the courtiers of Versailles. This novelty turned the light heads of the Frenchwomen. Elegant entertainments were given to Dr Franklin, who, to the reputation of a man of science, added the patriotic virtues which invested him with the character of an apostle of liberty. I was present at one of these entertainments, when the most beautiful woman out of 300 was selected to place a crown of laurels upon the white head of the American philosopher, and two kisses upon his cheeks. Even in the palace of Versailles, Franklin's medallion was sold under the King's eyes, in the exhibition of Sèvres porcelain. The legend of this medallion was:

Eripuit coelo fulmen, sceptrumque tyrannis

The King never declared his opinion upon an enthusiasm which his correct judgment no doubt led him to blame. The Queen spoke out more plainly about the part France was taking respecting the independence of the American colonies, and constantly opposed it. Far was she from foreseeing that a revolution at such a distance could excite one in which a misguided populace would drag her from her palace to a death equally unjust and cruel. She only saw something ungenerous in the method which France adopted, of checking the power of England.

However, as Queen of France, she enjoyed the sight of a whole people rendering homage to the prudence, courage, and good qualities of a young Frenchman; and she shared the enthusiasm inspired by the conduct and military success of the Marquis de La Fayette. The Queen granted him several audiences on his first return from America, and, until the 10th of August, on which day my house was plundered, I preserved some lines from Gaston and Bayard, in which the friends of M. de La Fayette saw the exact outline of his character, written by her own hand:

> … Why talk of youth,
> When all the ripe experience of the old
> Dwells with him? In his schemes profound and cool,
> He acts with wise precaution, and reserves
> For times of action his impetuous fire.
> To guard the camp, to scale the leaguered wall,
> Or dare the hottest of the fight, are toils
> That suit th' impetuous bearing of his youth;
> Yet like the gray-hair'd veteran he can shun
> The field of peril. Still before my eyes
> I place his bright example, for I love
> His lofty courage, and his prudent thought.
> Gifted like him, a warrior has no age.[15]

These lines had been applauded and encored at the French theatre; everybody's head was turned. There was no class of persons that did not heartily approve of the support given openly by the French Government to the cause of American independence. The constitution planned for the new nation was digested at Paris, and while liberty, equality, and the rights of man were commented upon by the Condorcets, Baillys, Mirabeaus, etc., the minister Ségur published the King's edict, which, by repealing that of 1st November 1750, declared all officers not noble by four generations incapable of filling the rank of captain, and denied all military rank to the *roturiers*, excepting sons of the Chevaliers de Saint Louis[16] The injustice and absurdity of this law was no doubt a secondary cause of the Revolution. To understand the despair and rage with which this law inspired the *tiers-état* one should have belonged to that honourable class. The provinces were full of *roturier* families, who for ages had lived as people of property upon their own domains, and paid the taxes. If these persons had several sons, they would place one in the King's service, one in the Church, another in the Order of Malta, as a *chevalier servent d'armes*, and one in the magistracy; while the eldest preserved the paternal manor, and if he were situated in a country celebrated for wine he would, besides selling his own produce, add a kind of commission trade in the wines of the canton. I have seen an individual of this justly respected class, who had been long employed in diplomatic business, and even honoured with the title of minister plenipotentiary, the son-in-law and nephew of colonels and town mayors, and, on his mother's side, nephew of a lieutenant-general with a *cordon rouge*, unable to introduce his sons as *sous-lieutenants* into a regiment of foot.

Another decision of the Court, which could not be announced by an edict, was that all ecclesiastical benefices, from the humblest priory up to the richest abbey, should in future be appanages of the nobility. Being the son of a village surgeon, the Abbé de Vermond, who had great influence in the disposition of benefices, was particularly struck with the justice of this decree.

During the absence of the Abbé in an excursion he made for his health, I prevailed on the Queen to write a postscript to the petition of a curate, one of my friends, who was soliciting a priory near his curacy, with the intention of retiring to it. I obtained it for him. On the Abbé's return he told me very harshly that I should act in a manner quite contrary to the King's wishes if I again obtained such a favour; that the wealth of the Church was for the future to be invariably devoted to the support of the poorer nobility; that it was the interest of the State that it should be so; and a plebeian priest, happy in a good curacy, had only to remain curate.

Can we be astonished at the part shortly afterwards taken by the deputies of the Third Estate, when called to the States-General?

1. The Queen's propitious delivery was celebrated throughout France. The birth of Madame inspired more than one poet. The following madrigal, by Imbert, was much admired:—

> A Dauphin we asked of our Queen;
> A Princess announces him near:
> Since one of the Graces is seen,
> Young Cupid will quickly appear.

> Pour toi, France, un Dauphin doit naître,
> Une Princesse vient pour en être témoin;
> Sitot qu'on voit une Grâce paraître,
> Croyez que l'Amour n'est pas loin.
> —*Note by the Editor.*

2. The acts of benevolence performed by the officers of the city did not prevent them from amusing the people with the usual fêtes. There were illuminations, *feux de joie*, fireworks, fountains of wine, and distributions of bread and sausages. All the theatres of Paris were open *gratis*—which was a new treat to the public. Every theatre was full before noon, and the performance began at two o'clock. The French comedians performed *Zaira*, and the little piece called *Le Florentin*. In spite of all the precautions taken to preserve the King's box for the charcoal vendors, who were accustomed to occupy it on similar occasions, as the *poissardes*, or market-women did that of the Queen, their places were occupied when they arrived. They were informed of this, and thought it very strange. These two chief classes of the lower orders were seen disputing upon etiquette, with almost as much pertinacity as noblemen or sovereign courts. They demanded to know why the boxes appropriated to them by custom

had been suffered to be occupied. It was necessary to call the officer for the week, and the histrionic senate being assembled in consultation, the registers were inspected, and the legitimacy of the claim was acknowledged. An offer was then made to the charcoal vendors to go upon the stage, and they all sat there on the King's side, upon benches prepared for them, The *poissardes* followed, and placed themselves on the opposite side.—*Note by the Editor.*

3. "The Duchesse de Polignac," says Montjoie, in the *Life of Marie Antoinette*, "sank under the fatigues of the life which her devotion to the Queen had imposed upon her, and which was little to her taste: Her health declined alarmingly: the physicians ordered her the Bath waters. As it was the established custom of the Court that the governess of the children of France should never be absent from them, the Duchess tendered her resignation to the Queen, who, having listened to her in silence, her eyes wet with tears, replied: 'You ought not to part from me, nor can you do it; your heart could not suffer it. In the rank I fill it is difficult to meet with a friend; and yet it is so useful—so happy—to confide in an estimable person! You do not judge me as the common herd do—you know that the splendour which surrounds me adds nothing to happiness—you are not ignorant that my soul, full of bitterness and troubles which I must conceal, feel the necessity for a heart that sympathises with them. Ought I not, then, to thank Heaven for having given me a friend like you, faithful, feeling, attached to myself and not to my rank? The benefit is inestimable! in the name of God, do not deprive me of it!'"—*Note by the Editor.*

4. Without desiring to lessen the high estimation in which the character of Maria Theresa may be held, it cannot be denied that certain acts of her policy were censurable. The complaisance or the weakness of the other cabinets of Europe did not excuse her. "A bishop of Saint Brieuc, in a funeral oration upon Maria Theresa," says Chamfort, "got over the partition of Poland very easily: 'France,' said he, 'having taken no notice of the partition in question, I will do as France did, and be silent about it likewise.'"—*Note by the Editor.*

5. The first Dauphin, Louis, born 1781, died 1789.

6. Eldest son of the Comte d'Artois, and till the birth of the Dauphin with near prospects of the succession.

7. M. Merard de Saint Just made a quatrain on the birth of the Dauphin to the following effect:—

> This infant Prince our hopes are centred in,
> Will doubtless make us happy, rich, and free;
> And since with *somebody* he must begin,
> My fervent prayer is—that it may be me!

> Le fils qui vient de naître au roi,
> Fera la bonheur de la France.
> Par quelqu'un il faut qu'il commence,
> S'il voulait commencer par moi.
> —*Note by the Editor*

8. Proofs of nobility, or at least of being noble in the third degree, were required for the office of *maître d'hôtel.*—*Madame Campan.*

9. "The well-known antagonism between Marie Antoinette and Madame de Genlis dated," says Madame Campan, "from the birth of the Dauphin, when the Duchesse de Chartres made the authoress' excuses for not appearing to offer her congratulations; indisposition had prevented her. The Queen replied that the Duchesse de Chartres would have caused an apology to be made in such a case; that the celebrity of Madame de Genlis might have occasioned her absence to be noticed; but that she was not of a rank to send an apology for it. This proceeding on the part of the Princess, influenced by the talents of the governess of her children, proves that at the time she still desired the regard and the friendship of the Queen; and from this moment unfavourable reflections on the habits and inclinations of the sovereign, and sharp criticisms on the works and the conduct of the female author, were continually interchanged between Marie Antoinette and Madame de Genlis."

10. Bachaumont in his Memoirs (tome xii, p. 189), which are often satirical and always somewhat questionable, speaks of the singular precautions taken at play at Court. "The bankers at the Queen's table," says he, "in order to prevent the mistakes [I soften the harshness of his expression] which daily happen, have obtained permission from her Majesty that before beginning to play the table shall be bordered by a ribbon entirely round it, and that no other money than that upon the cards beyond the ribbon shall be considered as staked."—*Note by the Editor.*

11. A contemptuous expression, meaning literally "as a scamp" or "rascal".

12. Madame Elizabeth had this house for several years; but the King arranged that she should not sleep there, until she was twenty-five years of age. The Revolution broke out before that time.—*Madame Campan.*

13. The extreme simplicity of the Queen's toilette began to be strongly censured, at first among the courtiers, and afterwards throughout the kingdom; and through one of those inconsistencies more common in France than elsewhere, while the Queen was blamed, she was blindly imitated. There was not a woman but would have the same undress, the same cap, and the same feathers as she had been seen to wear. They crowded to Mademoiselle Bertin, her milliner; there was an absolute revolution in the dress of our ladies, which gave importance to that woman. Long trains, and all those fashions which confer a certain nobility on dress, were discarded; and at last a duchess could not be distinguished from an actress. The men caught the mania; the upper classes had long before given up to their lacqueys feathers, tufts of ribbon, and laced hats. They now got rid of red heels and embroidery; and walked about our streets in plain cloth, short thick shoes, and with knotty cudgels in their hands. Many humiliating scrapes were the consequence of this metamorphosis. Bearing no mark to distinguish them from the common herd, some of the lowest classes got into quarrels with them, in which the nobles had not always the superiority ...

The Queen showed herself as little the slave of ceremony in her choice of amusements; theatrical performances took place in her apartments; she condescended to take characters not always of the most dignified description; she also played in comic operas. This sort of amusement was, like her plainness in dress, both blamed and imitated: all classes of society imbibed a taste for theatrical representations; there was not a man of rank, a financier, nor even a citizen in easy circumstances who would be without his theatre. Formerly a private gentleman would have been disgraced if suspected of metamorphosing himself into an actor, even in a private house. The Queen having by her example put an end to this prejudice, the head of the magistracy, unmindful of the dignity of his place, performed the lowest comic parts. The Queen got through the characters she assumed indifferently enough; she could hardly be ignorant of this, as her performances evidently excited little pleasure. Indeed, one day while she was thus exhibiting, somebody ventured to say, by no means inaudibly, "Well, this is royally ill played!" The lesson was thrown away upon her, for never did she sacrifice to the opinion of another that which she thought permissible. When she was told that her extreme plainness in dress, the nature of her amusements, and her dislike to that splendour which ought always to attend a queen, had an appearance of levity, which was misinterpreted by a portion of the public, she replied with Madame de Maintenon: "I am upon the stage, and of course I shall be either hissed or applauded." Louis XIV had a similar taste; he danced upon the stage; but he had shown by brilliant actions that he knew how to enforce respect; and besides, he unhesitatingly gave up the amusement from the moment he heard those beautiful lines in which Racine pointed out how very unworthy of him such pastimes were.—*History of Marie Antoinette*, by Montjoie.

14. These performances, in which Marie Antoinette delighted in taking a part, have been repeatedly censured. Montjoie reproaches the Queen almost with severity, and makes observations which appear not to be quite correct. "Formerly," says he, "any private gentleman would have been disgraced upon its being known that he had turned actor, even in a family party." We will not decide whether it would have been more disgraceful in a private gentleman to act in a play, or, for instance, like the Comte de Grammont, to back with a detachment of cavalry a game of piquet, in which art had corrected fortune; but we will observe that in 1701 J.B. Rousseau's *Ceinture Magique* was played by the Princes of the blood before the Duchess of Burgundy.—*Memoirs of Voltaire*, Amsterdam, 1785. Voltaire gives still more minute particulars of these performances, in which private gentlemen would no doubt have consented to figure. "There was," says he (tome xxi, p. 157), "a small theatre erected in the apartments of Madame de Maintenon. The Duchesse de Bourgogne, and the Duc d'Orléans, with such persons of the Court as were most conspicuous for talent, performed there. The famous actor Baron instructed them and played with them. The majority of Duché's tragedies were composed for this theatre." We shall add but one word to these positive facts, which is, that the young and amiable Marie Antoinette might well see nothing wrong in an amusement tolerated by Madame de Maintenon in the austere, hypocritical, and bigoted Court of the latter years of Louis XIV—*Note by the Editor.*

15. During the American war a general officer in the service of the United States advanced with a score of men under the English batteries to reconnoitre their position. His *aide-de-camp*, struck by a ball, fell at his side. The officers and orderly dragoons fled precipitately. The general, though under the fire of the cannon, approached the wounded man to see whether any help could be afforded him. Finding the wound had been mortal, he slowly rejoined the group which had got out of the reach of the cannon. This instance of courage and humanity took place at the battle of Monmouth. General Clinton, who commanded the English troops, knew that the Marquis de La Fayette generally rode a white horse; it was upon a white horse that the general officer who retired so slowly was mounted; Clinton desired the gunners not to fire. This noble forbearance probably saved M. de La Fayette's life, for he it was. At that time he was but twenty-two years of age.—*Historical Anecdotes of the Reign of Louis XVI.*

16. "M. de Ségur," says Chamfort, "having published an ordinance which prohibited the admission of any other than gentlemen into the artillery corps, and, on the other hand, none but well-educated persons being proper for admission, a curious scene took place: the Abbé Bossat, examiner of the pupils, gave certificates only to plebeians, while Cherin gave them only to gentlemen. Out of 100 pupils, there were not above four or five who were qualified in both respects."

X

Visit of the Grand Duke of Russia and his Duchess to France—
Entertainment and supper at Trianon—Cardinal de Rohan—Cold
reception given to Comte d'Haga (Gustavus III, King of Sweden)—Peace
with England—The English flock into France —Conduct to be observed
at Court—Mission of the Chevalier de Bressac to the Queen—Court of
Naples—Queen Caroline—The Minister Acton—Debates between the
Courts of Naples and Madrid—Insolent reply of the Spanish Ambassador
to Queen Caroline—Interference of France—MM. de Ségur and de
Castries appointed ministers through the Queen's influence—Treachery of
M. de Maurepas towards M. Necker—Appointment of M. de
Calonne—Observations of Marie Antoinette

About the close of the last century several of the Northern sovereigns took a fancy for travelling. Christian III, King of Denmark, visited the Court of France in 1763, during the reign of Louis XV. We have seen the King of Sweden and Joseph II at Versailles. The Grand Duke of Russia (afterwards Paul I), son of Catherine II, and the Princess of Wirtemberg, his wife, likewise resolved to visit France. They travelled under the titles of the Comte and Comtesse du Nord. They were presented on the 10th of May 1782. The Queen received them with grace and dignity. On the day of their arrival at Versailles they dined in private with the King and Queen.

The plain unassuming appearance of Paul I pleased Louis XVI. He spoke to him with more confidence and cheerfulness than he had done to Joseph II. The Comtesse du Nord was not at first so successful with the Queen. This lady was of a fine height, very fat for her age, with all the German stiffness, well informed, and perhaps displaying her acquirements with rather too much confidence. When the Comte and Comtesse du Nord were presented the Queen was exceedingly nervous. She withdrew into her closet before she went into the room where she was to dine with the illustrious travellers, and asked for a glass of water, confessing "she had just experienced how much more difficult it was to play the part of a Queen in the presence of other sovereigns, or of Princes born to become so, than before courtiers". She soon recovered from her confusion, and reappeared with ease and confidence. The dinner was tolerably cheerful, and the conversation very animated.

Brilliant entertainments were given at Court in honour of the King of Sweden and the Comte du Nord. They were received in private by the King and Queen, but they were treated with much more ceremony than the Emperor, and their Majesties always appeared to me to be very cautious before these personages. However, the King one day asked the Russian Grand Duke if it were true that he could not rely on the fidelity of any one of those who accompanied him. The Prince answered him without hesitation, and before a considerable number of persons, that he should be very sorry to have with him even a poodle that was much attached to him, because his mother would take care to have it thrown into the Seine, with a stone round its neck, before he should leave Paris. This reply, which I myself heard, horrified me, whether it depicted the disposition of Catherine, or only expressed the Prince's prejudice against her.

The Queen gave the Grand Duke a supper at Trianon, and had the gardens illuminated as they had been for the Emperor. The Cardinal de Rohan very indiscreetly ventured to introduce himself there without the Queen's knowledge. Having been treated with the utmost coolness ever since his return from Vienna, he had not dared to ask her himself for permission to see the illumination; but he persuaded the porter of Trianon to admit him as soon as the Queen should have set off for Versailles, and his Eminence engaged to remain in the porter's lodge until all the carriages should have left the Château. He did not keep his word, and while the porter was busy in the discharge of his duty, the Cardinal, who wore his red stockings and had merely thrown on a greatcoat, went down into the garden, and, with an air of mystery, drew up in two different places to see the royal family and suite pass by.

Her Majesty was highly offended at this piece of boldness, and next day ordered the porter to be discharged. There was a general feeling of disgust at the Cardinal's conduct, and of commiseration towards the porter for the loss of his place. Affected at the misfortune of the father of a family, I obtained his forgiveness; and since that time I have often regretted the feeling which induced me to interfere. The notoriety of the discharge of the porter of Trianon, and the odium that circumstance would have fixed upon the Cardinal, would have made the Queen's dislike to him still more publicly known; and would probably have prevented the scandalous and notorious intrigue of the necklace.

The Queen, who was much prejudiced against the King of Sweden, received him very coldly.[1] All that was said of the private character of that sovereign, his connection with the Comte de Vergennes, from the time of the Revolution of Sweden, in 1772, the character of his favourite Armsfeld, and the prejudices of the monarch himself against the Swedes who were well received at the Court of Versailles, formed the grounds of this dislike. He came one day uninvited and unexpected, and requested to dine with the Queen. The Queen received him in the little closet, and desired me to send for her clerk of the kitchen, that she might be informed whether there was a proper dinner to set before Comte d'Haga, and add to it if necessary. The King of Sweden assured her that there would be enough for him; and I could not help smiling when I thought of the length of the menu of the dinner of the King and Queen, not half of which would have made its appearance had they dined in private. The Queen looked significantly at me, and I withdrew. In the evening she asked me why I had seemed so astonished when she ordered me to add to her dinner; saying that I ought instantly to have seen that she was giving the King of Sweden a lesson for his presumption. I owned to her that the scene had appeared to me so much in the bourgeois style, that I involuntarily thought of the cutlets on the gridiron, and the omelette, which in families in humble circumstances serve to piece out short commons. She was highly diverted with my answer, and repeated it to the King, who also laughed heartily at it.

The peace with England satisfied all classes of society interested in the national honour. The departure of the English commissary from Dunkirk, who had been fixed at that place ever since the shameful peace of 1763 as inspector of our navy, occasioned an ecstasy of joy. The Government communicated to the Englishman the order for his departure before the treaty was made public. But for that precaution the populace would have probably committed some excess or other, in order to make the agent of English power feel the effects of the resentment which had constantly increased during his stay at that port. Those engaged in trade were the only persons dissatisfied with the treaty of 1783. That article which provided for the free admission of English goods, annihilated at one blow the trade of Rouen, and the other manufacturing towns throughout the kingdom. The English swarmed into Paris. A considerable number of them were presented at Court. The Queen paid them marked attention; doubtless she wished them to distinguish between the esteem she felt for their noble nation and the political views of the Government in the support it had afforded to the Americans. Discontent was, however, manifested at Court in consequence of the favour bestowed by the Queen on the English noblemen; these attentions were called infatuations. This was illiberal; and the Queen justly complained of such absurd jealousy.

The journey to Fontainebleau and the winter at Paris and at Court were extremely brilliant. The spring brought back those amusements which the Queen began to prefer to the splendour of fêtes. The most perfect harmony subsisted between the King and Queen; I never saw but one cloud between them. It was soon dispelled, and the cause of it is perfectly unknown to me.

My father-in-law, whose penetration and experience I respected greatly, recommended me, when he saw me placed in the service of a young Queen, to shun all kinds of confidence. "It procures," said he, "but a very fleeting, and at the same time, dangerous sort of favour; serve with zeal to the best of your judgment, but never do more than obey. Instead of setting your wits to work to discover why an order or a commission which may appear of consequence are given to you, use them to prevent the possibility of your knowing anything of the matter." I had occasion to act on this wise advice. One morning at Trianon I went into the Queen's chamber; there were letters lying upon the bed, and she was weeping bitterly. Her tears and sobs were occasionally interrupted by exlamations of "*Ah! that I were dead!—wretches! Monsters! What have I done to them?*" I offered her orange-flower water and ether. "*Leave me,*" said she, "*if you love me: it would be better to kill me at once.*" At this moment she threw her arm over my shoulder and began weeping afresh. I saw that some weighty trouble oppressed her heart, and that she wanted a confidante. I suggested sending for Duchesse de Polignac; this she strongly opposed. I renewed my arguments, and her opposition grew weaker. I disengaged myself from her arms, and ran to the antechamber, where I knew that an outrider always waited, ready to mount and start at a moment's warning for Versailles. I ordered him to go full speed, and tell the Duchesse de Polignac that the Queen was very uneasy, and desired to see her instantly. The Duchess always had a carriage ready.

In less than ten minutes she was at the Queen's door. I was the only person there, having been forbidden to send for the other women. Madame de Polignac came in; the Queen held out her arms to her, the Duchess rushed towards her. I heard her sobs renewed and withdrew.

A quarter of an hour afterwards the Queen, who had become calmer, rang to be dressed. I sent her woman in; she put on her gown and retired to her boudoir with the Duchess. Very soon afterwards the Comte d'Artois arrived from Compiègne, where he had been with the King. He eagerly inquired where the Queen was; remained half an hour with her and the Duchess; and on coming out told me the Queen asked for me. I found her seated on the couch by the side of her friend; her features had resumed their usual cheerful and gracious appearance. She held out her hand to me, and said to the Duchess, "I know I have made her so uncomfortable this morning that I must set her poor heart at ease." She then added, "You must have seen, on some fine summer's day, a black cloud suddenly appear and threaten to pour down upon the country and lay it waste. The lightest wind drives it away, and the blue sky and serene weather are restored. This is just the image of what has happened to me this morning." She afterwards told me that the King would return from Compiègne after hunting there, and sup with her; that I must send for her purveyor, to select with him from his bills of fare all such dishes as the King liked best; that she would have no others served up in the evening at her table; and that this was a mark of attention that she wished the King to notice. The Duchesse de Polignac also took me by the hand, and told me how happy she was that she had been with the Queen at a moment when she stood in need of a friend. I never knew what could have created in the Queen so lively and so transient an alarm; but I guessed from the particular care she took respecting the King that attempts had been made to irritate him against her; that the malice of her enemies had been promptly discovered and counteracted by the King's penetration and attachment; and that the Comte d'Artois had hastened to bring her intelligence of it.

It was, I think, in the summer of 1787, during one of the Trianon excursions, that the Queen of Naples[2] sent the Chevalier de Bressac to her Majesty on a secret mission relative to a projected marriage between the Hereditary Prince, her son, and Madame, the King's daughter; in the absence of the lady of honour he addressed himself to me. Although he said a great deal to me about the close confidence with which the Queen of Naples honoured him, and about his letters of credit, I thought he had the air of an adventurer.[3] He had, indeed, private letters for the Queen, and his mission was not feigned; he talked to me very rashly even before his admission, and entreated me to do all that lay in my power to dispose the Queen's mind in favour of his sovereign's wishes; I declined, assuring him that it did not become me to meddle with State affairs. He endeavoured, but in vain, to prove to me that the union contemplated by the Queen of Naples ought not to be looked upon in that light.

I procured M. de Bressac the audience he desired, but without suffering myself even to seem acquainted with the object of his mission. The Queen told me what it was; she thought him a person ill chosen for the occasion; and yet she thought that the Queen, her sister, had done wisely in not sending a man worthy to be avowed; it being impossible that what she solicited should take place. I had an opportunity on this occasion, as indeed on many others, of judging to what extent the Queen valued and loved France and the dignity of our Court. She then told me that Madame,[4] in marrying her cousin, the Duc d'Angoulême, would not lose her rank as daughter of the Queen; and that her situation would be far preferable to that of Queen of any other country; that there was nothing in Europe to be compared to the Court of France; and that it would be necessary, in order to avoid exposing a French Princess to feelings of deep regret, in case she should be married to a foreign Prince, to take her from the Palace of Versailles at seven years of age, and send her immediately to the Court in which she was to dwell; and that at twelve would be too late; for recollections and comparisons would ruin the happiness of all the rest of her life. The Queen looked upon the destiny of her sisters as far beneath her own; and frequently mentioned the mortifications inflicted by the Court of Spain upon her sister, the Queen of Naples; and the necessity she was under of imploring the mediation of the King of France.

She showed me several letters that she had received from the Queen of Naples relative to her differences with the Court of Madrid respecting the Minister Acton. She thought him useful to her people, inasmuch as he was a man of considerable information and great activity. In these letters she minutely acquainted her Majesty with the nature of the affronts she had received, and represented Mr Acton to her as a man whom malevolence itself could not suppose capable of interesting her otherwise than by his services. She had had to suffer the impertinences of a Spaniard named Las Casas, who had been sent to her by the King, her father-in-law, to persuade her to dismiss Mr Acton from the business of the State, and from her intimacy. She complained bitterly to the Queen, her sister, of the insulting proceedings of this *chargé d'affaires*, whom she told, in order to convince him of the nature of the feelings which attached her to Mr Acton, that she would have portraits and busts of him executed by the most eminent artists of Italy, and that she would then send them to the King of Spain, to prove that nothing but the desire to retain a man of superior capacity had induced her to bestow on him the favour he enjoyed. This Las Casas dared to answer her, that it would be useless trouble; that the ugliness of a man did not always render him displeasing; and that the King of Spain had too much experience not to know that there was no accounting for the caprices of a woman.

This audacious reply filled the Queen of Naples with indignation, and her emotion caused her to miscarry on the same day. In consequence of the mediation of Louis XVI the Queen of Naples obtained complete satisfaction, and Mr Acton continued Prime Minister.

Among the characteristics which denoted the goodness of the Queen, her respect for personal liberty should have a place. I have seen her put up with the most troublesome importunities from people whose minds were deranged rather than have them arrested. Her patient kindness was put to a very disagreeable trial by an ex-councillor of the Bordeaux Parliament, named Castelnaux; this man declared himself the lover of the Queen, and was generally known by that appellation. For ten successive years did he follow the Court in all its excursions. Pale and wan, as people who are out of their senses usually are, his sinister appearance occasioned the most uncomfortable sensations. During the two hours that the Queen's public card-parties lasted, he would remain opposite her Majesty. He placed himself in the same manner before her at chapel, and never failed to be at the King's dinner or the dinner in public. At the theatre he invariably seated himself as near the Queen's box as possible. He always set off for Fontainebleau or Saint Cloud the day before the Court, and when her Majesty arrived at her various residences, the first person she met on getting out of her carriage was this melancholy madman, who never spoke to any one. When the Queen stayed at Petit Trianon the passion of this unhappy man became still more annoying. He would hastily swallow a morsel at some eating-house, and spend all the rest of the day, even when it rained, in going round and round the garden, always walking at the edge of the moat. The Queen frequently met him when she was either alone or with her children; and yet she would not suffer any violence to be used to relieve her from this intolerable annoyance. Having one day given M. de Sèze permission to enter Trianon, she sent to desire he would come to me, and directed me to inform that celebrated advocate of M. de Castelnaux's derangement, and then to send for him that M. de Sèze might have some conversation with him. He talked to him nearly an hour, and made considerable impression upon his mind; and at last M. de Castelnaux requested me to inform the Queen positively that, since his presence was disagreeable to her, he would retire to his province. The Queen was very much rejoiced, and desired me to express her full satisfaction to M. de Sèze. Half an hour after M. de Sèze was gone the unhappy madman was announced. He came to tell me that he withdrew his promise, that he had not sufficient command of himself to give up seeing the Queen as often as possible. This new determination was a disagreeable message to take to her Majesty; but how was I affected at hearing her say, "Well, let him annoy me! but let him not be deprived of the blessing of freedom."[5]

The direct influence of the Queen on affairs during the earlier years of the reign was only shown in her exertions to obtain from the King a revision of the decrees in two celebrated causes. It was contrary to her principles to interfere in matters of justice, and never did she avail herself of her influence to bias the tribunals. The Duchesse de Praslin, through a criminal caprice, carried her enmity to her husband so far as to disinherit her children in favour of the family of M. de Guéménée. The Duchesse de Choiseul, who was warmly interested in this affair, one day entreated the Queen, in my presence, at least to condescend to ask the first President when the cause would be called on; the Queen replied that she could not even do that, for it would manifest an interest which it was her duty not to show.

If the King had not inspired the Queen with a lively feeling of love, it is quite certain that she yielded him respect and affection for the goodness of his disposition and the equity of which he gave so many proofs throughout his reign. One evening she returned very late; she came out of the King's closet, and said to M. de Misery and myself, drying her eyes, which were filled with tears, "You see me weeping, but do not be uneasy at it: these are the sweetest tears that a wife can shed; they are caused by the impression which the justice and goodness of the King have made upon me; he has just complied with my request for a revision of the proceedings against Messieurs de Bellegarde and de Monthieu, victims of the Duc d'Aiguillon's hatred to the Duc de Choiseul. He has been equally just to the Duc de Guines in his affair with Tort. It is a happy thing for a

Queen to be able to admire and esteem him who has admitted her to a participation of his throne; and as to you, I congratulate you upon your having to live under the sceptre of so virtuous a sovereign."

The Queen laid before the King all the memorials of the Duc de Guines, who, during his embassy to England, was involved in difficulties by a secretary, who speculated in the public funds in London on his own account, but in such a manner as to throw a suspicion of it on the ambassador. Messieurs de Vergennes and Turgot, bearing but little goodwill to the Duc de Guines, who was the friend of the Duc de Choiseul, were not disposed to render the ambassador any service. The Queen succeeded in fixing the King's particular attention on this affair, and the innocence of the Duc de Guines triumphed through the equity of Louis XVI.

An incessant underhand war was carried on between the friends and partisans of M. de Choiseul, who were called the Austrians, and those who sided with Messieurs d'Aiguillon, de Maurepas, and de Vergennes, who, for the same reason, kept up the intrigues carried on at Court and in Paris against the Queen. Marie Antoinette, on her part, supported those who had suffered in this political quarrel, and it was this feeling which led her to ask for a revision of the proceedings against Messieurs de Bellegarde and de Monthieu. The first, a colonel and inspector of artillery, and the second, proprietor of a foundry at Saint Étienne, were, under the ministry of the Duc d'Aiguillon, condemned to imprisonment for twenty years and a day for having withdrawn from the arsenals of France, by order of the Duc de Choiseul, a vast number of muskets, as being of no value except as old iron, while in point of fact the greater part of those muskets were immediately embarked and sold to the Americans. It appears that the Duc de Choiseul imparted to the Queen, as grounds of defence for the accused, the political views which led him to authorise that reduction and sale in the manner in which it had been executed. It rendered the case of Messieurs de Bellegarde and de Monthieu more unfavourable that the artillery officer who made the reduction in the capacity of inspector was, through a clandestine marriage, brother-in-law of the owner of the foundry, the purchaser of the rejected arms. The innocence of the two prisoners was nevertheless made apparent; and they came to Versailles with their wives and children to throw themselves at the feet of their benefactress. This affecting scene took place in the grand gallery, at the entrance to the Queen's apartment. She wished to restrain the women from kneeling, saying that they had only had justice done them; and that she ought to be congratulated upon the most substantial happiness attendant upon her station, that of laying just appeals before the King.[6]

On every occasion, when the Queen had to speak in public, she used the most appropriate and elegant language, notwithstanding the difficulty a foreigner might be expected to experience. She answered all addresses herself, a custom which she learned at the Court of Maria Theresa. The Princesses of the House of Bourbon had long ceased to take the trouble of speaking in such cases. Madame Adelaide blamed the Queen for not doing as they did, assuring her that it was quite sufficient to mutter a few words that might sound like an answer, while the addressers, occupied with what they had themselves been saying, would always take it for granted that a proper answer had been returned. The Queen saw that idleness alone dictated such a proceeding, and that as the practice even of muttering a few words showed the necessity of answering in some way, it must be more proper to reply simply but clearly, and in the best style possible. Sometimes indeed, when apprised of the subject of the address, she would write down her answer in the morning, not to learn it by heart, but in order to settle the ideas or sentiments she wished to introduce.

The influence of the Comtesse de Polignac increased daily; and her friends availed themselves of it to effect changes in the ministry. The dismissal of M. de Montbarrey, a man without talents or character, was generally approved of. It was rightly attributed to the Queen. He had been placed in administration by M. de Maurepas, and maintained by his aged wife; both, of course, became more inveterate than ever against the Queen and the Polignac circle.

The appointment of M. de Ségur to the place of Minister of War, and of M. de Castries to that of Minister of Marine, were wholly the work of that circle. The Queen dreaded making ministers; her favourite often wept when the men of her circle compelled her to interfere. Men blame women for meddling in business, and yet in courts it is continually the men themselves who make use of the influence of the women in matters with which the latter ought to have nothing to do.

When M. de Ségur was presented to the Queen on his new appointment, she said to me, "You have just seen a minister of my making. I am very glad, so far as regards the King's service, that he is appointed, for I think the selection a very good one; but I almost regret the part I have taken in it. I take a responsibility upon myself. I was fortunate in being free from any; and in order to relieve myself from this as much as possible I have just promised M. de Ségur, and that upon my word of honour, not to back any petition, nor to hinder any of his operations by solicitations on behalf of my protégés."

During the first administration of M. Necker, whose ambition had not then drawn him into schemes repugnant to his better judgment, and whose views appeared to the Queen to be very judicious, she indulged in hopes of the restoration of the finances. Knowing that M. de Maurepas wished to drive M. Necker to resign, she urged him to have patience until the death of an old man whom the King kept about him from a fondness for his first choice, and out of respect for his advanced age. She even went so far as to tell him that M. de Maurepas was always ill, and that his end could not be very distant. M. Necker would not wait for that event. The Queen's prediction was fulfilled. M. de Maurepas ended his days immediately after a journey to Fontainebleau in 1781.[7]

M. Necker had retired. He had been exasperated by a piece of treachery in the old minister, for which he could not forgive him. I knew something of this intrigue at the time; it has since been fully explained to me by Madame la Maréchale de Beauvau. M. Necker saw that his credit at Court was declining, and fearing lest that circumstance should injure his financial operations, he requested the King to grant him some favour which might show the public that he had not lost the confidence of his sovereign. He concluded his letter by pointing out five requests—such an office, or such a mark of distinction, or such a badge of honour, and so on, and handed it to M. de Maurepas. The *ors* were changed into *ands*; and the King was displeased at M. Necker's ambition, and the assurance with which he displayed it.

Madame la Maréchale de Beauvau assured me that the Maréchal de Castries saw the minute of M. Necker's letter, and that he likewise saw the altered copy.

The interest which the Queen took in M. Necker died away during his retirement, and at last changed into strong prejudice against him. He wrote too much about the measures he would have pursued, and the benefits that would have resulted to the State from them. The ministers who succeeded him thought their operations embarrassed by the care that M. Necker and his partisans incessantly took to occupy the public with his plans; his friends were too ardent. The Queen discerned a party spirit in these combinations, and sided wholly with his enemies.

After those inefficient comptrollers-general, Messieurs Joly de Fleury and d'Ormesson, it became necessary to resort to a man of more acknowledged talent, and the Queen's friends, at that time combining with the Comte d'Artois and with M. de Vergennes, got M. de Calonne appointed. The Queen was highly displeased, and her close intimacy with the Duchesse de Polignac began to suffer for this. It was at this period she said that when sovereigns chose favourites they raised powers about them which, being flattered at first for their masters' sake, were afterwards flattered for their own; formed a party in the State, acted alone, and caused the odium of their actions to fall upon the sovereigns to whom they owed their influence.

The inconveniences attendant on the private life of a sovereign then struck the Queen in all their bearings. She talked to me about them in confidence, and often told me that I was the only person aware of the vexations that her social habits brought upon her; but that she must bear the anxieties of which she herself was the sole author: that the appearance of fickleness in a friendship such as that which she had contracted with the Duchess, or a total rupture, could only produce fresh calamities. It was not that she had to reproach Madame de Polignac with a single fault which could make her regret the choice she had made of her for a friend, but she had not foreseen the inconvenience of having to support the friends of our friends, which society obliges one to do.

Her Majesty, continuing to converse with me upon the difficulties she had met with in private life, told me that ambitious men without merit sometimes found means to gain their ends by dint of importunity, and that she had to blame herself for having procured M. d'Adhémar's appointment to the London Embassy, merely because he teased her into it at the Duchess' house. She added, however, that it was at a time of perfect peace with the English; that the minister knew the inefficiency of M. d'Adhémar as well as she did, and that he could do neither harm nor good.

Often in conversations of unreserved frankness the Queen owned that she had purchased rather dearly a piece of experience which would make her carefully watch over the conduct of her daughters-in-law; and that she would be particularly scrupulous about the qualifications of the ladies who might attend them; that no consideration of rank or favour should bias her in so important a choice. She attributed several of her youthful mistakes to a lady of great levity, whom she found in her palace on her arrival in France. She also determined to forbid the Princesses coming under her control the practice of singing with professors, and said candidly, and with as much severity as her slanderers could have done, "I ought to have heard Garat sing, and never to have sung duets with him."

The indiscreet zeal of Monsieur Augéard contributed to the public belief that the Queen disposed of all the offices of finance. He had, without any authority for doing so, required the committee of *fermiers-général* to inform him of all vacancies, assuring them that they would be meeting the wishes of the Queen. The members complied, but not without murmuring. When the Queen became aware of what her secretary had done, she highly disapproved of it, caused her resentment to be made known to the *fermiers-général*, and abstained from asking for appointments; only making one request of the kind as a marriage portion for one of her attendants, a young woman of good family.

1. Gustavus III, King of Sweden, travelled in France under the title of Comte d'Haga. Upon his accession to the throne, he managed the Revolution which prostrated the authority of the senate with equal skill, coolness, and courage. He was assassinated in 1792 at a masked ball by Ankarstroem.—*Note by the Editor.*

2. Caroline, sister of Marie Antoinette.

3. He afterwards spent several years shut up in the Château de l'Œuf.—*Madame Campan.*

4. The Princess Marie Thérèse Charlotte, daughter of Louis XVI, who married her cousin, the Duc d'Angoulême, son of the Comte d'Artois, in 1799.

5. On the arrest of the King and Queen at Varennes, this unfortunate Castelnaux attempted to starve himself to death. The people in whose house he lived, becoming uneasy at his absence, had the door of his room forced open, when he was found stretched senseless on the floor. I do not know what became of him after the 10th of August.—*Madame Campan.*

6. There is a contemporary engraving which represents this scene of gratitude and kindness tolerably well, reproducing accurately places, costumes, and the likenesses of the principal personages. Among the latter we recognise M. the Comte de Provence (his Majesty Louis XVIII), Madame the Comtesse de Provence, M. the Comte and Madame the Comtesse d'Artois, and the Emperor Joseph II.—*Note by the Editor.*

7. Louis XVI deeply regretted Maurepas. During his last illness he went himself to inform him of the birth of the Dauphin, *to announce it to his friend and rejoice with him*; these were his very expressions. The day after his funeral he said, with an air of great affliction, "Ah! I shall no longer hear my friend overhead every morning."—*Biographie Universelle.*

XI

The Queen is dissatisfied with the appointment of M. de Calonne—Acts of benevolence—Purchase of Saint Cloud—Regulations of internal police—State of France—Beaumarchais—Marriage of Figaro—Character of M. de Vaudreuil

The Queen did not sufficiently conceal the dissatisfaction she felt at having been unable to prevent the appointment of M. de Calonne; she even one day went so far as to say at the Duchess', in the midst of the partisans and protectors of that minister, that the finances of France passed alternately from the hands of an honest man without talent into those of a skilful knave. M. de Calonne was thus far from acting in concert with the Queen all the time that he continued in office; and, while dull verses were circulated about Paris describing the Queen and her favourite dipping at pleasure into the coffers of the comptroller-general, the Queen was avoiding all communication with him.

During the long and severe winter of 1783–4 the King gave 3 millions of livres for the relief of the indigent. M. de Calonne, who felt the necessity of making advances to the Queen, caught at this opportunity of showing her respect and devotion. He offered to place in her hands one million of the three, to be distributed in her name and under her direction. His proposal was rejected: the Queen answered that the charity ought to be wholly distributed in the King's name, and that she would this year debar herself of even the slightest enjoyments, in order to contribute all her savings to the relief of the unfortunate.

The moment M. de Calonne left the closet the Queen sent for me: "Congratulate me, my dear," said she; "I have just escaped a snare, or at least a matter which eventually might have caused me much regret." She related the conversation which had taken place word for word to me, adding, "That man will complete the ruin of the national finances. It is said that I placed him in his situation. The people are made to believe that I am extravagant; yet I have refused to suffer a sum of money from the royal treasury, although destined for the most laudable purpose, even to pass through my hands."

The Queen making monthly retrenchments from the expenditure of her privy purse, and not having spent the gifts customary at the period of her confinement, was in possession of from 5–600,000 francs, her own savings. She made use of from 2–300,000 francs of this, which her first women sent to M. Lenoir, to the curés of Paris and Versailles, and to the *Soeurs Hospitalières*, and so distributed them among families in need.

Desirous to implant in the breast of her daughter not only a desire to succour the unfortunate but those qualities necessary for the due discharge of that duty, the Queen incessantly talked to her, though she was yet very young, about the sufferings of the poor during a season so inclement. The Princess already had a sum of from 8–10,000 francs for charitable purposes, and the Queen made her distribute part of it herself.

Wishing to give her children yet another lesson of beneficence, she desired me on New Year's Eve to get from Paris, as in other years, all the fashionable playthings, and have them spread out in her closet. Then taking her children by the hand she showed them all the dolls and mechanical toys which were ranged there, and told them that she had intended to give them some handsome New Year's gifts, but that the cold made the poor so wretched that all her money was spent in blankets and clothes to protect them from the rigour of the season, and in supplying them with bread; so that this year they would only have the pleasure of looking at the new playthings. When she returned with her children into her sitting-room, she said there was still an unavoidable expense to be incurred; that assuredly many mothers would at that season think as she did; that the toy man must lose by it; and therefore she gave him fifty *louis* to repay him for the cost of his journey, and console him for having sold nothing.

The purchase of Saint Cloud, a matter very simple in itself, had, on account of the prevailing spirit, unfavourable consequences to the Queen.

The Palace of Versailles, pulled to pieces in the interior by a variety of new arrangements, and mutilated in point of uniformity by the removal of the ambassadors' staircase, and of the peristyle of columns placed at the end of the marble court, was equally in want of substantial and ornamental repair. The King therefore desired M. Micque to lay before him several plans for the repairs of the palace. He consulted me on certain arrangements analogous to some of those adopted in the Queen's establishment, and in my presence asked M. Micque how much money would be wanted for the execution of the whole work, and how many years he would be in completing it. I forget how many millions were mentioned: M. Micque replied that six years would be sufficient time if the Treasury made the necessary periodical advances without any delay, "And how many years shall you require," said the King, "if the advances are not punctually made?"—"Ten, Sire," replied the architect. "We must then reckon upon ten years," said his Majesty, "and put off this great undertaking until the year 1790; *it will occupy the rest of the century*." The King afterwards talked of the depreciation of property which took place at Versailles, whilst the Regent removed the Court of Louis XV to the Tuileries, and said that he must consider how to prevent that inconvenience: it was the desire to do this that promoted the purchase of Saint Cloud. The Queen first thought of it one day when she was riding out with the Duchesse de Polignac and the Comtesse Diana; she mentioned it to the King, who was much pleased with the thought; the purchase confirming him in the intention, which he had entertained for ten years, of quitting Versailles.

The King determined that the ministers, public officers, pages, and a considerable part of his stabling should remain at Versailles. Messieurs de Breteuil and de Calonne were instructed to treat with the Duc d'Orléans for the purchase of Saint Cloud; at first they hoped to be able to conclude the business by a mere exchange. The value of the Château de Choisy, La Muette, and a forest, was equivalent to the sum demanded by the House of Orléans; and in the exchange which the Queen expected she only saw a saving to be made instead of an increase of expense. By this arrangement the government of Choisy, in the hands of the Duc de Coigny, and that of La Muette, in the hands of the Maréchal de Soubise, would be suppressed. At the same time the two concierges, and all the servants employed in these two royal houses, would be reduced; but while the treaty was going forward Messieurs de Breteuil and de Calonne gave up the point of exchange, and some millions in cash were substituted for Choisy, and La Muette.

The Queen advised the King to give her Saint Cloud, as a means of avoiding the establishment of a governor; her plan being to have merely a concierge there, by which means the governor's expenses would be saved. The King agreed, and Saint Cloud was purchased for the Queen. She provided the same liveries for the porters at the gates and servants at the Château as for those at Trianon. The concierge at the latter place had put up some regulations for the household, headed: "*By order of the Queen.*" The same thing was done at Saint Cloud. The Queen's livery at the door of a palace where it was expected none but that of the King would be seen, and the words, "By order of the Queen," at the head of the printed papers pasted near the iron gates, caused a great sensation, and produced a very unfortunate effect, not only among the common people but also among persons of a superior class. They saw in it an attack upon the customs of monarchy, and customs are nearly equal to laws. The Queen heard of this, but she thought that her dignity would be compromised if she made any change in the form of these regulations, though they might have been altogether superseded without inconvenience. "My name is not out of place," said she, "in gardens belonging to myself; I may give orders there without infringing on the rights of the State." This was her only answer to the representations which a few faithful servants ventured to make on the subject. The discontent of the Parisians on this occasion probably induced M. d'Esprémenil, upon the first troubles about the Parliament, to say that it was *impolitic* and *immoral* to see palaces belonging to a Queen of France.[1]

The Queen was very much dissatisfied with the manner in which M. de Calonne had managed this matter. The Abbé de Vermond, the most active and persevering of that minister's enemies, saw with delight that the expedients of those from whom alone new resources might be expected were gradually becoming exhausted, because the period when the Archbishop of Toulouse would be placed over the finances was thereby hastened.

The royal navy had resumed an imposing attitude during the war for the independence of America; a glorious peace with England had compensated for the former attacks of our enemies upon the fame of France; and the throne was surrounded by numerous heirs. The sole ground of uneasiness was in the finances, but that uneasiness related only to the manner in which they were administered. In a word, France felt confident in its own strength and resources, when two events, which seem scarcely worthy of a place in history, but which have nevertheless an important one in that of the French Revolution, introduced a spirit of ridicule and contempt, not only against the highest ranks, but even against the most august personages. I allude to a comedy and a great swindling transaction.

Portrait of Beaumarchais

Beaumarchais had long possessed a reputation in certain circles in Paris for his wit
and musical talents, and at the theatres for dramas more or less indifferent, when his
Barber of Seville procured him a higher position among dramatic writers. His memoirs
against M. Goësman had amused Paris by the ridicule they threw upon a parliament
which was disliked; and his admission to an intimacy with M. de Maurepas procured
him a degree of influence over important affairs. He then became ambitious of influencing public opinion by a kind of drama, in which established manners and customs
should be held up to popular derision and the ridicule of the new philosophers. After
several years of prosperity the minds of the French had become more generally critical;
and when Beaumarchais had finished his monstrous but diverting *Marriage of Figaro*

all people of any consequence were eager for the gratification of hearing it read, the censors having decided that it should not be performed. These readings of *Figaro* grew so numerous that people were daily heard to say, "I have been (or I am going to be) at the reading of Beaumarchais' play." The desire to see it performed became universal: an expression that he had the art to use compelled, as it were, the approbation of the nobility, or of persons in power, who aimed at ranking among the magnanimous; he made his *Figaro* say that "*none but little minds dreaded little books*". The Baron de Breteuil, and all the men of Madame de Polignac's circle, entered the lists as the warmest protectors of the comedy. Solicitations to the King became so pressing that his Majesty determined to judge for himself of a work which so much engrossed public attention, and desired me to ask M. Le Noir, lieutenant of police, for the manuscript of the *Marriage of Figaro*. One morning I received a note from the Queen ordering me to be with her at three o'clock, and not to come without having dined, for she should detain me some time. When I got to the Queen's inner closet I found her alone with the King; a chair and a small table were ready placed opposite to them, and upon the table lay an enormous manuscript in several books. The King said to me, "There is Beaumarchais' comedy; you must read it to us. You will find several parts troublesome on account of the erasures and references. I have already run it over, but I wish the Queen to be acquainted with the work. You will not mention this reading to any one."

I began. The King frequently interrupted me by praise or censure, which was always just. He frequently exclaimed, "That's in bad taste; this man continually brings the Italian concetti on the stage." At that soliloquy of Figaro in which he attacks various points of government, and especially at the tirade against State prisons, the King rose up and said indignantly, "That's detestable that shall never be played; the Bastille must be destroyed before the licence to act this play can be any other than an act of the most dangerous inconsistency. This man scoffs at everything that should be respected in a government." "It will not be played, then?" said the Queen. "No, certainly," replied Louis XVI; "you may rely upon that."

Still it was constantly reported that *Figaro* was about to be performed; there were even wagers laid upon the subject; I never should have laid any myself, fancying that I was better informed as to the probability than anybody else; if I had, however, I should have been completely deceived. The protectors of Beaumarchais, feeling certain that they would succeed in their scheme of making his work public in spite of the King's prohibition, distributed the parts in the *Marriage of Figaro* among the actors of the Théâtre Français. Beaumarchais had made them enter into the spirit of his characters, and they determined to enjoy at least one performance of this so-called *chef d'oeuvre*. The first gentleman of the chamber agreed that M. de la Ferté should lend the theatre of the Hôtel des Menus Plaisirs, at Paris, which was used for rehearsals of the opera; tickets were distributed to a vast number of leaders of society; and the day for the performance was fixed. The King heard of all this only on the very morning, and signed a *lettre de cachet*,[2] which prohibited the performance. When the messenger who brought the order arrived, he found a part of the theatre already filled with spectators, and the streets leading to the Hôtel des Menus Plaisirs filled with carriages; the piece was not performed. This prohibition of the King's was looked upon as an attack on public liberty.

The disappointment produced such discontent that the words *oppression* and *tyranny* were uttered with no less passion and bitterness at that time than during the days which immediately preceded the downfall of the throne. Beaumarchais was so far put off his guard by rage as to exclaim, "Well! gentlemen, he won't suffer it to be played here; but I swear it shall be played—perhaps in the very choir of Notre Dame!" There was something prophetic in these words.[3] It was generally insinuated shortly afterwards that Beaumarchais had determined to suppress all those parts of his work which could be obnoxious to Government; and on pretence of judging of the sacrifices made by the author, M. de Vaudreuil obtained permission to have this far-famed *Marriage of Figaro* performed at his country house. M. Campan was asked there; he had frequently heard the work read, and did not now find the alterations that had been announced; this he observed to several persons belonging to the Court, who maintained that the author had made all the sacrifices required. M. Campan was so astonished at these persistent assertions of an obvious falsehood that he replied by a quotation from Beaumarchais himself, and assuming the tone of Basilio in the *Barber of Seville*, he said, "Faith, gentlemen, I don't know who is deceived here; everybody is in the secret." They then came to the point, and begged him to tell the Queen positively that all which had been pronounced reprehensible in M. de Beaumarchais' play had been cut out. My father-in-law contented himself with replying that his situation at Court would not allow of his giving an opinion unless the Queen should first speak of the piece to him. The Queen said nothing to him about the matter. Shortly afterwards permission to perform this play was at length obtained. The Queen thought the people of Paris would be finely tricked when they saw merely an ill-conceived piece, devoid of interest, as it must appear when deprived of its satire.[4] Under the persuasion that there was not a passage left capable of malicious or dangerous application, Monsieur attended the first performance in a public box. The mad enthusiasm of the public in favour of the piece and Monsieur's just displeasure are well known. The author was sent to prison soon afterwards, though his work was extolled to the skies, and though the Court durst not suspend its performance.

The Queen testified her displeasure against all who had assisted the author of the *Marriage of Figaro* to deceive the King into giving his consent that it should be represented. Her reproaches were more particularly directed against M. de Vaudreuil for having had it performed at his house. The violent and domineering disposition of her favourite's friend at last became disagreeable to her.

One evening on the Queen's return from the Duchess's, she desired her *valet de chambre* to bring her billiard cue into her closet, and ordered me to open the box that contained it. I was surprised at not finding the padlock belonging to it, the key of which the Queen wore on her watch chain. I opened the box and took out the cue, broken in two. It was of ivory and formed of one single elephant's tooth; the butt was of gold and very tastefully wrought. "There," said she, "that is the way M. de Vaudreuil has treated a thing I valued so highly. I had laid it upon the couch while I was talking to the Duchess in the salon; he had the assurance to make use of it, and in a fit of passion about a blocked ball, he struck the cue so violently against the table that he broke it in two. The noise brought me back into the billiard room; I did not say a word to him, but my looks showed him how angry I was. He is the more provoked at the accident, as he already aspires to the post of Governor to the Dauphin, and with that object in view it is not wise to display passion. I never thought of him for the place. It is quite enough to have consulted my heart only in the choice of a governess; and I will not suffer that of a Governor to the Dauphin to be at all affected by the influence of my friends. I should be responsible for it to the nation. The poor man does not know that my determination is taken; for I have never expressed it to the Duchess. Therefore, judge of the sort of evening he must have passed! This is not the first occurrence that has shown me that if Queens are bored in their own circle, they are compromised in the circles of others."

1. The Queen never forgot this affront of M. d'Esprémenil's; she said that as it was offered at a time when social order had not yet been disturbed, she had felt the severest mortification at it. Shortly before the downfall of the throne M. d'Esprémenil, having openly espoused the King's side, was insulted in the gardens of the Tuileries by the Jacobins, and so ill-treated that he was carried home very ill. Somebody recommended the Queen, on account of the royalist principles he then professed, to send and inquire for him. She replied that she was truly grieved at what had happened to M. d'Esprémenil, but that mere policy should never induce her to show any particular solicitude about the man who had been the first to make so insulting an attack upon her character.—*Madame Campan.*

2. A *lettre de cachet* was any written order proceeding from the King. The term was not confined merely to orders for arrest.—*Madame Campan.*

3. The Keeper of the Seals had constantly opposed the performance of this play. The King said in his presence one day, "You will see that Beaumarchais will have more weight than the Keeper of the Seals."—*Note by the Editor.*

4. "The King," says Grimm, "made sure that the public would judge unfavourably of the work. He said to the Marquis de Montesquiou, who was going to see the first representation, 'Well, what do you augur of its success?' 'Sire, I hope the piece will fail.' 'And so do I,' replied the King."

"There is something still more ridiculous than my piece," said Beaumarchais himself; "that is, its success." Mademoiselle Arnould foresaw it the first day, and exclaimed, "It is a production that will fail fifty nights successively." There was as crowded an audience on the seventy-second night as on the first. The following is extracted from Grimm's *Correspondence:*—

"Answer of M. de Beaumarchais to the Duc de Villequier, who requested the use of his private box for some ladies who wished to see 'Figaro', without being seen:

'I have no respect, M. le Duc, for women who indulge themselves in seeing any play which they think indecorous, provided they can do so in secret. I lend myself to no such fancies. I have given my piece to the public, to amuse, and not to instruct, not to give any compounding prudes the pleasure of going to admire it in a private box, and balancing their account with conscience by censuring it in company. To indulge in the pleasure of vice and assume the credit of virtue is the hypocrisy of the age. My piece is not of a doubtful nature; it must be patronised in good earnest, or avoided altogether; therefore, with all respect to you, M. le Duc, I shall keep my box.' This letter was circulated all over Paris for a week. At first it was said to be addressed to the Duc de Villequier, and afterwards to the Duc d'Aumont. It got in

Marie Antoinette.

Gravé par Morse, sous la direction d'Henriquel Dupont, d'après le portrait
peint sur nature par Werthmüller premier peintre du Roi de Suède Gustave III.

Portrait of Marie Antoinette by Werthmüller

this form as far as Versailles, where it was pronounced an extraordinary piece of impertinence. It seemed the more insolent inasmuch as it was well known that certain very great ladies had declared that if they did go to see the *Marriage of Figaro*, it should be only in a private box. The most zealous partisans of M. de Beaumarchais did not dare even to attempt to vindicate him. After having enjoyed this new flash of celebrity owing either to his own consideration or to the threats of his enemies, M. de Beaumarchais was compelled to announce publicly that his famous letter never was written to a duke or peer, but to one of his own friends, and that upon the first spur of dissatisfaction. It was proved that the letter was written to a President of one of the parliaments, whereupon indignation subsided; for that which appeared impertinent when addressed to men of the Court, was deemed so no longer when addressed to one of the long robe."—*Note by the Editor.*

XII

The diamond necklace—Account of Bœhmer the jeweller—His interview with Madame Campan—The Cardinal de Rohan interrogated in the King's Cabinet—Particulars relative to Madame de Lamotte and her family—Steps taken by the Cardinal's relations—The prosecution—The clergy remonstrate—Decree of the Parliament—The Queen's grief—Remark of Louis XVI

Shortly after the public mind had been thrown into agitation by the performance of the *Marriage of Figaro* an obscure plot, contrived by swindlers and matured in a corrupted society, attacked the Queen's character in a vital point and assailed the majesty of the throne.

I am about to speak of the notorious affair of the necklace purchased, as it was said, for the Queen by Cardinal de Rohan.[1] I will narrate every circumstance that has come to my knowledge relating to this business; the most minute particulars will prove how little reason the Queen had to apprehend the blow by which she was threatened; and which must be attributed to a fatality that human prudence could not have foreseen; but from which, to say the truth, she might have extricated herself with more skill.[2]

I have already said that in 1774 the Queen purchased jewels of Bœhmer to the value of 360,000 francs, that she paid for them herself out of her own private funds, and that it required several years to enable her to complete the payment. The King afterwards presented her with a set of rubies and diamonds of a fine water, and subsequently with a pair of bracelets worth 200,000 francs. The Queen, after having her diamonds reset in new patterns, told Bœhmer that she found her jewel-case rich enough, and was not desirous of making any addition to it.[3] Still, this jeweller busied himself for some years in forming a collection of the finest diamonds circulating in the trade, in order to compose a necklace of several rows, which he hoped to induce her Majesty to purchase; he brought it to M. Campan, requesting him to mention it to the Queen, that she might ask to see it, and thus be induced to wish to possess it. This M. Campan refused to do, telling him that he should be stepping out of the line of his duty were he to propose to the Queen an expense of 1,600,000 francs, and that he believed neither the lady of honour nor the tire-woman would take upon herself to execute such a commission. Bœhmer persuaded the King's first gentleman for the year to show this superb necklace to his Majesty, who admired it so much that he himself wished to see the Queen adorned with it and sent the case to her; but she assured him she should much regret incurring so great an expense for such an article, that she had already very beautiful diamonds, that jewels of that description were now worn at Court not more than four or five times a year, that the necklace must be returned, and that the money would be much better employed in building a man-of-war.[4] Bœhmer, in sad tribulation at finding his expectations delusive, endeavoured for some time, it is said, to dispose of his necklace among the various Courts of Europe. A year after his fruitless attempts, Bœhmer again caused his diamond necklace to be offered to the King, proposing that it should be paid for partly by instalments, and partly in life annuities; this proposal was represented as highly advantageous, and the King, in my presence, mentioned the matter once more to the Queen. I remember the Queen told him that if the bargain really was not bad, he might make it, and keep the necklace until the marriage of one of his children; but that, for her part, she would never wear it, being unwilling that the world should have to reproach her with having coveted so expensive an article. The King replied that their children were too young to justify such an expense, which would be greatly increased by the number of years the diamonds would remain useless, and that he would finally decline the offer. Bœhmer complained to everybody of his misfortune, and all reasonable people blamed him for having collected diamonds to so considerable an amount without any positive order for them. This man had purchased the office of jeweller to the Crown, which gave him some rights of entry at Court. After several months spent in ineffectual attempts to carry his point, and in idle complaints, he obtained an audience of the Queen, who had with her the young Princess her daughter; her Majesty did not know for what purpose Bœhmer sought this audience, and had not the slightest idea that it was to speak to her again about an article twice refused by herself and the King.

Bœhmer threw himself upon his knees, clasped his hands, burst into tears, and exclaimed, "Madame, I am ruined and disgraced if you do not purchase my necklace. I cannot outlive so many misfortunes. When I go hence I shall throw myself into the river." "Rise, Bœhmer," said the Queen, in a tone sufficiently severe to recall him to himself; "I do not like these rhapsodies; honest men have no occasion to fall on their knees to make their requests. If you were to destroy yourself I should regret you as a madman in whom I had taken an interest, but I should not be in any way responsible for that misfortune. Not only have I never ordered the article which causes your present despair, but whenever you have talked to me about fine collections of jewels I have told you that I should not add four diamonds to those which I already possessed. I told you myself that I declined taking the necklace; the King wished to give it to me, but I refused him also; never mention it to me again. Divide it, and try to sell it piecemeal, and do not drown yourself. I am very angry with you for acting this scene of despair in my presence and before this child. Let me never see you behave thus again. Go." Bœhmer withdrew, overwhelmed with confusion, and nothing farther was then heard of him.

When Madame Sophie was born the Queen told me M. de Sainte James, a rich financier, had apprised her that Bœhmer was still intent upon the sale of his necklace, and that she ought, for her own satisfaction, to endeavour to learn what the man had done with it; she desired me the first time I should meet him to speak to him about it, as if from the interest I took in his welfare. I spoke to him about his necklace and he told me he had been very fortunate, having sold it at Constantinople for the favourite

Sultana. I communicated this answer to the Queen, who was delighted with it, but could not comprehend how the Sultan came to purchase his diamonds in Paris.

The Queen long avoided seeing Bœhmer, being fearful of his rash character; and her *valet de chambre*, who had the care of her jewels, made the necessary repairs to her ornaments unassisted. On the baptism of the Duc d'Angoulême in 1785 the King gave him a diamond epaulette and buckles, and directed Bœhmer to deliver them to the Queen. Bœhmer presented them on her return from mass, and at the same time gave into her hands a letter in the form of a petition. In this paper he told the Queen that he was happy to see her "in possession of the finest diamonds known in Europe", and entreated her not to forget him. The Queen read Bœhmer's address to her aloud, and saw nothing in it but a proof of mental aberration; she lighted the paper at a wax taper standing near her, as she had some letters to seal, saying, "It is not worth keeping." She afterwards much regretted the loss of this enigmatical memorial. After having burnt the paper, her Majesty said to me, "That man is born to be my torment; he has always some mad scheme in his head; remember, the first time you see him, to tell him that I do not like diamonds now, and that I will buy no more so long as I live; that if I had any money to spare, I would rather add to my property at Saint Cloud by the purchase of the land surrounding it; now, mind you enter into all these particulars and impress them well upon him." I asked her whether she wished me to send for him; she replied in the negative, adding that it would be sufficient to avail myself of the first opportunity afforded by meeting him; and that the slightest advance towards such a man would be misplaced.

On the 1st of August I left Versailles for my country house at Crespy; on the 3rd came Bœhmer, extremely uneasy at not having received any answer from the Queen, to ask me whether I had any commission from her to him; I replied that she had entrusted me with none; that she had no commands for him, and I faithfully repeated all she had desired me to say to him. "But," said Bœhmer, "the answer to the letter I presented to her—to whom must I apply for that?" "To nobody," answered I; "her Majesty burnt your memorial without even comprehending its meaning." "Ah! madame," exclaimed he, "that is impossible; the Queen knows that she has money to pay me!" "Money, M. Bœhmer? Your last accounts against the Queen were discharged long ago." "Madame, you are not in the secret. A man who is ruined for want of payment of 1,500,000 francs cannot be said to be satisfied." "Have you lost your senses?" said I; "for what can the Queen owe you so extravagant a sum!" "For my necklace, madame," replied Bœhmer coolly. "How!" returned I, "that necklace again, which you have teased the Queen about so many years! Did you not tell me you had sold it at Constantinople?" "The Queen desired me to give that answer to all who should speak to me on the subject," said the wretched dupe. He then told me that the Queen wished to have the necklace, and had had it purchased for her by Monseigneur the Cardinal de Rohan. "You are deceived," I exclaimed; "the Queen has not once spoken to the Cardinal since his return from Vienna; there is not a man at her Court less favourably looked upon." "You are deceived yourself, madame," said Bœhmer; "she sees him so much in private, that it was to his Eminence she gave 30,000 francs, which were paid me as an instalment; she took them, in his presence, out of the little *secrétaire* of Sèvres porcelain next the fireplace in her boudoir." "And the Cardinal told you all this?" "Yes, madame, himself." "What a detestable plot!" cried I.—"Indeed, to say the truth, madame, I begin to be much alarmed, for his Eminence assured me that the Queen would wear the necklace on Whit-Sunday, but I did not see it upon her, and it was that which induced me to write to her Majesty." He then asked me what he ought to do. I advised him to go on to Versailles, instead of returning to Paris, whence he had just arrived; to obtain an immediate audience from the Baron de Breteuil, who, as head of the King's household, was the minister of the department which Bœhmer belonged, and to be circumspect; and I added, that he appeared to me extremely culpable, not as a diamond merchant, but because being a sworn officer it was unpardonable of him to have acted without the direct orders of the King, the Queen, or the minister. He answered, that he had not acted without direct orders; that he had in his possession all the notes signed by the Queen, and that he had even been obliged to show them to several bankers in order to induce them to extend the time for his payments. I urged his departure for Versailles, and he assured me he would go there immediately. Instead of following my advice, he went to the Cardinal, and it was of this visit of Bœhmer's that his Eminence made a memorandum, found in a drawer overlooked by the Abbé Georgel when he burnt, by order of the Cardinal, all the papers which the latter had at Paris. The memorandum was thus worded: "On this day, 3rd August, Bœhmer went to Madame Campan's country house, and she told him that the Queen had never had his necklace, and that he had been deceived."

When Bœhmer was gone, I wanted to follow him, and go to the Queen; my father-in-law prevented me, and ordered me to leave the minister to elucidate such an important affair, observing that it was an infernal plot; that I had given Bœhmer the best advice, and had nothing more to do with the business. Bœhmer never said one word to me about the woman De Lamotte, and her name was mentioned for the first time by the Cardinal in his answers to the interrogatories put to him before the King. After seeing the Cardinal, Bœhmer went to Trianon, and sent a message to the Queen, purporting that I had advised him to come and speak to her. His very words were repeated to her Majesty, who said, "He is mad; I have nothing to say to him, and will not see him." Two or tree days afterwards the Queen sent for me to Petit Trianon, to rehearse with me the part of Rosina, which she was to perform in the *Barber of Seville*. I was alone with her, sitting upon her couch; no mention was made of anything but the part. After we had spent an hour in the rehearsal, her Majesty asked me why I had sent Bœhmer to her; saying he had been in my name to speak to her, and that she would not see him. It was in this manner I learnt that he had not followed my advice in the slightest degree. The change of my countenance, when I heard the man's name, was very perceptible; the Queen perceived it, and questioned me. I entreated her to see him, and assured her it was of the utmost importance for her peace of mind; that there was a plot going on, of which she was not aware; and that it was a serious one, since engagements signed by herself were shown about to people who had lent Bœhmer money. Her surprise and vexation were excessive. She desired me to remain at Trianon, and sent off a courier to Paris, ordering Bœhmer to come to her upon some pretext which has escaped my recollection. He came next morning; in fact it was the day on which the play was performed, and that was the last amusement the Queen allowed herself at that retreat.

The Queen made him enter her closet, and asked him by what fatality it was that she was still doomed to hear of his foolish pretence of selling her an article which she had steadily refused for several years? He replied, that he was compelled, being unable to pacify his creditors any longer. "What are your creditors to me?" said her Majesty. Bœhmer then regularly related to her all that he had been made to believe had passed between the Queen and himself through the intervention of the Cardinal. She was equally incensed and surprised at each thing she heard. In vain did she speak; the jeweller, equally importunate and dangerous, repeated incessantly, "Madame, there is no longer time for feigning; condescend to confess that you have my necklace, and let some assistance be given to me, or my bankruptcy will soon bring the whole to light."

It is easy to imagine how the Queen must have suffered. On Bœhmer's going away, I found her in an alarming condition; the idea that any one could have believed that such a man as the Cardinal possessed her full confidence; that she should have employed him to deal with a tradesman without the King's knowledge, for a thing which she had refused to accept from the King himself, drove her to desperation. She sent first for the Abbé de Vermond, and then for the Baron de Breteuil. Their hatred and contempt for the Cardinal made them too easily forget that the lowest vices do not prevent the higher orders of the empire from being defended by those to whom they have the honour to belong; that a Rohan, a Prince of the Church, however culpable he might be, would be sure to have a considerable party which would naturally be joined by all the discontented persons of the Court, and all the *frondeurs* of Paris.

They too easily believed that he would be stripped of all the advantages of his rank and order, and given up to the disgrace due to his irregular conduct; they deceived themselves.

I saw the Queen after the departure of the Baron and the Abbé; her agitation made me shudder. "Hideous vices must be unmasked," said she; "when the Roman purple and the title of Prince cover a money-seeker, a cheat who dares to compromise the wife of his sovereign, France and all Europe should know it." It is evident that from that moment the fatal plan was decided on. The Queen perceived my alarm; I did not conceal it from her. I knew too well that she had many enemies not to be apprehensive on seeing her attract the attention of the whole world to an intrigue that they would try to complicate still more. I entreated her to seek the most prudent and moderate advice. She silenced me by desiring me to make myself easy, and to rest satisfied that no imprudence would be committed.

On the following Sunday, the 15th of August, being the Assumption, at twelve o'clock, at the very moment when the Cardinal, dressed in his pontifical garments, was about to proceed to the chapel, he was sent for into the King's closet, where the Queen then was. The King said to him, "You have purchased diamonds of Bœhmer?"—"Yes, Sire."— "What have you done with them?"—"I thought they had been delivered to the Queen."— "Who commissioned you?"—"A lady called the Comtesse de Lamotte-Valois, who handed me a letter from the Queen; and I thought I was gratifying her Majesty by taking this business on myself." The Queen here interrupted him and said, "How, sir, could you believe that I should select you, to whom I have not spoken for eight years, to negotiate anything for me, and especially through the mediation of a woman whom I do not even know?"—"I see plainly," said the Cardinal, "that I have been duped; I will pay for the necklace; my desire to please your Majesty blinded me; I suspected no trick in the affair, and I am sorry for it." He then took out of his pocket-book a letter from the Queen to Madame de Lamotte, giving him this commission. The King took it, and holding it towards the Cardinal, said, "This is neither written nor signed by the Queen; how could a Prince of the House of Rohan, and a Grand Almoner of France, ever think that the Queen would sign *Marie Antoinette de France?* Everybody knows that Queens sign only by their baptismal names.[5] But, sir," pursued the King, handing him a copy of his letter to Bœhmer, "have you ever written such a letter as this?" Having glanced over it, the Cardinal said, "I do not remember having written it."—"But what if the original, signed by yourself, were shown to you?"—"If the letter be signed by myself it is genuine." He was extremely confused, and repeated several times, "I have been deceived, Sire; I will pay for the necklace. I ask pardon of your Majesties."—"Then explain to me," resumed the King, "the whole of this enigma. I do not wish to find you guilty; I had rather you would justify yourself. Account for all the manœuvres with Bœhmer, these assurances and these letters." The Cardinal then, turning pale, and leaning against the table, said, "Sire, I am too much confused to answer your Majesty in a way—" "Compose yourself, Cardinal, and go into my cabinet, you will there find paper, pens, and ink, write what you have to say to me." The Cardinal went into the King's cabinet, and returned a quarter of an hour afterwards with a document as confused as his verbal answers had been. The King then said, "Withdraw, sir." The Cardinal left the King's chamber, with the Baron de Breteuil, who gave him in custody to a lieutenant of the Body Guard, with orders to take him to his apartment. M. d'Agoult, aide-major of the Body Guard, afterwards took him into custody, and conducted him to his hotel, and from there to the Bastille. But while the Cardinal had with him only the young lieutenant of the Body Guard, who was much embarrassed at having such an order to execute, his Eminence met his *heyduc* at the door of the Salon of Hercules; he spoke to him in German, and then asked the lieutenant if he could lend him a pencil; the officer gave him that which he carried about him, and the Cardinal wrote to the Abbé Georgel, his grand vicar and friend, instantly to burn all Madame de Lamotte's correspondence, and all his other letters.[6] This commission was executed before M. de Crosne, lieutenant of police, had received an order from the Baron de Breteuil to put seals upon the Cardinal's papers. The destruction of all his Eminence's correspondence, and particularly that with Madame de Lamotte, threw an impenetrable cloud over the whole affair.[7]

From that moment all proofs of this intrigue disappeared. Madame de Lamotte was apprehended at Bar-sur-Aube; her husband had already gone to England. From the beginning of this fatal affair the proceedings of the Court appear to have been prompted by imprudence and want of foresight; the obscurity resulting left free scope for the fables of which the voluminous memorials written on one side and the other consisted. The Queen so little imagined what could have given rise to the intrigue, of which she was about to become the victim, that at the moment when the King was interrogating the Cardinal, a terrific idea entered her mind. With that rapidity of thought caused by personal interest and extreme agitation, she fancied that if a design to ruin her in the

The arrest of the Cardinal de Rohan

eyes of the King and the French people were the concealed motive of this intrigue, the Cardinal would, perhaps, affirm that she had the necklace; that he had been honoured with her confidence for this purchase, made without the King's knowledge; and point out some secret place in her apartment, where he might have got some villain to hide it. Want of money and the meanest swindling were the sole motives for this criminal affair. The necklace had already been taken to pieces and sold, partly in London, partly in Holland, and the rest in Paris.

The moment the Cardinal's arrest was known a universal clamour arose. Every memorial that appeared during the trial increased the outcry. On this occasion the clergy took that course which a little wisdom and the least knowledge of the spirit of such a body ought to have foreseen. The Rohans and the House of Condé, as well as the clergy, made their complaints heard everywhere. The King consented to having a legal judgment, and early in September he addressed letters patent to the Parliament, in which he said that he was "penetrated with the most just indignation on seeing the means which, by the confession of his Eminence the Cardinal, had been employed in order to inculpate his most dear spouse and companion".

Fatal moment! in which the Queen found herself, in consequence of this highly impolitic step, on trial with a subject, who ought to have been dealt with by the power of the King alone. Mistaken ideas of equity, ignorance and hatred, united ill-digested advice to dictate a course of conduct injurious at the same time to the royal authority and to public morals.

The Princes and Princesses of the House of Condé, and of the Houses of Rohan, Soubise, and Guéménée, put on mourning, and were seen ranged in the way of the members of the Grand Chamber to salute them as they proceeded to the palace, on the days of the Cardinal's trial; and Princes of the blood openly canvassed against the Queen of France.

The Pope wished to claim, on behalf of the Cardinal de Rohan, the right belonging to his ecclesiastical rank, and demanded that he should be judged at Rome. The Cardinal de Berris, ambassador from France to his Holiness, formerly Minister for Foreign Affairs, blending the wisdom of an old diplomatist with the principles of a Prince of the Church, wished that this scandalous affair should be hushed up.

The King's aunts, who were on very intimate terms with the ambassador, adopted his opinion, and the conduct of the King and Queen was equally and loudly censured in the apartments of Versailles and in the hotels and coffee-houses of Paris.

It is easy to refer to this transaction, alike fatal and unexpected, as wickedly planned as it was weakly and injudiciously punished, disorders which furnished many weapons to the party opposed to authority.

Madame, the King's sister-in-law, had been the sole protectress of De Lamotte, and had confined her patronage to granting her a pension of 1,2–1,500 francs. Her brother was in the navy, but the Marquis de Chabert, to whom he had been recommended, could never train a good officer. The Queen in vain endeavoured to call to mind the features of this person, of whom she had often heard as an intriguing woman, who came frequently on Sundays to the gallery of Versailles. At the time when all France was engrossed by the prosecution against the Cardinal, the portrait of the Comtesse de

Lamotte-Valois was publicly sold. Her Majesty desired me one day, when I was going to Paris, to buy her the engraving, which was said to be a tolerable likeness, that she might ascertain whether she could recognise in it any person whom she might have seen in the gallery[8]'

The woman De Lamotte's father was a peasant at Auteuil, though he called himself Valois. Madame de Boulainvilliers once saw from her terrace two pretty little peasant girls, each labouring under a heavy bundle of sticks. The priest of the village, who was walking with her, told her that the children possessed some curious papers, and that he had no doubt they were descendants of a Valois, an illegitimate son of one of the Princes of that name.[9]

The family of Valois had long ceased to appear in the world. Hereditary vices had gradually plunged them into the deepest misery. I have heard that the last Valois then known of occupied the estate called Gros Bois; that as he seldom came to Court, Louis XIII asked him what he was about that he remained so constantly in the country; and that this M. de Valois merely answered, "*Sire, I only do there what I ought.*"[10] It was shortly afterwards discovered that he was *coining*.

Neither the Queen herself nor any one near her ever had the slightest connection with the woman De Lamotte; and during her prosecution she could point out but one of the Queen's servants, named Desclos, a valet of the Queen's bed-chamber, to whom she pretended she had delivered Bœhmer's necklace. This Desclos was a very honest man; upon being confronted with the woman De Lamotte, it was proved that she had never seen him but once, which was at the house of the wife of a *surgeon-accoucheur* at Versailles, the only person she visited at Court; and that she had not given him the necklace. Madame de Lamotte married a private in Monsieur's Body Guard; she lodged at Versailles at the Belle Image, a very inferior furnished house; and it is inconceivable how so obscure a person could succeed in making herself believed to be a friend of the Queen, who, though so extremely affable, seldom granted audiences, and only to titled persons.

The trial of the Cardinal is too generally known to require me to repeat its details here.[11] The point most embarrassing to him was the interview he had in February 1785 with M. de Sainte James, to whom he confided the particulars of the Queen's pretended commission, and showed the contract approved and signed *Marie Antoinette de France*. The memorandum found in a drawer of the Cardinal's bureau, in which he had himself written what Bœhmer told him after having seen me at my country house, was likewise an unfortunate document for his Eminence.

I offered to the King to go and declare that Bœhmer had told me that the Cardinal assured him he had received from the Queen's own hand the 30,000 francs given on account upon the bargain being concluded, and that his Eminence had seen her Majesty take that sum in bills from the porcelain *secrétaire* in her boudoir. The King declined my offer, and said to me, "Were you alone when Bœhmer told you this?" I answered that I was alone with him in my garden. "Well!" resumed he, "the man would deny the fact; he is now sure of being paid his sixteen hundred thousand francs, which the Cardinal's family will find it necessary to make good to him;[12] we can no longer rely upon his sincerity; it would look as if you were sent by the Queen, and that would not be proper."

The *procureur-général's* information was severe on the Cardinal. The Houses of Condé and Rohan and the majority of the nobility saw in this affair only an attack on the Prince's rank, the clergy only a blow aimed at the privileges of a Cardinal. The clergy demanded that the unfortunate business of the Prince Cardinal de Rohan should be submitted to ecclesiastical jurisdiction, and the Archbishop of Narbonne, then President of the Convocation, made representations upon the subject to the King;[13] the bishops wrote to his Majesty to remind him that a private ecclesiastic implicated in the affair then pending would have a right to claim his constitutional judges, and that this right was refused to a cardinal, his superior in the hierarchical order.[14] In short, the clergy and the greater part of the nobility were at that time outrageous against authority, and chiefly against the Queen.

The *procureur-général's* conclusions, and those of a part of the heads of the magistracy, were as severe towards the Cardinal as the information had been; yet he was fully acquitted by a majority of three voices; the woman De Lamotte was condemned to be whipped, branded, and imprisoned; and her husband, for contumacy, was condemned to the galleys for life.

As soon as I heard of the sentence passed on the Cardinal I went to the Queen. She heard my voice in the anteroom. She called to me; I found her very much agitated. In a faltering voice she said, "Condole with me; the intriguer who wished to ruin me, or get money by misusing my name, adopting my signature, has just been fully acquitted; but," added she, with warmth, "as a Frenchwoman let me pity you. Unfortunate indeed are a people who have for their supreme tribunal a set of men who consult only their passions; some of whom are capable of being corrupted, and others of an audacity which they have always manifested against authority, and which they have just suffered to break out against those who are invested with it."[15] At this moment the King entered, and I wished to withdraw. "Stay," said he to me; "you are one of those who sincerely participate in the grief of your mistress." He went up to the Queen and took her by the hand. "This affair," said he, "has been decided outrageously; however, that is very easily accounted for. To be able to cut this Gordian knot it is not necessary to be an Alexander. In the Cardinal the Parliament saw only a Prince of the Church, a Prince de Rohan, the near relation of a Prince of the blood; while they ought to have seen in him a man unworthy of his ecclesiastical character, a great nobleman degraded by his shameful connections, a young spendthrift trying expedients, like many in Paris, and grasping at everything. He thought he would pay Bœhmer, on account, sums large enough to discharge the price of the necklace within a moderate time; but he knew the customs of the Court enough, and was not so silly as to believe that Madame de Lamotte was received by the Queen and deputed to execute such a commission."

In giving the King's opinion, I do not pretend to speak decisively on the Cardinal's credulity or dishonesty; but it got abroad, and I am bound to report the exact terms of a conversation in which he declared it with so little reserve. He still continued to speak of that dreadful trial, and condescended to say to me, "I have saved you a mortification, which you would have experienced, without any advantage to the Queen; all the Cardinal's papers were burnt, with the exception of a little note written by him, which was found by itself at the bottom of a drawer; it is dated in the latter end of July, and says that Bœhmer has seen Madame Campan, who told him to beware of the intrigue of which he would become the victim; that she would lay her head upon the block to maintain that the Queen had never wished to have the necklace, and that she had certainly not purchased it secretly. Had you any such conversation with the man?" concluded the King. I answered that I remembered having said nearly those very words to him, and that I had informed the Queen of it. "Well!" he resumed, "I was asked whether it would be agreeable to me that you should be summoned to appear; and I replied that, if it were not absolutely indispensable, I should be obliged by their not summoning a person so intimately connected with the Queen as yourself. How could it, for instance, be explained that this man wrote the note in question three weeks before the day on which I spoke to him, without taking any step towards approaching either the Queen or myself?"

M. Pierre de Laurencel, the *procureur-général's* substitute, sent the Queen a list of the names of the members of the Grand Chamber, with the means made use of by the friends of the Cardinal to gain their votes during the trial. I had this list to keep among the papers which the Queen deposited in the house of M. Campan, my father-in-law, and which at his death, she ordered me to preserve. I burnt this statement, but I remember ladies performed a part not very creditable to their principles; it was by them, in consideration of large sums which they received, that some of the oldest and most respected members were won over. I did not see a single name amongst the whole Parliament that was gained directly.

The belief confirmed by time is, that the Cardinal was completely duped by the woman De Lamotte and Cagliostro. The King may have been in error in thinking him an accomplice in this miserable and criminal scheme, but I have faithfully repeated his Majesty's judgment about it.

However, the generally received opinion that the Baron de Breteuil's hatred for the Cardinal was the cause of the scandal and the unfortunate result of this affair contributed to the disgrace of the former still more than his refusal to give his granddaughter in marriage to the son of the Duc de Polignac.

The Abbé de Vermond threw the whole blame of the imprudence and impolicy of the affair of the Cardinal de Rohan upon the minister, and ceased to be the friend and supporter of the Baron de Breteuil with the Queen.

In the early part of the year 1786 the Cardinal, as has been said, was fully acquitted, and came out of the Bastille, while Madame de Lamotte was condemned to be whipped, branded, and imprisoned. The Court, persisting in the erroneous views which had hitherto guided its measures, conceived that the Cardinal and the woman De Lamotte were equally culpable and unequally punished, and sought to restore the balance of justice by exiling the Cardinal to La Chaise-Dieu, and suffering Madame de Lamotte to escape a few days after she entered l'Hôpital. This new error confirmed the Parisians in the idea that the wretch De Lamotte, who had never been able to make her way so far as to the room appropriated to the Queen's women, had really interested the Queen herself.[16]

1. For full details of the affair of the diamond necklace, see the work by M. Émile Campardon, *Marie Antoinette et le Procès du Collier* (Paris, Plon, 1863). The *Memoirs* of Madame Campan are frequently quoted in this work, in which the answers of the Cardinal and of the other persons implicated to the interrogations made are given, with an engraving of the too celebrated collar.

2. In order to comprehend the account about to be given by Madame Campan, and to appreciate the importance of her historical testimony on this wretched intrigue, the reader should be in possession of the leading facts. There are many remarkable circumstances which, though connected with Madame Campan's narrative, do not form part of it, because she speaks only of what she knew well. A great number of persons acted culpable parts in this shameful drama; it is necessary to be acquainted with them. No one knew the whole affair better than the Abbé Georgel, but at the same time no one was more devoted to the Cardinal de Rohan, or showed more ingenuity in discovering means of defending him, or greater skill in throwing, with artfully affected delicacy, a false light upon the irreproachable conduct of a Princess made the victim of shocking suspicions through either the blind credulity or the corruption of a Prince of the Church. The Abbé reveals in this part of his *Memoirs* a respectful hatred against Marie Antoinette. He supposes the Queen to be aware of the transaction, while she was still wrapped in all the security of a woman whose imagination could not even conceive the idea of such a masterpiece of intrigue. The reader will do well to glance at his statement [see Appendix] and observe how far the assertions it contains are weakened or disproved by Madame Campan.—*Note by the Editor.*

3. Except on those days when the assemblies at Court were particularly attended, such as the 1st of January and the 2nd of February, devoted to the procession of the Order of the Holy Ghost, and on the festivals of Easter, Whitsuntide, and Christmas, the Queen no longer wore any dresses but muslin or white Florentine taffety. Her head-dress was merely a hat; the plainest were preferred; and her diamonds never quitted their caskets but for the dresses of ceremony, confined to the days I have mentioned. Before the Queen was five-and-twenty she began to apprehend that she might be induced to make too frequent use of flowers and of ornaments, which at that time were exclusively reserved for youth. Madame Bertin having brought a wreath for the head and neck, composed of roses, the Queen feared that the brightness of the flowers might be disadvantageous to her complexion. She was unquestionably too severe upon herself, her beauty having as yet experienced no alteration; it is easy to conceive the concert of praise and compliment that replied to the doubt she had expressed. The Queen, approaching me, said, "I charge you, from this day, to give me notice when flowers shall cease to become me." "I shall do no such thing," I replied immediately; "I have not read *Gil Blas* without profiting in some degree from it, and I find your Majesty's order too much like that given him by the Archbishop of Granada, to warn him of the moment when he should begin to fall off in the composition of his homilies." "Go," said the Queen; "you are less sincere than *Gil Blas*; and I would have been more amenable than the Archbishop."— *Madame Campan.*

4. Messrs Bœhmer and Bassange, jewellers to the Crown, were proprietors of a superb diamond necklace, which had, as it was said, been intended for the Comtesse du Barry. Being under the necessity of selling it, they offered it, during the last war, to the King and Queen; but their Majesties made the following prudent answer: "*We stand more in need of ships than of jewels.*"—*Secret Correspondence of the Court of Louis XVI.*

5. The Cardinal ought, it has been said, to have detected the forgery of the approbations and signature to the instructions; his place of Grand Almoner gave him the opportunity of knowing both her Majesty's writing and her manner of signing her name. To this important objection it is answered, that it was long since M. de Rohan had seen her writing; that he did not recollect it; that, besides, not being at all suspicious, he had no inducement to endeavour to verify it; and that the Crown jewellers, to whom he showed the instrument, had not, any more than himself, detected the imposition.—*Secret Correspondence of the Court of Louis XVI.*

6. The *Secret Correspondence* thus explains the officer's conduct and confusion:—

> The lieutenant being reprimanded for suffering the Cardinal to write, replied that his orders did not forbid it; and that, besides, he had been much disconcerted by the unusual address of the Baron de Breteuil—'*Sir, in the King's name follow me;*' that he had not recovered himself and did not perfectly know what he was about. This excuse is not very satisfactory, though it is true that this officer, who was very irregular in his conduct, was much in debt, and at first feared that the order concerned himself personally.

The Abbé Georgel relates the circumstance in a very different manner:—

> The Cardinal, at that dreadful moment, gave an astonishing proof of his presence of mind: notwithstanding the escort which surrounded him, favoured by the attendant crowd, he stopped, and stooping down with his face towards the wall, as if to fasten his buckle, snatched out his pencil and hastily wrote a few words upon a scrap of paper placed under his hand in his square red cap. He rose again and proceeded. On entering his house, his people formed a lane; he slipped this paper, unperceived, into the hand of a confidential *valet de chambre*, who waited for him at the door of his apartment.

This story is scarcely credible: it is not at the moment of a prisoner's arrest, when an inquisitive crowd surrounds and watches him, that he can stop and write mysterious words. However, the *valet de chambre* posts off to Paris. He arrives at the palace of the Cardinal between twelve and one o'clock; and his horse falls dead in the stable. "I was in my apartment," says the Abbé Georgel, "the *valet de chambre* entered wildly, with a deadly paleness on his countenance, and exclaimed, '*All is lost; the Prince is arrested.*' He instantly fell, fainting, and dropped the note of which he was the bearer."

The portfolio containing the papers which might compromise the Cardinal was immediately placed beyond the reach of all search.—*Note by the Editor.*

7. Madame de Lamotte was foolishly allowed sufficient time after she heard of the arrest of the Cardinal to burn all the letters she had received from him. Assisted by Beugnot, she completed this at three the same morning that she was arrested at four.—*Memoirs of Count Beugnot*, vol. i, p. 74.

8. The public, with the exception of the lowest class, were admitted into the gallery and larger apartments of Versailles, as they were into the park.—*Madame Campan.*

9. Madame de Lamotte (Jeanne de Saint Rémi de Valois) was born at Fontette, in the department of the Aube, 22nd July 1756. She was the second child of Jacques de Saint Rémi de

Valois, who at first called himself De Luz, and later De Valois, Baron de Saint Rémi, the
seventh in descent from Henri de Saint Rémi, the son of Henry II, King of France, and of
Nicole de Savigny, Dame de Saint Rémi, de Fontette, du Chatelier, and de Noëz.—*Marie
Antoinette et le Procès du Collier*, by Campardon, p. 14.

10. "*Je n'y fait que ce que je dois*", which also means, "I only make what I owe," and in that sense
    was a true answer.

11. The letters patent which gave the Parliament cognisance of the process were couched in these
    terms:—

> Louis, etc. having been informed that the Sieurs Bœhmer and Bassange sold the
> Cardinal de Rohan a necklace of brilliants; that the said Cardinal de Rohan, with-
> out the knowledge of the Queen our beloved spouse and consort, told them he was
> authorised by her to purchase it at the price of sixteen hundred thousand livres, payable
> by instalments, and showed them false instructions to that effect, which he exhibited
> as approved by the Queen; that the said necklace having been delivered by the said
> Bœhmer and Bassange to the said Cardinal, and the first payment agreed on between
> them not having been made good, they had recourse to the Queen; we could not
> without just indignation see an august name, dear to us on so many accounts, thus
> daringly used, and the respect due to majesty violated with such unheard-of temerity.
> We therefore have deemed it incumbent to cite before us the said Cardinal, and upon
> his declaration to us that he had been deceived by a woman named Lamotte, called De
> Valois, we judged it indispensable to secure his person and that of the said Lamotte,
> called De Valois, and to take those steps suggested to us by our wisdom for the discov-
> ery of the authors or accomplices of an attempt of this nature; and we have thought fit
> to refer the matter to you, that the process may be instituted and decided by you, the
> great chamber and criminal court assembled.
> —*Note by the Editor.*

12. The guilty woman no sooner knew that all was about to be discovered than she sent for the
    jewellers, and told them the Cardinal had perceived that the agreement, which he believed
    to have been signed by the Queen, was a false and forged document. "However," added she,
    "the Cardinal possesses a considerable fortune, *and he can very well pay you.*" These words
    reveal the whole secret. The Countess had taken the necklace to herself and flattered herself
    that M. de Rohan, seeing himself deceived and cruelly imposed upon, would determine to
    pay and make the best terms he could, rather than suffer a matter of this nature to become
    public.—*Secret Correspondence of the Court of Louis XVI.*

13. The clergy, then assembled, embraced this opportunity to assert its rights. The Archbishop of
    Narbonne spoke:—

> My lords and gentlemen, no one among us is unaware that Cardinal de Rohan has
> had the misfortune to incur the King's displeasure. Without doubt, we have reason to
> fear that his guilt has been great, since his Majesty has thought proper to arrest him in
> a public manner, to secure his person and his papers. But Cardinal de Rohan is both a
> cardinal and a grand almoner, as well as bishop of the kingdom. This latter title, com-

mon to ourselves as well as to him, obliges us to claim the observance of the regulations which prescribe that a bishop must be tried by those of his own rank. God forbid that by so doing we should pretend to render our order exempt from punishment, and seduce it from the obedience due to the King!

—*Note by the Editor.*

14. The Sovereign Pontiff assembled a consistory, which unanimously declared that the Cardinal de Rohan had erred against his dignity as a member of the sacred college in recognising the authority of Parliament, that he was suspended for six months, and that if he persisted he should be struck out of the list of cardinals. An Abbé Lemoine, a doctor of the Sorbonne, had to be sent to Rome to prove to the Pope that M. de Rohan had made the protests required by his dignity, and that he had only accepted the judgment of a secular tribunal because he had to yield to the will of his King.—*Marie Antoinette et le Procès du Collier*, by Campardon, p. 53.

15. The following extract is from the Memoirs of the Abbé Georgel:—"M. d'Epremésnil, a counsellor of the Parliament, but who was not a judge in the affair, found secret means to inform us of very interesting particulars, the knowledge of which was of the greatest utility to us." He adds in another place, speaking of the moment in which the decree was pronounced: "The sittings were long and multiplied; it was necessary to read the whole proceedings; more than fifty judges sat; a master of requests, a friend of the Prince, wrote down all that was there, and sent it to his advisers, who found means to inform the Cardinal of it, and to add the plan of conduct he ought to pursue." D'Epremésnil, and other young counsellors, showed upon that occasion but too much audacity in braving the Court, too much eagerness in seizing an opportunity of attacking it. They were the first to shake that authority which their function made it a duty in them to respect.—*Note by the Editor.*

16. Further particulars will be found in the *Memoirs of the Comte de Beugnot* (London: Hurst and Blackett, 1871), as he knew Madame de Lamotte from the days of her early childhood (when the three children, the Baron de Valois, who died captain of a frigate, and the two Mademoiselles de Saint Rémi, the last descendants of the Baron de Rémi, a natural son of Henry II, were almost starving), to the time of her temporary prosperity. In fact, he was with her when she burnt the correspondence of the Cardinal, in the interval the Court foolishly allowed between his arrest and her capture, and De Beugnot believed he had met at her house, at the moment of their return from their successful trick, the whole party engaged in deluding the Cardinal. It worth noting that he was then struck by the face of Mademoiselle d'Oliva, who had just personated the Queen in presenting a rose to the Cardinal. It may also be cited as a pleasing quality of Madame de Lamotte that she, "in her ordinary conversation, used the words *stupid* and *honest* as synonymous".—See *Beugnot*, vol. i, p. 60.

XIII

The Archbishop of Sens is appointed to the Ministry—The Abbé de Vermond's joy on the occasion—The Queen is obliged to take a part in business—Money sent to Vienna contrary to her inclination—Anecdotes—The Queen supports the Archbishop of Sens in office—Public rejoicings on his dismissal—Opening of the States-General—Cries of "Vive le Duc d'Orléans!"—Their effect upon the Queen—Mirabeau—He requests an embassy—Misfortunes induce the Queen to yield to superstitious fears—Anecdotes—Prejudices of the provincial deputies of the tiers-état—Causes of these prejudices—Death of the first Dauphin—Anecdotes

The Abbé de Vermond could not suppress his exultation when he succeeded in getting the Archbishop of Sens appointed head of the Council of finance. I have more than once heard him say that seventeen years of patience were not too long a term for success in a Court; that he spent all that time in gaining the end he had in view; but that at length the Archbishop was where he ought to be for the good of the State. The Abbé from this time in the Queen's private circle no longer concealed his credit and influence; nothing could equal the confidence with which he displayed the extent of his pretensions. He requested the Queen to order that the apartments appropriated to him should be enlarged, telling her that being obliged to give audiences to bishops, cardinals, and ministers he required a residence suitable to his present circumstances. The Queen continued to treat him as she did before the Archbishop's arrival at Court; but the household showed him increased consideration: the word *Monsieur* preceded that of Abbé; and from that moment not only the livery servants but also the people of the antechambers rose when *Monsieur l'Abbé* was passing, though there never was, to my knowledge, any order given to that effect.

The Queen was obliged, on account of the King's disposition, and the very limited confidence he placed in the Archbishop of Sens, to take a part in public affairs. While M. de Maurepas lived she kept out of that danger, as may be seen by the censure which the Baron de Besenval passes on her in his memoirs for not availing herself of the conciliation he had promoted between the Queen and that minister, who counteracted the ascendancy which the Queen and her intimate friends might otherwise have gained over the King's mind.

The Queen has often assured me that she never interfered respecting the interests of Austria but once; and that was only to claim the execution of the treaty of alliance at the time when Joseph II was at war with Prussia and Turkey; that she then demanded that an army of 24,000 men should be sent to him instead of 15 millions, an alternative which had been left to option in the treaty, in case the Emperor should have a just war to maintain; that she could not obtain her object, and M. de Vergennes, in an interview which she had with him upon the subject, put an end to her importunities by observing that he was answering the mother of the Dauphin and not the sister of the Emperor. The 15 millions were sent. There was no want of money at Vienna, and the value of a French army was fully appreciated.

"But how," said the Queen, "could they be so wicked as to send off those fifteen millions from the general post-office, diligently publishing, even to the street porters, that they were loading carriages with money that I was sending to my brother—whereas it is certain that the money would equally have been sent if I had belonged to another house; and, besides, it was sent contrary to my inclination."[1]

When the Comte de Moustier set out on his mission to the United States, after having had his public audience of leave, he came and asked me to procure him a private one. I could not succeed with the strongest solicitations: the Queen desired me to wish him a good voyage, but added that none but ministers could have anything to say to him in private, since he was going to a country where the names of King and Queen must be detested.

Marie Antoinette had then no direct influence over State affairs until after the deaths of M. de Maurepas and M. de Vergennes, and the retreat of M. de Calonne. She frequently regretted her new situation, and looked upon it as a misfortune which she could not avoid. One day, while I was assisting her to tie up a number of memorials and reports, which some of the ministers had handed to her to be given to the King, "Ah!" said she, sighing, "there is an end of all happiness for me, since they have made an intriguer of me." I exclaimed at the word. "Yes," resumed the Queen, "that is the right term; every woman who meddles with affairs above her understanding or out of her line of duty is an intriguer and nothing else; you will remember, however, that it is not my own fault, and that it is with regret I give myself such a title; the Queens of France are happy only so long as they meddle with nothing, and merely preserve influence sufficient to advance their friends and reward a few zealous servants. Do you know what happened to me lately? One day since I began to attend private committees at the King's, while crossing the *Œil de Bœuf*, I heard one of the musicians of the chapel say so loud that I lost not a single word, 'A Queen who does her duty will remain in her apartment to knit.' I said within myself, 'Poor wretch, thou art right: but thou knowest not my situation; I yield to necessity and my evil destiny.'" This situation was the more painful to the Queen inasmuch as Louis XVI had long accustomed himself to say nothing to her respecting State affairs; and when, towards the close of his reign, she was obliged to interfere in the most important matters, the same habit in the King frequently kept from her particulars which it was necessary she should have known. Obtaining, therefore, only insufficient information, and guided by persons more ambitious than skilful, the Queen could not be useful in great affairs; yet, at the same time, her ostensible interference drew upon her, from all parties and all classes of society, an unpopularity, the rapid progress of which alarmed all those who were sincerely attached to her.[2]

Carried away by the eloquence of the Archbishop of Sens, and encouraged in the confidence she placed in that minister by the incessant eulogies of the Abbé de Vermond on his abilities, the Queen unfortunately followed up her first mistake of bringing him into office in 1787 by supporting him at the time of his disgrace, which was obtained by the despair of a whole nation. She thought it was due to her dignity to give him some marked proof of her regard at the moment of his departure; misled by her feelings she sent him her portrait enriched with jewellery, and a brevet for the situation of lady of the palace for Madame de Canisy, his niece, observing that it was necessary to indemnify a minister sacrificed to the intrigues of the Court and the factious spirit of the nation; that otherwise none would be found willing to devote themselves to the interests of the sovereign. However, on the day of the Archbishop's departure the public joy was universal, both at Court and at Paris: there were bonfires; the attorneys' clerks burnt the Archbishop in effigy, and on the evening of his disgrace more than a hundred couriers were sent out from Versailles to spread the happy tidings among the country seats. I have seen the Queen shed bitter tears at the recollection of the errors she committed at this period, when subsequently, a short time before her death, the Archbishop had the audacity to say, in a speech which was printed, that the sole object of one of his operations, during his administration, was the salutary crisis which the Revolution produced.

The benevolence and generosity shown by the King and Queen during the severe winter of 1788, when the Seine was frozen over and the cold was more intense than it had been for eighty years, procured them some fleeting popularity. The gratitude of the Parisians for the succour their Majesties poured forth was lively if not lasting. The snow was so abundant that since that period there has never been seen such a prodigious quantity in France. In different parts of Paris pyramids and obelisks of snow were erected with inscriptions expressive of the gratitude of the people. The pyramid in the Rue d'Angiviller was supported on a base six feet high by twelve broad; it rose to the height of fifteen feet, and was terminated by a globe. Four blocks of stone, placed at the angles, corresponded with the obelisk, and gave it an elegant appearance. Several inscriptions, in honour of the King and Queen, were affixed to it. I went to see this singular monument, and recollect the following inscription:—

TO MARIE ANTOINETTE

Lovely and good, to tender pity true,
Queen of a virtuous King, this trophy view;
Cold ice and snow sustain its fragile form,
But ev'ry grateful heart to thee is warm.
Oh, may this tribute in your hearts excite,
Illustrious pair, more pure and real delight,
Whilst thus your virtues are sincerely prais'd,
Than pompous domes by servile flatt'ry rais'd.

The theatres generally rang with praises of the beneficence of the sovereigns: *La Partie de Chasse de Henri IV* was represented for the benefit of the poor. The receipts were very considerable.

When the fruitless measure of the Assembly of the Notables,[3] and the rebellious spirit in the Parliaments, had created the necessity for States-General, it was long discussed in Council whether they should be assembled at Versailles or at forty or sixty leagues from the capital; the Queen was for the latter course, and insisted to the King that they ought to be far away from the immense population of Paris. She feared that the people would influence the deliberations of the deputies; several memorials were presented to the King upon that question; but M. Necker prevailed, and Versailles was the place fixed upon.

The day on which the King announced that he gave his consent to the convocation of the States-General, the Queen left the public dinner, and placed herself in the recess of the first window of her bed-chamber, with her face towards the garden. Her chief butler followed her to present her coffee, which she usually took standing, as she was about to leave the table. She made me a sign to come close to her. The King was engaged in conversation with some one in his room. When the attendant had served her he retired; and she addressed me, with the cup still in her hand: "Great Heavens! what fatal news goes forth this day! The King assents to the convocation of the States-General." Then she added, raising her eyes to heaven, "I dread it; this important event is a first fatal signal of discord in France." She cast her eyes down, they were filled with tears. She could not take the remainder of her coffee, but handed me the cup, and went to join the King. In the evening, when she was with me, she spoke only of this momentous decision. "It is the Parliament," said she, "that has compelled the King to have recourse to a measure long considered fatal to the repose of the kingdom. These gentlemen wish to restrain the power of the King; but they give a great shock to the authority of which they make so bad a use, and they will bring on their own destruction."

The double representation granted to the *tiers-état* was now the chief topic of conversation. The Queen favoured this plan, to which the King had agreed; she thought the hope of obtaining ecclesiastical favours would secure the clergy of the second order, and that M. Necker felt assured that he possessed the same degree of influence over the lawyers and other people of that class. The Comte d'Artois, holding the contrary opinion, presented a memorial in the names of himself and several Princes of the blood to the King against the double representation. The Queen was displeased with him for this; her confidential advisers infused into her apprehensions that the Prince was made the tool of a party; but his conduct was approved of by Madame de Polignac's circle, which the Queen thenceforward only frequented to avoid the appearance of a change in her habits. She almost always returned unhappy; she was treated with the profound respect due to a Queen, but the devotion of friendship had vanished, to make way for the coldness of etiquette, which wounded her deeply. The alienation between her and the Comte d'Artois was very painful to her, for she had loved him as tenderly as if he had been her own brother.

The opening of the States-General took place on the 4th of May 1789. The Queen on that occasion appeared for the last time in her life in regal magnificence. During the procession some low women, seeing the Queen pass, cried out, "*Vive le Duc d'Orléans!*"

in so threatening a manner that she nearly fainted. She was obliged to be supported, and those about her were afraid it would be necessary to stop the procession. The Queen, however, recovered herself, and much regretted that she had not been able to command more presence of mind.[4]

The first sitting of the States took place on the following day. The King delivered his speech with firmness and dignity; the Queen told me that he had taken great pains about it, and had repeated it frequently. His Majesty gave public marks to attachment and respect for the Queen, who was applauded; but it was easy to see that this applause was in fact rendered to the King alone.

It was evident, during the first sittings, that Mirabeau would be very dangerous to Government. It is affirmed that at this period he communicated to the King, and still more fully to the Queen, part of his schemes for abandoning them. He brandished the weapons afforded him by his eloquence and audacity, in order to make terms with the party he meant to attack. This man played the game of revolution to make his own fortune. The Queen told me that he asked for an embassy, and, if my memory does not deceive me, it was that of Constantinople. He was refused with well-deserved contempt, though policy would doubtless have concealed it, could the future have been foreseen.[5]

The enthusiasm prevailing at the opening of this Assembly, and the debates between the *tiers-état,* the nobility, and even the clergy, daily increased the alarm of their Majesties, and all who were attached to the cause of monarchy. The Queen went to bed late, or rather she began to be unable to rest. One evening, about the end of May, she was sitting in her room, relating several remarkable occurrences of the day; four wax candles replaced upon her toilette table; the first went out of itself; I re-lighted it; shortly afterwards the second, and then the third went out also; upon which the Queen, squeezing my hand in terror, said to me: "Misfortune makes us superstitious; if the fourth taper should go out like the rest, nothing can prevent my looking upon it as a sinister omen." The fourth taper went out. It was remarked to the Queen that the four tapers had probably been run in the same mould, and that a defect in the wick had naturally occurred at the same point in each, since the candles had all gone out in the order in which they had been lighted.

The deputies of the *tiers-état* arrived at Versailles full of the strongest prejudices against the Court. They believed that the King indulged the pleasures of the table to a shameful excess and that the Queen was draining the treasury of the State in order to satisfy the most unbridled luxury. They almost all determined to see Petit Trianon. The extreme plainness of the retreat in question not answering the ideas they had formed, some of them insisted upon seeing the very small closets, saying that the richly furnished apartments were concealed from them. They particularised one which, according to them, was ornamented with diamonds, and with wreathed columns studded with sapphires and rubies. The Queen could not get these foolish ideas out of her mind, and spoke to the King on the subject. From the description given of this room by the deputies to the keepers of Trianon, the King concluded that they were looking for the scene enriched with paste ornaments, made in the reign of Louis XV for the theatre of Fontainebleau.[6]

The King supposed that his Body Guards, on their return to the country, after their quarterly duty at Court, related what they had seen, and that their exaggerated accounts being repeated became at last totally perverted. This idea of the King, after the search for the diamond chamber, suggested to the Queen that the report of the King's propensity for drinking also sprang from the guards who accompanied his carriage when he hunted at Rambouillet. The King, who disliked sleeping out of his usual bed, was accustomed to leave that hunting seat after supper; he generally slept soundly in his carriage, and awoke only on his arrival at the courtyard of his palace; he used to get down from his carriage in the midst of his Body Guards, staggering, as a man half awake will do, which was mistaken for intoxication.[7]

The majority of the deputies who came imbued with prejudices produced by error or malevolence went to lodge with the most humble private individuals of Versailles, whose inconsiderate conversation contributed not a little to nourish such mistakes. Everything, in short, tended to render subservient to the schemes of the leaders of the rebellion.

Shortly after the opening of the States-General the first Dauphin died. That young Prince suffered from the rickets, which in a few months curved his spine, and rendered his legs so weak that he could not walk without being supported like a feeble old man.[8] How many maternal tears did his condition draw from the Queen, already overwhelmed with apprehensions respecting the state of the kingdom! Her grief was enhanced by intrigues, which, when frequently renewed, became intolerable. An open quarrel between the families and friends of the Duc d'Harcourt, the Dauphin's governor, and those of the Duchesse de Polignac, his governess, added greatly to the Queen's affliction. The young Prince showed a strong dislike to the Duchesse de Polignac, who attributed it either to the Duc or the Duchesse d'Harcourt, and came to make her complaints respecting it to the Queen. The Dauphin twice sent her out of his room, saying to her, with that maturity of manner which long illness always gives to children: "Go out, Duchess, you are so fond of using perfumes, and they always make me ill;" and yet she never used any. The Queen perceived, also, that his prejudices against her friend extended to herself; her son would no longer speak in her presence. She knew that he had become fond of sweetmeats, and offered him some marsh-mallow and jujube lozenges. The under-governors and the first *valet de chambre* requested her not to give the Dauphin anything, as he was to receive no food of any kind without the consent of the faculty. I forbear to describe the wound this prohibition inflicted upon the Queen; she felt it the more deeply because she was aware it was unjustly believed she gave a decided preference to the Duke of Normandy, whose ruddy health and amiability did, in truth, form a striking contrast to the languid look and melancholy disposition of his elder brother. She could not doubt that a plot had for some time existed to deprive her of the affection of a child whom she loved as a good and tender mother ought. Previous to the audience by the King on the 10th August 1788 to the envoy of the Sultan Tippoo Sahib, she had begged the Duc d'Harcourt to divert the Dauphin, whose deformity was already apparent, from his intention to be present at that ceremony, being unwilling to expose him to the gaze of the crowd of inquisitive Parisians who would be in the gallery. Notwithstanding this injunction the Dauphin was suffered to write to his mother, requesting her permission to be present at the audience. The Queen was obliged to refuse him, and warmly reproached the governor, who merely answered that he could not oppose the wishes of a sick child. A year before the death of the Dauphin the Queen lost the Princesse Sophie; this was, as the Queen said, the first of a series of misfortunes.[9]

1. This was not the first time the Queen had become unpopular in consequence of financial support afforded by France to her brother. The Emperor Joseph II made, in November 1783 and in May 1784, startling claims on the republic of the United Provinces; he demanded the opening of the Scheldt, the cession of Maëstricht with its dependencies, of the country beyond the Meuse, the county of Vroenhoven, and a sum of 70 millions of florins. The first gun was fired by the Emperor on the Scheldt on 5th November 1784. Peace was concluded on 8th November 1785, through the mediation of France. The singular part was the indemnification granted to the Emperor: this was a sum of 10 millions of Dutch florins; the articles 15, 16 and 17 of the treaty stipulated the quotas of it. Holland paid 5.5 millions and France, under the direction of M. de Vergennes, 4.5 millions of florins, that is to say, 9,045,000 francs, according to M. Soulavie. M. de Ségur, in his *Policy of Cabinets* (vol. iii), says relative to this affair:—

> M. de Vergennes has been much blamed for having terminated, by a sacrifice of seven millions, the contest that existed between the United Provinces and the Emperor. In that age of philosophy men were still very uncivilised; in that age of commerce they made very erroneous calculations; and those who accused the Queen of sending the gold of France to her brother would have been better pleased if, to support a republic devoid of energy, the blood of two hundred thousand men, and three or four hundred millions of francs, had been sacrificed, and at the same time the risk run of losing the advantage of peace dictated to England.
> —*Madame Campan.*

2. In a caricature of the time the King was represented at table with his consort. He had a glass in his hand; the Queen was raising a morsel to her lips; the people were crowding round with their mouths open. Below was written, "The King drinks; the Queen eats; the people cry out."—*Anecdotes of the Reign of Louis XVI*, vol. i.

3. The Assembly of the Notables, as may be seen in Weber's *Memoirs*, vol. i, overthrew the plans and caused the downfall of M. de Calonne. A Prince of the blood presided over each of the meetings of that Assembly. Monsieur, afterwards Louis XVIII, presided over the first meeting.

    "Monsieur," says a contemporary, "gained great reputation at the Assembly of the Notables in 1787. He did not miss attending his meeting a single day, and he displayed truly patriotic virtues. His care in discussing the weighty matters of administration, in throwing light upon them, and in defending the interests and the cause of the people, was such as even to inspire the King with some degree of jealousy. Monsieur only said, 'That a respectful resistance to the orders of the Monarch was not blameable, and that authority might be met by argument, and forced to receive information without any offence whatever.'"—*Note by the Editor.*

4. The rapidly increasing distrust of the King and Queen shown by the populace was greatly attributable to incessant corruption by English gold, and the projects, either of revenge or of ambition, of the Duc d'Orléans. Let it not be thought that this accusation is founded on what has been so often repeated, by the heads of the French Government since the Revolution. Twice, between the 14th July and the 6th October 1789, the day on which the Court was dragged to Paris, the Queen prevented me from making little excursions thither of business or pleasure, saying to me, "Do not go on such a day to Paris; the English have been scattering gold, we shall have some disturbance." The repeated visits of the Duc d'Orléans to England had excited the *Anglomania* to such a pitch that Paris was no longer distinguishable from London. The French, formerly imitated by the whole of Europe, became on a sudden a nation of imitators, without considering the evils that arts and manufactures must suffer in consequence of the change. Since the treaty of commerce made with England at the peace of 1783, not merely equipages, but everything, even to ribands and common earthenware, were of English make. If this predominance of English fashions had been confined to filling our drawing-rooms with young men in English frock-coats, instead of the French dress, good taste and commerce might alone have suffered; but the principles of English government had taken possession of these young heads—*Constitution, Upper House, Lower House, national guarantee, balance of power, Magna Carta, Law of Habeas Corpus*, all these words were incessantly repeated, and seldom understood; but they were of fundamental importance to a party which was then forming.—*Madame Campan.*

5. For further information on this subject the reader is referred to the *Memoirs of Madame Junot (Duchesse d'Abrantès),* vol. i, pp. 48–52 of the English edition, published in 1883.

6. "An idea may be formed," says Montjoie, "of the life led by the Queen after the opening of the States-General by what she described to the Duchesse de Polignac. In one letter she writes: 'My health still lasts, but my mind is overwhelmed with troubles, annoyances, and alarms; every day I learn new misfortunes, and for me one of the greatest is to be parted from all my friends. No longer do I meet hearts that sympathise with me.' In another she wrote: 'All your letters to M——— give me great pleasure: I see at least your writing, I read that you love me, and that does me good. Be tranquil: adversity has not diminished my strength and my courage, and it has increased my prudence.'"—*Note by the Editor.*

7. Boursault's play of *Æsop at Court* contains a scene in which the prince permits the courtiers to tell him his failings. They all chorus in praising him beyond measure, with the exception of one, who reproaches him with getting intoxicated, a dangerous vice in any one, but especially in a King. Louis XV, in whom that disgusting propensity had almost grown into a habit from the year 1739, found fault with Boursault's piece, and forbade its performance at Court. After the death of that King, Louis XVI commanded *Æsop at Court* for performance, found the play full of good sense, and directed that it should be often performed before him. —*Note by the Editor.*

8. Louis, Dauphin of France, who died at Versailles on the 4th of June 1789, gave promise of intellectual precocity. The following particulars, which convey some idea of his disposition, and of the assiduous attention bestowed upon him by the Duchess de Polignac, will be found in a work of that time:—"At two years old the Dauphin was very pretty: he articulated well, and answered questions put to him intelligently. While he was at the Château de la Muette everybody was at liberty to see him. Having received, in the presence of the visitors, a box of

sweetmeats sent to him by the Queen with her portrait upon it, he said, "*Ah! That's mamma's picture.*" The Dauphin was dressed plainly, like a sailor; there was nothing to distinguish him from other children in external appearance but the cross of Saint Louis, the blue ribbon, and the Order of the Fleece, decorations that are the distinctive signs of his rank. The Duchesse Jules de Polignac, his governess, scarcely ever left him for a single instant: she gave up all the Court excursions and amusements in order to devote her whole attention to him. The Prince always manifested a great regard for M. de Bourset, his *valet de chambre*. During the illness of which he died, he one day asked for a pair of scissors; that gentleman reminded him that they were forbidden. The child insisted mildly, and they were obliged to yield to him. Having the scissors, he cut off a lock of his hair, which he wrapped in a sheet of paper: 'There, sir,' said he to his *valet de chambre*, 'there is the only present I can make you, having nothing at my command; but when I am dead you will present this pledge to papa and mamma; and while they remember me, I hope they will not forget you.'"—*Note by the Editor.*

9. The article on Louis XVI in the *Biographie Universelle* makes no mention of the Princesse Sophie. "This Prince," says the work in question, "had three children: Louis, the Dauphin who died in 1789; Louis XVII; and Marie Thérèse Charlotte, now Duchesse d'Angoulême." The omission is of little importance; but we are surprised, when the family of Louis XVI is spoken of, to meet with a mistake in an article signed Bonald.—*Note by the Editor.*

XIV

*"Oath of the Tennis Court"—Insurrection of the 14th of July—The
King goes to the National Assembly—Anecdotes—Spectacle presented by
the courtyards of the Château of Versailles—Report that the National
Assembly is threatened—The King's speech rebutting these suspicions—
Anecdotes—Disposition of the troops—Departure of the Comte d'Artois,
the Prince de Condé, and the Duc and Duchesse de Polignac—The
latter is recognised by a postilion, who saves her—The King goes to
Paris—Alarm at Versailles—The Queen determines to go to the National
Assembly—Speech prepared by her—The King's return—Bailly's speech—
Assassination of Messieurs Foulon and Berthier—Plans presented by
Foulon to the King for arresting the progress of the Revolution—Remark
by Barnave—His repentance*

The ever memorable oath of the States-General, taken at the Tennis Court of Versailles,
was followed by the royal sitting of the 23rd of June.[1] The Queen looked on M. Necker's
not accompanying the King as treachery or criminal cowardice: she said that he had
converted a remedy into poison; that being in full popularity his audacity, in openly
disavowing the step taken by his sovereign, had emboldened the factious, and led away
the whole Assembly; and that he was the more culpable inasmuch as he had the evening
before given her his word to accompany the King. In vain did M. Necker endeavour to
excuse himself by saying that his advice had not been followed.

Soon afterwards the insurrections of the 11th, 12th, and 14th of July[2] opened the
disastrous drama with which France was threatened. The massacre of M. de Flesselles
and M. de Launay drew bitter tears from the Queen, and the idea that the King had lost
such devoted subjects wounded her to the heart.

The character of the movement was no longer merely that of a popular insurrection; cries of "*Vive la Nation! Vive la Roi! Vive la Liberté!*" threw the strongest light
upon the views of the reformers. Still the people spoke of the King with affection, and
appeared to think him favourable to the national desire for the reform of what were
called abuses; but they imagined that he was restrained by the opinions and influence of the Comte d'Artois and the Queen; and those two august personages were
therefore objects of hatred to the malcontents. The dangers incurred by the Comte
d'Artois determined the King's first step with the States-General. He attended their
meeting on the morning of the 15th of July with his brothers, without pomp or escort;
he spoke standing and uncovered, and pronounced these memorable words: "I trust

myself to you; I only wish to be at one with my nation, and, counting on the affection and fidelity of my subjects, I have given orders to the troops to remove from Paris and Versailles." The King returned on foot from the chamber of the States-General to his palace; the deputies crowded after him, and formed his escort, and that of the Princes who accompanied him. The rage of the populace was pointed against the Comte d'Artois, whose unfavourable opinion of the double representation was an odious crime in their eyes. They repeatedly cried out, "*The King for ever, in spite of you and your opinions, Monseigneur!*" One woman had the impudence to come up to the King and ask him whether what he had been doing was done sincerely, and whether he would not be forced to retract it.

The courtyards of the Château were thronged with an immense concourse of people; they demanded that the King and Queen, with their children, should make their appearance in the balcony. The Queen gave me the key of the inner doors, which led to the Dauphin's apartments, and desired me to go to the Duchesse de Polignac to tell her that she wanted her son, and had directed me to bring him myself into her room, where she waited to show him to the people. The Duchess said this order indicated that she was not to accompany the Prince. I did not answer; she squeezed my hand, saying, "Ah! Madame Campan, what a blow I receive!" She embraced the child and me with tears. She knew how much I loved and valued the goodness and the noble simplicity of her disposition. I endeavoured to reassure her by saying that I should bring back the Prince to her; but she persisted, and said she understood the order, and knew what it meant. She then retired to her private room, holding her handkerchief to her eyes. One of the under-governesses asked me whether she might go with the Dauphin; I told her the Queen had given no order to the contrary, and we hastened to her Majesty, who was waiting to lead the Prince to the balcony.

Having executed this sad commission, I went down into the courtyard, where I mingled with the crowd. I heard a thousand vociferations; it was easy to see, by the difference between the language and the dress of some persons among the mob, that they were in disguise. A woman, whose face was covered with a black lace veil, seized me by the arm with some violence, and said, calling me by my name, "I know you very well; tell your Queen not to meddle with government any longer; let her leave her husband and our good States-General to effect the happiness of the people." At the same moment a man, dressed much in the style of a market man, with his hat pulled down over his eyes, seized me by the other arm, and said, "Yes, yes; tell her over and over again that it will not be with these States as with the others which produced no good to the people; that the nation is too enlightened in 1789 not to make something more of them; and that there will not now be seen a deputy of the *tiers-état* making a speech with one knee on the ground; tell her this, do you hear?" I was struck with dread; the Queen then appeared in the balcony. "Ah!" said the woman in the veil, "the Duchess is not with her." "No," replied the man, "but she is still at Versailles; she is working underground, mole-like; but we shall know how to dig her out." The detestable pair moved away from me, and I re-entered the palace, scarcely able to support myself. I thought it my duty to relate the dialogue of these two strangers to the Queen; she made me repeat the particulars to the King.

About four in the afternoon I went across the terrace to Madame Victoire's apartments; three men had stopped under the windows of the throne-chamber. "Here is that throne," said one of them aloud, "the vestiges of which will soon be sought for." He added a thousand invectives against their Majesties. I went in to the Princess, who was at work alone in her closet, behind a canvas blind, which prevented her from being seen by those without. The three men were still walking upon the terrace; I showed them to her, and told her what they had said. She rose to take a nearer view of them, and informed me that one of them was named Saint Huruge; that he was sold to the Duc d'Orléans, and was furious against government, because he had been confined once under a *lettre de cachet* as a bad character.

The King was not ignorant of these popular threats; he also knew the days on which money was scattered about Paris, and once or twice the Queen prevented my going there, saying there would certainly be a riot the next day, because she knew that a quantity of crown pieces had been distributed in the faubourgs.[3]

On the evening of the 14th of July the King came to the Queen's apartments, where I was with her Majesty alone: he conversed with her respecting the horrid report disseminated by the factious, that he had had the Chamber of the National Assembly undermined, in order to blow it up; but he added that it became him to treat such absurd assertions with contempt, as usual; I ventured to tell him that I had the evening before supped with M. Begouen, one of the deputies, who said that there were very respectable persons who thought that this horrible contrivance had been proposed without the King's knowledge. "Then," said his Majesty, "as the idea of such an atrocity was not revolting to so worthy a man as M. Begouen, I will order the chamber to be examined early to-morrow morning." In fact, it will be seen by the King's speech to the National Assembly, on the 15th of July, that the suspicions excited obtained his attention. "I know," said he in the speech in question, "that unworthy insinuations have been made; I know there are those who have dared to assert that your persons are not safe; can it be necessary to give you assurances upon the subject of reports so culpable, denied beforehand by my known character?"

The proceedings of the 15th of July produced no mitigation of the disturbances. Successive deputations of *poissardes* came to request the King to visit Paris, where his presence alone would put an end to the insurrection.

On the 16th a committee was held in the King's apartments, at which a most important question was discussed: whether his Majesty should quit Versailles and set off with the troops whom he had recently ordered to withdraw, or go to Paris to tranquillise the minds of the people. The Queen was for the departure. On the evening of the 16th she made me take all her jewels out of their cases, to collect them in one small box, which she might carry off in her own carriage. With my assistance she burnt a large quantity of papers; for Versailles was then threatened with an early visit of armed men from Paris.

The Queen, on the morning of the 16th, before attending another committee at the King's, having got her jewels ready, and looked over all her papers, gave me one folded up but not sealed, and desired me not to read it until she should give me an order to do so from the King's room; and that then I was to execute its contents; but she returned herself about ten in the morning; the affair was decided; the army was to go away without the King; all who were in imminent danger were to go at the same time. "The King will go to the Hôtel de Ville to-morrow," said the Queen to me; "he did not choose this course for himself; there were long debates on the question; at last the King put an end to them by rising and saying, '*Well gentlemen, we must decide, am I to go or am I to stay? I am ready to do either.*' The majority were for the King's stay; time will show whether the right choice has been made." I returned the Queen the paper she had given me, which was now useless: she read it to me; it contained her orders for the departure; I was to go with her, as well on account of my office about her person as to serve as a teacher to Madame. The Queen tore the paper, and said, with tears in her eyes, "When I wrote this I thought it would be useful, but fate has ordered otherwise, to the misfortune of us all, as I much fear."

After the departure of the troops the new administration received thanks; M. Necker was recalled. The artillery soldiers were undoubtedly corrupted. "Wherefore all these guns?" exclaimed the crowds of women who filled the streets: "Will you kill your mothers, your wives, your children?"—"Don't be afraid," answered the soldiers; "these guns shall rather be levelled against the tyrant's palace than against you!"

The Comte d'Artois, the Prince de Condé, and their children set off at the same time with the troops. The Duc and Duchesse de Polignac, their daughter, the Duchesse de Guiche, the Comtesse Diana de Polignac, sister of the Duke, and the Abbé de Balivière, also emigrated on the same night. Nothing could be more affecting than the parting of the Queen and her friend; extreme misfortune had banished from their minds the recollection of references to which political opinions alone had given rise. The Queen several times wished to go and embrace her once more after their sorrowful *adieu,* but she was too closely watched. She desired M. Campan to be present at the departure of the Duchess, and gave him a purse of 500 *louis,* desiring him to insist upon her allowing the Queen to lend her that sum to defray her expenses on the road. The Queen added that she knew her situation; that she had often calculated her income, and the expenses occasioned by her place at Court; that both husband and wife having no other fortune than their official salaries, could not possibly have saved anything, however differently people might think at Paris. M. Campan remained till midnight with the Duchess to see her enter her carriage. She was disguised as a *femme de chambre*, and got up in front of the berlin; she requested M. Campan to speak of her frequently to the Queen, and then quitted for ever that palace, that favour, and that influence which had raised her up such cruel enemies. On their arrival at Sens the travellers found the people in a state of insurrection; they asked all those who came from Paris whether the Polignacs were still with the Queen. A group of inquisitive persons put that question to the Abbé de Balivière, who answered them in the firmest tone, and with the most cavalier air, that they were far enough from Versailles, and that we had got rid of all such bad people. At the following stage the postilion got on the doorstep and said to the Duchess, "Madame, there are some good people left in the world: I recognised you all at Sens." They gave the worthy fellow a handful of gold.

On the breaking out of these disturbances an old man above seventy years of age gave the Queen an extraordinary proof of attachment and fidelity. M. Péraque, a rich inhabitant of the colonies, father of M. d'Oudenarde, was coming from Brussels to

Paris; while changing horses he was met by a young man who was leaving France, and who recommended him if he carried any letters from foreign countries to burn them immediately, especially if he had any for the Queen. M. Péraque had one from the Archduchess, the Gouvernante of the Low Countries, for her Majesty. He thanked the stranger, and carefully concealed his packet; but as he approached Paris the insurrection appeared to him so general and so violent, that he thought no means could be relied on for securing this letter from seizure. He took upon him to unseal it, learned it by heart, which was a wonderful effort for a man at his time of life, as it contained four pages of writing. On his arrival at Paris he wrote it down, and then presented it to the Queen, telling her that the heart of an old and faithful subject had given him courage to form and execute such a resolution. The Queen received M. Péraque in her closet, and expressed her gratitude in an affecting manner most honourable to the worthy old man. Her Majesty thought the young stranger who had apprised him of the state of Paris was Prince George of Hesse-Darmstadt, who was very devoted her, and who left Paris at that time.

The Marquise de Tourzel replaced the Duchesse Polignac.[4] She was selected by the Queen as being the mother of a family and a woman of irreproachable conduct, who had superintended the education her own daughters with the greatest success.

The King went to Paris on the 17th of July, accompanied by the Maréchal de Beauvau, the Duc de Villeroi, and the Duc de Villequier; he also took the Comte d'Estaing, and the Marquis de Nesle, who were then very popular, in his carriage. Twelve Body Guards, and the town guard of Versailles, escorted him to the Pont du Jour, near Sèvres, where the Parisian guard was waiting for him. His departure caused equal grief and alarm to his friends, notwithstanding the calmness he exhibited. The Queen restrained her tears, and shut herself up in her private rooms with her family. She sent for several persons belonging to her Court; their doors were locked. Terror had driven them away. The silence of death reigned throughout the palace; they hardly dared hope that the King would return.[5] The Queen had a robe prepared for her, and sent orders to her stables to have all her equipages ready. She wrote an address of a few lines for the Assembly, determining to go there with her family, the officers of her palace, and her servants, if the King should be detained prisoner at Paris. She got this address by heart; it began with these words: "Gentlemen, I come to place in your hands the wife and family of your sovereign; do not suffer those who have been united in Heaven to be put asunder on earth." While she was repeating this address she was often interrupted by tears, and sorrowfully exclaimed: "*They will not let him return!*"

It was past four when the King, who had left Versailles at ten in the morning, entered the Hôtel de Ville. At length, at six in the evening M. de Lastours, the King's first page, arrived; he was not half an hour in coming from the Barrière de la Conférence to Versailles. Everybody knows that the moment of calm in Paris was that in which the unfortunate sovereign received the tri-coloured cockade from M. Bailly, and placed it in his hat. A shout of "*Vive le Roi!*" arose on all sides; it had not been once uttered before. The King breathed again, and with tears in his eyes exclaimed that his heart stood in need of such greetings from the people. One of his equerries (M. de Cubières) told him the people loved him, and that he could never have doubted it. The King replied in accents of profound sensibility: "Cubières, the French loved Henri IV, and what King ever better deserved to be so beloved?"[6]

His return to Versailles filled his family with inexpressible joy; in the arms of the Queen, his sister, and his children, he congratulated himself that no accident had happened; and he repeated several times, "Happily no blood has been shed, and I swear that never shall a drop of French blood be shed by my order,"—a determination full of humanity, but too openly avowed in such factious times!

The King's last measure raised a hope in many that general tranquillity would soon enable the Assembly to resume its labours, and promptly bring its session to a close. The Queen never flattered herself so far; M. Bailly's speech to the King had equally wounded her pride and hurt her feelings—"Henri IV conquered his people, and here are the people conquering their King." The word *conquest* offended her; she never forgave M. Bailly for this fine academical phrase.

Five days after the King's visit to Paris, the departure of the troops, and the removal of the Princes and some of the nobility whose influence seemed to alarm the people, a horrible deed committed by hired assassins proved that the King had descended the steps of his throne without having effected a reconciliation with his people.

M. Foulon, *adjoint* to the administration while M. de Broglie was commanding the army assembled at Versailles, had concealed himself at Viry. He was there recognised, and the peasants seized him, and dragged him to the Hôtel de Ville. The cry for death was heard; the electors, the members of committee, and M. de La Fayette, at that time the idol of Paris, in vain endeavoured to save the unfortunate man. After tormenting him in a manner which makes humanity shudder, his body was dragged about the streets, and to the Palais Royal, and his heart was carried by *women* in the midst of a bunch of white carnations![7]

M. Berthier, M. Foulon's son-in-law, intendant of Paris, was seized at Compiègne, at the same time that his father-in-law was seized at Viry, and treated with still more relentless cruelty.

The Queen was always persuaded that this horrible deed was occasioned by some piece of indiscretion; and she informed me that M. Foulon had drawn up two memorials for the direction of the King's conduct at the time of his being called to Court on the removal of M. Necker; and that these memorials contained two schemes of totally different nature for extricating the King from the dreadful situation in which he was placed. In the first of these projects M. Foulon expressed himself without reserve respecting the criminal views of the Duc d'Orléans; said that he ought to be put under arrest, and that no time should be lost in commencing a prosecution against him, while the criminal tribunals were still in existence; he likewise pointed out such deputies as should be apprehended, and advised the King not to separate himself from his army until order was restored.

His other plan was that the King should make himself master of the Revolution before its complete explosion; he advised his Majesty to go to the Assmbly, and there, in person, to demand the *cahiers*,[8] and to make the greatest sacrifices to satisfy the legitimate wishes of the people, and not give the factious time to enlist them in aid of their criminal designs. Madame Adelaide had M. Foulon's two memorials read to her in the presence of four or five persons. One of them[9] was very intimate with Madame de Staël, and that intimacy gave the Queen reason to believe that the opposite party had gained information of M. Foulon's schemes.

It is known that young Barnave, during an aberration of mind, since expiated by sincere repentance, and even by death, uttered these atrocious words: "*Is then the blood now flowing so pure?*" when M. Berthier's son came to the Assembly to implore the eloquence of M. de Lally to entreat that body to save his father's life. I have since been informed that a son of M. Foulon, having returned to France after these first ebullitions of the Revolution, saw Barnave, and gave him one of those memorials, in which M. Foulon advised Louis XVI to prevent the revolutionary explosion by voluntarily granting all that the Assembly required before the 14th of July. "Read this memorial," said he; "I have brought it to increase your remorse: it is the only revenge I wish to inflict on you." Barnave burst into tears, and said to him all that the profoundest grief could dictate.

1. In this *séance* the King declared that the orders must vote separately, and threatened, if further obstacles were met with, to himself act for the good of the people.

2. The Bastille was taken on the 14th July 1789.

3. I have seen a six-franc crown piece, which certainly served to pay some wretch on the night of the 12th of July; the words "*Midnight, 12th July, three pistols,*" were rather deeply engraven on it. They were no doubt a password for the first insurrection.—*Madame Campan.*

4. The *Memoirs* of the Marquise de Tourzel, edited by the Duc des Cars, have just been published in Paris, and are noteworthy also as containing the last authentic portrait of the unhappy Queen, in facsimile from a striking crayon drawing by one of her attendants found after her execution hidden behind a door in the prison.

5. See Ferrières' *Memoirs.*—*Note by the Editor.*

6. Louis XVI cherished the memory of Henri IV: at that moment he thought of his deplorable end; but he long before regarded him as a model. Soulavie says on the subject: "A tablet with the inscription *Resurrexit* placed upon the pedestal of Henri IV's statue on the accession of Louis XVI flattered him exceedingly. '*What a fine compliment,*' said he, '*if it were true! Tacitus himself never wrote anything so concise or so happy.*'" Louis XVI wished to take the reign of that Prince for a model. In the following year the party that raised a commotion among the people on account of the dearness of corn removed the tablet inscribed *Resurrexit* from the statue of Henri IV and placed it under that of Louis XV, whose memory was then detested, as he was believed to have traded on the scarcity of food. Louis XVI, who was informed of it, withdrew into his private apartments, where he was found in a fever shedding tears; and during the whole of that day he could not be prevailed upon either to dine, walk out, or sup. From this circumstance we may judge what he endured at the commencement of the Revolution, when he was accused of not loving the French people."[a]—*Note by the Editor.*

a. This phrase, *Resurrexit*, may be compared with the *Ludovico Reduce, Henricus Redivivus,* prepared by Beugnot for a copy of the same statue on the arrival of Louis XVIII at Paris in 1814.—See *Beugnot*, vol. ii, p. 137.

7. This horrible circumstance is related nowhere else. No record of the time makes any mention of it. —*Note by the Editor*.

8. *Cahiers*, the memorials or lists of complaints, grievances, and requirements of the electors drawn up by the primary assemblies and sent with the deputies.

9. Comte Louis de Narbonne.

XV

Creation of the national guard—Departure of the Abbé de Vermond—The
Queen desires Madame Campan to portray his character—The French
guards quit Versailles—Entertainment given by the Body Guards to the
regiment of Flanders—The King, the Queen, and the Dauphin are present
at it—Proceedings of the 5th and 6th of October—Detestable threats
against the Queen—Devotedness of one of the Body Guard—The life of
Marie Antoinette in danger—The Queen is required to appear on the
balcony—The royal family repair to Paris—Residence at the Tuileries—
Change of feeling—The Queen applauded with enthusiasm by the women
of the populace—Private life—Ingenuous observations of the Dauphin—It
is proposed that the Queen shall quit her family and France—Her noble
refusal—She devotes herself to the education of her children—Picture of
the Court—Anecdote of Luckner—Exasperated state of feeling

After the 14th of July, by a manœuvre for which the most skilful factions of any age
might have envied the Assembly, the whole population of France was armed and organised into a national guard. A report was spread throughout France on the same day, and
almost at the same hour, that 4,000 brigands were marching towards such towns or
villages as it was wished to induce to take arms.[1] Never was any plan better laid; terror
spread at the same moment all over the kingdom. In 1791 a peasant showed me a steep
rock in the mountains of the Mont d'Or on which his wife concealed herself on the day
when the 4,000 brigands were to attack their village, and told me they had been obliged
to make use of ropes to let her down from the height which fear alone had enabled her
to climb.

Versailles was certainly the place where the national military uniform appeared
most offensive. All the King's valets, even of the lowest class, were metamorphosed
into lieutenants or captains; almost all the musicians of the chapel ventured one day to
make their appearance at the King's mass in a military costume; and an Italian soprano
adopted the uniform of a grenadier captain. The King was very much offended at this
conduct, and forbade his servants to appear in his presence in so unsuitable a dress.

The departure of the Duchesse de Polignac naturally left the Abbé de Vermond
exposed to all the dangers of favouritism. He was already talked of as an adviser dangerous to the nation. The Queen was alarmed at it, and recommended him to remove to
Valenciennes, where Count Esterhazy was in command. He was obliged to leave that
place in a few days and set off for Vienna, where he remained.

On the night of the 17th of July the Queen, being unable to sleep, made me watch by her until three in the morning. I was extremely surprised to hear her say that it would be a very long time before the Abbé de Vermond would make his appearance at Court again, even if the existing ferment should subside, because he would not readily be forgiven for his attachment to the Archbishop of Sens;[2] and that she had lost in him a very devoted servant. Then, on a sudden, she remarked to me, that although he was not much prejudiced against me I could not have much regard for him, because he could not bear my father-in-law to hold the place of secretary of the closet. She went on to say that I must have studied the Abbé's character, and, as I had sometimes drawn her portraits of living characters, in imitation of those which were fashionable in the time of Louis XIV, she desired me to sketch that of the Abbé, without any reserve. My astonishment was extreme; the Queen spoke of the man who, the day before, had been in the greatest intimacy with her with the utmost coolness, and as a person whom, perhaps, she might never see again! I remained petrified; the Queen persisted, and told me that he had been the enemy of my family for more than twelve years, without having been able to injure it in her opinion; so that I had no occasion to dread his return, however severely I might depict him. I promptly summarised my ideas about the favourite; but I only remember that the portrait was drawn with sincerity, except that everything which could denote antipathy was kept out of it. I shall make but one extract from it: I said that he had been born talkative and indiscreet, and had assumed a character of singularity and abruptness in order to conceal those two failings. The Queen interrupted me by saying, "Ah! how true that is!" I have since discovered that, notwithstanding the high favour which the Abbé de Vermond enjoyed, the Queen took precautions to guard herself against an ascendancy the consequences of which she could not calculate.

On the death of my father-in-law his executors placed in my hands a box containing a few jewels deposited by the Queen with M. Campan on the departure from Versailles of the 6th of October, and two sealed packets, each inscribed, "*Campan will take care of these matters for me.*" I took the two packets to her Majesty, who kept the jewels and the larger packet, and returning me the smaller, said, "Take care of that for me as your father-in-law did."

After the fatal 10th of August 1792,[3] when my house was about to be surrounded, I determined to burn the most interesting papers of which I was the depositary; I thought it my duty, however, to open this packet, which it might perhaps be necessary for me to preserve at all hazards. I saw that it contained a letter from the Abbé de Vermond to the Queen. I have already related that in the earlier days of Madame de Polignac's favour he determined to remove from Versailles, and that the Queen recalled him by means of the Comte de Mercy. This letter contained nothing but certain conditions for his return; it was the most whimsical of treaties; I confess I greatly regretted being under the necessity of destroying it. He reproached the Queen for her infatuation for the Comtesse Jules, her family, and society; and told her several truths about the possible consequences of a friendship which ranked that lady among the favourites of the Queens of France, a title always disliked by the nation. He complained that his advice was neglected; and then came to the conditions of his return to Versailles; after strong assurances that he would never, in all his life, aim at the higher church dignities, he said that he delighted in an unbounded confidence, and that he asked but two things of her Majesty as essential: the first was, not to give him her orders through any third person, and to write to him herself; he complained much that he had had no letter in her own hand since he had left Vienna; then he demanded of her an income of 80,000 livres, in ecclesiastical benefices; and concluded by saying that if she condescended to assure him herself that she would set about procuring him what he wished, her letter would be sufficient in itself to show him that her Majesty had accepted the two conditions he ventured to make respecting his return. No doubt the letter was written; at least it is very certain that the benefices were granted, and that his absence from Versailles lasted only a single week.

In the course of July 1789 the regiment of French guards, which had been in a state of insurrection from the latter end of June, abandoned its colours. One single company of grenadiers remained faithful to its post at Versailles. M. the Baron de Leval was the captain of this company. He came every evening to request me to give the Queen an account of the disposition of his soldiers; but M. de La Fayette having sent them a note, they all deserted during the night and joined their comrades, who were enrolled in the Paris guard; so that Louis XVI on rising saw no guard whatever at the various posts entrusted to them.

The decrees of the 4th of August, by which all privileges were abolished, are well known.[4] The King sanctioned all that tended to the diminution of his own personal gratifications, but refused his consent to the other decrees of that tumultuous night; this refusal was one of the chief causes of the ferments of the month of October.

In the early part of September meetings were held at the Palais Royal, and propositions made to go to Versailles: it was said to be necessary to separate the King from his evil counsellors, and keep him, as well as the Dauphin, at the Louvre. The proclamations by the officers of the Commune for the restoration of tranquillity were ineffectual; but M. de La Fayette succeeded this time in dispersing the populace. The Assembly declared itself permanent; and during the whole of September, in which no doubt the preparations were made for the great insurrections of the following month, the Court was not disturbed.

The King had the Flanders regiment removed to Versailles; unfortunately the idea of the officers of that regiment fraternising with the Body Guards was conceived, and the latter invited the former to a dinner, which was given in the great theatre of Versailles, and not in the Salon of Hercules, as some chroniclers say. Boxes were appropriated to various persons who wished to be present at this entertainment. The Queen told me she had been advised to make her appearance on the occasion; but that, under existing circumstances, she thought such a step might do more harm than good; and that, moreover, neither she nor the King ought directly to have anything to do with such a festival. She ordered me to go, and desired me to observe everything closely, in order to give a faithful account of the whole affair.

The tables were set out upon the stage; at them were placed one of the Body Guard and an officer of the Flanders regiment alternately. There was a numerous orchestra in the room, and the boxes were filled with spectators. The air, "*O Richard! o mon Roi!*" was played, and shouts of "*Vive le Roi*" shook the roof for several minutes. I had with me one of my nieces, and a young person brought up with Madame by her Majesty. They were crying "*Vive le Roi*" with all their might when a deputy of the Third Estate, who was in the next box to mine, and whom I had never seen, called to them, and reproached them for their exclamations; it hurt him, he said, to see young and handsome Frenchwomen brought up in such servile habits, screaming so outrageously for the life of one man, and with true fanaticism exalting him in their hearts above even their dearest relations: he told them what contempt worthy American women would feel on seeing Frenchwomen thus corrupted from their earliest infancy. My niece replied with tolerable spirit, and I requested the deputy to put an end to the subject, which could by no means afford him any satisfaction, inasmuch as the young persons who were with me lived, as well as myself, for the sole purpose of serving and loving the King. While I was speaking what was my astonishment at seeing the King, the Queen, and the Dauphin enter the chamber! It was M. de Luxembourg who had effected this change in the Queen's determination.

The enthusiasm became general; the moment their Majesties arrived the orchestra repeated the air I have just mentioned, and afterwards played a song in the Deserter, "*Can we grieve those whom we love?*" which also made a powerful impression upon those present: on all sides were heard praises of their Majesties, exclamations of affection, expressions of regret for what they had suffered, clapping of hands, and shouts of the "*Vive le Roi, vive la Reine, vive le Dauphin!*" It has been said that white cockades were worn on this occasion; that was not the case; the fact is, that a few young men belonging to the national guard of Versailles, who were invited to the entertainment, turned the white lining of their national cockades outwards. All the military men quitted the hall, and re-conducted the King and his family to their apartments. There was intoxication in these ebullitions of joy: a thousand extravagances were committed by the military, and many of them danced under the King's windows; a soldier belonging to the Flanders regiment climbed up to the balcony of the King's chamber in order to shout "*Vive le Roi!*" nearer his Majesty; this very soldier, as I have been told by several officers of the corps, was one of the first and most dangerous of their insurgents in the riots of the 5th and 6th of October. On the same evening another soldier of that regiment killed himself with a sword. One of my relations, chaplain to the Queen, who supped with me, saw him stretched out in a corner of the Place d'Armes; he went to him to give him spiritual assistance, and received his confession and his last sighs. He destroyed himself out of regret at having suffered himself to be corrupted by the enemies of his King, and said that, since he had seen him and the Queen and the Dauphin, remorse had turned his brain.

I returned home, delighted with all that I had seen. I found a great many people there. M. de Beaumetz, deputy for Arras, listened to my description with a chilling air, and when I had finished, told me that all that had passed was terrific; that he knew the disposition of the Assembly, and that the greatest misfortunes would follow the drama of that night; and he begged my leave to withdraw that he might take time for deliberate reflection whether he should on the very next day emigrate, or pass over to the left side of the Assembly. He adopted the latter course, and never appeared again among my associates.

On the 2nd of October the military entertainment was followed up by a breakfast given at the hotel of the Body Guards. It is said that a discussion took place whether they should not march against the Assembly; but I am utterly ignorant of what passed at that breakfast. From that moment Paris was constantly in commotion; there were continual mobs, and the most virulent proposals were heard in all public places; the conversation was invariably about proceeding to Versailles. The King and Queen did not seem apprehensive of such a measure, and took no precaution against it; even when the army had actually left Paris, on the evening of the 5th of October, the King was shooting at Meudon, and the Queen was alone in her gardens at Trianon, which she then beheld for the last time in her life. She was sitting in her grotto absorbed in painful reflection, when she received a note from the Comte de Saint Priest, entreating her to return to Versailles. M. de Cubières at the same time went off to request the King to leave his sport and return to the palace; the King did so on horseback, and very leisurely. A few minutes afterwards he was informed that a numerous body of women, which preceded the Parisian army, was at Chaville, at the entrance of the avenue from Paris.

The scarcity of bread and the entertainment of the Body Guards were the pretexts for the insurrection of the 5th and 6th of October 1789; but it is clear to demonstration that this new movement of the people was a part of the original plan of the factious, insomuch as, ever since the beginning of September, a report had been industriously circulated that the King intended to withdraw, with his family and ministers, to some stronghold; and at all the popular assemblies there had been always a great deal said about going to Versailles to seize the King.

At first only women showed themselves; the latticed doors of the Château were closed, and the Body Guard and Flanders regiment were drawn up in the Place d'Armes. As the details of that dreadful day are given with precision in several works, I will only observe that consternation and disorder reigned throughout the interior of the palace.

I was not in attendance on the Queen at this time. M. Campan remained with her till two in the morning. As he was leaving her she condescendingly, and with infinite kindness, desired him to make me easy as to the dangers of the moment, and to repeat to me M. de La Fayette's own words, which he had just used on soliciting the royal family to retire to bed, undertaking to answer for his army.

The Queen was far from relying upon M. de La Fayette's loyalty; but she has often told me that she believed on that day that La Fayette, having affirmed to the King, in the presence of a crowd of witnesses, that he would answer for the army of Paris, would not risk his honour as a commander, and was sure of being able to redeem his pledge. She also thought the Parisian army was devoted to him, and that all he said about his being forced to march upon Versailles was mere pretence.

On the first intimation of the march of the Parisians the Comte de Saint Priest prepared Rambouillet for the reception of the King, his family, and suite, and the carriages were even drawn out; but a few cries of "*Vive le Roi!*" when the women reported his Majesty's favourable answer, occasioned the intention of going away to be given up, and orders were given to the troops to withdraw.[5] The Body Guards were, however, assailed with stones and musketry while they were passing from the Place d'Armes to their hotel. Alarm revived; again it was thought necessary that the royal family should go away; some carriages still remained ready for travelling; they were called for; they were stopped by a wretched player belonging to the theatre of the town, seconded by the mob: the opportunity for flight had been lost.

The insurrection was directed against the Queen in particular; I shudder even now at the recollection of the *poissardes*, or rather furies, who wore white aprons, which they screamed out were intended to receive the bowels of Marie Antoinette, and that they would make cockades of them, mixing the most obscene expressions with these horrible threats.

The Queen went to bed at two in the morning, and even slept, tired out with the events of so distressing a day. She had ordered her two women to go to bed, imagining there was nothing to dread, at least, for that night; but the unfortunate Princess was indebted for her life to that feeling of attachment which prevented their obeying her. My sister who was one of the ladies in question, informed me next day of all that I am about to relate.

On leaving the Queen's bed-chamber these ladies called their *femmes de chambre*, and all four remained sitting together against her Majesty's bedroom door. About half-past four in the morning they heard horrible yells and discharges of firearms; one ran to the Queen to awaken her and get her out of bed; my sister flew to the place from which the tumult seemed to proceed; she opened the door of the antechamber which leads to the great guard-room, and beheld one of the Body Guard holding his musket across the door, and attacked by a mob, who were striking at him; his face was covered with blood; he turned round and exclaimed: "*Save the Queen, madame; they are come to assassinate her.*" She hastily shut the door upon the unfortunate victim of duty, fastened it with the great bolt, and took the same precaution on leaving the next room. On reaching the Queen's chamber she cried out to her, "*Get up, Madame; don't stay to dress yourself; fly to the King's apartment.*" The terrified Queen threw herself out of bed; they put a petticoat upon her without tying it, and the two ladies conducted her towards the *Œil de Bœuf.*[6] A door, which led from the Queen's dressing-room to that apartment, had never before been fastened but on her side. What a dreadful moment! it was found to be secured on the other side. They knocked repeatedly with all their strength; a servant of one of the King's *valets de chambre* came and opened it; the Queen entered the King's chamber, but he was not there. Alarmed for the Queen's life, he had gone down the staircases and through the corridors under the *Œil de Bœuf*, by means of which he was accustomed to go to the Queen's apartments without being under the necessity of crossing that room. He entered her Majesty's room and found no one there but some Body Guards, who had taken refuge in it. The King, unwilling to expose their lives, told them to wait a few minutes, and afterwards sent to desire them to go to the *Œil de Bœuf*. Madame de Tourzel, at that time governess of the children of France, had just taken Madame and the Dauphin to the King's apartments. The Queen saw her children again. The reader must imagine this scene of tenderness and despair.

It is not true that the assassins penetrated to the Queen's chamber and pierced the bed with their swords. The fugitive Body Guards were the only persons who entered it; and if the crowd had reached so far they would all have been massacred. Besides, when the rebels had forced the doors of the antechamber the footmen and officers on duty, knowing that the Queen was no longer in her apartments, told them so with that air of truth which always carries conviction. The ferocious horde instantly rushed towards the Œil de Bœuf hoping, no doubt, to intercept her on her way.

Many have asserted that they recognised the Duc d'Orléans in a greatcoat and slouched hat, at half-past four in the morning, at the top of the marble staircase, pointing out with his hand the guard-room, which led to the Queen's apartments. This fact was deposed to at the Châtelet by several individuals in the course of the inquiry instituted respecting the transactions of the 5th and 6th of October.

The prudence and honourable feeling of several officers of the Parisian guards, and the judicious conduct of M. de Vaudreuil, lieutenant-general of marine, and of M. de Chevanne, one of the King's guards, brought about an understanding between the grenadiers of the national guard of Paris and the King's guard. The doors of the Œil de Bœuf were closed, and the antechamber which precedes that room was filled with grenadiers who wanted to get in to massacre the guards. M. de Chevanne offered himself to them as a victim if they wished for one, and demanded what they would have. A report had been spread through their ranks that the Body Guards set them at defiance, and that they all wore black cockades. M. de Chevanne showed them that he wore, as did the corps, the cockade of their uniform; and promised that the guards should exchange it for that of the nation. This was done; they even went so far as to exchange the grenadiers' caps for the hats of the Body Guards; those who were on guard took off their shoulder-belts; embraces and transports of fraternisation instantly succeeded to the savage eagerness to murder the band which had shown so much fidelity to its sovereign. The cry was now "*Vivent le Roi, la Nation, et les Gardes-du-corps!*"

The army occupied the Place d'Armes, all the courtyards of the Château, and the entrance to the avenue. They called for the Queen to appear in the balcony: she came forward with Madame and the Dauphin. There was a cry of "*No children.*" Was this with a view to deprive her of the interest she inspired, accompanied as she was by her young family, or did the leaders of the democrats hope that some madman would venture to aim a mortal blow at her person? The unfortunate Princess certainly was impressed with the latter idea, for she sent away her children, and with her hands and eyes raised towards Heaven, advanced upon the balcony like a self-devoted victim.

A few voices shouted "*To Paris!*" The exclamation soon became general. Before the King agreed to this removal he wished to consult the National Assembly and caused that body to be invited to sit at the Château. Mirabeau opposed this measure. While these discussions were going forward it became more and more difficult to restrain the immense disorderly multitude. The King, without consulting any one, now said to the people: "You wish, my children, that I should follow you to Paris: I consent, but on condition that I shall not be separated from my wife and family." The King added that he required safety also for his guards; he was answered by shouts of "*Vive le Roi, vivent les Gardes-du-corps!*" The guards, with their hats in the air, turned so as to exhibit the cockade, shouted "*Vive le Roi, vive la Nation!*" shortly afterwards a general discharge of all the muskets took place, in token of joy. The King and Queen set off from Versailles at one o'clock. The Dauphin, Madame, the King's daughter, Monsieur, Madame,[7] Madame Elizabeth, Madame de Tourzel, were

Portrait of Louis XVI

in the carriage; the Princesse de Chimay, and the ladies of the bed-chamber for the week, the King's suite and servants, followed in Court carriages; a hundred deputies in carriages, and the bulk of the Parisian army, closed the procession.

The *poissardes* went before and around the carriage of their Majesties, crying "We shall no longer want bread—we have the baker, the baker's wife, and the baker's boy with us." In the midst of this troop of cannibals the heads of two murdered Body Guards were carried on poles. The monsters, who made trophies of them, conceived the horrid idea of forcing a wigmaker of Sèvres to dress them up, and powder their bloody locks. The unfortunate man who was forced to perform this dreadful work died in consequence of the shock it gave him.[8]

The progress of the procession was so slow that it was near six in the evening when this august family, made prisoners by their own people, arrived at the Hôtel de Ville.[9] Bailly received them there; they were placed upon a throne, just when that of their ancestors had been overthrown. The King spoke in a firm yet gracious manner; he said that he always came with pleasure and confidence among the inhabitants of his good city of Paris. M. Bailly repeated this observation to the representatives of the Commune, who came to address the King; but he forgot the word confidence. The Queen instantly and loudly reminded him of the omission. The King and Queen, their children, and

Madame Elizabeth, retired to the Tuileries. Nothing was ready for their reception there. All the living rooms had been long given up to persons belonging to the Court; they hastily quitted them on that day, leaving their furniture, which was purchased by the Court. The Comtesse de la Marck, sister to the Maréchals de Noailles and de Mouchy, had occupied the apartments now appropriated to the Queen. Monsieur and Madame retired to the Luxembourg.

The Queen had sent for me on the morning of the 6th of October, to leave me and my father-in-law in charge of her most valuable property. She took away only her casket of diamonds. Comte Gouvernet de la Tour-du-Pin, to whom the military government of Versailles was entrusted *pro tempore,* came and gave orders to the national guard, which had taken possession of the apartments, to allow us to remove everything that we should deem necessary for the Queen's accommodation.

I saw her Majesty alone in her private apartments a moment before her departure for Paris; she could hardly speak; tears bedewed her face, to which all the blood in her body seemed to have rushed; she condescended to embrace me, gave her hand to M. Campan[10] to kiss, and said to us, "Come immediately and settle at Paris; I will lodge you at the Tuileries; come, and do not leave me henceforward; faithful servants at moments like these become useful friends; we are lost, dragged away, perhaps to death; when kings become prisoners they are very near it."

I had frequent opportunities during the course of our misfortunes of observing that the people never obey factions with steadiness, but easily escape their control when some cause reminds them of their duty. As soon as the most violent Jacobins had an opportunity of seeing the Queen near at hand, of speaking to her, and of hearing her voice, they became her most zealous partisans; and even when she was in the prison of the Temple several of those who had contributed to place her there perished for having attempted to get her out again.

On the morning of the 7th of October the same women who the day before surrounded the carriage of the august prisoners riding on cannons and uttering the most abusive language, assembled under the Queen's windows upon the terrace of the Château, and desired to see her. Her Majesty appeared. There are always among mobs of this description orators, that is to say, beings who have more assurance than the rest; a woman of this description told the Queen that she must now remove far from her all such courtiers as ruin kings, and that she must love the inhabitants of her good city. The Queen answered that she had loved them at Versailles, and would likewise love them at Paris. "*Yes, yes,*" said another; "*but on the 14th of July you wanted to besiege the city and have it bombarded: and on the 6th of October you wanted to fly to the frontiers.*" The Queen replied affably that they had been told so, and had believed it; that there lay the cause of the unhappiness of the people and of the best of kings. A third addressed a few words to her in German: the Queen told her she did not understand it; that she had become so entirely French as even to have forgotten her mother tongue. This declaration was answered with "*Bravos!*" and clapping of hands; they then desired her to make a compact with them: "Ah," said she, "how can I make a compact with you, since you have no faith in that which my duty points out to me; and which I ought for my own happiness to respect?" They asked her for the ribbons and flowers out of her hat; her

Majesty herself unfastened them and gave them; they were divided among the party, which for above half an hour cried out, without ceasing, "*Marie Antoinette for ever! our good Queen for ever!*"

Two days after the King's arrival at Paris, the city and the national guard sent to request the Queen to appear at the theatre, and prove by her presence and the King's that it was with pleasure they resided in their capital. I introduced the deputation which came to make this request. Her Majesty replied that she should have infinite pleasure in acceding to the invitation of the city of Paris; but that time must be allowed her to soften the recollection of the distressing events which had just occurred, and from which she had suffered too much. She added, that having come into Paris preceded by the heads of the faithful guards who had perished before the door of their sovereign, she could not think that such an entry into the capital ought to be followed by rejoicings, but that the happiness she had always felt in appearing in the midst of the inhabitants of Paris was not effaced from her memory, and that she should enjoy it again as soon as she found herself able to do so.

Their Majesties[11] found some consolation in their private life: from Madame's[12] gentle manners and filial affection, from the accomplishments and vivacity of the little Dauphin, and the attention and tenderness of the pious Princess Elizabeth, they still derived moments of happiness. The young Prince daily gave proofs of sensibility and penetration; he was not yet beyond female care; but a private tutor, Abbé Davout, gave him all the instruction suitable to his age; his memory was highly cultivated, and he recited verses with much grace and feeling.

The day after the arrival of the Court at Paris, terrified at hearing some noise in the gardens of the Tuileries, he threw himself into the arms of the Queen, crying out, "*Grand Dieu, mamma! will it be yesterday over again?*" A few days after this affecting exclamation he went up to the King, and looked at him with a pensive air. The King asked him what he wanted; he answered, that he had some thing very serious to say to him. The King having prevailed on him to explain himself, the young Prince asked why his people, who formerly loved him so well, were all at once angry with him; and what he had done to irritate them so much. His father took him upon his knees, and spoke to him nearly as follows: "I wished, child, to render the people still happier than they were; I wanted money to pay the expenses occasioned by wars. I asked my people for money, as my predecessors have always done; magistrates, composing the Parliament, opposed it, and said that my people alone had a right to consent to it. I assembled the principal inhabitants of every town, whether distinguished by birth, fortune, or talents, at Versailles; that is what is called the *States-General*. When they were assembled they required concessions of me which I could not make, either with due respect for myself or with justice to you, who will be my successor; wicked men inducing the people to rise have occasioned the excesses of the last few days; the people must not be blamed for them."

The Queen made the young Prince clearly comprehend that he ought to treat the commanders of battalions, the officers of the national guard, and all the Parisians who were about him, with affability; the child took great pains to please all those people, and when he had had an opportunity of replying obligingly to the Mayor or members of the Commune he came and whispered in his mother's ear, "*Was that right?*"

He requested M. Bailly to show him the shield of Scipio, which is in the royal library; and M. Bailly, asking him which he preferred, Scipio or Hannibal, the young Prince replied without hesitation that he preferred him who had defended his own country. He gave frequent proofs of ready wit. One day, while the Queen was hearing Madame repeat her exercises in ancient history, the young Princess could not at the moment recollect the name of the Queen of Carthage; the Dauphin was vexed at his sister's want of memory, and though he never spoke to her in the second person singular, he bethought himself of the expedient of saying to her, "But *dis donc* the name of the queen, to mamma; *dis donc* what her name was."

Shortly after the arrival of the King and his family at Paris the Duchesse de Luynes came, in pursuance of the advice of a committee of the Constitutional Assembly, to propose to the Queen a temporary retirement from France, in order to leave the constitution to perfect itself: so that the patriots should not accuse her of influencing the King to oppose it. The Duchess knew how far the scheme of the factious extended, and her attachment to the Queen was the principal cause of the advice she gave her. The Queen perfectly comprehended Duchesse de Luynes' motive; but replied that she would never leave either the King or her son; that if she thought herself alone obnoxious to public hatred she would instantly offer her life as a sacrifice; but that it was the throne which was aimed at, and that, in abandoning the King, she should be merely committing an act of cowardice, since she saw no other advantage in it than that of saving her own life.

One evening, in the month of November 1790, I returned home rather late; I there found the Prince de Poix; he told me he came to request me to assist him in regaining his peace of mind; that at the commencement of the sittings of the National Assembly he had suffered himself to be seduced into the hope of a better order of things; that he blushed for his error, and that he abhorred plans which had already produced such fatal results; that he broke with the reformers for the rest of his life; that he had just given in his resignation as a deputy of the National Assembly; and finally, that he was anxious that the Queen should not sleep in ignorance of his sentiments. I undertook his commission, and acquitted myself of it in the best way I could; but I was totally unsuccessful. The Prince de Poix remained at Court, he there suffered many mortifications, never ceasing to serve the King in the most dangerous commissions with that zeal for which his house has always been distinguished.

When the King, the Queen, and the children were suitably established at the Tuileries, as well as Madame Elizabeth and the Princesse de Lamballe, the Queen resumed her usual habits; she employed her mornings in superintending the education of Madame, who received all her lessons in her presence, and she herself began to work large pieces of tapestry. Her mind was too much occupied with passing events and surrounding dangers to admit of her applying herself to reading; the needle was the only employment which could divert her.[13] She received the Court twice a week before going to mass, and on those days dined in public with the King; she spent the rest of the time with her family and children; she had no concert, and did not go to the play until 1791, after the acceptation of the constitution.[14] The Princesse de Lamballe, however, had some evening parties in her apartments at the Tuileries, which were tolerably brilliant, in consequence of the great number of persons who attended them. The Queen was present at a few of these assemblies; but being soon convinced that her present situation forbade her appearing much in public, she remained at home, and conversed as she sat at work.[15] The sole topic of her discourse was, as may well be supposed, the Revolution. She sought to discover the real opinions of the Parisians respecting her, and how she could have so completely lost the affections of the people, and even of many persons in the higher ranks.[16] She well knew that she ought to impute the whole to the spirit of party, to the hatred of the Duc d'Orléans, and the folly of the French, who desired to have a total change in the constitution; but she was not the less desirous of ascertaining private feelings of all the people in power.

From the very commencement of the Revolution General Luckner indulged in violent sallies against her. Her Majesty, knowing that I was acquainted with a lady who had been long connected with the general, desired me to discover through that channel what was the private motive on which Luckner's hatred against her was founded. On being questioned upon this point, he answered that Maréchal de Ségur had assured him he had proposed him for the command of a camp of observation, but that the Queen had made a bar against his name; and that this *par*, as he called it, in his German accent, he could not forget. The Queen ordered me to repeat this reply to the King myself, and said to him, "See, Sire, whether I was not right in telling you that your ministers, in order to give themselves full scope in the distribution of favours, persuaded the French that I interfered in everything; there was not a single licence given out in the country for the sale of salt or tobacco but the people believed it was given to one of my favourites."—"That is very true," replied the King; "but I find it very difficult to believe that Maréchal de Ségur ever said any such thing to Luckner; he knew too well that you never interfered in the distribution of favours. That Luckner is a good-for-nothing fellow, and Ségur is a brave and honourable man who never uttered such a falsehood, however, you are right; and because you provided for a few dependants, you are most unjustly reported to have disposed of all offices, civil and military."

All the nobility who had not left Paris made a point of presenting themselves assiduously to the King, and there was a considerable influx to the Tuileries. Marks of attachment were exhibited even in external symbols; the women wore enormous bouquets of lilies in their bosoms, and upon their heads, and sometimes even bunches of white ribbon. At the play there were often disputes between the pit and the boxes about removing these ornaments, which the people thought dangerous emblems. National cockades were sold in every corner of Paris; the sentinels stopped all who did not wear them; the young men piqued themselves upon breaking through this regulation, which was in some degree sanctioned by the acquiescence of Louis XVI. Frays took place, which were to be regretted, because they excited a spirit of rebellion. The King adopted conciliatory measures with the Assembly in order to promote tranquillity; the revolutionists were but little disposed to think him sincere; unfortunately the royalists encouraged this incredulity by incessantly repeating that the King was not free, and that all that he did was completely null, and in no way bound him for the time to come. Such was the heat and violence of party spirit that persons the most sincerely attached to the King were not even permitted to use the language of reason, and recommend greater reserve in conversation. People would talk and argue at table without considering that all the servants belonged to the hostile army; and it may duly be said there was as much imprudence and levity in the party assailed as there was cunning, boldness, and perseverance in that which made the attack.

1. For an account of the local effects of this strange general panic, see the *Memoirs of Beugnot,* vol. i, p. 120.

2. Cardinal Loménie de Brienne, the dismissed minister.

3. The day of the attack on the Tuileries, slaughter of the Swiss guard, and suspension of the King from his functions.

4. "It was during the night of the 4th of August," says Rivarol, "that the demagogues of the nobility, wearied with a protracted discussion upon the rights of man, and burning to signalise their zeal, rose all at once, and with loud exclamations called for the last sighs of the feudal system. This demand electrified the Assembly. All heads were frenzied. The younger sons of good families, having nothing, were delighted to sacrifice their too fortunate elders upon the altar of the country; a few country curés felt no less pleasure in renouncing the benefices of others; but what posterity will hardly believe is that the same enthusiasm infected the whole nobility; zeal walked hand in hand with malevolence; they made sacrifice upon sacrifice. And as in Japan the point of honour lies in a man's killing himself in the presence of the person who has offended him, so did the deputies of the nobility vie in striking at themselves and their constituents. The people who were present at this noble conflict increased the intoxication of their new allies by their shouts; and the deputies of the commons, seeing that this memorable night would only afford them profit without honour, consoled their self-love by wondering at what Nobility, grafted upon the Third Estate, could do. They named that night the *night of dupes*; the nobles called it the *night of sacrifices.*" —*Note by the Editor.*

5. Compare this account with the particulars given in the *Memoirs* of Ferrières, Weber, and Bailly.—*Note by the Editor.*

6. The celebrated antechamber at Versailles, lighted by a bull's eye or circular window.

7. Madame, here, the wife of Monsieur le Comte de Provence.

8. Thiers' *History of the French Revolution*, vol. i, p. 85, says-that La Fayette "had given orders for disarming the brigands who carried the heads of two of the Body Guards at the end of their pikes. This horrible trophy was torn from them, and it is not true that it preceded the King's carriage." The Duc d'Orléans in his account says, "In going to Versailles at eight in the morning all seemed quiet till I got to the Bridge of Sèvres, there I met the heads of those unhappy victims of the fury of the people."—*Anecdotes of the Reign of Louis XVI.*

9. The King did not leave Versailles till one o'clock. The Queen, the Dauphin, Madame Royale, Monsieur, Madame Elizabeth, and Madame de Tourzel were in his Majesty's carriage. The hundred deputies in their carriages came next. A detachment of brigands, bearing the heads of the two Body Guards in triumph, formed the advance guard, and set out two hours earlier. These cannibals stopped a moment at Sèvres, and carried their cruelty to the length of forcing an unfortunate hairdresser to dress the gory heads; the bulk of the Parisian army followed them closely. The King's carriage was preceded by the *poissardes*, who had arrived the day before from Paris, and a whole rabble of prostitutes, the vile refuse of their sex, still drunk with fury and wine. Several of them rode astride upon cannons, boasting, in the most

horrible songs, of the crimes they had committed themselves, or seen others commit. Those who were nearest the King's carriage sang ballads, the allusions in which by means of their vulgar gestures they applied to the Queen. Waggons, full of corn and flour, which had been brought into Versailles, formed a train escorted by grenadiers, and surrounded by women and bullies, some armed with pikes, and some carrying long branches of poplar. At some distance this part of the procession had a most singular effect: it looked like a moving forest amidst which shone pike-heads and gun-barrels. In the paroxysms of their brutal joy the women stopped passengers, and pointing to the King's carriage howled in their ears: "Cheer up, friends; we shall no longer be in want of bread: we bring you the baker, the baker's wife, and the little baker's boy." Behind his Majesty's carriage were several of his faithful guards, some on foot, and some on horseback, most of them uncovered, all unarmed, and worn out with hunger and fatigue; the dragoons, the Flanders regiment, the hundred Swiss, and the national guards, preceded, accompanied, or followed the file of carriages. I witnessed this heartrending spectacle; I saw the ominous procession. In the midst of all the tumult, clamour, and singing, interrupted by frequent discharges of musketry, which the hand of a monster or a bungler might so easily render fatal, I saw the Queen preserving most courageous tranquillity of soul, and an air of nobleness and inexpressible dignity, and my eyes were suffused with tears of admiration and grief.—*Memoirs of Bertrand de Molleville.*

10. In the course of that one night my father-in-law declined from perfect health into a languishing condition, which brought him to the grave in September 1791.—*Madame Campan.*

11. On the 19th of October, that is to say, thirteen days after he had taken up his abode at Paris, the King went, on foot and almost alone, to review some detachments of the national guard. After the review, Louis XVI met with a child sweeping the street who asked him for money. The child called the King *M. le Chevalier.* His Majesty gave him six francs. The little sweeper, surprised at receiving so large a sum, cried out, "Oh! I have no change, you will give me money another time." A person who accompanied the monarch said to the child, "Keep it all, my friend, the gentleman is not *chevalier,* he is the eldest of the family."—*Note by the Editor.*

12. Madame, here, the Princess Marie Thérèse, daughter of Marie Antoinette.

13. There was long preserved at Paris, in the house of Mademoiselle Dubuquois, a tapestry-worker, a carpet worked by the Queen and Madame Elizabeth for the large room of her Majesty's ground-floor apartments at the Tuileries. The Empress Josephine saw and admired this carpet, and desired it might be taken care of, in the hope of one day sending it to Madame.—*Madame Campan.*

14. A judgment may be formed of the situation in which the Queen found herself placed during the earlier part of her residence in Paris, from the following letter written by her to the Duchesse de Polignac:—"I shed tears of affection on reading your letters. You talk of my courage: it required much less to go through that dreadful crisis which I had to suffer than is daily necessary to endure our situation, our own griefs, those of our friends, and those of the persons who surround us. This is a heavy weight to sustain; and but for the strong ties by which my heart is bound to my husband, my children, and my friends, I should wish to sink under it. But you bear me up: I ought to sacrifice such feelings to your friendship. But it is I who bring misfortune on you all, and your troubles are on my account." (*History of Marie Antoinette,* by Montjoie.)—*Note by the Editor.*

15. The Queen returned one evening from one of these assemblies very much affected: an English nobleman, who was playing at the same table with her Majesty, ostentatiously displayed an enormous ring in which was a lock of Oliver Cromwell's hair.—*Madame Campan.*

16. This is somewhat inconsistent with the following extract from a letter written by Madame Campan in the latter part of 1789:—"Since the Queen has been at Paris her Court is numerous; she dines three times a week in public with the King; her card-rooms are open on those days. Though the apartments are small, all Paris is to be found there; she converses with the commanders of districts; she finds familiar opportunities of saying obliging things even to the private soldiers, among whom citizens of the first class are to be found, as well as the lowest artisans: mildness, resignation, courage, affability, popularity, everything is made use of, and sincerely, to reconcile people's minds, and promote re-establishment of order. Every one gives the credit due to such affecting attentions; and that is a reparation for the very cruel sufferings that have been endured, for the dreadful risks that have been encountered. Upon the whole, nothing is more prudent, or more consistent, than the conduct of the King and Queen; and therefore the number of their partisans increases daily. They are spoken of with enthusiasm in almost every company. In moments of adversity the Queen has displayed a character generous and elevated; she is an angel of mildness and of goodness; she is a woman particularly gifted with courage. She has given proofs of it in the most critical moments; and Paris, replete with the most seditious opinions—Paris, continually reading the most disgusting libels, could not refuse her the admiration due to bravery, presence of mind, and courtesy. Her bitterest enemies confine themselves to saying, 'It must be confessed that she is a woman of strong mind.'"

ANNEX TO CHAPTER XV

It will be useful to compare the following full and minute narrative with the details of the same events furnished by Madame Campan. The writer, François E. Guignard, Comte de Saint Priest (1735–1821), was at the time Minister of the Interior. He emigrated in 1790, and returned to France in 1814.

ACCOUNT OF THE DEPARTURE OF LOUIS XVI FOR PARIS ON THE 6TH OF OCTOBER 1789, BY M. DE SAINT PRIEST[1]

I commence the narrative of what took place at Versailles or the 5th and 6th of October 1789 by relating the contents of a letter written to me by M. de La Fayette a few days before. I was unable to preserve it, as my papers were burned in France during my emigration: but I have copied it from Bailly's journal printed after his death.

"The Duc de la Rochefoucauld will have informed you of the idea put into the grenadiers' heads of going to Versailles this night. I wrote to you not to be uneasy about it, because I rely upon their confidence in me, in order to divert them from this project. I owe them the justice to say that they had intended to ask my permission to do so, and that many of them thought it was a very proper step, and one ordered by me. Their very slight inclination has been destroyed by four words which I said to them. The affair is off my mind, except as to the idea of the inexhaustible resources of the plotters of mischief. You should not consider this circumstance as anything more than an indication of a design, and by no means as dangerous."

M. de La Fayette did not rely so much as he told me he did upon the obedience of these grenadiers, who had formerly belonged to the French guards, since he posted detachments of the paid national guard at Sèvres and at Saint Cloud to guard those passages of the river Seine. He informed me of it, and ordered the commandant of those posts to apprise me if there should be any occasion.

These arrangements appeared to me insufficient for the safety of the royal residence. I took M. de La Fayette's letter to the Council of State, and made it the ground of a proposal to reinforce Versailles with some regular troops. I observed that M. de La Fayette's letter afforded a plausible reason for it, and offered the means of literally complying with the decree sanctioned by the King, which gave the municipal authorities the first right to direct the action of regular troops. The King, by the advice of his Council, approved of my proposal, and charged me to execute it. I consequently forwarded M. de La Fayette's letter to the municipality of Versailles, after having apprised the Mayor of it. This document was entered in the register, and a resolution was made for demanding a reinforcement of troops for the executive power. Invested with this authority I observed to the Minister at War that the Flanders regiment of foot, being on the march, escorting a convoy of arms destined for the Parisian national guard from Douay to Paris, it would be well to withdraw that body to Versailles as soon as its mission should be fulfilled, in order to prevent, at least in part, the ferment which the arrival of a corps of soldiers of the line in the royal residence would not fail to occasion at Paris and in the National Assembly. This measure was adopted by the Council. Bailly says, in his journal, that he wrote to me respecting the uneasiness it gave the districts of Paris. He adds, that I replied "that the arrival of armed men in the royal residence, announced by circumstantial reports, had determined the King to call in the Flanders regiment, and to take military measures upon the subject."

I am the less able to recollect what I could have meant by that, insomuch as I am certain I never took any step of a military nature beyond desiring the Flanders regiment to march in a military manner, without turning aside from their destination.

It is true that the civic authorities of Paris, in pursuance of my answer to Bailly, had the insolence to send four deputies to Versailles to learn from the King's ministers their reasons for calling in the Flanders regiment. These deputies alighted, at my house, and one of them, M. Dusaulx, a member of the Académie des Belles Lettres, was the spokesman. He interrogated me upon the matter in question in the most imperious manner, informing me that carrying it into execution would be followed by fatal consequences. I answered, with all the moderation I could command, that this demand of a regiment of the line was a natural consequence of the information communicated by a letter from M. de La Fayette. I added that I gave him this answer as from myself; the King not having authorised me to answer a question which his Majesty could never have imagined any one would dare to put to his minister. M. Dusaulx and his three brother deputies returned much dissatisfied. M. de Condorcet was one of them. Some factious members of the National Assembly likewise meddled in the matter. M. Alexandre Lameth and M. Barnave spoke to me, and endeavoured to persuade me to induce the King to revoke his call for this regiment of the line. I answered them in such a manner as to leave them no hope of it. The regiment arrived at Versailles without meeting the smallest obstacle. The conspirators gave the former French guards to understand that they were destined to guard the King in their stead, which was untrue; but that served to make them resume their project of coming to Versailles. I am ignorant whether they had any other view than to take their post again or whether they had already determined to bring the King back to Paris. However that may have been, the explosion soon took place.

The Body Guards gave a regimental entertainment to the officers of the Flanders regiment, and invited some *sous-officiers* and soldiers, as well as some of the national guards of Versailles. It was an old custom for the military corps quartered at any place to pay this compliment to others which arrived there. Upon such occasions many healths will, of course, be drunk, and the repasts must of necessity be always noisy; and this was the case with the present. The regimental band had been invited, and the air, beginning "*O Richard! o mon Roi!*" from the play of Richard Cœur de Lion, excited the liveliest enthusiasm. It was thought right to go and fetch the Queen to increase the fervour. And her Majesty came with the Dauphin, which prompted fresh acclamation. When the company left the dining-hall a few soldiers, perhaps affected by wine, appeared in the marble court below the apartments of the King, who had returned from hunting. Shouts of "*Vive le Roi!*" were heard, and one of the soldiers, with the assistance of his comrades, climbed up on the outside, as high as the balcony of the chamber of his Majesty, who did not show himself. I was in my closet, and I sent to know what occasioned the noise. I have, however, no reason to believe that the national cockade was trampled under foot; and it is the less likely because the King wore it at that time, and it would have been a want of respect to his Majesty himself. It was a lie invented to irritate the minds of the Parisian national guard.

The Comte d'Estaing commanded the national guard of Versailles at that time. The King gave him also the command of all the regular troops there. They consisted of the two battalions of the Flanders regiment, 200 Chasseurs des Évêchés, 800 mounted Body Guards, and the Swiss guard on duty. On the 5th of October, at about eleven in the morning, one of my *valets de chambre* came from Paris to apprise me that the Parisian national guard, both paid and unpaid, accompanied by a numerous concourse of men and women, had set out for Versailles. The King was hunting on the heights of Meudon, and I wrote to tell him of it. His Majesty returned promptly, and ordered that the Council of State should be summoned for half-past three. The Council then consisted of eight ministers: the Maréchal de Beauvau, the Archbishop of Vienne, the Archbishop of Bordeaux, Keepers of the Seals, M. Necker, Minister of the Finances, and the Comtes de Montmorin, de la Luzerne, de la Tour-du-Pin, and de Saint Priest, Secretaries of State.

I laid before the Council the information I had received, and which had been subsequently confirmed by several other reports. I represented the danger that would attend the waiting for this multitude at Versailles, and I proposed measures to be pursued on this emergency. They were, that detachments should be sent to guard the bridges across the Seine; a battalion of the Flanders regiment for that at Sèvres; another for that at Saint Cloud; and the Swiss guard for that at Neuilly; and that the King should send the Queen and the royal family to Rambouillet, where the chasseurs of the regiment of Lorraine were; while his Majesty himself should go and meet the Parisians with the 200 Chasseurs des Évêchés, and his 800 Body Guards. The thousand horse being drawn up in order of battle beyond the bridge of Sèvres, the King was to order the Parisian band to retire, and, in case they should disobey, was to make a few charges of cavalry to endeavour to disperse them. Then, if this should be unsuccessful, the King would have time to regain Versailles at the head of his troops, and march immediately to Rambouillet. My advice was approved by the Maréchal de Beauvau, M. de la Luzerne, and M. de la Tour-du-Pin; and warmly opposed by M. Necker, seconded by Comte de Montmorin, and the Archbishops of Vienne and Bordeaux. M. Necker insisted that there was no danger in suffering the multitude to come to Versailles, where its object was probably only to present some petition to the King; and, should the worst happen, if his Majesty should find it necessary to reside in Paris, he would be venerated and respected there by his people, who adored him.

I replied by opposing to this reasoning the origin and the features of this proceeding, which completely contradicted the alleged loyalty of the people of Paris.

The King did not declare the course he should pursue; he broke up the Council, and we knew that he went to consult the Queen. She declared that she would not, upon any consideration, separate herself from him and her children; which rendered the execution of the measure I had proposed impossible. Thus perplexed, we did nothing but wait. However, I sent an order to the Swiss barracks at Courbevoie, that all belonging to the regiment of guards who were then there should immediately repair to Versailles, which was promptly done.

The National Assembly was sitting when information of the march of the Parisians was given to it by one of the deputies who came from Paris. A certain number of the members were no strangers to this movement. It appears that Mirabeau wished to avail himself of it to raise the Duc d'Orléans to the throne. Mounier, who presided over the National Assembly, rejected the idea with horror: "*My good man,*" said Mirabeau to him, "*what difference will it make to you to have Louis XVII for your King instead of Louis XVI?*" [The Duc d'Orléans was baptized Louis.]

Mounier, seeing the urgency of the case, proposed that the Assembly should declare itself permanent and inseparable from his Majesty, which was decreed. Mirabeau then insisted that the deputation which should carry up this decree to the King should demand his sanction to some which had remained in arrear; among others that of the rights of man, in which some alterations were desired. But existing circumstances carried the King's sanction. A few female citizens then presented themselves to offer civic gifts; it seems they were sent to keep the Assembly employed until the arrival of the Parisians. They were admitted, and the scene was ridiculous enough.

The Comte d'Estaing had ordered the mounted Body Guards to horse, and stationed them in the Place d'Armes, in advance of the post of the French guard, which was occupied by a detachment of the national guard of Versailles, commanded by a man named Lecointre, a draper, and of very bad disposition. He was displeased that the

Body Guards left his soldiers in the second line, and tried to raise some quarrel in order to dislodge them. For that purpose he sent persons who slipped between the ranks of the soldiers to annoy the horses. M. de Savonnières, an officer of the Body Guards, while giving chase to these wretches, received a musket shot from the national guard, of which he died. A short time afterwards M. d'Estaing, who had received a secret order from the King not to permit any violence, sent the Body Guards back to their hotel. They were saluted as they went off by a few musket shots from the national guard of Versailles, by which some men and horses were wounded. When they reached their hotel they found it pillaged by the populace of Versailles, which made them return to their former position.

The Flanders regiment was under arms at the end of the avenue of Versailles. Mirabeau and some other deputies mingled among the ranks of the soldiery; it is asserted that they distributed money to them. The soldiers dispersed themselves in the public-houses of the town, and reassembled in the evening, when they were shut up in the King's stables.

As to the Body Guards, M. d'Estaing knew not what to do beyond bringing them into the courtyard of the ministers, and shutting the *grilles*. Thence they proceeded to the terrace of the Château, then to Trianon, and lastly to Rambouillet.

I could not refrain from expressing to M. d'Estaing when he came to the King my astonishment at not seeing him make any military disposition. "*Sir,*" replied he, "*I await the orders of the King*" (who did not open his mouth). "*When the King gives no orders,*" pursued I, "*a general should decide for himself in a soldier-like manner.*" This observation remained unanswered. About seven o'clock in the evening a kind of advanced guard from Paris, consisting of ill-armed men and women of the rabble, arrived at the gates of the minister's courtyard, which those within refused to open. The mob then demanded that a few women should be permitted to go and present a supplication to the King. His Majesty ordered that six should be let in, and desired me to go into the *Œil de Bœuf* and there hear what they had to say. I accordingly went. One of these women told me that a famine existed in Paris, and that the people came to ask bread of his Majesty. I answered that the King had taken all the steps which could depend on him for preventing the injurious effects of the failure in the last harvest; and I added that calamities of this nature ought to be borne with patience, as drought was borne when there was a dearth of rain. I dismissed the women, telling them to return to Paris, and to assure their fellow-citizens of the King's affection for the people of his capital. It was then that the Marquis de Favras, whom I did not know at the time, proposed to me to mount a number of gentlemen on horses from the King's stables; and that they should meet the Parisians, and force them to retreat. I answered that the King's horses not being trained to the kind of service which he proposed would be but ill adapted to it, and would only endanger their riders without answering any purpose. I returned to the King to give him an account of my conversation with the women. Shortly afterwards the King assembled the Council; it was dark; we were scarcely seated when an *aide-de-camp* of M. de La Fayette, named Villars, brought me a letter written to me by that general from near Auteuil, half a league from Paris: he informed me that he was on his march with the national guard of Paris, both paid and unpaid, and a part of the people of Paris, who came to make remonstrances to the King. He begged me to assure his Majesty that he vouched for it that no disorder would take place. Notwithstanding this tone of confidence, it is certain that La Fayette had been dragged to Versailles against his will at the moment when he endeavoured to stop the former French guards, who were already on their march upon the Pont Royal. It is not the less true that he had become familiar with the idea of marching to Versailles since the first time he had written to me about it. He had even spoken to me on the subject, believing it at that time preferable that the King should reside at Paris; but undoubtedly he would have preferred the adoption of some other method of taking his Majesty thither.

After I had read M. de La Fayette's letter to the Council I recapitulated my advice of the afternoon, observing, however, that it was now impossible to resort to the measures I had then proposed; but that it was of importance that the King, with his family and regular troops, should set off for Rambouillet. The contest between M. Necker and myself now grew warmer than upon the former occasion. I explained the risks which the King and his family would incur if they did not avoid them by departing. I dwelt upon the advantages that would be gained by quitting Versailles for Rambouillet, and I concluded by saying to the King, "*Sire, if you are taken to Paris to-morrow your crown is lost!*" The King was shaken, and he arose to go and speak to the Queen, who this time consented to the departure. M. Necker says in one of his works: "*He alone* [the King] *was to determine, and he determined to remain at Versailles. Out of a considerable number of persons, one alone, so far as I remember, was for the departure and without any modification.*"

It is probably to myself that M. Necker attributes this isolated opinion, but his memory has failed him, for it is a fact that M. de Beauvau, M. de la Luzerne, and M. de la Tour-du-Pin were always of my opinion.

M. Necker passes over in silence the order which the King gave me on re-entering the Council chamber, to have his carriages got ready, which broke up the Council. I told his Majesty that I would execute his orders, send off his wife and children to Rambouillet, and proceed thither myself, to be ready to receive him upon his arrival. I deputed the Chevalier de Cubières, equerry in charge of the stable, to carry the order for getting the carriages ready to the stables, and I went home to make my own arrangements. After regulating everything with Madame de Saint Priest for her departure, I got on horseback, wrapped up in my cloak that I might not be observed, and succeeded in keeping myself concealed. I had scarcely proceeded half a league when my wife's carriage overtook me. She informed me that M. de Montmorin had sent her word that the King was no longer willing to set out; "but," added she, "I would not countermand the arrangements you had made." I begged she would proceed on her journey, most happy in the reflection that she and my children would be far from the scene which I then anticipated would take place on the morrow. As for myself, I retraced my steps and re-entered by one of the park gates, where I dismissed my horses, and went through the gardens to the King's apartments. There I found M. de La Fayette, who had just arrived. He personally confirmed to his Majesty all the assurances which he had by letter desired me to give him, and went to bed extremely fatigued by the events of the day, without making any fresh arrangement for the safety of the Château. The King as he withdrew gave orders to the captain of his guards to prohibit his subalterns from any violence.

I never knew perfectly what made the King change his mind: respecting his departure. I returned home in great anxiety, and threw myself, dressed as I was, upon my bed. It was impossible for me to close my eyes on account of the noise made by the mob from Paris, with which the streets of Versailles were filled. At daybreak I went into my closet, the windows of which commanded the courtyard of the ministers. At that very moment I saw the gates open, and a frenzied multitude, armed with pikes and bludgeons, and some of them with sabres and muskets, rush in and run with the utmost speed to the courtyard of the Princes, where the staircase leading to the apartments of their Majesties is situated. They all passed below my windows without seeing me. I waited about a quarter of an hour, and saw a considerable number of them bringing back a dozen of the Body Guards, whom they had seized in the Queen's guard-room, and were going to massacre in the Place d'Armes. Fortunately for these unhappy men M. de La Fayette appeared with some soldiers of the guards, whom he employed to drive off the assailants. It is known that they immediately went up to the Queen's apartments; that the Body Guard suffered them to enter their guard-room without opposition, in pursuance of the King's orders; that, however, those who stood sentinels at the door of the Queen's antechamber made some resistance, and gave the footmen on duty inside time to awaken the Queen and barricade the door with trunks and chairs; and that her Majesty, alarmed by the noise, took refuge in the King's rooms through the communication between their apartments. The rioters then made their way in, and finding their prey escaped, committed no violence in the apartments. But they had assassinated two of the Body Guards, and wounded many others in the guard-room, which was the result of the King's order of the preceding day to make no resistance. M. de La Fayette went up to the King's rooms, and found the door of the antechamber, called the *Œil de Bœuf*, closed and barricaded. He parleyed with the Body Guards who had taken refuge there to preserve his Majesty's apartments. Upon M. de Lafayette's assurances the door was opened. He then stationed there some grenadiers, who, in conjunction with the Body Guards, kept that entry closed until the King's departure for Paris. The door by which the King generally went out to get into his carriage remained free; the people of Paris were not aware of its existence. I wrapped myself in a greatcoat to make my way through the crowd which filled the courtyard, and went up to the King's apartments. I found him with the Queen and the Dauphin in the balcony of his bedroom, protected by M. de La Fayette, who harangued the rabble from time to time; but all his speeches could not stop their shouts of "*To Paris, to Paris!*" There were even a few musket-shots fired from the courtyard, which fortunately struck nobody. The King occasionally withdrew into his room to sit down and rest himself; he was in a state of stupefaction, which it is difficult to describe, or even to imagine. I accosted him repeatedly, and represented to him the delay in yielding to the wishes of the mob was useless and dangerous; that it was necessary he should promise to go to Paris; and that this was the only way of getting rid of these savages, who might the very next moment proceed to the utmost extremities, to which there were not wanting persons to excite them. To all this the King did not answer one single word. The Queen, who was present, said to me, "*Ah! Monsieur de Saint Priest, why did we not go away last night!*" I could not refrain from replying, "*It was no fault of mine.*"—"*I know that well,*" answered she. These remarks proved to me that she had no share in his Majesty's change of determination. He made up his mind at last, about eleven o'clock, to promise to go to Paris. Some cries of "*Vive le Roi!*" were then heard, and the mob began to quit the courtyards and take the road to the capital. Care had been taken to send cart-loads of bread from Paris during the night to feed the multitude. I left the King in order to be at the Tuileries before him; and as I took the Saint Cloud road, I met with no obstacle. I dined with the Ambassador of the Two Sicilies, and proceeded to the Tuileries, ready for the arrival of their Majesties. I had not calculated that their unfortunate journey, which was a real martyrdom, would have occupied so much time. Their carriage was preceded by the heads of two murdered Body Guards, carried upon pikes. The carriage was surrounded by ill-looking fellows, who contemplated the royal personages with a brutal curiosity. A few of the Body Guards on foot and unarmed, protected by the former French guards, followed dejectedly; and to complete the climax, after six or seven hours spent in travelling from Versailles to Paris, their Majesties were led to the Hôtel de Ville, as if to make the *amende honorable*. I know not who ordered this. The King ascended the Hôtel de Ville, and said that he came freely to reside in his capital. As he spoke in a low tone of voice, "Tell them, then," said the Queen, "that the King comes freely to reside in his capital." "You are more fortunate than if I had uttered it," said Bailly; "since the Queen herself has given you this favourable assurance." This was a falsehood, in which his Majesty was obviously contradicted by facts; never had he acted less freely. It was near ten at night when the King reached the Tuileries. As he got out of his carriage I told him that if I had known he was going to the Hôtel de Ville I would have waited for him there. "*I did not know it myself,*" replied the King, in a tone of dejection.

On the morrow the Body Guards, who had passed the night upon benches in the Château of the Tuileries, were dismissed. M. de La Fayette filled up all the posts with the national guard of Paris, which was commanded by himself, and hence he became the keeper of the royal family.

When I reflect how many favourable consequences would have resulted from a more steadfast resolution to quit Versailles, I feel myself, even at this day, filled with regret. In the first place, M. de Villars, M. de La Fayette's *aide-de-camp*, who brought me the letter from the latter to Versailles on the 5th of October, told me that he had been sent by his general to the bridge of Sèvres to know whether it was defended; and that if it had been, he would have retreated. Secondly, Madame de Saint Priest, on her arrival at Rambouillet, saw there a deputation from the city of Chartres, which is in its neighbourhood; they came in the name of their fellow-citizens to entreat his Majesty to make their city his asylum; to assure him they abhorred the insolence of the Parisians, and that they would lay down their lives and property in support of his Majesty's authority—an example which would infallibly have been followed by the other towns, and in particular by Orléans, which was wholly devoted to the royal cause. The Mayor of Rambouillet has since assured me that the request of the deputation from Chartres was transcribed into the registers of the municipality of Rambouillet. Thirdly, the National Assembly, under the Presidency of Mounier, a man of integrity, who had the welfare of the State at heart, had declared itself inseparable from his Majesty. It would therefore have followed him to Rambouillet and Chartres. It is probable, moreover, that the factious leaders would not have ventured there; that the National Assembly, purified by their absence, would have united itself to the King, whose intentions were pure; and that useful reforms would have resulted without an overthrow of the monarchy. Fourthly, and lastly, if it had been necessary to come to extremities for the reduction of Paris, what advantages would not the royal party have possessed over that city, which at that time subsisted only upon the corn carried up the Seine! By stopping the convoys at Pontoise, Paris would have starved. Besides, the King would easily have collected round him 10,000 men in four days, and 40,000 in five, secure of being able to concentrate still more considerable forces if circumstances should require it. The army under M. de Bouillé in his district of Metz, would have been ready to march in a very short time; and, under such a general, the insurgents would speedily have been subdued.[2]

Such is the correct narrative which I determined to give as an eye-witness, and even as an actor, on the days of the 5th and 6th of October; it may one day contribute to the history of that remarkable period which, by its consequences, has perhaps decided the fate of the universe.

1. We recommend the reader to collate this interesting account with those contained in the *Memoirs* of Ferrières, Dusaulx, and Bailly, and the explanations annexed to Weber's book.— *Note by the Editor.*

2. The Marquis de Bouillé writes of this period: "During these transactions I resided at Metz, hated by the people, but having the most perfect reliance on my army, between which and the inhabitants of the town I maintained a constant jealousy, inspiring it at the same time with contempt for the lower class of the people" (p. 98). It was only in July 1790 that the troops of De Bouillé became untrustworthy, see *Bouillé*, p. 167.

Affair of Favras—His prosecution and death—His children are imprudently presented to the Queen—Plan laid for carrying off the royal family—Singular letter from the Empress Catherine to Louis XVI—The Queen is unwilling to owe the re-establishment of the throne to the émigrés—Death of the Emperor Joseph II—First negotiation between the Court and Mirabeau—Louis XVI and his family inhabit Saint Cloud—New plans for escaping

In February 1790 the affair of the unfortunate Favras gave the Court much uneasiness; this individual had conceived the scheme of carrying off the King, and effecting what was then called a counter-revolution. Monsieur, probably out of mere benevolence, gave him some money, and thence arose a report that he thereby wished to favour the execution of the enterprise. The step taken by Monsieur in going to the Hôtel de Ville to explain himself on this matter was unknown to the Queen; it is more than probable that the King was acquainted with it. When judgment was pronounced upon M. de Favras the Queen did not conceal from me her fears about the confessions of the unfortunate man in his last moments.

I sent a confidential person to the Hôtel de Ville; she came to inform the Queen that the condemned had demanded to be taken from Notre Dame to the Hôtel de Ville to make a final declaration, and give some particulars verifying it. These particulars compromised nobody; Favras corrected his last will after writing it, and went to the scaffold with heroic courage and coolness. The judge who read his condemnation to him told him that his life was a sacrifice which he owed to public tranquillity. It was asserted at the time that Favras was given up as a victim in order to satisfy the people and save the Baron de Besenval, who was a prisoner in the Abbaye.[1]

On the morning of the Sunday following this execution, M. de la Villeurnoy[2] came to my house to tell me that he was going that day to the public dinner of the King and Queen to present Madame Favras and her son, both of them in mourning for the brave Frenchman who fell a sacrifice for his King; and that all the royalists expected to see the Queen load the unfortunate family with favours. I did all that lay in my power to prevent this proceeding: I foresaw the effect it would have upon the Queen's feeling heart, and the painful constraint she would experience, having the horrible Santerre, the commandant of a battalion of the Parisian guard, behind her chair during dinner-time. I could not make M. de la Villeurnoy comprehend my argument; the Queen was gone to mass, surrounded by her whole Court, and I had not even means of apprising her of his intention.

When dinner was over I heard a knocking at the door of my apartment, which opened into the corridor next that of the Queen; it was herself. She asked me if there was anybody with me; I was alone; she threw herself into an arm-chair, and told me she came to weep with me over the foolish conduct of the ultras of the King's party. "We must fall," said she, "attacked as we are by men who possess every talent and shrink from no crime, while we are defended only by those who are no doubt very estimable, but have no adequate idea of our situation. They have exposed me to the animosity of both parties by presenting the widow and son of Favras to me. Were I free to act as I wish I should take the child of the man who has just sacrificed himself for us and place him at table between the King and myself, but surrounded by the assassins who have destroyed his father, I did not dare even to cast my eyes upon him. The royalists will blame me for not having appeared interested in this poor child; the revolutionists will be enraged at the idea that his presentation should have been thought agreeable to me." However, the Queen added that she knew Madame de Favras was in want, and that she desired me to send her next day, through a person who could be relied on, a few rouleaus of fifty *louis*, and to direct that she should be assured her Majesty would always watch over the fortunes of herself and her son.

In the month of March following I had an opportunity of ascertaining the King's sentiments respecting the schemes which were continually proposed to him for making his escape. One night at about ten o'clock Comte d'Inisdal, who was deputed by the nobility, came to request that I would see him in private, as he had an important matter to communicate to me. He told me that on that very night the King was to be carried off; that the section of the national guard that day commanded by M. Aumont,[3] was gained over, and that sets of horses, furnished by some good royalists, were placed in relays at suitable distances; that he had just left a party of nobles assembled for the execution of this scheme, and that he had been sent to me that I might, through the medium of the Queen, obtain the King's positive consent to it before midnight; that the King was aware of their plan, but that his Majesty never would speak decidedly, and that it was necessary he should consent to the undertaking. I greatly displeased Comte d'Inisdal by expressing my astonishment that the nobility at the moment of the execution of so important a project should send to me, the Queen's first woman, to obtain a consent which ought to have been the basis of any well-concerted scheme. I told him, also, that it would be impossible for me to go at that time to the Queen's apartments without exciting the attention of the people in the antechambers; that the King was at cards with the Queen and his family, and that I never broke in upon their privacy unless I was called for. I added, however, that M. Campan could enter without being called; and if the Count chose to give him his confidence he might rely upon him. My father-in-law, to whom Comte d'Inisdal repeated what he had said to me, took the commission upon himself, and went to the Queen's apartments. The King was playing at whist with the Queen, Monsieur, and Madame; Madame Elizabeth was kneeling on a stool near the table. M. Campan informed the Queen of what had been communicated to me; nobody uttered a word. The Queen broke silence and said to the King, "Do you hear, Sire, what Campan says to us?"—"Yes, I hear," said the King, and continued his game. Monsieur, who was in the habit of introducing passages from plays into his conversation, said to my father-in-law, "M. Campan, that pretty little couplet again, if you please;" and pressed the King to reply. At length the Queen said, "But something must be said to Campan." The King then spoke to my father-in-law in these words "*Tell M. d'Inisdal that I cannot consent to be carried off!*" The Queen enjoined M. Campan to take care and report this answer faithfully. "*You understand,*" added she, "*the King cannot consent to be carried off.*" Comte d'Inisdal was very much dissatisfied with the King's answer, and went out, saying, "I understand; he wishes to throw all the blame, beforehand, upon those who are to devote themselves for him." He went away, and I thought the enterprise would be abandoned. However, the Queen remained alone with me till midnight, preparing her cases of valuables, and ordered me not to go to bed. She imagined the King's answer would be understood as a tacit consent, and merely a refusal to participate in the design. I do not know what passed in the King's apartments during the night; but I occasionally looked out at the windows: I saw the garden clear; I heard no noise in the palace, and day at length confirmed my opinion that the project had been given up. "*We must, however, fly,*" said the Queen to me shortly afterwards: "*who knows how far the factious may go? The danger increases every day.*"⁴ This Princess received advice and memorials from all quarters. Rivarol addressed several to her, which I read to her. They were full of ingenious observations; but the Queen did not find that they contained anything of essential service under the circumstances in which the royal family was placed. Comte du Moustier also sent memorials and plans of conduct. I remember that in one of his writings he said to the King, "Read *Telamachus* again, Sire; in that book which delighted your Majesty in infancy you will find the first seeds of those principles which, erroneously followed up by men of ardent imaginations, are bringing on the explosion we expect every moment." I read so many of these memorials that I could hardly give a faithful account of them, and I am determined to note in this work no other events than such as I witnessed; no other words than such as (notwithstanding the lapse of time) still in some measure vibrate in my ears.

Comte de Ségur,⁵ on his return from Russia, was employed some time by the Queen, and had a certain degree of influence over her; but that did not last long. Comte Augustus de la Marck likewise endeavoured to negotiate for the King's advantage with the leaders of the factious. M. de Fontanges, Archbishop of Toulouse, possessed also the Queen's confidence; but none of the endeavours which were made at home produced any beneficial result. The Empress Catherine II also conveyed her opinion upon the situation of Louis XVI to the Queen, and her Majesty made me read a few lines in the Empress's own handwriting, which concluded with these words: "Kings ought to proceed in their career undisturbed by the cries of the people, as the moon pursues her course unimpeded by the howling of dogs." This maxim of the despotic sovereign of Russia was very inapplicable to the situation of a captive King.

Meanwhile the revolutionary party followed up its audacious enterprise in a determined manner, without meeting any opposition. The advice from without, as well as from Coblentz as from Vienna, made various impressions upon the members of the royal family, and those cabinets were not in accordance with each other. I often had reason to infer from what the Queen said to me that she thought the King, by leaving all the honour of restoring order to the Coblentz party,⁶ would, on the return of the emigrants, be put under a kind of guardianship which would increase his own misfortunes. She frequently said to me, "If the emigrants succeed, they will give the law for a long time; it will be impossible to refuse them anything: to owe the Crown to them would be contracting too great an obligation." It always appeared to me that she wished her own family to counterbalance the claims of the emigrants by disinterested services. She was fearful of M. de Calonne, and with good reason. She had proof that this minister was her bitterest enemy, and that he made use of the most criminal means in order to blacken her reputation. I can testify that I have seen in the hands of the Queen a manuscript copy of the infamous memoirs of the woman De Lamotte, which had been brought to her from London, and in which all those passages where a total ignorance of the customs of Courts had occasioned that wretched woman to make blunders which would have been too palpable, were corrected in M. de Calonne's own handwriting.

The two King's Guards who were wounded at her Majesty's door on the 6th of October were M. du Repaire and M. de Miomandre de Sainte Marie; on the dreadful night of the 6th of October the latter took the post of the former the moment he became incapable of maintaining it.

M. de Miomandre was at Paris, living on terms of friendship with another of the guards, who, on the same day, received a gunshot wound from the brigands in another part of the Château. These two officers, who were attended and cured together at the infirmary of Versailles,[7] were almost constant companions; they were recognised at the Palais Royal, and insulted. The Queen thought it necessary for them to quit Paris. She desired me to write to M. de Miomandre de Sainte Marie, and tell him to come to me at eight o'clock in the evening; and then to communicate to him her wish to hear of his being in safety; and ordered me, when he had made up his mind to go, to tell him in her name that gold could not repay such a service as he had rendered; that she hoped some day to be in sufficiently happy circumstances to recompense him as she ought; but that for the present her offer of money was only that of a sister to a brother situated as she then was, and that she requested he would take whatever might be necessary to discharge his debts at Paris and defray the expenses of his journey. She told me also to desire he would bring his friend Bertrand with him, and to make him the same offer.

The two Guards came at the appointed hour, and accepted, I think, each one or two hundred *louis*. A moment afterwards the Queen opened my door; she was accompanied by the King and Madame Elizabeth; the King stood with his back against the fireplace; the Queen sat down upon a sofa and Madame Elizabeth sat near her; I placed myself behind the Queen, and the two Guards stood facing the King. The Queen told them that the King wished to see before they went away two of the brave men who had afforded him the strongest proofs of courage and attachment. Miomandre said all that the Queen's affecting observations were calculated to inspire. Madame Elizabeth spoke of the King's gratitude; the Queen resumed the subject of their speedy departure, urging the necessity of it; the King was silent; but his emotion was evident, and his eyes were suffused with tears. The Queen rose, the King went out, and Madame Elizabeth followed him; the Queen stopped and said to me, in the recess of a window, "I am sorry

I brought the King here! I am sure Elizabeth thinks with me; if the King had but given utterance to a fourth part of what he thinks of those brave men they would have been in ecstasies; but he cannot overcome his diffidence."

The Emperor Joseph died about this time. The Queen's grief was not excessive; that brother of whom she had been so proud, and whom she had loved so tenderly, had probably suffered greatly in her opinion; she reproached him sometimes, though with moderation, for having adopted several of the principles of the new philosophy, and perhaps she knew that he looked upon our troubles with the eye of the sovereign of Germany rather than that of the brother of the Queen of France.[8]

Mirabeau had not lost the hope of becoming the last resource of the oppressed Court; and at this time some communications passed between the Queen and him. The question was about an office to be conferred upon him. This transpired, and it must have been about this period that the Assembly decreed that no deputy could hold an office as a minister of the King until the expiration of two years after the cessation of his legislative functions. I know that the Queen was much hurt at this decision, and considered that the Court had lost a promising opening.[9]

The Palace of the Tuileries was a very disagreeable residence during the summer, which made the Queen wish to go to Saint Cloud. The removal was decided on without any opposition; the national guard of Paris followed the Court thither. At this period new plans of escape were presented; nothing would have been more easy than to execute them. The King had obtained leave (!) to go out without guards, and to be accompanied only by an *aide-de camp* of M. de La Fayette. The Queen also had one on duty with her, and so had the Dauphin. The King and Queen often went out at four in the afternoon, and did not return until eight or nine.

I will relate one of the plans of emigration which the Queen communicated to me, the success of which seemed infallible. The royal family were to meet in a wood four leagues from Saint Cloud; some persons who could be fully relied on were to accompany the King, who was always followed by his equerries and pages; the Queen was to join him with her daughter and Madame Elizabeth: these Princesses, as well as the Queen, had equerries and pages, of whose fidelity no doubt could be entertained. The Dauphin likewise was to be at the place of rendezvous with Madame de Tourzel;[10] a large berlin and a chaise for the attendants were sufficient for the whole family; the *aides-de-camp* were to have been gained over or mastered. The King was to leave a letter for the President of the National Assembly on his bureau at Saint Cloud. The people in the service of the King and Queen would have waited until nine in the evening without anxiety, because the family sometimes did not return until that hour. The letter could not be forwarded to Paris until ten o'clock at the earliest. The Assembly would not then be sitting; the President must have been sought for at his own house or elsewhere; it would have been midnight before the Assembly could have been summoned and couriers sent off to have the royal family stopped; but the latter would have been six or seven hours in advance, as they would have started at six leagues' distance from Paris; and at this period travelling was not yet impeded in France. The Queen approved of this plan; but I did not venture to interrogate her, and I even thought if it was put in execution she would leave me in ignorance of it. One evening in the month of June the people of the Château, finding the King did not return by nine o'clock, were walking about the courtyards in a state of great anxiety. I thought the family was gone, and I could scarcely breathe amidst the confusion of my good wishes, when I heard the sound of the carriages.¹¹ I confessed to the Queen that I thought she had set off; she told me she must wait until Mesdames the King's aunts had quitted France, and afterwards see whether the plan agreed with those formed abroad.

1. Favras (Thomas Mahy, Marquis de), born at Blois in 1745, entered the service first in the corps of *mousquetaires*, and made the campaign in 1761 with them; he was afterwards captain and adjutant of Belsunce's regiment, and subsequently lieutenant of the Swiss guard of Monsieur, the King's brother; he resigned that commission in 1775 to go to Vienna, where his wife was acknowledged the only and legitimate daughter of the Prince d'Anhalt-Schauenbourg. He commanded a legion in Holland on the insurrection against the Stadtholder in 1787. Possessing a warm imagination and a head fertile in expedients, Favras always had something to propose. He presented a great number of plans on the subject of finance; and at the breaking out of the Revolution he tendered some upon political measures, which rendered him an object of suspicion to the revolutionary party. Favras was accused in the month of December 1789 of having conspired against the Revolution. Having been arrested by order of the committee of inquiry of the National Assembly, he was transferred to the Châtelet, where he defended himself with much coolness and presence of mind, repelling the accusations brought against him by Morel, Turcati, and Marquié, with considerable force. These witnesses declared he had imparted his plan to them; it was to be carried into execution by 12,000 Swiss and 12,000 Germans, who were to be assembled at Montargis, thence to march upon Paris, carry off the King, and assassinate Bailly, La Fayette, and Necker. The greater number of these charges he denied, and declared that the rest related only to the levy of a troop intended to favour the Revolution preparing in Brabant. The judge having refused to disclose who had denounced him, he complained to the Assembly, which passed to the order of the day. His death was obviously inevitable. During the whole time of the proceedings the populace never ceased threatening the judges and shouting, "*A la lanterne!*" It was even necessary to keep numerous troops and artillery constantly ready to act in the courtyard of the Châtelet. The judges, who had just acquitted M. de Besenval in an affair nearly similar, doubtless dreaded the effects of this fury. When they refused to hear Favras' witnesses in exculpation, he compared them to the tribunal of the Inquisition. The principal charge against him was founded on a letter from M. de Foucault, asking him, "Where are your troops? In which direction will they enter Paris? I should like to be employed among them." Favras was condemned to make the *amende honorable* in front of the cathedral, and to be hanged at the Place de Grève. He heard this sentence with wonderful calmness, and said to his judges, "I pity you much if the testimony of two men is sufficient to induce you to condemn." The judge having said to him, "I have no other consolation to hold out to you than that which religion affords," he replied nobly, "My greatest consolation is that which I derive from my innocence."—*Biographie Universelle, Ancienne et Moderne*, vol. xiv, p. 221.

2. M. de la Villeurnoy, master of the requests, was deported to Sinamary on the 18th Fructidor, 4th September 1797—the *coup d'état* made by the Directory against the royalist party—and there died.—*Madame Campan*.

3. A brother of the Duc de Villequier, who had joined the revolutionary party; a man of no weight or respectability, who desired he might be called *Jacques Aumont*; a far different man from his brave brother, who always proved himself entirely devoted to the cause of his King.—*Madame Campan.*

4. The disturbances of the 13th of April 1790, occasioned by the warmth of the discussions upon Dom Gerle's imprudent motion in the National Assembly, having afforded room for apprehension that the enemies of the country would endeavour to carry off the King from the capital, M. de La Fayette promised to keep watch, and told Louis XVI that if he saw any alarming movement among the disaffected he would give him notice of it by the discharge of a cannon from Henri IV's battery on the Pont Neuf. On the same night a few casual discharges of musquetry were heard from the terrace of the Tuileries. The King, deceived by the noise, flew to the Queen's apartments, he did not find her; he ran to the Dauphin's room, where he found the Queen holding her son in her arms. "Madame," said the King to her, "I have been seeking you; and you have made me uneasy." The Queen, showing her son, said to him, "I was at my post."—*Anecdotes of the Reign of Louis XVI.*

5. Louis Philippe, Comte de Ségur (1753–1830), son of the Maréchal and Minister of War, Philippe Henri, Marquis de Ségur.

6. The Princes and the chief of the emigrant nobility assembled at Coblentz, and the name was used to designate the reactionary party.

7. A considerable number of the Body Guards, who were wounded on the 6th of October, betook themselves to the infirmary at Versailles. The brigands wanted to make their way into the infirmary in order to massacre them. M. Voisin, head surgeon of that infirmary, ran to the entrance hall, invited the assailants to refresh themselves, ordered wine to be brought, and found means to direct the Sister Superior to remove the guards into a ward appropriated to the poor, and dress them in the caps and greatcoats furnished by the institution. The good sisters executed this order so promptly that the guards were removed, dressed as paupers, and their beds made, while the assassins were drinking. They searched all the wards, and fancied they saw no persons there but the sick poor; thus the guards were saved.—*Madame Campan.*

8. The Emperor Joseph sent the Queen an engraving which represented unfrocked nuns and monks. The first were trying on fashionable dresses, the latter were having their hair arranged; this engraving was always left in a closet, and never hung up. The Queen told me to have it taken away; for she was hurt to see how much influence the philosophers had over her brother's mind and actions.—*Madame Campan.*

9. See Thiers' *History of the French Revolution*, vol. i, p. 89.

10. The *Memoirs* of Madame de Tourzel have since been published (Paris, 1883), edited by the Duc des Cars.

11. On his return from one of the visits to Saint Cloud the King wrote to the Duchesse de Polignac:—"I have returned from the country; the air has been of service to us; but how changed did the place appear! How desolate was the breakfast-room! Neither of you were there. I do not give up the hope of our meeting there again; but when? I know not. How many things we shall have to say to one another! The health of your friend keeps up in spite of all the misfortunes which press upon her. Adieu, Duchess! speak of me to your husband and all around you; and understand that I shall not be happy until the day I find myself with my old friends again."

"The farther the first National Assembly advanced in its labours," adds Montjoie (*History of Marie Antoinette*, p. 262), "the more unhappy the Queen found herself. We have a proof of this in these few words from another note from Louis XVI to the Duchesse de Polignac: 'For the last eighteen months we have seen and heard nothing but what was disagreeable; we do not lose our temper, but we are hurt and rendered melancholy at being thwarted in everything, and particularly at being misrepresented.'"

In a former letter from the King to the Duchess the following passage occurs: "Your friend is unhappy and exceedingly misrepresented; but I flatter myself that justice will one day be done to her. Still, the wicked are very active; they are more readily believed than the good; you are a striking proof of it."—*Note by the Editor*.

XVII

*First Federation—Attempts to assassinate the Queen—Affecting
scene—Account of the affair of Nancy, written by Madame Campan,
at night, in the Council chamber, by the King's dictation—Madame
Campan becomes the subject of calumnious denunciation—Marks
of confidence bestowed upon her by the Queen—Interview between
the Queen and Mirabeau in the gardens of Saint Cloud—He treats
with the Court—Ridicule of the revolutionary party—Stones of the
Bastille offered to the Dauphin—The Queen feels her aversion to
M. de La Fayette increase—Plan formed by the Princess for re-entering
France through Lyons—Imprudence of persons attached to the
Queen—Anecdote relative to M. de La Fayette—Departure of the
King's aunts—Death of Mirabeau*

There was a meeting at Paris for the first federation on the 14th of July 1790, the anniversary of the taking of the Bastille. What an astonishing assemblage of 4,000 men, of whom there were not perhaps 200 who did not believe that the King found happiness and glory in the order of things then being established. The love which was borne him by all, with the exception of those who meditated his ruin, still reigned in the hearts of the French in the departments; but if I may judge from those whom I had an opportunity of seeing, it is totally impossible to enlighten them; they were as much attached to the King as to the constitution, and to the constitution as to the King; and it impossible to separate the one from the other in their hearts and minds.[1]

The Court returned to Saint Cloud after the federation. A wretch, named Rotondo, made his way into the palace with the intention of assassinating the Queen. It is known that he penetrated to the inner gardens: the rain prevented her Majesty from going out on that day. M. de La Fayette, who was aware of this plot, gave all the sentinels the strictest orders, and a description of the monster was distributed throughout the palace by order of the general. I do not know how he was saved from punishment. The police belonging to the King covered that there was likewise a scheme on foot for poisoning the Queen. She spoke to me, as well as to her head physician, M. Vicq-d'Azyr, about it, without the slightest emotion, but both he and myself considered what precautions it would be proper to take. He relied much upon the Queen's temperance; yet he recommended me always to have a bottle of oil of sweet almonds within reach, and to renew it occasionally, that oil and milk being, as it is known, the most certain antidotes to the divellications of corrosive poisons. The Queen had a habit which rendered

Saint Cloud

M. Vicq-d'Azyr particularly uneasy: there was always some pounded sugar upon the table in her Majesty's bed-chamber; and she frequently, without calling anybody, put spoonfuls of it to a glass of water when she wished to drink. It was agreed that I should get a considerable quantity of sugar powdered; that I should always have some papers of it in my bag, and that three or four times a day, when alone in the Queen's room, I should substitute it for that in her sugar-basin. We knew that the Queen would have prevented all such precautions, but we were not aware of her reason. One day she caught me alone making this exchange, and told me she supposed it was agreed on between myself and M. Vicq-d'Azyr, but that I gave myself very unnecessary trouble. "Remember," added she, "that not a grain of poison will be put in use against me. The Brinvilliers do not belong to this century: this age possesses calumny, which is a much more convenient instrument of death; and it is by that I shall perish."

Even while melancholy presentiments afflicted this unfortunate Princess, manifestations of attachment to her person, and to the King's cause, would frequently raise agreeable illusions in her mind, or present to her, the affecting spectacle of tears shed for her sorrows. I was one day, during this same visit to Saint Cloud, witness of a very touching scene, which we took great care to keep secret. It was four in the afternoon; the guard was not set; there was scarcely anybody at Saint Cloud that day, and I was reading to the Queen, who was at work in a room, the balcony of which hung over the courtyard. The windows were closed, yet we heard a sort of inarticulate murmur from a great number of voices. The Queen desired me to go and see what it was; I raised the muslin curtain, and perceived more than fifty persons beneath the balcony: this group consisted of women, young and old, perfectly well dressed in the country costume, old chevaliers of Saint Louis, young knights of Malta and a few ecclesiastics. I told the Queen it was probably an assemblage of persons residing in the neighbourhood who wished to see her. She rose, opened the window, and appeared in the balcony; immediately all these worthy people said to her, in an undertone: "Courage, Madame; good French men suffer for you, and with you; they pray for you; Heaven will hear their prayers: we love you, we respect you, we will continue to venerate our virtuous King." The Queen burst into tears, and held her handkerchief to her eyes. "Poor Queen! she weeps!" said the women and young girls; but the dread of exposing her Majesty, and even the persons who showed so much affection for her, to observation, prompted me to take her hand, and prevail upon her to retire into her room; and, raising my eyes, I gave the excellent people to understand that my conduct was dictated by prudence. They comprehended me, for I heard, "*That lady is right*;" and afterwards, "*Farewell Madame!*" from several of them; and all this in accents of feeling so true and so mournful, that I am affected at the recollection of them even after a lapse of twenty years.

A few days afterwards the insurrection of Nancy took place.[2] Only the ostensible cause is known; here was another, of which I might have been in full possession, if the great confusion I was in upon the subject had not deprived me of the power of paying attention to it: I will endeavour to make myself understood. In the early part of September the Queen, as she was going to bed, desired me to tell all her people to go, and to remain with her myself: when we were alone she said to me, "The King will come here at midnight. You know that he has always shown you marks of distinction; he now proves his confidence in you by selecting you to write down the whole affair of Nancy from his dictation. He must have several copies of it." At midnight the King came to the Queen's apartments, and said to me, smiling, "You did not expect to become my secretary, and that, too, during the night." I followed the King into the Council chamber. I found there sheets of paper, an inkstand, and pens all ready prepared. He sat down by my side and dictated to me the report of the Marquis de Bouillé, which he himself copied at the same time. My hand trembled; I wrote with difficulty, my reflections scarcely left me sufficient power of attention to listen to the King. The large table, the velvet cloth, seats which ought to have been filled by none but the King's chief counsellors; what that chamber had been, and what it was at that moment, when the King was employing a woman in an office which had so little affinity with her ordinary functions; the misfortunes which had brought him to the necessity of doing so—all these ideas made such an impression upon me that when I had returned to the Queen's apartments I could not sleep for the remainder of the night, nor could I remember what I had written.

The more I saw that I had the happiness to be of some use to my employers, the more scrupulously careful was I to live entirely with my family; and I never indulged in any conversation which could betray the intimacy to which I was admitted; nothing at Court remains long concealed, and I saw I had numerous enemies. The means of injuring others in the minds of sovereigns are but too easily obtained, and they had become still more so, since the mere suspicion of communication with partisans of the Revolution was sufficient to forfeit the esteem and confidence of the King and Queen: happily my conduct protected me, with them, against calumny. I had left Saint Cloud two days, when I received at Paris a note from the Queen, containing these words: "Come to Saint Cloud immediately: I have something concerning you to communicate." I set off without loss of time. Her Majesty told me she had a sacrifice to request of me: I answered that it was made. She said it went so far as the renunciation of a friend's society; that such a renunciation was always painful, but that it must be particularly so to me; that, for her own part, it might have been very useful that a deputy, a man of talent, should be constantly received at my house; but at this moment she thought only of my welfare. The Queen then informed me that the ladies of the bed-chamber had, the preceding evening, assured her that M. de Beaumetz, deputy from the nobility of Artois, who had taken his seat on the left of the Assembly, spent his whole time at my house. Perceiving on what false grounds the attempt to injure me was based, I replied respectfully, but at the same time smiling, that it was impossible for me to make the sacrifice exacted by her Majesty; that M. de Beaumetz, a man of great judgment, had not determined to cross over to the left of the Assembly with the intention of afterwards making himself unpopular by spending his time with the Queen's first woman; and that, ever since the 1st of October 1789, I had seen him nowhere but at the play, or in the public walks, and even then without his ever coming to speak to me; that this line of conduct had appeared to me perfectly consistent: for whether he was desirous to please the popular party, or to be sought after by the Court, he could not act in any other way towards me. The Queen closed this explanation by saying, "Oh! it is clear, as clear as the day! this opportunity for trying to do you an injury is very ill chosen, but be cautious in your slightest actions; you perceive that the confidence placed in you by the King and myself raises you up powerful enemies."

The private communications which were still kept up between the Court and Mirabeau at length procured him an interview with the Queen, in the gardens of Saint Cloud.[3] He left Paris on horseback, on pretence of going into the country; to M de Clavières, one of his friends; but he stopped at one of the gates of the gardens of Saint Cloud, and was led to a spot situated in the highest part of the private garden, where the Queen was waiting for him. She told me she accosted him by saying, "With a common enemy, with a man who has sworn to destroy monarchy without appreciating its utility among a great people, I should at this moment be guilty of a most ill-advised step; but in speaking to a Mirabeau," etc. The poor Queen was delighted at having discovered this method of exalting him above all others of his principles; and in imparting the particulars of this interview to me she said, "Do you know that those words, 'a Mirabeau', appeared to flatter him exceedingly." On leaving the Queen he said to her with warmth, "Madame, the monarchy is saved!" It must have been soon afterwards that Mirabeau received considerable sums of money. He showed it too plainly by the increase of his expenditure. Already did some of his remarks upon the necessity of arresting the progress of the democrats circulate in society. Being once invited to meet a person at dinner who was very much attached to the Queen, he learned that that person withdrew on hearing that he was one of the guests; the party who invited him told him this with some degree of satisfaction; but all were very much astonished when they heard Mirabeau eulogise the absent guest, and declare that in his place he would have done the same; but, he added, they had only to invite that person again in a few months, and he would then dine with the restorer of the monarchy. Mirabeau forgot that it was more easy to do harm than good, and thought himself the political Atlas of the whole world.

Outrages and mockery were incessantly mingled with the audacious proceedings of the revolutionists. It was customary to give serenades under the King's windows on New Year's Day. The band of the national guard repaired thither on that festival in 1791; in allusion to the liquidation of the debts of the State, decreed by the Assembly, they played solely, and repeatedly, that air from the comic opera of the *Debts*, the burthen of which is, "*But our creditors are paid, and that makes us easy.*"

On the same day some *conquerors of the Bastille*, grenadiers of the Parisian guard, preceded by military music, came to present to the young Dauphin, as a New Year's gift, a box of dominoes, made of some of the stone and marble of which that state prison was built. The Queen gave me this inauspicious curiosity, desiring me to preserve it, as it would be a curious illustration of the history of the Revolution. Upon the lid were engraved some bad verse the purport of which was as follows, "*Stones from those walls, which enclosed the innocent victims of arbitrary power, have been converted into a toy, to be presented to you, Monseigneur, as a mark of the people's love and to teach you their power.*"

The Queen said that M. de La Fayette's thirst for popularity induced him to lend himself, with discrimination, to all popular follies. Her distrust of the general increased daily, and grew so powerful that when, towards the end of the Revolution, he seemed willing to support the tottering throne, she could never bring herself to incur so great an obligation to him.

M. de J——, a colonel attached to the staff of the army, was fortunate enough to render several services to the Queen, and acquitted himself with discretion and dignity of various important missions.[5] Their Majesties had the highest confidence him, although it frequently happened that his prudence, when inconsiderate projects were under discussion, brought upon him the charge of adopting the principles of the constitutionals. Being sent to Turin, he had some difficulty in dissuading the Princes from a scheme they had formed at that period of re-entering France, with a very weak army, by way of Lyons; and when, in a Council which lasted till three o'clock in the morning, he showed his instructions, and demonstrated that the measure would endanger the King, the Comte d'Artois alone declared against the plan, which emanated from the Prince de Condé.

Among the persons employed in subordinate situations, whom the critical circumstances of the times involved in affairs of importance, was M. de Goguelat, a geographical engineer at Versailles, and an excellent draughtsman. He made plans of Saint Cloud and Trianon for the Queen; she was very much pleased with them, and had the engineer admitted into the staff of the army. At the commencement of the Revolution he was sent to Count Esterhazy, at Valenciennes, in the capacity of *aide-de-camp*. The latter rank was given him solely to get him away from Versailles, where his rashness endangered the Queen during the earlier months of the Assembly of the States-General. Making a parade of his devotion to the King's interests, he went repeatedly to the tribunes of the Assembly and there openly railed at all the motions of the deputies, and then returned to the Queen's antechamber, where he repeated all that he had just heard, or had had the imprudence to say. Unfortunately at the same time that the Queen sent away M. de Goguelat she still believed that, in a dangerous predicament, requiring great self-devotion, the man might be employed advantageously. In 1791 he was commissioned to act in concert with the Marquis de Bouillé in furtherance of the King's intended escape.[6]

Projectors in great numbers endeavoured to introduce themselves not only to the Queen, but to Madame Elizabeth, who had communications with many individuals who took upon themselves to make plans for the conduct of the Court. The Baron de Gilliers and M. de Vanoise were of this description; they went to the Baroness de Mackau's, where the Princess spent almost all her evenings. The Queen did not like these meetings, where Madame Elizabeth might adopt views in opposition to the King's intentions or her own.

The Queen gave frequent audiences to M. de La Fayette. One day, when he was in her inner closet, his *aides-de-camp*, who waited for him, were walking up and down the great room where the persons in attendance remained. Some imprudent young women were thoughtless enough to say, with the intention of being overheard by those officers, that it was very alarming to see the Queen alone with a rebel and a brigand. I was annoyed at their indiscretion, and imposed silence on them. One of them persisted in the appellation "brigand". I told her that M. de La Fayette well deserved the name of rebel, but that the title of leader of a party was given by history to every man commanding 40,000 men, a capital, and forty leagues of country; that kings had frequently treated with such leaders, and if it was convenient to the Queen to do the same, it remained for us only to be silent and respect her actions. On the morrow the Queen, with a serious air, but with the greatest kindness, asked what I had said respecting M. de La Fayette on the preceding day; adding that she had been assured I had enjoined her women silence, because they did not like him, and that I had taken his part. I repeated what had passed to the Queen, word for word. She condescended to tell me that I had done perfectly right.

Whenever any false reports respecting me were conveyed to her she was kind enough to inform me of them; and they had no effect on the confidence with which she continued to honour me, and which I am happy to think I have justified even at the risk of my life.

Mesdames, the King's aunts, set out from Bellevue in the beginning of the year 1791.[7] I went to take leave of Madame Victoire.[8] I little thought that I was then seeing her for the last time. She received me alone in her closet, and assured me that she hoped, as well as wished, soon to return to France; that the French would be much to be pitied if the excesses of the Revolution should arrive at such a pitch as to force her to prolong her absence. I knew from the Queen that the departure of Mesdames was deemed necessary, in order to leave the King free to act when he should be compelled to go away with his family. It being impossible that the constitution of the clergy should be otherwise than in direct opposition to the religious principles of Mesdames, they thought their journey to Rome would be attributed to piety alone. It was, however, difficult to deceive an Assembly which weighed the slightest actions of the royal family, and from that moment they were more than ever alive to what was passing at the Tuileries.

Mesdames were desirous of taking Madame Elizabeth to Rome. The free exercise of religion, the happiness of taking refuge with the head of the Church, and the prospect of living in safety with her aunts, whom she tenderly loved, were sacrificed by that virtuous Princess to her attachment to the King.

The oath required of priests by the civil constitution of the clergy introduced into France a division which added to the dangers by which the King was already surrounded.[9] Mirabeau spent a whole night with the Curé of Saint Eustache, confessor of the King and Queen, to persuade him to take the oath required by that constitution. Their Majesties chose another confessor, who remained unknown.

A few months afterwards (2nd April 1791) the too celebrated Mirabeau, the mercenary democrat and venal royalist, terminated his career. The Queen regretted him, and was astonished at her own regret; but she had hoped that he who had possessed adroitness and weight enough to throw everything into confusion would have been able by the same means to repair the mischief he had caused. Much has been said respecting the cause of Mirabeau's death. M. Cabanis, his friend and physician, denied that he was poisoned. M. Vicq-d'Azyr assured the Queen that the *procès-verbal* drawn up on the state of the intestines would apply just as well to a case of death produced by violent remedies as to one produced by poison. He said, also, that the report had been faithful; but that it was prudent to conclude it by a declaration of natural death, since, in the critical state in which France then was, if a suspicion of foul play were admitted, a person innocent of any such crime might be sacrificed to public vengeance.

1. Two deputies from Nantes, sent to England to cement the fraternal union between the London revolutionary club and all the friends of the French constitution, wrote the following letter:—

> From all that we have seen and known, we can assure you that the people of London are at least as enthusiastic on the subject of the French Revolution as the people of France. We went yesterday to see the opera of *The Confederation of the French at the Champ de Mars*. This piece has been played daily for six weeks. The house is filled by five o'clock, though the performance does not begin till seven. When we arrived there was no room; but as soon as they heard us speak French they hastened to place us in the front of the boxes; they paid every possible attention, and forced refreshments upon us. The first act of this opera represents the arrival of several people at Paris for the federation. The second, the works of the Champ de Mars. The third, the Confederation itself. In the second act Capuchins are seen in grenadier caps, girls are caressing abbés, the King comes in, and chops with a hatchet; everybody is at work, and singing: "*Ça ira, ça ira.*" In the third act you see the municipal officers in scarfs, the National Assembly, the national guard, officiating ministers in pontifical dresses, and priests singing. A regiment of children sing, "*Moi je suis soldat pour la patrie!*" in French and English. All this appears to us something new upon the banks of the Thames, and every verse is encored and applauded to delirium.
> —*Anecdotes of the Reign of Louis XVI*, vol. iv, pp. 93–4.

2. The insurrection of the troops at Nancy broke out in August 1790, and was put down by Maréchal de Bouillé on the last day of that month. See *Bouillé*, p. 195.
3. It was not in her apartments, as is asserted by M. de Lacretelle, that the Queen received Mirabeau; his person was too generally known.—*Madame Campan.*
4. See an anecdote in Weber's *Memoirs*, vol. ii, on the subject of this interview.—*Note by the Editor.*
5. During the Queen's detention in the Temple he introduced himself into that prison in the dress of a lamplighter, and there discharged his duty unrecognised.—*Madame Campan.*

6. See the *Memoirs* of M. de Bouillé, those of the Duc de Choiseul, and the account of the journey to Varennes, by M. de Fontanges, in Weber's *Memoirs.—Note by the Editor.*

7. Alexander Berthier, Prince de Neufchâtel, then a colonel on the staff of the army, and commandant of the national guard of Versailles, favoured the departure of Mesdames. The Jacobins of that town procured his dismissal, and he ran the greatest risk, on account of having rendered this service to these Princesses. *—Madame Campan.*

8. The departure of Mesdames was an important event. It was an actual experiment made by the Court of the means to be taken to quit Paris. We will here relate from the memoirs of these Princesses what concerns General Berthier, and the part he took in their departure.

A crowd of women collected at Bellevue to oppose the setting out of Mesdames. On their arrival at the Château they were told that Mesdames were no longer there, that they had gone with a suite of twenty persons. The intelligence of this departure caused a great ferment at the Palais Royal. All the clubs who were apprised of it gave orders to the leaders to put the light troops in motion. The Department of Seine and Oise came to a resolution that there were no grounds for retaining the property of Mesdames. The municipality of Versailles was charged to require the commandant of the national guard and the troops of the line to aid and assist. It was to have an understanding with the municipalities of Sèvres and Meudon to put down all obstacles. General Berthier justified the monarch's confidence by a firm and prudent line of conduct which entitled him to the highest military honours, and to the esteem of the warrior whose fortune, dangers, and glory he afterwards shared. He went to Bellevue at midnight of the day on which the order was made. As soon as the municipalities of Sèvres and Meudon were informed of his arrival at the Château they both came to a resolution, by which they left the General full liberty to act for the department; but in order to leave no doubt as to their own sentiments relative to Mesdames, these two municipalities made the arrangement which provided that no search should be made in either the Château or its dependencies. The posts were relieved quietly enough; but when it was necessary to send off the carriages murmurs broke out, and violent resistance was made. Part of the armed force and the unarmed mob declared that Mesdames should not go, and uttered horrible imprecations against them. A sapper of the national guard of Sèvres, an officer of the same guard, and an officer of chasseurs of the first division, distinguished themselves by formal and obstinate disobedience; several gunners, instead of keeping the refractory in awe by remaining at their guns, cut the traces of one of the carriages. Such was the impotence of the laws that General Berthier, although invested with full powers by reiterated acts of the departments and municipalities of Versailles and Meudon, could not send off the equipages. This officer, full of honour, and gifted with the highest courage, was shut into the courtyard of Bellevue by his own troops, and ran the great risk of being murdered. It was not until the 14th of March that he succeeded in executing the law.

—(*Memoirs of Mesdames by Montigny,* vol. i.)—*Note by the Editor.*

9. The priests were required to swear to the civil constitution of the clergy of 1790, by which all the former bishoprics and parishes were remodelled, and the priests and

bishops elected by the people. Most refused, and under the name of *prêtres insermentés* (as opposed to the few who took the oath, *prêtres assermentés*) were bitterly persecuted. A simple promise to obey the constitution of the State was substituted by Napoleon as soon as he came to power.

ANNEX TO CHAPTER XVII

A full report of the proceedings taken by the National Assembly after the departure of the King's aunts will be found in Montigny's *Memoires des Mesdames*, tome i, from which the following account is somewhat condensed.

THE FLIGHT OF MESDAMES

The King informed the Assembly of the departure of his aunts, which caused much excitement in Paris, in the following letter:—

> Gentlemen,—Having learned that the National Assembly had referred a question arising upon a journey intended by my aunts to the committee for matters concerning the constitution, I think it right to inform the Assembly that I was this morning apprised of their departure at ten o'clock last night. As I am persuaded they could not be deprived of the liberty, which every one possesses of going wherever he chooses, I felt that I neither ought to, nor could, offer any obstacle to their setting off, although I witness their separation from me with much regret.
> (Signed)   LOUIS

The two parties which divided the Assembly were in the highest state of excitement when intelligence was received that Mesdames had been stopped by the municipality of Moret. It was at the same time announced that they had been liberated by the chasseurs of Lorraine. It was known that individuals had preceded Mesdames, spreading among the people the reports with which the newspapers were filled by the conspirators. They scattered handfuls of money among the most brutalised men, as most likely to plunge into the greatest excesses; consequently the lives of Mesdames were in imminent danger. One scoundrel, who grossly insulted the Princesses, talked of hanging them up to a street lamp. The money lavished by the persons unknown was not furnished by the Duc d'Orléans; his finances were then exhausted—it was English money.[1] The Parliament granted the minister all the supplies he asked for, and dispensed with any account from him. The purpose served by these funds is no longer problematical.

The Assembly soon received the following *procès-verbal* from the municipality of Moret:—"On the 20th of February 1791 certain carriages attended by a retinue, and escorted in a manner announcing rank, appeared at Moret. The municipal officers, who had heard of the departure of Mesdames, and of the uneasiness it had occasioned in Paris, stopped these carriages, and would not suffer them to pass until they should have exhibited their passports. They produced two—one was from the King, and counter-signed *Montmorin*, to go to Rome; the other was a declaration from the municipality of Paris, acknowledging that it possessed no right to prevent these *citoyennes* from trav-elling in such parts of the kingdom as they should think fit. The municipal officers of Moret, on inspection of these two passports, between which they think they see some contradiction, are disposed to believe that it is their duty to consult the National Assembly, and to await the answer of that body with Mesdames; but while they are hesitating as to the course they are to pursue, certain chasseurs of the regiment of Lorraine come up, with arms in their hands, and by force open the gates to Mesdames, who proceed on their way."

The reading of this *procès-verbal* was hardly ended when the ex-director Rewbell exhibited great surprise. How could the Minister for Foreign Affairs have signed a pass-port when he was well aware that their departure had been the ground for demanding a new decree, which the committee for affairs concerning the constitution was drawing up? As everything was a *scandal* and a *reproach* in that impious age, the speaker said it was *scandalous* that the chasseurs of Lorraine should have so conducted themselves. "If such acts of violence," said he, in conclusion, "are permitted to remain unpunished, the belief that we have a constitution is a strange illusion: no, there are no laws, and we live under the dominion of the sword." Being compelled to defend himself, the Minister at War declared that he had given no orders to the chasseurs of Lorraine; and that, after all, they had done nothing in the affair. The decree passed upon Rewbell's motion was supported by the Duc d'Aiguillon, and it was found, from M. de Ségur's letter, *that they were chasseurs of Hagueneau, and not chasseurs of Lorraine, who had had the honour of forming the escort of Mesdames at Fontainebleau and Moret.* This letter, which was signed by M. de Ségur, was inserted in the journals at his own request. He prided himself upon having given the order. "The ancient ordinances are not abrogated," said the colonel of the chasseurs of Hagueneau, and not of Lorraine; "the officer commanding did no more than conform to them, and if he did enter the town armed, it was but in observ-ance of the custom among soldiers to say that mark of respect to cities."

Still M. de Montmorin could not avoid justifying himself. He did it triumphantly, by the following letter:—

M. le President—I have just learned that, upon the reading of the *procès-verbal* sent by the municipality of Moret, some members of the Assembly appeared astonished at my having countersigned the passport given to Mesdames by the King. If this circumstance requires explanation, I entreat the Assembly to reflect that the opinion of the King and his ministers upon the point is sufficiently well known. This passport would be a permission to quit the kingdom if any law forbade the passing of its limits; but no such law ever existed. Down to the present moment a passport is to be looked upon as merely an attestation of the quality of the persons who bear it. In this light it was impossible to refuse one to Mesdames, either their journey must be opposed or their possible arrest by a municipality to which they were unknown must be prevented. There were ancient laws against emigration; they had fallen into disuse, and the principles of liberty, established by the decrees of the Assembly, had wholly abrogated them. These, sir, are the grounds upon which I countersigned the passports granted to Mesdames. I request you will have the kindness to communicate them to the Assembly, on whose justice I shall always rely with the utmost confidence.

The fate of Mesdames depended on the resolution to which the National Assembly was about to come; the two parties were ready, and well prepared. The Abbé Maury, whose merit has placed him at the head of Catholicism, was eager for the honour of being the first to speak. He eulogised the principles of order, without which no government can subsist, and there can be neither peace nor prosperity for the people. Several orators spoke, and all of them acknowledged that there was no law which forbade the departure of Mesdames. But an unknown member, remarkable only for his gigantic form and his strength of voice, rose and roared out—"You profess that no law exists, and I maintain that a law does exist—it is the safety of the people." General Menou put an end to the debate by one of those caustic observations which seldom fail to take effect when they are happily introduced, that is to say, when the audience begin to be tired by the discussion. "Europe," said he, "will be greatly astonished, no doubt, on hearing that the National Assembly spent four hours in deliberating upon the departure of two ladies who preferred hearing mass at Rome rather than at Paris." The debate was thus terminated, and the decree, conformably to the opinion of Mirabeau, was as follows:—

The National Assembly, inasmuch as there exists no law of the realm to forbid the free journeying of Mesdames, the King's Aunts, declares that there is no ground for deliberating on it, and refers the matter to the executive power.

1. This statement hardly requires refutation.—*Note by the Editor.*

XVIII

Preparations for the Journey to Varennes—The Queen watched and betrayed—Madame Campan's departure for Auvergne precedes that of the royal family for Versailles—Madame Campan hears of the King's arrest—Note written to her by the Queen immediately upon her return to Paris—Anecdotes—Measures taken for keeping the King at the Tuileries—Barnave gains the esteem and confidence of Marie Antoinette during the return from Varennes—His honourable and respectful conduct—She contrasts it with that of Pétion—Bravery of Barnave—His advice to the Queen—Particulars respecting the Varennes journey

In the beginning of the spring of 1791 the King, tired of remaining at the Tuileries, wished to return to Saint Cloud. His whole household had already gone, and his dinner was prepared there. He got into his carriage at one; the guard mutinied, shut the gates, and declared they would not let him pass. This event certainly proceeded from some suspicion of a plan for escape. Two persons who drew near the King's carriage were very ill treated. My father-in-law was violently laid hold of by the guards, who took his sword from him. The King and his family were obliged to alight and return to their apartments. They did not much regret this outrage in their hearts; they saw in it a justification, even in the eyes of the people, of their intention to leave Paris.

So early as the month of March in the same year the Queen began to busy herself in preparing for her departure. I spent that month with her, and executed a great number of secret orders which she gave me respecting the intended event. It was with uneasiness that I saw her occupied with cares which seemed to me useless, and even dangerous, and I remarked to her that the Queen of France would find linen and gowns everywhere. My observations were made in vain; she determined to have a complete wardrobe with her at Brussels, as well for her children as herself. I went out alone and almost disguised to purchase the articles necessary and have them made up.

I ordered six chemises at the shop of one seamstress, six at that of another, gowns, combing cloths, etc. My sister had a complete set of clothes made for Madame, by the measure of her eldest daughter, and I ordered clothes for the Dauphin from those of my son. I filled a trunk with these things, and addressed them, by the Queen's orders, to one of her women, my aunt, Madame Cardon—a widow living at Arras, by virtue of an unlimited leave of absence—in order that she might be ready to start for Brussels, or any other place, as soon as she should be directed to do so. This lady had landed property in Austrian Flanders, and could at any time quit Arras unobserved.

The Queen was to take only her first woman in attendance with her from Paris. She apprised me that if I should not be on duty at the moment of departure she would make arrangements for my joining her. She determined also to take her travelling dressing-case. She consulted me on her idea of sending it off, under pretence of making a present of it to the Archduchess Christina, Gouvernante of the Netherlands. I ventured to oppose this plan strongly, and observed that, amidst so many people who watched her slightest actions, there would be found a sufficient number sharp-sighted enough to discover that it was only a pretext for sending away the property in question before her own departure; she persisted in her intention, and all I could arrange was that the dressing-case should not be removed from her apartment, and that M. de——, *chargé d'affaires* from the Court of Vienna during the absence of the Comte de Mercy, should come and ask her at her toilette, before all her people, to order one like her own for Madame the Gouvernante of the Netherlands. The Queen, therefore, commanded me before the *chargé d'affaires* to order the article in question. This occasioned only an expense of 500 *louis*, and appeared calculated to lull suspicion completely.

About the middle of May 1791, a month after the Queen had ordered me to bespeak the dressing case, she asked me whether it would soon be finished. I sent for the ivory-turner who had it in hand. He could not complete it for six weeks. I informed the Queen of this, and she told me she should not be able to wait for it, as she was to set out in the course of June. She added that, as she had ordered her sister's dressing-case in the presence of all her attendants, she had taken a sufficient precaution, especially by saying that her sister was out of patience at not receiving it, and that therefore her own must be emptied and cleaned, and taken to the *chargé d'affaires*, who would send it off. I executed this order without any appearance of mystery. I desired the wardrobe woman to take out of the dressing-case all that it contained, because that intended for the Archduchess could not be finished for some time; and to take great care to leave no remains of the perfumes which might not suit that Princess.

The woman in question executed her commission punctually; but, on the evening of that very day, the 15th of May 1791, she informed M. Bailly, the Mayor of Paris, that preparations were making at the Queen's residence for a departure; and that the dressing-case was already sent off, under pretence of its being presented to the Archduchess Christina.[1]

It was necessary, likewise, to send off the whole of the diamonds belonging to the Queen. Her Majesty shut herself up with me in a closet in the *entresol*, looking into the garden of the Tuileries, and we packed all the diamonds, rubies, and pearls she possessed in a small chest. The cases containing these ornaments, being altogether of considerable bulk, had been deposited, ever since the 6th of October 1789, with the *valet de chambre* who had the care of the Queen's jewels. That faithful servant, himself detecting the use that was to be made of the valuables, destroyed all the boxes, which were, as usual, covered with red morocco, marked with the cipher and arms of France. It would have been impossible for him to hide them from the eyes of the popular inquisitors during the domiciliary visits in January 1793, and the discovery might have formed a ground of accusation against the Queen.

I had but a few articles to place in the box when the Queen was compelled to desist from packing it, being obliged to go down to cards, which began at seven precisely. She therefore desired me to leave all the diamonds upon the sofa, persuaded that, as she took the key of her closet herself, and there was a sentinel under the window, no danger was to be apprehended for that night, and she reckoned upon returning very early next day to finish the work.

The same woman who had given information of the sending away of the dressing-case was also deputed by the Queen to take care of her more private rooms. No other servant was permitted to enter them; she renewed the flowers, swept the carpets, etc. The Queen received back the key, when the woman had finished putting them in order, from her own hands; but, desirous of doing her duty well, and sometimes having the key in her possession for a few minutes only, she had probably on that account ordered one without the Queen's knowledge. It is impossible not to believe this, since the despatch of the diamonds was the subject of a second accusation which the Queen heard of after the return from Varennes. She made a formal declaration that her Majesty, with the assistance of Madame Campan, had packed up the whole of her jewellery some time before the departure; that she was certain of it, as she had found the diamonds, and the cotton which served to wrap them, scattered upon the sofa in the Queen's closet in the *entresol,* and most assuredly she could only have seen these preparations in the interval between seven in the evening and seven in the morning. The Queen having met me next day, at the time appointed, the box was handed over to Léonard, her Majesty's hair-dresser, who left the country with the Duc de Choiseul.[2] The box remained a long time at Brussels, and at length got into the hands of Madame the Duchesse d'Angoulême, being delivered to her by the Emperor on her arrival at Vienna.

In order not to leave out any of the Queen's diamonds, I requested the first tire-woman to give me the body of the full dress, and all the assortment which served for the stomacher of the full dress on days of state, articles which always remained at the wardrobe.

The superintendent and the *dame d'honneur* being absent, the first tire-woman required me to sign a receipt, the terms of which she dictated, and which acquitted her of all responsibility for these diamonds. She had the prudence to burn this document on the 10th of August 1792.[3] The Queen having determined, upon the arrest at Varennes, not to have her diamonds brought back to France, was often anxious about them during the year which elapsed between that period and the 10th of August, and dreaded above all things that such a secret should be discovered.

In consequence of a decree of the Assembly, which deprived the King of the custody of the Crown diamonds, the Queen had at this time already given up those which she generally used.

She preferred the twelve brilliants called *Mazarins* from the name of the Cardinal who had enriched the treasury with them, a few rose-cut diamonds, and the *Sanci.* She determined to deliver, with her own hands, the box containing them to the commissioner nominated by the National Assembly to place them with the Crown diamonds. After giving them to him, she offered him a row of pearls of great beauty, saying to him, "that it had been brought into France by Anne of Austria; that it was invaluable, on account of its rarity; that having been appropriated by that Princess to the use of the Queens and Dauphinesses, Louis XV had placed it in her hands on her arrival in France; but that she considered it national property."—"That is an open question, Madame," said the commissary.—"Sir," replied the Queen, "it is one for me to decide, and is now settled."

My father-in-law, who was dying of the grief he felt for the misfortunes of his master and mistress, strongly interested and occupied the thoughts of the Queen. He had been saved from the fury of the populace in the courtyard of the Tuileries.

On the day on which the King was compelled by an insurrection to give up a journey to Saint Cloud, her Majesty looked upon this trusty servant as inevitably lost, if, on going away, she should leave him in the apartment he occupied in the Tuileries. Prompted by her apprehensions, she ordered M. Vicq-d'Azyr, her physician, to recommend him the waters of Mont d'Or in Auvergne, and to persuade him to set off at the latter end of May. At the moment of my going away the Queen assured me that the grand project would be executed between the 15th and the 20th of June; that, as it was not my month to be on duty, Madame Thibaut would take the journey; but that she had many directions to give me before I went. She then desired me to write to my aunt, Madame Cardon, who was by that time in possession of the clothes which I had ordered, that as soon as she should receive a letter from M. Auguié, the date of which should be accompanied with a B, an L, or an M, she was to proceed with her property to Brussels, Luxembourg, or Montmédy. She desired me to explain the meaning of these three letters clearly to my sister, and to leave them with her in writing, in order that at the moment of my going away she might be able to take my place in writing to Arras.

The Queen had a more delicate commission for me; it was to select from among my acquaintance a prudent person of obscure rank, wholly devoted to the interests of the Court, who would be willing to receive a portfolio which she was to give up only to me, or some one furnished with a note from the Queen. She added that she would not travel with this portfolio, and that it was of the utmost importance that my opinion of the fidelity of the person to whom it was to be entrusted should be well founded. I proposed to her Madame Vallayer Coster, a painter of the Academy, and an amiable and worthy artist, whom I had known from my infancy. She lived in the galleries of the Louvre. The choice seemed a good one. The Queen remembered that she had made her marriage by giving her a place in the financial offices, and added that gratitude ought sometimes to be reckoned on. She then pointed out to me the valet belonging to her toilette, whom I was to take with me, to show him the residence of Madame Coster, so that he might not mistake it when he should take the portfolio to her. The day before her departure the Queen particularly recommended me to proceed to Lyons and the frontiers as soon as she should have started. She advised me to take with me a confidential person, fit to remain with M. Campan when I should leave him, and assured me that she would give orders to M.—— to set off as soon as she should be known to be at the frontiers in order to protect me in going out. She condescended to add that having a long journey to make in foreign countries she determined to give me 300 *louis*.

I bathed the Queen's hands with tears at the moment of this sorrowful separation; and having money at my disposal I declined accepting her gold. I did not dread the road I had to travel in order to rejoin her; all my apprehension was that by treachery or miscalculation a scheme, the safety of which was not sufficiently clear to me, should fail. I could answer for all those who belonged to the service immediately about the Queen's person, and I was right; but her wardrobe woman gave me well-founded reason for alarm. I mentioned to the Queen many revolutionary remarks which this woman had made to me a few days before. Her office was directly under the control of the first *femme de chambre,* yet she had refused to obey the directions I gave her, talking insolently to me about *hierarchy overturned, equality among men,* of course more especially among persons holding offices at Court; and this jargon, at that time in the mouths of all the partisans of the Revolution, was terminated by an observation which frightened me. "You know many important secrets, madame," said this woman to me, "and I have guessed quite as many. I am not a fool; I see all that is going forward here in consequence of the bad advice given to the King and Queen; I could frustrate it all if I chose." This argument, in which I had been promptly silenced, left me pale and trembling. Unfortunately, as I began my narrative to the Queen with particulars of this woman's refusal to obey me, and sovereigns are all their lives importuned with complaints upon the rights of places, she believed that my own dissatisfaction had much to do with the step I was taking; and she did not sufficiently fear the woman. Her office, although a very inferior one, brought her in nearly 15,000 francs a year. Still young, tolerably handsome, with comfortable apartments in the *entresols* of the Tuileries, she saw a great deal of company, and in the evening had assemblies, consisting of deputies of the revolutionary party. M. de Gouvion, major-general of the national guard, passed almost every day with her; and it is to be presumed that she had long worked for the party in opposition to the Court. The Queen asked her for the key of a door which led to the principal vestibule of the Tuileries, telling her she wished to have a similar one, that she might not be under the necessity of going out through the pavilion of Flora. M. de Gouvion and M. de La Fayette would, of course, be apprised of this circumstance, and well-informed persons have assured me that on the very night of the Queen's departure this wretched woman had a spy with her, who saw the royal family set off.

As for myself, after I had executed all the Queen's orders, on the 30th of May 1791, I set out for Auvergne. I was settled in the gloomy narrow valley of Mont d'Or, when, about four in the afternoon of the 25th of June, I heard the beat of a drum to call the inhabitants of the hamlet together. When it had ceased I heard a hairdresser from Bresse proclaim in the provincial dialect of Auvergne: "The King and Queen were taking flight in order to ruin France, but I come to tell you that they are stopped, and are well guarded by a hundred thousand men under arms." I still ventured to hope that he was repeating only a false report, but he went on: "The Queen, with her well-known haughtiness, lifted up the veil which covered her face, and said to the citizens who were upbraiding the King, '*Well, since you recognise your sovereign, respect him.*'" Upon hearing these expressions, which the Jacobin club of Clermont could not have invented, I exclaimed, "*The news is true!*"

I immediately learnt that a courier being come from Paris to Clermont, the *procureur de la Commune* had sent off messengers to the chief places of the canton; these again sent couriers to the districts, the districts in like manner informed the villages and hamlets which they contained. It was through this ramification, arising from the establishment of clubs, that the afflicting intelligence of the misfortune of my sovereigns reached me in the wildest part of France, and in the midst of the snows by which we were environed.

On the 28th I received a note written in a hand which I recognised as that of M. Diet,[4] usher of the Queen's chamber, but dictated by her Majesty. It contained these words: "I am this moment arrived; I have just got into my bath; I and my family exist, that is all. I have suffered much. Do not return to Paris until I desire you. Take good care of my poor Campan, soothe his sorrow. Look for happier times."

This note was for greater safety addressed to my father-in-law's *valet de chambre*. What were my feelings on perceiving that after the most distressing crisis we were among the first objects of the kindness of that unfortunate Princess!

M. Campan having been unable to use the waters of Mont d'Or, and the first popular effervescence having subsided, I thought I might return to Clermont. The committee of surveillance, that of general safety, had resolved to arrest me there; but the Abbé Louis, formerly a parliamentary counsellor, and then a member of the Constituent Assembly, was kind enough to affirm that I was in Auvergne solely for the purpose of attending my father-in-law, who was extremely ill. The precautions relative to my absence from Paris were limited to placing us under the surveillance of the *procureur de la Commune*, who was at the same time President of the Jacobin club; but he was also a physician of repute, and without having any doubt that he had received secret orders relative to me, I thought it would favour our quiet if I selected him to attend my patient. I paid him according to the rate given to the best Paris physicians, and I requested him to visit us every morning and every evening. I took the precaution to subscribe to no other newspaper than the *Moniteur.* Doctor Monestier (for that was the physician's name) frequently took upon himself to read it to us. Whenever he thought proper to speak of the King and Queen in the insulting and brutal terms at that time unfortunately adopted throughout France, I used to stop him and say coolly, "Sir, you are here in company with the servants of Louis XVI and Marie Antoinette. Whatever may be the wrongs with which the nation believes it has to reproach them, our principles forbid our losing sight of the respect due to them from us." Notwithstanding that he was an inveterate patriot he felt the force of this remark, and even procured the revocation of a second order for our arrest, becoming responsible for us to the committee of the Assembly, and to the Jacobin society.

The two chief women about the Dauphin, who had accompanied the Queen to Varennes, Diet her usher, and Camot her *garçon de toilette*—the females on account of the journey, and the men in consequence of the denunciation of the woman belonging to the wardrobe—were sent to the prisons of the Abbaye. After my departure the *garçon de* toilette whom I had taken to Madame Vallayer Coster's was sent there with the portfolio she had agreed to receive. This commission could not escape the detestable spy upon the Queen. She gave information that a portfolio had been carried out on the evening of the departure, adding that the King had placed it upon the Queen's easy-chair, that the *garçon de toilette* wrapped it up in a napkin and took it under his arm, and that she did not know where he had carried it. The man, who was remarkable for his fidelity, underwent three examinations without making the slightest disclosure. M. Diet, a man of good family, a servant on whom the Queen placed particular reliance, likewise experienced the severest treatment. At length, after a lapse of three weeks, the Queen succeeded in obtaining the release of her servants.

The Queen, about the 15th of August, had me informed by letter that I might come back to Paris without being under any apprehension of arrest there, and that she greatly desired my return. I brought my father-in-law back in a dying state, and on the day preceding that of the acceptation of the constitutional act, I informed the Queen that he was no more. "The loss of Lassonne and Campan," said she, as she applied her handkerchief to her streaming eyes, "has taught me how valuable such subjects are to their masters. I shall never find their equals."

I resumed my functions about the Queen on the 1st of September 1791. She was unable then to converse with me on all the lamentable events which had occurred since the time of my leaving her, having on guard near her an officer whom she dreaded more than all the others. She merely told me that I should have some secret services to perform for her, and that she would not create uneasiness by long conversations with me, my return being a subject of suspicion. But next day the Queen, well knowing the discretion of the officer who was to be on guard that night, had my bed placed very near hers, and having obtained the favour of having the door shut, when I was in bed she began the narrative of the journey, and the unfortunate arrest at Varennes. I asked her permission to put on my gown, and kneeling by her bedside I remained until three o'clock in the morning, listening with the liveliest and most sorrowful interest to the account I am about to repeat, and of which I have seen various details, of tolerable exactness, in papers of the time.

The King entrusted the Comte de Fersen with all the preparations for departure. The carriage was ordered by him; the passport, in the name of Madame de Korf, was procured through his connection with that lady, who was a foreigner. And he himself drove the royal family, as their coachman, as far as Bondy, where the travellers got into their berlin. Madame Brunier and Madame Neuville, the first women of Madame and the Dauphin, there joined the principal carriage. They were in a cabriolet. Monsieur and Madame set out from the Luxembourg and took another road. They as well as the King were recognised by the master of the last post in France; but this man, devoting himself to the fortune of the Prince, left the French territory, and drove them himself as postilion. Madame Thibaut, the Queen's first woman, reached Brussels without the slightest difficulty. Madame Cardon, from Arras, met with no hindrance; and Léonard, the Queen's hairdresser, passed through Varennes a few hours before the royal family. Fate had reserved all its obstacles for the unfortunate monarch.

Nothing worthy of notice occurred in the beginning of the journey. The travellers were detained a short time, about twelve leagues from Paris, by some repairs which the carriage required. The King chose to walk up one of the hills, and there two circumstances caused a delay of three hours, precisely at the time when it was intended that the berlin should have been met, just before reaching Varennes, by the detachment commanded by M. de Goguelat. This detachment was punctually stationed upon the spot fixed on, with orders to wait there for the arrival of certain treasure, which it was to escort; but the peasantry of the neighbourhood, alarmed at the sight of this body of troops, came armed with staves, and asked several questions, which manifested their anxiety. M. de Goguelat, fearful of causing a riot, and not finding the carriage arrive as he expected, divided his men into two companies, and unfortunately made them leave the highway in order to return to Varennes by two crossroads.[5] The King looked out of the carriage at Sainte Menehould, and asked several questions concerning the road. Drouet, the postmaster, struck by the resemblance of Louis to the impression of his head upon the assignats, drew near the carriage, felt convinced that he recognised the Queen also, and that the remainder of the travellers consisted of the royal family and their suite, mounted his horse, reached Varennes by crossroads before the royal fugitives, and gave the alarm.[6]

The Queen began to feel all the agonies of terror; they were augmented by the voice of a person unknown, who, passing close to the carriage in full gallop, cried out, bending towards the window without slackening his speed, "You are recognised!" They arrived with beating hearts at the gates of Varennes without meeting one of the horsemen by whom they were to have been escorted into the place. They were ignorant where to find their relays, and some minutes were lost in waiting, to no purpose. The cabriolet had preceded them, and the two ladies in attendance found the bridge already blocked up with old carts and lumber. The town guards were all under arms. The King at last entered Varennes. M. de Goguelat had arrived there with his detachment. He came up to the King and asked him *if he chose to effect a passage by force*! What an unlucky question to put to Louis XVI, who from the very beginning of the Revolution had shown in every crisis the fear he entertained of giving the least order which might cause an effusion of blood! "Would it be a brisk action?" said the King. "It is impossible that it should be otherwise, Sire," replied the *aide-de-camp*. Louis XVI was unwilling to expose his family. They therefore went to the house of a grocer, Mayor of Varennes. The King began to speak, and gave a summary of his intentions in departing, analogous to the declaration he had made at Paris. He spoke with warmth and affability, and endeavoured to demonstrate to the people around him that he had only put himself, by the step he had taken, into a fit situation to treat with the Assembly, and to sanction with freedom the constitution which he would maintain, though many of its articles were incompatible with the dignity of the throne, and the force by which it was necessary that the sovereign should be surrounded. Nothing could be more affecting, added the Queen, than this moment, in which the King communicated to the very humblest class of his subjects his principles, his wishes for the happiness of his people, and the motives which had determined him to depart.

Whilst the King was speaking to this Mayor, whose name was Sauce, the Queen, seated at the farther end of the shop, among parcels of soap and candles, endeavoured to make Madame Sauce understand that if she would prevail upon her husband to make use of his municipal authority to cover the flight of the King and his family, she would have the glory of having contributed to restore tranquillity to France. This woman was moved; she could not, without streaming eyes, see herself thus solicited by her Queen; but she could not be got to say anything more than, "Bon Dieu, Madame, it would be the destruction of M. Sauce; I love my King, but I love my husband too, you must know, and he would be answerable, you see." Whilst this strange scene was passing in the shop, the people, hearing that the King was arrested, kept pouring in from all parts. M. de Goguelat, making a last effort, demanded of the dragoons whether they would protect the departure of the King; they replied only by murmurs, dropping the points of their swords. Some person unknown fired a pistol at M. de Goguelat; he was slightly wounded by the ball. M. Romeuf, *aide-de-camp* to M. de La Fayette, arrived at that moment. He had been chosen, after the 6th of October 1789, by the commander of the Parisian guard to be in constant attendance about the Queen. She reproached him bitterly with the object of his mission. "If you wish to make your name remarkable, sir," said the Queen to him, "you have chosen strange and odious means, which will produce the most fatal consequences." This officer wished to hasten their departure. The Queen, still cherishing the hope of seeing M. de Bouillé arrive with a sufficient force to extricate the King from his critical situation, prolonged her stay at Varennes by every means in her power.

The Dauphin's first woman pretended to be taken ill with a violent colic, and threw herself upon a bed, in the hope of aiding the designs of her superiors; she wept and implored for assistance. The Queen understood her perfectly well, and refused to leave one who had devoted herself to follow them in such a state of suffering. But no delay in departing was allowed. The three Body Guards (Valory, Du Moustier, and Maiden) were gagged and fastened upon the seat of the carriage.

A horde of national guards, animated with fury, and the barbarous joy with which their fatal triumph inspired them, surrounded the carriage of the royal family.

The three commissioners sent by the Assembly to meet the King, MM. de Latour-Maubourg, Barnave, and Pétion joined them in the environs of Epernay. The two last mentioned got into the King's carriage. The Queen astonished me by the favourable opinion she had formed of Barnave. When I quitted Paris a great many persons spoke of him only with horror. She told me he was much altered, that he was full of talent and noble feeling. "A feeling of pride which I cannot much blame in a young man belonging to the *tiers-état*," she said, "made him applaud everything which smoothed the road to rank and fame for that class in which he was born. And if we get the power in our own hands again, Barnave's pardon is already written on our hearts." The Queen added, that she had not the same feeling towards those nobles who had joined the revolutionary party, who had always received marks of favour, often to the injury of those beneath them in rank, and who, born to be the safe guard of the monarchy, could never be pardoned for having deserted it. She then told me that Barnave's conduct upon the road was perfectly correct, while Pétion's republican rudeness was disgusting; that the latter ate and drank in the King's berlin in a slovenly manner, throwing the bones of the fowls out through the window at the risk of sending them even into the King's face; lifting up his glass, when Madame Elizabeth poured him out wine, to show her that there was enough, without saying a word; that this offensive behaviour must have been intentional, because the man was not without education; and that Barnave was hurt at it. On being pressed by the Queen to take something— "Madame," replied Barnave, "on so solemn an occasion the deputies of the National Assembly ought to occupy your Majesties solely about their mission, and by no means

Portrait of Louis XVII

about their wants." In short, his respectful, his considerate attentions, and all that he did, gained the esteem not only of the Queen but of Madame Elizabeth also.

The King began to talk to Pétion about the situation of France, and the motives of his conduct, which were founded upon the necessity of giving to the executive power a strength necessary for its action, for the good even of the constitutional act, since France could not be a republic. "Not yet, 'tis true," replied Pétion, "because the French are not ripe enough for that." This audacious and cruel answer silenced the King, who said no more until his arrival at Paris. Pétion held the little Dauphin upon his knees, and amused himself with curling the beautiful light hair of the interesting child round his fingers, and, as he spoke with much gesticulation, he pulled his locks hard enough to make the Dauphin cry out. "Give me my son," said the Queen to him, "he is accustomed to tenderness and delicacy; which render him little fit for such familiarity."

The Chevalier de Dampierre was killed near the King's carriage upon leaving Varennes. A poor village curé, some leagues from the place where the crime was committed, was imprudent enough to draw near to speak to the King; the cannibals who surrounded the carriage rushed upon him. "Tigers," exclaimed Barnave, "have you ceased to be

Frenchmen? Nation of brave men, are you become a set of assassins?" These words alone saved the curé, who was already upon the ground, from certain death. Barnave, as he spoke to them, threw himself almost out of the coach window, and Madame Elizabeth, affected by this noble burst of feeling, held him by the skirt of his coat. The Queen, while speaking of this event, said that on the most momentous occasions whimsical contrasts always struck her, and that even at such a moment the pious Elizabeth holding Barnave by the flap of his coat was a ludicrous sight. The deputy was astonished in another way. Madame Elizabeth's comments upon the state of France, her mild and persuasive eloquence, and the ease and simplicity with which she talked to him, yet without sacrificing her dignity in the slightest degree, appeared to him celestial, and his heart, which was doubtless inclined to right principles though he had followed the wrong path, was overcome by admiration. The conduct of the two deputies convinced the Queen of the total separation between the republican and constitutional parties. At the inns where she alighted she had some private conversation with Barnave. The latter said a great deal about the errors committed by the royalists during the Revolution, adding that he had found the interest of the Court so feebly and so badly defended that he had been frequently tempted to go and offer it, in himself, a courageous wrestler, who knew the spirit of the age and nation. The Queen asked him what was the weapon he would recommend her to use. "Popularity, Madame."—"And how could I use that," replied her Majesty, "of which I had been deprived?"—"Ah! Madame, it was much more easy for you to regain it, than for me to acquire it."

The Queen mainly attributed the arrest at Varennes to M. de Goguelat; she said he calculated the time that would be spent in the journey erroneously. He performed that from Montmédy to Paris before taking the King's last orders, alone in a post-chaise, and he founded all his calculations upon the time he spent thus. The trial has been made since, and it was found that a light carriage without any courier was nearly three hours less in running the distance than a heavy carriage preceded by a courier.[7]

The Queen also blamed him for having quitted the high road at Pont-de-Sommevelle, where the carriage was to meet the forty hussars commanded by him. She thought that he ought to have dispersed the very small number of people at Varennes, and not have asked the hussars whether they were for the King or the nation; that, particularly, he ought to have avoided taking the King's orders, as he was aware of the reply M. d'Inisdal had received when it was proposed to carry off the King.

After all that the Queen had said to me respecting the mistakes made by M. de Goguelat, I thought him of course disgraced. What was my surprise when, having been set at liberty after the amnesty which followed the acceptance of the constitution, he presented himself to the Queen, and was received with the greatest kindness. She said he had done what he could, and that his zeal ought to form an excuse for all the rest.[8]

When the royal family was brought back from Varennes to the Tuileries, the Queen's attendants found the greatest difficulty in making their way to her apartments; everything had been arranged so that the wardrobe woman, who had acted as spy, should have the service; and she was to be assisted in it only by her sister and her sister's daughter.

M. de Gouvion, M. de La Fayette's *aide-de-camp*, had this woman's portrait placed at the foot of the staircase which led to the Queen's apartments, in order that the sentinel should not permit any other women to make their way in. As soon as the Queen was informed of this contemptible precaution she told the King of it, who sent to ascertain the fact. His Majesty then called for M. de La Fayette, claimed freedom in his household, and particularly in that of the Queen, and ordered him to send a woman in whom no one but himself could confide out of the palace. M. de La Fayette was obliged to comply.[9]

The measures adopted for guarding the King were rigorous with respect to the entrance into the palace, and insulting as to his private apartments. The commandants of battalion, stationed in the saloon called the *grand cabinet*, and which led to the Queen's bed-chamber, were ordered to keep the door of it always open, in order that they might have their eyes upon the royal family. The King shut the door one day, the officer of the guard opened it, and told him such were his orders, and that he would always open it; so that his Majesty in shutting it gave himself useless trouble. It remained open even during the night, when the Queen was in bed; and the officer placed himself in an arm-chair between the two doors, with his head turned towards her Majesty. They only obtained permission to have the inner door shut when the Queen was rising. The Queen had the bed of her first *femme de chambre* placed very near her own; this bed, which ran on castors, and was furnished with curtains, hid her from the officer's sight.

Madame de Jarjaye, my companion, who continued her functions during the whole period of my absence, told me that one night the commandant of battalion, who slept between the two doors, seeing that she was sleeping soundly, and that the Queen was awake, quitted his post and went close to her Majesty, to advise her as to the line of conduct she should pursue. Although she had the kindness to desire him to speak lower in order that he might not disturb Madame de Jarjaye's rest, the latter awoke, and nearly died with fright at seeing a man in the uniform of the Parisian guard so near the Queen's bed. Her Majesty comforted her, and told her not to rise; that the person she saw was a good Frenchman, who was deceived respecting the intentions and situation of his sovereign and herself, but whose conversation showed sincere attachment to the King. There was a sentinel in the corridor which runs behind the apartments in question, where there is a staircase, which was at that time an inner one, and enabled the King and Queen to communicate freely. This post, which was very onerous, because it was to be kept four-and-twenty hours, was often claimed by Saint Prix, an actor belonging to the Théâtre Français. He took it upon himself in some measure to favour short interviews between the King and Queen in this corridor. He left them at a distance, and gave them notice if he heard the slightest noise. M. Collot, commandant of battalion of the national guard, who was charged with the military duty of the Queen's household, in like manner softened down, so far as he could with prudence, all the revolting orders he received; for instance, one to follow the Queen to the very door of her wardrobe was never executed. An officer of the Parisian guard dared to speak insolently of the Queen in her own apartment. M. Collot wished to make a complaint to M. de La Fayette and have him dismissed. The Queen opposed it, and condescended to say a few words of explanation and kindness to the man; he instantly became one of her most devoted partisans.

The first time I saw her Majesty after the unfortunate catastrophe of the Varennes journey, I found her getting out of bed; her features were not very much altered; but after the first kind words she uttered to me she took off her cap and desired me to observe the effect which grief had produced upon her hair. It had become, in one single night, as white as that of a woman of seventy Her Majesty showed me a ring she had just had mounted for the Princesse de Lamballe, it contained a lock of her whitened hair, with the inscription, "*Blanched by sorrow.*" At the period of the acceptance of the constitution the Princess wished to return to France. The Queen, who had no expectation that tranquillity would be restored, opposed this; but the attachment of Madame de Lamballe to the royal family impelled her to come and seek death.

When I returned to Paris most of the harsh precautions were abandoned; the doors were not kept open; greater respect was paid to the sovereign; it was known that the constitution soon to be completed would be accepted, and a better order of things was hoped for.

1. After the return from Varennes M. Bailly put this woman's deposition into the Queen's hands. —*Madame Campan.*

2. This unfortunate man, after having emigrated for some time, returned to France, and perished upon the scaffold.—*Note by the Editor.*

3. The sack of the Tuileries and slaughter of the Swiss guard.

4. This officer was massacred in the Queen's chamber on the 10th of August 1792.—*Madame Campan.*

5. Madame Campan here attributes to M. de Goguelat the steps taken by the Duc de Choiseul, the motives for which he explains in his *Memoirs*, p. 84.—*Note by the Editor.*

6. Varennes lies between Verdun and Montmédy, and not far from the French frontier.

7. The affair of Varennes, the event of the Revolution which it is the more important to clear up because it was one of the most decisive, has given birth to a mass of accounts which contradict or corroborate one another, but all of which have their own interest. The accounts of the Marquis de Bouillé, of M. de Fontanges (*Mémoires de Weber*), of M. le Duc de Choiseul, have already appeared in the *Collection des Mémoires sur la Révolution.* The second volume of that collection contains also the private memoirs of M. le Comte Louis, afterwards Marquis de Bouillé, and the accounts of the Comtes de Raigecourt, de Damas, and de Valory, who have all been actors or witnesses in this historical scene.—*Note by the Editor.*

8. Full details of the preparations for the flight to Varennes will be found in *Le Comte de Fersen et La Cour de France* (Paris, Didot et Cie, 1878)—a review of which was given in the *Quarterly Review* for July 1880—and in the *Memoirs of the Marquis de Bouillé* (London: Cadell and Davis, 1797); the Comte de Fersen being the person who planned the actual escape, and de Bouillé being in command of the army which was to receive the King. The plan was excellent, and would certainly have succeeded, if it had not been for the royal family themselves. Marie Antoinette, it will have been seen by Madame Campan's account, nearly wrecked the plan from inability to do without a dressing or travelling case. The King did a more fatal thing. De Bouillé had pointed out the necessity for having in the King's carriage an officer knowing the route, and able to show himself to give all directions, and a proper person had been provided.

The King, however, objected, as "he could not have the Marquis d'Agoult in the same carriage with himself; the governess of the royal children, who was to accompany them having refused to abandon her privilege of constantly remaining in her charge." See *Bouillé*, pp. 307 and 334. Thus, when Louis was recognised at the window of the carriage by Drouet, he was lost by the very danger that had been foreseen, and this wretched piece of etiquette led to his death.

9. On the day when the return of the royal family was expected, there were no carriages in motion in the streets of Paris. Five or six of the Queen's women, after being refused admittance at all the other gates, went with one of my sisters to that of the Feuillans, insisting that the sentinel should admit them. The *poissardes* attacked them for their boldness in resisting the order excluding them. One of them seized my sister by the arm, calling her the slave of the Austrian. "Hear me," said my sister to her, "I have been attached to the Queen ever since I was fifteen years of age; she gave me my marriage portion; I served her, when she was powerful and happy. She is now unfortunate. Ought I to abandon her?"—"She is right," cried the *poissardes;* "she ought not to abandon her mistress; let us make an entry for them." They instantly surrounded the sentinel, forced the passage, and introduced the Queen's women, accompanying them to the terrace of the Feuillans. One of these furies, whom the slightest impulse would have driven to tear my sister to pieces, taking her under her protection, gave her advice by which she might reach the palace in safety. "But of all things, my dear friend," said she to her, "pull off that green ribbon sash; it is the colour of that d'Artois, whom we will never forgive."—*Madame Campan.*

XIX

*Acceptance of the constitution—Opinion of Barnave and his friends
approved by the Court of Vienna—Secret policy of the Court—The
Legislative Assembly deliberates upon the ceremony to be observed on
receiving the King—Offensive motion—Louis XVI is received by the
Assembly with transport—He gives way to profound grief when with his
family—Public fêtes and rejoicings—M. de Montmorin's conversation with
Madame Campan upon the continual indiscretions of the people about
the Court—The royal family go to the Théâtre Français—Play changed—
Personal conflicts in the pit of the Italiens—Double correspondence of the
Court with foreign powers—Maison Civile —The Queen's misfortunes
do not alter the sweetness of her disposition—Method adopted by the
Queen respecting her secret correspondence—Madame Campan's conduct
when attacked by both parties—Particulars respecting M. Genet, her
brother, chargé d'affaires from France to Russia—Written testimony of
the Queen in favour of Madame Campan's zeal and fidelity—The King
comes to see her, and confirms these marks of confidence and satisfaction—
Projected interview between Louis XVI and Barnave—Attempts to
poison Louis XVI—Precautions taken—The Queen consults Pitt about
the Revolution—His reply—The émigrés oppose all alliance with the
constitutionals—Letter from Barnave to the Queen*

On my arrival at Paris on the 25th of August I found the state of feeling there much more
temperate than I had dared to hope. The conversation generally ran upon the acceptance
of the constitution, and the fêtes which would be given in consequence. The struggle
between the Jacobins and the constitutionals on the 17th of July 1791 nevertheless had
thrown the Queen into great terror for some moments; and the firing of the cannon
from the Champ de Mars upon a party which called for a trial of the King, and the
leaders of which were in the very bosom of the Assembly, left the most gloomy impressions upon her mind.

The constitutionals, the Queen's connection with whom was not slackened by the
intervention of the three members already mentioned, had faithfully served the royal
family during their detention.

"We still hold the wire by which this popular mass is moved," said Barnave to
M. de J—— one day, at the same time showing him a large volume, in which the

names of all those who were influenced by the power of gold alone were registered. It was at that time proposed to hire a considerable number of persons in order to secure loud acclamations when the King and his family should make their appearance at the play upon the acceptance of the constitution. That day, which afforded a glimmering hope of tranquillity, was the 14th of September; the fêtes were brilliant; but already new anxieties forbade the royal family to encourage hope.

The Legislative Assembly, which had just succeeded the Constituent Assembly (October 1791), founded its conduct upon the wildest republican principles; created from the midst of popular assemblies, it was wholly inspired by the spirit which animated them. The constitution, as I have said, was presented to the King on the 3rd of September 1791. The ministers, with the exception of M. de Montmorin, insisted upon the necessity of accepting the constitutional act in its entirety. The Prince de Kaunitz[1] was of the same opinion. Malouet wished the King to express himself candidly respecting any errors or dangers that he might observe in the constitution. But Duport and Barnave, alarmed at the spirit prevailing in the Jacobin Club,[2] and even in the Assembly, where Robespierre had already denounced them as traitors to the country, and dreading still greater evils, added their opinions to those of the majority of the ministers and M. de Kaunitz; those who really desired that the constitution should be maintained advised that it should not be accepted thus literally; and of this number, as I have already said, were M. Montmorin and M. Malouet. The King seemed inclined to this advice; and this is one of the strongest proofs of his sincerity.[3]

Alexandre Lameth, Duport, and Barnave, still relying on the resources of their party, hoped to have credit for directing the King through the influence they believed they had acquired over the mind of the Queen. They also consulted people of acknowledged talent, but belonging to no council nor to any assembly. Among these was M. Dubucq, formerly intendant of the marine and of the colonies. He answered in one phrase: "*Prevent disorder from organising itself.*"

Opinions such as those of the sententious and laconic M. Dubucq emanated from the aristocratic party, who preferred anything, even the Jacobins, to the establishment of the constitutional laws; and who, in fact, believed that any acceptance which should have any other appearance than that of compulsion would amount to a sanction sufficient to uphold the new government. The most unbridled disorders seemed preferable, because they gave hope of a total change; and twenty times over, upon occasions when persons but little acquainted with the secret policy of the Court expressed the apprehensions they entertained of the popular societies, the initiated answered that a sincere royalist ought to favour the Jacobins. My avowal of the terror with which they inspired me often brought this answer upon me, and often procured me the epithet of "constitutional"; while all the time I was intent only upon diligently serving the unfortunate Princess with whom my destiny was united.

The letter written by the King to the Assembly, claiming to accept the constitution in the very place where it had been created, and where he announced he would be on the 14th September at mid-day, was received with transport, and the reading was repeatedly interrupted by plaudits. The sitting terminated amidst the greatest enthusiasm, and M. de La Fayette obtained the release of all those who were detained on account of the King's journey [to Varennes], the abandonment of all proceedings relative to the events of the Revolution, and the discontinuance of the use of passports and of temporary restraints upon free travelling, as well in the interior as without. The whole was conceded by acclamation. Sixty members were deputed to go to the King and express to him fully the satisfaction his Majesty's letter had given. The Keeper of the Seals quitted the chamber, in the midst of applause, to precede the deputation to the King.

The King answered the speech addressed to him, and concluded by saying to the Assembly that a decree of that morning, which had abolished the Order of the Holy Ghost, had left him and his son alone permission to be decorated with it; but that an order having no value in his eyes, save for the power of conferring it, he would not use it.

The Queen, her son, and Madame, were at the door of the chamber into which the deputation was admitted. The King said to the deputies, "You see there my wife and children, who participate in my sentiments;" and the Queen herself confirmed the King's assurance. These apparent marks of confidence were very inconsistent with the agitated state of her mind. "These people want no sovereigns," said she. "We shall fall before their treacherous though well-planned tactics; they are demolishing the monarchy stone by stone."

Next day the particulars of the reception of the deputies by the King were reported to the Assembly, and excited warm approbation. But the President having put the question whether the Assembly ought not to remain seated while the King took the oath—"Certainly," was repeated by many voices; "*and the King, standing, uncovered.*" M. Malouet observed that there was no occasion on which the nation, assembled in the presence of the King, did not acknowledge him as its head; that the omission to treat the head of the State with the respect due to him would be an offence to the nation, as well as to the monarch. He moved that the King should take the oath standing, and that the Assembly should also stand while he was doing so. M. Malouet's observations would have carried the decree, but a deputy from Brittany exclaimed, with a shrill voice, "that he had an amendment to propose which would render all unanimous. Let us decree," said he, "that M. Malouet, and whoever else shall so please, may have leave to receive the King upon their knees; but let us stick to the decree."

The King repaired to the chamber at mid-day. His speech was followed by plaudits which lasted several minutes. After the signing of the constitutional act all sat down. The President rose to deliver his speech; but after he had begun, perceiving that the King did not rise to hear him, he sat down again. His speech made a powerful impression; the sentence with which it concluded excited fresh acclamations, cries of "*Bravo!*" and "*Vive le Roi!*" "Sire," said he, "how important in our eyes, and how dear to our hearts—how sublime a feature in our history—must be the epoch of that regeneration which gives citizens to France, and a country to Frenchmen—to you, as a King, a new title of greatness and glory, and, as a man, a source of new enjoyment." The whole Assembly accompanied the King on his return, amidst the people's cries of happiness, military music, and salvoes of artillery.

At length I hoped to see a return of that tranquillity which had so long vanished from the countenances of my august master and mistress. Their suite left them in the salon;

the Queen hastily saluted the ladies, and returned much affected; the King followed her, and, throwing himself into an arm-chair, put his handkerchief to his eyes. "Ah! Madame," cried he, his voice choked by tears, "why were you present at this sitting? To witness——." I heard these words, and no more, respecting their affliction. I withdrew, struck with the contrast between the shouts of joy without the palace, and the profound grief which oppressed the sovereigns within.[4] Half an hour afterwards the Queen sent for me. She desired to see M. de Goguelat, to announce to him his departure on that very night for Vienna. The new attacks upon the dignity of the throne which had been made during the sitting; the spirit of an Assembly worse than the former; the monarch put upon a level with the President, without any deference to the throne—all this proclaimed but too loudly that the sovereignty itself was aimed at. The Queen no longer saw any ground for hope from the interior of the country. The King wrote to the Emperor; she told me that she would herself, at midnight, bring the letter which M. de Goguelat was to bear to the Emperor, to my room. During all the remainder of the day the Château and the Tuileries were crowded; the illuminations were magnificent. The King and Queen were requested to take an airing in their carriage in the Champs-Elysées, escorted by the *aides-de-camp* and leaders of the Parisian army, the constitutional guard not being at that time organised. Many shouts of "*Vive le Roi!*" were heard; but as often as they ceased, one of the mob, who never quitted the door of the King's carriage for a single instant, exclaimed with a stentorian voice, "*No, don't believe them; Vive la Nation!*" This ill-omened cry struck terror into the Queen.

A few days afterwards M. de Montmorin sent to say he wanted to speak to me; that he would come to me, if he were not apprehensive his doing so would attract observation; and that he thought it would appear less particular if he should see me in the Queen's great closet at a time which he specified, and when nobody would be there. I went. After having made some polite observations upon the services I had already performed, and those I might yet perform, for my master and mistress, he spoke to me of the King's imminent danger; of the plots which were hatching, and of the lamentable composition of the Legislative Assembly; but he particularly dwelt upon the necessity of appearing, by prudent remarks, determined as much as possible to abide by the act the King had just recognised. I told him that could not be done without committing ourselves in the eyes of the royalist party, with which moderation was a crime; that it was painful to hear ourselves taxed with being constitutionals, at the same time that it was our opinion that the only constitution which was consistent with the King's honour, and the happiness and tranquillity of his people, was the entire power of the sovereign; that this was my creed, and it would pain me to give any room for suspicion that I was wavering in it. "Could you ever believe," said he, "that I should desire any other order of things? Have you any doubt of my attachment to the King's person, and the maintenance of his rights?"—"I know it, Count," replied I; "but you are not ignorant that you lie under the imputation of having adopted revolutionary ideas."—"Well, Madame, have resolution enough to dissemble and to conceal your real sentiments; dissimulation was never more necessary. Endeavours are being made to paralyse the evil intentions of the factious as much as possible; but we must not be counteracted here by certain dangerous expressions which are circulated in Paris as coming from the King and Queen." I told him that I had been already struck with apprehension of the evil which might be done by the intemperate observations of persons who had no power to act; and that I had felt ill consequences from having repeatedly enjoined silence on those in the Queen's service. "I know that," said the Count; "the Queen informed me of it, and that determined me to come and request you to cherish, as much you can, that spirit of discretion which is so necessary."

While the household of the King and Queen were a prey to all these fears, the festivities in celebration of the acceptance of the constitution proceeded. Their Majesties went to the opera; the audience consisted entirely of persons who sided with the King, and on that day the happiness of seeing him for a short time surrounded by faithful subjects might be enjoyed. The acclamations were then sincere.

La Coquette Corrigée had been selected for presentation at the Théâtre Français solely because it was the piece in which Mademoiselle Contat shone most. Yet the notions propagated by the Queen's enemies coinciding in my mind with the name of the play, I thought the choice very ill-judged. I was at a loss, however, how to tell her Majesty so; but sincere attachment gives courage. I explained myself; she was obliged to me, and desired that another play might be performed. They accordingly acted *La Gouvernante*.

The Queen, Madame the King's daughter, and Madame Elizabeth, were all well received on this occasion. It is true that the opinions and feelings of the spectators in the boxes could not be otherwise than favourable, and great pains had been taken, previously to these two performances, to fill the pit with proper persons. But, on the other hand, the Jacobins took the same precautions on their side at the Théâtre Italien, and the tumult was excessive there. The play was Grétry's *Les Événemens imprévus*. Unfortunately, Madame Dugazon thought proper to bow to the Queen as she sung the words, "Ah, how I love my mistress!" in a duet. Above twenty voices immediately exclaimed from the pit, "*No mistress! no master! liberty!*" A few replied from the boxes and slips, "*Vive le Roi! vive la Reine!*" Those in the pit answered, "*No master! no Queen!*" The quarrel increased; the pit formed into parties; they began fighting, and the Jacobins were beaten; tufts of their black hair flew about the theatre.[5] A strong guard arrived. The Faubourg Saint Antoine, hearing of what was going forward at the Théâtre Italien, flocked together, and began to talk of marching towards the scene of action. The Queen preserved the calmest demeanour; the commandants of the guard surrounded and encouraged her; they conducted themselves promptly and discreetly. No accident happened. The Queen was highly applauded as she quitted the theatre: it was the last time she was ever in one.

While couriers were bearing confidential letters from the King to the Princes, his brothers, and the foreign sovereigns, the Assembly invited him write to the Princes in order to induce them to return to France. The King desired the Abbé Montesquiou to write the letter he was to send; this letter, which was admirably composed in a simple and affecting style, suited to the character of Louis XVI, and filled with very powerful arguments in favour of the advantages to be derived from adopting the principles of the constitution, was confided to me by the King, who desired me to make him a copy of it.

At this period M. M——, one of the intendants of Monsieur's household, obtained a passport from the Assembly to join that Prince on business relative to his domestic concerns. The Queen selected him to be the bearer of this letter. She determined to give it to him herself, and to inform him of its object. I was astonished at her choice of this courier. The Queen assured me he was exactly the man for her purpose, that she relied even upon his indiscretion, and that it was merely necessary that the letter from the King to his brothers should be known to exist. The Princes were doubtless informed beforehand on the subject by the private correspondence. Monsieur nevertheless manifested some degree of surprise, and the messenger returned more grieved than pleased at this mark of confidence, which nearly cost him his life during the Reign of Terror.

Among the causes of uneasiness to the Queen there was one which was but too well founded—the thoughtlessness of the French whom she sent to foreign Courts. She used to say that they had no sooner passed the frontiers than they disclosed the most secret matters relative to the King's private sentiments, and that the leaders of the Revolution were informed of them through their agents, many of whom were Frenchmen who passed themselves off as emigrants in the cause of their King.

After the acceptance of the constitution the formation of the King's household, as well military as civil, formed a subject of attention. The Duc de Brissac had the command of the constitutional guard, which was composed of officers and men selected from the regiments, and of several officers drawn from the national guard of Paris. The King was satisfied with the feelings and conduct of this band, which, as is well known, existed but a very short time.

The new constitution abolished what were called honours, and the prerogatives belonging to them. Duchesse de Duras resigned her place of lady of the bed-chamber, not choosing to lose her right to the tabouret at Court. This step hurt the Queen, who saw herself forsaken for lost privileges at a time when her own rights were so hotly attacked. Many ladies of rank left the Court for the same reason. However, the King and Queen did not dare to form the civil part of their household, lest by giving the new names of the posts they should acknowledge the abolition of the old ones, and also lest they should admit into the highest positions persons not calculated to fill them well. Some time was spent in discussing the question, *whether the household should be formed without chevaliers and without ladies of honour.* The Queen's constitutional advisers were of opinion that the Assembly, having decreed a civil list adequate to uphold the splendour of the throne, would be dissatisfied at seeing the King adopting only a military household, and not forming his civil household upon the new constitutional plan. "How is it, Madame," wrote Barnave to the Queen, "that you will persist in giving these people even the smallest doubt as to your sentiments? When they decree you a civil and a military household, you, like young Achilles among the daughters of Lycomedes, eagerly seize the sword and scorn the mere ornaments." The Queen persisted in her determination to have no household. "If," said she, "this household be formed, not a single person of rank will remain with us, and upon a change of affairs we should be obliged to discharge the persons received into their place."

"Perhaps," added she, "perhaps I might find one day that I had saved the nobility, if I now had resolution enough to afflict them for a time: I have it not. When any measure which injures them is wrested from us they sulk with me; nobody comes to my card party; the King goes unattended to bed. No allowance is made for political necessity; we are punished for our very misfortunes."

The Queen wrote almost all day, and spent part of the night in reading: her courage supported her physical strength; her disposition was not at all soured by misfortune, and she was never seen in an ill-humour for a moment. She was, however, held up to the people as a woman absolutely furious and mad whenever the rights of the Crown were in any way attacked.

I was with her one day at one of her windows. We saw a man plainly dressed, like an ecclesiastic, surrounded by an immense crowd. The Queen imagined it was some Abbé whom they were about to throw into the basin of the Tuileries; she hastily opened her window and sent a *valet de chambre* to know what was going forward in the garden. It was Abbé Grégoire, whom the men and women of the tribunes were bringing back in triumph, on account of a motion he had just made in the National Assembly against the royal authority. On the following day the democratic journalists described the Queen as witnessing this triumph, and showing, by expressive gestures at her window, how highly she was exasperated by the honours conferred upon the patriot.

The correspondence between the Queen and the foreign powers was carried on in cipher. That to which she gave the preference can never be detected; but the greatest patience is requisite for its use. Each correspondent must have a copy of the same edition of some work. She selected *Paul and Virginia*. The page and line in which the letters required, and occasionally a monosyllable, are to be found are pointed out in ciphers agreed upon. I assisted her in finding the letters, and frequently I made an exact copy for her of all that she had ciphered, without knowing a single word of its meaning.

There were always several secret committees in Paris occupied in collecting information for the King respecting the measures of the factions, and in influencing some of the committees of the Assembly.

M. Bertrand de Molleville was in close correspondence with the Queen. The King employed M. Talon and others; much money was expended through the latter channel for the secret measures. The Queen had no confidence in them. M. de Laporte, minister of the civil list and of the household, also attempted to give a bias to public opinion by means of hireling publications; but these papers influenced none but the royalist party, which did not need influencing. M. de Laporte had a private police, which gave him some useful information.

I determined to sacrifice myself to my duty, but by no means to any intrigue, and I thought that circumstanced as I was, I ought to confine myself to obeying the Queen's orders. I frequently sent off couriers to foreign countries, and they were never discovered, so many precautions did I take. I am indebted for the preservation of my own existence to the care I took never to admit any deputy to my abode, and to refuse all interviews which even people of the highest importance often requested of me; but this line of conduct exposed me to every species of ill-will, and on the same day I saw myself denounced by Prudhomme, in his *Gazette Révolutionnaire*, as capable of making an aristocrat of the mother of the Gracchi, if a person so dangerous as myself could have got into her household; and by Gauthier's *Gazette Royaliste*, as a *monarchist*, a *constitutionalist*, more dangerous to the Queen's interests than a Jacobin.

At this period an event with which I had nothing to do placed me in a still more critical situation. My brother, M. Genet, began his diplomatic career successfully. At eighteen he was attached to the embassy to Vienna; at twenty he was appointed chief secretary of Legation in England, on occasion of the peace of 1783. A memorial which he presented to M. de Vergennes upon the dangers of the treaty of commerce then entered into with England gave offence to M. de Calonne, a patron of that treaty, and particularly to M. Gérard de Rayneval, chief clerk for Foreign Affairs. So long as M. de Vergennes lived, having upon my father's death declared himself the protector of my brother, he supported him against the enemies his memorial had raised up. But on his death M. de Montmorin, being much in need of the long experience in business which he found in M. de Rayneval, was guided solely by the latter. The office of which my brother was the head was suppressed. He then went to St Petersburg, strongly recommended to the Comte de Ségur, minister from France to that Court, who appointed him secretary of Legation. Some time afterwards the Comte de Ségur left him at St Petersburg, charged with the affairs of France.[6]

When my brother quitted Versailles he was much hurt at being deprived of a considerable income for having penned a memorial which his zeal alone had dictated, and the importance of which was afterwards but too well understood. I perceived from his correspondence that he inclined to some of the new notions. He told me it was right he should no longer conceal from me that he sided with the constitutional party; that the King had in fact commanded it, having himself accepted the constitution; that he would proceed firmly in that course, because in this case disingenuousness would be fatal, and that he took that side of the question because he had had it proved to him that the foreign powers would not serve the King's cause without advancing pretensions prompted by long-standing interests, which always would influence their Councils; that he saw no salvation for the King and Queen but from within France, and that he would serve the constitutional King as he served him before the Revolution. And lastly, he requested me to impart to the Queen the real sentiments of one of his Majesty's agents at a foreign Court. I immediately went to the Queen and gave her my brother's letter, she read it attentively, and said, "This is the letter of a young man led astray by discontent and ambition. I know you do not think as he does; do not fear that you will lose the confidence of the King and myself." I offered to discontinue all correspondence with my brother; she opposed that, saying it would be dangerous. I then entreated she would permit me in future to show her my own and my brother's letters, to which she consented. I wrote warmly to my brother against the course he had adopted. I sent my letters by sure channels; he answered me by the post, and no longer touched upon anything but family affairs. Once only he informed me that if I should write to him respecting the affairs of the day he would give me no answer. "Serve your august mistress with the unbounded devotion which is due from you," said he, "and let us each do our duty. I will only observe to you that at Paris the fogs of the Seine often prevent people from seeing that immense capital, even from the Pavilion of Flora, and I see it more

The Grand Trianon

clearly from St Petersburg." The Queen said, as she read this letter, "Perhaps he speaks but too truly; who can decide upon so disastrous a position as ours has become?"

The day on which I gave the Queen my first letter to read she had several audiences to give to ladies and other persons belonging to the Court, who came on purpose to inform her that my brother was an avowed constitutional and revolutionist. The Queen replied, "I know it; Madame Campan has been to tell me so." Persons jealous of my situation having subjected me to mortifications, and these unpleasant circumstances recurring daily, I requested the Queen's permission to withdraw from Court. She exclaimed against the very idea, represented it to me as extremely dangerous for my own reputation, and had the kindness to add that, for my sake as well as for her own, she never would consent to it. After this conversation I retired to my apartment. A few minutes later a footman brought me this note from the Queen:—"I have never ceased to give you and yours proofs of attachment; I wish to tell you in writing that I have full faith in your honour and fidelity, as well as in your other good qualities; and that I ever rely on the zeal and address you exert to serve me."[7]

At the moment that I was going to express my gratitude to the Queen I heard a tapping at the door of my room, which opened upon the Queen's inner corridor; I opened it: it was the King. I was confused; he perceived it, and said to me kindly, "I alarm you, Madame Campan; I come, however, to comfort you; the Queen has told me how much she is hurt at the injustice of several persons towards you. But how is it that you complain of injustice and calumny when you see that we are victims of them? In some of your companions it is jealousy; in the people belonging to the Court, it is anxiety. Our situation is so disastrous, and we have met with so much ingratitude and treachery, that the apprehensions of those who love us are excusable! I could quiet them by telling them all the secret services you perform for us daily; but I will not do it. Out of goodwill to you they would repeat all I should say, and you would be lost with the Assembly. It is much better, both for you and for us, that you should be thought a constitutional. It has been mentioned to me a hundred times already; I have never contradicted it; but I come to give you my word that if we are fortunate enough to see an end of all this, I will, at the Queen's residence, and in the presence of my brothers, relate the important services you have rendered us, and I will recompense you and your son for them." I threw myself at the King's feet and kissed his hand. He raised me up, saying, "Come, come, do not grieve; the Queen, who loves you, confides in you as I do."

Down to the day of the acceptance it was impossible to introduce Barnave into the interior of the palace; but when the Queen was free from the inner guard she said she would see him. The very great precautions which it was necessary for the deputy to take in order to conceal his connection with the King and Queen compelled them to spend two hours waiting for him in one of the corridors of the Tuileries, and all in vain. The first day that he was to be admitted, a man whom Barnave knew to be dangerous having met him in the courtyard of the palace, he determined to cross it without stopping, and walked in the gardens in order to lull suspicion. I was desired to wait for Barnave at a little door belonging to the *entresols* of the palace, with my hand upon the open lock. I was in that position for an hour. The King came to me frequently, and always to speak to me of the uneasiness which a servant belonging to the Château, who was a patriot, gave him. He came again to ask me whether I had heard the door called *de Decret* opened. I assured him nobody had been in the corridor, and he became easy. He was dreadfully apprehensive that his connection with Barnave would be discovered. "It would," said the King, "be a ground for grave accusations, and the unfortunate man would be lost." I then ventured to remind his Majesty that as Barnave was not the only one in the secret of the business which brought him in contact with their Majesties, one of his colleagues might be induced to speak of the association with which they were honoured, and that in letting them know by my presence that I also was informed of it, a risk was incurred of removing from those gentlemen part of the responsibility of the secret. Upon this observation the King quitted me hastily and returned a moment afterwards with the Queen. "Give me your place," said she, "I will wait for him in my turn. You have convinced the King. We must not increase in their eyes the number of persons informed of their communications with us."

The police of M. de Laporte, intendant of the civil list, apprised him, as early as the latter end of 1791, that a man belonging to the King's offices who had set up as a pastry-cook at the Palais Royal was about to resume the duties of his situation, which had devolved upon him again on the death of one who held it for life; that he was so furious a Jacobin that he had dared to say it would be a good thing for France if the King's days were shortened. His duty was confined to making the pastry; he was closely watched by the head officers of the kitchen, who were devoted to his Majesty; but it is so easy to introduce a subtle poison into made dishes that it was determined the King and Queen should eat only plain roast meat in future; that their bread should be brought to them by M. Thierry de Ville d'Avray, intendant of the smaller apartments, and that he should likewise take upon himself to supply the wine. The King was fond of pastry; I was directed to order some, as if for myself; sometimes of one pastry-cook, and sometimes of another. The pounded sugar, too, was kept in my room. The King, the Queen, and Madame Elizabeth ate together, and nobody remained to wait on them. Each had a dumb waiter and a little bell to call the servants when they were wanted. M. Thierry used himself to bring me their Majesties' bread and wine, and I locked them up in a private cupboard in the King's closet on the ground floor. As soon as the King sat down to table I took in the pastry and bread. All was hidden under the table lest it might be necessary to have the servants in. The King thought it dangerous as well as distressing to show any apprehension of attempts against his person, or any mistrust of his officers of the kitchen. As he never drank a whole bottle of wine at his meals (the Princesses drank nothing but water), he filled up that out of which he had drunk about half from the bottle served up by the officers of his butlery. I took it away after dinner. Although he never ate any other pastry than that which I brought, he took care in the same manner that it should seem that he had eaten of that served at table. The lady who succeeded me found this duty all regulated, and she executed it in the same manner; the public never was in possession of these particulars, nor of the apprehensions which gave rise to them. At the end of three or four months the police of M. de Laporte gave notice that nothing more was to be dreaded from that sort of plot against the King's life; that the plan was entirely changed; and that all the blows now to be struck would be directed as much against the throne as against the person of the sovereign.

There are others besides myself who know that at this time one of the things about which the Queen most desired to be satisfied was the opinion of the famous Pitt. She would sometimes say to me, "I never pronounce the name of *Pitt* without feeling a chill like that of death" (I repeat here her very expressions). "That man is the mortal enemy of France; and he takes a dreadful revenge for the impolitic support given by the cabinet of Versailles to the American insurgents. He wishes by our destruction to guarantee the maritime power of his country for ever against the efforts made by the King to improve his marine power and their happy results during the last war. He knows that it is not only the King's policy but his private inclination to be solicitous about his fleets, and that the most active step he has taken during his whole reign was to visit the port of Cherbourg. Pitt has served the cause of the French Revolution from the first disturbances; he will perhaps serve it until its annihilation. I will endeavour to learn to what point he intends to lead us, and I am sending M. —— to London for that purpose. He has been intimately connected with Pitt, and they have often had political conversations respecting the French Government. I will get him to make him speak out, at least so far as such a man can speak out."

Some time afterwards the Queen told me that her secret envoy was returned from London, and that all he had been able to wring from Pitt, whom he found alarmingly reserved, was that *he would not suffer the French monarchy to perish*; that to suffer the revolutionary spirit to erect an organised republic in France would be a great error, affecting the tranquillity of Europe. "Whenever," said she, "Pitt expressed himself upon the necessity of supporting *monarchy* in France, he maintained the most profound silence upon what concerns the monarch. The result of these conversations is anything but encouraging; but, even as to that monarchy which he wishes to save, will he have means and strength to save it if he suffers us to fall?"

The death of the Emperor Leopold took place on the 1st of March 1792. When the news of this event reached the Tuileries the Queen was gone out. Upon her return I put the letter containing it into her hands. She exclaimed that the Emperor had been poisoned; that she had remarked and preserved a newspaper, in which, in an article upon the sitting of the Jacobins, at the time when the Emperor Leopold declared for the coalition, it was said, speaking of him, that a *piecrust* would settle that matter. The Queen lamented her brother. However, the education of Francis II, which had been superintended by the Emperor Joseph, inspired her with new hopes: she thought he must have inherited sentiments of affection for her, and did not doubt that he had, under the care of his uncle, imbibed that valiant spirit so necessary for the support of a crown. At this period Barnave obtained the Queen's consent that he should read all the letters she should write. He was fearful of private correspondences that might hamper the plan marked out for her; he mistrusted her Majesty's sincerity on this point; and the diversity of counsels, and the necessity of yielding, on the one hand, to some of the views of the constitutionalists, and on the other, to those of the French Princes, and even of foreign Courts, were unfortunately the circumstances which most rapidly impelled the Court towards its ruin.

The Queen wished she could have shown Barnave the letter of condolence she wrote to Francis II. This letter was to be shown to her *triumvirate* (as she sometimes designated the three deputies whom I have named). She would not use a single word which, by clashing with their plans, might prevent its going; she was also fearful of introducing anything not in accordance with her sentiments which the Emperor might learn by other means. "Sit down at that table," said she to me, "and sketch me out a letter: dwell upon the idea that I see in my nephew the pupil of Joseph. If yours be better than mine you shall dictate it to me." I wrote a letter; she read it and said, "It is the very thing, the matter concerned me too nearly to admit of my keeping the true line as you have done."

The party of the Princes was much alarmed on being informed of the communication between the remnant of the constitutional party and the Queen, who, on her part, always dreaded the party of the Princes. She did justice to the Comte d'Artois, and often said that his party would act in contradiction to his feelings towards the King, his brother, and herself; but that he would be led away by people over whom Calonne had a most lamentable ascendancy. She reproached Count Esterhazy, whom she had loaded with favours, for having sided with Calonne so entirely that she had reason to consider him an enemy.

However, the emigrants showed great apprehensions of the consequences which might follow in the interior from a connection with the constitutionalists, whom they described as a party existing only in idea, and totally without means of repairing their errors. The Jacobins were preferred to them, because, said they, there would be no treaty to be made with any one at the moment of extricating the King and his family from the abyss in which they were plunged.

I frequently read to the Queen the letters written to her by Barnave. One struck me forcibly, and I think I have retained the substance of it sufficiently well to enable me to give a faithful account of it. He told the Queen he did not rely enough upon the strength remaining in the constitutional party; that their flag was indeed torn, but the word *constitution* was legible upon it; that this word would recover its virtue if the King and his friends would rally round it sincerely; that the authors of the constitution, enlightened with respect to their own errors, might yet amend it, and restore to the throne all its splendour; that the Queen must not believe the public mind was favourably disposed towards the Jacobins, that the weak joined them because there was no strength elsewhere, but the general opinion was for the constitution; that the party of the French Princes, unfortunately shackled by the policy of foreign courts, ought not to be depended on; that the majority of the emigrants had already destroyed by misconduct much of the interest excited by their misfortunes; that entire confidence ought not to be reposed in the foreign powers, guided, as they were, by the policy of their cabinets, and not by the ties of blood; and that the interior alone was capable of supporting the integrity of the kingdom. He concluded the letter by saying that he laid at her Majesty's feet the only national party still in existence; that he feared to name it; but that she ought not to forget that Henri IV was not assisted by foreign Princes in regaining his dominions, and that he ascended a Catholic throne after having fought at the head of a Protestant party.

Barnave and his friends presumed too far upon their strength; it was exhausted in the contest with the Court. The Queen was aware of this, and if she seemed to have any confidence in them, she was probably prompted by a policy which, it must be confessed, could only prove injurious to her.

1. Chief minister of Austria.

2. The extreme revolutionary party, so called from the club, originally "Breton", then "Amis de la Constitution", sitting at the convent of the Dominicans (called in France Jacobins) of the Rue Saint Honoré.

3. The first time I ever had the honour of being *tête-à-tête* with the King, diffidence so completely overcame me, that if it had been my duty to speak first it would have been impossible for me to have framed a single phrase; but I took courage when I saw the King still more embarrassed than myself, and, with difficulty, stammering out a few unconnected words; he, in his turn, grew composed on seeing me at ease, and our conversation soon became highly interesting. After a few general observations upon the perplexities of the existing state of things, the King said to me, "Well! have you any objection remaining?"—"No, Sire; a desire to obey and gratify your Majesty is the only feeling I am sensible of; but, in order that I may be able really to serve you, it is necessary that your Majesty should have the goodness to inform me what is your intention with regard to the constitution, and what is the line of conduct you would wish your ministers to adopt."—"That is true," replied the King; "this is my opinion: I do not consider the constitution by any means a masterpiece; I think there are very great errors in it, and if I had been at liberty to comment upon it, advantageous alterations would have been made. But the time is now gone by: such as it is, I have sworn to maintain it; I ought to be, and I will be, strictly true to my oath, and the rather, as I think the utmost exactness in executing the mandates of the constitution is the most certain way to draw the attention of the nation to the alterations that ought to be made in it. I neither can, nor ought to have, any other plan than this; I certainly will not abandon it, and I wish my ministers to conform to it."—"Your scheme appears infinitely judicious, Sire; I feel myself in a condition to accomplish it, and I engage to

do so. I have not sufficiently studied the constitution as a whole, and in all its parts, to form a decided opinion, and I will refrain from forming one, until the operation of the constitution shall have enabled the nation to estimate it by its effects. But may I venture to ask your Majesty whether the Queen's opinion upon this point is in accordance with your own?"—"Yes, certainly it is; she will tell you so herself." Immediately afterwards I went to the Queen, who, after assuring me with the greatest kindness how truly she felt the obligation under which the King lay to me for having accepted the administration at so perplexing a juncture, added, "The King has informed you of his views with regard to the constitution; do you not think the only way is to be faithful to the oath?"—"Yes, certainly, Madame."—"Well, then, be assured that we shall not be induced to swerve. Come, come, M. Bertrand, courage; I hope with patience, firmness, and consistency, all is not yet lost."—*Private Memoirs of the Latter End of the Reign of Louis XVI*, by M. Bertrand de Molleville, Minister and Secretary of State, vol. i, pp. 101–3.

4. Madame Campan, in one of her manuscripts, relates this anecdote in a somewhat different manner:—

> The Queen attended the sitting in a private box. I remarked her total silence, and the deep grief which was depicted in her countenance on her return. The King came to her apartment the private way: he was pale, his features were much changed. The Queen uttered an exclamation of surprise at his appearance. I thought he was ill; but what was my affliction when I heard the unfortunate monarch say, as he threw himself into a chair and put his handkerchief to his eyes, "All is lost! Ah! Madame, and you are witness to this humiliation! What! you are come into France to see—" these words were interrupted by sobs. The Queen threw herself upon her knees before him, and pressed him in her arms. I remained with them, not from any blameable curiosity, but from a stupefaction which rendered me incapable of determining what I ought to do. The Queen said to me "*Oh! go, go!*" with an accent which expressed, "*Do not remain to see the dejection and despair of your sovereign!*"
> —Note by the Editor.

5. At this time none but the Jacobins had discontinued the use of hair-powder.—*Madame Campan.*

6. After his return from Russia, M. Genet was appointed ambassador to the United States by the party called Girondists, the deputies who headed it being from the department of the Gironde. He was recalled by the Robespierre party, which overthrew the former faction, on the 31st of May 1793, and condemned to appear before the Convention. Vice-President Clinton, at that time Governor of New York, offered him an asylum in his house and the hand of his daughter, and M. Genet established himself prosperously in America.—*Madame Campan.*

7. I had just received this letter from the Queen when M. de la Chapelle, commissary general of the King's household, and head of the offices of M. de Laporte, minister of the civil list, came to see me. The palace having been already forced by the brigands on the 20th of June 1792, he proposed that I should entrust the paper to him, that he might place it in a safer situation than the apartments of the Queen. When he returned into his offices he placed the letter she had condescended to write to me behind a large picture in his closet; but on the 10th of August M. de la Chapelle was thrown into the prisons of the Abbaye, and the committee

of public safety established themselves in his offices, whence they issued all their decrees of death. There it was that a villanous servant belonging to M. de Laporte went to declare that in the minister's apartment, under a board in the floor, a number of papers would be found. They were brought forth, and M. de Laporte was sent to the scaffold, where he suffered *for having betrayed the State by serving his master and sovereign*. M. de la Chapelle was saved, as if by a miracle, from the massacres of the 2nd of September. The committee of public safety having removed to the King's apartments at the Tuileries, M. de la Chapelle had permission to return to his closet to take away some property belonging to him. Turning round the picture, behind which he had hidden the Queen's letter, he found it in the place into which he had slipped it, and, delighted to see that I was safe from the ill consequences the discovery of this paper might have brought upon me, he burnt it instantly. In times of danger a mere nothing may save life or destroy it.—*Madame Campan.*

ANNEX TO CHAPTER XIX

Madame Campan refers in the preceding chapter to "secret measures" and "expenditure." Bertrand de Molleville, in the second volume of his *Memoirs*, thus explains this systematic and extensive mode of bribery.

HOW THE TRIBUNES WERE INFLUENCED

M. de Laporte, to whom I had some time previously communicated my opinion on the subject of the tribunes, or galleries, told me that in the course of eight or nine months the King had been induced to spend more than 2,500,000 livres upon the tribunes alone; and that they had, all along, been for the Jacobins; that the persons to whom the operation had been entrusted were strongly suspected of having diverted a considerable part of the money, perhaps the whole of it, to their own purposes; but that this inconvenience was unavoidable in an expenditure of that sort, which, from its nature, was not susceptible of any control or check whatever; and that this consideration had determined the King to discontinue it.

I will not insist, as a certain fact, that the two chief agents in this service (MM. T—— and S——) did really apply the fund committed to them to their own use, although it was a matter of public notoriety that since their being entrusted with it one of them made purchases to the extent of from 1,2–1,500,000 livres, and the other to the extent of from 7–800,000 livres; but I have no hesitation in asserting that they can rebut the reproach of signal knavery only by proving that they managed the operation with a want of skill and a degree of negligence almost equally culpable; for nothing was more easy than to secure the tribunes by paying them. I had made the experiment once only during my administration, but then I was completely successful; it was on the day on which I was to make, in the Assembly, my full reply to the denunciations which had been made against me. I was informed two days beforehand by my spies that the secret committee of the Jacobins had determined on that day to augment the number of their hirelings in the tribunes, to ensure my being hooted; I immediately sent for one of the victors of the Bastille, to whom I had before the Revolution rendered some important services, who was entirely devoted to me, and who was a man of great weight in the Faubourg Saint Antoine. Him I directed to select from among the working men of the Faubourg 200 staunch and sturdy men on whom he could rely, and to take them next day to the Assembly, at six o'clock in the morning, in order that they might be the first there before the opening of the chamber, and so fill the front places in the tribune at the two ends of the chamber; and to give them no other order than merely to applaud or hoot according to a signal which was agreed on.

This manœuvre was as successful as I could wish; my speech was repeatedly interrupted by applause, which was doubled when I ceased speaking; the Jacobins were thunderstruck at this and could not at all understand it. A quarter of an hour afterwards I was still in the Assembly, as well as all the ministers who had made it their duty to attend me on the emergency in question, when the Abbé Fauchet rose to notice a fact which he declared to be of great importance. "I have this moment," said he, "received a letter informing me that a considerable proportion of the citizens in the tribunes have been paid to applaud the Minister of Marine."

Although this was true enough, my unaltered countenance, and the reputation of the Abbé Fauchet, who was known to be an unblushing liar, caused his denunciation to be ridiculed; and it was considered a calumny the more stupid inasmuch as it was nothing unusual to hear my speeches applauded by the tribunes. True, I had always taken care to introduce into them some of those phrases which the people never failed to applaud mechanically, when they were uttered with a certain emphasis, without troubling themselves to examine the sense in which they were used. This victory, gained in the tribunes over the Jacobins, cost me no more than 270 livres in assignats, because a considerable number of my champions, out of regard for their leader, would receive nothing more from him than a glass of brandy.

I gave the King all these particulars in my reply to his Majesty's latter notes, and I again entreated him to permit me to make a second experiment upon the tribunes for one single week only, upon a plan which I annexed to my letter, and the expense of which did not exceed 800 livres *per diem*. This plan consisted in filling the front rows of the two tribunes with 262 trusty fellows, whose pay was fixed at the following rates:—

		Liv. per diem
1st	To a leader, who alone was in the secret	50
2ndly	To a sub-leader, chosen by the former	25
3rdly	To ten assistants, selected by the leader and sub-leader, having no knowledge of each other, and each deputed to recruit twenty-five men, and take them daily to the Assembly, ten livres a piece; total	100
4thly	To two hundred and fifty men, each fifty sous a day; total	625

| | Total | 800 livres |

The leader and sub-leader were to be placed, one in the middle of the front row of one tribune, and the other in the same situation in the other tribune; each of them was known only to the five assistants whom he had under his orders in the tribune in which he took his seat; the sub-leader received his directions by a signal concerted between themselves alone; they had a second signal for the purpose of passing the order to the adjutants, each of whom again transmitted it to his twenty-five men by a third signal. All of them, with the exception of the leader and sub-leader, were to be engaged in the name of Pétion, for the support of the constitution against the aristocrats and republicans. Each assistant was to pay his own recruits, and was to receive the funds from the leader or the sub-leader, in proportion to the number of men he brought with him.

The leader alone was to correspond with a friend of a captain of the King's constitutional guard, named Piquet, a man of courage, and entirely devoted to his Majesty's service. This captain was to receive from me daily the funds necessary for the expenditure of the day following, with directions for the conduct of the tribunes according to what had passed on the day preceding; he was to communicate the whole to his friend, who, in his turn, was to transmit to the leader of the operation. By means of these various subdivisions this man might get wind by treachery or otherwise without any serious inconvenience resulting from it, because it cut off the possibility of all ultimate discovery, and prevented inquiries from being directed to me; nothing more was necessary than to remove any one of the intermediaries. Besides, in order so far as possible to watch the fidelity of the agents of this enterprise, and in some measure to keep a check upon the expense, I had agreed with Buob, *a juge de la paix*, that he should daily send five of his runners, whose salary I was to pay him, into each of the tribunes to see what was going forward there, especially in the front rows; to calculate as exactly as they could the number of persons shouting or applauding, and give him an account accordingly. We had not neglected to apprise the assistants that this inspection was regularly made by agents of Pétion.

The King returned me this plan after reflecting upon it for four-and-twenty hours, and authorised me to try it in the course of the following week; this was the result:—
The first and second days our people contented themselves with silencing all marks of disapprobation and applause under pretence of hearing better, and that was one great point gained. On the third day, they began slightly to applaud constitutional motions and opinions, and continued to prevent contrary motions and opinions from being heard. On the fourth day, the same line of conduct was continued, only the applauses were warmer, and longer persevered in. The Assembly could not make it out; several of the members looked towards the tribunes frequently and with attention, and made themselves easy on seeing them filled with individuals whose appearance and dress were as usual. On the fifth day, the marks of applause became stronger, and they began to murmur a little against anti-constitutional motions and remarks. At this the Assembly appeared somewhat disconcerted; but one of the assistants, on being interrogated by a deputy, replying that he was for the constitution and for Pétion, it was supposed that the disapprobation which had been heard was the effect of some mistake. On the sixth day, the sounds of approbation and disapprobation were still conducted in the same way, but with a degree of violence considerable enough to give offence to the Assembly;

a motion was made against the tribunes, who repelled it by violent clamours, insults, and threats. Some of the men employed carried their audacity so far as to raise their sticks, as if to strike the deputies who were near them, and repeated, over and over again, that the Assembly consisted of a pack of beggars, who ought to be knocked on the head. The President, no doubt thinking that it was not quite prudent to wait till the majority of those who filled the tribunes should declare themselves of that opinion, broke up the sitting.

As the members of the Assembly quitted the hall, several of the deputies accosted a considerable number of individuals coming down from the tribunes, and, by dint of questions and cajolery, drew from them that they were employed by Pétion. They immediately went to complain to him on the subject, under a conviction that he had been deceived in the choice of his men and would dismiss them. Pétion, who as yet knew nothing of what had been going forward in the Assembly, swore truly that he had no hand in it. He insisted that it was a manœuvre of his enemies, and promised to leave no stone unturned to find out its authors. I was informed that in the evening several of his emissaries had been all over the faubourgs, and had questioned a great many working men; but, fortunately, all these inquiries ended in nothing.

The letter which I addressed to the King every morning informed him of the orders I had issued for the next day with regard to the management of the tribunes; and as he had always some confidential person at the Assembly, in order that he might be accurately informed of what was going forward there, he was enabled to judge with what success the directions I gave were executed; and consequently his Majesty in almost all his answers to the letters of that week observed: "The tribunes go on well—better and better—admirable." But the scene of violence on Saturday gave him some uneasiness. On the following day, when I made my appearance at the *levée*, their Majesties and Madame Elizabeth looked at me in the most gracious manner. After mass the King, passing close by me, said without turning, and low enough to be heard by nobody but myself—"Very well, only too rapidly. I will write to you." In fact, in the letter which the King returned to me the same day, he observed: "That the experiment had succeeded beyond his hopes, but that it would be dangerous, especially to myself, to pursue it. That this resource ought to be reserved for a time of need, and that he would apprise me when that time arrived."

XX

*Fresh libel by Madame de Lamotte—The Queen refuses to purchase
the manuscript—The King buys it—The Queen performs her
Easter devotions secretly in 1792—She dares not confide in General
Dumouriez—Barnave's last advice—Insults offered to the royal family
by the mob—The King's dejection—20th of June—The King's kindness
to Madame Campan—Iron closet—Louis XVI entrusts a portfolio
to Madame Campan—Importance of the documents it contained—
Procedure of M. de La Fayette—Why it was unsuccessful —An assassin
conceals himself in the Queen's apartments*

In the beginning of the year 1792 a worthy priest requested a private interview with me. He had learned the existence of a new libel by Madame de Lamotte. He told me that the people who came from London to get it printed in Paris only desired gain, and that they were ready to deliver the manuscript to him for 1,000 *louis*, if he could find any friend of the Queen disposed to make that sacrifice for her peace; that he had thought of me, and if her Majesty would give him the 24,000 francs, he would hand the manuscript to me.

I communicated this proposal to the Queen, who rejected it, and desired me to answer that at the time when she had power to punish the hawkers of these libels she deemed them so atrocious and incredible that she despised them too much to stop them; that if she were imprudent and weak enough to buy a single one of them, the Jacobins might possibly discover the circumstance through their espionage; that were this libel bought up, it would be printed nevertheless, and would be much more dangerous when they apprised the public of the means she had used to suppress it.

Baron d'Aubier, gentleman-in-ordinary to the King, and my particular friend, had a good memory and a clear way of communicating the substance of the debates and decrees of the National Assembly. I went daily to the Queen's apartments to repeat all this to the King, who used to say, on seeing me, "Ah! here's the *Postillon par Calais*"—a newspaper of the time.

M. d'Aubier one day said to me, "The Assembly has been much occupied with an information laid by the workmen of the Sèvres manufactory. They brought to the President's office a bundle of pamphlets which they said were the life of Marie Antoinette. The director of the manufactory was ordered up to the bar, and declared he had received orders to burn the printed sheets in question in the furnaces used for baking his china."

While I was relating this business to the Queen, the King coloured and held his head down over his plate. The Queen said to him, "Do you know anything about this, Sire?" The King made no answer. Madame Elizabeth requested him to explain what all this meant. Still silent. I withdrew hastily. A few minutes afterwards the Queen came to my room and informed me that the King, out of regard for her, had purchased the whole edition struck off from the manuscript which I had mentioned to her; and that M. de Laporte had not been able to devise any more secret way of destroying the work than that of having it burnt at Sèvres among 200 workmen, 180 of whom must, in all probability, be Jacobins! She told me she had concealed her vexation from the King; that he was in consternation, and that she could say nothing, since his good intentions and his affection for her had been the cause of the mistake.[1]

Some time afterwards the Assembly received a denunciation against M. de Montmorin. The ex-minister was accused of having neglected forty despatches from M. Genet, the *chargé d'affaires* from France in Russia, not having even unsealed them, because M. Genet acted on constitutional principles. M. de Montmorin appeared at the bar to answer this accusation. Whatever distress I might feel in obeying the order I had received from the King to go and give him an account of the sitting, I thought I ought not to fail in doing so. But instead of giving my brother his family name, I merely said *your Majesty's chargé d'affaires at St Petersburg.*

The King did me the favour to say that he noticed a reserve in my account of which he approved. The Queen condescended to add a few obliging remarks to those of the King. However, my office of journalist gave me in this instance so much pain that I took an opportunity, when the King was expressing his satisfaction to me at the manner in which I gave him this daily account, to tell him that its merit belonged wholly to M. d'Aubier; and I ventured to request the King to suffer that excellent man to give him an account of the sittings himself. I assured the King that if he would permit it, that gentleman might proceed to the Queen's apartments through mine unseen; the King consented to the arrangement. Thenceforward M. d'Aubier gave the King repeated proofs of zeal and attachment.

The Curé of Saint Eustache ceased to be the Queen's confessor when he took the constitutional oath. I do not remember the name of the ecclesiastic who succeeded him; I only know that he was conducted into her apartments with the greatest mystery. Their Majesties did not perform their Easter devotions in public, because they could neither declare for the constitutional clergy, nor act so as to show that they were against them.

The Queen did perform her Easter devotions in 1792; but she went to the chapel attended only by myself. She desired me beforehand to request one of my relations, who was her chaplain, to celebrate a mass for her at five o'clock in the morning. It was still dark; she gave me her arm, and I lighted her with a taper. I left her alone at the chapel door. She did not return to her room until the dawn of day.

Dangers increased daily. The Assembly were strengthened in the eyes of the people by the hostilities of the foreign armies and the army of the Princes. The communication with the latter party became more active; the Queen wrote almost every day. M. de Goguelat possessed her confidence for all correspondence with the foreign parties, and I was obliged to have him in my apartments; the Queen asked for him very frequently, and at times which she could not previously appoint.

All parties were exerting themselves either to ruin or to save the King. One day I found the Queen extremely agitated; she told me she no longer knew where she was; that the leaders of the Jacobins offered themselves to her through the medium of Dumouriez; or that Dumouriez, abandoning the Jacobins, had come and offered himself to her; that she had granted him an audience; that when alone with her, he had thrown himself at her feet, and told her that he had drawn the *bonnet rouge* over his head to the very ears; but that he neither was nor could be a Jacobin; that the Revolution had been suffered to extend even to that rabble of destroyers who, thinking of nothing but pillage, were ripe for anything, and might furnish the Assembly with a formidable army, ready to undermine the remains of a throne already but too much shaken. Whilst speaking with the utmost ardour he seized the Queen's hand and kissed it with transport, exclaiming, "*Suffer yourself to be saved.*" The Queen told me that the protestations of a traitor were not to be relied on; that the whole of his conduct was so well known, that undoubtedly the wisest course was not to trust to it;[2] that moreover, the Princes particularly recommended that no confidence should be placed in any proposition emanating from within the kingdom; that the force without became imposing; and that it was better to rely upon their success, and upon the protection due from Heaven to a sovereign so virtuous as Louis XVI and to so just a cause.

The constitutionalists, on their part, saw that there had been nothing more than a pretence of listening to them. Barnave's last advice was as to the means of continuing, a few weeks longer, the constitutional guard, which had been denounced to the Assembly, and was to be disbanded. The denunciation against the constitutional guard affected *only its staff and the Duc de Brissac.* Barnave wrote to the Queen that the staff of the guard was already attacked; that the Assembly was about to pass a decree to reduce it; and he entreated her to prevail on the King, the very instant the decree should appear, to form the staff afresh of persons whose names he sent her. Barnave said that all who were set down in it passed for decided Jacobins, but were not so in fact; that they, as well as himself, were in despair at seeing the monarchical government attacked; that they had learned to dissemble their sentiments, and that it would be at least a fortnight before the Assembly could know them well, and certainly before it could succeed in making them unpopular; that it would be necessary to take advantage of that short space of time to get away from Paris, immediately after their nomination. The Queen was of opinion that she ought not to yield to this advice. The Duc de Brissac was sent to Orléans, and the guard was disbanded.

Barnave, seeing that the Queen did not follow his counsel in anything, and convinced that she placed all her reliance on assistance from abroad, determined to quit Paris. He obtained a last audience. "Your misfortunes, Madame," said he, "and those which I anticipate for France, determine me to sacrifice myself to serve you. I see that my advice does not agree with the views of your Majesties. I augur but little advantage from the plan you are induced to pursue—you are too remote from your succours; you will be lost before they reach you. Most ardently do I wish I may be mistaken in so lamentable a prediction; but I am sure to pay with my head for the interest your misfortunes have raised in me, and the services I have sought to render you. I request, for my sole reward, the honour of kissing your hand." The Queen, her eyes suffused with tears, granted him that favour, and remained impressed with a favourable idea of his sentiments. Madame Elizabeth participated in this opinion, and the two Princesses frequently spoke of Barnave. The Queen also received M. Duport several times, but with less mystery. Her connection with the constitutional deputies transpired. Alexandre de Lameth was the only one of the three who survived the vengeance of the Jacobins.[3]

The national guard, which succeeded the King's guard, having occupied the gates of the Tuileries, all who came to see the Queen were insulted with impunity. Menacing cries were uttered aloud even in the Tuileries; they called for the destruction of the throne, and the murder of the sovereign; the grossest insults were offered by the very lowest of the mob.

About this time the King fell into a despondent state, which amounted almost to physical helplessness. He passed ten successive days without uttering a single word, even in the bosom of his family, except, indeed, when playing at backgammon after dinner with Madame Elizabeth. The Queen roused him from this state, so fatal at a critical period, by throwing herself at his feet, urging every alarming idea, and employing every affectionate expression. She represented also what he owed to his family; and told him that if they were doomed to fall they ought to fall honourably, and not wait to be smothered upon the floor of their apartment.

About the 15th of June 1792 the King refused his sanction to the two decrees ordaining the deportation of priests, and the formation of a camp of 20,000 men under the walls of Paris. He himself wished to sanction them, and said that general insurrection only waited for a pretence to burst forth.[4] The Queen insisted upon the veto, and reproached herself bitterly when this last act of the constitutional authority had occasioned the day of the 20th of June.

A few days previously above 20,000 men had gone to the Commune to announce that, on the 20th, they would plant the tree of liberty at the door of the National Assembly, and present a petition to the King respecting the veto which he had placed upon the decree for the deportation of the priests. This dreadful army crossed the garden of the Tuileries, and marched under the Queen's windows; it consisted of people who called themselves the citizens of the Faubourgs Saint Antoine and Saint Marceau. Covered with filthy clothes, they bore a most terrifying appearance, and even infected the air. People asked each other where such an army could come from; nothing so disgusting had ever before appeared in Paris.

On the 20th of June this mob thronged about the Tuileries in still greater numbers, armed with pikes, hatchets, and murderous instruments of all kinds, decorated with ribbons of the national colours, shouting, "*The nation for ever! Down with the veto!*" The King was without guards. Some of these desperadoes rushed up to his apartment; the door was about to be forced in, when the King commanded that it should be opened. Messieurs de Bougainville, d'Hervilly, de Parois, d'Aubier, Acloque,[5] Gentil, and other courageous men who were in the apartment of M. de Septeuil, the King's first *valet de chambre,* instantly ran to his Majesty's apartment. M. de Bougainville, seeing the torrent furiously advancing, cried out, "Put the King in the recess of the window, and place benches before him." Six royalist grenadiers of the battalion of the Filles Saint Thomas made their way by an inner staircase, and ranged themselves before the benches.

The order given by M. de Bougainville saved the King from the blades of the assassins, among whom was a Pole named Lazousky, who was to strike the first blow. The King's brave defenders said, "Sire, fear nothing." The King's reply is well known—"Put your hand upon my heart, and you will perceive whether I am afraid." M. Vanot, commandant of battalion, warded off a blow aimed by a wretch against the King; a grenadier of the Filles Saint Thomas parried a sword-thrust made in the same direction. Madame Elizabeth ran to her brother's apartments; when she reached the door she heard loud threats of death against the Queen: they called for the head of the Austrian. "Ah! let them think I am the Queen," she said to those around her, "that she may have time to escape." The Queen could not join the King; she was in the Council chamber, where she had been placed behind the great table to protect her, as much as possible, against the approach of the barbarians. Preserving a noble and becoming demeanour in this dreadful situation, she held the Dauphin before her, seated upon the table. Madame was at her side; the Princesse de Lamballe, the Princesse de Tarente, Madame de la Roche-Aymon, Madame de Tourzel, and Madame de Mackau, surrounded her. She had fixed a tri-coloured cockade, which one of the national guard had given her, upon her head. The poor little Dauphin was, like the King, shrouded in an enormous red cap.[6] The horde passed in files before the table; the sort of standards which they carried were symbols of the most atrocious barbarity. There was one representing a gibbet, to which a dirty doll was suspended; the words "*Marie Antoinette à la lanterne*" were written beneath it. Another was a board, to which a bullock's heart was fastened, with "*Heart of Louis XVI*" written round it. And a third showed the horn of an ox, with an obscene inscription.

One of the most furious Jacobin women who marched with these wretches stopped to give vent to a thousand imprecations against the Queen. Her Majesty asked whether she had ever seen her. She replied that she had not. Whether she had done her any personal wrong. Her answer was the same; but she added, "It is you who have caused the misery of the nation." "You have been told so," answered the Queen; "you are deceived. As the wife of the King of France, and mother of the Dauphin, I am a Frenchwoman; I shall never see my own country again—I can be happy or unhappy only in France; I was happy when you loved me." The fury began to weep, asked her pardon, and said, "It was because I did not know you; I see that you are good."

Santerre, the monarch of the faubourgs, made his subjects file off as quickly as he could; and it was thought at the time that he was ignorant of the object of this insurrection, which was the murder of the royal family. However, it was eight 'o'clock in the evening before the palace was completely cleared. Twelve deputies, impelled by attachment to the King's person, ranged themselves near him at the commencement of the insurrection; but the deputation from the Assembly did not reach the Tuileries until six in the evening; all the doors of the apartments were broken. The Queen pointed out to the deputies the state of the King's palace, and the disgraceful manner in which his asylum had been violated under the very eyes of the Assembly: she saw that Merlin de Thionville was so much affected as to shed tears while she spoke. "You weep, M. Merlin," said she to him, "at seeing the King and his family so cruelly treated by a people whom he always wished to make happy." "True, Madame," replied Merlin; "I weep for the misfortunes of a beautiful and feeling woman, the mother of a family; but do not mistake, not one of my tears falls for either King or Queen; I hate kings and queens: it is my religion." The Queen could not understand this madness, and saw all that was to be apprehended from persons who evinced it.

All hope was gone, and nothing was thought of but succour from abroad. The Queen appealed to her family and the King's brothers; her letters probably became more pressing, and expressed apprehensions upon the tardiness of relief. Her Majesty read me one to herself from the Archduchess Christina, Gouvernante of the Low Countries: she reproached the Queen for some of her expressions, and told her that those out of France were at least as much alarmed as herself at the King's situation and her own; but that the manner of attempting to assist her might either save her or endanger her safety; and that the members of the coalition were bound to act prudently, entrusted as they were with interests so dear to them.

The 14th of July 1792, fixed by the constitution as the anniversary of the independence of the nation, drew near. The King and Queen were compelled to make their appearance on the occasion; aware that the plot of the 20th of June had their assassination for its object, they had no doubt but that their death was determined on for the day of this national festival. The Queen was recommended, in order to give the King's friends time to defend him if the attack should be made, to guard him against the first stroke of a dagger by making him wear a breastplate. I was directed to get one made in my apartments: it was composed of fifteen folds of Italian taffety, and formed into an under-waistcoat and a wide belt. This breastplate was tried; it resisted all thrusts of the dagger, and several balls were turned aside by it. When it was completed the difficulty was to let the King try it on without running the risk of being surprised. I wore the immense heavy waistcoat as an under-petticoat for three days without being able to find a favourable moment. At length the King found an opportunity one morning to pull off his coat in the Queen's chamber and try on the breastplate.

The Queen was in bed; the King pulled me gently by the gown, and drew me as far as he could from the Queen's bed, and said to me, in a very low tone of voice: "It is to satisfy her that I submit to this inconvenience: they will not assassinate me; their scheme is changed; they will put me to death another way." The Queen heard the King whispering to me, and when he was gone out she asked me what he had said. I hesitated to answer; she insisted that I should, saying that nothing must be concealed from her, and that she was resigned upon every point. When she was informed of the King's remark she told me she had guessed it, that he had long since observed to her that all which was going forward in France was an imitation of the Revolution in England in the time of Charles I, and that he was incessantly reading the history of that unfortunate monarch in order that he might act better than Charles had done at a similar crisis.[7] "I begin to be fearful of the King's being brought to trial," continued the Queen; "as to me, I am a foreigner; they will assassinate me. What will become of my poor children?" These sad ejaculations were followed by a torrent of tears.[8] I wished to give her an antispasmodic; she refused it, saying that only happy women could feel nervous; that the cruel situation to which she was reduced rendered these remedies useless. In fact the Queen, who during her happier days was frequently attacked by hysterical disorders, enjoyed more uniform health when all the faculties of her soul were called forth to support her physical strength.

I had prepared a corset for her, for the same purpose as the King's under-waistcoat, without her knowledge; but she would not make use of it; all my entreaties, all my tears, were in vain. "If the factions assassinate me," she replied, "it will be a fortunate event for me; they will deliver me from a most painful existence." A few days after the King had tried on his breastplate I met him on a back staircase. I drew back to let him pass. He stopped and took my hand; I wished to kiss his; he would not suffer it, but drew me towards him by the hand, and kissed both my cheeks without saying a single word.

The fear of another attack upon the Tuileries occasioned scrupulous search among the King's papers: I burnt almost all those belonging to the Queen. She put her family letters, a great deal of correspondence which she thought it necessary to preserve for the history of the era of the Revolution, and particularly Barnave's letters and her answers, of which she had copies, into a portfolio, which she entrusted to M. de J——. That gentleman was unable to save this deposit, and it was burnt. The Queen left a few papers in her *secrétaire*. Among them were instructions to Madame de Tourzel, respecting the dispositions of her children and the characters and abilities of the sub-governesses under that lady's orders. This paper, which the Queen drew up at the time of Madame de Tourzel's appointment, with several letters from Maria Theresa, filled with the best advice and instructions, were printed after the 10th of August by order of the Assembly in the collection of papers found in the *secrétaires* of the King and Queen.

Her Majesty had still, without reckoning the income of the month, 140,000 francs in gold. She was desirous of depositing the whole of it with me; but I advised her to retain 1,500 *louis*, as a sum of rather considerable amount might be suddenly necessary for her. The King had an immense quantity of papers, and unfortunately conceived the idea of privately making, with the assistance of a locksmith, who had worked with him above ten years, a place of concealment in an inner corridor of his apartments. The place of concealment, but for the man's information, would have been long undiscovered.[9] The wall in which it was made was painted to imitate large stones, and the opening was entirely concealed among the brown grooves which formed the shaded part of these painted stones. But even before this locksmith had denounced what was afterwards called *the iron closet* to the Assembly, the Queen was aware that he had talked of it to some of his friends; and that this man, in whom the King from long habit placed too much confidence, was a Jacobin. She warned the King of it, and prevailed on him to fill a very large portfolio with all the papers he was most interested in preserving, and entrust it to me. She entreated him in my presence to leave nothing in this closet; and the King, in order to quiet her, told her that he had left nothing there. I would have taken the portfolio and carried it to my apartment, but it was too heavy for me to lift. The King said he would carry it himself; I went before to open the doors for him. When he placed the portfolio in my inner closet he merely said, "The Queen will tell you what it contains." Upon return to the Queen I put the question to her, deeming, from what the King had said, that it was necessary I should know. "They are," the Queen answered me, "such documents as would be most dangerous to the King should they go so far as to proceed to a trial against him. But what he wishes me to tell you is, that the portfolio contains a *procès-verbal* of a cabinet Council, in which the King gave his opinion against the war. He had it signed by all the ministers, and, in case of a trial, he trusts that this document will be very useful to him." I asked the Queen to whom she thought I ought to commit the portfolio. "To whom you please," answered she, "*you alone are answerable for it.* Do not quit the palace even during your vacation months: there may be circumstances under which it would be very desirable that we should be able to have it instantly."

At this period M. de La Fayette, who had probably given up the idea of establishing a republic in France similar to that of the United States, and was desirous to support the first constitution which he had sworn to defend, quitted his army and came to the Assembly for the purpose of supporting by his presence and by an energetic speech a petition signed by 20,000 citizens against the late violation of the residence of the King and his family. The General found the constitutional party powerless, and saw that he himself had lost his popularity. The Assembly disapproved of the step he had taken; the King, for whom it was taken, showed no satisfaction at it, and he saw himself compelled to return to his army as quickly as he could. He thought he could rely on the national guard; but on the day of his arrival those officers who were in the King's interest inquired of his Majesty whether they were to forward the views of General de La Fayette by joining him in such measures as he should pursue during his stay at Paris. The King enjoined them not to do so. From this answer M. de La Fayette perceived that he was abandoned by the remainder of his party in the Paris guard.

On his arrival a plan was presented to the Queen, in which it was proposed by a junction between La Fayette's army and the King's party to rescue the royal family and convey them to Rouen. I did not learn the particulars of this plan; the Queen only said to me upon the subject that M. de La Fayette was offered to them as a resource; but that it would be better for them to perish than to owe their safety to the man who had done them the most mischief, or to place themselves under the necessity of treating with him.

I passed the whole month of July without going to bed; I was fearful of some attack by night. There was one plot against the Queen's life which has never been made known. I was alone by her bedside at one o'clock in the morning; we heard somebody walking softly down the corridor, which passes along the whole line of her apartments, and which was then locked at each end. I went out to fetch the *valet de chambre*; he entered the corridor, and the Queen and myself soon heard the noise of two men fighting. The unfortunate Princess held me locked in her arms, and said to me, "What a situation! insults by day and assassins by night!" The *valet de chambre* cried out to her from the corridor, "Madame, it is a wretch that I know; I have him!" "Let him go," said the Queen; "open the door to him; he came to murder me; the Jacobins would carry him about in triumph tomorrow." The man was a servant of the King's toilette, who had taken the key of the corridor out of his Majesty's pocket after he was in bed, no doubt with the intention of committing the crime suspected. The *valet de chambre,* who was a very strong man, held him by the wrists, and thrust him out at the door. The wretch did not speak a word. The *valet de chambre* said, in answer to the Queen, who spoke to him gratefully of the danger to which he had exposed himself, that he feared nothing; and that he had always a pair of excellent pistols about him for no other purpose than to defend her Majesty.

Next day M. de Septeuil had all the locks of the King's inner apartments changed. I did the same by those of the Queen.

We were every moment told that the Faubourg Saint Antoine was preparing to march against the palace. At four o'clock one morning towards the latter end of July a person came to give me information to that effect. I instantly sent off two men, on whom I could rely, with orders to proceed to the usual places for assembling, and to come back speedily and give me an account of the state of the city. We knew that at least an hour must elapse before the populace of the faubourgs assembled on the site of the Bastille could reach the Tuileries. It seemed to me sufficient for the Queen's safety that all about her should be awakened. I went softly into her room; she was asleep; I did not awaken her. I found General de W—— in the great closet; he told me the meeting was, for this once, dispersing. The General had endeavoured to please the populace by the same means as M. de La Fayette had employed. He saluted the lowest *poissarde*, and lowered his hat down to his very stirrup. But the populace, who had been flattered for three years, required far different homage to its power, and the poor man was unnoticed. The King had been awakened, and so had Madame Elizabeth, who had gone to him. The Queen, yielding to the weight of her griefs, slept till nine o'clock on that day, which was very unusual with her. The King had already been to know whether she was awake: I told him what I had done, and the care I had taken not to disturb her. He thanked me and said, "I was awake, and so was the whole palace; she ran no risk. I am very glad to see her take a little rest—Alas! her griefs double mine!" What was my chagrin, when upon awaking and learning what had passed, the Queen burst into tears from regret at not having been called, and to upbraid me, on whose friendship she ought to have been able to rely, for having served her so ill under such circumstances! In vain did I reiterate that it had been only a false alarm, and that she required to have her strength recruited. "It is not diminished," said she: "misfortune gives us additional strength. Elizabeth was with the King, and I was asleep—I who am determined to perish by his side! I am his wife; I will not suffer him to incur the smallest risk without my sharing it."

1. M. de Laporte had by order of the King bought up the whole edition of the *Memoirs* of the notorious Madame de Lamotte against the Queen. Instead of destroying them immediately, he shut them up in one of the closets in his house. The alarming and rapid growth of the rebellion, the arrogance of the crowd of brigands, who in great measure composed the populace of Paris, and the fresh excesses daily resulting from it, rendered the intendant of the civil list apprehensive that some mob might break into his house, carry off these *Memoirs*, and spread them among the public. In order to prevent this he gave orders to have the *Memoirs* burnt with every necessary precaution; and the clerk who received the order entrusted the execution of it to a man named Riston, a dangerous intriguer, formerly an advocate of Nancy, who had a twelve month before escaped the gallows by favour of the new principles and the patriotism of the new tribunals, although convicted of forging the great seal, and fabricating decrees of the Council, in a proceeding instituted at the insistence of the tribunal of the King's palace, in which I examined and confronted the parties, at the risk of attempts at assassination not only by the accused, who during one of the sittings was so enraged that he rushed

at me with a knife in his hand, but also by the brigands in his pay, who filled the court. This Riston, finding himself entrusted with a commission which concerned her Majesty, and the mystery attending which bespoke something of importance, was far less anxious to execute it faithfully than to make a parade of this mark of confidence. On the 30th of May, at ten in the morning, he had the sheets carried to the porcelain manufactory at Sèvres, in a cart which he himself accompanied, and made a large fire of them before all the workmen, who were expressly forbidden to approach it. All these precautions, and the suspicions to which they gave rise, under such critical circumstances, gave so much publicity to this affair that it was denounced to the Assembly that very night. Brissot, and the whole Jacobin party, with equal effrontery and vehemence, insisted that the papers thus secretly burnt could be no other than the registers and documents of the correspondence of the Austrian committee. M. de Laporte was ordered to the bar, and there gave the most exact account of the circumstances. Riston was also called up, and confirmed M. de Laporte's deposition. But these explanations, however satisfactory, did not calm the violent ferment raised in the Assembly by this affair.—*Memoirs of Bertrand de Molleville.*

2. The sincerity of General Dumouriez cannot be doubted in this instance. The second volume of his *Memoirs* shows how unjust the mistrust and reproaches of the Queen were. By rejecting his services, Marie Antoinette deprived herself of her only remaining support. He who saved France in the defiles of Arne would perhaps have saved France before the 20th of June had he obtained the full confidence of Louis XVI and the Queen.—*Note by the Editor.*

3. When, after the revolution of the 10th of August 1792, the iron closet of the Château of the Tuileries had been discovered and forced, a considerable number of documents, which had been imprudently preserved in it, and which were communicated to the Convention by Gohier, who had just succeeded Danton in the ministry of justice, proved that the Court had established and maintained during the latter months of the session of the Constituent Assembly, and from the time of the meeting of the Legislative Assembly, constant communication with the most powerful members of those Assemblies. Being decreed as accused, on the 15th of August 1792, with Alexandre de Lameth, ex-member of the Constituent Assembly, Bertrand de Molleville, Duport du Tertre, Duportail, Montmorin, and Tarbé, ex-ministers of the marine, of justice, of war, of foreign affairs, and of public contributions, Barnave was arrested at Grenoble. He remained in prison in that town for fifteen months, and his friends began to hope that he would be forgotten, when an order arrived that he should be removed to Paris. At first he was imprisoned in the Abbaye, but transferred to the Conciergerie, and almost immediately taken before the Revolutionary Tribunal. He appeared there with wonderful firmness, summed up the services he had rendered to the cause of liberty with his usual eloquence, and made such an impression upon the numerous auditors that, although accustomed to behold only conspirators worthy of death in all those who appeared before the tribunal, they themselves considered his acquittal certain. The decree of death was read amidst the deepest silence; but Barnave's firmness was immovable. When he left the court, he cast upon the judges, the jurors, and the public looks expressive of contempt and indignation. He was led to his fate with the respected Duport du Tertre, one of the last ministers of Louis XVI. When he had ascended the scaffold, Barnave stamped, raised his eyes to heaven, and said—"This, then, is the reward of

all that I have done for liberty!" He fell on the 29th of October 1793, in the thirty-second year of his age; his bust was placed in the Grenoble Museum. The Consular Government placed his statue next to that of Vergniaud, on the great staircase of the palace of the Senate.—*Biographie de Bruxelles.*

4. This assertion contradicts the almost unanimous testimony of historians. To say nothing of Dumouriez, who tells us precisely the contrary, Bertrand de Molleville enters into particulars upon the subject which leave no room for doubt. "The Assembly," he says, "which kept up its credit by acts of violence, passed a decree against non-constitutional priests, to oblige them to take a fresh oath, or quit the kingdom. The bishops then in Paris met to draw up a petition against this decree, under a conviction that the King, who had already shown the deepest regret at having sanctioned the decrees relating to the clergy, would rejoice at having grounds pointed out to him for refusing his sanction to this. When the petition was drawn up they asked leave to put it into his Majesty's hands, and the Bishop of Uzes had a private correspondence with me on this occasion; for at this period no minister could have received a bishop publicly without becoming an object of suspicion *to the nation.* The King appeared much moved on reading the petition, and said to me, with the energy which always warmed him when religion was under discussion,—'They may be very sure I will never sanction it. But the question is, whether I ought to assign a reason for my refusal, or give it plainly and simply according to the usual formula; or whether, under all circumstances, it is not more prudent to temporise. Try to find out what your colleagues think about it before it is discussed in Council.' I observed that the constitution dispensed with any reason for the King's refusal to sanction, and that although the Assembly ought to be pleased at seeing his Majesty waive so important a prerogative, they were capable of carrying their insolence so far as to refuse to hear his reasons, and would even reproach him for this departure from the constitution as a violation of his oath; that, as to temporising, it would be showing weakness, and inviting the Assembly to become still more audacious; and therefore that a plain unexplained refusal of the sanction was the safest course. This matter was discussed next day at the Council of the ministers. They all saw the necessity for refusing the sanction; and at the following Council they unanimously recommended that course to the King, who determined upon it with the greatest satisfaction. But this gleam of happiness was clouded by a proposal made to him by the Minister of the Interior immediately to form his chapel, and that of the Queen, of constitutional priests, as the most certain way to convince the people of his sincere attachment to the constitution. 'No, sir, no,' replied the King in the firmest tone; 'do not speak of that to me; let me be left at rest upon that point. When liberty of worship was established, it was established for all; I ought, therefore, to enjoy it.' The warmth with which the King spoke surprised us all, and silenced M. Cahier de Gerville."—*Note by the Editor.*

5. A citizen of Paris, commandant of battalion, who during the whole of the Revolution was in direct opposition to the regicide Santerre.—*Madame Campan.*

6. One of the circumstances of the 20th of June which most vexed the King's friends being that of his wearing the *bonnet rouge* nearly three hours, I ventured to ask him for some explanation of a fact so strikingly in contrast with the extraordinary intrepidity shown by his Majesty during that horrible day. This was his answer: "The cries of '*The nation for ever!*' violently increasing around me, and seeming to be addressed to me, I replied that

the nation had not a warmer friend than myself. Upon this an ill-looking man, making his way through the crowd, came up to me and said, rather roughly, '*Well, if you speak the truth, prove it by putting on this red cap.*' 'I consent,' replied I. One or two of them immediately came forward and placed the cap upon my hair, for it was too small for my head. I was convinced, I knew not why, that his intention was merely to place the cap upon my head for a moment, and then to take it off again; and I was so completely taken up with what was passing before me that I did not feel whether the cap did or did not remain upon my hair. I was so little aware of it that when I returned to my room I knew only from being told so that it was still there. I was very much surprised to find it upon my head, and was the more vexed at it because I might have taken it off immediately without the smallest difficulty. But I am satisfied that if I had hesitated to consent to its being placed upon my head the drunken fellow who offered it to me would have thrust his pike into my stomach."—*Memoirs of Bertrand de Molleville.*

7. The King's usual book was the *History of Charles I*, and his principal attention was directed to avoiding, in all his actions, everything that might serve as a pretence for a judicial accusation. He would readily have sacrificed his life, but not the glory of France, which an assassination, that would have been only the crime of a few individuals, would not have tarnished. To all my congratulations upon his good fortune in escaping the dangers of the 20th June his Majesty answered with the utmost indifference: "All my uneasiness was about the Queen and my sister; for as to myself—" "But it appears to me," said I, "this insurrection was directed chiefly against your Majesty." "I know it well; I saw that they wished to assassinate me, and I cannot tell how it was they did not do so. But I shall not escape them another time, so that I am no better off: there is but little difference in being assassinated two months earlier or later." "Good heavens! Sire," exclaimed I, "can your Majesty, then, so steadfastly believe that you will be assassinated?" "Yes, I am certain of it; I have long expected it, and have made up my mind. Do you think I fear death?" "No, surely; but I should be glad to see your Majesty less determined to expect that event, and more disposed to adopt vigorous measures, which are now become the only means by which the King can look to be rescued." "I believe that, but still there would be many chances against me, and I am not fortunate. I should be at no loss if I had not my family with me. It would soon be seen that I am not so weak as they think me; but what will become of my wife and children if I do not succeed?" "But does your Majesty think that if you were assassinated your family would be more secure?" "Yes, I do think so, at least I hope so; and if it happened otherwise I should not have to reproach myself with being the cause of their misfortunes. Besides, what could I do?" "I think your Majesty might at this moment leave Paris with greater ease than ever, because the events of yesterday but too clearly prove that your life is not safe in the capital." "Oh! I will not fly a second time: I suffered too much before." "I am of opinion, too, that your Majesty should not think of it, at least at this moment: but it seems to me that existing circumstances; and the general indignation which the affair of yesterday appears to have excited, present the King with the most favourable opportunity that can possibly offer for leaving Paris publicly, not only with the consent of the great majority of the citizens, but with their approbation. I ask your Majesty's permission to reflect upon this step, and to give you my ideas upon the mode and means of executing it." "Do so, but it is a more difficult matter than you imagine."—*Memoirs of Bertrand de Molleville.*

8. These distressing scenes were often renewed. There is nothing in history to which the misfortunes of Marie Antoinette can be compared but those of Henriette de France, the daughter of Henri IV, wife of Charles I, and mother of Charles II. Like Henriette, she was accused of having exercised too much control over the King's mind; like her, she was haunted by continual fears for the lives of her husband and her children: but she had not, like Henriette, the consolation, after protracted misfortunes, of seeing her family re-ascend the throne. The tragic and deplorable end of Mary Stuart awaited her who had experienced all the griefs of Henriette de France.—*Note by the Editor.*

9. See p. 127.

XXI

Madame Campan's communications with M. Bertrand de Molleville for the King's service—Hope of a speedy deliverance—The Queen's reflections upon the character of Louis XVI—Insults—Inquiry set on foot by the Princesse de Lamballe respecting the persons of the Queen's household—The 10th of August—Curious particulars—Battle—Scenes of carnage—The royal family at the Feuillans

During July the correspondence of M. Bertrand de Molleville with the King and Queen was most active. M. de Marsilly, formerly a lieutenant of the *Cent Suisses* of the guard, was the bearer of the letters.[1] He came to me the first time with a note from the Queen directed to M. Bertrand himself. In this note the Queen said: "Address yourself with full confidence to Madame Campan; the conduct of her brother in Russia has not at all influenced her sentiments; she is wholly devoted to us; and if, hereafter, you should have anything to say to us verbally, you may rely entirely upon her devotion and discretion."

The mobs which gathered almost nightly in the faubourgs alarmed the Queen's friends; they entreated her not to sleep in her room on the ground floor of the Tuileries. She removed to the first floor, to a room which was between the King's apartments and those of the Dauphin. Being awake always from daybreak, she ordered that neither the shutters nor the window blinds should be closed, that her long sleepless nights might be the less weary. About the middle of one of these nights, when the moon was shining into her bed-chamber, she gazed at it, and told me that in a month she should not see that moon unless freed from her chains, and beholding the King at liberty. She then imparted to me all that was concurring to deliver them; but said that the opinions of their intimate advisers were alarmingly at variance; that some vouched for complete success, while others pointed out insurmountable dangers. She added that she possessed the itinerary of the march of the Princes and the King of Prussia: that on such a day they would be at Verdun, on another day at such a place, that Lille was about to be besieged, but that M de J——, whose prudence and intelligence the King, as well as herself, highly valued, alarmed them much respecting the success of that siege, and made them apprehensive that, even were the commandant devoted to them, the civil authority, which by the constitution gave great power to the mayors of towns, would overrule the military commandant. She was also very uneasy as to what would take place at Paris during the interval, and spoke to me of the King's want of energy, but always in terms expressive of her veneration for his virtues and her attachment to himself. "The King," said she, "is not a coward; he possesses abundance of passive courage, but he is overwhelmed by an awkward shyness, a mistrust of himself, which proceeds from his education as much as from his disposition He is afraid to command, and, above all things, dreads speaking to assembled numbers. He lived like a child, and always ill at ease under the eyes of Louis XV, until the age of twenty-one. This constraint confirmed his timidity.[2] Circumstanced as we are, a few well-delivered words addressed to the Parisians, who are devoted to him, would multiply the strength of our party a hundredfold: he will not utter them. What can we expect from those addresses to the people which he has been advised to post up? Nothing but fresh outrages. As for myself, I could do anything, and would appear on horseback if necessary. But if I were really to begin to act, that would be furnishing arms to the King's enemies; the cry against the Austrian, and against the sway of a female, would become general in France; and, moreover, by showing myself, I should render the King a mere nothing. A Queen who is not regent ought, under these circumstances, to remain passive and prepare to die."

The garden of the Tuileries was full of maddened men, who insulted all who seemed to side with the Court. *The Life of Marie Antoinette* was cried under the Queen's windows, infamous plates were annexed to the book, the hawkers showed them to the passers-by. On all sides were heard the jubilant outcries of a people in a state of delirium almost as frightful as the explosion of their rage. The Queen and her children were unable to breathe the open air any longer. It was determined that the garden of the Tuileries should be closed: as soon as this step was taken the Assembly decreed that the whole length of the Terrace des Feuillans belonged to it, and fixed the boundary between what was called the *national ground* and the *Coblentz ground* by a tri-coloured ribbon stretched from one end of the terrace to the other. All good citizens were ordered, by notices affixed to it, not to go down into the garden, under pain of being treated in the same manner as Foulon and Berthier.[3] The shutting up of the Tuileries did not enable the Queen and her children to walk in the garden. The people on the terrace sent forth dreadful howls, and she was twice compelled to return to her apartments.

In the early part of August many zealous persons offered the King money; he refused considerable sums, being unwilling to injure the fortunes of individuals. M. de la Ferté, intendant of the *menus plaisirs*, brought me 1,000 *louis*, requesting me to lay them at the feet of the Queen. He thought she could not have too much money at so perilous a time, and that every good Frenchman should hasten to place all his ready money in her hands. She refused this sum, and others of much greater amount which were offered to her.[4] However, a few days afterwards, she told me she would accept M. de la Ferté's 24,000 francs, because they would make up a sum which the King had to expend. She therefore directed me to go and receive those 24,000 francs, to add them to the 100,000 francs she had placed in my hands, and to change the whole into assignats to increase their amount. Her orders were executed, and the assignats were delivered to the King. The Queen informed me that Madame Elizabeth had found a well-meaning man who had engaged to gain over Pétion by the bribe of a large sum of money, and that deputy would, by a preconcerted signal, inform the King of the success of the project. His Majesty soon had an opportunity of seeing Pétion, and on the Queen asking him before me if he was satisfied with him, the King replied, "Neither more nor less satisfied than usual; he did not make the concerted signal, and I believe I have been cheated." The Queen then condescended to explain the whole of the enigma to me. "Pétion," said she, "was, while talking to the King, to have kept his finger fixed upon his right eye for at least two seconds." "He did not even put his hand up to his chin," said the King; "after all, it is but so much money stolen: the thief will not boast of it, and the affair will remain a secret. Let us talk of something else." He turned to me and said, "Your father was an intimate friend of Mandat, who now commands the national guard; describe him to me; what ought I to expect from him?" I answered that he was one of his Majesty's most faithful subjects, but that with a great deal of loyalty he possessed very little sense, and that he was involved in the constitutional vortex. "I understand," said the King; "he is a man who would defend my palace and my person, because that is enjoined by the constitution which he has sworn to support, but who would fight against the party in favour of sovereign authority: it is well to know this with certainty."

On the next day the Princesse de Lamballe sent for me very early in the morning. I found her on a sofa facing a window that looked upon the Pont Royal. She then occupied that apartment of the Pavilion of Flora which was on a level with that of the Queen. She desired me to sit down by her. Her Highness had a writing-desk upon her knees. "You have had many enemies," said she; "attempts have been made to deprive you of the Queen's favour; they have been far from successful. Do you know that even I myself, not being so well acquainted with you as the Queen, was rendered suspicious of you; and that upon the arrival of the Court at the Tuileries I gave you a companion to be a spy upon you; and that I had another belonging to the police placed at your door! I was assured that you received five or six of the most virulent deputies of the *tiers-état*; but it was that wardrobe woman whose rooms were above you. In short," said the Princess, "persons of integrity have nothing to fear from the evil-disposed when they belong to so upright a prince as the King. As to the Queen, she knows you, and has loved you ever since she came into France. You shall judge of the King's opinion of you: it was yesterday evening decided in the family circle that at a time when the Tuileries is likely to be attacked it was necessary to have the most faithful account of the opinions and conduct of all the individuals composing the Queen's service. The King takes the same precaution on his part respecting all who are about him. He said there was with him a person of great integrity, to whom he would commit this inquiry; and that, with regard to the Queen's household, you must be spoken to; that he had long studied your character, and that he esteemed your veracity."

The Princess had a list of the names of all who belonged to the Queen's chamber on her desk. She asked me for information respecting each individual. I was fortunate in having none but the most favourable information to give. I had to speak of my avowed enemy in the Queen's chamber; of her who most wished that I should be responsible for my brother's political opinions. The Princess, as the head of the chamber, could not be ignorant of this circumstance; but as the female in question, who idolised the King and Queen, would not have hesitated to sacrifice her life in order to save theirs, and as possibly her attachment to them, united to considerable narrowness of intellect and a limited education, contributed to her jealousy of me, I spoke of her in the highest terms.

Portrait of Princesse de Lamballe

The Princess wrote as I dictated, and occasionally looked at me with astonishment. When I had done I entreated her to write in the margin that the lady alluded to was my declared enemy. She embraced me, saying, "Ah! do not write it! we should not record an unhappy circumstance which ought to be forgotten." We came to a man of genius who was much attached to the Queen, and I described him as a man born solely to contradict, showing himself an aristocrat with democrats, and a democrat among aristocrats; but still a man of probity, and well disposed to his sovereign. The Princess said she knew many persons of that disposition, and that she was delighted I had nothing to say against this man, because she herself had placed him about the Queen.

The whole of her Majesty's chamber, which consisted entirely of persons of fidelity, gave throughout all the dreadful convulsions of the Revolution proofs of the greatest prudence and self-devotion. The same cannot be said of the antechambers. With the exception of three or four, all the servants of that class were outrageous Jacobins; and I saw on those occasions the necessity of composing the private household of Princes of persons completely separated from the class of the people.

The situation of the royal family was so unbearable during the months which immediately preceded the 10th of August that the Queen longed for the crisis whatever might be its issue. She frequently said that a long confinement in a tower by the seaside would seem to her less intolerable than those feuds in which the weakness of her party daily threatened an inevitable catastrophe.[5]

Not only were their Majesties prevented from breathing the open air, but they were also insulted at the very foot of the altar. The Sunday before the last day of the monarchy, while the royal family went through the gallery to the Chapel, half the soldiers of the national guard exclaimed, "*Long live the King!*" and the other half, "*No; no King! down with the veto!*" and on that day at vespers the choristers preconcerted to use loud and threatening emphasis when chanting the words "*Deposuit potentes de sede,*" in the *Magnificat*. Incensed at such an irreverent proceeding, the royalists in their turn thrice exclaimed, "*Et reginam*" after the "*Domine salvum fac regem*". The tumult during the whole time of divine service was excessive.

At length the terrible night of the 10th of August 1792 arrived. On the preceding evening Pétion went to the Assembly and informed it that preparations were making for an insurrection on the following day; that the tocsin would sound at midnight; and that he feared he had not sufficient means for resisting the attack which was about to take place. Upon this information the Assembly passed to the order of the day. Pétion, however, gave an order for repelling force by force.[6] M. Mandat was armed with this order; and finding his fidelity to the King's person supported by what he considered the law of the State, he conducted himself in all his operations with the greatest energy. On the evening of the 9th I was present at the King's supper. While his Majesty was giving me various orders we heard a great noise at the door of the apartment. I went to see what was the cause of it, and found the two sentinels fighting. One said, speaking of the King, that he was hearty in the cause of the constitution, and would defend it at the peril of his life; the other maintained that he was an encumbrance to the only constitution suitable to a free people. They were almost ready to cut one another throats. I returned with a countenance which betrayed my emotion. The King desired to know what was going forward at his door; I could not conceal it from him. The Queen said she was not at all surprised at it, and that more than half the guard belonged to the Jacobin party.

The tocsin sounded at midnight. The Swiss were drawn up like walls; and in the midst of their soldier-like silence, which formed a striking contrast with the perpetual din of the town guard, the King informed M. de J——, an officer of the staff, of the plan of defence laid down by General Vioménil. M. de J—— said to me, after this private conference, "Put your jewels and money into your pockets; our dangers are unavoidable; the means of defence are null; safety might be obtained by some degree of energy in the King, but that is the only virtue in which he is deficient."

An hour after midnight the Queen and Madame Elizabeth said they would lie down on a sofa in a closet in the *entresols*, the windows of which commanded the courtyard of the Tuileries.

The Queen told me the King had just refused to put on his quilted under-waistcoat; that he had consented to wear it on the 14th of July because he was merely going to a ceremony where the blade of an assassin was to be apprehended, but that on a day on which his party might fight against the revolutionists he thought there was something cowardly in preserving his life by such means.

During this time Madame Elizabeth disengaged herself from some of her clothing which encumbered her in order to lie down on the sofa: she took a cornelian pin out of her cape, and before she laid it down on the table she showed it to me, and desired me to read a motto engraved upon it round a stalk of lilies. The words were, "*Oblivion of injuries— pardon for offences.*" "I much fear," added that virtuous Princess, "this maxim has but little influence among our enemies; but it ought not to be less dear to us on that account."[7]

The Queen desired me to sit down by her; the two Princesses could not sleep; they were conversing mournfully upon their situation when a musket was discharged in the courtyard. They both quitted the sofa, saying, "There is the first shot, unfortunately it will not be the last; let us go up to the King." The Queen desired me to follow her; several of her women went with me.

At four o'clock the Queen came out of the King's chamber and told us she had no longer any hope; that M. Mandat, who had gone to the Hôtel de Ville to receive further orders, had just been assassinated, and that the people were at that time carrying his head about the streets. Day came. The King, the Queen, Madame Elizabeth, Madame, and the Dauphin went down to pass through the ranks of the sections of the national guard; the cry of "*Vive le Roi!*" was heard from a few places. I was at a window on the garden side; I saw some of the gunners quit their posts, go up to the King, and thrust their fists in his face, insulting him by the most brutal language. Messieurs de Salvert and de Bridges drove them off in a spirited manner. The King was as pale as a corpse. The royal family came in again. The Queen told me that all was lost; that the King had shown no energy; and that this sort of review had done more harm than good.

I was in the billiard-room with my companions; we placed ourselves upon some high benches. I then saw M. d'Hervilly with a drawn sword in his hand, ordering the usher to open the door to the French *noblesse*. Two hundred persons entered the room nearest to that in which the family were; others drew up in two lines in the preceding rooms. I saw a few people belonging to the Court, many others whose features were unknown to me, and a few who figured groundlessly enough among what was called the *noblesse*, but whose self-devotion ennobled them at once. They were all so badly armed that even in that situation the indomitable French liveliness indulged in jests. M. de Saint Souplet, one of the King's equerries, and a page, carried on their shoulders instead of muskets the tongs belonging to the King's antechamber, which they had broken and divided between them. Another page, who had a pocket-pistol in his hand, stuck the end of it against the back of the person who stood before him, and who begged he would be good enough to rest it elsewhere. A sword and a pair of pistols were the only arms of those who had had the precaution to provide themselves with arms at all. Meanwhile, the numerous bands from the faubourgs, armed with pikes and cutlasses, filled the Carrousel and the streets adjacent to the Tuileries. The sanguinary Marseillais were at their head, with cannon pointed against the Château. In this emergency the

King's Council sent M. Dejoly, the Minister of Justice, to the Assembly to request they would send the King a deputation which might serve as a safeguard to the executive power. His ruin was resolved on; they passed to the order of the day. At eight o'clock the department repaired to the Château. The *procureur-syndic*, seeing that the guard within was ready to join the assailants, went into the King's closet and requested to speak to him in private. The King received him in his chamber; the Queen was with him. There M. Rœderer told him that the King, all his family, and the people about them would inevitably perish unless his Majesty immediately determined to go to the National Assembly. The Queen at first opposed this advice, but the *procureur-syndic* told her that she rendered herself responsible for the deaths of the King, her children, and all who were in the palace. She no longer objected. The King then consented to go to the Assembly. As he set out he said to the minister and persons who surrounded him, "*Come, gentlemen, there is nothing more to be done here.*"[8] The Queen said to me as she left the King's chamber, "Wait in my apartments; I will come to you, or I will send for you to go I know not whither." She took with her only the Princesse de Lamballe and Madame de Tourzel. The Princesse de Tarente and Madame de la Roche-Aymon were inconsolable at being left at the Tuileries; they, and all who belonged to the chamber, went down into the Queen's apartments.

We saw the royal family pass between two lines formed by the Swiss grenadiers and those of the battalions of the Petits-Pères and the Filles Saint Thomas. They were so pressed upon by the crowd that during that short passage the Queen was robbed of her watch and purse. A man of great height and horrible appearance, one of such as were to be seen at the head of all the insurrections, drew near the Dauphin, whom the Queen was leading by the hand, and took him up in his arms. The Queen uttered a scream of terror, and was ready to faint. The man said to her, "Don't be frightened, I will do him no harm;" and he gave him back to her at the entrance of the chamber

I leave to history all the details of that too memorable day, confining myself to retracing a few of the frightful scenes acted in the interior of the Tuileries after the King had quitted the palace.

The assailants did not know that the King and his family had betaken themselves to the Assembly; and those who defended the palace from the side of the courts were equally ignorant of it. It is supposed that if they had been aware of the fact the siege would never have taken place.

The Marseillais began by driving from their posts several Swiss, who yielded without resistance; a few of the assailants fired upon them; some of the Swiss officers seeing their men fall, and perhaps thinking the King was still at the Tuileries, gave the word to a whole battalion to fire. The aggressors were thrown into disorder, and the Carrousel was cleared in a moment; but they soon returned, spurred on by rage and revenge. The Swiss were but 800 strong; they fell back into the interior of the Château; some of the doors were battered in by the guns, others broken through with hatchets; the populace rushed from all quarters into the interior of the palace; almost all the Swiss were massacred; the nobles, flying through the gallery which leads to the Louvre, were either stabbed or shot, and the bodies thrown out of the windows. M. Pallas and M. de Marchais, ushers of the King's chamber, were killed in defending the door of the Council chamber; many others of the King's servants fell victims to their fidelity. I mention these two persons in particular because, with their hats pulled over their brows and their swords in their hands, they exclaimed, as they defended themselves with unavailing courage, "We will not survive—this is our post; our duty is to die at it." M. Diet behaved in the same manner at the door of the Queen's bed-chamber; he experienced the same fate. The Princesse de Tarente had fortunately opened the door of the apartments; otherwise, the dreadful band seeing several women collected in the Queen's salon would have fancied she was among us, and would have immediately massacred us had we resisted them. We were, indeed, all about to perish, when a man with a long beard came up, exclaiming, in the name of Pétion, "*Spare the women; don't dishonour the nation!*" A particular circumstance placed me in greater danger than the others. In my confusion I imagined, a moment before the assailants entered the Queen's apartments, that my sister was not among the group of women collected there; and I went up into an *entresol*, where I supposed she had taken refuge, to induce her to come down, fancying it safer that we should not be separated. I did not find her in the room in question; I saw there only our two *femmes de chambre* and one of the Queen's two *heyducs*, a man of great height, and military aspect. I saw that he was pale, and sitting on a bed. I cried out to him, "Fly! the footmen and our people are already safe." "I cannot," said the man to me; "I am dying of fear." As he spoke I heard a number of men rushing hastily up the staircase; they threw themselves upon him, and I saw him assassinated. I ran towards the staircase, followed by our women. The murderers left the *heyduc* to come to me. The women threw themselves at their feet, and held their sabres. The narrowness of the staircase impeded the assassins; but I had already felt a horrid hand thrust into my back to seize me by my clothes, when some one called out from the bottom of the staircase, "*What are you doing above there? We don't kill women.*"

I was on my knees; my executioner quitted his hold of me, and said, "*Get up, you jade; the nation pardons you.*"

The brutality of these words did not prevent my suddenly experiencing an indescribable feeling which partook almost equally of the love of life and the idea that I was going to see my son, and all that was dear to me, again. A moment before I had thought less of death than of the pain which the steel, suspended over my head, would occasion me. Death is seldom seen so close without striking his blow. I heard every syllable uttered by the assassins, just as if I had been calm.

Five or six men seized me and my women, and having made us get up on benches placed before the windows, ordered us to call out, "*The nation for ever!*"

I passed over several corpses; I recognised that of the old Vicomte de Broves, to whom the Queen had sent me at the beginning of the night to desire him and another old man in her name to go home. These brave men desired I would tell her Majesty that they had but too strictly obeyed the King's orders in all circumstances under which they ought to have exposed their own lives in order to preserve his; and that for this once they would not obey, though they would cherish the recollection of the Queen's goodness.

Near the *grille,* on the side next the bridge, the men who conducted me asked whither I wished to go. Upon my inquiring, in my turn, whether they were at liberty to take me wherever I might wish to go, one of them, a Marseillais, asked me, giving me at the same time a push with the butt end of his musket, whether I still doubted the power of the people? I answered *"No,"* and I mentioned the number of my brother-in-law's house. I saw my sister ascending the steps of the parapet of the bridge, surrounded by members of the national guard. I called to her, and she turned round. "Would you have her go with you?" said my guardian to me. I told him I did wish it. They called the people who were leading my sister to prison; she joined me.

Madame de la Roche-Aymon and her daughter, Mademoiselle Pauline de Tourzel, Madame de Ginestoux, lady to the Princesse de Lamballe, the other women of the Queen, and the old Comte d'Affry, were led off together to the Abbaye.

Our progress from the Tuileries to my sister's house was most distressing. We saw several Swiss pursued and killed and musket-shots were crossing each other in all directions. We passed under the walls of the Louvre; they were firing from the parapet into the windows of the gallery, to hit the *knights of the dagger*, for thus did the populace designate those faithful subjects who had assembled at the Tuileries to defend the King.

The brigands broke some vessels of water in the Queen's first antechamber; the mixture of blood and water stained the skirts of our white gowns. The *poissardes* screamed after us in the streets that we were attached to the *Austrian*. Our protectors then showed some consideration for us, and made us go up a gateway to pull off our gowns; but our petticoats being too short, and making us look like persons in disguise, other *poissardes* began to bawl out that we were young Swiss dressed up like women. We then saw a tribe of female cannibals enter the street, carrying the head of poor Mandat. Our guards made us hastily enter a little public-house, called for wine, and desired us to drink with them. They assured the landlady that we were their sisters, and good patriots. Happily the Marseillais had quitted us to return to the Tuileries. One of the men who remained with us said to me in a low voice—"I am a gauze-worker in the faubourg. I was forced to march; I am not for all this; I have not killed anybody, and have rescued you. You ran a great risk when we met the mad women who are carrying Mandat's head. These horrible women said yesterday at midnight, upon the site of the Bastille, that they must have their revenge for the 6th of October, at Versailles, and that they had sworn to kill the Queen and all the women attached to her; the danger of the action saved you all."

As I crossed the Carrousel, I saw my house in flames; but as soon as the first moment of affright was over, I thought no more of my personal misfortunes. My ideas turned solely upon the dreadful situation of the Queen.

On reaching my sister's we found all our family in despair, believing they should never see us again. I could not remain in her house; some of the mob, collected round the door, exclaimed that Marie Antoinette's confidante was in the house, and that they must have her head. I disguised myself, and was concealed in the house of M. Morel, secretary for the lotteries. On the morrow I was inquired for there, in the name of the Queen. A deputy, whose sentiments were known to her, took upon himself to find me out.

I borrowed clothes, and went with my sister to the Feuillans.[9] We got there at the same time with M. Thierry de Ville d'Avray, the King's first *valet de chambre*. We were taken into an office, where we wrote down our names and places of abode, and we received tickets for admission into the rooms belonging to Camus, the keeper of the Archives, where the King was with his family.

Portrait of Madame Elizabeth

As we entered the first room, a person who was there said to me, "Ah! you are a brave woman; but where is that Thierry,[10] that man loaded with his master's bounties?" "He is here," said I; "he is following me. I perceive that even scenes of death do not banish jealousy from among you."

Having belonged to the Court from my earliest youth, I was known to many persons whom I did not know. As I traversed a corridor above the cloisters which led to the cells inhabited by the unfortunate Louis and his family, several of the grenadiers called me by name. One of them said to me, "Well, the poor King is lost! The Comte d'Artois would have managed it better." "Not at all," said another.

The royal family occupied a small suite of apartments consisting of four cells, formerly belonging to the ancient monastery of the Feuillans. In the first were the men who had accompanied the King: the Prince de Poix, the Baron d'Aubier, M. de Saint Pardou, equerry to Madame Elizabeth, MM. de Goguelat, de Chamilly, and de Huë. In the second we found the King; he was having his hair dressed; he took two locks of it, and gave one to my sister and one to me. We offered to kiss his hand; he opposed it, and embraced us without saying anything. In the third was the Queen, in bed, and in indescribable affliction. We found her accompanied only by a stout woman, who appeared tolerably civil; she was the keeper of the apartments. She waited upon the Queen, who as yet had none of her own people about her. Her Majesty stretched out her arms to us, saying, "Come, unfortunate women; come, and see one still more unhappy than yourselves, since she has been the cause of all your misfortunes. We are ruined," continued she; "we have arrived at that point to which they have been leading us for three years, through all possible outrages; we shall fall in this dreadful Revolution, and many others will perish after us. All have contributed to our downfall; the reformers have urged it like mad people, and others through ambition, for the wildest Jacobin seeks wealth and office, and the mob is eager for plunder. There is not one lover of his country among all this infamous horde. The emigrant party had their intrigues and schemes; foreigners sought to profit by the dissensions of France; every one had a share in our misfortunes."

The Dauphin came in with Madame and the Marquise de Tourzel. On seeing them the Queen said to me, "Poor children! how heartrending it is, instead of handing down to them so fine an inheritance, to say it ends with us!" She afterwards conversed with me about the Tuileries and the persons who had fallen; she condescended also to mention the burning of my house. I looked upon that loss as a mischance which ought not to dwell upon her mind, and I told her so. She spoke of the Princesse de Tarente, whom she greatly loved and valued, of Madame de la Roche-Aymon and her daughter, of the other persons whom she had left at the palace, and of the Duchesse de Luynes, who was to have passed the night at the Tuileries. Respecting her she said, "Hers was one of the first heads turned by the rage for that mischievous philosophy, but her heart brought her back, and I again found a friend in her."[II] I asked the Queen what the ambassadors from foreign powers had done under existing circumstances? She told me that they could do nothing; and that the wife of the English ambassador had just given her a proof of the personal interest she took in her welfare by sending her linen for her son.

I informed her that, in the pillaging of my house, all my accounts with her had been thrown into the Carrousel, and that every sheet of my month's expenditure was signed by her, sometimes leaving four or five inches of blank paper above her signature, a circumstance which rendered me very uneasy, from an apprehension that an improper use might be made of those signatures. She desired me to demand admission to the committee of general safety, and to make this declaration there. I repaired thither instantly and found a deputy, with whose name I have never become acquainted. After hearing me he said that he would not receive my deposition; that Marie Antoinette was now nothing more than any other Frenchwoman; and that if any of those detached papers bearing her signature should be misapplied she would have, at a future period, a right to make a complaint, and to support her declaration by the facts which I had just related. The Queen regretted having sent me, and feared that she had, by her very caution, pointed out a method of fabricating forgeries which might be dangerous to her; then again she exclaimed, "My apprehensions are as absurd as the step I made you take. They need nothing more for our ruin; all has been told." She gave us details of what had taken place subsequently to the King's arrival at the Assembly. They are all well known, and I have no occasion to record them; I will merely mention that she told us, though with much delicacy, that she was not a little hurt at the King's conduct since he had been at the Tuileries; that his habit of laying no restraint upon his great appetite had prompted him to eat as if he had been at his palace; that those who did not know him as she did, did not feel the piety and the magnanimity of his resignation, all which produced so bad an effect that deputies who were devoted to him had warned him of it; but that no change could be effected.

I still see in imagination, and shall always see, that narrow cell at the Feuillans, hung with green paper, that wretched couch whence the dethroned Queen stretched out her arms to us, saying that our misfortunes, of which she was the cause, increased her own. There, for the last time, I saw the tears, I heard the sobs of her whom high birth, natural endowments, and, above all, goodness of heart, had seemed to destine to adorn any throne, and be the happiness of any people! It is impossible for those who lived with Louis XVI and Marie Antoinette not to be fully convinced, while doing full justice to the King's virtues, that if the Queen had been from the moment of her arrival in France the object of the care and affection of a Prince of decision and authority she would have only added to the glory of his reign.

What affecting things I have heard the Queen say in the affliction caused her by the belief of part of the Court and the whole of the people that she did not love France! How did that opinion shock those who knew her heart and her sentiments! Twice did I see her on the point of going from her apartments in the Tuileries into the gardens, to address the immense throng constantly assembled there to insult her. "Yes," exclaimed she, as she paced her chamber with hurried steps; "I will say to them—Frenchmen, they have had the cruelty to persuade you that I do not love France!—I! the mother of a Dauphin who will reign over this noble country!—I! whom Providence has seated upon the most powerful throne of Europe! Of all the daughters of Maria Theresa am I not that one whom fortune has most highly favoured? And ought I not to feel all these advantages? What should I find at Vienna? Nothing but sepulchres! what should I lose in France? Everything which can confer glory!"

I protest I only repeat her own words; the soundness of her judgment soon pointed out to her the dangers of such a proceeding. "I should descend from the throne," said she, "merely, perhaps, to excite a momentary sympathy, which the factious would soon render more injurious than beneficial to me."

Yes, not only did Marie Antoinette love France, but few women took greater pride in the courage of Frenchmen. I could adduce a multitude of proofs of this; I will relate two traits which demonstrate the noblest enthusiasm: The Queen was telling me that at the coronation of the Emperor Francis II, that Prince, bespeaking the admiration of a French general officer, who was then an emigrant, for the fine appearance of his troops, said to him, "*There are the men to beat your sans culottes!*"—"*That remains to be seen, Sire,*" instantly replied the officer. The Queen added, "I don't know the name of that brave Frenchman, but I will learn it; the King ought to be in possession of it." As she was reading the public papers a few days before the 10th of August she observed that mention was made of the courage of a young man who died in defending the flag he carried, and shouting, "*Vive la Nation!*" "Ah! the fine lad!" said the Queen; "what a happiness it would have been for us if such men had never left off crying, '*Vive le Roi!*'"[12]

In all that I have hitherto said of this most unfortunate of women and of Queens, those who did not live with her, those who knew her but partially, and especially the majority of foreigners, prejudiced by infamous libels, may imagine I have thought it my duty to sacrifice truth on the altar of gratitude. Fortunately I can invoke unexceptionable witnesses; they will declare whether what I assert that I have seen and heard appears to them either untrue or improbable.

1. I received by night only the King's answer, written with his own hand, in the margin of my letter. I always sent him back with the day's letter that to which he had replied the day before, so that my letters and his answers, of which I contented myself with taking notes only, never remained with me twenty-four hours. I proposed this arrangement to his Majesty to remove all uneasiness from his mind; my letters were generally delivered to the King or the Queen by M. de Marsilly, captain of the King's Guard, whose attachment and fidelity were known to their Majesties. I also sometimes employed M. Bernard de Marigny, who had left Brest for the purpose of facing the dangers which threatened the King, and sharing with all his Majesty's faithful servants the honour of forming a rampart round him with their bodies.—*Memoirs of Bertrand de Molleville*, vol. ii, p. 12.

2. One of the most remarkable features of the King's character and the nature of his mind was that his natural timidity and the difficulty which he generally felt in expressing himself were never perceptible when religion, the relief of the people, or the welfare of the French were the subjects in question; he would then speak with a facility and an energy which astonished new ministers in particular, who almost invariably came at first to the Council possessed with the generally received opinion that the King had a very limited intellect. I do not mean to say that Louis XVI was a genius; but I am convinced that if he had received a different education, and his abilities had been cultivated and exercised, he could have shown as much talent as those princes who have had the reputation of possessing the most. We saw him daily, and with the greatest ease, read a letter, a newspaper, or a memorial, and at the same time listen to the relation of some affair, and yet understand both perfectly well.

The King's constant practice was to come to the Council with the evening paper, and the letters or memorials which had been presented to him during the day, in his hand. He spent the first half hour of each sitting in reading them, handed the memorials which required attention to the proper ministers, lit the others and the newspaper at the taper next to him, and threw them on the floor. All this time the ministers reported the business of their respective departments, and the King understood them so well that in an affair of some delicacy, reported while he was reading by M. Cahier de Gerville, and adjourned for a week for consideration, his Majesty astonished us upon the second report of the same affair by the exactness with which he fixed upon the omission of a fact extremely important to the decision, and which M. Cahier de Gerville no longer remembered. None of us could cope with the King in point of memory. His judgment was not less sound, not only in business, but in the composition of proclamations, or of letters, or speeches addressed to the Assembly. All the important documents of that nature which appeared during my administration were submitted to the King's examination in particular, after having been discussed and frequently settled at the committee of the ministers, and there are few of them in which his Majesty did not make some valuable corrections.—*Memoirs of Bertrand de Molleville,* vol. i.

3. A young man who did not observe this written order went down into the garden; furious outcries, threats of *la lanterne,* and the crowd of people which collected upon the terrace warned him of his imprudence, and the danger which he ran. He immediately pulled off his shoes, took out his handkerchief and wiped the dust from their soles. The people cried out, "*Bravo! The good citizen for ever!*" He was carried off in triumph.—*Madame Campan.*

4. M. Auguié, my brother-in-law, receiver-general of the finances, offered her, through his wife, a portfolio containing 100,000 crowns in paper money. On this occasion the Queen said the most affecting things to my sister, expressive of her happiness at having contributed to the fortunes of such faithful subjects as herself and her husband, but declined her offer.—*Madame Campan.*

5. A few days before the 10th of August the squabbles between the royalists and the Jacobins, and between the Jacobins and the constitutionalists, increased in warmth; among the latter those men who defended the principles they professed with the greatest talent, courage, and constancy were at the same time the most exposed to danger. Montjoie says: "The question of dethronement was discussed with a degree of frenzy in the Assembly. Such of the deputies as voted against it were abused, ill-treated, and surrounded by assassins. They had a battle to fight at every step they took; and at length they did not dare to sleep in their own houses. Of this number were Regnault de Beaucaron, Froudiere, Girardin, and Vaublanc. Girardin complained of having been struck in one of the lobbies of the Assembly. A voice cried out to him, '*Say where you were struck.*'—'*Where?*' replied Girardin, '*what a question! Behind. Do assassins ever strike otherwise?*" (*History of Marie Antoinette*)—Note by the Editor.

6. Pétion was the Mayor of Paris, and Mandat on this day was commandant of the national guard. Mandat was assassinated that night.—*Thiers,* vol. i, p. 260.

7. The exalted piety of Madame Elizabeth gave to all she said and did a noble character, descriptive of that of her soul. On the day on which this worthy descendant of Saint Louis was sacrificed the executioner, in tying her hands behind her, raised up one of the ends of her handkerchief. Madame Elizabeth, with calmness, and in a voice which seemed not to belong to earth, said to him, "In the name of modesty, cover my bosom." I learned this from Madame de Serilly, who was condemned the same day as the Princess, but who obtained a respite at the moment of the execution, Madame de Montmorin, her relation, declaring that her cousin was *enceinte.*—*Madame Campan.*

8. The informant, cited by Montjoie, thus relates the efforts made by M. Rœderer with the people and the national guard, and the conversation he afterwards had with the King in his closet: "M. Rœderer, it must be said to his praise, tried all means. At last, being unable to subdue the fury of the people, he calmed it for a few minutes; they granted him half an hour, and the depositaries of the law instantly returned into the court of the Château. Here they met with obstacles of another kind; the national guard seemed perfectly resolute and well disposed. M. Rœderer called their attention to the extent of the danger; he made them promise to remain firm at their posts; he exhorted them not to attack their fellow-citizens, their brethren, as long

as they should remain inactive; but he foresaw the approaching moment when the Château would be attacked. He explained to them the principles of lawful defence, and made the requisition prescribed by the law of the month of May 1791 relative to the public safety. The national guard, however, remained silent, and the gunners unloaded their cannon. What could the authorities of the department then do? They joined the King's ministers, and all with one consent conjured him to save himself with his family, and take refuge in the bosom of the National Assembly. 'There, only, Sire,' said M. Rœderer, 'in the midst of the representatives of the people, can your Majesty, the Queen, and the royal family be in safety. Come, let us fly; in another quarter of an hour, perhaps, we shall not be able to command a retreat.'

"The King hesitated, the Queen manifested the highest dissatisfaction. 'What!' said she, 'are we alone; is there nobody who can act?' 'Yes, Madame, alone; action is useless—resistance is impossible.' One of the members of the department, M. Gerdrot, insisted on the prompt execution of the proposed measure. 'Silence, sir,' said the Queen to him; 'silence; you are the only person who ought to be silent here; when the mischief is done, those who did it should not pretend to wish to remedy it.' …

"Before my return to the Château I visited the hall of the department. The authorities of the department were to remain assembled the whole night. The *procureur-général* offered to pass it himself in the Château if the King thought it necessary. The King wished it should be so; I informed M. Rœderer who instantly proceeded to the King; it was then near midnight. About one in the morning, the tocsin having only begun to sound after the Mayor had quitted the King, his Majesty desired me to inform M. Pétion of it, and to communicate to him his wish that the gates of the terrace called Des Feuillans should be closed … He went to the National Assembly, gave the explanations required of him, but said nothing about the Terrace des Feuillans. The terrace had been declared part of the area of the National Assembly; that body alone could dispose of it; therefore I pressed M. Pétion to demand what the King required of the National Assembly. The Mayor could do this with the more propriety because the tocsin had sounded, and the *générale* had been beaten; it was certain the meeting was assembling, and that the National Assembly had recalled the Mayor to their bar fully three quarters of an hour.

"M. Pétion heard the King's observations. He felt the force of them. Even before he went to the National Assembly he used the gate which commands the riding-house yard to be shut; the Swiss received a verbal order for it in the presence of all the municipal officers, and of several grenadiers who were with the Mayor. The moment afterwards M. Pétion returned to the garden, and proceeded to the terrace. I saw him walking there in the midst of the same group, accompanied by the same municipal officers, and by a still greater number of national guards. I am a witness that the *commandant de bataillon* accosted the Mayor opposite the principal gate of the Château, and said to him that everything was quiet, and that there was nothing to fear; that the commissioners of the sections, who had met at the Faubourg Saint Antoine, had separated and adjourned to Friday morning early, at the Hôtel de Ville, with the intention of coming to a final resolution; but that until that time there was no ground for apprehension. This intelligence was too agreeable not to be readily believed. The Mayor announced that he should soon retire. However, several persons pointed out to him that the account of the *commandant de bataillon* might be true, and still the danger might be pressing.

"It has been observed that the commandant came from the section of the Croix Rouge; that the commissioners spoken of had separated at eleven o'clock; that since, and notwithstanding their pretended resolution, the tocsin had been sounded, the alarm-gun had been fired, the assemblage had taken place, and everything seemed to announce that the people would put themselves in motion about five o'clock in the morning.

"The Queen resumed her watch; the King remained mute; nobody spoke. It was reserved for me to give the last piece of advice. I had the firmness to say, 'Let us go, and not deliberate; honour commands it, the good of the State requires it. Let us go to the National Assembly; this step ought to have been taken long ago.'—'Let us go,' said the King, raising his right hand; 'let us start; let us give this last mark of self-devotion, since it is necessary.' The Queen was persuaded. Her first anxiety was for the King, the second for her son; the King had none. 'M. Rœderer—gentlemen,' said the Queen, 'you answer for the person of the King; you answer for that of my son.'—'Madame,' replied M. Rœderer, 'we pledge ourselves to die at your side; that is all we can engage for.'"—"Historical narrative of the transactions at the Château of the Tuileries during the night of the 9th and 10th August 1792, and the morning of the 10th"; from Montjoie's *History of Marie Antoinette*.

9. A former monastery near the Tuileries, so called from the Bernardines, one of the Cistercian orders; later, a revolutionary club.

10. M. Thierry, who never ceased to give his sovereign proofs of unalterable attachment, was one of the victims of the 2nd of September.—*Madame Campan*.

11. During the Reign of Terror I withdrew to the Château de Coubertin, near that of Dampierre. The Duchesse de Luynes frequently came to ask me to tell her what the Queen had said about her at the Feuillans. She would say as she went away, "I have often need to request you to repeat those words of the Queen."—*Madame Campan*.

12. In reading this account of the 10th August 1792 the reader must remember that there was hardly any armed force to resist the mob. The regiments that had showed signs of being loyal to the King had been removed from Paris by the Assembly. The Swiss had been deprived of their own artillery, and the Court had sent one of their battalions into Normandy at a time when there was an idea of taking refuge there. The national guard were either disloyal or disheartened, and the gunners, especially, of that force at the Tuileries sympathised with the mob. Thus the King had about 800 or 900 Swiss and little more than one battalion of the national guard. Mandat, one of the six heads of the legions of the national guard, to whose turn the command fell on that day, was true to his duty, but was sent for to the Hôtel de Ville and assassinated. Still the small force, even after the departure of the King, would have probably beaten off the mob had not the King given the fatal order to the Swiss to cease firing.—See Thiers' *History of the French Revolution*, vol. i, chap. xi. Bonaparte's opinion of the mob may be judged by his remarks on the 20th June 1792, when, disgusted at seeing the King appear with the red cap on his head, he exclaimed, "Che coglione! Why have they let in all that rabble? why don't they sweep off four or five hundred of them with the cannon? the rest would then set off."—*Bourrienne*, vol. i, p. 13 (London: Bentley, 1836). Bonaparte carried out his own plan against a far stronger force of assailants on the Jour des Sections, 4 October 1795.

XXII

Pétion refuses Madame Campan permission to be imprisoned in the Temple with the Queen—She excites the suspicions of Robespierre — Domiciliary visits—Madame Campan opens the portfolio she had received from the King—Papers in it, with the seals of State—Mirabeau's secret correspondence with the Court—Destroyed as well as the other papers— The only document preserved—It is delivered to M. de Malesherbes on the trial of the unfortunate Louis XVI—End of the Memoirs

The Queen having lost her watch and purse as she was passing from the Tuileries to the Feuillans, requested my sister to lend her twenty-five *louis*.[1]

I spent part of the day at the Feuillans, and her Majesty told me she would ask Pétion to let me be with her in the place which the Assembly should decree for her prison. I then returned home to prepare everything that might be necessary for me to accompany her. On the same day (11th August) at nine in the evening I returned to the Feuillans. I found there were orders at all the gates forbidding my being admitted. I claimed a right to enter by virtue of the first permission which had been given to me; I was again refused. I was told that the Queen had as many people as were requisite about her. My sister was with her as well as one of my companions, who came out of the prisons of the Abbaye on the 11th. I renewed my solicitations on the 12th; my tears and entreaties moved neither the keepers of the gates, nor even a deputy, to whom I addressed myself.

I soon heard of the transfer of Louis XVI and his family to the Temple. I went to Pétion accompanied by M. Valadon, for whom I had procured a place in the post-office, and who was devoted to me. He determined to go up to Pétion alone; he told him that those who requested to be confined could not be suspected of evil designs, and that no political opinion could afford a ground of objection to these solicitations. Seeing that the well-meaning man did not succeed I thought to do more in person; but Pétion persisted in his refusal, and threatened to send me to La Force. Thinking to give me a kind of consolation, he added I might be certain that all those who were then with Louis XVI and his family would not stay with them long. And in fact two or three days afterwards the Princesse de Lamballe, Madame de Tourzel, her daughter, the Queen's first woman, the first woman of the Dauphin and of Madame, M. de Chamilly and M. de Huë were carried off during the night and transferred to La Force. After the departure of the King and Queen for the Temple my sister was detained a prisoner in the apartments their Majesties had quitted for twenty-four hours.

From this time I was reduced to the misery of having no further intelligence of my august and unfortunate mistress but through the medium of the newspapers or the national guard, who did duty at the Temple.

The King and Queen said nothing to me at the Feuillans about the portfolio which had been deposited with me; no doubt they expected to see me again. The minister Roland and the deputies composing the provisional government were very intent on a search for papers belonging to their Majesties. They had the whole of the Tuileries ransacked. The infamous Robespierre bethought himself of M. Campan, the Queen's private secretary, and said that his death was feigned, that he was living unknown in some obscure part of France, and was doubtless the depositary of all the important papers. In a great portfolio belonging to the King there had been found a solitary letter from the Comte d'Artois, which, by its date, and the subjects of which it treated, indicated the existence of a continued correspondence. (This letter appears among the documents used on the trial of Louis XVI.) A former preceptor of my son's had studied with Robespierre; the latter meeting him in the street, and knowing the connection which had subsisted between him and the family of M. Campan, required him to say, upon his honour, whether he was certain of the death of the latter. The man replied that M. Campan had died at La Briche in 1791, and that he had seen him interred in the cemetery of Epinay. "Well, then!" resumed Robespierre, "bring me the certificate of his burial at twelve to-morrow; it is a document for which I have pressing occasion." Upon hearing the deputy's demand I instantly sent for a certificate of M. Campan's burial, and Robespierre received it at nine o'clock the next morning. But I considered that, in thinking of my father-in-law, they were coming very near me, the real depositary of these important papers. I passed days and nights in considering what I could do for the best under such circumstances.

I was thus situated when the order to inform against those who had been denounced as suspected on the 10th of August led to domiciliary visits. My servants were told that the people of the quarter in which I lived were talking much of the search that would be made in my house, and came to apprise me of it. I heard that fifty armed men would make themselves masters of M. Auguié's house, where I then was. I had just received this intelligence when M. Gougenot, the King's *maître d'hôtel* and receiver-general of the taxes, a man much attached to his sovereign, came into my room wrapped in a riding-cloak, under which, with great difficulty, he carried the King's portfolio, which I had entrusted to him. He threw it down at my feet, and said to me, "There is your deposit; I did not receive it from our unfortunate King's own hands; in delivering it to you I have executed my trust." After saying this he was about to withdraw. I stopped him, praying him to consult with me what I ought to do in such a trying emergency. He would not listen to my entreaties, or even hear me describe the course I intended to pursue. I told him my abode was about to be surrounded; I imparted to him what the Queen had said to me about the contents of the portfolio. To all this he answered, "There it is; decide for yourself; I will have no hand in it." Upon that I remained a few seconds thinking, and my conduct was founded upon the following reasons. I spoke aloud, although to myself; I walked about the room with agitated steps; M. Gougenot was thunderstruck. "Yes," said I, "when we can no longer communicate with our King and receive his orders, however attached we may be to him, we can only serve him according to the best of our own judgment. The Queen said to me, 'This portfolio contains scarcely anything but documents of a most dangerous description in the event of a trial taking place, if it should fall into the hands of revolutionary persons.' She mentioned, too, a single document which would, under the same circumstances, be useful. It is my duty to interpret her words, and consider them as orders. She meant to say, 'You will save such a paper, you will destroy the rest if they are likely to be taken from you.' If it were not so, was there any occasion for her to enter into any detail as to what the portfolio contained? The order to keep it was sufficient. Probably it contains, moreover, the letters of that part of the family which has emigrated; there is nothing which may have been foreseen or decided upon that can be useful now; and there can be no political thread which has not been cut by the events of the 10th of August and the imprisonment of the King. My house is about to be surrounded, I cannot conceal anything of such bulk; I might then, through want of foresight, give up that which would cause the condemnation of the King. Let us open the portfolio, save the document alluded to, and destroy the rest." I took a knife and cut open one side of the portfolio. I saw a great number of envelopes endorsed by the King's own hand. M. Gougenot found there the former seals of the King,[2] such as they were before the Assembly had changed the inscription. At this moment we heard a great noise; he agreed to tie up the portfolio, take it again under his cloak, and go to a safe place to execute what I had taken upon me to determine. He made me swear, by all I held most sacred, that I would affirm, under every possible emergency, that the course I was pursuing had not been dictated to me by anybody; and that whatever might be the result, I would take all the credit or all the blame upon myself. I lifted up my hand and took the oath he required; he went out. Half an hour afterwards a great number of armed men came to my house; they placed sentinels at all the outlets; they broke open *secrétaires* and closets, of which they had not the keys; they searched the flower-pots and boxes; they examined the cellars; and the commandant repeatedly said, "Look particularly for papers." In the afternoon M. Gougenot returned. He had still the seals of France about him, and he brought me a statement of all that he had burnt.

The portfolio contained twenty letters from Monsieur, eighteen or nineteen from the Comte d'Artois, seventeen from Madame Adelaide, eighteen from Madame Victoire, a great many letters from Comte Alexandre de Lameth, and many from M. de Malesherbes, with documents annexed to them. There were also some from M. de Montmorin and other ex-ministers or ambassadors. Each correspondence had its title written in the King's own hand upon the blank paper which contained it. The most voluminous was that from Mirabeau. It was tied up with a scheme for an escape, which he thought necessary. M. Gougenot, who had skimmed over these letters with more attention than the rest, told me they were of so interesting a nature that the King had no doubt kept them as documents exceedingly valuable for a history of his reign, and that the correspondence with the Princes, which was entirely relative to what was going forward abroad, in concert with the King, would have been fatal to him if it had been seized. After he had finished he placed in my hands the *procès-verbal*, signed by all the ministers to which the King attached so much importance, because he had given his opinion against the declaration of war; a copy of the letter written by the King to the Princes, his brothers, inviting them to return to France; an account of the diamonds which the Queen had sent to Brussels (these two documents were in my handwriting); and a receipt for 400,000 francs, under the hand of a celebrated banker. This sum was part of the 800,000 francs which the Queen had gradually saved during her reign out of her pension of 300,000 francs per annum, and out of the 100,000 francs given by way of present on the birth of the Dauphin. This receipt, written on a very small piece of paper, was in the cover of an almanac. I agreed with M. Gougenot, who was obliged by his office to reside in Paris, that he should retain the *procès-verbal* of the Council and the receipt for the 400,000 francs, and that we should wait either for orders or for the means of transmitting these documents to the King or Queen; and I set out for Versailles.

The strictness of the precautions taken to guard the illustrious prisoners was daily increased. The idea that I could not inform the King of the course I had adopted of burning his papers, and the fear that I should not be able to transmit to him that which he had pointed out as necessary, tormented me to such a degree that it is wonderful my health endured the strain.

The dreadful trial drew near. Official advocates were granted to the King; the heroic virtue of M. de Malesherbes induced him to brave the most imminent dangers, either to save his master or to perish with him. I hoped also to be able to find some means of informing his Majesty of what I had thought it right to do. I sent a man, on whom I could rely, to Paris, to request M. Gougenot to come to me at Versailles: he came immediately. We agreed that he should see M. de Malesherbes without availing himself of any intermediate person for that purpose.

M. Gougenot awaited his return from the Temple at the door of his hotel, and made a sign that he wished to speak to him. A moment afterwards a servant came to introduce him into the magistrates' room. He imparted to M. de Malesherbes what I had thought it right to do with respect to the King's papers, and placed in his hands the *procès-verbal* of the Council, which his Majesty had preserved in order to serve, if occasion required it, for a ground of his defence. However, that paper is not mentioned in either of the speeches of his advocate; probably it was determined not to make use of it.

I stop at that terrible period which is marked by the assassination of a King whose virtues are well known; but I cannot refrain from relating what he deigned to say in my favour to M. de Malesherbes: "Let Madame Campan know that she did what I should myself have ordered her to do; I thank her for it; she is one of those whom I regret I have it not in my power to recompense for their fidelity to my person, and for their good services." I did not hear of this until the morning after he had suffered, and I think I should have sunk under my despair if this honourable testimony had not given me some consolation.

* * *

[Madame Campan's narrative suddenly ceases with the end of her personal attendance on Marie Antoinette, probably in pursuance of the rule she laid down for herself in writing her *Memoirs,* not to relate anything concerning the royal family which she had not either witnessed, or been informed of by eye-witnesses. Madame Campan's share in the horrors of the Revolution through the violent death of her sister, Madame Auguié, and her own life after parting from the Queen, are detailed in the Prefatory Memoir.]

1. On being interrogated the Queen declared that these five and-twenty *louis* had been lent to her by my sister; this formed a pretence for arresting her and myself, and led to her death.— *Madame Campan.*

2. No doubt it was in order to have the ancient seals ready at a moment's notice, in case of a counter-revolution, that the Queen desired me not to quit the Tuileries. M. Gougenot threw the seals into the river, one from above the Pont Neuf; and the other from near the Pont Royal.—*Madame Campan.*

ANNEX TO CHAPTER XXII

Madame Campan's narrative breaking off abruptly at the time of the painful end met with by her sister, we have supplemented it by abridged accounts of the chief incidents in the tragedy which overwhelmed the royal house she so faithfully served, taken from contemporary records and the best historical authorities.

THE ROYAL FAMILY IN THE TEMPLE

The Assembly having, at the instance of the Commune of Paris, decreed that the royal family should be immured in the Temple, they were removed thither from the Feuillans on the 13th of August 1792, in the charge of Pétion, Mayor of Paris, and Santerre, the commandant-general. Twelve commissioners of the general Council were to keep constant watch at the Temple, which had been fortified by earthworks and garrisoned by detachments of the national guard, no person being allowed to enter without permission from the municipality.[1]

The Temple, formerly the headquarters of the Knight Templars in Paris, consisted of two buildings—the palace, facing the Rue de Temple, usually occupied by one of the Princes of the blood;[2] and the Tower, standing behind the palace.[3] The Tower was a square building, with a round tower at each corner and a small turret on one side, usually called the Tourelle. In the narrative of the Duchesse d'Angoulême she says that the soldiers who escorted the royal prisoners wished to take the King alone to the Tower, and his family to the Palace of the Temple, but that on the way Manuel[4] received an order to imprison them all in the Tower, where so little provision had been made for their reception that Madame Elizabeth slept in the kitchen. The royal family were accompanied by the Princesse de Lamballe, Madame de Tourzel and her daughter Pauline, Mesdames de Navarre, de Saint Brice, Thibaut, and Bazire, MM. de Huë and de Chamilly, and three men servants.[5] An order from the Commune soon removed these devoted attendants, and M. de Huë alone was permitted to return. In spite of the frightful ordeal so recently passed through at the Tuileries and in the Assembly, and the distracting uncertainty as to the fate awaiting them, the royal family at once adopted a quiet and studious routine. "We all passed the day together," says Madame Royale. "My father taught my brother geography; my mother history, and to learn verses by heart; and my aunt gave him little lessons in arithmetic. My father had fortunately found a library which amused him, and my mother worked tapestry … We went every day to walk in the garden, for the sake of my brother's health, though the King was always insulted by the guard. On the Feast of Saint Louis *Ça Ira* was sung under the walls of the Temple. Manuel that evening brought my aunt a letter from her aunts at Rome.[6] It was the last the family received from without. My father was no longer called King. He was treated with no kind of respect; the officers always sat in his presence and never took off their hats. They deprived him of his sword and searched his pockets … Pétion sent as turnkey and gaoler the horrible man[7] who had broken open my father's door on the 20th June 1792, and who had been near assassinating him. This man never left the Tower, and was indefatigable in endeavouring to torment him. One time he would sing the *Carmagnole*, and a thousand other horrors, before us; again, knowing that my mother disliked the smoke of tobacco, he would puff it in her face, as well as in that of my father, as they happened to pass him. He took care always to be in bed before we went to supper, because he knew that we must pass through his room. Sometimes, even, he would be in bed as we went to dinner; in short, there was no species of torment or insult that he did not practise. My father suffered it all with gentleness, forgiving the man from the bottom of his heart. My mother bore it with a dignity that frequently repressed his insolence."[8] The only occasion, Madame Royale says, on which the Queen showed any impatience at the conduct of the officials, was when a municipal officer woke the Dauphin suddenly in the night to make certain that he was safe, as though the sight of the peacefully sleeping child would not have been in itself the best assurance.

Clery, the *valet de chambre* of the Dauphin,[9] having with difficulty obtained permission to resume his duties, entered the Temple on 24th August, and for eight days shared with M. de Huë the personal attendance; but on the 2nd September De Huë was arrested, seals were placed on the little room he had occupied, and Clery passed the night in that of the King. On the following morning Manuel arrived, charged by the Commune to inform the King that M. de Huë would not be permitted to return, and to offer to send another person. "I thank you," answered the King. "I will manage with the *valet de chambre* of my son; and if the Council refuse I will serve myself. I am determined to do it."[10] On the 3rd September Manuel visited the Temple and assured the King that Madame de Lamballe and all the other prisoners who had been removed to La Force were well, and safely guarded. "But at three o'clock," says Madame Royale, "just after dinner, and as the King was sitting down to tric-trac with my mother (which he played for the purpose of having an opportunity of saying a few words to her unheard by the keepers), the most horrid shouts were heard. The officer who happened to be on guard in the room behaved well. He shut the door and the window, and even drew the curtains to prevent their seeing anything; but outside the workmen and the gaoler Rocher joined the assassins and increased the tumult. Several officers of the guard and the municipality now arrived, and on my father's asking what was the matter, a young officer replied, 'Well, since you will know, it is the head of Madame de Lamballe that they want to show you.' At these words my mother was overcome with horror; it was the only occasion on which her firmness abandoned her. The municipal officers were very angry with the young man; but the King, with his usual goodness, excused him, saying that it was his own fault since he had questioned the officer. The noise lasted till five o'clock. We learned that the people had wished to force the door, and that the municipal officers had been enabled to prevent it only by putting a tri-coloured scarf[11] across it, and allowing six of the murderers to march round our prison with the head of the Princess, leaving at the door her body, which they would have dragged in also."

Clery was not so fortunate as to escape the frightful spectacle. He had gone down to dine with Tison and his wife, employed as servants in the Temple, and says: "We were hardly seated when a head, on the end of a pike, was presented at the window. Tison's wife gave a great cry; the assassins fancied they recognised the Queen's voice, and responded by savage laughter. Under the idea that his Majesty was still at table, they placed their dreadful trophy where it must be seen. It was the head of the Princesse de Lamballe; although bleeding, it was not disfigured, and her light hair, still in curls, hung about the pike."

The republicans were at this time infuriated by reports of the rapid approach of the Prussians. Rocher drew his sabre and threatened the King with it, crying, "If they come, I shall kill you!" For some hours it seemed impossible that the prisoners of the Temple should escape the fate of those slaughtered at La Force, the Conciergerie, and the other prisons, for the Commissioners of the Commune addressed a letter to the Assembly beginning with these ominous words: "The sanctuary of Louis XVI is threatened. *Resistance would be impolitic and dangerous, perhaps unjust.* Harmony between the representatives of the people and the Commissioners of the Commune might prevent excess."[12] At length, however, the immense mob that surrounded the Temple gradually withdrew, "to follow the head of the Princesse de Lamballe to the Palais Royal".[13] Meanwhile the royal family could scarcely believe that for the time their lives were saved. "My aunt and I heard the drums beating to arms all night," says Madame Royale; "my unhappy mother did not even attempt to sleep. We heard her sobs."

In the comparative tranquillity which followed the September massacres, the royal family resumed the regular habits they had adopted on entering the Temple. "The King usually rose at six in the morning," says Clery. "He shaved himself, and I dressed his hair; he then went to his reading-room, which being very small, the municipal officer on duty remained in the bed-chamber with the door open, that he might always keep the King in sight. His Majesty continued praying on his knees for some time, and then read till nine. During that interval, after putting his chamber to rights and preparing the breakfast, I went down to the Queen, who never opened her door till I arrived, in order to prevent the municipal officer from going into her apartment. At nine o'clock the Queen, the children, and Madame Elizabeth went up to the King's chamber to breakfast. At ten the King and his family went down to the Queen's chamber, and there passed the day. He employed himself in educating his son, made him recite passages from Corneille and Racine, gave him lessons in geography, and exercised him in colouring the maps. The

Queen, on her part, was employed in the education of her daughter, and these different lessons lasted till eleven o'clock. The remaining time till noon was passed in needle-work, knitting, or making tapestry. At one o'clock, when the weather was fine, the royal family were conducted to the garden by four municipal officers and the commander of a legion of the national guard. As there were a number of workmen in the Temple employed in pulling down houses and building new walls, they only allowed a part of the chestnut-tree walk for the promenade, in which I was allowed to share, and where I also played with the young Prince at ball, quoits, or races. At two we returned to the Tower, where I served the dinner, at which time Santerre regularly came to the Temple, attended by two *aides-de-camp*. The King sometimes spoke to him—the Queen never.

"After the meal the royal family came down into the Queen's room, and their Majesties generally played a game of picquet or tric-trac. At four o'clock the King took a little repose, the Princesses round him, each with a book … When the King woke the conver-sation was resumed, and I gave writing lessons to his son, taking the copies, according to his instructions, from the works of Montesquieu and other celebrated authors. After the lesson I took the young Prince into Madame Elizabeth's room, where we played at ball, and battledore and shuttlecock. In the evening the family sat round a table, while the Queen read to them from books of history, or other works proper to instruct and amuse the children. Madame Elizabeth took the book in her turn, and in this manner they read till eight o'clock. After that I served the supper of the young Prince, in which the royal family shared, and the King amused the children with charades out of a collection of French papers which he found in the library. After the Dauphin had supped, I undressed him, and the Queen heard him say his prayers. At nine the King went to supper, and afterwards went for a moment to the Queen's chamber, shook hands with her and his sister for the night, kissed his children, and then retired to the turret-room, where he sate reading till midnight. The Queen and the Princesses locked themselves in, and one of the municipal officers remained in the little room which parted their chamber, where he passed the night; the other followed his Majesty. In this manner was the time passed as long as the King remained in the small tower."

But even these harmless pursuits were too often made the means of further insulting and thwarting the unfortunate family. Commissary Le Clerc interrupted the Prince's writing lessons, proposing to substitute Republican works for those from which the King selected his copies. A smith who was present when the Queen was reading the history of France to her children denounced her to the Commune for choosing the period when the Connétable de Bourbon took arms against France, and said she wished to inspire her son with unpatriotic feelings; a municipal officer asserted that the multi-plication table the Prince was studying would afford a means of "speaking in cipher", so arithmetic had to be abandoned.[14] Much the same occurred even with the needlework: the Queen and Princess finished some chair-backs, which they wished to send to the Duchesse de Serente; but the officials considered that the patterns were hieroglyphics, intended for carrying on a correspondence, and ordered that none of the Princesses' work should leave the Temple. The short daily walk in the garden was also embittered by the rude and cruel buffoonery of the military and municipal gaolers; sometimes, however, it afforded an opportunity for marks of sympathy to be shown. People would station themselves at the windows of houses overlooking the Temple gardens, and evince by gestures their loyal affection, and some of the sentinels showed, even by tears, that their duty was painful to them.

On the 21st September the National Convention was constituted, Pétion being made President and Collot d'Herbois moving the "abolition of royalty" amidst transports of applause. That afternoon a municipal officer, attended by *gendarmes à cheval* and followed by a crowd of people, arrived at the Temple, and, after a flourish of trumpets, proclaimed the establishment of the French Republic. "The man," says Clery, "had the voice of a stentor." The royal family could distinctly hear the announcement of the King's deposition. "Hebert, so well known under the title of Père Duchêne, and Destournelles were on guard. They were sitting near the door, and turned to the King with meaning smiles. He had a book in his hand, and went on reading without changing countenance. The Queen showed the same firmness. The proclamation finished, the trumpets sounded afresh. I went to the window; the people took me for Louis XVI, and I was overwhelmed with insults."

After the new decree the prisoners were treated with increased harshness. Pens, paper, ink, and pencils were taken from them. The King and Madame Elizabeth gave up all, but the Queen and her daughter each concealed a pencil. "In the beginning of October," says Madame Royale, "after my father had supped, he was told to stop, that he was not to return to his former apartments, and that he was to be separated from his family. At this dreadful sentence the Queen lost her usual courage. We parted from him with abundance of tears, though we expected to see him again in the morning.[15] They brought in our breakfast separately from his, however. My mother would take nothing. The officers, alarmed at her silent and concentrated sorrow, allowed us to see the King, but at meal-times only, and on condition that we should not speak low, nor in any foreign language, but loud and in 'good French'.[16] We went down, therefore, with the greatest joy to dine with my father. In the evening, when my brother was in bed, my mother and my aunt alternately sat with him or went with me to sup with my father. In the morning, after breakfast, we remained in the King's apartments while Clery dressed our hair, as he was no longer allowed to come to my mother's room, and this arrangement gave us the pleasure of spending a few moments more with my father."[17]

The royal prisoners had no comfort except their affection for each other. At that time even common necessaries were denied them. Their small stock of linen had been lent them by persons of the Court during the time they spent at the Feuillans.[18] The Princesses mended their clothes every day, and after the King had gone to bed Madame Elizabeth mended his. "With much trouble," says Clery, "I procured some fresh linen for them. But the workwomen having marked it with crowned letters, the Princesses were ordered to pick them out." The room in the great tower to which the King had been removed contained only one bed, and no other article of furniture. A chair was brought on which Clery spent the first night; painters were still at work on the room, and the smell of the paint, he says, was almost unbearable. This room was afterwards furnished by collecting from various parts of the Temple a chest of drawers, a small bureau, a few odd chairs, a chimney-glass, and a bed hung with green damask, which had been used by the Captain of the Guard to the Comte d'Artois. A room for the Queen was being prepared over that of the King, and she implored the workmen to finish it quickly, but it was not ready for her occupation for some time, and when she was allowed to remove to it the Dauphin was taken from her and placed with his father. When their Majesties met again in the great Tower, says Clery, there was little change in the hours fixed for meals, reading, walking, and the education of their children. They were not allowed to have mass said in the Temple, and therefore commissioned Clery to get them the breviary in use in the diocese of Paris. Among the books read by the King while in the Tower were Hume's *History of England* (in the original), Tasso, and the *De Imitatione Christi*. The jealous suspicions of the municipal officers led to the most absurd investigations; a draught-board was taken to pieces lest the squares should hide treasonable papers; macaroons were broken in half to see that they did not contain letters; peaches were cut open and the stones cracked; and Clery was compelled to drink the essence of soap prepared for shaving the King, under the pretence that it might contain poison.

In November the King and all the family had feverish colds, and Clery had an attack of rheumatic fever. On the first day of his illness he got up and tried to dress his master, but the King, seeing how ill he was, ordered him to lie down, and himself dressed the Dauphin. The little Prince waited on Clery all day, and in the evening the King contrived to approach his bed, and said in a low voice, "I should like to take care of you myself, but you know how we are watched. Take courage; to-morrow you shall see my doctor."[19] Madame Elizabeth brought the valet cooling draughts, of which she deprived herself; and after Clery was able to get up, the young Prince one night with great difficulty kept awake till eleven o'clock in order to give him a box of lozenges when he went to make the King's bed.

On 7th December a deputation from the Commune brought an order that the royal family should be deprived of "knives, razors, scissors, penknives, and all other cutting instruments". The King gave up a knife, and took from a morocco case a pair of scissors and a penknife; and the officials then searched the room, taking away the little toilette implements of gold and silver, and afterwards removing the Princesses' working materials. Returning to the King's room, they insisted on seeing what remained in his pocket-case. "Are these toys which I have in my hand also cutting instruments?" asked the King, showing them a cork-screw, a turn-screw, and a steel for lighting. These also were taken from him. Shortly afterwards Madame Elizabeth was mending the King's coat, and, having no scissors, was compelled to break the thread with her teeth. "What a contrast!" he exclaimed, looking at her tenderly. "You wanted nothing in your pretty house at Montreuil."—"Ah, brother," she answered, "how can I have any regret when I partake your misfortunes?"[20]

The Queen had frequently to take on herself some of the humble duties of a servant. This was especially painful to Louis XVI when the anniversary of some State festival brought the contrast between past and present with unusual keenness before him. "Ah, Madame," he once exclaimed, "what an employment for a Queen of France! Could they see that at Vienna! Who would have foreseen that, in uniting your lot to mine, you would have descended so low?"—"And do you esteem as nothing," she replied, "the glory of being the wife of one of the best and most persecuted of men? Are not such misfortunes the noblest honours?"[21]

Meanwhile the Assembly had decided that the King should be brought to trial. Nearly all parties, except the Girondists, no matter how bitterly opposed to each other, could agree in making him the scapegoat; and the first rumour of the approaching ordeal was conveyed to the Temple by Clery's wife,[22] who, with a friend, had permission occasionally to visit him. "I did not know how to announce this horrid news to the King," he says; "but time was pressing, and he had forbidden my concealing anything from him. In the evening, while undressing him, I gave him an account of all I had learnt, and added that there were only four days to concert some plan of corresponding with the Queen. The arrival of the municipal officer would not allow me to say more. Next morning, when the King rose, I could not get a moment for speaking with him. He went up with his son to breakfast with the Princesses, and I followed. After breakfast he talked long with the Queen, who, by a look full of trouble, made me understand that they were discussing what I had told the King. During the day I found an opportunity of describing to Madame Elizabeth how much it had cost me to augment the King's distresses by informing him of his approaching trial. She reassured me, saying that the King felt this as a mark of attachment on my part, and added, 'That which most troubles him is the fear of being separated from us.' In the evening the King told me how satisfied he was at having had warning that he was to appear before the Convention. 'Continue,' he said, 'to endeavour to find out something as to what they want to do with me. Never fear distressing me. I have agreed with my family not to seem pre-informed, in order not to compromise you.'"

Soon after this conversation Clery had to appear before a committee sent to the Temple to audit the expenses of the royal prisoners, and he then learnt from a municipal officer that it had not yet been decided to separate the King from his family; but a newspaper was given him containing the decree which ordered that the King should appear before the Convention.

On the 11th December, at five o'clock in the morning, the prisoners heard the *générale* beaten throughout Paris, and cavalry and cannon entered the Temple gardens. At nine the King and the Dauphin went as usual to breakfast with the Queen. They were allowed to remain together for an hour, but constantly under the eyes of their republican guardians. "Not being able to pour out their hearts freely, or express the many fears agitating them, was," says Clery, "perpetual torture to the royal family." At last they were obliged to part, doubtful whether they would ever see each other again. The little Prince, who remained with his father, and was ignorant of the new cause for anxiety, begged hard that the King would play at ninepins with him as usual. Twice the Dauphin could not get beyond a certain number. "Each time that I get up to *sixteen*," he said, with some vexation, "I lose the game." The King did not reply, but Clery fancied the words made some impression on him.[23]

At eleven, while the King was giving the Dauphin a reading lesson, two municipal officers entered and said they had come "to take young Louis to his mother". The King inquired why, but was only told that such were the orders of the Council. At one o'clock the Mayor of Paris, Chambon, accompanied by Chaumette, *procureur de la Commune*, Santerre, commandant of the national guard, and others, arrived at the Temple and read a decree to the King, which ordered that "Louis Capet" should be brought before the Convention. "Capet is not my name," he replied, "but that of one of my ancestors. I could have wished," he added, "that you had left my son with me during the last two hours. But this treatment is consistent with all I have experienced here. I follow you, not because I recognise the authority of the Convention, but because I can be compelled to obey it." He then followed the Mayor to a carriage which waited, with a numerous escort, at the gate of the Temple. The family left behind were overwhelmed with grief and apprehension. "It is impossible to describe the anxiety we suffered," says Madame Royale. "My mother used every endeavour with the officer who guarded her to discover what was passing; it was the first time she had condescended to question any of these men. He would tell her nothing."

Madame Elizabeth beckoned to Clery to follow her to her room, while the Queen talked with the municipal officer. "We are prepared for the worst," she said; "we encourage no false hopes about the King's fate. He will die the victim of his goodness and his love for the people, for whose happiness he has laboured ever since he came to the throne. How cruelly are they deceived! The King's religion will support him even in this terrible adversity." For an hour the Princess talked to the faithful servant, asking, after a time, with obvious agitation, "Have you heard them speak of the Queen? Alas! what can they reproach *her* with?"—"No, Madame; but what can they reproach the King with?"—"Oh, with nothing, with nothing! But perhaps they look on the King as a victim necessary for their safety. The Queen and her children could not be an obstacle to their ambition."

This long and sad interview was their last. At six o'clock Clery received the Commune's orders to have no further communication with the Dauphin and the three Princesses, as he was set apart to wait on the King only. By a refinement of cruelty, when the prisoners felt most intense anxiety for tidings of each other, they were to be most strictly guarded from receiving them; and the hours already numbered were no longer to be passed together.

TRIAL OF THE KING—HIS WILL—DEBATE ON THE SENTENCE—PARTING OF THE ROYAL FAMILY—EXECUTION

The crowd was immense as, on the morning of 11th December 1792, Louis XVI was driven slowly from the Temple to the Convention, escorted by cavalry, infantry, and artillery. Paris looked like an armed camp: all the posts were doubled; the muster-roll of the national guard was called over every hour; a piquet of 200 men watched in the court of each of the right sections; a reserve with cannon was stationed at the Tuileries, and strong detachments patrolled the streets and cleared the road of all loiterers. The trees that lined the boulevards, the doors and windows of the houses, were alive with gazers, and all eyes were fixed on the King. He was much changed since his people last beheld him. The beard he had been compelled to grow after his razors were taken from him covered cheeks, lips, and chin with light-coloured hair, which concealed the melancholy expression of his mouth; he had become thin, and his garments hung loosely on him; but his manner was perfectly collected and calm, and he recognised and named to the Mayor the various quarters through which he passed. On arriving at the Feuillans he was taken to a room to await the orders of the Assembly. During this brief interval the members debated on how their illustrious prisoner should be received. Barère, the President, said, "Citizens of the tribunes, Louis is at the bar. You are about to give a great lesson to kings, a great and useful example to nations. Bethink you of the silence that accompanied Louis from Varennes—a silence that was the precursor of the judgment of kings by the people." "Let the silence of the grave affright the guilty,"[24] exclaimed Légendie. "As the Convention is not condemned to attend to-day to nothing but a King," said Manuel, "I think it would be proper to employ ourselves on some important business, even though we should make Louis wait when he arrives."[25] His motion was adopted, and a discussion began on a law concerning the emigrants.

It was about half-past two when the King appeared at the bar. The Mayor and Generals Santerre and Wittengoff were at his side. Profound silence pervaded the Assembly. All were touched by the King's dignity and the composure of his looks under so great a reverse of fortune. By nature he had been formed rather to endure calamity with patience than to contend against it with energy. The approach of death could not disturb his serenity.

"Louis, you may be seated," said Barère. "Answer the questions that shall be put to you." The King seated himself and listened to the reading of the *acte énonciatif*, article by article.[26] All the faults of the court were there enumerated and imputed to Louis XVI personally. He was charged with the interruption of the sittings of the 20th of June 1789, with the Bed of Justice held on the 23rd of the same month, the aristocratic conspiracy thwarted by the insurrection of the 14th of July, the entertainment of the life-guards, the insults offered to the national cockade, the refusal to sanction the declaration of rights, as well as several constitutional articles; lastly, all the facts which indicated a new conspiracy in October, and which were followed by the scenes of the 5th and 6th; the speeches of reconciliation which had succeeded all these scenes, and which promised a change that was not sincere; the false oath taken at the Federation of the 14th of July; the secret practices of Talon and Mirabeau to effect a counter-revolution; the money spent in bribing a great number of deputies; the assemblage of the *knights of the dagger* on the 28th of February 1791; the flight to Varennes; the fusillade of the Champ de Mars; the silence observed respecting the treaty of Pilnitz; the delay in the promulgation of the decree which incorporated Avignon with France; the commotions at Nîmes, Montauban, Mende, and Jalès; the continuance of their pay to the emigrant life-guards and to the disbanded constitutional guard; the insufficiency of the armies assembled on the frontiers; the refusal to sanction the decree for the camp of 20,000 men; the disarming of the fortresses; the organisation of secret societies in the interior of Paris; the review of the Swiss and the garrison of the palace on the 10th August; the summoning the Mayor to the Tuileries; and lastly, the effusion of blood which had resulted from these military dispositions. After each article the President paused, and said, "What have you to answer?" The King, in a firm voice, denied some of the facts, imputed others to his ministers, and always appealed to the constitution, from which he declared he had never deviated.[27] His answers were very temperate, but on the charge —"You spilt the blood of the people on the 10th of August," he exclaimed with emphasis, "No, sir, no; it was not I."[28]

All the papers on which the act of accusation was founded were then shown to the King, and he disavowed some of them and disputed the existence of the iron chest; this produced a bad impression, and was worse than useless, as the fact had been proved.[29] Throughout the examination the King showed great presence of mind. He was careful in his answers never to implicate any members of the Constituent and Legislative Assemblies; many who then sat as his judges trembled lest he should betray them. The Jacobins beheld with dismay the profound impression made on the Convention by the firm but mild demeanour of the sovereign. The most violent of the party proposed that he should be hung that very night; a laugh as of demons followed the proposal from the benches of the Mountain, but the majority, composed of the Girondists and the neutrals, decided that he should be formally tried.[30]

After the examination Santerre took the King by the arm and led him back to the waiting-room of the Convention, accompanied by Chambon and Chaumette. Mental agitation and the length of the proceedings had exhausted him, and he staggered from weakness. Chaumette inquired if he wished for refreshment, but the King refused it. A moment after, seeing a grenadier of the escort offer the *procureur de la Commune* half a small loaf, Louis XVI approached and asked him, in a whisper, for a piece. "Ask aloud for what you want," said Chaumette, retreating as though he feared being suspected of pity. "I ask for a piece of your bread," replied the King. "Divide it with me," said Chaumette. "It is a Spartan breakfast. If I had a root I would give you half."[31]

Soon after six in the evening the King returned to the Temple. "He seemed tired," says Clery simply, "and his first wish was to be led to his family. The officers refused, on the plea that they had no orders. He insisted that at least they should be informed of his return, and this was promised him. The King ordered me to ask for his supper at half-past eight. The intervening hours he employed in his usual reading, surrounded by four municipals. When I announced that supper was served, the King asked the commissaries if his family could not come down. They made no reply. 'But at least,' the King said, 'my son will pass the night in my room, his bed being here?' The same silence. After supper the King again urged his wish to see his family. They answered that they must await the decision of the Convention. While I was undressing him the King said, 'I was far from expecting all the questions they put to me.' He lay down with perfect calmness. The order for my removal during the night was not executed." On the King's return to the Temple being known, "my mother asked to see him instantly," writes Madame Royale. "She made the same request even to Chambon, but received no answer. My brother passed the night with her; and as he had no bed, she gave him hers, and sat up all the night in such deep affliction that we were afraid to leave her; but she compelled my aunt and me to go to bed. Next day she again asked to see my father, and to read the newspapers, that she might learn the course of the trial. She entreated that if she was to be denied this indulgence, his children, at least, might see him. Her requests were referred to the Commune. The newspapers were refused; but my brother and I were to be allowed to see my father on condition of being *entirely separated from my mother*. My father replied that, great as his happiness was in seeing his children, the important business which then occupied him would not allow of his attending altogether to his son, and that his daughter could not leave her mother."[32]

The Assembly having, after a violent debate, resolved that Louis XVI should have the aid of counsel, a deputation was sent to the Temple to ask whom he would choose. The King named MM. Target and Tronchet: the former refused his services on the ground that he had discontinued practice since 1785; the latter complied at once with the King's request; and while the Assembly was considering who to nominate in Target's place, the President received a letter from the venerable Malesherbes,[33] then seventy years old, and "the most respected magistrate in France", in the course of which he said, "I have been twice called to be counsel for him who was my master, in times when that duty was coveted by every one. I owe him the same service now that it is a duty which many people deem dangerous. If I knew any possible means of acquainting him with my desires, I should not take the liberty of addressing myself to you." Other citizens made similar proposals, but the King, being made acquainted with them by a deputation from the Commune, while expressing his gratitude for all the offers, only accepted that of Malesherbes.[34]

On 14th December M. Tronchet was allowed to confer with the King, and later in the same day M. de Malesherbes was admitted to the Tower. "The King ran up to this worthy old man, whom he clasped in his arms," says Clery, "and the former minister melted into tears at the sight of his master."[35] Another deputation brought the King the Act of Accusation and the documents relating to it, numbering more than a hundred, and taking from four o'clock till midnight to read. During this long process the King had refreshments served to the deputies, taking nothing himself till they had left, but considerately reproving Clery for not having supped. From the 14th to the 26th December the King saw his counsel and their colleague M. de Sèze every day. At this time a means of communication between the royal family and the King was devised; a man named Turgi, who had been in the royal kitchen, and who contrived to obtain employment in the Temple, when conveying the meals of the royal family to their apartments, or articles he had purchased for them, managed to give Madame Elizabeth news of the King. Next day the Princess, when Turgi was removing the dinner, slipped into his hand a bit of paper on which she had pricked with a pin a request for a word from her brother's own hand. Turgi gave this paper to Clery, who conveyed it to the King the same evening; and he, being allowed writing materials while preparing his defence, wrote Madame Elizabeth a short note. An answer was conveyed in a ball of cotton, which Turgi threw under Clery's bed while passing the door of his room. Letters were also passed between the Princess' room and that of Clery, who lodged beneath her, by means of a string let down and drawn up at night. This communication with his family was a great comfort to the King, who nevertheless constantly cautioned his faithful servant. "Take care," he would say kindly, "you expose yourself too much."[36]

During his separation from his family the King refused to go into the garden. When it was proposed to him he said, "I cannot make up my mind to go out alone; the walk was agreeable to me only when I shared it with my family." But he did not allow himself to dwell on painful reflections. He talked freely to the municipals on guard, and surprised them by his varied and practical knowledge of their trades, and his interest in their domestic affairs. On the 19th December the King's breakfast was served as usual; but, being a fast-day, he refused to take anything. At dinner-time the King said to Clery, "Fourteen years ago you were up earlier than you were to-day; it is the day my daughter was born—to-day, her birthday," he repeated with tears, "and to be prevented from seeing her!" Madame Royale had wished for a calendar; the King ordered Clery to buy her the *Almanac of the Republic*, which had replaced the *Court Almanac*, and ran through it, marking with a pencil many names.

"On Christmas Day," says Clery, "the King wrote his will.[37] I read and copied it at the time, when it was given to the Council." It was as follows:—

THE LAST WILL AND TESTAMENT OF HIS MOST CHRISTIAN MAJESTY

In the name of the Holy Trinity, the Father, Son, and Holy Ghost: This day, December 25, 1792, I, Louis XVI, King of France, having been for more than four months shut up with my family in the Tower of the Temple at Paris by those who were my subjects, and deprived of every kind of communication with my family since the 11th of this month; and being moreover involved in a trial, of which, from the passions of mankind, it is impossible to foresee the event, and for which neither pretext nor precedent can be found in any existing law; having no witness of my thoughts but God, and no one but Him to whom I can address myself I here declare in His presence, my last Will and sentiments.

I leave my soul to God, my Creator: I implore Him to receive it in His mercy, and not to judge it according to its merits but according to those of our Lord Jesus Christ, who offered Himself as a sacrifice to God, His Father, for us men, unworthy as we were, and especially myself. I die in the communion of our Catholic, Apostolic, and Roman Mother Church, which holds its powers by an uninterrupted succession from St Peter, to whom Jesus Christ had entrusted them. I firmly believe, and I confess, all that is contained in the commandments of God and the Church—in the sacraments and mysteries which the Church teaches and has always taught. I have never presumed to make myself a judge as to the different manners of explaining the doctrines which divide the Church of Jesus Christ; but I have always referred myself; and shall always refer myself, if God shall grant me life, to the decisions which the superior ecclesiastics give, and shall give conformably to the discipline of the Church followed since Jesus Christ. I lament with my whole heart for our brethren who may be in error, but I do not presume to judge them; and I do not the less love them in Jesus Christ agreeably to what Christian charity teaches us.

I implore God to pardon me all my sins. I have endeavoured scrupulously to know them, to detest them, and to humble myself in His presence.

Not having it in my power to avail myself of the ministry of a Catholic Priest, I implore God to receive the confession I have made to Him; and, above all, my profound repentance for having put my name (although it was contrary to my will) to those acts which may be contrary to the discipline and the belief of the Catholic Church, to which I have always remained sincerely united in my heart. I implore God to receive the firm resolution I entertain, should He grant me life, to avail myself, as soon as it shall be in my power, of the ministry of a Catholic Priest, to accuse myself of all my sins, and to receive the sacrament of penitence.

I beseech all those whom by inadvertence I may have offended (for I do not recollect ever knowingly to have committed an offence against any one), or those to whom I may have given a bad example, or occasion for scandal, to pardon me the evil which they think I may have done them.

I beseech all those who have charity to unite their prayers to my own, to obtain from God the pardon of my sins.

I pardon with my whole heart those who have made themselves my enemies, without my having given them any cause; and I pray to God that he will pardon them, as well as those who, by a false zeal, or by a zeal ill-understood, have done me much evil.

I recommend to God my wife, my children, my sister, my aunts, my brother, and all those who are attached to me by the ties of blood, or in any other manner whatsoever.

I especially implore God to cast the eyes of His mercy upon my wife, my children, and my sister, who have for so long a time suffered with me, to support them by His grace, should they happen to lose me, so long as they shall remain in this perishable world.

I recommend my children to my wife; I have never doubted of her maternal tenderness for them. I recommend her to make them good Christians and honest; to induce them to consider the grandeurs of this world (should they be condemned to make trial of them) as no other than dangerous and perishable possessions; and to turn their view to the only solid and durable glory of eternity.

I beseech my sister to be pleased to continue her tenderness to my children and to supply to them the place of a mother, should they have the misfortune to lose their own.

I beseech my wife to forgive me all those evils which she suffers for me, and the uneasiness which I may have given her in the course of our union; as she may be assured that I retain nothing in my mind respecting her, should she imagine that she has any reason to reproach herself with respect to me.

I earnestly recommend to my children, after what they owe to God, which they ought to consider as prior to everything else, to remain always united among themselves, submissive and obedient to their mother, and grateful to her for all the pains she takes for them, and in memory of me.

I beseech them to consider my sister as a second mother. I recommend to my son, should he have the misfortune to become a King, to reflect that he owes himself entirely to the happiness of his fellow-citizens, that he ought to forget all hatred and resentment, and especially all which has a reference to the misfortunes and miseries which I experience; that he cannot effect the happiness of his people but by reigning according to the laws; that, at the same time, a King cannot make those respected or do the good which is in his heart unless he possess the necessary authority; and that otherwise being confined in his operations, and commanding no respect, he is more hurtful than useful.

I recommend to my son to take care of all those persons who have been attached to me, as far as the circumstances in which he may find himself shall give him an opportunity; to reflect that this is a sacred debt which I have contracted towards the children, or the relations of those who have perished for my sake, and towards those who have become miserable on my account.

I know there are several persons in the number of those who were attached to me who have not behaved towards me as they ought to have done, and who have even shown ingratitude towards me; but I forgive them (for in the moments of trouble and effervescence one is not always master of one's self); and I beseech my son, should he find an opportunity, to reflect only on their misfortunes. I wish I could here testify my thankfulness to those who have manifested towards me a true and disinterested attachment. On the one hand, if I have been sensibly affected by the ingratitude and disloyalty of those to whom I have never acted but with kindness, as well to themselves as to their relations and friends; on the other, I have had the consolation to see the voluntary attachment and interest which many persons have shown me. I beseech them to receive all my thanks for this. In the situation in which things yet are I should fear to commit them were I to speak more explicitly; but I especially recommend to my son to seek opportunity of being able to acknowledge them.

I should, however, conceive that I calumniated the sentiments of the nation were I not openly to recommend to my son MM. de Chamilly and de Huë, whose sincere attachment to me has induced them to shut themselves up with me in this sorrowful abode, and who have been in danger of becoming the unhappy victims of that attachment. I also recommend to him Clery, with whose attention I have every reason to be satisfied since he has been with me to the end. I beseech MM. de la Commune to deliver to him my effects, my books, my watch, and the other little articles of my property which have been deposited with the Conseil de Commune.

I moreover fully pardon those who have imprisoned me, the ill-treatment and harshness which they have thought it their duty to use towards me. I have found some feeling and compassionate souls. May these enjoy in their hearts that tranquillity to which their mode of thinking should entitle them!

I beseech MM. de Malesherbes, Tronchet, and de Sèze to receive here my utmost thanks, and the expression of my sensibility for all the pains and trouble they have been at on my account. I conclude, by declaring before God, and being ready to appear before Him, that I do not reproach myself with any of those crimes which have been charged against me.

This instrument made in duplicate at the Tower of the Temple, the 25th of December 1792.

(Signed)   LOUIS

(Inscribed)   BAUDRAIS
                                                           Municipal Officer

On the 26th December 1792 the King appeared a second time before the Convention. M. de Sèze, labouring night and day, had completed his defence. The King insisted on excluding from it all that was too rhetorical, and confining it to the mere discussion of essential points.[38] At half-past nine in the morning the whole armed force was in motion to conduct him from the Temple to the Feuillans, with the same precautions and in the same order as had been observed on the former occasion. Riding in the carriage of the Mayor, he conversed, on the way, with the same composure as usual, and talked of Seneca, of Livy, of the hospitals. Arrived at the Feuillan he showed great anxiety for his defenders; he seated himself beside them in the Assembly, surveyed with great composure the benches where his accusers and his judges sat, seemed to examine their faces with the view of discovering the impression produced by the pleading of M. de Sèze, and more than once conversed smilingly with Tronchet and Malesherbes. The Assembly received his defence in sullen silence, but without any tokens of disapprobation. The advocate concluded with this brief and just tribute to the virtues of the King:—

Louis ascended the throne at the age of twenty, and at the age of twenty he gave, upon the throne, an example of morality. He carried to it no culpable weakness, no corrupting passion. In that station he was economical, just, and severe, and proved himself the constant friend of the people. The people wished for the abolition of a disastrous impost which oppressed them;—he abolished it. The people demanded the abolition of servitude;—he began by abolishing it himself in his domains. The people solicited reforms in the criminal legislation to alleviate the condition of accused persons;—he made those reforms. The people desired that thousands of Frenchmen, whom the rigour of our customs had till then deprived of the rights belonging to citizens, might either acquire or be restored to those rights;—he extended that benefit to them by his laws. The people wanted liberty; and he conferred it. He even anticipated their wishes by his sacrifices; and yet it is in the name of this very people that men are now demanding—Citizens, I shall not finish—I pause before history. Consider that it will judge your judgment, and that its judgment will be that of ages!

As soon as his advocate had finished Louis XVI delivered a few observations which he had written. "My means of defence," said he, "are now before you. I shall not repeat them. In addressing you, perhaps for the last time, I declare that my conscience reproaches me with nothing, and that my defenders have told you the truth.

"I was never afraid that my conduct should be publicly examined; but it wounds me to the heart to find in the act of accusation the imputation that I caused the blood of the people to be spilt, and above all, that the calamitous events of the 10th of August are attributed to me.

"I confess that the multiplied proofs which I have given at all times of my love for the people, and the manner in which I have always conducted myself, ought in my opinion to demonstrate that I was not afraid to expose myself in order to prevent bloodshed, and to clear me for ever from such an imputation."

The President then asked Louis XVI if he had anything more to say in his defence. Louis having declared that he had not, the President informed him that he might retire.

Being conducted to an adjoining room with his counsel, the King showed great anxiety about M. de Sèze, who seemed fatigued by the long defence. While riding back to the Temple he conversed with his companions with the same serenity as he had shown on leaving it.

No sooner had the King left the hall of the Convention than a violent tumult arose there. Some were for opening the discussion. Others, complaining of the delays which postponed the decision of this process, demanded the vote immediately, remarking that in every court, after the accused had been heard, the judges proceed to give their opinion. Lanjuinais had from the commencement of the proceedings felt an indignation, which his impetuous disposition no longer suffered him to repress. He darted to the tribune, and, amidst the cries excited by his presence, demanded the annulling of the proceedings altogether. He exclaimed that the days of ferocious men were gone by, that the Assembly ought not to be so dishonoured as to be made to sit in judgment on Louis XVI, that no authority in France had that right, and the Assembly in particular had no claim to it; that if it resolved to act as a political body, it could do no more than take measures of safety against the *ci-devant* King; but that if it was acting as a court of justice it was overstepping all principles, for it was subjecting the vanquished to be tried by the conquerors; since most of the present members had declared themselves the conspirators of the 10th of August. At the word *conspirators*, a tremendous uproar arose on all sides. Cries of "*Order!*" "*To the Abbaye!*" "*Down with the Tribune!*" were heard. Lanjuinais strove in vain to justify the word conspirators, saying that he meant it to be taken in a favourable sense, and that the 10th of August was a glorious conspiracy. He concluded by declaring that he would rather die a thousand deaths than condemn, contrary to all laws, even the most execrable of tyrants.

A great number of speakers followed, and the confusion kept continually increasing. The members, determined not to hear any more, mingled together, formed groups, abused and threatened one another. After a tempest of an hour's duration tranquillity was at last restored, and the Assembly, adopting the opinion of those who demanded the discussion on the trial of Louis XVI, declared that it was opened, and that it should be continued, to the exclusion of all other business, till sentence should be passed.

The discussion was accordingly resumed on the 27th, and there was a constant succession of speakers from the 28th to the 31st. Vergniaud at length ascended the tribune for the first time, and an extraordinary eagerness was manifested to hear the Girondists express their sentiments by the lips of their greatest orator, and break that silence of which Robespierre was not the only one to accuse them. Vergniaud asked if, to form a majority suitable to the wishes of certain persons, it was right to employ banishment and death, to change France into a desert, and thus deliver her up to the schemes of a handful of villains? Having avenged the majority and France, he avenged himself and his friends, whom he represented as resisting constantly, and with equal courage, all sorts of despotisms, the despotism of the Court, as well as that of the brigands of September. He represented them during the commotion of the 10th of August, sitting amidst the pealing of the cannon of the palace, pronouncing the forfeiture of the Crown before the victory of the people, while those Brutuses now so eager to take the lives of prostrate tyrants, were hiding their terrors in the bowels of the earth, and thus awaiting the issue of the uncertain battle which liberty was fighting with despotism. He strenuously urged that there was no danger of the appeal to the people, which he claimed as a right, leading to civil war. "Civil war!" he cried, "for having invoked the sovereignty of the people! … In July 1791 ye were more modest. Ye had no desire to paralyse it, and to reign in its stead. Ye circulated a petition for consulting the people on the judgment to be passed upon Louis on his return from Varennes! Ye then wished for the sovereignty of the people, and did not think that invoking it was capable of exciting civil war. Was it that then it favoured your secret views, and that now it is hostile to them?"[39]

"Who," he concluded, "will guarantee to me that these seditious outcries of anarchical turbulence will not have the effect of rallying the aristocracy eager for revenge, poverty eager for change, and even pity itself, which inveterate prejudices will have excited for the fate of Louis? Who will guarantee to me that, amid this tempest, in which we shall see the murderers of the 2nd of September issuing from their lairs, there will not be presented to you, dripping with blood, and by the title of liberator, that defender, that chief who is said to be so indispensable? A chief! The instant he appeared he would be pierced by a thousand wounds! But to what horrors would not Paris be consigned—Paris, whose heroic courage against kings posterity will admire, while it will be utterly incapable of conceiving her ignominious subjection to a handful of brigands, the scum of mankind, who rend her bosom by the convulsive movements of their ambition and their fury! Who could dwell in a city where terror and death would hold sway? And ye, industrious citizens, whose labour is all your wealth, and for whom the means of labour would be destroyed; ye, who have made such great sacrifices at the Revolution, and who would be deprived of the absolute necessaries of life; ye, whose virtues, whose ardent patriotism, and whose sincerity have rendered your seduction so easy, what would become of you? What would be your resources? What hand would dry your tears and carry relief to your perishing families?

"Would you apply to those false friends, those treacherous flatterers, who would have plunged you into the abyss? Ah! shun them rather! Dread their answer! I will tell you what it would be. You would ask them for bread; they would say to you, 'Go to the quarries, and dispute with the earth the possession of the mangled flesh of the victims whom ye have slaughtered!' Or, 'Do you want blood? here it is, take it—blood and carcases. We have no other food to offer you!' … Ye shudder, citizens! O my country, I call upon thee in my turn to attest the efforts that I make to save thee from this deplorable crisis!"[40]

This extempore speech of Vergniaud produced a deep impression on all his hearers. Robespierre was thunderstruck by his earnest and persuasive eloquence. Vergniaud, however, had but shaken, not convinced, the Assembly, which wavered between the two parties. Several members were successively heard, for and against the appeal to the people. Brissot, Gensonné, Pétion, supported it in their turn. One speaker at length had a decisive influence on the question. This was Barère. By his suppleness, and his cold and evasive eloquence, he was the model and oracle of the centre. He spoke at great length on the trial, reviewed it in all its bearings—of facts, of laws, and of policy—and furnished all those weak minds who only wanted specious reasons for yielding, with motives for the condemnation of the King. From that moment the unfortunate King was condemned. The discussion lasted till the 7th, and nobody would listen any longer to the continual repetition of the same facts and arguments. It was therefore declared to be closed without opposition, but the proposal of a fresh adjournment excited a commotion among the most violent, and ended in a decree which fixed the 14th of January for putting the questions to the vote.

Meantime the King did not allow the torturing suspense to disturb his outward composure, or lessen his kindness to those around him. On the morning after his second appearance at the bar of the Convention, the commissary Vincent, who had undertaken secretly to convey to the Queen a copy of the King's printed defence, asked for something which had belonged to him, to treasure as a relic; the King took off his neck handkerchief and gave it him; his gloves he bestowed on another municipal, who had made the same request. "On January 1st," says Clery, "I approached the King's bed and asked permission to offer him my warmest prayers for the end of his misfortunes. 'I accept your good wishes with affection,' he replied, extending his hand to me. As soon as he had risen, he requested a municipal to go and inquire for his family, and present them his good wishes for the new year. The officers were moved by the tone in which these words, so heartrending, considering the position of the King, were pronounced … The correspondence between their Majesties went on constantly. The King being informed that Madame Royale was ill, was very uneasy for some days. The Queen, after begging earnestly, obtained permission for M. Brunnier, the medical attendant of the royal children, to come to the Temple. This seemed to quiet him."[41]

The nearer the moment which was to decide the King's fate approached, says Thiers, the greater became the agitation in Paris. At the theatres voices favourable to Louis XVI had been raised on the performance of *L'Ami des Lois*. "The Commune had ordered all the playhouses to be shut up; but the executive Council had revoked that measure as a violation of the liberty of the press, in which was comprehended the liberty of the theatre. Deep consternation pervaded the prisons. A report was circulated that the atrocities of September were to be repeated there, and the prisoners and their relatives beset the deputies with supplications that they would snatch them from destruction. The Jacobins, on their part, alleged that conspiracies were hatching in all quarters to save Louis XVI from punishment, and to restore royalty. Their anger, excited by delays and obstacles, assumed a more threatening aspect; and the two parties thus alarmed one another by supposing that each harboured sinister designs."

The debates of the 14th, 15th and 16th January 1793 were so important to the royal family and the nation, that it will be of interest to reproduce the actual words of some of the speakers, as reported at the time.

On the 14th January the Convention called for the order of the day, being

THE FINAL JUDGMENT OF LOUIS XVI

M. Lebardi. There is a great variety of opinions in this Assembly relative to the conduct of Louis XVI, but there is one fact which we all ought to recognise, and that is that his judgment ought to be sanctioned by the people.

M. Denou presented a series of questions to be decided upon by the Convention.

M. Louvet wished to know, previous to his passing sentence on Louis XVI, whether there was to be an appeal to the Primary Assemblies?

Cambacérès, Gaudet, and *Quenette* argued on the mode of decision.

The President then summed up what had been said by the various members, and put the question twice without effect. The *Appel Nominal* was then called for, and after much noise, riot, and confusion, it was decided that the following order should be observed relative to the questions about to be discussed:—

(1) Is Louis guilty?

(2) Shall the judgment be committed to the sanction of the people?

(3) What punishment shall be inflicted upon him?

On 15th January, during profound silence, M. Manuel read the first question with an audible voice:

"Is Louis guilty of a conspiracy against the liberty of the Nation and the safety of the State?"

The subject of deliberation being thus enounced, *Salles*, another of the secretaries, commenced the *Appel Nominal.*

Each member in his turn ascended the tribune and expressed his opinion by saying "Yes" or "No". At the same time his declaration was registered exactly opposite his name, in order that printed lists might be made out and transmitted to the 34 departments.

The *Appel Nominal* being finished, the President examined the register and made the following report:—

"Of 745 members that form the Convention, 693 have voted for the affirmative, 26 are absent upon public business, 26 have made different declarations, but not a single person has voted for the negative."

The third series of votes was postponed till the following day, which drew together a still greater concourse. It was the decisive sitting; the tribunes were early occupied by the Jacobins, whose eyes were fixed on the bureau at which every member was to deliver his vote. Great part of the day was taken up by measures of public order, and it was decided that the sitting should be permanent till the voting was over. It began at half-past seven in the evening, and lasted all night.[42]

As each deputy ascended the steps of the bureau silence was observed in order that he might be heard; but after he had given his vote, tokens of approbation or disapprobation burst forth, and accompanied his return to his seat. The tribunes received with murmurs all votes that were not for death; and they frequently addressed threatening gestures to the Assembly itself. The deputies replied to them from the interior of the hall, and hence resulted a tumultuous exchange of menaces and abusive epithets. This fearfully ominous scene shook all minds, and changed many resolutions.[43] Lecointe, of Versailles, whose courage was undoubted, and who had not ceased to respond to the gesticulation of the tribunes, advanced to the bureau, hesitated, and at length dropped from his lips the unexpected and terrible word *Death.* Vergniaud, who had appeared deeply affected by the fate of Louis XVI, and who had declared to his friends that he never could condemn that unfortunate Prince,—Vergniaud, on beholding this tumultuous scene, imagined that he saw civil war kindled in France, and pronounced sentence of death, with the addition, however, of Mailhe's amendment, that they should inquire whether it was not expedient to stay the execution. On being questioned respecting his change of opinion, Vergniaud replied that he thought he beheld civil war on the point of breaking out, and that he durst not balance the life of an individual against the welfare of France.

We shall here repeat the observations of some of those who did not decide directly on the question.

M. Rouzet. I cannot divide my opinion: I think that Louis and his family ought to be confined during the present war, unless some extraordinary circumstance occurs.

M. Wandelaincourt (*a bishop*). My holy functions do not permit me to pronounce in criminal matters.

M. Lalande (*a bishop*). I am exactly in the same predicament.

M. Offelin. I declare Louis guilty, and I beg leave to observe that although he asserted, through the medium of his defender, that the Body Guard was only paid up to January 1792, yet they actually received their appointments until the middle of July in that year.

M. Conté. I vote in the affirmative as a legislator, but as a judge I have not anything to say.

M. Noel. I cannot vote at all, because I have lost a son during a war that Louis has raised up against my country.

MM. Fauchet, Dubois, Dubain, Larvière, and *Doucée* said they were convinced of the guilt of Louis Capet; but they could not vote, on account of the manner in which the questions had been put.

M. Chambon. Louis is guilty; but this vote is conditional— that is, if you appeal to the people.

MM. Girouett and *Baraillon* begged leave to be excused from giving their opinion.

M. Egalité. Louis Capet is guilty.[44]

The President at the close of the *Appel Nominal* arose, and taking off his hat spoke as follows:—

"I hereby declare that the National Convention has found Louis Capet guilty of a conspiracy against the liberty of the Nation and the safety of the State."

A secretary now read the second question, "Shall the decree relative to the fate of Louis Capet be submitted to the judgment of the people?"

During the second *Appel Nominal* all the members in succession ascended the tribune. Those who voted for the appeal to the people declared themselves swayed by the dread of tumults in the Primary Assemblies.

M. Robespierre. I vote that the sentence of Louis Capet be decided by the Convention.

M. Manuel. I see legislators, not judges in this Assembly. I appeal to the people. I was shocked to observe Philippe Egalité, a relation of the late King, deciding upon his guilt!

Philippe Egalité. I thought of my duty, and of nothing else, when I declared Louis Capet guilty. I now vote that his judgment be not submitted to the people.[45]

M. Camille Desmoulins. The King of Prussia was formerly bribed by Russia, and I am afraid that some persons here are bought over by England and Holland. I vote for a final decision.

This member was instantly called to order, and censured by the President.

M. Dufraulx. An appeal to the people. (This member having been insulted by a stranger on going out, the latter was instantly arrested.)

M. Pons. I have altered my opinion. I now vote against the appeal.

M. Barbaroux. I also wish the appeal to the people, and that because it has been negatived by Philippe d'Orléans. I vote for this also, because I dread lest an usurper should succeed a tyrant.

M. Chambon. I too appeal to the people, because I behold a powerful faction, in the midst of whom is Philippe d'Orléans.

The President having examined the register, the result of the scrutiny was proclaimed as follows:—

For an appeal to the people   283
Against an appeal to the people   480
Majority for final judgment   197

The President, taking off his hat, then said "I do hereby declare, in the name of the Convention, that the decree concerning the punishment of Louis Capet shall not be referred to the sanction of the people."

On the morning of the 16th, Clery says that M. de Malesherbes remained some time with the King, and on going out promised to give him the result of the voting as soon as it was known. At six o'clock in the evening four municipals entered the King's room with an order from the Commune to the effect that they should keep him constantly in sight, and that two of them should pass the night at the side of his bed. The King asked if his sentence was pronounced; one of the municipals seated himself in an armchair by which the King was standing, and then replied that he did not concern himself about what passed at the Convention, but he had heard that they were still voting.

On the following day (January 17) the *Appel Nominal* for declaring the punishment to be inflicted upon Louis XVI was continued.

M. Ysabeau. It is repugnant to my nature to pronounce sentence of death against a fellow-creature. It is now my consolation that I pronounce it upon a tyrant!

F.B. Lacoste. A living tyrant is a beacon of our enemies. His death will terminate all our troubles and divisions, give peace to the Republic, and destroy the growth of prejudice. I vote for death.

Manuel. We talk of the Romans: let us imitate them. I vote that Louis be imprisoned during the war, and expelled on the return of peace.

Robert. I vote for death! Ah! could we but as easily dispose of all tyrants!

Heron. If the majority ordain banishment, I shall move that the statue of Junius Brutus be erected. My sentence is, Death.

Sillery. I vote for the detention and not the death of Louis, as I am convinced that in that case it will be impossible to re-establish royalty.

Lasource. Let Louis die; but recollect that you will merit the opprobrium of posterity if you do not smite the first ambitious man who pretends to succeed him.

Isnard. I said in the Legislative Assembly that if I commanded the thunder, I should overwhelm the first man who dared to attempt the liberty of my country. I now vote for the death of Louis; but as his brothers are not less guilty than himself, I demand that they may be tried within twenty-four hours after his demise, and executed in effigy.

Goupilleaux. I vote for instant death.

Lakanal. A Republican speaks but little (*placing his hand upon his breast*)—Death!

Barbaroux. I now vote for the death of the tyrant, and shall soon move the expulsion of all his family.

M. Ducos. The forms of the proceeding have been extraordinary, and so has been the occasion; were they employed against an ordinary individual I should denounce them to mankind. I consent to the death of Louis.

Russet. It were to have been wished that the punishment to be inflicted upon Louis had been pronounced by the people; this would have afforded the surest means of acquiring the approbation of neighbouring nations, and also of defeating the projects of the tyrants of Europe, who desire the punishment of the *ci-devant* King in order to excite the hatred and indignation of mankind against the National Convention, but as the Assembly has thought proper to reject the appeal to the people, I now am of opinion that the sole mode of avoiding the dangers which at present menace us is to pronounce the sentence of death against Louis, and to defer the execution of it until that moment when the people shall have sanctioned the constitution which we are about to submit to their acceptance.

Thomas Paine did not vote, but sent his opinion to the President, to the effect that Louis Capet should be banished, but not until the end of the war, during the continuance of which he should be kept in prison.

The President having announced that he was about to declare the result of the scrutiny, a profound silence ensued, and he then gave in the following declaration, that out of 719 votes 366 were for DEATH, 319 were for imprisonment during the war, 2 for perpetual imprisonment, 8 for a suspension of the execution of the sentence of death until after the expulsion of the family of the Bourbons, 23 were for not putting him to death until the French territory was invaded by any foreign power, and 1 was for a sentence of death, but with power of commutation of the punishment.[46]

After this enumeration the President took off his hat, and lowering his voice said, "In consequence of this expression of opinion. I declare that the punishment pronounced by the National Convention against Louis Capet is DEATH!"

Previous to the passing of the sentence the President announced on the part of the Foreign Minister the receipt of a letter from the Spanish Minister relative to that sentence. The Convention, however, refused to hear it. [It will be remembered that a similar remonstrance was forwarded by the English Government.]

M. de Malesherbes, according to his promise to the King, went to the Temple at nine o'clock on the morning of the 17th.[47] "All is lost," he said to Clery. "The King is condemned." The King, who saw him arrive, rose to receive him.[48] M. de Malesherbes threw himself at his feet choked by sobs. The King raised him up and affectionately embraced him. When he could control his voice, De Malesherbes informed the King of the decree sentencing him to death; he made no movement of surprise or emotion, but seemed only affected by the distress of his advocate, whom he tried to comfort.[49]

When M. de Malesherbes returned to the Convention the three advocates of the King were admitted to the bar. M. de Sèze then said, "Citizens, Representatives, the Law and Decrees have entrusted to us the sacred function of the defence of Louis. We come with regret to present to you the last act of our function. Louis has given to us his express charge to read to you a letter signed with his own hand, of which the following is a copy:—

LETTER FROM LOUIS

I owe to my own honour, I owe to my family, not to subscribe to a sentence which declares me guilty of a crime of which I cannot accuse myself.

In consequence I appeal to the Nation from the sentence of its Representatives, and I commit by these presents to the fidelity of my defenders to make known to the National

Convention this appeal by all the means in their power, and to demand that mention of it be made in the minutes of their sittings.

(Signed)   LOUIS

M de Sèze then prayed the National Convention in the name of his colleagues to consider by what a small majority the punishment of death was pronounced against Louis. "Do not afflict France," added the worthy citizen, "by a judgment that will appear to her to be terrible when five (?) voices only were thought sufficient to carry it." He invoked Eternal Justice and Sacred Humanity to determine the Convention to refer their judgment to the tribunal of the people.

"We declare," said *M. Tronchet*, "that it is inconceivable that the greatest number of voters have invoked the Penal Code to justify their judgment, and that they have forgotten the indulgence of the law in favour of the accused. They have forgotten that the law requires two-thirds of the voices for the decision."

M. de Malesherbes demanded of the Assembly to give him until the following day to make such reflections as crowded upon his imagination.

After the defenders of Louis had finished their observations they were invited to the honours of the sitting.

M. Robespierre opposed the inserting in the *procès-verbal* of the appeal to the people demanded by Louis. He claimed that such appeal should be declared contrary to the principles of public justice and an invasion of the authority of the National Convention, and that those ought to be considered as conspirators who thought otherwise.

M. Gaudet was also against the appeal to the people; but he demanded an adjournment until after *M. de Malesherbes* had been heard upon the question, whether it is for the interest of the French people that the execution of the judgment pronounced against Louis ought to be delayed or accelerated.

The decision upon the question rejected the appeal to the people and the observations to be made by *M. de Malesherbes*, and it was decreed that the National Convention "should examine whether the national interest did or did not require an arrest of judgment in the execution of the sentence pronounced against Louis".

Thus after thirty-six hours the sitting was concluded—a sitting that the latest posterity will never forget!

The executive Council was charged with the melancholy commission of carrying the sentence into execution. Garat, as Minister of Justice, had the most painful of all tasks imposed upon him, that of acquainting Louis XVI with the decrees of the Convention.[50] He repaired to the Temple, accompanied by Santerre, by a deputation of the Commune and of the criminal tribunal, and by the secretary of the executive Council. On the 20th of January, at two in the afternoon, Louis XVI was awaiting his advocates, when he heard the approach of a numerous party. He stopped with dignity at the door of his apartment, apparently unmoved. Garat then told him sorrowfully that he was commissioned to communicate to him the decrees of the Convention. Grouvelle, secretary of the executive Council, read them to him. The first declared Louis XVI guilty of treason against the general safety of the State; the second condemned him to death; the third rejected any appeal to the people; and the fourth and last ordered his execution in twenty-four hours. Louis, looking calmly round, took the paper from Grouvelle, and read Garat a letter, in which he demanded from the Convention three days to prepare for death, a confessor to assist him in his last moments, liberty to see his family, and permission for them to leave France. Garat took the letter, promising to submit it immediately to the Convention.

Louis XVI then went back into his room with great composure, ordered his dinner, and ate as usual. There were no knives on the table, and his attendants refused to let him have any. "Do they think me so cowardly," he exclaimed, "as to lay violent hands on myself? I am innocent, and I am not afraid to die."

The Convention refused the delay, but granted the other demands which he had made. Garat sent for Edgeworth de Firmont, the ecclesiastic whom Louis XVI had chosen, and took him in his own carriage to the Temple.[51] M. Edgeworth, on being ushered into the presence of the King, would have thrown himself at his feet, but Louis instantly raised him, and both shed tears of emotion. He then, with eager curiosity, asked various questions, concerning the clergy of France, several bishops, and particularly the Archbishop of Paris, requesting him to assure the latter that he died faithfully attached to his communion. The clock having struck eight, he rose, begged M. Edgeworth to wait, and retired with emotion, saying that he was going to see his family. The municipal officers, unwilling to lose sight of the King, even while with his family, had decided that he should see them in the dining-room, which had a glass door, through which they could watch all his motions without hearing what he said. At half-past eight the door opened. The Queen, holding the Dauphin by the hand, Madame Elizabeth, and Madame Royale, rushed sobbing into the arms of Louis XVI. The door was closed, and the municipal officers, Clery, and M. Edgeworth placed themselves behind it. During the first moments, it was but a scene of confusion and despair. Cries and lamentations prevented those who were on the watch from distinguishing anything. At length the conversation became more calm, and the Princesses, still holding the King clasped in their arms, spoke with him in a low tone. "He related his trial to my mother," says Madame Royale, "apologising for the wretches who had condemned him. He told her that he would not consent to any attempt to save him, which might excite disturbance in the country. He then gave my brother some religious advice, and desired him, above all, to forgive those who caused his death; and he gave us his blessing. My mother was very desirous that the whole family should pass the night with my father, but he opposed this, observing to her that he much needed some hours of repose and quiet." After a long conversation, interrupted by silence and grief, the King put an end to the painful meeting, agreeing to see his family again at eight the next morning. "Do you promise that you will?" earnestly inquired the Princesses. "Yes, yes," sorrowfully replied the King.[52] At this moment the Queen held him by one arm, Madame Elizabeth by the other, while Madame Royale clasped him round the waist, and the Dauphin stood before him, with one hand in that of his mother. At the moment of retiring Madame Royale fainted; she was carried away, and the King returned to M. Edgeworth deeply depressed by this painful interview. The King retired to rest about midnight; M. Edgeworth threw himself upon a bed, and Clery took his place near the pillow of his master.

Next morning, the 21st of January, at five, the King awoke, called Clery, and dressed with great calmness. He congratulated himself on having recovered his strength by sleep. Clery kindled a fire, and moved a chest of drawers, out of which he formed an altar. M. Edgeworth put on his pontifical robes, and began to celebrate mass. Clery waited on him, and the King listened, kneeling with the greatest devotion. He then received the communion from the hands of M. Edgeworth, and after mass rose with new vigour, and awaited with composure the moment for going to the scaffold. He asked for scissors that Clery might cut his hair; but the Commune refused to trust him with a pair.

At this moment the drums were beating in the capital. All who belonged to the armed sections repaired to their company with complete submission. It was reported that four or five hundred devoted men were to make a dash upon the carriage, and rescue the King. The Convention, the Commune, the executive Council, and the Jacobins were sitting. At eight in the morning, Santerre, with a deputation from the Commune, the department, and the criminal tribunal, repaired to the Temple. Louis XVI, on hearing them arrive, rose and prepared to depart. He desired Clery to transmit his last farewell to his wife, his sister, and his children; he gave him a sealed packet, hair, and various trinkets, with directions to deliver these articles to them.[53] He then clasped his hand and thanked him for his services. After this he addressed himself to one of the municipal officers, requesting him to transmit his last will to the Commune. This officer, who had formerly been a priest, and was named Jacques Roux, brutally replied that his business was to conduct him to execution, and not to perform his commissions. Another person took charge of it, and Louis, turning towards the party, gave with firmness the signal for starting.

Officers of *gendarmerie* were placed on the front seat of the carriage. The King and M. Edgeworth occupied the back. During the ride, which was rather long, the King read in M. Edgeworth's breviary the prayers for persons at the point of death; the two *gendarmes* were astonished at his piety and tranquil resignation. The vehicle advanced slowly, and amidst universal silence. At the Place de la Révolution an extensive space had been left vacant about the scaffold. Around this space were planted cannon; the most violent of the Federalists were stationed about the scaffold; and the vile rabble, always ready to insult genius, virtue, and misfortune, when a signal is given it to do so, crowded behind the ranks of the Federalists, and alone manifested some outward tokens of satisfaction.

At ten minutes past ten the carriage stopped. Louis XVI, rising briskly, stepped out into the Place. Three executioners came up; he refused their assistance, and took off his clothes himself. But, perceiving that they were going to bind his hands, he made a movement of indignation, and seemed ready to resist. M. Edgeworth gave him a last look, and said, "Suffer this outrage, as a last resemblance to that God who is about to be your reward." At these words the King suffered himself to be bound and conducted to the scaffold. All at once Louis hurriedly advanced to address the people. "Frenchmen," said he, in a firm voice, "I die innocent of the crimes which are imputed to me; I for-give the authors of my death, and I pray that my blood may not fall upon France."[54] He would have continued, but the drums were instantly ordered to beat: their rolling drowned his voice; the executioners laid hold of him, and M. Edgeworth took his leave in these memorable words: "Son of Saint Louis, ascend to heaven!"[55] As soon as the blood flowed, furious wretches dipped their pikes and handkerchiefs in it, then dispersed throughout Paris, shouting "*Vive la République! Vive la Nation!*" and even went to the gates of the Temple to display brutal and factious joy.[56]

THE ROYAL PRISONERS—SEPARATION OF THE DAUPHIN FROM HIS FAMILY—REMOVAL OF THE QUEEN

On the morning of the King's execution, according to the narrative of Madame Royale, his family rose at six: "The night before, my mother had scarcely strength enough to put my brother to bed. She threw herself, dressed as she was, on her own bed, where we heard her *shivering with cold and grief all night long*. At a quarter past six the door opened; we believed that we were sent for to the King, but it was only the officers looking for a prayer-book for him. We did not, however, abandon the hope of seeing him, till shouts of joy from the infuriated populace told us that all was over. In the afternoon my mother asked to see Clery, who probably had some message for her; we hoped that seeing him would occasion a burst of grief which might relieve the state of silent and choking agony in which we saw her." The request was refused, and the officers who brought the refusal said Clery was in "a frightful state of despair" not being allowed to see the royal family; shortly afterwards he was dismissed from the Temple.

"We had now a little more freedom," continues the Princess; "our guards even believed that we were about to be sent out of France; but nothing could calm my mother's agony; no hope could touch her heart; and life or death became indifferent to her. Fortunately my own affliction increased my illness so seriously that it distracted her thoughts ... My mother would go no more to the garden, because she must have passed the door of what had been my father's room, and that she could not bear. But fearing lest want of air should prove injurious to my brother and me, about the end of February she asked permission to walk on the leads of the Tower, and it was granted." The Council of the Commune becoming aware of the interest which these sad promenades excited, and the sympathy with which they were observed from the neighbouring houses, ordered that the spaces between the battlements should be filled up with shutters, which intercepted the view. But while the rules for the Queen's captivity were again made more strict, some of the municipal commissioners tried slightly to alleviate it, and by means of M. de Huë, who was at liberty in Paris, and the faithful Turgi, who remained in the Tower, some communications passed between the royal family and their friends. The wife of Tison, who waited on the Queen, suspected and finally denounced these more lenient guardians,[57] who were executed, the royal prisoners being subjected to a close examination.

"On the 20th of April," says Madame Royale, "my mother and I had just gone to bed when Hebert arrived with several municipals. We got up hastily, and these men read us a decree of the Commune directing that we should be searched. My poor brother was asleep; they tore him from his bed under the pretext of examining it.

My mother took him up, shivering with cold. All they took were a shopkeeper's card which my mother had happened to keep, a stick of sealing-wax from my aunt, and from me *une sacré cœur de Jésus* and a prayer for the welfare of France. The search lasted from half-past ten at night till four o'clock in the morning." The next visit of the officials was to Madame Elizabeth alone; they found in her room a hat which the King had worn during his imprisonment, and which she had begged him to give her as a souvenir. They took it from her in spite of her entreaties: "It was suspicious," said the cruel and contemptible tyrants.

The Dauphin became ill with fever, and it was long before his mother, who watched by him night and day, could obtain medicine or advice for him. When Thierry was at last allowed to see him his treatment relieved the most violent symptoms, but, says Madame Royale, "his health was never re-established. Want of air and exercise did him great mischief, as well as the kind of life which this poor child led, who at eight years old passed his days amidst the tears of his friends, and in constant anxiety and agony."

While the Dauphin's health was causing his family such alarm they were deprived of the services of Tison's wife, who became ill, and finally insane, and was removed to the Hôtel Dieu, where her ravings were reported to the Assembly and made the ground of accusations against the royal prisoners.[58] No woman took her place, and the Princesses themselves made their beds, swept their rooms, and waited upon the Queen.

Far worse punishments than menial work were prepared for them. On 3rd July a decree of the Convention ordered that the Dauphin should be separated from his family and "placed in the most secure apartment of the Tower". As soon as he heard this decree pronounced, says his sister, "he threw himself into my mother's arms, and with violent cries entreated not to be parted from her. My mother would not let her son go, and she actually defended against the efforts of the officers the bed in which she had placed him. The men threatened to call up the guard and use violence. My mother exclaimed that they had better kill her than tear her child from her. At last they threatened our lives, and my mother's maternal tenderness forced her to the sacrifice. My aunt and I dressed the child, for my poor mother had no longer strength for anything. Nevertheless, when he was dressed, she took him up in her arms and delivered him herself to the officers, bathing him with her tears, foreseeing that she was never to behold him again. The poor little fellow embraced us all tenderly, and was carried away in a flood of tears. My mother's horror was extreme when she heard that Simon, a shoemaker by trade, whom she had seen as a municipal officer in the Temple, was the person to whom her child was confided ... The officers now no longer remained in my mother's apartment; they only came three times a day to bring our meals and examine the bolts and bars of our windows; we were locked up together night and day. We often went up to the Tower, because my brother went, too, from the other side. The only pleasure my mother enjoyed was seeing him through a crevice as he passed at a distance. She would watch for hours together to see him as he passed. It was her only hope, her only thought."

The Queen was soon deprived even of this melancholy consolation. On 1st August 1793 it was resolved that she should be tried. Robespierre opposed the measure, but Barère roused into action that deep-rooted hatred of the Queen which not even the sacrifice of

her life availed to eradicate. "Why do the enemies of the Republic still hope for success?" he asked. "Is it because we have too long forgotten *the crimes of the Austrian?* The
children of Louis the Conspirator are hostages for the Republic ... but behind them
lurks a woman who has been the cause of all the disasters of France."[59] At two o'clock
on the morning of the following day the municipal officers "awoke us", says Madame
Royale, "to read to my mother the decree of the Convention, which ordered her removal
to the Conciergerie,[60] preparatory to her trial. She heard it without visible emotion, and
without speaking a single word. My aunt and I immediately asked to be allowed to
accompany my mother, but this favour was refused us. All the time my mother was
making up a bundle of clothes to take with her these officers never left her. She was
even obliged to dress herself before them, and they asked for her pockets, taking away
the trifles they contained. She embraced me, charging me to keep up my spirits and
my courage, to take tender care of my aunt, and obey her as a second mother. She then
threw herself into my aunt's arms, and recommended her children to her care; my aunt
replied to her in a whisper, and she was then hurried away. In leaving the Temple she
struck her head against the wicket, not having stooped low enough.[61] The officers asked
whether she had hurt herself. 'No,' she replied, '*nothing can hurt me now.*'"

THE LAST MOMENTS OF MARIE ANTOINETTE

We have already seen what changes had been made in the Temple. Marie Antoinette
had been separated from her sister, her daughter, and her son,[62] by virtue of a decree
which ordered the trial and exile of the last members of the family of the Bourbons.
She had been removed to the Conciergerie, and there alone in a narrow prison she was
reduced to what was strictly necessary, like the other prisoners. The imprudence of a
devoted friend had rendered her situation still more irksome. Michonnis, a member of
the municipality, in whom she had excited a warm interest, was desirous of introducing
to her a person who, he said, wished to see her out of curiosity. This man, a courageous
emigrant, threw to her a carnation, in which was enclosed a slip of very fine paper
with these words: "*Your friends are ready*"—false hope, and equally dangerous for her
who received and for him who gave it! Michonnis and the emigrant were detected,
and forthwith apprehended; and the vigilance exercised in regard to the unfortunate
prisoner became from that day more rigorous than ever.[63] *Gendarmes* were to mount
guard incessantly at the door of her prison, and they were expressly forbidden to answer
anything that she might say to them.

That wretch Hebert, the deputy of Chaumette, and editor of the disgusting paper of
Père Duchêne, a writer of the party of which Vincent, Ronsin, Varlet, and Leclerc were
the leaders—Hebert had made it his particular business to torment the unfortunate
remnant of the dethroned family. He asserted that the family of the tyrant ought not to
be better treated than any *sans-culotte* family; and he had caused a resolution to be passed
by which the sort of luxury in which the prisoners in the Temple were maintained was
to be suppressed. They were no longer to be allowed either poultry or pastry; they were
reduced to one sort of aliment for breakfast, and to soup or broth and a single dish for

dinner, to two dishes for supper and half a bottle of wine apiece. Tallow candles were to be furnished instead of wax, pewter instead of silver plate, and delft ware instead of porcelain. The wood and water carriers alone were permitted to enter their room, and that only accompanied by two commissioners. Their food was to be introduced to them by means of a turning box. The numerous establishment was reduced to a cook and an assistant, two men-servants, and a woman-servant to attend to the linen.

As soon as this resolution was passed Hebert had repaired to the Temple and inhumanly taken away from the unfortunate prisoners even the most trifling articles to which they attached a high value. Eighty *louis* which Madame Elizabeth had in reserve, and which she had received from Madame de Lamballe, were also taken away. No one is more dangerous, more cruel, than the man without acquirements, without education, clothed with a recent authority. If, above all, he possess a base nature, if, like Hebert, who was check-taker at the door of a theatre, and embezzled money out of the receipts, he be destitute of natural morality, and if he leap all at once from the mud of his condition into power, he is as mean as he is atrocious. Such was Hebert in his conduct at the Temple. He did not confine himself to the annoyances which we have mentioned. He and some others conceived the idea of separating the young Prince from his aunt and sister. A shoemaker named Simon and his wife were the instructors to whom it was deemed right to consign him for the purpose of giving him a *sans-culotte* education. Simon and his wife were shut up in the Temple, and, becoming prisoners with the unfortunate child, were directed to bring him up in their own way.[64] Their food was better than that of the Princesses, and they shared the table of the municipal commissioners who were on duty. Simon was permitted to go down, accompanied by two commissioners, to the court of the Temple for the purpose of giving him a little exercise.

Hebert conceived the infamous idea of wringing from this boy revelations to criminate his unhappy mother. Whether this wretch imputed to the child false revelations or abused his tender age amid his condition to extort from him what admissions soever he pleased, he obtained a revolting deposition and as the youth of the Prince did not admit of his being brought before the tribunal Hebert appeared and detailed the infamous particulars which he had himself either dictated or invented.

It was on the 14th of October that Marie Antoinette appeared before her judges. Dragged before the sanguinary tribunal by inexorable revolutionary vengeance, she appeared there without any chance of acquittal, for it was not to obtain her acquittal that the Jacobins had brought her before it. It was necessary, however, to make some charges. Fouquier therefore collected the rumours current among the populace ever since the arrival of the Princess in France, and, in the act of accusation, he charged her with having plundered the exchequer, first for her pleasures, and afterwards in order to transmit money to her brother the Emperor. He insisted on the scenes of the 5th and 6th of October, and on the dinners of the life-guards, alleging that she had at that period framed a plot, which obliged the people to go to Versailles to frustrate it. He afterwards accused her of having governed her husband, interfered in the choice of ministers, conducted the intrigues with the deputies gained by the Court, prepared the journey to Varennes, provoked the war, and transmitted to the enemy's generals all our plans of campaign. He further accused her of having prepared a new conspiracy on the 10th of August, of having on that day caused the people to be fired upon, of having induced her husband to defend himself by taxing him with cowardice; lastly, of having never ceased to plot and correspond with foreigners since her captivity in the Temple, and of having there treated her young son as King. We here observe how, on the terrible day of long-deferred vengeance, when subjects at length break forth and strike such of their princes as have not deserved the blow, everything is distorted and converted into crime. We see how the profusion and fondness for pleasure, so natural to a young Princess, how her attachment to her native country, her influence over her husband, her regrets, always more indiscreet in a woman than a man, nay, even her bolder courage, appeared to their inflamed or malignant imaginations.

It was necessary to produce witnesses. Lecointre, deputy of Versailles, who had seen what had passed on the 5th and 6th of October, Hebert, who had frequently visited the Temple, various clerks in the ministerial offices, and several domestic servants of the old Court, were summoned. Admiral d'Estaing, formerly commandant of the guard of Versailles; Manuel, the ex-*procureur de la Commune*; Latour-du-Pin, Minister at War in 1789; the venerable Bailly, who, it was said, had been, with La Fayette, an accomplice in the journey to Varennes; lastly, Valazé, one of the Girondists destined to the scaffold; were taken from their prisons and compelled to give evidence.

No precise fact was elicited. Some had seen the Queen in high spirits when the life-guards testified their attachment; others had seen her vexed and dejected while being conducted to Paris, or brought back from Varennes; these had been present at splendid festivities which must have cost enormous sums; those had heard it said in the ministerial offices that the Queen was adverse to the sanction of the decrees. An ancient waiting-woman of the Queen had heard the Duc de Coigny say, in 1788, that the Emperor had already received 200 millions from France to make war upon the Turks.

The cynical Hebert, being brought before the unfortunate Queen, dared at length to prefer the charges wrung from the young Prince. He said that Charles Caper had given Simon an account of the journey to Varennes, and mentioned La Fayette and Bailly as having co-operated in it. He then added that this boy was addicted to odious and very premature vices for his age; that he had been surprised by Simon, who, on questioning him, learned that he derived from his mother the vices in which he indulged. Hebert said that it was no doubt the intention of Marie Antoinette, by weakening thus early the physical constitution of her son, to secure to herself the means of ruling him in case he should ever ascend the throne.

The rumours which had been whispered for twenty years by a malicious Court had given the people a most unfavourable opinion of the morals of the Queen. That audience, however, though wholly Jacobin, was disgusted at the accusations of Hebert.[65] He nevertheless persisted in supporting them.[66] The unhappy mother made no reply. Urged anew to explain herself, she said with extraordinary emotion, "I thought that human nature would excuse me from answering such an imputation, but I appeal from it to the heart of every mother here present." This noble and simple reply affected all who heard it. In the depositions of the witnesses, however, all was not so bitter for Marie Antoinette. The brave d'Estaing, whose enemy she had been, would not say anything to inculpate her, and spoke only of the courage which she had shown on the 5th and

6th of October, and of the noble resolution which she had expressed, to die beside her husband rather than fly. Manuel, in spite of his enmity to the Court during the time of the Legislative Assembly, declared that he could not say anything against the accused. When the venerable Bailly was brought forward, who formerly had so often predicted to the Court the calamities which its imprudence must produce, he appeared painfully affected; and when he was asked if he knew the wife of Capet, "Yes," said he, bowing respectfully, "I have known Madame." He declared that he knew nothing, and maintained that the declarations extorted from the young Prince relative to the journey to Varennes were false. In recompense for his deposition he was assailed with outrageous reproaches, from which he might judge what fate would soon be awarded to himself.

In the whole of the evidence there appeared but two serious facts, attested by Latour-du-Pin and Valazé who deposed to them because they could not help it. Latour-du-Pin declared that Marie Antoinette had applied to him for an accurate statement of the armies while he was Minister at War. Valazé, always cold, but respectful towards misfortune, would not say anything to criminate the accused; yet he could not help declaring that, as a member of the commission of twenty-four, being charged with his colleagues to examine the papers found at the house of Septeuil, treasurer of the civil list, he had seen bonds for various sums signed Antoinette, which was very natural; but he added that he had also seen a letter in which the minister requested the King to transmit to the Queen the copy of the plan of campaign which he had in his hands. The most unfavourable construction was immediately put upon these two facts, the application for a statement of the armies, and the communication of the plan of campaign; and it was concluded that they could not be wanted for any other purpose than to be sent to the enemy; for it was not supposed that a young Princess should turn her attention, merely for her own satisfaction, to matters of administration and military plans. After these depositions, several others were received respecting the expenses of the Court, the influence of the Queen in public affairs, the scene of the 10th of August, and what had passed in the Temple; and the most vague rumours and most trivial circumstances, were eagerly caught at as proofs.[67]

Marie Antoinette frequently repeated with presence of mind and firmness that there was no precise fact against her;[68] that, besides, though the wife of Louis XVI, she was not answerable for any of the acts of his reign. Fouquier nevertheless declared her to be sufficiently convicted; Chaveau-Lagarde made unavailing efforts to defend her; and the unfortunate Queen was condemned to suffer the same fate as her husband.

Conveyed back to the Conciergerie, she there passed in tolerable composure the night preceding her execution, and, on the morning of the following day, the 16th of October,[69] she was conducted, amidst a great concourse of the populace, to the fatal spot where ten months before, Louis XVI had perished. She listened with calmness to the exhortations of the ecclesiastic who accompanied her, and cast an indifferent look at the people who had so often applauded her beauty and her grace, and who now as warmly applauded her execution. On reaching the foot of the scaffold she perceived the Tuileries, and appeared to be moved; but she hastened to ascend the fatal ladder, and gave herself up with courage to the executioner.[70] The infamous wretch exhibited her head to the people, as he was accustomed to do when he had sacrificed an illustrious victim.—Thiers, *History of the French Revolution,* vol. iii, p. 225 *et seq.*

THE LAST LETTER OF MARIE ANTOINETTE

On the morning of the Queen's execution she wrote the following letter to Madame Elizabeth, having obtained paper, pen, and ink from her gaoler:—

This 15th October, at half-past four in the morning.

I write to you, my sister, for the last time. I have been condemned, not to an ignominious death—that only awaits criminals—but to go and rejoin your brother. Innocent as he, I hope to show the same firmness as he did in his last moments.[71] I grieve bitterly at leaving my poor children; you know that I existed but for them and you—you who have by your friendship sacrificed all to be with us. In what a position do I leave you! I have learned, by the pleadings on my trial, that my daughter is separated from you. Alas! poor child—I dare not write to her; she would not receive my letter; I know not even if this may reach you. Receive my blessing for both. I hope one day, when they are older, they may rejoin you, and rejoice in liberty at your tender care. May they both think on what I have never ceased to inspire them with! May their friendship and mutual confidence form their happiness! May my daughter feel that at her age she ought always to aid her brother with that advice with which the greater experience she possesses, and her friendship, should inspire her! May my son, on his part, render to his sister every care and service which affection can dictate! May they, in short, both feel, in whatever position they may find themselves, that they can never be truly happy but by their union! Let them take example by us. How much consolation has our friendship given us in our misfortunes! and in happiness to share it with a friend is doubly sweet. Where can one find any more tender or dearer than in one's own family? Let my son never forget the last words of his father. I repeat them to him expressly: '*Let him never attempt to avenge our death.*' I must now speak to you of a matter most painful to my heart. I know how much trouble this child must have given you. Pardon him, my dear sister; think of his age, and how easy it is to make a child say what one wishes, and what he even does not comprehend. A day will arrive, I hope, when he will the better feel all the value of your kindness and affection for them both. It still remains to me to confide to you my last thoughts. I had desired to write them from the commencement of the trial; but, exclusively of their not permitting me to write, the proceedings have been so rapid that I should really not have had the time. I die in the Catholic, Apostolic, and Roman religion; in that of my fathers; in that in which I have been bred, and which I have always professed, having no spiritual consolation to expect, not knowing if priests of this religion still exist here—and even the place in which I am would expose them too much, were they once to enter it. I sincerely ask pardon of God for all the errors I may have committed during my life. I hope that in His kindness He will accept my last vows, as well as those I have long since made, that He may vouchsafe to receive my soul in His mercy and goodness. I ask pardon of all those with whom I am acquainted, and of you, my sister, in particular, for all the trouble which, without desiring it, I may have caused you. I forgive all my enemies the evil they have done me. I say here adieu to my aunts and to all my brothers and sisters. I had friends, and the idea of being separated for ever from them and their sorrows causes me the greatest regret I experience in dying. Let them, at least, know that in my last moments

I have thought of them. Adieu, my good and kind sister! May this letter reach you! Think of me always! I embrace you with all my heart, as well as those poor dear children. My God, how heartrending it is to quit them for ever! Adieu! ... Adieu! ... I ought no longer to occupy myself but with my spiritual duties. As I am not mistress of my actions, they may bring me perhaps a priest. But I here protest that I will not tell him one word, and that I will treat him absolutely as a stranger.

When the letter was finished the Queen kissed each page repeatedly, then folded without sealing it, and gave it to the concierge Bault. Her presentiment that it would never reach those to whom it would have afforded a melancholy consolation was fulfilled. Bault remitted it to Fouquier-Tinville, and it was ultimately found among the papers of Couthon, to whom Fouquier-Tinville had transmitted many relics of royalty.—See Lamartine's *History of the Girondists* (edit. 1864), vol. iii, pp. 153–4.

THE LAST SEPARATION—EXECUTION OF MADAME ELIZABETH—DEATH OF THE DAUPHIN

The two Princesses left in the Temple were now almost inconsolable; they spent days and nights in tears, whose only alleviation was that they were shed together. "The company of my aunt whom I loved so tenderly," says Madame Royale, "was a great comfort to me. But alas! all that I loved was perishing around me, and I was soon to lose her also ... In the beginning of September I had an illness caused solely by my anxiety about my mother; I never heard a drum beat that I did not expect another 2nd of September."[72] In the course of the month the rigour of their captivity was much increased. The Commune ordered that they should only have one room; that Tison (who had done the heaviest of the household work for them, and since the kindness they showed to his insane wife had occasionally given them tidings of the Dauphin) should be imprisoned in the turret; that they should only be supplied with the barest necessaries; and that no one should enter their room save to carry water and firewood. Their quantity of firing was reduced, and they were not allowed candles. They were also forbidden to go on the leads, and their large sheets were taken away, "lest"—notwithstanding the gratings!—"they should escape from the windows." Madame Royale heard that attempts were made to save the life of the Queen, and she observes that they did not surprise her, for "all honest men took an interest in her fate, and, with the exception of vile and ferocious wretches, who were, alas! too numerous, every one who was permitted to speak to her, to approach her or to see her, was touched with pity and respect, so well did her affability temper the dignity of her manners."

On 8th October 1793 Madame Royale was ordered to go downstairs that she might be interrogated by some municipal officers. "My aunt, who was greatly affected, would have followed, but they stopped her. She asked whether I should be permitted to come up again; Chaumette assured her that I should. 'You may trust,' said he, 'the word of an honest republican. She shall return.' I soon found myself in my brother's room, whom I embraced tenderly; but we were torn asunder, and I was obliged to go into another room.[73] ... Chaumette then questioned me about a thousand shocking things of which they accused my mother and aunt; I was so indignant at hearing such horrors that, terrified as I was, I could not help exclaiming that they were infamous falsehoods. But in spite of my tears they still pressed their questions. There were some things which I did not comprehend, but of which I understood enough to make me weep with indignation and horror ... They then asked me about Varennes, and other things. I answered as well as I could without implicating anybody. I had always heard my parents say that it were better to die than to implicate anybody." When the examination was over the Princess begged to be allowed to join her mother, but Chaumette said he could not obtain permission for her to do so. She was then cautioned to say nothing about her examination to her aunt, who was next to appear before them. Madame Elizabeth, her niece declares, "replied with still more contempt to their shocking questions."

The only intimation of the Queen's fate which her daughter and her sister-in-law were allowed to receive was through hearing her sentence cried by the newsman. But, "we could not persuade ourselves that she was dead," writes Madame Royale. "A hope, so natural to the unfortunate, persuaded us that she must have been saved. For eighteen months I remained in this cruel suspense. We learnt also by the cries of the newsman the death of the Duc d'Orléans.[74] It was the only piece of news that reached us during the whole winter." The severity with which the prisoners were treated was carried into every detail of their life. The officers who guarded them took away their chessmen and cards because some of them were named kings and queens, and all the books with coats of arms on them; they refused to get ointment for a gathering on Madame Elizabeth's arm; they would not allow her to make a herb-tea which she thought would strengthen her niece; they declined to supply fish or eggs on fast days or during Lent, bringing only coarse fat meat, and brutally replying to all remonstrances, "None but fools believe in that stuff nowadays." Madame Elizabeth never made the officials another request, but reserved some of the bread and *café-au-lait* from her breakfast for her second meal.[75] The time during which she could be thus tormented was growing short.

On 9th May 1794, as the Princesses were going to bed, the outside bolts of the door were unfastened and a loud knocking was heard. "When my aunt was dressed," says Madame Royale, "she opened the door, and they said to her, '*Citoyenne*, come down.'— 'And my niece?'—'We shall take care of her afterwards.' She embraced me, and to calm my agitation promised to return. ' No, *citoyenne*,' said the men, 'bring your bonnet, you shall not return.' They overwhelmed her with abuse, but she bore it patiently, embracing me, and exhorting me to trust in Heaven, and never to forget the last commands of my father and mother."

Madame Elizabeth was then taken to the Conciergerie, where she was interrogated by the Vice-President at midnight,[76] and then allowed to take some hours' rest on the bed on which Marie Antoinette had slept for the last time. In the morning she was brought before the tribunal, with twenty other prisoners, of varying ages and both sexes, some of whom had once been frequently seen at Court. "Of what has Elizabeth to complain?" Fouquier-Tinville satirically asked; "at the foot of the guillotine, surrounded by faithful nobility, she may imagine herself again at Versailles." "You call my brother a tyrant," the Princess replied to her accuser, "if he had been what you say, you would not be where you are, nor I before you!" She was sentenced to death, and showed neither surprise nor grief. "I am ready to die," she said, "happy at the prospect of rejoining in a better world those whom I loved on earth."[77] On being taken to the room where those condemned to suffer at the same time as herself were assembled, she spoke to them with so much piety and resignation that they were encouraged by her example to show calmness and resignation like her own. The women, on leaving the cart, begged to embrace her, and she said some words of comfort to each in turn as they mounted the scaffold, which she was not allowed to ascend till all her companions had been executed before her eyes.[78]

"It is impossible to imagine my distress at finding myself separated from my aunt," says Madame Royale. "Since I had been able to appreciate her merits, I saw in her nothing but religion, gentleness, meekness, modesty, and a devoted attachment to her family; she sacrificed her life for them, since nothing could persuade her to leave the King and Queen. I never can be sufficiently grateful to her for her goodness to me, which ended only with her life. She looked on me as her child, and I honoured and loved her as a second mother. I was thought to be very like her in countenance, and I feel conscious that I have something of her character.[79] Would to God I might imitate her virtues, and hope that I may hereafter deserve to meet her, as well as my dear parents, in the bosom of our Creator, where I cannot doubt that they enjoy the reward of their virtuous lives and meritorious deaths." Madame Royale vainly begged to be allowed to rejoin her mother or her aunt, or at least to know their fate. The municipal officers would tell her nothing, and rudely refused her request to have a woman placed with her. "I asked nothing but what seemed indispensable, though it was often harshly refused," she says. "But I at least could keep myself clean. I had soap and water, and carefully swept out my room every day. I had no light, but in the long days I did not feel this privation much ... I had some religious works and travels, which I had read over and over. I had also some knitting, *qui m'ennuyait beaucoup.*" Once, she believes, Robespierre visited her prison:[80] "The officers showed him great respect; the people in the Tower did not know him, or at least would not tell me who he was. He stared insolently at me, glanced at my books, and, after joining the municipal officers in a search, retired."[81]

When Laurent was appointed by the Convention to the charge of the young prisoners, Madame Royale was treated with more consideration. "He was always courteous," she says; he restored her tinder-box, gave her fresh books, and allowed her candles and as much firewood as she wanted, "which pleased me greatly." This simple expression of relief gives a clearer idea of what the delicate girl must have suffered than a volume of complaints.

But however hard Madame Royale's lot might be, that of the Dauphin was infinitely harder. Though only eight years old when he entered the Temple, he was by nature and education extremely precocious, "his memory retained everything, and his sensitiveness comprehended everything". His features "recalled the somewhat effeminate look of Louis XV and the Austrian hauteur of Maria Theresa; his blue eyes, aquiline nose, elevated nostrils, well-defined mouth, pouting lips, chestnut hair parted in the middle and falling in thick curls on his shoulders, resembled his mother before her years of tears and torture. All the beauty of his race, by both descents, seemed to reappear in him."[82] For some time the care of his parents preserved his health and cheerfulness even in the Temple; but his constitution was weakened by the fever recorded by his sister, and his jailors were determined that he should never regain strength. "What does the Convention intend to do with him?" asked Simon when the innocent victim was placed in his clutches. "Transport him?"—"No."—"Kill him?"—"No."—"Poison him?"—"No."—"What then?" "Why, *get rid of him.*" For such a purpose they could not have chosen their instruments better. "Simon and his wife cut off all those fair locks that had been his youthful glory and his mother's pride. This worthy pair stripped him of the mourning he wore for his father; and as they did so they called it 'playing at the game of the spoiled king'. They alternately induced him to commit excesses, and then half starved him. They beat him mercilessly; nor was the treatment by night less brutal than that by day. As soon as the weary boy had sunk into his first profound sleep, they would loudly call him by name, 'Capet, Capet.' Startled, nervous, bathed in perspiration, or sometimes trembling with cold, he would spring up, rush through the dark, and present himself at Simon's bedside, murmuring tremblingly, 'I am here, citizen.' 'Come nearer; let me feel you.' He would approach the bed as he was ordered, although he knew the treatment that awaited him. Simon would buffet him on the head, or kick him away, adding the remark, 'Get to bed again, wolf's cub; I only wanted to know that you were safe.' On one of these occasions, when the child had fallen half stunned upon his own miserable couch, and lay there groaning and faint with pain, Simon roared out with a laugh, 'Suppose you were king, Capet, what would you do to me?' The child thought of his father's dying words, and said, 'I would forgive you.'"[83] The change in the young Prince's mode of life and the cruelties and caprices to which he was subjected soon made him fall ill, says his sister. "Simon forced him to eat to excess, and to drink large quantities of wine, which he detested … He grew extremely fat without increasing in height or strength." His aunt and sister, deprived of the pleasure of tending him, had the pain of hearing his childish voice raised in the abominable songs his gaolers taught him. The brutality of Simon "depraved at once the body and soul of his pupil. He called him the young wolf of the Temple. He treated him as the young of wild animals are treated when taken from the mother and reduced to captivity—at once intimidated by blows and enervated by taming. He punished for sensibility; he rewarded meanness; he encouraged vice; he made the child wait on him at table, sometimes striking him on the face with a knotted towel, sometimes raising the poker and threatening to strike him with it."[84]

Yet when Simon was removed[85] the poor young Prince's condition became even worse. His horrible loneliness induced an apathetic stupor to which any suffering would have been preferable. "He passed his days without any kind of occupation; they did not allow him light in the evening. His keepers never approached him but to give him food;" and on the rare occasions when they took him to the platform of the Tower he was unable or unwilling to move about. When, in November 1794, a commissary named Gomin arrived at the Temple, disposed to treat the little prisoner with kindness, it was too late. "He took extreme care of my brother," says Madame Royale. "For a long time the unhappy child had been shut up in darkness, and he was dying of fright. He was very grateful for the attentions of Gomin, and became much attached to him." But his physical condition was alarming, and owing to Gomin's representations a commission was instituted to examine him. "The commissioners appointed were Harmond, Mathieu, and Reverchon, who visited 'Louis Charles', as he was now called, in the month of February 1795. They found the young Prince seated at a square deal table, at which he was playing with some dirty cards, making card houses and the like,—the materials having been furnished him, probably, that they might figure in the report as evidences of indulgence. He did not look up from the table as the commissioners entered. He was in a slate-coloured dress, bare headed; the room was reported as clean, the bed in good condition, the linen fresh; his clothes were also reported as new; but, in spite of all these assertions, it is well known that his bed had not been made for months, that he had not left his room, nor was permitted to leave it for any purpose whatever, that it was consequently uninhabitable, and that he was covered with vermin and with sores. The swellings at his knees alone were sufficient to disable him from walking. One of the commissioners approached the young Prince respectfully. The latter did not raise his head. Harmond in a kind voice begged him to speak to them. The eyes of the boy remained fixed on the table before him. They told him of the kindly intentions of the Government, of their hopes that he would yet be happy, and their desire that he would speak unreservedly to the medical man that was to visit him. He seemed to listen with profound attention, but not a single word passed his lips. It was an heroic principle that impelled that poor young heart to maintain the silence of a mute in the presence of these men. He remembered too well the days when three other commissaries waited on him, regaled him with pastry and wine, and obtained from him that hellish accusation against the mother that he loved. He had learnt by some means the import of the act, so far as it was an injury to his mother. He now dreaded seeing again three commissaries, hearing again kind words, and being treated again with fine promises. Dumb as death itself he sat before them, and remained motionless as stone, and as mute."[86]

His disease now made rapid progress, and Gomin and Lasne, superintendents of the Temple, thinking it necessary to inform the Government of the melancholy condition of their prisoner, wrote on the register: "Little Capet is unwell." No notice was taken of this account, which was renewed next day in more urgent terms: "Little Capet is dangerously ill". Still there was no word from beyond the walls. "We must knock harder," said the keepers to each other, and they added, "It is feared he will not live," to the words "dangerously ill." At length on Wednesday, 6th May 1795, three days after the first report, the authorities appointed M. Desault to give the invalid the assistance of his art. After having written down his name on the register he was admitted to see the Prince. He made a long and very attentive examination of the unfortunate child, asked him many questions without being able to obtain an answer, and contented himself with prescribing a decoction of hops, to be taken by spoonfuls every half hour, from six o'clock in the morning till eight in the evening. On the first day the Prince steadily refused to take it. In vain Gomin several times drank off a glass of the potion in his presence; his example proved as ineffectual as his words. Next day Lasne renewed his solicitations. "Monsieur knows very well that I desire nothing but the good of his health, and he distresses me deeply by thus refusing to take what might contribute to it. I entreat him as a favour not to give me this cause of grief." And as Lasne, while speaking, began to taste the potion in a glass, the child took what he offered him out of his hands. "You have, then, taken an oath that I should drink it," said he firmly; "well, give it me, I *will* drink it." From that moment he conformed with docility to whatever was required of him, but the policy of the Commune had attained its object; help had been withheld till it was almost a mockery to supply it. The Prince's weakness was excessive, his keepers could scarcely drag him to the top of the Tower; walking hurt his tender feet, and at every step he stopped to press the arm of Lasne with both hands upon his breast. At last he suffered so much that it was no longer possible for him to walk, and his keeper carried him about, sometimes on the platform, and sometimes in the little tower, where the royal family had lived at first. But the slight improvement to his health occasioned by the change of air scarcely compensated for the pain which his fatigue gave him. On the battlement of the platform nearest the left turret the rain had, by perseverance through ages, hollowed out a kind of basin. The water that fell remained there for several days; and as, during the spring of 1795, storms were of frequent occurrence, this little sheet of water was kept constantly supplied. Whenever the child was brought out upon the platform he saw a little troop of sparrows, which used to come to drink and bathe in this reservoir. At first they flew away at his approach, but from being accustomed to see him walking quietly there every day, they at last grew more familiar, and did not spread their wings for flight till he came up close to them. They were always the same, he knew them by sight, and perhaps like himself they were inhabitants of that ancient pile. He called them *his* birds; and his first action, when the door into the terrace was opened, was to look towards that side,—and the sparrows were always there. He delighted in their chirping, and he must have envied them their wings!

Though so little could be done to alleviate his sufferings, a moral improvement was taking place in him. He was touched by the lively interest displayed by his physician, who never failed to visit him at nine o'clock every morning. He seemed pleased with the attention paid him, and ended by placing entire confidence in M. Desault. Gratitude loosened his tongue; brutality and insult had failed to extort a murmur, but kind treatment restored his speech: he had no words for anger, but he found them to express his thanks. M. Desault prolonged his visits as long as the officers of the municipality would permit. When they announced the close of the visit, the child, unwilling to beg them to allow a longer time, held back M. Desault by the skirt of his coat.[87] Suddenly M. Desault's visits ceased. Several days passed and nothing was heard of him. The keepers wondered at his absence, and the poor little invalid was much distressed at it. The commissary on duty (M. Benoist) suggested that it would be proper to send to the physician's house to make inquiries as to the cause of so long an absence. Gomin and Lasne had not yet ventured to follow this advice, when next day M. Benoist was relieved by M. Bidault, who hearing M. Desault's name mentioned as he came in, immediately said, "You must not expect to see him any more; he died yesterday."

M. Pelletan, head surgeon of the Grand Hospice de l'Humanité was next directed to attend the prisoner, and in June he found him in so alarming a state that he at once asked for a coadjutor, fearing to undertake the responsibility alone. The physician—sent for form's sake to attend the dying child, as an advocate is given by law to a criminal condemned beforehand—blamed the officers of the municipality for not having removed the blind which obstructed the light, and the numerous bolts, the noise of which never failed to remind the victim of his captivity. That sound, which always caused him an involuntary shudder, disturbed him in the last mournful scene of his unparalleled tortures. M. Pelletan said authoritatively to the municipal on duty, "If you will not take these bolts and casings away at once, at least you can make no objection to our carrying the child into another room, for I suppose we are sent here to take charge of him." The Prince being disturbed by these words, spoken as they were with great animation, made a sign to the physician to come nearer. "Speak lower, I beg of you," said he; "I am afraid they will hear you upstairs, and I should be very sorry for them to know that I am ill, as it would give them much uneasiness."

At first the change to a cheerful and airy room revived the Prince and gave him evident pleasure, but the improvement did not last. Next day M. Pelletan learned that the Government had acceded to his request for a colleague. M. Dumangin, head physician of the Hospice de l'Unité, made his appearance at his house on the morning of Sunday, 7th June, with the official despatch sent him by the committee of public safety. They repaired together immediately to the Tower. On their arrival they heard that the child, whose weakness was excessive, had had a fainting fit, which had occasioned fears to be entertained that his end was approaching. He had revived a little, however, when the physicians went up at about nine o'clock. Unable to contend with increasing exhaustion, they perceived there was no longer any hope of prolonging an existence worn out by so much suffering, and that all their art could effect would be to soften the last stage of this lamentable disease. While standing by the Prince's bed, Gomin noticed that he was quietly crying, and asked him kindly what was the matter. "I am always alone," he said. "My dear mother remains in the other tower." Night came—his last night—which the regulations of the prison condemned him to pass once more in solitude, with suffering, his old companion, only at his side. This time, however, death too stood at his pillow. When Gomin went up to the child's room on the morning of 8th June, he said, seeing him calm, motionless, and mute, "I hope you are not in pain just now?"—"Oh yes, I am still in pain, but not nearly so much—the music is so beautiful!" Now there was no music to be heard, either in the Tower or anywhere near. Gomin, astonished, said to him, "From what direction do you hear this music?"—"From above!"—"Have you heard it long?"— "Since you knelt down. Do you not hear it? Listen! Listen!" And the child, with a nervous motion, raised his faltering hand, as he opened his large eyes, illuminated by delight. His poor keeper, unwilling to destroy this last sweet illusion, appeared to listen also. After a few minutes of attention the child again started, and cried out in intense rapture, "Amongst all the voices I have distinguished that of my mother!"

These were almost his last words. At a quarter past two[88] he died, Lasne only being in the room at the time.[89] Lasne acquainted Gomin and Damont, the commissary on duty, with the event, and they repaired to the chamber of death. The poor little royal corpse was carried from the room into that where he had suffered so long—where for two years he had never ceased to suffer. From this apartment the father had gone to the scaffold, and thence the son must pass to the burial-ground. The remains were laid out on the bed, and the doors of the apartment were set open—doors which had remained closed ever since the Revolution had seized on a child, then full of vigour, and grace, and life, and health! Gomin then repaired to the committee of general safety; there he saw M. Gauthier, one of the members, who said to him, "You did very right to take charge of this message yourself; and promptly; but, notwithstanding your diligence, it has arrived too late, and the sitting is over. The report cannot be made to the National Convention. Keep the news secret till to-morrow, and till I have taken all proper measures. I will send M. Bourguignon, one of the secretaries of the committee of general safety, to the Temple, in order to convince himself of the truth of your declaration." Accordingly, M. Bourguignon followed Gomin to the Tower. He verified the event, and renewed the exhortation of keeping it secret, and of carrying on the service as usual. At eight o'clock next morning (9th June) four members of the committee of general safety came to the Tower to make sure that the Prince was really dead. When they were admitted to the death-chamber by Lasne and Damont they affected the greatest indifference. "The event is not of the least importance," they repeated, several times over; "the police commissary of the section will come and receive the declaration of the decease; he will acknowledge it, and proceed to the interment without any ceremony; and the committee will give the necessary directions." As they withdrew, some officers of the Temple guard asked to see the remains of little Capet. Damont having observed that the guard would not permit the bier to pass without its being opened, the deputies decided that the officers and non-commissioned officers of the guard going off duty, together with those coming on, should be all invited to assure themselves of the child's death. All having assembled in the room where the body lay, he asked them if they recognised it as that of the ex-Dauphin, son of the last King of France. Those who had seen the young prince at the Tuileries, or at the Temple (and most of them had), bore witness to its being the body of Louis XVII. When they were come down into the Council-room Darlot drew up the minutes of this attestation, which was signed by a score of persons. These minutes were inserted in the journal of the Temple tower, which was afterwards deposited in the office of the Minister of the Interior. During this visit the surgeons entrusted with the autopsy arrived at the outer gate of the Temple. These were Dumangin, head physician of the Hospice de l'Unité; Pelletan, head surgeon of the Grand Hospice de l'Humanité; Jeanroy, professor in the medical schools of Paris; and Lassus, professor of legal medicine at the École de Santé of Paris. The two last were selected by Dumangin and Pelletan because of the former connection of M. Lassus with Mesdames de France, and of M. Jeanroy with the House of Lorraine, which gave a peculiar weight to their signature. Gomin received them in the Council-room and detained them until the national guard, descending from the second floor, entered to sign the minutes prepared by Darlot. This done, Lasne, Darlot, and Bouquet went up again with the surgeons, and introduced them into the apartment of Louis XVII, whom they at first examined as he lay on his deathbed; but M. Jeanroy, observing that the dim light of this room was but little favourable to the accomplishment of their mission, the commissaries prepared a table in the first room near the window, on which the corpse was laid, and the surgeons began their melancholy operation.

While these things were passing at the Temple, Achille-Sévestre, the deputy from Ile-et-Vilaine, who had voted for the death of Louis XVI, and who had said, in speaking of the Dauphin (13th April 1794), "*This child will never attain his majority!*" made the following report to the National Convention, in the name of the committee of general safety:—"Citizens, for some time past the son of Capet had been troubled with swellings on the right knee and left wrist; on the 15th Floréal his pain increased, the invalid lost his appetite, and was attacked by fever. The celebrated Desault, medical officer, was appointed to see and attend him, as we were convinced by his talents and probity that he would not fail to exercise that care which is due to humanity. Still the disease assumed a very serious character. On the 16th of this month Desault died, and the committee appointed in his stead citizen Pelletan, a well-known medical man, and citizen Dumangin as his coadjutor. Their bulletin of yesterday, at eleven o'clock AM, announced symptoms which gave cause of alarm for the life of the invalid, and at a quarter past two PM we received the intelligence of the death of the son of Capet. The committee of general safety has desired me to inform you of the event. All is verified, and here are the reports, which will remain in your archives."

The National Convention heard this announcement with apparent indifference. It was part of their policy not to take much notice of the Prince's last hour, though it was the welcome result of a plan they had long pursued. The news of the death announced to the Convention had already spread in Paris. The event was discussed by some fanatics with joy, but by the mass of the people with pity and commiseration, as they recollected the beauty, the graceful ways, and the generous heart of the young Prince.

At seven o'clock the police commissary ordered the body to be taken up, and that they should proceed to the cemetery. It was the season of the longest days, and therefore the interment did not take place in secrecy and at night as some misinformed narrators have said or written; it took place in broad daylight, and attracted a great concourse of people before the gates of the Temple palace. One of the municipals wished to have the coffin carried out secretly by the door opening into the chapel enclosure; but M. Dusser, police commissary, who was specially entrusted with the arrangement of the ceremony, opposed this indecorous measure, and the procession passed out through the great gate. The crowd that was pressing round was kept back, and compelled to keep a line by a tri-coloured ribbon, held at short distances by *gendarmes*. Compassion and sorrow were impressed on every countenance. A small detachment of the troops of the line from the garrison of Paris, sent by the authorities, was waiting to serve as an escort. The bier, still covered with the pall, was carried on a litter on the shoulders of four men, who relieved each other two at a time; it was preceded by six or eight men, headed by a sergeant. Dusser walked behind, with Lasne and the civic commissary before mentioned; Damont, who was on duty the day of the death; Darlot, Guérin, and Bigot. With them were also Goddet, Biard, and Arnoult, whom the Temple section had appointed to assist Dusser in making the official report of the decease, and superintending the interment. Then came six or eight more men and a corporal. They entered the cemetery of Sainte Marguerite by the Rue Saint Bernard. The procession was accompanied a long way by the crowd, and a great number of persons followed it even to the cemetery. In particular, there was a marked movement of interest in a numerous group that had formed at the corner of the Boulevard and the Rue Pont-aux-Choux, and which was mainly composed of women. The name of "Little Capet", and the more popular title of Dauphin spread from lip to lip, with exclamations of pity and compassion. Further on, in the Rue Popincourt, a few children of the common people in rags took off their caps in token of respect and sympathy before this coffin that contained a child who had died poorer than they themselves were to live. The procession entered the cemetery of Sainte Marguerite, not by the church, as some accounts assert, but by the old gate of the cemetery. The interment was made in the corner, on the left, at a distance of eight or nine feet from the enclosure wall, and at an equal distance from a small house, which subsequently served as a class-room for a Christian school. The grave was filled up—no mound marked its place—and not even a trace remained of the interment! Not till then did the commissaries of police and the municipality withdraw. They departed by the same gate of the cemetery, and entered the house opposite the church to draw up the declaration of interment. It was nearly nine o'clock, and still daylight.—See "Illustrations" to Thiers' *History of the French Revolution.*

THE EMIGRANT ROYALISTS—PROCLAMATION OF THE REGENT—LETTER OF LOUIS XVIII TO THE FRENCH NATION—RELEASE OF MADAME ROYALE—HER MARRIAGE TO THE DUC D'ANGOULÊME—RETURN TO FRANCE—DEATH

The last person to hear of the sad events in the Temple was the one for whom they had the deepest and most painful interests. After her brother's death the captivity of Madame Royale was much lightened. She was allowed to walk in the Temple gardens, and to receive visits from some ladies of the old Court, and from Madame de Chantereine, who at last, after several times evading her questions, ventured cautiously to tell her of the deaths of her mother, aunt, and brother. Madame Royale wept bitterly, but had much difficulty in expressing her feelings. "She spoke so confusedly," says Madame de la Ramière in a letter to Madame de Vernéuil, "that it was difficult to understand her. It took her more than a month's reading aloud, with careful study of pronunciation, to make herself intelligible—so much had she lost the power of expression." She was dressed with plainness amounting to poverty, and her hands were disfigured by exposure to cold and by the menial work she had been so long accustomed to do for herself and which it was difficult to persuade her to leave off. When urged to accept the services of an attendant, she replied, with a sad prevision of the vicissitudes of her future life, that she did not like to form a habit which she might have again to abandon. She suffered herself, however, to be persuaded gradually to modify her recluse and ascetic habits. It was well she did so, as a preparation for the great changes about to follow.

At the time of the deposition of Louis XVI, his brothers were nominally the heads of a court composed of fugitives and an army of emigrants. But during the counter-revolutionary campaign they seldom showed themselves in the field, the Princes of the House of Condé really taking the lead in all military matters. When news of the King's execution reached the emigrant royalists the Comte de Provence issued the following proclamation:—

DECLARATION OF THE REGENT OF FRANCE

LOUIS STANISLAUS XAVIER[90] de France, son of France, uncle to the present King, and Regent of the Kingdom,—To all those who may peruse these presents, greeting:

WHEREAS the most criminal of men have, by the perpetration of the most atrocious of crimes, completed the burthen of their iniquities; we, struck with horror on receiving the information, have invoked the Almighty to enable us, by His gracious assistance, to suppress the emotions of our just indignation, caused by the sentiments of profound grief which had overwhelmed us; to the end that we might the better fulfil those essential duties that are, in circumstances so weighty, the first in order among those obligations which the unchangeable laws of the French monarchy impose upon us.

The sanguinary usurpers of the sovereign authority in France having, on the 21st day of the present month of January, laid violent hands on, and barbarously murdered our dearly beloved and highly honoured brother and sovereign the KING, Louis XVI by name,—We declare that the Dauphin, Louis CHARLES, born the 27th day of March, the year of our Lord 1785, is KING OF FRANCE AND NAVARRE, under the name of **Louis XVII**. We furthermore declare, in virtue of our birthright, and the fundamental laws of the Kingdom of France, that we are, and will act as REGENT OF FRANCE during the minority of the King, our nephew and Sovereign Lord.

Thus invested with the exercise of the rights and powers of the sovereignty in France, and of the supreme administration of royal justice, we, in consequence of our obligations and duties so to do, take upon ourselves the said office of Regent.

We are therefore determined, with the assistance of Divine Providence and that of our good and loyal subjects of all ranks and orders, aided by the powerful succours of the allied sovereigns for the same purpose, to do our utmost endeavours to recover the liberty of our royal nephew, King Louis XVII; of Her Majesty, his august mother and guardian; of Madame Royale, Maria Theresa, his sister and our niece; and of her Royal Highness the Princess Elizabeth, his aunt and our dearest sister; all held in the severest captivity by the chiefs of a faction.

We are likewise determined and resolved to effect the re-establishment of the French monarchy on the unalterable basis of the French Constitution, with a reform of those abuses that may have been introduced in the public administration. We will likewise exert ourselves in the restoration of the religion of our forefathers to its original purity, according to the canonical discipline of the Church. We will, moreover, re-establish the magistrature, so essential to the revival of good order and the due and regular administration of justice. We also promise to reinstate all and every description of persons in the full enjoyment of their property, now usurped; and in the free exercise of their lawful rights, of which they may have been illegally deprived. In order to enforce the law we shall punish crimes with severity, and in an exemplary manner.

In fine, for the fulfilling of this solemn engagement, we have thought proper to assume the reins of government, in conjunction with our dearest brother Charles Philippe de France, Comte d'Artois,[91] with whom are united our dear nephews, grandsons of France, their Royal Highnesses Louis Antoine, Duc d'Angoulême, and Charles Ferdinand, Duc de

Berri; and our cousins, their Royal Highnesses Louis Henri de Bourbon, Prince de Condé; Louis Henri Joseph de Bourbon, Duc de Bourbon; and Louis Antoine Henri de Bourbon, Due d'Enghien; Princes of the blood royal—conformably to the declaration we conjointly addressed to the late King, the 10th of September 1791, and every other act signed by us, to be considered as the declarations of our uniform principles and sentiments; and we invariably maintain these our said acts for the purposes and ends aforesaid.

We therefore order and direct all the natives of France, singly and collectively, to obey the commands they may and will receive from us on the part of the King. We furthermore enjoin all the loving subjects of this our kingdom to show obedience to the orders that may and will be issued by our dearest brother, Charles Philippe de France, Comte d'Artois, named and constituted by us Lieutenant-General of the Kingdom in the name and on the part of the King and Regent of France.

In fine, we direct and enjoin all the King's officers, whether military or magisterial, to publish and notify this our present declaration to all those to whom it may pertain, authorising and empowering them to make it known in France; and when circumstances permit the several courts of justice to reassume their function in their respective jurisdictions, the said declaration, as soon as conveniently may be, is to be immediately legalised, published, and executed.

Given at Ham, in Westphalia, under our Seal; which is what we make use of in the signing of sovereign acts, till the Seals of the Kingdom, destroyed by the ruling faction, are re-made; to be likewise countersigned by the Maréchals de Broglie and de Castries, our Ministers of State, the 28th day of January, in the year of grace 1793, and the 1st of the reign of Louis XVII.

(Signed)   **LOUIS STANISLAUS XAVIER**

And at the same time he professed to share his authority with his more popular brother by appointing him Lieutenant-General:

LETTER PATENT issued by the Regent of France for the naming of a Lieutenant-General of the Kingdom.

LOUIS STANISLAUS XAVIER, son of France, uncle to the King, and Regent of the Kingdom, to our dear brother Charles Philippe de France, son of France, Comte d'Artois, greeting:

The God of our fathers, the God of St Louis, who has so long protected the French monarchy, will certainly not permit its final destruction by the hands of a set of factious men, as execrable by their impious audacity as by the enormity of the crimes they have committed. Heaven has assuredly, and it is our greatest hope, destined us to be the ministers of His justice, to revenge the blood of the King our brother, which these monsters have dared to spill with the most appalling ferocity. It is therefore to place our nephew and sovereign on the throne of his father, to reinstate and maintain him in the possession of all the rights and prerogatives of his crown, that we call upon you, Charles Philippe de France, Comte d'Artois, to aid and assist us.

This first act of the Regency we assume displays, according to the wish of our heart, the full confidence we have in you.

On these causes, and for these honourable ends and purposes, we have appointed and constituted you by these presents Lieutenant-General of the Kingdom of France, investing you with all those powers that the Regent of France can delegate, and particularly of commanding in our absence and in our presence under our authority the armies of the King.

Be it understood that all the officers of his Majesty in the military or magisterial capacity, as well as all Frenchmen the subjects of the King, are to obey your commands given by you in the name of the King or Regent of France. It is our pleasure that you assist at all the Councils of State, Justice, and Administration, and others that it may be judged necessary to establish; the same to be presided over by you in our absence; all of which powers shall continue in force as long as our Regency lasts, unless restrained or annulled by our authority.

In virtue of these presents, all letters patent issued in the ordinary form, and addressed to the courts of justice of the kingdom, when re-established in their respective jurisdictions, are to be therein legalised, registered, published, and executed.

Given at Ham, in Westphalia, under our hand and common Seal, and countersigned by the Maréchals de Broglie and de Castries, our Ministers of State, the 28th day of the month of January, anno 1793, and the first year of the reign of his present Majesty.

(Signed)   **LOUIS STANISLAUS XAVIER**

(Undersigned, by order of   Maréchal de Brogue
the Regent of France)—   Maréchal de Castries

This "ideal authority" was recognised by the army of Condé, and liberally supported by the Empress of Russia; it had representatives and sympathisers at all the European Courts; but it was long before it exercised any practical influence. The Regent, Lamartine says, "reigned by correspondence". He was ready with a manifesto on all occasions. When the death of the Dauphin, or Louis XVII, as the emigrants called him, was announced, his uncle addressed the French nation in the following terms:—

In depriving you of a King who has only reigned in fetters, but whose infancy promised a worthy successor to the best of Kings, the inscrutable decrees of Providence have transmitted to us with the Crown the necessity of snatching it from the hands of revolt, and the duty of saving the country, which a disastrous revolution has placed on the verge of ruin. A terrible experience has but too well enlightened you on your misfortunes and on their causes. Impious and factious men, after having seduced you by lying declarations and by deceitful promises, have drawn you into irreligion and revolt. From that moment a deluge of calamities has poured upon you from all parts … Your property became the prey of robbers the moment the Throne became the prey of usurpers. Servitude and tyranny invaded you when the royal authority ceased to cover you with its ægis. Property, safety, and liberty all disappeared with monarchical government. You must return to that holy religion which had conferred upon France the blessing of Heaven; you must re-establish that government which during fourteen centuries was the glory of France and the delight of the French nation,—which had made of your country the most flourishing of kingdoms and of yourselves the happiest of people. The implacable tyrants who keep you enslaved alone retard this happy moment. After having taken from you everything, they paint us in your eyes as an implacable avenger! But learn to know the heart of your King, and entrust to us the duty of saving you! We not only see no crimes in simple errors, but even the crimes that errors may have caused shall find mercy at our hands. All French people who, abjuring fatal opinions, shall come and throw themselves at the foot of the Throne, shall be received by it. Those still under the influence of a cruel obstinacy, who shall hasten to return to reason and duty, shall be our children. We are French! This title the crimes of villainy shall not be sufficient to debase. There are crimes, however, the atrocity of which has passed the bounds of clemency—those of the regicides. Posterity will not name these monsters without horror. France, universal France, invokes upon their heads the sword of justice. The feeling which now makes us restrain the vengeance of the laws within such narrow bounds is a certain pledge to you that we shall suffer no private revenge. Who will dare to avenge himself when the King pardons?

"Universal France" was in no immediate hurry to accept this olive branch held out by its titular monarch, but it did begin to show some commiseration for his orphan niece. Nine days after the death of her brother the city of Orléans interceded for the daughter of Louis XVI, and sent deputies to the Convention to pray for her deliverance and restoration to her family. Nantes followed this example; and Charette, on the part of the Vendéans, demanded as a condition of the pacification of La Vendée, that the Princess should be allowed to join her relations. At length the Convention decreed that Madame Royale should be exchanged with Austria for the representatives and ministers whom Dumouriez had given up to the Prince of Cobourg—Drouet, Semonville, Maret, and other prisoners of importance. At midnight on 19th December 1795, which was her birthday, the Princess was released from prison, the Minister of the Interior, M. Benezech, to avoid attracting public attention and possible disturbance, conducting her on foot from the Temple to a neighbouring street, where his carriage awaited her.[92] She made it her particular request that Gomin, who had been so devoted to her brother, should be the commissary appointed to accompany her to the frontier; Madame de Soucy, formerly under-governess to the children of France, was also in attendance; and the Princess took with her a dog named Coco, which had belonged to Louis XVI.[93] She was frequently recognised on her way through France, and always with marks of pleasure and respect.

It might have been supposed that the Princess would rejoice to leave behind her the country which had been the scene of so many horrors and such bitter suffering. But it was her birthplace, and it held the graves of all she loved; and as she crossed the frontier she said to those around her, "I leave France with regret, for I shall never cease to consider it my country." She arrived in Vienna on 9th January 1796, and her first care was to attend a memorial service for her murdered relatives. After many weeks of close retirement she occasionally began to appear in public, and people looked with interest at the pale grave slender girl of seventeen, dressed in the deepest mourning, over whose young head such terrible storms had swept.[94] The Emperor wished her to marry the Archduke Charles of Austria, but her father and mother had, even in the cradle, destined her hand for her cousin, the Duc d'Angoulême, son of the Comte d'Artois, and the memory of their slightest wish was law to her.

Her quiet determination entailed anger and opposition amounting to persecution. Every effort was made to alienate her from her French relations. She was urged to claim Provence, which had become her own if Louis XVIII was to be considered King of France. A pressure of opinion was brought to bear upon her which might well have overawed so young a girl. "I was sent for to the Emperor's cabinet," she writes, "where I found the Imperial family assembled. The ministers and chief Imperial counsellors were also present ... When the Emperor invited me to express my opinion, I answered that to be able to treat fittingly of such interests I thought I ought to be surrounded not only by my mother's relatives, but also by those of my father ... Besides, I said, I am above all things French, and in entire subjection to the laws of France, which had rendered me alternately the subject of the King my father, the King my brother, and the King my uncle, and that I would yield obedience to the latter, whatever might be his commands. This declaration appeared very much to dissatisfy all who were present, and when they observed that I was not to be shaken, they declared that my right being independent of my will, my resistance would not be the slightest obstacle to the measures they might deem it necessary to adopt for the preservation of my interests." In their anxiety to make a German Princess of Marie Thérèse her Imperial relations suppressed her French title as much as possible. When, with some difficulty, the Duc de Grammont succeeded in obtaining an audience of her, and used the familiar form of address, she smiled faintly, and bade him beware. "Call me Madame de Bretagne, or de Bourgogne, or de Lorraine," she said, "for here I am so identified with these provinces[96] that I shall end in believing in my own transformation." After these discussions she was so closely watched, and so many restraints were imposed upon her, that she was scarcely less a prisoner than in the old days of the Temple, though her cage was this time gilded. Rescue, however, was at hand. In 1798 Louis XVIII accepted a refuge offered to him at Mittau by the Czar Paul, who had promised that he would grant his guest's first request, whatever it might be. Louis begged the Czar to use his influence with the Court of Vienna to allow his niece to join him. "Sir, my brother," was Paul's answer, "Madame Royale shall be restored to you, or I shall cease to be Paul."[97] Next morning the Czar despatched a courier to Vienna with a demand for the Princess, so energetically worded that refusal must have been followed by war. Accordingly, in May 1799, Madame Royale was allowed to leave the capital which she had found so uncongenial an asylum.

In the old ducal castle of Mittau, the capital of Courland, Louis XVIII and his wife, with their nephews the Ducs d'Angoulême[98] and de Berri, were awaiting her, attended by the Abbé Edgeworth, as chief ecclesiastic, and a little Court of refugee nobles and officers. With them were two men of humbler position, who must have been even more welcome to Madame Royale—De Malden, who had acted as courier to Louis XVI during the flight to Varennes, and Turgi, who had waited on the Princesses in the Temple. It was a sad meeting, though so long anxiously desired, and it was followed on 10th June 1799 by an equally sad wedding—exiles, pensioners on the bounty of the Russian monarch, fulfilling an engagement founded not on personal preference but on family policy and reverence for the wishes of the dead, the bride and bridegroom had small cause for rejoicing. During the eighteen months of tranquil seclusion which followed her marriage the favourite occupation of the Duchess was visiting and relieving the poor. In January 1801 the Czar Paul, in compliance with the demand of Napoleon, who was just then the object of his capricious enthusiasm, ordered the French royal family to leave Mittau. Their wanderings commenced on the 21st, a day of bitter memories; and the young Duchess led the King to his carriage through a crowd of men, women, and children, whose tears and blessings attended them on their way.[99] The exiles asked permission from the King of Prussia to settle in his dominions, and while awaiting his answer at Munich they were painfully surprised by the entrance of five old soldiers of noble birth, part of the bodyguard they had left behind at Mittau, relying on the protection of Paul. The "mad Czar" had decreed their immediate expulsion, and, penniless and almost starving, they made their way to Louis XVIII. All the money the royal family possessed was bestowed on these faithful servants, who came to them in detachments for relief; and then the Duchess offered her diamonds to the Danish Consul for an advance of 2,000 ducats, saying she pledged her property "that in our common distress it may be rendered of real use to my uncle, his faithful servants, and myself". The Duchess' consistent and unselfish kindness procured her from the King, and those about him who knew her best, the name of "our angel".

Warsaw was for a brief time the resting-place of the wanderers, but there they were disturbed in 1803 by Napoleon's attempt to threaten and bribe Louis XVIII into abdication. It was suggested that refusal might bring upon them expulsion from Prussia. "We are accustomed to suffering," was the King's answer, "and we do not dread poverty. I would, trusting in God, seek another asylum." In 1808, after many changes of scene, this asylum was sought in England, Gosfield Hall, Essex, being placed at their disposal by the Marquis of Buckingham. From Gosfield, the King moved to Hartwell Hall, a fine old Elizabethan mansion rented from Sir George Lee for £500 a year.[100] A yearly grant of £24,000 was made to the exiled family by the British Government, out of which 140 persons were supported, the royal dinner-party generally numbering two dozen. At Hartwell, as in her other homes, the Duchess was most popular amongst the poor. In general society she was cold and reserved, and she disliked the notice of strangers. In March 1814 the royalist successes at Bordeaux paved the way for the restoration of royalty in France, and amidst general sympathy and congratulation, with the Prince Regent himself to wish them good fortune, the King, the Duchess, and their suite left Hartwell in April 1814. The return to France was as triumphant as a somewhat half-hearted and doubtful enthusiasm could make it, and most of such cordiality as there was fell to the share of the Duchess. As she passed to Notre Dame in May 1814, on entering Paris, she was vociferously greeted.[101] The feeling of loyalty, however, was not much longer lived than the applause by which it was expressed; the Duchess had scarcely effected one of the strongest wishes of her heart—the identification of what remained of her parents' bodies, and the magnificent ceremony with which they were removed from the cemetery of the Madeleine to the Abbey of Saint Denis—when the escape of Napoleon from Elba in February 1815 scattered the royal family and their followers like chaff before the wind. The Duc d'Angoulême, compelled to capitulate at Toulouse, sailed from Cette in a Swedish vessel. The Comte d'Artois, the Duc de Berri, and the Prince de Condé withdrew beyond the frontier. The King fled from the capital. The Duchesse d'Angoulême, then at Bordeaux celebrating the anniversary of the proclamation of Louis XVIII, alone of all her family made any stand against the general panic. Day after day she mounted her horse and reviewed the national guard. She made personal and even passionate appeals to the officers and men, standing firm, and prevailing on a handful of soldiers to remain by her, even when the Imperialist troops were on the other side of the river and their cannon were directed against the square where the Duchess was reviewing her scanty followers.[102] With pain and difficulty she was convinced that resistance was vain; Napoleon's banner soon floated over Bordeaux; the Duchess issued a farewell proclamation to her "brave Bordelais", and on 1st April 1815 she started for Pouillac, whence she embarked for Spain. During a brief visit to England she heard that the reign of a hundred days was over, and the 27th of July 1815 saw her second triumphal return to the Tuileries. She did not take up her abode there with any wish for State ceremonies or Court gaieties. Her life was as secluded as her position would allow. Her favourite retreat was the Pavilion, which had been inhabited by her mother, and in her little oratory she collected relics of her family, over which on the anniversaries of their deaths she wept and prayed. In her daily drives through Paris she scrupulously avoided the spot on which they had suffered; and the memory of the past seemed to rule all her sad and self-denying life, both in what she did and what she refrained from doing.[103] Her somewhat austere goodness was not of a nature to make her popular. The few who really understood her loved her, but the majority of her pleasure-seeking subjects regarded her either with ridicule or dread. She is said to have taken no part in politics, and to have exerted no influence in public affairs, but her sympathies were well known, and "the very word liberty made her shudder"; like Madame Roland, she had seen "so many crimes perpetrated under that name".

The claims of three pretended Dauphins—Hervagault, the son of the tailor of Saint Lo; Bruneau, son of the shoemaker of Vergin; and Naundorf or Norndorff, the watchmaker—somewhat troubled her peace, but never for a moment obtained her sanction. Of the many other pseudo-Dauphins (said to number a dozen and a half) not even the names remain.[104] In February 1820 a fresh tragedy befell the royal family in the assassination of the Duc de Berri, brother-in-law of the Duchesse d'Angoulême, as he was seeing his wife into her carriage at the door of the opera-house. He was carried into the theatre, and there the dying Prince and his wife were joined by the Duchess, who remained till he breathed his last, and was present when he too was laid in the Abbey of Saint Denis. She was present also when his son the Duc de Bordeaux was born, and hoped that she saw in him a guarantee for the stability of royalty in France. In September 1824 she stood by the deathbed of Louis XVIII, and thenceforward her chief occupation was directing the education of the little Duc de Bordeaux, who generally resided with her at Villeneuve l'Etang, her country house near Saint Cloud. Thence she went in July 1830 to the baths of Vichy, stopping at Dijon on her way to Paris, and visiting the theatre on the evening of the 27th. She was received with "a roar of execrations and seditious cries", and knew only too well what they signified. She instantly left the theatre and proceeded to Tonnerre, where she received news of the rising in Paris, and quitting the town by night was driven to Joigny with three attendants. Soon after leaving that place it was thought more prudent that the party should separate and proceed on foot, and the Duchess and M. de Foucigny, disguised as peasants, entered Versailles arm-in-arm, to obtain tidings of the King. The Duchess found him at Rambouillet with her husband the Dauphin, and the King met her with a request for "pardon", being fully conscious, too late, that his unwise decrees and his headlong flight had destroyed the last hopes of his family. The Act of Abdication followed, by which the prospect of royalty passed from the Dauphin and his wife, as well as from Charles X—Henri V being proclaimed King, and the Duc d'Orléans (who refused to take the boy monarch under his personal protection) Lieutenant-General of the Kingdom.

Then began the Duchess' third expatriation. At Cherbourg the royal family, accompanied by the little King without a kingdom, embarked in the *Great Britain*, which stood out to sea. The Duchess, remaining on deck for a last look at the coast of France, noticed a brig which kept, she thought, suspiciously near them. "Who commands that vessel?" she inquired. "Captain Thibault."—"And what are his orders?"—"To fire into and sink the vessels in which we sail should any attempt be made to return to France." Such was the farewell of their subjects to the House of Bourbon. The fugitives landed at Weymouth; the Duchesse d'Angoulême under the title of Comtesse de Marne, the Duchesse de Berri as Comtesse de Rosny, and her son Henri de Bordeaux as Comte de Chambord, the title he retained till his death, originally taken from the estate presented to him in infancy by his enthusiastic people. Holyrood, with its royal and gloomy associations, was their appointed dwelling. The Duc and Duchesse d'Angoulême, and the daughter of the Duc de Berri, travelled thither by land, the King and the young Comte de Chambord by sea. "I prefer my route to that of my sister," observed the latter, "because I shall see the coast of France again, and she will not."

The French Government soon complained that at Holyrood the exiles were still too near their native land, and accordingly in 1832 Charles X, with his son and grandson, left Scotland for Hamburg, while the Duchesse d'Angoulême and her niece repaired to Vienna. The family were reunited at Prague in 1833, where the birthday of the Comte de Chambord was celebrated with some pomp and rejoicing, many Legitimists flocking thither to congratulate him on attaining the age of thirteen, which the old law of monarchical France had fixed as the majority of her Princes. Three years later the wanderings of the unfortunate family recommenced; the Emperor Francis II was dead, and his successor Ferdinand must visit Prague to be crowned, and Charles X feared that the presence of a discrowned monarch might be embarrassing on such an occasion. Illness and sorrow attended the exiles on their new journey, and a few months after they were established in the Château of Graffenburg at Goritz, Charles X died of cholera, in his eightieth year. At Goritz, also, on 31st May 1844, the Duchesse d'Angoulême, who had sat beside so many deathbeds, watched over that of her husband. Theirs had not been a marriage of affection in youth, but they respected each other's virtues, and to a great extent shared each other's tastes; banishment and suffering had united them very closely, and of late years they had been almost inseparable—walking, riding, and reading together.[105] When the Duchesse d'Angoulême had seen her husband laid by his father's side in the vault of the Franciscan convent, she, accompanied by her nephew and niece, removed to Fröhsdorf, where they spent seven tranquil years. Here she was addressed as "Queen" by her household for the first time in her life, but she herself always recognised Henri, Comte de Chambord, as her sovereign. The Duchess lived to see the overthrow of Louis Philippe, the usurper of the inheritance of her family. Her last attempt to exert herself was a characteristic one. She tried to rise from a sick-bed in order to attend the memorial service held for her mother, Marie Antoinette, on 16th October, the anniversary of her execution. But her strength was not equal to the task; on the 19th she expired, with her hand in that of the Comte de Chambord, and on 28th October 1851 Marie Thérèse Charlotte, Duchesse d'Angoulême, was buried in the Franciscan convent. "Her youth was passed in captivity and her age in exile," says her biographer, "but she accepted every visitation with dignity towards man, and with meekness towards God."

THE CEREMONY OF EXPIATION

About this time [the spring of 1814] a ceremony took place in Paris, at which I was present, because there was nothing in it that could be mortifying to a French heart. The death of Louis XVI had long been admitted to be one of the most serious misfortunes of the Revolution. The Emperor Napoleon never spoke of that sovereign but in terms of the highest respect, and always prefixed the epithet *unfortunate* to his name. The ceremony to which I allude was proposed by the Emperor of Russia and the King of Prussia. It consisted of a kind of expiation and purification of the spot on which Louis XVI and his Queen were beheaded. I went to see the ceremony, and I had a place at a window in the Hôtel of Madame de Rémusat, next to the Hôtel de Crillon, and what was termed the Hôtel de Courlande.

The Expiation took place on the 10th of April. The weather was extremely fine, and warm for the season. The Emperor of Russia and King of Prussia, accompanied by Prince Schwartzenberg, took their station at the entrance of the Rue Royale; the King of Prussia being on the right of the Emperor Alexander, and Prince Schwartzenberg on his left. There was a long parade, during which the Russian, Prussian, and Austrian military bands vied with each other in playing the air—"*Vive Henri IV!*" The cavalry defiled past, and then withdrew into the Champs Elysées; but the infantry ranged themselves round an altar which was raised in the middle of the Place, and which was elevated on a platform having twelve or fifteen steps. The Emperor of Russia alighted from his horse, and, followed by the King of Prussia, the Grand Duke Constantine, Lord Cathcart, and Prince Schwartzenberg, advanced to the altar. When the Emperor had nearly reached the altar the *Te Deum* commenced. At the moment of the benediction, the sovereigns and persons who accompanied them, as well as the 25,000 troops who covered the Place, all knelt down. The Greek priest presented the cross to the Emperor Alexander, who kissed it; his example was followed by the individuals who accompanied him, though they were not of the Greek faith.[106] On rising, the Grand Duke Constantine took off his hat, and immediately salvoes of artillery were heard.—*Memoirs of Madame Junot (Duchesse d'Abrantès), vol. iii, pp. 416–7 of English edition of 1883.*

1. See Thiers' *History of the French Revolution*, translated by Frederick Shoberl. (Edit. 1854), vol. ii, p. 53.

2. The Comte d'Artois had been the last royal resident.

3. Clery gives a more minute description of this singular building: "The small tower of the Temple in which the King was then confined stood with its back against the great tower, without any interior communication, and formed a long square, flanked by two turrets. In one of these turrets there was a narrow staircase that lead from the first floor to a gallery on the platform; in the other were small rooms, answering to each story of the tower. The body of the building was four stories high. The first consisted of an antechamber, a dining-room, and a small room in the turret, where there was a library containing from twelve to fifteen hundred volumes. The second story was divided nearly in the same manner. The largest room was the Queen's bed-chamber, in which the Dauphin also slept; the second, which was separated from the Queen's by a small antechamber almost without light, was occupied by Madame Royale and Madame Elizabeth. The King's apartments were on the third story. He slept in the great room, and made a study of the turret closet. There was a kitchen separated from the King's chamber by a small dark room, which had been successively occupied by M. de Chamilly and M. de Huë. The fourth story was shut up; and on the ground floor there were kitchens of which no use was made."—*Journal*, p. 96.

4. *Procureur de la Commune.* He moved that the King should be sent to the Temple, and volunteered to be his gaoler; but his intercourse with the royal family modified his feelings towards them; he voted against the King's death, paid a high tribute to the Queen at her trial, and was himself executed by order of the Revolutionary Tribunal in November 1793.—See Thiers, vol. i.

5. *Royal Memoirs of the French Revolution* (Murray, 1823), p. 159.

6. Mesdames Adelaide and Victoire.

7. Rocher, a saddler by trade.

8. *Royal Memoirs*, pp. 166–70.

9. Clery we have seen and known, and the form and manners of that model of pristine faith and loyalty can never be forgotten. Gentleman-like and complaisant in his manners, his deep gravity and melancholy features announced that the sad scenes in which he had acted a part so honourable were never for a moment out of his memory.—Scott's *Life of Napoleon* (edit. 1827), vol. ii, p. 148.

10. Clery's *Journal*.

11. Madame Royale says later in her narrative: "The municipal officer who had given his scarf to tie across the door took care to make my father pay him its value." Clery says that he himself "paid the forty-five sous".

12. Bertrand de Molleville's *Annals of the French Revolution* (English edit. 1802), vol. vii, p. 377.

13. The pike that bore the head was fixed before the Duc d'Orléans' window as he was going to dinner. It is said that he looked at this horrid sight without horror, went into the dining-room,

sat down to table, and helped his guests without saying a word. His silence and coolness left it doubtful whether the assassins, in presenting him this bloody trophy, intended to offer him an insult or to pay him homage.—*Ibid,* p. 388.

14. "When I took my lessons," says Madame Royale, "and my mother made extracts from books for me, a municipal officer continually looked over my shoulder, thinking we were engaged in conspiracies."

15. At nine o'clock, says Clery, the King asked to be taken to his family, but the municipal officers replied that they had "no orders for that". Shortly afterwards a boy brought the King some bread and a decanter of lemonade for his breakfast. The King gave half the bread to Clery, saying, "It seems they have forgotten your breakfast; take this, the rest is enough for me." Clery refused, but the King insisted. "I could not contain my tears," he adds; "the King perceived them, and his own fell also."

16. Madame Elizabeth was violently rebuked by one of the officers for addressing her brother in a low tone.

17. When the first deputation from the Council of the Commune visited the Temple, and formally inquired whether the King had any complaint to make, he replied, "No; while he was permitted to remain with his family he was happy."

18. Madame Campan says the Queen told her while at the Feuillans that the wife of the English Ambassador (the Countess of Sutherland) had provided linen for the use of the Dauphin. (See *ante,* p. 329.)

19. M. Le Monnier, who had been allowed to attend the royal family during their slight illnesses.

20. Clery's *Journal.*

21. Alison's *History of Europe,* vol. ii, p. 299.

22. The Convention was fatigued by long discussions. Members not interested in them, and the two parties not in the first rank, felt the need of concord, and wished to see men occupy themselves with the Republic. There was an apparent truce, and the attention of the Assembly was directed for a moment to the new constitution, which the Mountain caused it to abandon in order to decide on the fate of the fallen Prince. The leaders of the Extreme Left did not want the Girondists and the moderate members of the Plain to organise the Republic. They would have established the system of the Bourgeoisie, a little more democratic than that of 1791 … but they could only accomplish their end by power, and they could only obtain power by protracting the revolutionary state in France. The condemnation of Louis XVI would arouse all passions, rally round them the violent parties, and, by exposing the desire of the Girondists to save Louis XVI, ruin them in the estimation of the multitude. A dethroned king was dangerous to a young democracy; but the party of the Mountain would have been more clement had it not hoped to ruin the Gironde at the same time.—Mignet's *History of the French Revolution* (Bell and Daldy, 1868), p. 178.

23. In such crises the royal family naturally saw evil omens in things too trivial for notice at other times.—See *ante,* Madame Campan's story of the Queen's alarm about the candles on her toilette table, p. 215.

24. See Lamartine's *History of the Girondists* (English edit. 1870), vol. ii, pp. 309–10.

25. De Molleville's *Annals,* vol. viii, p. 243.

26. The King sat down with an intrepid air; no signs of emotion appeared on his countenance. The dignity and calmness of his presence were such that the Girondists were melted to tears,

and the fanaticism of Saint Just, Robespierre, and Marat for a moment yielded to the feelings of humanity.—Alison's *History of Europe.*

27. The King listened unmoved to the act of accusation, only at one or two passages, where it passed the bounds of even injustice and falsehood, and where he was reproached with shedding the blood of the people, which he had so religiously spared during his reign, he could not prevent himself from betraying his indignation by a bitter smile and a shrug of his shoulders. It was evident that he expected everything but to be called a sanguinary Prince. He lifted his eyes to heaven as though invoking God to witness his innocence.—Lamartine's *History of the Girondists*, vol. ii, p. 355.

28. Thiers' *History of the French Revolution*, vol. ii, pp. 198–200.

29. A secret closet which the King had directed to be constructed in a wall in the Tuileries. The door was of iron, whence it was afterwards known by the name of the *iron chest.* The workman employed to construct it gave information to Roland, who, being anxious to ascertain the truth of the statement, had the imprudence to hasten to the spot unaccompanied by witnesses selected from the Assembly, which gave his enemies occasion to assert that he had abstracted some of the papers. One important document the Jacobins turned into an implement against the Girondists. It was an overture from that party to Louis XVI, shortly before the 10th of August, engaging to oppose the motion for his forfeiture, provided he would recall to his Councils the three discarded ministers of the Girondist party.—See *Thiers* and *Scott.*

30. Alison's *History of Europe*, 10th edit., vol. ii, p. 301.

31. Lamartine's *History of the Girondists*, vol. ii, p. 353.

32. The substance of the decree as to the King's intercourse with his family was as follows:—"That the Queen and Madame Elizabeth should not communicate with the King at all during the course of the trial; that his children should come to him if he wished, on condition that they should not see their mother nor their aunt again until after the last examination. 'You see,' said the King, 'the cruel alternative in which they have just placed me. I cannot make up my mind to have my children with me. As to my daughter, it is impossible; and as to my son, I know by myself the pain the Queen would feel. I must therefore submit to this fresh sacrifice.' His Majesty ordered me to take away the young Prince's bed; but I kept his linen and clothes, and every other day sent what was necessary, as I had agreed with Madame Elizabeth."—Clery's *Journal.* During their last interview Madame Elizabeth had given Clery one of her handkerchiefs, saying, "You shall keep it so long as my brother continues well; if he becomes ill, send it to me among my nephew's things."

33. Christian Guillaume de Lamoignon de Malesherbes, an eminent French statesman, son of the Chancellor of France, was born at Paris in 1721. In 1750 he succeeded his father as President of the Court of Aids, and was also made superintendent of the press. On the banishment of the Parliaments and the suppression of the Court of Aids, Malesherbes was exiled to his country-seat. In 1775 he was appointed Minister of State. On the decree of the Convention for the King's trial, he emerged from his retreat to become the voluntary advocate of his sovereign. Malesherbes was guillotined in 1794, and almost his whole family were extirpated by their merciless persecutors.—*Encyclopaedia Americana.*

34. The Citoyenne Olympia Degouges, calling herself *a free and loyal Republican without spot or blame,* and declaring that the cold and selfish cruelty of Target had inflamed her heroism and roused her sensibility, asked permission to assist M. de Malesherbes in defending the

King. The Assembly passed to the order of the day on this request.—Bertrand de Molleville's *Annals*, vol. viii, p. 254.

35. According to M. de Huë: "The first time M. de Malesherbes entered the Temple the King clasped him in his arms and said, 'Ah, is it you, my friend? You fear not to endanger your own life to save mine; but all will be useless. They will bring me to the scaffold. No matter; I shall gain my cause if I leave an unspotted memory behind me.'"

36. The King's natural benevolence was constantly shown while in the Temple. His own dreadful position never prevented him from sympathy with the smaller troubles of others. A servant in the Temple named Marchand, the father of a family, was robbed of 200 francs—his wages for two months. The King observed his distress, asked its cause, and gave Clery the amount to be handed to Marchand, with a caution not to speak of it to any one, and, above all, not to thank the King, lest it should injure him with his employers.

37. Madame Royale says: "On the 26th December, St Stephen's Day, my father made his will, because he expected to be assassinated that day on his way to the bar of the Convention. He went thither, nevertheless, with his usual calmness."—*Royal Memoirs*, p. 195.

38. When the pathetic peroration of M. de Sèze was read to the King, the evening before it was delivered to the Assembly, "I have to request of you," he said, "to make a painful sacrifice; strike out of your pleading the peroration. It is enough for me to appear before such judges, and show my entire innocence; I will not move their feelings."—*Lacretelle.*

39. The Girondists, said Napoleon, condemned the King to death, and yet the majority of them had voted for the appeal to the people, which was intended to save him. This forms the inexplicable part of their conduct. Had they wished to preserve his life, they had the power to do so; nothing more would have been necessary than to adjourn the sentence, or condemn him to exile or transportation. But to condemn him to death, and at the same time endeavour to make his fate depend on a popular vote, was the height of imprudence and absurdity; it was, after having destroyed the monarchy, to endeavour to tear France in pieces by a civil war. It was this false combination which ruined them. Vergniaud, their main pillar, was the very man who proclaimed, as President, the death of Louis; and he did this at the moment when the force of their party was such in the Assembly that it required several months' labour, and more than one popular insurrection, to overturn it. That party might have ruled the Convention, destroyed the Mountain, and governed France if they had at once pursued a manly, straightforward conduct. It was the refinement of metaphysicians which occasioned their fall.—*Las Casas.*

40. It is known that throughout the King's trial the deputy Vergniaud seemed in despair, and passed the whole night after the monarch's condemnation in tears; and it is probable that the same night was as dreadful to all his colleagues, if we except a small number who, in their absurd ferocity, declared in the National Assembly that Louis XVI deserved death for the single crime of being a King, and condemned him merely because they wished to destroy royalty.—*Bertrand de Molleville.*

41. "I had something the matter with my foot," writes Madame Royale, "and my father, having heard of it, was, with his usual tenderness, very uneasy, and made constant inquiries."

42. The sitting of the Convention which concluded the trial lasted seventy-two hours. It might naturally be supposed that silence, restraint, a sort of religious awe, would have pervaded the scene. On the contrary, everything bore the marks of gaiety, dissipation, and the most

grotesque confusion. The farther end of the hall was converted into boxes, where ladies, in a studied *déshabillé* swallowed ices, oranges, liqueurs, and received the salutations of the members who went and came, as on ordinary occasions. Here the door keepers on the Mountain side opened and shut the boxes reserved for the mistresses of the Duc d'Orléans; and there, though every sound of approbation or disapprobation was strictly forbidden, you heard the long and indignant "Ha, ha's!" of the mother-duchess, the patroness of the bands of female Jacobins, whenever her ears were not loudly greeted with the welcome sounds of death. The upper gallery, reserved for the people, was during the whole trial constantly full of strangers of every description drinking wine as in a tavern. Bets were made as to the issue of the trial in all the neighbouring coffee-houses. Ennui, impatience, disgust sat on almost every countenance. The figures passing and re-passing, rendered more ghastly by the pallid lights, and who in a slow, sepulchral voice only pronounced the word—Death; others calculating if they should have time to go to dinner before they gave their verdict; women pricking cards with pins in order to count the votes; some of the deputies fallen asleep, and only waking up to give their sentence; all this had the appearance rather of a hideous dream than of a reality.—Hazlitt's *Life of Napoleon.*

43. Many great and good men mournfully inclined to the severer side, from an opinion of its absolute necessity to annihilate a dangerous enemy, and establish an unsettled republic. Among these must be reckoned Carnot, who, when called on for his opinion, gave it in these words "Death; and never did word weigh so heavily on my heart!"—*Alison.*

44. "I cannot express the horror which was painted on the countenance of every individual in the National Convention when the Duke gave his votes for the death of his King and relation."—*From the narrative of an eye witness.*

The Duc d'Orléans, when called on to give his vote, walked with a faltering step, and a face paler than death itself, to the appointed place, and there read these words: "Exclusively governed by my duty, and convinced that all those who have resisted the sovereignty of the people deserve death, my vote is for death!" Important as the accession of the first Prince of the blood was to the terrorist faction, his conduct in this instance was too obviously selfish and atrocious not to excite a general feeling of indignation; the agitation of the Assembly became extreme; it seemed as if by this single vote the fate of the monarch was irrevocably sealed.—*History of the Convention.*

45. The Duc d'Orléans lived in Paris, striving in vain to hide himself in the bosom of the Convention. This place most assuredly was not suited to him amidst furious demagogues. But whither was he to fly? In Europe the emigrants were ready for him, and insult, nay, perhaps even death, threatened this kinsman of royalty, who had repudiated his birthright and his rank. In France he strove to disguise that rank under the humblest titles, and he called himself *Egalité.* But still there remained the ineffaceable remembrance of his former existence, and the ever-present testimony of his immense wealth. Unless he were to put on rags, and render himself contemptible by cynicism, how was he to escape suspicion? In the ranks of the Girondists he would have been undone the very first day, and all the charges of royalism preferred against them would have been justified. In those of the Jacobins he would have the violence of Paris for a support, but he could not have escaped the accusations of the Girondists; and this it was that actually befell him. The latter, never forgiving him for having joined the ranks of their enemies, supposed that, to make himself endurable, he lavished his wealth on anarchists, and lent them the aid of his mighty fortune.—*Thiers.*

46. The analysis of votes given by Thiers slightly differs from this, and is as follows:—

    The Assembly was composed of seven hundred and forty-nine members: fifteen were absent on commissions, eight from illness, five had refused to vote, which reduced the number of deputies present to seven hundred and twenty-one, and the absolute majority to three hundred and sixty-one votes. Two hundred and eighty-six had voted for detention or banishment with different conditions. Two had voted for imprisonment; forty-six for death with reprieve either till peace, or till the ratification of the constitution. Twenty-six had voted for death, but, with Mailhe, they had desired that the Assembly should consider whether it might not be expedient to stay the execution. Their vote was nevertheless independent of the latter clause. Three hundred and sixty-one had voted for death unconditionally.—*History of the French Revolution*, vol. ii, p. 231.

47. Louis was fully prepared for his fate. During the calling of the votes he asked M. de Malesherbes, "Have you not met near the Temple the White Lady?"—"What do you mean?" replied he. "Do you not know," resumed the King with a smile, "that when a prince of our house is about to die, a female dressed in white is seen wandering about the palace? My friends," added he to his defenders, "I am about to depart before you for the land of the just, but there, at least, we shall be reunited." In fact, his Majesty's only apprehension seemed to be for his family.—*Alison*.

48. When M. de Malesherbes went to the Temple to announce the result of the vote, he found Louis with his forehead resting on his hands, and absorbed in a deep reverie. Without inquiring concerning his fate, he said, "For two hours I have been considering whether, during my whole reign, I have voluntarily given any cause of complaint to my subjects; and with perfect sincerity I declare that I deserve no reproach at their hands, and that I have never formed a wish but for their happiness."—*Lacretelle*.

49. Madame Royale says that M. de Malesherbes added, after telling her father the nature of his sentence, "Every honest man will endeavour to save your Majesty, or die at your feet;" but the King replied, "Such proceedings would excite a civil war in Paris—*I had rather die*. You will, therefore, I entreat you, command them from me to make no effort to save me."—*Royal Memoirs*, p. 197.

50. The sentence of death was announced by Garat. No alteration took place in the King's countenance; I observed only at the word "conspiracy", a smile of indignation appear on his lips; but at the words "shall suffer the punishment of death", the expression of his face, when he looked on those around him, showed that death had no terrors for him.—*Clery*.

51. Henry Essex Edgeworth de Firmont, father-confessor of Louis XVI, was born in Ireland in 1745, in the village of Edgeworthstown. His father, an episcopalian clergyman, adopted the Catholic faith with his family, and went to France. His piety and good conduct obtained him the confidence of Madame Elizabeth, who chose him for her confessor, and made him known to Louis. M. Edgeworth arrived in England in 1796. Pitt offered him a pension, which he declined. He soon after followed Louis XVIII to Blankenburg in Brunswick, and thence to Mittau. M. Edgeworth died in 1807, of a fever caught in attending to some French emigrants. The Duchesse d'Angoulême waited on him in his last moments, the royal family followed him to the tomb, and Louis XVIII wrote his epitaph.—*Encyclopædia Americana*.

52. "But when we were gone," says his daughter, "he requested that we might not be permitted to return, as our presence afflicted him too much."

53. In the course of the morning the King said to me, "You will give this seal to my son and this ring to the Queen, and assure her that it is with pain I part with it. This little packet contains the hair of all my family; you will give her that too. Tell the Queen, my dear sister, and my children that, although I promised to see them again this morning, I have resolved to spare them the pang of so cruel a separation. Tell them how much it costs me to go away without receiving their embraces once more!" He wiped away some tears, and then added in the most mournful accents, "I charge you to bear them my last farewell."—*Clery*.

54. Thiers' *History of the French Revolution*.

55. Thus perished, at the age of thirty-nine, after a reign of sixteen years and a half, spent in endeavouring to do good, the best but weakest of monarchs. His ancestors bequeathed him a revolution. He was better calculated than any of them to prevent or terminate it; for he was capable of becoming a reformer-king before it broke out, or of becoming a constitutional king afterwards. He is, perhaps, the only prince who, having no other passion, had not that of power, and who united the two qualities which make good kings—fear of God, and love of the people.He perished, the victim of passions which he did not share; of those of the persons about him to which he was a stranger, and of those of the multitude which he had not excited.—Mignet's *French Revolution*, p. 189.

56. The body of Louis was, immediately after the execution, removed to the ancient cemetery of the Madeleine. Large quantities of quicklime were thrown into the grave, which occasioned so rapid a decomposition that, when his remains were sought for in 1815, it was with difficulty any part could be recovered. Over the spot where he was interred Napoleon commenced the splendid Temple of Glory, after the battle of Jena; and the superb edifice was completed by the Bourbons, and now forms the church of the Madeleine, the most beautiful structure in Paris. Louis was executed on the same ground where the Queen, Madame Elizabeth, and so many other noble victims of the Revolution perished; where Robespierre and Danton afterwards suffered; and where the Emperor Alexander and the allied sovereigns took their station, when their victorious troops entered Paris in 1814! The history of modern Europe has not a scene fraught with equally interesting recollections to exhibit. It is now marked by the colossal obelisk of blood-red granite which was brought from Thebes, in Upper Egypt, in 1833, by the French Government.—*Alison*.

57. Toulan, Lepitre, Vincent, Bruno, and others.

58. This woman, troubled by remorse, lost her reason, threw herself at the feet of the Queen, implored her pardon, and disturbed the Temple for many days with the sight and the noise of her madness. The Princesses, forgetting the denunciations of this unfortunate being, in consideration of her repentance and insanity, watched over her by turns, and deprived themselves of their own food to relieve her.—Lamartine, *History of the Girondists*, vol. iii, p. 140. The first time Tison's wife showed signs of madness, "she began to talk to herself," says Madame Royale simply; "alas! that made me laugh; and my poor mother and aunt looked at me as though they saw with pleasure that short moment of gaiety."

59. Alison's *History of Europe*, vol. iii, p. 162.

60. The Conciergerie was originally, as its name implies, the porter's lodge of the ancient Palace of Justice, and became in time a prison, from the custom of confining there persons who had committed trifling offences about the Court.

61. Mathieu, the gaoler, used to say, "I make Madame Veto and her sister and daughter, proud though they are, salute me; for the door is so low they cannot pass without bowing."

62. The Queen's separation from her son, for whose sake alone she had consented to endure the burden of existence, was so touching, so heartrending that the very gaolers who witnessed the scene confessed, when giving an account of it to the authorities, that they could not refrain from tears.—Weber's *Memoirs of Marie Antoinette.*

63. The Queen was lodged in a room called the Council chamber, which was considered as the most unwholesome apartment in the Conciergerie on account of its dampness and the bad smells by which it was continually affected. Under pretence of giving her a person to wait upon her they placed near her a spy—a man of a horrible countenance and hollow sepulchral voice. This wretch, whose name was Barassin, was a robber and murderer by profession. Such was the chosen attendant on the Queen of France! A few days before her trial this wretch was removed and a *gendarme* placed in her chamber, who watched over her night and day, and from whom she was not separated, even when in bed, but by a ragged curtain. In this melancholy abode Marie Antoinette had no other dress than an old black gown, stockings with holes, which she was forced to mend every day; and she was entirely destitute of shoes.—*Du Broca.*

64. Simon, who was entrusted with the bringing up of the Dauphin, had had the cruelty to leave the poor child absolutely alone. Unexampled barbarity to leave an unhappy and sickly infant eight years old in a great room, locked and bolted in, with no other resource than a broken bell which he never rang, so greatly did he dread the people whom its sound would have brought to him! He preferred wanting everything to the sight of his persecutors. His bed had not been touched for six months, and he had not strength to make it himself; it was alive with bugs, and vermin still more disgusting. His linen and his person were covered with them. For more than a year he had had no change of shirt or stockings; every kind of filth was allowed to accumulate in his room. His window was never opened, and the infectious smell of this horrid apartment was so dreadful that no one could bear it. He passed his days wholly without occupation. They did not even allow him light in the evening. This situation affected his mind as well as his body; and he fell into a frightful atrophy.—*Duchesse d'Angoulême.*

65. Can there be a more infernal invention than that made against the Queen by Hebert—namely, that she had had an improper intimacy with her own son? He made use of this sublime idea of which he boasted in order to prejudice the women against the Queen, and to prevent her execution from exciting pity. It had, however, no other effect than that of disgusting all parties.—*Prudhomme.*

66. Hebert did not long survive her in whose sufferings he had taken such an infamous part. He was executed on 26th March 1794. "Hébert," says the *Rapport d'un Détenu dans les Prisons,* "montra jusqu'au bout une extrême faiblesse. Pendant le trajet de la Conciergerie à l'échafaud, le spectacle de son agonie empêcha que l'on prêt être attentif à la contenance de ses compagnons. La dernière nuit dans la prison il a eu des accès de désespoir."

67. Yet even Robespierre, so inveterate against the King, would have saved the Queen. "Revolutions are very cruel," he said. "They regard neither sex nor age. Ideas are pitiless, but the people should also know how to forgive. If my head were not necessary to the Revolution, there are moments when I would offer that head to the people in exchange for one of those which they demand of us."—Lamartine's *Girondists,* vol. iii, p. 137.

68. At first the Queen, consulting only her own sense of dignity, had resolved on her trial to make no other reply to the questions of her judges than—"Assassinate me as you have already assassinated my husband!" Afterwards, however, she determined to follow the example of

the King, exert herself in her defence, and leave her judges without any excuse or pretext for putting her to death.—Weber's *Memoirs of Marie Antoinette*.

69. The Queen, after having written and prayed, slept soundly for some hours. On her waking, Bault's daughter dressed her and adjusted her hair with more neatness than on other days. Marie Antoinette wore a white gown, a white handkerchief covered her shoulders, a white cap her hair; a black ribbon bound this cap round her temples … The cries, the looks, the laughter, the jests of the people overwhelmed her with humiliation; her colour, changing continually from purple to paleness, betrayed her agitation … On reaching the scaffold she inadvertently trod on the executioner's foot. "Pardon me," she said courteously. She knelt for an instant and uttered a half-audible prayer; then rising and glancing towards the towers of the Temple— "Adieu, once again, my children," she said, "I go to rejoin your father."—*Lamartine*.

70. Sorrow had blanched the Queen's once beautiful hair; but her features and air still commanded the admiration of all who beheld her; her cheeks, pale and emaciated, were occasionally tinged with a vivid colour at the mention of those she had lost. When led out to execution, she was dressed in white; she had cut off her hair with her own hands. Placed in a tumbrel, with her arms tied behind her, she was taken by a circuitous route to the Place de la Révolution, and she ascended the scaffold with a firm and dignified step, as if she had been about to take her place on a throne by the side of her husband.—*Lacretelle*.

71. Since the King's captivity all the defects of his youth had gradually disappeared; the somewhat rough *bonhommie* of his character was changed into grace and sensibility towards those who were about him. His *brusquerie* was no longer perceptible, and all the trifling blemishes in his character were effaced by the grandeur of his resignation. His children adored, his sister admired him, while the Queen was astonished at his tenderness and courage. His very gaolers could not recognise the vulgar and sensual man public prejudice had described to them.—*Lamartine*.

72. It seems probable that Madame Royale must have been thinking of 3rd September 1792, when the head of the Princesse de Lamballe was carried to the Temple.

73. This was the last time the brother and sister met.

74. The Duc d'Orléans, the early and interested propagator of the Revolution, was its next victim. Billaud Varennes said in the Convention, "The time has come when all the conspirators should be known and struck. I demand that we no longer pass over in silence a man whom we seem to have forgotten, despite the numerous facts against him. I demand that D'Orléans be sent to the Revolutionary Tribunal." The Convention, once his hireling adulators, unanimously supported the proposal. In vain he alleged his having been accessory to the disorders of 5th October, his support of the revolt on 10th August 1792, his vote against the King on 17th January 1793. His condemnation was pronounced. He then asked only for a delay of twenty-four hours, and had a repast carefully prepared, on which he feasted with avidity. When led out for execution he gazed with a smile on the Palais Royal, the scene of his former orgies. He was detained for a quarter of an hour before that palace by the order of Robespierre, who had asked his daughter's hand, and promised in return to excite a tumult in which the Duke's life should be saved. Depraved though he was, he would not consent to such a sacrifice, and he met his fate with stoical fortitude.—*Alison*, vol. iii, p. 172.

75. Duchesse d'Angoulême, *Royal Memoirs*, p. 254.

76. "It has been said," Lamartine observes, "that the day did not contain sufficient hours for the impatience of the tribunal."

77. Duchesse d'Angoulême, *Royal Memoirs*, p. 261.

78. Madame Elizabeth was one of those rare personages only seen at distant intervals during the course of ages; she set an example of steadfast piety in the palace of kings, she lived amid her family the favourite of all and the admiration of the world … When I went to Versailles Madame Elizabeth was twenty-two years of age. Her plump figure and pretty pink colour must have attracted notice, and her air of calmness and contentment even more than her beauty. She was fond of billiards, and her elegance and courage in riding were remarkable. But she never allowed these amusements to interfere with her religious observances. At that time her wish to take the veil at Saint Cyr was much talked of, but the King was too fond of his sister to endure the separation. There were also rumours of a marriage between Madame Elizabeth and the Emperor Joseph. The Queen was sincerely attached to her brother, and loved her sister-in-law most tenderly; she ardently desired this marriage as a means of raising the Princess to one of the first thrones in Europe, and as a possible means of turning the Emperor from his innovations. She had been very carefully educated, had talent in music and painting, spoke Italian and a little Latin, and understood mathematics. Her last moments were worthy of her courage and virtue.—D'Hézecques' *Recollections*, pp. 72–5.

79. Pensive as her father, proud as her mother, pious as her aunt, Madame Royale's mind bore the impress of the three minds amidst which it had been nurtured. Hers was a shadowy, pale, ideal beauty. Never quitting the side of her mother or her aunt, she seemed to shrink from life. Her light hair, still hanging over her shoulders, almost concealed her features; her expression was timid and reserved.—*Lamartine*.

80. It has been said that Robespierre vainly tried to obtain the hand of Mademoiselle d'Orléans. It was also rumoured that Madame Royale herself owed her life to his matrimonial ambition. "Dans ces tems cette jeune infortunée n'avait du son salut qu'à l'ambition de Robespierre. Et si sous la règne de la Terreur elle n'avait point suivie sa famille à l'échafaud, c'est que ce monstre avait des vues sur elle, et se promettait de l'épouser pour affermir sa puissance."—*Deux Amis*, xiv, p. 173.

81. On another occasion "three men in scarves", who entered the Princess' room, told her that they did not see why she should wish to be released, as she seemed very comfortable! "'It is dreadful,' I replied, 'to be separated for more than a year from one's mother without even hearing what has become of her or of my aunt.'—'You are not ill?'—'No, sir, but the cruel illness is that of the heart.'—'We can do nothing for you. Be patient, and submit to the justice and goodness of the French people.' I had nothing more to say."—Duchesse d'Angoulême, *Royal Memoirs*, p. 273.

82. Lamartine.

83. Thiers.

84. Lamartine.

85. Simon left the Temple to become a municipal officer. He was involved in the overthrow of Robespierre, and guillotined the day after him, 29th July 1794.

86. Thiers.

87. Others would gladly have shared this work of mercy. As rumours of the Prince's critical state spread within and without the prison, Madame Royale renewed her entreaties to be allowed to nurse her brother, or at least to see him once more, and M. de Huë offered to share his imprisonment; but both were refused.

88. Madame Royale says at three o'clock on 9th June. The confusion as to the day and hour probably arose from the death being at first kept secret.

89. Lamartine says: "He died at length without pain, but without uttering a word, on 9th June 1795. The doctors who attended him in his last moments had never seen him till the final hour." This is entirely contrary to the statement of Gomin, quoted in the "Illustrations" to Thiers' *History of the French Revolution*. Lamartine also speaks of several visits paid by Madame Royale to her brother, of which there is no mention in her own narrative.—*History of the Restoration of Monarchy in France* (Bell and Daldy, 1865), vol. i, pp. 306–10.

90. Afterwards Louis XVIII.

91. Afterwards Charles X.

92. A short time after Madame Royale left the Temple, Rœderer, who had voted for the death of the King, entered her room, and looked curiously round. Some lines pencilled on the wall caught his eye: the first inscription he read was, "Oh my father, watch over me from your place in heaven!" the second, "Oh God, pardon those through whom my parents died!" He gazed for a moment stupefied, and then rushed out of the apartment, impelled, he confesses in his *Memoirs*, by the fiercest remorse.—*Filia Dolorosa: Memoirs of the Duchesse d'Angoulême* (Bentley, 1852), vol. i, p. 355.

93. The mention of the little dog taken from the Temple by Madame Royale reminds me how fond all the family were of these creatures. Each Princess kept a different kind. Mesdames had beautiful spaniels, little greyhounds were preferred by Madame Elizabeth. Louis XVI was the only one of all his family who had no dogs in his room. I remember one day waiting in the great gallery for the King's retiring, when he entered with all his family and the whole pack, who were escorting him. All at once all the dogs began to bark, one louder than another, and ran away, passing like ghosts along those great dark rooms, which rang with their hoarse cries. The Princesses shouting, calling them, running everywhere after them, completed a ridiculous spectacle, which made those august persons very merry.—*D'Hézecques*, p. 49.

94. Madame Royale inherited all the pride of blood peculiar to the Houses of Bourbon and Hapsburg. Naturally reflecting and reserved, she evinced a gravity even in her earliest years which is rarely the characteristic of childhood. It was remarked of her that "elle n'avait jamais été enfant, toujours grande dame." Without being precisely of a melancholy disposition, all her tendencies were serious and meditative. In all respects she resembled Louis XVI more than Marie Antoinette. She took no pleasure in noisy games, but early showed a taste for reading, and that inherent piety and reverence for religion which so strongly characterised Madame Elizabeth.—*Filia Dolorosa*, vol. i, p. 14.

95. According to the *Memoirs of Louis XVIII*, "l'Impératrice regnante ne craignant pas de la maltraiter pas des voies de fait."

96. Which the Emperor wished her to claim from her uncle Louis XVIII.

97. *Filia Dolorosa*, vol. ii, p. 12.

98. The Duc d'Angoulême was quiet and reserved. He loved hunting as a means of killing time; was given to early hours and innocent pleasures. He was a gentleman, and brave as became one. He had not the "gentlemanly vices" of his brother, and was all the better for it. He was ill-educated, but had natural good sense, and would have passed for having more than that had he cared to put forth pretensions. Of all his family he was the one most ill-spoken of and least deserving of it.—*Dr Doran*.

99. The Queen was too ill to travel. The Duc d'Angoulême took another route to join a body of French gentlemen in arms for the Legitimist cause.

100. It pleased the King to notice a fleur-de-lis in the old carving on each side of the porch.

101. She needed all the strength that He who is the source of it could give; for on leaving the Cathedral she had to repair to the Tuileries, which she had not seen since the fatal 10th of August, when she left it with those who were never to cross its threshold again, and traverse the garden which was to them as the valley of the shadow of death … Here memory was too much for her, and she fell to the ground in a swoon.—*Dr Doran.*

102. "It was the Duchesse d'Angoulême who saved you," said General Clauzel, after these events, to a royalist volunteer; "I could not bring myself to order such a woman to be fired upon, at the moment when she was providing material for the noblest page in her history."—*Filia Dolorosa*, vol. ii, p. 131.

103. She was so methodical and economical, though liberal, in her charities, that one of her regular evening occupations was to tear off the seals from the letters she had received during the day, in order that the wax might be melted down and sold; the produce made one poor family "passing rich with forty pounds a year".—*Filia Dolorosa*, vol. ii, p. 239.

104. Except that of the latest and perhaps best known—Augustus Mèvès. See *Memoirs of Louis Charles, Dauphin of France* (Ridgway, 1868); and *The Dauphin, Louis XVII* (Bentley, 1876).

105. See *Filia Dolorosa*, vol. ii.

106. The King of Prussia was a Protestant, Prince Schwartzenberg a Catholic, and the Emperor Alexander belonged to the Greek communion.

APPENDIX

CONTEMPORARY REMINISCENCES OF MARIE ANTOINETTE

The following extracts from the correspondence of the Comte de la Marck with the Comte de Mirabeau will possess interest as containing the views of one fully conversant with the affairs of the period:—

The influence which the Queen is said to have exercised in directing the King's choice of his ministers is altogether imaginary; I have it in my power to prove that this charge also was quite without foundation, except in one instance, which I have before mentioned, when she exerted herself on behalf of the Marquis de Ségur. Far from desiring to mix herself up in State affairs, she manifested a strong distaste to anything like important business; in this respect, perhaps, she only exhibits what is natural to the character of a woman's mind. I have not the slightest hesitation, therefore, in declaring that all that has been said on this subject is utterly false, as well concerning the part which the Abbé de Vermond is stated to have taken with regard to the relations of France with Austria, as in the cases which I have already enumerated, and which were of little importance.

I here take the opportunity of mentioning some facts in support of my opinion, and shall begin with one which first suggests itself to my memory, though it occurred after others which I shall subsequently relate. When M. Necker was dismissed from office the first time, I happened to be at Brussels, as well as the Emperor Joseph; I saw him almost every day, and he seemed to take pleasure in conversing with me about France and the Queen; it was from him that I heard of M. Necker's dismissal, for he had just received the news in a letter from his sister. He spoke in the warmest terms of this Minister, and of the talents with which he considered him endowed, and seriously blamed the King for dismissing him. He remarked, "that the Queen was also very much vexed at this step; *she wrote to me*," he added, "*to assure me that she had nothing to do with this change of Ministry.*" But I must proceed to mention some other facts.

At the death of Louis XV the Court of Vienna was very anxious that the Duc de Choiseul should be placed at the head of the new King's Ministry. He had ever shown himself the most zealous upholder of the Treaty of 1756, that is to say, of the close alliance between France and Austria. The most explicit and urgent instructions were therefore despatched to the Comte de Mercy on the subject, and he readily found an instrument for his purpose in the Abbé de Vermond, who was devoted to M. de Choiseul; for, as I have previously observed, he was partly indebted to him for the post he had obtained at Vienna. The Choiseul party, which was exceedingly numerous, did not either remain inactive; its members lost no opportunity in endeavouring to interest the Queen in M. de Choiseul's nomination to the Ministry. They even went so far as to say that it was to them she owed the successful issue of the negotiation for her marriage, as if the Archduchess was not at that period the most fitting match for the Dauphin, and as if there had been a better choice left for him! But M. de Choiseul and his party were not very scrupulous about the means they employed; they sought only to turn everything they could to their own advantage.

After the death of his grandfather Louis XVI consulted Mesdames his aunts about the person whom he should place at the head of the Ministry, and it was in consequence of their advice that he fixed upon M. de Maurepas, though he was at first undecided whether he should select him or M. de Machault.

The young Queen was pleased at the respect which the King had shown for Mesdames' advice. At a later period, however, when she found herself surrounded by those who strove to get M. de Choiseul created minister, she began to share their desire that he might be elected. There is little doubt but that she spoke to the King on the subject, but she discovered immediately on broaching it that Louis XVI entertained the most decided aversion to M. de Choiseul, which may be accounted for by the great dislike which his father, the Dauphin, even till his death, experienced towards this minister. But this I know for certain, as I learnt it from the Comte de Mercy, but a few months after the death of Louis XV, the Queen expressed herself very clearly with regard to the reception with which her petition in M. de Choiseul's favour had met, and declared that she had resolved never to speak to the King again on the subject.

M. de Maurepas, who did not desire to have M. de Choiseul associated with himself in the Ministry, was accused at the time of strengthening the King's dislike to him. But however the case stood, M. de Maurepas was getting very old, so that the Choiseul party did not give up its ultimate aim, and only awaited the death of the minister to renew all its former intrigues. When this event happened, however, all manœuvres were useless, for the Queen resolutely refused to move in the matter, and the Abbé de Vermond, who was well acquainted with her sentiments, warned M. de Mercy that it would be impossible to make her alter her determination. The ambassador, accordingly, placed this view of the case before the Court of Vienna, and induced it to relinquish all hopes of M. de Choiseul being raised to the Ministry. Meanwhile another ambitious and intriguing person was working silently, yet actively, in order that he might one day, by the influence of the Court of Vienna, and through the medium of the Abbé de Vermond, be placed at the head of the Ministry,—this was M. de Brienne, Archbishop of Toulouse. He humoured and managed the Abbé with great judgment. It was by his (the Abbé's) means that he had broached the subject to the Comte de Mercy, and that he had succeeded in persuading him that were he once minister he would firmly uphold the Treaty of 1756. The ambassador did not omit to inform the Court of Vienna of this circumstance, who from that time seriously entertained the project of raising M. de Brienne to the Ministry through the influence of the Queen. But as long as M. de Maurepas lived they kept their scheme secret; the great age of the minister gave birth to the same feelings in the minds of its authors, as in those of the Choiseul camp. They resolved to wait patiently; they contented themselves with enumerating to the Queen the various merits of the Archbishop; they represented him to her as a man endowed with great intelligence, with a strong and comprehensive mind, and as likely one day to make a first-rate minister.

The Comte de Mercy sometimes spoke to her on this subject, and he found himself warmly seconded by the Abbé de Vermond, who, being deluded by his attachment to the Archbishop, really considered him the greatest man in France. The Queen, whose mental vision was somewhat blinded by these subtle insinuations, began at length to form a high opinion of M. de Brienne.

On the death of M. de Maurepas these intrigues and M. de Mercy's support caused the Archbishop to entertain great hopes of success, but this time they were soon overthrown; the King bestowed his confidence at once on M. de Vergennes, a man who was a perfect stranger to those persons who habitually surrounded the Queen. As soon as Marie Antoinette became acquainted with the King's choice, she not only gave up all thoughts of endeavouring to change his resolution, but she also immediately relinquished the idea of further exerting her influence in M. de Brienne's cause, in whose favour it must be confessed she had previously spoken to the King on several occasions. Even the answer which the King made her on this point I can positively state; he replied as follows, "that it would not do to make an archbishop or a bishop, minister, for as soon as they had attained this position they would be eagerly looking forward to the cardinal's hat, and when once this dignity had been bestowed on them they would put forth pretensions to precedence and importance in Council which would inevitably lead to their being created Prime Minister; and for this very reason he would not have M. de Brienne in the Ministry, as he did not intend to have a Prime Minister."

When this reply came to M. de Mercy's and the Abbé de Vermond's ears it vexed them exceedingly, but they did not attempt to challenge it. They still, every now and then, used fresh exertions, but they could never succeed in inducing the Queen to speak to the King on the subject, though she still maintained her good opinion of M. de Brienne. He in fact at a later period did attain his end, but owing to circumstances which had nothing whatever to do with the Queen, and which I shall here relate.

In 1787 M. de Calonne, then Minister of Finance, had persuaded the King to convoke an Assembly of the Notables. This measure had been arranged with the greatest secrecy between the King, the Comte de Vergennes, M. de Calonne, and the Keeper of the Seals, M. de Miroménil. The Queen was not even informed of it by the King until a few days after the letters of convocation were issued, which is yet another proof of how little she mixed herself up in political questions, and that at this time the King certainly did not consult her with regard to State affairs, for which I again declare she had very little taste. If at a later period she interfered in them, it was rather, as I shall afterwards show, as the King's *confidante*, and in circumstances so serious that she was only too well justified in mixing herself up in them.

The Notables were scarcely assembled when the frivolity, the thoughtlessness, and the inconsistency of M. de Calonne's proceedings, and above all the death of M. de Vergennes, placed the King in the most embarrassing situation. He found himself compelled, on account of the general feeling of animosity which was displayed towards M. de Calonne, to dismiss him; but being deprived of the able advice of M. de Vergennes, he scarcely knew to whom to apply to assist him in his choice of a successor to M. de Calonne.

And now intrigue went forward with greater activity than ever. One party was eager that M. Necker should be Minister of Finance, and another the Archbishop of Toulouse.

Meanwhile, till a fitting person could be fixed upon, the post was given to M. de Fourqueux, and M. de Lamoignon was made Keeper of the Seals.

In all these proceedings, however, the Queen took no share. But the rival parties of MM. de Brienne and Necker were still on the stage, and employed themselves in negotiating with each other. Madame la Maréchale de Beauvau, a great friend of Necker's, was the most active person in endeavouring to bring about a reconciliation between the two aspirants. She held also close relations with the Archbishop, therefore she persuaded him to unite his exertions to those of M. Necker's friends, with the view of their both being raised to the Ministry.

As Louis XVI's dislike to M. Necker was well known, it was agreed that the Archbishop should be first appointed minister, and when he was once installed in this position that M. Necker should be chosen to the like office.

While these intrigues were going forward the Archbishop, who did not hesitate to make promises which cost him little, in order that he might obtain the power which he desired, bound himself that M. Necker should be placed at the head of the financial department three months after he (M. de Brienne) had been created minister.

These two parties completely beset the King, who at last began to be deceived by these reiterated addresses in their favour, and who at length thought that the election of M. de Brienne was generally desired by the public. He determined to fix upon him, therefore, and it was only after he had come to this decision that he spoke to the Queen on the subject. She answered, "*I have always heard M. de Brienne mentioned as a man of distinguished merit; and I confess it gives me pleasure to learn that he is about to form part of the Ministry.*" The Archbishop was elected head of the *conseil des finances*, which was left vacant by the death of the Comte de Vergennes, but far from keeping the promise which he had given to M. Necker, he did all he could to injure him in the King's opinion. M. de Villedeuil consequently took M. de Fourqueux's place as superintendent of the financial department, and M. Necker's hopes, therefore, were for the present overthrown.

Everybody is well acquainted with the manner in which M. de Brienne conducted himself during the short time he remained in the Ministry. His utter incapacity rendered it absolutely impossible for the King to retain him in office, so that Louis XVI found himself once more plunged into fresh difficulties and uncertainty as to the person who should fill his place. On all sides he was again told that public opinion was universally in favour of M. Necker. The poor King, therefore, only imagined that he was yielding to the general wish in endeavouring to overcome his personal dislike to M. Necker, and in electing him. He fancied that M. Necker might be disinclined to accept the office on account of his being aware of the King's antipathy to him, and when he remembered the discussions they had together at the time he was first in office: the King, however, took the best means to remove any unpleasant feeling. He sent to the Comte de Mercy and begged him to come to the Queen. On his arriving the King explained to him the awkward position in which he was placed, and asked him to act as intermediary between himself (the King) and M. Necker. M. de Mercy, who thoroughly understood M. Necker's character, hastened to remove all doubts from the King's mind, but he refused at first to undertake the mission that was confided to him. The King, however, insisted on his executing it, consequently he was obliged to accede to his request. Accordingly he set out for Saint Ouen in order to sound M. Necker. His conjectures were quite correct; he met with few obstacles, and after a few vague remarks as to the state of public affairs, and the necessity of the King's not opposing his views, M. Necker accepted the office, and did not attempt to disguise the satisfaction he felt at the cause of M. de Mercy's visit.

The circumstances which I have just related are known only to a few persons, but I can vouch for the truth of all I have stated, and I trust that in mentioning these facts I shall have completely vindicated the Queen from the reproach of having meddled with the internal politics of the country, as I have previously endeavoured to do with regard to Foreign Affairs. What the Queen eagerly strove for, and felt pleasure in obtaining, was some place or other for those persons whom she liked, or who sought her protection; but her wishes were chiefly confined to the object of procuring some post in diplomacy, or in a regiment, or some few advantages at Court for her friends. If the minister to whom she applied on such occasions assured her that in bestowing the place on her *protégé* he should be guilty of injustice to somebody else who possessed more merit and more claims to it, she never pursued the matter. If errors of this kind were committed, it is not the Queen who ought to be blamed, for she only imagined she was doing a good action in soliciting a position for her friend; but those servile ministers who were only too eager to please the Queen, who did not refuse to grant her desire, and did not represent the true state of the case to her, to which she would certainly have listened. Under what rule, however, has not favouritism triumphed over merit? When a King or Queen has not bestowed protection and favours on an object who has little deserved them, has not a minister perhaps, or his wife, or mistress, or even an agent, or some one in a still lower degree?

On looking back to the time of which I am speaking, and in reflecting what the position of a Queen of France was at that period, ought she not to be viewed with impartial indulgence, when she is known to have solicited offices for her friends, or for those whom she deemed worthy of the favours they asked for themselves? But in fact, the *coryphées* of the Polignac society often found that the Queen refused their demands, consequently they coaxed and flattered the Comte d'Artois much more than herself, because he lent himself much more willingly to assist them in their plans.

I cannot resist mentioning another fact, which will serve to prove that the King knew how to set limits to the influence which the Queen was supposed to exercise, on occasions when it was necessary to elect somebody to an important post.

The place of *grand mâitre des postes et relais* had been left vacant ever since Louis XV had deprived the Duc de Choiseul of it, at the time of this minister's disgrace and exile. M. d'Ogny, a magistrate of great integrity and worth, fulfilled its duties, but he was invested with a subordinate rank. This post, which was very lucrative, was also one of great importance, as it concerned the opening of letters, this being one of its duties. In fact, it has been declared that this opening of letters served to feed the King's curiosity with regard to private matters in families, and that it furnished him with a kind of chronicle of scandal. But I am quite certain that when Louis XVI came to the throne this particular portion of the police's surveillance was abolished, except as far as the interests of the kingdom and of public tranquillity were concerned; yet this still left the place one of great confidential importance. When the family of the Polignacs had reached the height of the King's and Queen's favour, the Duchesse de Polignac entreated the Queen to procure the *grand maîtrise des postes* for her husband. Marie Antoinette made several attempts to interest the King in the Duc de Polignac's favour, but did not succeed in gaining her point; still she was continually importuned by the Duchess, and therefore she was ever seeking to change the King's determination. At length Louis XVI had the weakness to yield, and promised that the place should be bestowed on the Duc de Polignac; nevertheless he did not fulfil his word till several weeks afterwards, and then, unable to resist any longer the frequent solicitations which were made to him on the subject, he suddenly created the Duc de Polignac *grand maître des relais de France*, but did not invest him with that portion of the office which concerned the letters which arrived by post. The Polignacs, who were very disappointed and discontented at the division of the duties of this position, urged the Queen to speak again to the King on this head, in order that everything might go on as it did during the time of the Duc de Choiseul, but in this instance Louis XVI would not allow his resolution to be shaken. He observed to the Queen that the business of opening letters was too important to be confided to anybody who lived in the great world, that this particular duty ought to be left in the hands of that person who had already proved himself to possess sufficient tact and discretion, to avoid all the embarrassments of so delicate an office. The Queen, who was thoroughly convinced of the justice of the King's remarks, declared to the discontented Polignacs that she would not permit the subject to be further discussed.

M. and Madame de Polignac were not always careful to assemble about them those persons whom the Queen liked to meet, and she was often pained when she noticed this circumstance. The Comte de Mercy, who was well aware of this peculiarity in the society of the Polignacs, joined it as seldom as possible, and only visited them occasionally, to prevent his absence from being too much remarked.

The Comte de Fersen, influenced by the Queen, declined to frequent their circle, though they had made all kinds of advances to induce him to do so. At length, four years before the Revolution—that is to say, in 1785—things had come to such a point that the Queen, previously to visiting Madame de Polignac, always sent one of her *valets de chambre* to inquire the names of those persons whom she should find in her society, and very frequently on learning them she gave up the idea of joining it. She had taken a profound dislike to M. de Calonne, and had begun to entertain the same feeling towards M. de Vaudreuil, whose imperious and exacting disposition had extremely displeased her. M. de Calonne, however, took great pains to get into her good graces; he seemed to guess her least wish and to know beforehand what she was going to ask. It was this superfluity of attention on his part, I think, which disgusted the Queen with him; at any rate, she seemed scarcely to endure it with patience. He was very anxious to be of some importance in the Polignac's society, in order that he might obtain the Queen's favour and support. Consequently he had formed an intimacy with the Duc de Vaudreuil, and lent a willing ear to this man's incessant demands for money, so that when M. de Calonne left the Ministry, bills of 800,000 francs, which Vaudreuil owed him, were found in his possession. Upon one occasion the Queen ventured to express to Madame de Polignac the dislike she felt for many persons whom she found in her society. Madame de Polignac, who was quite submissive to those who ruled her, did not hesitate, in spite of her habitual easiness and sweet temper, to say to the Queen, "I do not think, because your Majesty does me the honour to visit my salon, that you have a right to exclude my friends from it." The Queen herself related this circumstance to me in 1790, and she remarked, "*I do not lay blame on Madame de Polignac for this answer, for she is in the main a good creature, and loves me, but the people who surround her completely manage her.*"

As the Queen discovered that no advantage was likely to accrue to her from joining the society of Madame de Polignac, she gradually withdrew from her salon, and soon fell into the habit of going frequently and unceremoniously to the Comtesse d'Ossun, who was her lady-in-waiting, and whose apartments were close to those of her Majesty. Marie Antoinette would take dinner with her, accompanied by four or five other persons; she would get up little concerts, at which she would sing herself; in short, she seemed to be much more at ease, and was much more full of gaiety, than she ever appeared to be at Madame de Polignac's.

The Comtesse d'Ossun was neither very striking nor gifted with fascinating manners, nor was she remarkably intelligent; but the want of these endowments was amply compensated for by a good heart and sweet disposition, and she was a most estimable woman. She was devoted, heart and soul, to the Queen, and was the last person in the world to mix herself up in intrigue of any kind; she did not strive to gain the Queen's favour, she was only anxious that the Queen should be amused when in her society, and that she should be pleased with her. Her fortune was exceedingly small, and would not, without serious embarrassment, permit her to receive the Queen often at dinner, nor to give *soirées* in her honour, upon which occasions there was always a ball or concert, so she frankly explained this circumstance to her Majesty, and begged that expenses of this kind might be defrayed from the King's funds. Marie Antoinette preferred offering to give entertainments, in order that she might not lose anything by these royal visits. Many people in Madame d'Ossun's place would have taken advantage of such a proposal, and would have asked more than was necessary to cover the expense of the Queen's visit, but she did not act in this manner, and only begged that she might receive 6,000 livres monthly, which was a very moderate request, for the Queen was frequently in the habit of going to her when she felt her conscience easy about the cost to which she was putting her lady-in-waiting; the result was, that Madame d'Ossun spent much more than she received.

The preference which the Queen showed to Madame d'Ossun was naturally displeasing to the Polignac society; it placed the latter, too, in a peculiarly delicate position, for she was connected with them by marriage; her brother, the Duc de Guiche, afterwards Duc de Grammont, had married the daughter of the Duchesse de Polignac, and it was in consequence of this match that he had the reversion of the company of the *gardes du corps* conferred on him, which at this time was under the command of the Duc de Villeroi. Madame d'Ossun conducted herself with great propriety in this awkward dilemma; she was particularly careful to avoid saying anything which might be likely to injure the Polignacs in the Queen's opinion; she was very reserved on this point, and only exerted herself to please the Queen, without harming anybody else, and without, be it said to her honour, taking advantage of the Queen's partiality to her in order to obtain favours for herself, her family, or her friends.

How very different was the conduct of the Polignacs! They seemed to find pleasure in giving vent to the most angry feelings against the Queen. Some of these might be natural, but there are others which can scarcely be understood,—namely, that they should have carried their ill-temper to such a pitch as to spread the most atrocious reports about her. They spoke maliciously of the Queen's delight in dancing *Écossaises* with young Lord Strathaven at the little balls which were given at Madame d'Ossun's. A frequenter of the Polignac salon, who ought, on the contrary, to have been moved by profound respect and gratitude to the Queen, wrote some very slanderous verses against her; these verses, which were founded on a most infamous falsehood, were destined to be circulated in Paris.

It is painful to remark that the unfortunate Marie Antoinette met with some very dangerous enemies among those who ought to have been her most faithful, devoted, and grateful followers. They were the more dangerous because it was they who caused the vile calumny to be propagated which alighted so cruelly upon this poor Princess's head at the outbreak of the French Revolution. From these wicked and false reports, which were spread by the Court in 1785 and 1788, the Revolutionary Tribunal found pretexts for the accusations they brought against Marie Antoinette in 1793.

These observations of the Comte de la Marck with regard to the Queen give us, I think, a very truthful and precise idea of the character of this Princess, and of the life she led before the French Revolution.

The author of these sketches possesses at least the merit of being thoroughly informed, as to all that he relates, of having known most of the persons whom he brings on the stage, and of having judged them with impartiality and without bitter feeling, for it must be remarked that he had no reason to view them otherwise. His position at Court raised him above those petty and absorbing jealousies which at this period were continually creating disputes for Court favours or influence.

PRIVATE DIARY OF LOUIS XVI

Without holding ourselves responsible for its authenticity, we are tempted to reproduce here some passages from what is alleged to have been the private memoranda of the King brought to light by an accidental discovery about forty years after the assassination of the unhappy monarch.

M. Alby gives the following account of this discovery. After a graphic description of the innumerable shops and stalls for old books in several quarters of Paris, particularly along the Quais, and in the oldest parts of the *Cité*, the multitudes of which are so surprising to strangers, and furnish such inexhaustible food to book-collectors, he says:

"At the corner of the Rue du Marché-aux-Fleurs and the Rue Gervais-Laurent, one of these old bookshops attracts the eyes of the book-hunter. About five years ago a friend of mine, strolling one day along the Quai aux Fleurs, happened to go into this shop. The shopkeeper the day before had bought several hundreds weight of old paper at a private sale, and my friend set about exploring their contents. After a long search, which produced nothing of any consequence, he was about to give it up, when he came upon a number of paper books, the appearance and preservation of which excited his curiosity. He began to examine them, and was not a little surprised to find a regular journal, drawn up year by year, month by month, day by day, the contents of which, apparently, could relate only to Louis XVI. He bought the manuscripts, and when he went home compared the handwriting with autographs of this sovereign. His satisfaction may be imagined when he ascertained that these papers, of which chance had made him the possessor, were all written by the hand of Louis XVI, and that he had in his custody a most precious manuscript, the perusal of which must necessarily afford curious information respecting the habits, tastes, and dispositions of a Prince whose tragical fate has not yet silenced his enemies, or expiated the faults laid to his charge— faults which should be ascribed to a state of social organisation antiquated and worn out by his predecessors. The question occurred to my friend, how these memoirs had found their way into this old bookshop; and his inquiries afforded an answer. When the populace, in 1792, broke open and ransacked the iron cabinets in which papers were kept in the Palace of the Tuileries, several members of the Convention took possession of the papers which were carried off. These memoirs fell into the hands of a member of the Convention, who kept them concealed during his life. His family, ignorant of their value and importance, got rid of them at his death as useless rubbish, no doubt, and they found their way into the hands of the old book-vendor."

M. Alby goes on to say that, on hearing of this adventure, he entreated his friend to give him a perusal of these manuscripts; but his friend had already shown them to more prudent people, by whom he had permitted them to be torn up (*lacérés*). M. Alby, however, was able to make notes and extracts from them, which he has given to the world through the medium of a newspaper entitled *La Presse*. By presenting to our readers a few of these passages, and exhibiting them in connection with the passing occurrences and circumstances in which Louis was placed at the moments when he wrote them, we may afford some curious glimpses of his character.

The diary began on the 1st of January 1766 (when Louis was yet Dauphin), and was continued down to the 31st of July 1792, only ten days before the fatal 10th of August, which consummated his fall.

In phrenological language, he seems to have possessed in a very remarkable degree the organ of *order*. He put down his petty receipts and disbursements with extreme minuteness, and the smallest mistake in his entries annoyed him excessively. Many instances are mentioned of his exactness in regard to accounts and figures. One day in particular (we are told by Soulavie) an account was laid before him by one of the ministers, in which there appeared among the disbursements an item which had been inserted in the preceding year's account. "There is a double charge here," said the King; "bring me last year's account, and I will show it you there."

The King thus begins his diary for the year 1779:—

I have in my cash-box on 1st January—

	liv.	*s.*	*d.*
42 rouleaus of 1,200 livres	50,400	0	0
In my purse	549	0	0
17 24-sous pieces	20	8	0
46 12-sous pieces	27	12	0

99 6-sous pieces	29	14	0
88 2-sous pieces	8	16	0
136 6-farthing pieces	10	4	0
	51,045	14	0

The following are some of his disbursements:—

July 1772.—A watch-glass, 12 sous.
August.—To Testard, for postage of a letter, 6 sous.
September.—To L'Epinay, for a wash-hand basin, 6 sous.
January 1773.—For a quire of paper, 4 sous.
February.—For cotton, 6 sous.
May.—To L'Epinay for disbursement, 4 sous 3 deniers.

Many of these entries are important in themselves, or interesting from their simplicity. For example:—

27th December 1776.—Gave the Queen 25,000 livres.

And he adds in a note:—

These 25,000 livres are the first payment of a sum of 300,000 livres which I have engaged to pay to Bœhmer in six years, with interest, for the ear-rings bought by the Queen for 348,000 livres, and of which she has already paid 48,000 livres.

Bœhmer was the Court jeweller; the same person who afterwards furnished the celebrated "diamond necklace", which gave rise to so much scandal, and for a time so deeply involved the Queen's character. Under the date of 18th February 1777 there is a further entry on the same subject as the preceding:—

Paid the Queen, on account of the 162,660 livres which she owes Bœhmer for diamond bracelets, 24,000 livres.

There are various entries of gratuities given to courtiers and men of letters:—

15th January 1775.—Paid M. de Sartine [the chief of the police] 12,000 livres for a part of the expenses incurred by Beaumarchais in stopping the circulation of an improper book.
1st April 1775.—Paid M. de Sartine for Beaumarchais, 18,000 livres.

The celebrated author of *Figaro*, by the way, notwithstanding the bitterness of his political satires, and the ultra-liberalism of his sentiments, was for many years a regular and well-paid *employé* of the Court during the reigns of both Louis XV and Louis XVI.

Prince Esterhazy is put down annually for a sum of 15,000 livres, which the Queen was charged with paying him. He held some employment, we may presume, in the household of the Austrian Princess; but a salary of five or six hundred a year sounds odd to a member of a family whose revenues are equal to those of many a sovereign.

M. de Cubières, Court poet, had an allowance of 6,000 livres a year; and M. de Pezay, another Court poet, had 12,000 livres. These sums were paid through M. de Maurepas, the minister, or M. de Sartine.

Louis summed up his gains and losses at play, and entered them at the end of every month:—

October 1779.—Lost at play 59,394 livres.
March 1780.—My partners have lost at Marly, at lansquenet, 36,000 livres.
February 1781.—Lost at play 15 livres.

He was much given to the weakness—a common one in his day—of trying his fortune in the lottery. We find such entries as the following:—

28th December 1777.—To M. Necker for lottery tickets, 6,000 livres.
2nd January 1783.—Gained in the lottery 990 livres.
10th (same month).—Gained in the lottery 225 livres.

He was equally minute in recording the employment of his time as of his money. At the end of every year he drew up a general summary of the manner in which his days had been spent. The following is his *recapitulation* for the year 1775:—

	Days when I was out
Stag-hunting—	
Saint Germain	15
Versailles	17
The 'Grands Environs'	9
Alluerts and Besnet	7
Rambouillet	14
(I missed two hunts there)	
Saint Geneviève	1
Fontainebleau	9–72
Boar-hunting—	
Saint Germain	4
Alluerts	1
Compiègne	2
Fontainebleau	7–14
Roebuck-hunting	27
Harriers—	
Compiègne	2
Fontainebleau	2–4
Shooting	58

Journeys without hunting—

Going to Compiègne	I
to Fismes	I
to Rheims	I
Returning from Compiègne	I
from Versailles	I
Going to and returning from Choisy	2
Going to Fontainebleau	I
Returning from Fontainebleau	I
To Saint Denis, where dined	2–II
Reviews	3
Total	189
Hunting dinners	8
Dinners and suppers at Saint Hubert	26

He was careful, too, to mark down every month the quantity of game he killed, and summed up the whole at the end of the year. It thus appears that in the month of December 1775 he killed 1,564 head of game, and the total for the whole year amounted to 8,424.

"The only passion ever shown by Louis XVI," says Soulavie, "was for hunting. He was so much occupied by it that when I went up to his private apartments at Versailles, after the 10th of August, I saw upon the staircase six frames in which there were statements of all his hunting-parties both when Dauphin and when King. They contained the number, kind, and quality of the game he had killed every time he went out, with recapitulations for every, month, every season, and every year of his reign."

It is obvious that these statements, which the King seems to have had so much pleasure in making up and displaying, must have been drawn from the entries in his diary.

The following is the *whole* of Louis' diary for the eventful month of July 1789:—

Wednesday, 1.—Nothing. Deputation of the States.

Thursday, 2.—Got on horseback at the Porte du Main, for a stag-hunt at Port-Royal.
  One taken.

Friday, 3.—Nothing.

Saturday, 4.—Hunted the roebuck at Butart. One taken and twenty-nine killed.

Sunday, 5.—Vespers.

Monday, 6.—Nothing.

Tuesday, 7.—Stag-hunt at Port-Royal. Two taken.

Wednesday, 8.—Nothing.

Thursday, 9.—Nothing. Deputation of the States.

Friday, 10.—Nothing. Answer to the deputation of the States.

Saturday, 11.—Nothing. Departure of M. Necker.

Sunday, 12.—Vespers. Departure of Mess. Montmorenci, Saint Priest, and La Lucerne.

Monday, 13.—Nothing.

Tuesday, 14.—Nothing.

Wednesday, 15.—At a meeting in the hall of the States, and returned on foot.

Thursday, 16.—Nothing.

Friday, 17.—Went to Paris, to the Hôtel de Ville.

Saturday, 18.—Nothing.

Sunday, 19.—Vespers. Return of Messieurs Montmorenci and Saint Priest.

Monday, 20.—Airing on horseback, and shooting in the Little Park. Killed two.

Tuesday, 21.—Nothing. Return of M. de Lucerne. Stag-hunt at Butart. Cardinal
   Montmorenci's audience.

Wednesday, 22.—Nothing.

Thursday, 23.—Nothing.

Friday, 24.—Airing on horseback, and shooting at Butart. Killed thirteen.

Saturday, 25.—Nothing.

Sunday, 26.—Vespers.

Monday, 27.—Nothing. Stag-hunt at Marly.

Tuesday, 28.—Nothing. Prevented from going out by bad weather.

Wednesday, 29.—Return of M. Necker.

Thursday, 30.—Nothing.

Friday, 31.—Kept within doors by rain.

It was in this month of July 1789, in which we find such "an infinite deal of *nothing*",
that the Revolution actually commenced. The terrible day of the fourteenth, when the
Bastille was stormed by the populace, and the heads of its governor and some of its
defenders, paraded on pikes through the streets of Paris, is merely noticed by the word
"*Rien*", and in the momentous and agitating scenes which occupied the following days
Louis quietly records his stag-hunts and shooting-matches at Butart and the Little Park,
and the quantity of game he killed! Was this the depth of insensibility or the height of
philosophy?

   The following is the diary for the whole of another memorable month—June
1791:—

Wednesday, 1.—Nothing.

Thursday, 2.—Vespers.

Friday, 3.—Nothing.

Saturday, 4.—Nothing.

Sunday, 5.—Vespers.

Monday, 6.—Nothing.

Tuesday, 7.—Airing on horseback at half-past seven, by Grenelle, Sèvres, and Saint Cloud.

Wednesday, 8.—Nothing.

Thursday, 9.—Nothing.

Friday, 10.—Nothing.

Saturday, 11.—Airing on horseback at nine o'clock, by Mesnilmontant and Noisy-le-sec.
   There were no early vespers for want of orders.

Sunday, 12.—There have not been the regular ceremonies. High mass and vespers.
   Grand couvert.

Monday, 13.—Vespers.

Tuesday, 14.—Vespers.

Wednesday, 15.—Airing on horseback at half-past nine, all round the new enclosure.

Thursday, 16.—Nothing.

Friday, 17.—Nothing.

Saturday, 18.—On horseback at half-past nine to the Bois de Boulogne.

Sunday, 19.—Vespers.

Monday, 20.—Nothing.

Tuesday, 21.—Left Paris at midnight. Arrived and arrested at Varennes-en-Argonne, at eleven o'clock at night.

Wednesday, 22.—Left Varennes at five or six in the morning. Breakfasted at Saint Menehould. Arrived at ten in the evening at Châlons. Supped and slept.

Thursday, 23.—At half-past eleven mass interrupted to urge our setting off. Breakfasted at Châlons. Dined at Epernay. Met the Commissioners of the Assembly. Arrived at eleven o'clock at Dormans. Supped there. Slept three hours in an armchair.

Friday, 24.—Left Dormans at half-past seven. Dined at Ferté-sous-Jouarre. Arrived at ten o'clock at Meaux. Supped and slept at the Bishop's residence.

Saturday, 25.—Left Meaux at half-past six. Arrived at Paris at eight, without stopping.

Sunday, 26.—Nothing at all. Mass in the gallery. Conference with the Commissioners of the Assembly.

Monday, 27.—*Idem.*

Tuesday, 28.—*Idem.* Took whey.

Wednesday, 29.—*Idem.*

Thursday, 30.—*Idem.*

The whole of the following month (July 1791) is comprised in a bracket, opposite the middle of which is written, "*Nothing the whole month. Mass in the gallery.*" Some of the days, however, have special notes. The following are remarkable:—

Thursday, 14.—Was to have taken medicine.

Sunday, 17.—Affair of the Champ de Mars.

Thursday, 21.—Medicine at six; and the end of my whey.

There is something exceedingly striking in these trifling and insignificant entries, relating, apparently, to the most ordinary course of everyday life, when contrasted with the agitating and momentous occurrences which took place during the days and nights of the period which they embrace. The earlier part of this month of June 1791 was occupied on the part of the royal family with anxious discussions with some of their most attached adherents as to an escape from the dangers which now surrounded them and in secret preparations for their memorable attempt to fly from France. On the 10th (a day which the King commemorates by the word "*Rien*"), these preparations were completed through the energy and activity of the Queen (Louis himself being as passive as usual), and their flight, which the King expresses by the words "Left Paris", began at midnight.

"On the 20th of June," says Thiers, "about midnight the King, the Queen, Madame Elizabeth, Madame de Tourzel, the governess of the children of France, disguised themselves, and one by one left the palace. Madame de Tourzel, with the children, hastened to the Petit Carrousel, and got into a carriage driven by M. de Fersen, a young foreign nobleman, disguised as a coachman. The King immediately joined them. But the Queen, who had gone out accompanied by a *garde du corps*, gave them all the utmost alarm. Neither she nor her guide knew the way; they lost it, and did not get to the Petit Carrousel till an hour afterwards. On arriving there she met the carriage of M. de La Fayette, whose servants carried torches. She concealed herself under the gateway of the Louvre; and escaping this danger, reached the carriage where she was so anxiously waited for. Thus reunited, the family set out. After a long drive, and a second loss of their way, they arrived at the Porte Saint Martin, and got into a berlin with six horses, which was waiting to receive them. Madame de Tourzel, under the name of Madame Korff was to pass for a mother travelling with her children; the King was to personate her *valet de chambre*, and three *gardes du corps*, in disguise, were to precede the carriage as couriers, or follow it as servants. At length they got clear of Paris, accompanied by the prayers of M. de Fersen, who returned to Paris in order to take the road to Brussels."

The circumstances attending the arrest of the royal family at Varennes are too well known to require repetition. The King, it would appear, brought this misfortune upon himself by constantly putting his head out of the carriage window. In consequence of this imprudence he was recognised at Châlons; but the person who made the discovery, and who was at first disposed to reveal it, was persuaded by the Mayor, a zealous royalist, to say nothing. When the travellers got to Saint Menehould, the King, still with his head out of the window, was recognised by young Drouet, the postmaster's son, who immediately set off full speed to Varennes, the next stage, where he arrived before the King, and took measures to stop his further progress. In this extremity the Queen took the lead, and displayed so much energy in insisting on being allowed to proceed, that she seems at one time to have almost succeeded. The King at first wished to preserve his incognito, and a warm altercation took place; one of the municipal officers maintaining that he knew him to be the King. "Since you recognise him for your King, then," said the Queen, "address him with the respect which you owe him!"

"On Wednesday the 22nd," says the King in his diary, "left Varennes at five or six in the morning." And he proceeds on that and the three following days to chronicle his journey back to Paris, as if it were the most ordinary thing in the world, instead of being full of deep and even tragical interest.

About six in the morning M. Romeuf, an *aide-de-camp* of La Fayette, who had been sent after the fugitives, bearing a decree of the National Assembly for their arrest, arrived at Varennes, and found the carriage and six in readiness, and the horses' heads turned towards Paris. Romeuf, with an air of grief, handed the decree to the King. The whole family joined in exclaiming against La Fayette. Romeuf said that his general and himself had only done their duty in pursuing them, but had hoped they should not come up with them. The Queen seized the decree, threw it on her children's bed, and then snatched it up, and threw it away, saying it would sully them. "Madame," said Romeuf, who was devoted to her, "would you choose that any other than I should witness this violence?" The Queen instantly recovered herself, and resumed her wonted dignity.

Thiers and some other authorities say that the journey from Varennes to Paris took eight days; and this at first threw suspicion on the genuineness of the King's diary, according to which he left Varennes on the morning of Wednesday, the 22nd, and arrived in Paris on the morning of Saturday, the 25th; three days in all. But this is correct according to Thiers himself, who afterwards says: "The effect of the journey to Varennes was to destroy all respect for the King, to accustom the public to the idea of doing without him, and to produce the desire for a republic. On the very morning of his arrival (Saturday, the 25th of June) the Assembly had provided for everything by a decree, whereby Louis XVI was suspended from his functions, and a guard placed over his person, and those of the Queen and the Dauphin. Sentinels," adds this historian, "watched continually at their door, and never lost sight of them. One day the King, wishing to ascertain whether he was actually a prisoner, appeared at a door; the sentinel opposed his passage. 'Do you know me?' said the King. 'Yes, Sire,' answered the soldier. The King was allowed merely to walk in the Tuileries in the morning, before the garden was open to the public."

The following month—July 1791—is comprehensively disposed of in the diary by the words, "Nothing the whole month. Mass in the gallery." This month, however, was a momentous one for the King. The republican spirit now displayed itself, and the cry of "No King!" became, for the first time, general in the capital. On the 16th of July the Commissioners appointed by the Assembly to inquire into the affair of Varennes presented their report, exculpating the King, and declaring the inviolability of his person. This report produced a violent commotion among the Jacobin party, headed by Robespierre, Pétion, and others; and a petition against it was exhibited upon an altar in the Champ de Mars, to be signed by all who chose it. A great tumult ensued; La Fayette arrived at the head of a body of military, who fired upon the people, and dispersed them with great slaughter, though not till they had torn to pieces two or three soldiers. This sanguinary scene, arising out of a question involving the King's personal safety, is the "affair of the Champ de Mars" noted in the diary on the 17th of July, and is one of the occurrences comprised under the general entry of "Nothing the whole month. Mass in the gallery"![1]

There are only two occasions on which the King mentions his wife and children (we do not speak of the entries of money paid the Queen's jeweller), and quits his habitual conciseness to indulge in ampler details. There are accounts of the Queen's *accouchements*, more resembling the official reports of a Court chamberlain than the narrative of an anxious husband and father. They are in precisely the same style; and it is sufficient, therefore, to give that of the birth of the Dauphin,—not that poor boy whose fate it makes one's heart bleed to think of, but the King's eldest born, a child of extraordinary promise, who had the happiness to die in infancy.

Accouchement of the Queen, 22nd October 1781.

The Queen passed the night of the 21st–22nd October very well. She felt some slight pains when she awoke, which did not prevent her from taking the bath. I gave no orders for the shooting-party, which I was to have at Saclé, till noon. Between twelve and half-past twelve her pains increased; and at a quarter past one she was delivered very favourably of a boy. During the labour the only persons in the chamber were Madame de Lamballe, Monsieur the Comte d'Artois, my aunts, Madame de Chimay, Madame de Mailly, Madame d'Ossun, Madame de Tavannes, and Madame de Guéménée, who went alternately into the adjoining room, which had been left empty. In the great closet there were my household and the Queen's; and the persons having the *grandes entrées* and the *sous-gouvernantes*, who entered towards the end, kept themselves at the bottom of the room, without intercepting the air.

Of all the Princes to whom Madame de Lamballe had given notice, the Duc d'Orléans only arrived before the *accouchement*. He remained in the chamber, or in that adjoining. The Prince de Condé, M. de Penthièvre, the Duc de Chartres, the Princesse de Condé, and Mademoiselle de Condé arrived after the Queen was delivered, the Duc de Bourbon in the evening, and the Prince de Conti next day. The Queen saw all these Princes next day, one after the other. After the *accouchement* was over my son was carried into the great closet, where I saw him dressed, and delivered him into the hands of Madame de Guéménée, his governess. I announced to the Queen that it was a boy, and he was put upon her bed, and after she had seen him for a little while, everybody retired. I signed letters for the Emperor, the King of Spain, and the Prince of Piedmont, and gave orders for the despatch of the others which I had already signed. At three o'clock I was at chapel, where my son was baptized by Cardinal de Rohan, and held at the font by the Emperor and the Princess of Piedmont, represented by Monsieur and my sister Elizabeth. He was named Louis Joseph Xavier François. My brothers, my sisters, my aunts, the Duc d'Orléans, the Duc de Chartres, the Prince de Condé, and M. de Penthièvre signed the act of baptism. After the ceremony I heard the *Te Deum* performed with music, the Princesses not having had time to dress in the evening.

While I was looking at the fireworks on the parade the Chief President of the Chamber of Accounts came to pay me his compliments. The others, who were not at Paris, came the day following. Next day at my *levée t*he ambassadors came to pay their respects, with the nuncio at their head. At six I received the salutations of a hundred and twenty-five ladies; my brothers, sisters, aunts, and the Princesses were in the apartment.

On the 29th the Chapter of Notre Dame came to compliment me; as did the judges, the company of arquebusiers, and the *Dames de la Halle*.[2] For nine days all the trades and professions came into the marble court with violins, and everything they could imagine to testify their joy. I had about twelve thousand livres distributed among them. After my son's baptism M. de Vergennes, grand treasurer of the Order of the Holy Spirit, brought him the blue ribbon, and M. de Ségur the cross of Saint Louis. The Queen saw her ladies on the 29th, the Princes and Princesses on the 30th, my household on the 3rd, and the rest in succession. On Sunday, the 4th of November, there was a *Te Deum* at the parish church of Versailles, and an illumination throughout the city.

There is a good deal more to the same purpose, and the whole is as cold, stiff, and formal as a bulletin drawn up by the Court newsman. Such, however, is the only way in which the monarch ever mentions his wife or his children. He never makes the slightest allusion to any of those little family incidents which it might be supposed would occupy the mind of a husband and a parent, and would naturally have a prominent place in a private record of domestic occurrences. The total silence of his diary on such subjects is a proof of the extreme coldness of Louis' nature, and accords with the strange and unaccountable indifference with which he treated the beautiful Princess to whom he was married in the very flower of his age. Her charms, her graces, her talents, her accomplishments made no impression on her youthful husband. He remained for years a stranger to her society and to her couch; and it was more to his taste to spend his days in hunting and lock-making than to share in her elegant and intellectual pastimes. Gradually, however, she acquired the influence of a strong mind over a weak one; his indolence, vacillation, and timidity found resources in her courage, energy, and decision; and his original indifference, and even aversion, was at length succeeded by unbounded deference and submission, and by a degree of passive acquiescence in the dictates of her proud and impetuous spirit, which probably hastened the ruin of both.

But "sweet are the uses of adversity"; and the effect of calamity has never been more apparent in exalting and purifying the character than in the instances of Louis XVI and his Queen. Their latter days have thrown a radiance over their memory. Had the reign of Louis been tranquil, and had he ended his days in peace, what would have been his character with posterity? That of the most imbecile monarch who ever sat on the throne of France,—of a man without passions, affections, or capacity,—sunk in sloth, and making the most frivolous amusements the occupation of his life. The Queen, too, how would she have been described? As vain, haughty, and imperious, the votary alternately of pleasure and of ambition, and dividing her life between dissipation and intrigue. Their faults were nourished and their virtues blighted by the atmosphere of the most corrupted Court in Europe. The great and good qualities of which they themselves were probably unconscious, and of which the world would never have been aware, which in the season of prosperity were dormant and almost extinct, were roused into action by the rude hand of misfortune; and it was when this illustrious pair were "fallen from their high estate" that they presented one of the noblest as well as most affecting spectacles that ever has engaged the admiration and sympathy of the world.

THE EARLY DAYS OF MARIE ANTOINETTE

The following extract is taken from Sir Nathaniel Wraxall's *Posthumous Memoirs*, where this lively and spirited writer, whose reputation for accuracy has long since been vindicated from the unjust charges brought against him, gives an account of the early Court days of Marie Antoinette. In the height of her beauty that Queen attracted all men towards her, and with an innocent freedom she dispensed with those conventionalities to which the Court had been too much accustomed. This sometimes led to misconstruction, and her enemies made a base use of this latitude to rouse popular feeling against her.

"Two of the most interesting Princesses whom the eighteenth century produced, and who will be considered as such by posterity, were unquestionably Maria Theresa and Marie Antoinette of Austria—one, the mother; the other, the daughter; both endowed with qualities fitted to sustain the throne in times of the greatest difficulty. The former, when driven from her hereditary dominions by the French and Bavarians in 1741, found resources in her own mind which impelled her to resist, and ultimately enabled her to expel, her enemies ... With equal self devotion and fortitude, no man can doubt, would the late ill-fated Queen of France have conducted herself during the course of the French Revolution if, like her mother, she had reigned in her own right. To Louis she might have justly said, as Catherine de Foix did to her husband John d'Albret, King of Navarre, nearly three centuries earlier: 'Si nous fussions nés, vous, Catherine de Foix, et moi, Don Jean d'Albret, nous n'aurions jamais perdu la Navarre.' More unfortunate even than Margaret of Anjou, wife of our Henry VI, Marie Antoinette, after beholding, like the English Queen, her husband immolated, and her only son imprisoned by ferocious assassins, was ultimately conducted in a cart, with her hands tied behind her, as a common criminal to the place of execution. In the autumn of 1784 she had nearly completed her twenty-ninth year. Her beauty, like the mother of Æneas, '*incessu patuit*'. It consisted in her manner, air, and movements, all which were full of dignity as well as grace. No person could look at her without conceiving a favourable impression of her intelligence and spirit. The King was heavy and inert, destitute of activity or elasticity; wanting all the characteristic attributes of youth; who, though not corpulent, yet might be termed unwieldy, and who rather tumbled from one foot to the other than walked with firmness. His Queen could not move a step or perform an act in which majesty was not blended. She possessed all the vigour of mind, decision of character, and determination to maintain the royal authority, which were wanting in Louis. Nor does it demand any exertion of our belief to be convinced that she would have preferred death on the 10th of August 1792, as she loudly declared, rather than have fled for shelter to the intimidated Assembly which transferred her to the Temple. Her understanding was not highly cultivated, nor her acquaintance with works of literature extensive; but her heart could receive and cherish some of the best emotions of our nature. Friendship, gratitude, maternal affection, conjugal love, fortitude, contempt of danger and of death, all these and many other virtues, however they might be choked up by the rank soil of a court, yet manifested themselves under the pressure of calamity.

"While I do this justice to her distinguished intellectual endowments and natural disposition, the impartiality which I profess compels me to disclose her defects with the same unreserve. She had many, some of them belonging to the *Queen*, others more properly appertaining to the *woman*. Like the wife of Germanicus, she wanted caution and due command over her words and actions. Descended as she was from a house which during successive centuries had been the rival and the inveterate enemy of France, young, destitute of experience, surrounded by courtiers who dwelt upon her smiles, she did not sufficiently appreciate the dangers of such an elevation, and she violated frequently the most ordinary maxims of prudence. Her high and haughty temper, made for dominion, impelled her to regard the people as populace; and she seemed always to say while she looked round her:

Odi profanum vulgus, et arceo.

This well-known feature of her character aggravated all the errors or mistakes of her conduct, and enabled detraction to accuse her of the crime of being not only an

Austrian by birth, but such in heart and inclination. So long as she had not produced a son, the imputation wore at least a semblance of probability; and a similar charge had been made in the preceding century, with some reason, against Anne of Austria. Louis XIII's consort was, in fact, pursued criminally by the Cardinal de Richelieu for maintaining a treasonable correspondence with her brother, Philip IV, King of Spain. The birth of a Dauphin, who afterwards became Louis XIV, rescued Anne from ministerial prosecution; but Marie Antoinette, even after she had given an heir to the monarchy in 1781, and a second son in 1785, was still accused by popular malevolence, though most unjustly, of remitting pecuniary supplies to her brother, the Emperor Joseph II. Whatever might have been her predilections before she became a mother, we cannot doubt that subsequently to that event she beheld only the interests of France before her eyes. Her judgment did not, however, equal the elevation of her mind. The expensive purchase of the Palace of Saint Cloud from the Duc d'Orléans in her name was an act of great imprudence. Her contempt or disregard of appearances exposed her to severe comments; as did her strong partialities and preferences, manifested for various individuals of both sexes. The renunciation which she made of etiquette, and her emancipation from court form, though calculated to heighten the enjoyments of private society, broke down one of the barriers that surrounded the throne. Her personal vanity, not to say coquetry, was excessive and censurable. She passed more time in studying and adjusting the ornaments of her dress than became a woman placed upon the most dangerous eminence in Europe. Mademoiselle Bertin, who was her directress on this article, could indeed more easily obtain an audience of Marie Antoinette than persons of the first rank. Pleasure and dissipation offered for her irresistible charms.

"But was she, or was she not, it may be asked, a woman of gallantry? Did she ever violate her nuptial fidelity? Are we to rank her among the virtuous, or among the licentious princesses recorded in history? I am well aware that the illustrious female in question did not always restrain the marks of her predilection within prudent limits, and she thereby furnished ample matter for detraction. So did Anne Bullen; but I imagine there are very few, if any, persons who believe that the unfortunate mother of Elizabeth was false to Henry VIII's bed. I have personally known many of the individuals, commonly supposed or asserted to have been favoured lovers of the late Queen of France. Ignorance and malevolence furnished the principal or the only proofs of criminality. Some of these men, thus distinguished, were foreigners and Englishmen. At their head I might place the late Lord Hugh Seymour, then the Honourable Hugh Seymour Conway, a captain in the navy. After the peace of 1783, when he was about twenty-five, he visited Paris and Versailles. Like all his six brothers, he exceeded in height the ordinary proportion of mankind; and he possessed great personal advantages, sustained by most engaging manners. The Queen, who met him at the Duchesse de Polignac's, among the crowd of eminent and elegant strangers there assembled, honoured him with marks of her particular notice, appeared to take a pleasure in conversing with him, and unquestionably displayed towards him great partiality. On this foundation was raised the accusation. I believe the present Earl Whitworth made a similar impression on Marie Antoinette, about the same time. He too was highly favoured by nature, and his address exceeded even his figure. At every period of his life queens and duchesses and countesses have showered on him their regard. The Duke of Dorset, recently sent ambassador to France, being an intimate friend of Mr Whitworth, made him known to the Queen, who not only distinguished him by flattering marks of her attention, but interested herself in promoting his fortune, which then stood greatly in need of such a patronage. As Lord Whitworth is at this hour a British Earl, Lord-Lieutenant of Ireland, decorated with various orders of knighthood, and one of the most distinguished subjects of the Crown, I shall digress from Marie Antoinette for a short time in order to relate some particulars of his rise and elevation in life.

"Lord Whitworth is about three years younger than myself, and must have been born in, or towards, 1754. His father, who had received the honour of knighthood, and was likewise a member of the House of Commons, left at his decease a numerous family involved in embarrassed circumstances. Mr Whitworth, the eldest son, having embraced the military profession, served in the guards and attained the rank of lieutenant-colonel; but I believe was more distinguished during this period of his career by success in gallantries than by any professional merits or brilliant services. Soon after his thirtieth year he quitted the army; and as his fortune was very limited, he next aspired to enter the *corps diplomatique*. The circumstance becoming known to the Queen of France, she recommended his interests strongly to the Duke of Dorset, who, not without great difficulty, obtained at length in the year 1786, for his friend, the appointment of Minister Plenipotentiary to the Court of Warsaw. I know from good authority that when that nomination was bestowed on him, no little impediment to his departure arose from the want of a few hundred pounds to defray the unavoidable expenses of his equipment. The unfortunate Stanislaus Poniatowski then reigned over the nominal monarchy of Poland, and Mr Whitworth gave such satisfaction while residing at Warsaw in his public character, that on a vacancy occurring at St Petersburg about two years afterwards he was sent as British envoy to Russia. During his residence of eleven or more years on the banks of the Neva, he received the Order of the Bath, and was subsequently raised to the dignity of an Irish baron. But as very ample pecuniary resources were necessary for sustaining the dignity of his official situation, to support which in an adequate manner his salary as minister from the British Court was altogether unequal, he did not hesitate to avail himself of female aid. Among the distinguished ladies of high rank about Catherine's person at that time was the Countess Gerbetzow, who, though married, possessed a very considerable fortune at her own disposal. Such was her partiality for the English envoy that she, in a great measure provided, clothed, and defrayed his household from her own purse. In return for such solid proofs of attachment he engaged to give her his hand in marriage, a stipulation the accomplishment of which was necessarily deferred till she could obtain a divorce from her husband. Catherine's brilliant reign being closed, and her eccentric successor having adopted those pernicious measures which, within a short period of time, produced his destruction, Lord Whitworth returned in 1800 to this country. He was then about fifty years of age, and still possessed as many personal graces as are perhaps ever retained at that period of life …

"The late Duke of Dorset himself was by vulgar misrepresentation included in the list of the Princess's pretended lovers. Unquestionably he enjoyed much of her regard and confidence, with proofs of both which sentiments she honoured him during his embassy in France. He preserved a letter-case, which I have seen, full of her notes addressed to him. They were written on private concerns, commissions that she requested him to execute for her, principally regarding English articles of dress or ornament, and other innocent or unimportant matters. Colonel Edward Dillon, with whom I was particularly acquainted, was likewise highly distinguished by her. He descended, I believe, collaterally, from the noble Irish family of the Earls of Roscommon, though his father carried on the trade of a wine merchant at Bordeaux. But he was commonly denominated 'Le Comte Edouard Dillon', and 'Le beau Dillon'. In my estimation, he possessed little pretension to the latter epithet; but he surpassed most men in stature, like Lord Whitworth, Lord Hugh Seymour, and the other individuals on whom the French Queen cast a favourable eye. That she showed him some imprudent marks of predilection at a ball, which, when they took place, excited comment, is true; but they prove only indiscretion and levity on her part. Even the Comte d'Artois was enumerated among her lovers, by Parisian malignity; an accusation founded on his personal graces, his dissolute manners, and his state of separation, as well as of alienation from his own wife. The hatred of the populace towards the Queen became naturally inflamed by this supposed mixture of a species of incest with matrimonial infidelity; and it was to the base passions of the multitude that such atrocious fabrications were addressed by her enemies.

"If Marie Antoinette ever violated her nuptial vow (which, however, I am far from asserting), either Count Fersen or Monsieur de Vaudreuil were the favoured individuals. Of the former nobleman, who was a native of Sweden, though of Scottish descent, I may hereafter have occasion to make mention. Vaudreuil had received from nature many qualities, personal and intellectual, of the most ingratiating description. The Queen delighting much in his society, he was naturally invited to the parties at Madame de Polignac's, where her Majesty never failed to be present. But there were other parties in which Vaudreuil performed a conspicuous part, and respecting which I feel it impossible to observe a total silence; yet of which it is difficult to speak, without involuntarily awakening suspicions or reflections injurious to the memory of the Princess. They were called 'descampativos'; being held in the gardens of Versailles; where at a spot sheltered from view by lofty woods, about forty individuals, in equal numbers of both sexes, all selected or approved by the Queen, repaired at the appointed time. An altar of turf being erected, the election of a high priest followed, who, by virtue of his office, possessed the power of pairing the different couples for the space of one hour, at his arbitrary pleasure. On pronouncing the word 'descampativos', they all scampered off in different directions; being, however, bound by the compact to reassemble at the same place, when the hour should be expired. Those persons who maintained that the amusement was altogether innocent as far as Marie Antoinette had in it any participation, observed that the King repeatedly sanctioned it by his presence. They added that he appeared to enjoy the diversion not less than any other individual of the company, and was himself repeatedly paired with different ladies. Vaudreuil generally performed the function of pontiff; and as that office conferred the power, not only of associating the respective couples, but of nominating his own partner, he frequently chose the Queen. Her enemies, indeed, asserted that one of her principal objects in setting on foot the diversion was to overcome by temptation combined with opportunity the scrupulous as well as troublesome fidelity observed by Louis towards her person and bed. In this expectation they pretended she was successful; partners, such as would not interpose any impediments or delays to his Majesty's wishes, being selected for him by the high priest. That a *game*, or diversion, such as I have described, and other similar amusements which in common language we denominate *romps*, did occasionally take place at Versailles, or at Trianon during the first years after Marie Antoinette became Queen, when she was between twenty and twenty-five years of age, admits of no denial. I consider them, nevertheless, to have been exaggerated by her enemies, and to have been at least as free from stain or guilt as were the romping parties which we know our own Elizabeth permitted herself with Admiral Seymour, under her brother Edward's reign. Even Mary, Princess of Orange, afterwards Queen of William III, a most exemplary and virtuous woman, yet did not hesitate at two-and-twenty to receive instructions, from the Duke of Monmouth, as her dancing master, while he resided at the Hague, towards the end of Charles II's reign. The Duke, it must be remembered, was the handsomest man of his time; and if we may credit contemporary authority, the petticoats of the *scholar* were adapted to the *lesson*. But Louis XVI might exclaim with *the Moor*:

'Tis not to make me jealous,
To say—my wife is fair, feeds well, loves company,
Is free of speech, sings, plays, and dances well:
Where virtue is, these are more virtuous.

"I do not, indeed, mean to maintain that the virtue of the late Queen of France can be placed on the same level with the honour of her two immediate predecessors on the French throne, namely, Maria Theresa of Spain, consort of Louis XIV, or Maria Leczinska of Poland, the wife of Louis XV—Princesses so correct in their deportment that detraction never ventured to impute to either of them the slightest deviation from propriety of conduct. But, on the other hand, it ought not to be forgotten that these Queens, who fell far below Marie Antoinette in personal as well as in mental endowments, who wanted all her graces and powers of captivating mankind, were likewise, each of them, married to Princes highly adorned by nature, and cast in her finest mould. Louis XVI might inspire respect, or affection, or esteem, but did not appear, even at twenty, made to awaken sentiments of love. It demanded consequently a stronger principle of moral action to keep her in the right path than might have sufficed in the two former instances. With Anne of Austria she may be more justly compared, whose conjugal virtue forms a subject of historic doubt; neither above suspicion, nor yet abandoned to censure. Like her, Marie Antoinette remained many years a wife before she became a mother. The birth of Louis XIV, born after more than two-and-twenty years of marriage, especially if we reflect on the extenuated state of Louis XIII at the time, whose whole life was a perpetual disease, might well excite doubts of his Queen's fidelity in the minds of her contemporaries. Marie Antoinette brought into the world a daughter before the expiration of the ninth year from the celebration of her nuptials; and the cause of her not having sooner gratified the expectations of the French by giving heirs to the monarchy—a fact which was well known and ascertained—depended, not on her, but on the King, her husband. Both Princesses were handsome; both inclined to gallantry and coquetry. Anne of Austria manifested for Villiers, Duke of Buckingham, no less than for Mazarin, as strong a partiality, and committed acts as imprudent, as any which were ever attributed to the late Queen of France. She—I mean Anne of Austria—passed likewise a great part of her life in total separation from her unamiable husband; while the utmost external harmony, if not real affection, always subsisted between Louis XVI and his consort. The balance of reputation between the two Queens inclines in favour of the latter Princess. And how gloriously did she redeem the levities, or the indiscretions, committed at Trianon and at Versailles by the magnanimity which she displayed during her confinement in the Tuileries, at the Temple, and in the Conciergerie! What a display of conjugal duty and maternal tenderness did she not exhibit; what heroism and resources of mind, what superiority even to death, did she not manifest, while in the power of that atrocious mob of rebels and assassins, denominated the Republican Government! Whatever may have been the measure of her errors while in the splendour of royal prosperity, she will be ranked by posterity among the most illustrious, high-minded, and unfortunate Princesses who have appeared in modern ages."

THE QUEEN'S HOUSEHOLD

First Office: The Superintendent

Queen Maria Leczinska, the wife of Louis XV, had Mademoiselle de Clermont, a Princess of the blood, as the superintendent of her household. Mademoiselle de Clermont died, and the Queen requested the King not to have the vacancy filled up, the privileges of the office of superintendent being so extensive that they were felt as a restraint on the sovereign. They included a right to nominate to employments, to determine differences between the holders of offices, to dismiss[3] or suspend the servants, etc. There was therefore no superintendent after Mademoiselle de Clermont, and Queen Marie Antoinette had none at the time of her accession. But shortly afterwards the Queen, interesting herself for the young Princesse de Lamballe, who was left a widow and childless, determined to give her greater personal consideration by placing her at Court, and therefore appointed her superintendent of her household. She constantly resided at Versailles in the commencement of her service, and was very scrupulous in the punctual execution of all its duties. The Queen checked her a little in those which stood in the way of her inclinations; and after the intimacy between the Queen and Madame de Polignac had been formed, she attended Court with less assiduity. Her devoted attachment led her, at the moment when all the eminent persons in the kingdom were emigrating, to return to France and the Queen, who was then deprived of all her friends, and of that intimate connection which had occasioned a kind of distance between the Queen and the superintendent. The tragic end of the Princess must heighten the feeling excited by her zeal and fidelity. The Princess superintendent was, moreover, head of the Queen's Council; but her functions in that capacity could only become important in case of a regency.

Lady of Honour: The Princesse de Chimay

The place of lady of honour losing many of its advantages in consequence of the appointment of a superintendent, Madame la Maréchale de Mouchy gave in her resignation. When the Queen conferred the title of superintendent upon the Princesse de Lamballe, the lady of honour appointed to the offices administered the oaths in her absence, made presentations, and sent invitations in the Queen's name for the excursions to Marly, Choisy, and Fontainebleau, and for balls, suppers, and hunting parties. All changes in the furniture, and the linen and laces for the bed and toilette, were likewise made under her orders; the head woman of the Queen's wardrobe managed these matters jointly with the lady of honour. Up to the time when M. de Silhouette was appointed comptroller-general, cloths, napkins, body linen, and lace had been renewed every three years; that minister prevailed on Louis XV to decide that they should be renewed only once in five years. M. Necker, during his first administration, increased the interval of renewal by two years; so that it took place only every seven years. The whole of the old articles belonged to the lady of honour. When a foreign Princess was married to the heir presumptive, or a son of France, it was the etiquette to go and meet her with her wedding clothes. The young Princess was undressed in the pavilion usually built upon the frontiers for the occasion, and every article of her apparel, without exception, was changed; notwithstanding which the foreign courts furnished their Princesses also with rich wedding clothes, which were considered the lawful perquisites of the lady of honour and the tire-woman. It is to be observed that emoluments and profits of all kinds generally belonged to the great offices. On the death of Maria Leczinska, the whole of her chamber furniture was given up to the Comtesse de Noailles, afterwards Maréchale de Mouchy, with the exception of two large rock crystal lustres which Louis XV ordered should be preserved as appurtenances to the Crown. The tire-woman was entrusted with the care of ordering materials, robes, and court dresses, and of checking and paying bills; all accounts were submitted to her, and were paid only on her signature and by her order from shoes up to Lyons embroidered dresses. I believe the fixed annual sum for this department of expenditure was 100,000 francs; but there might be additional sums when the funds appropriated to this purpose were insufficient. The tire-woman sold the cast-off gowns and ornaments for her own benefit; the lace for head-dresses, ruffles, and gowns was provided by her, and kept distinct from those of which the lady of honour had the charge. There was a secretary of the wardrobe, to whom the care of keeping the books, accounts of payments, and correspondence relating to this department was confided.

The tire-woman had likewise under her order a principal under-tire-woman, charged with the care and preservation of all the Queen's dresses; two women to fold and press such articles as required it; two valets, and one porter of the wardrobe. The latter brought every morning into the Queen's apartments baskets covered with taffety, containing all that she was to wear during the day, and large cloths of green taffety covering the robes and the full dresses. The valet of the wardrobe on duty presented every morning a large book to the first *femme de chambre*, containing patterns of the gowns, full dresses, undresses, etc. Every pattern was marked, to show to which sort it belonged. The first *femme de chambre* presented this book to the Queen on her awaking, with a pin-cushion; her Majesty stuck pins in those articles which she chose for the day—one for the dress, one for the afternoon undress, and one for the full evening dress for card or supper parties in the private apartments. The book was then taken back to the wardrobe, and all that was wanted for the day was soon after brought in in large taffety wrappers. The wardrobe woman, who had the care of the linen, in her turn brought in a covered basket containing two or three chemises and handkerchiefs. The morning basket was called *prêt du jour*. In the evening she brought in one containing the night-gown and night-cap, and the stockings for the next morning; this basket was called *prêt de la nuit*. They were in the department of the lady of honour, the tire-woman having nothing to do with the linen. Nothing was put in order or taken care of by the Queen's women. As soon as the toilette was over, the valets and porter belonging to the wardrobe were called in, and they carried all away in a heap, in the taffety wrappers, to the tire-woman's wardrobe, where all were folded up again, hung up, examined, and cleaned with so much regularity and care that even the cast-off clothes scarcely looked as if they had been worn. The tire-woman's wardrobe consisted of three large rooms surrounded with closets, some furnished with drawers and others with shelves; there were also large tables in each of these rooms, on which the gowns and dresses were spread out and folded up.

For the winter the Queen had generally twelve full dresses, twelve undresses called fancy dresses, and twelve rich hoop petticoats for the card and supper parties in the smaller apartments.

She had as many for the summer; those for the spring served likewise for the autumn. All these dresses were discarded at the end of each season, unless, indeed, she retained some that she particularly liked. I am not speaking of muslin or cambric gowns, or others of the same kind—they were lately introduced; but such as these were not renewed at each returning season, they were kept several years. The chief women were charged with the care and examination of the diamonds; this important duty was formerly confided to the tire-woman, but for many years had been included in the business of the first *femmes de chambre*.

The Queen's Bed-Chamber

There was formerly but one first *femme de chambre*. The large income derived from the place, and the favour by which it was generally accompanied, rendered a division of it necessary.

The Queen had two, and two reversioners:

The incumbents were—Madame de Misery, a daughter of the Comte de Chemant, and by the side of her mother, who descended from a Montmorency, cousin to the Prince de Tingry, who always called her cousin, even before the Queen; Madame Thibaut, formerly *femme de chambre* of Queen Maria Leczinska.

The reversioners were—Madame Campan and Madame Regnier de Jarjaye, whose husband was a staff officer with the rank of colonel.

The duty of the chief *femmes de chambre* was to attend to the performance of the whole service of the bed-chamber, to receive the Queen's orders for her times of rising, dressing, going out, and making journeys; they were, moreover, charged with the Queen's privy purse, and the payment of pensions and gratuities. The diamonds, too, were entrusted to them. They did the honours of the service when the ladies of honour or tire-women were absent, and in the same manner acted for them in making presentations to the Queen. Their appointments did not exceed 12,000 francs; but all the wax candles of the bed-chamber, closets, and card-room belonged to them daily, whether lighted or not, and this perquisite raised their income to more than 50,000 francs each. The candles for the great closet of the salon of the nobility, the room preceding the Queen's chamber, and those for the antechambers and corridors, belonged to the servants of the chamber. The undress gowns were, whenever left off, carried by order of the tire-woman to the chief *femmes de chambre*. The court and full dresses, with all other accessories of the Queen's toilette, belonged to the tire-woman herself.

The Queens were very circumspect in the choice of their principal women; they generally took care to select them from among the twelve ordinary women whom they knew well in order to keep this confidential situation exempt from the intrigues of the Court and capital. Queen Marie Antoinette, who knew Madame Campan when she was reader to the daughters of Louis XV, and wished to have her as first woman, made her a promise of that place; but for several years she filled the situation of ordinary woman. A lady of noble family, much beloved by the Queen and distinguished by her upon her arrival in France, who flattered herself with the hopes of becoming first woman, was disappointed of the place in consequence of her imprudence in taking advantage of the kindness of the young Dauphiness, who twice paid her debts at the time she was expecting to be appointed first woman. The Dauphiness when she became Queen assigned as the reason for her refusal that it was very imprudent to entrust money to persons known to be extravagant and thoughtless, as it exposed the honour of families as well as the deposit to danger. The Queen, however, softened down her refusal by placing the lady's children at Saint Cyr and the military school and granting them pensions. At the period of the constitution, when it was proposed to reform the household by abolishing the titles of ladies of honour and gentlemen ushers, and the King determined to introduce the strictest economy into all parts of his own expenses and those of the Queen, it was decided that the daily renewal of the wax candles should be discontinued. The office of first woman was by this reduction deprived of its greatest revenue. The King, after consulting with M. de Laporte, fixed the income of the first women at 24,000 livres each, with the addition of the functions and perquisites of the tire-woman, whose office was suppressed. He observed at the same time that the first women ought to be selected from among persons of merit and good birth, and that their income ought to be sufficient to place them above intrigue or corruption. The plan of the household formed after the constitutional laws was decreed, but the military part was the only one put in execution.

The Queen had twelve women in ordinary.

The eight senior women of the Queen had incomes of 3,600 francs.

The other four had 2,400 livres.

They had 300 livres less when they had lodgings in the Château of Versailles, or apartments assigned them. When the King went to Compiègne in July and Fontainebleau in October, 300 livres a journey were added to their salaries to defray the expenses of moving. It must be observed that these journeys, even if economically performed, cost from 1,000 to 1,200 livres. But the husbands of these ladies had all honourable and lucrative situations, and the emoluments of places of this description were not at all thought of; the support and protection of the Queen were the only things that made them canvassed for. I remember when the poorest among them had an income of from 15–20,000 francs, and some of them from their husbands' circumstances had from 60–80,000 francs a year; but these fortunes came from financial employments or places of hereditary property, and were no way drawn from the royal treasury, the pensions granted being few and inconsiderable.

There was no pension granted to the first women; when they retired they retained the whole emoluments of their post, which was too considerable to admit of their being indemnified for it. Those who had the places in reversion acted for them, and received a salary of 6,000 livres.

The *femmes de chambre* in ordinary were allowed 4,000 livres pension after thirty years', 3,000 after twenty-five years', and 2,000 after twenty years' service.

The twelve women served in turns, four every week, two of these every day alternately; so that the four women who had served one week were the next fortnight at leisure, unless a substitute were wanted, and in the week of duty they had intervals of two or three days. There was no table appointed for the female service, except when the Court left Versailles; the first women had their kitchen and cook. The others had their dinners taken to them in their apartment.

Wardrobe Woman

A person named R—— was entrusted with all matters relating to this post, but as her service lasted all the year round she was very useful in several particulars of internal domestic service, which would have been otherwise but ill performed by women of the class who served the Queen. Her usefulness and the kindness of her mistress had unfortunately made her services but too indispensable. Some particulars relative to the departure for Varennes could not be concealed from her, and it appears clear that she betrayed the Queen's secret to some of the deputies or members of the Commune of Paris. She was under the immediate orders of the first *femme de chambre*, who frequently, in case of a vacancy, procured the place for her own *femme de chambre*. When the Queen, on her return from Varennes, dismissed this woman R——, she put the governess of Madame Campan's son in her place.

There were also two women, charged with all that belonged to the baths, who gave them their exclusive attention. The flowers, vases, porcelain, and all the ornaments of the apartment were arranged every morning by the wardrobe woman.

Master of the Wardrobe

This office, important as it may be about a Prince was but a mere name about a Princess, the tire-woman being charged with all that related to his department, and having under her orders a secretary of the wardrobe for correspondence and payment of demands. The income of the master of the wardrobe was, notwithstanding, 60,000 francs. The office was held by the Comte de la Mortiere, who died a general, and in reversion by M. Ponjaud, *fermier-général*. Its only prerogative was its right of entrance into the chamber.

First Valet de Chambre

The functions of first *femme de chambre* had in the same manner reduced this office to the mere title, and a right of entrance to the toilette. The salary was 40,000 francs.

Train-Bearer in Ordinary

This office had daily and assiduous duties attached to it. To hold it it was necessary to be either noble, the son of an ennobled person, or decorated with the cross of Saint Louis; the first gentleman usher being obliged to receive him into his carriage when attending the Court *en suite*, would not otherwise have consented to sit with him. This officer suffered continual mortification, being obliged by etiquette to give up the Queen's train to her page whenever her Majesty entered the chapel or the inner apartments of the King; so that after having borne the train in the great apartment and the mirror gallery, he gave it up to the page at the entrance to the chapel and the King's apartment. He kept the Queen's mantle or pelisse, but handed them to the first gentleman usher or the first equerry if the Queen wished to make use of them. This practice was called doing the honours of the service, and was always observed by the inferior officer to the superior.

Secretaries for Orders: Messieurs Augéard and Beaugéard

The business of these officers was to get orders for the payment of her household signed by the Queen; which she did punctually every three months at her dressing-hour.

These secretaries were also to answer letters of etiquette, such as those from sovereigns upon births, deaths, etc. The Queen merely signed letters of this nature.

The private secretary of the secretaries for orders took every Sunday from a table in the Queen's room the whole of the memorials which had been presented to her in the course of the week. He made an abstract of them, and they were sent to the different ministers. Generally the applicants got very little by them unless in some extraordinary cases of hardship; but they were, at all events, sure that the original certificates and family documents which are often imprudently annexed to memorials and petitions would be faithfully returned. The Queen took into her private closet all those memorials to which she intended to add postscripts, or which she wished to give to the ministers herself.

Superintendant of Finances, Demesnes, and Affairs: M. Bertier, Intendant of Paris

This office was almost entirely a sinecure.

Intendant of the Household and Finances: M. Gabriel de Saint Charles.

A sinecure.

Reader: The Abbé de Vermond

This modest title gives a very inadequate idea of the office and power of the man. Having been the Queen's tutor before her marriage he retained an absolute power over her mind. He was her private secretary, confidant, and (unfortunately) her adviser.

Readers: The Comtesse de Neuilly; Madame de La Borde, in reversion

This lady married M. de Rohan Chabot; her first husband fell a victim to the Revolution. He was first *valet de chambre* to Louis XV, and brother of the Comtesse d'Angiviller.

The office of female reader was a sinecure during the reign of Marie Antoinette, the Abbé de Vermond objecting to the female reader having the advantage of reading to the Queen. He did not, however, object to the women or first women officiating for her. Madame Campan generally had that honour.

Secretary of the Closet: M. Campan

He was entrusted with every part of the correspondence which did not belong to the secretaries for orders, or the Abbé de Vermond. He enjoyed the confidence of his mistress, and succeeded the Abbé de Vermond, who emigrated on the 17th of July 1789, until his death in September 1791. The Queen could not refrain from tears at his death, which was occasioned by the grief experienced by that faithful servant during the sanguinary scenes of the Revolution.

M. Campan was, besides, librarian to the Queen from the time of her arrival in France, though she suffered M. Moreau, historiographer of France, to retain the title. She came from Versailles strongly prepossessed against that literary man, whose political character had in truth suffered during the parliamentary troubles towards the close of the reign of Louis XV. She caused it to be intimated to him that she wished him to give up the keys of her library to M. Campan, but that out of respect to the King's appointment she left him his title and the salary of his office.

It is to be presumed that the Abbé de Vermond, while fulfilling his duties of tutor at Vienna, was startled at the appointment of a literary man to the situation of librarian to the young Dauphiness, more especially as M. Moreau, elated with his new honour, had printed a work entitled *Library of Madame the Dauphiness*, in which he traced out a course of history and general study for the Princess. The Abbé de Vermond, determined to have the sole charge of duties of that kind, planned Moreau's fall so skilfully long beforehand, that it took place on his very first step. M. Moreau died at an advanced age at his estate of Chambourcy, near Saint Germain. His disgrace, at which he was greatly hurt, probably preserved his life and fortune.

The Queen had—

Two *valets de chambre* in ordinary.

An usher in ordinary.

(The duty of the offices denominated ordinary was to act as substitutes for those who could not perform their quarterly service.)

Four ushers of the chamber serving by the quarter.

Two ushers of the closet.

Two ushers of the antechamber.

Eight *valets de chambre*, per quarter.

Six servants of the chamber, or rather, we may say (in order to convey a more accurate idea of this office), *valets de chambre of the sleeping room*. These six places about the King and Queen were greatly preferred to those of *valet de chambre*, because they were much more in the inner apartments. Those of the King were raised gradually to 80,000 francs.

An ordinary valet of the wardrobe.

Two valets of the wardrobe, each serving six months.

A porter of the wardrobe who carried the taffety wrappers, clothes, and baskets from the chamber to the tiring wardrobe.

An Ordinary Keeper of the Wardrobe of the Chamber: M. Bonnefri du Plan

He was also house steward of Petit Trianon. It was he who designed and executed the kind of secretary appropriated to the Queen's jewels, and which was transferred to Saint Cloud. His name and the year in which that piece of furniture, remarkable for its richness, and the paintings with which it was ornamented, was made are engraved upon a plate of copper, which was at the bottom of it. Boulard, an eminent upholsterer of Paris, was long a servant of the wardrobe under the orders of Bonnefri.

Four Valets de Chambre Upholsterers

They came to make the bed in the morning and turn it down in the evening.

The Queen had two hairdressers attached to her person. They were the brother and cousin of Léonard, the celebrated hairdresser. The latter also held a place as hairdresser, but did not quit Paris, and came only on Sundays at noon to the Queen's toilette. He also came to Versailles on holidays and at balls. He went to St. Petersburg.

His brother was guillotined at Paris; his cousin died an emigrant. They were very good and faithful servants.

Medical Department

A chief physician: M. Vicq-d'Azyr, after the death of M. de Lassone.

A physician in ordinary: M. de Lassone, the son.

A chief surgeon: M. de Chairgnac.

A surgeon in ordinary officiating for the household.

Two common surgeons to attend to the livery servants, kitchen servants, and stable servants.

A body apothecary.

A common apothecary.

A well-furnished dispensary, from which the inferior servants received the necessary drugs and remedies. All above the class of footmen, or kitchen servants, thought it beneath them to avail themselves of this right, but they had liberty to do so.

Officers of the Table

A chief *maître d'hôtel:* the Marquis de Talaru.

A *maître d'hôtel* in ordinary: M. Chalut de Verin; M. de Guimps, in reversion.

Messieurs Dufour and Campan the son, in reversion.

Cosson de Guimps.

De Malherbe, in reversion.

Despriez, Moreau d'Olibois, in reversion.

Clement de Ris.

These places required nobility. The *maître d'hôtel* officiated for the gentlemen ushers in case the Queen should happen to want them when going in grand procession. Quarterly at Versailles, as well as on journeys, they did the honours of a table to which were admitted the lieutenant and exempt of the guards upon duty, the gentleman usher in ordinary, as well as the one for the quarter, and the Queen's almoner.

The Queen had—

One gentleman serving in ordinary.

Twelve gentlemen serving by the quarter.

Their duty was to serve up at the dinners of the King and Queen, and at the *grand couvert*. Notwithstanding the title gentleman, this place did not require nobility.

A Comptroller-General of the Queen's Household: M. Mercier de la Source

This officer inspected and regulated all the expenses of the table, being a kind of medium between the Queen's household and the royal treasury; he had power upon the Queen's mere demand in case of extraordinary expense to draw for additional supplies; the Queen availed herself of this privilege but very seldom, and then only for things relative to the arts which she patronised. It was accordingly M. de la Source who fixed the sum granted for the quarto edition of Metastasio: a tribute which the Queen thought due from her to that celebrated author, her old Italian master at the Court of Vienna.

Four comptrollers of the table serving by the quarter.

A comptroller in ordinary, specially charged with the Queen's table.

Stables

Chief equerry: the Comte de Tessé.

The Duc de Polignac, in reversion.

Processional equerry: M. de Salvost.

Governor of the pages: M. de Perdreauville.

A preceptor.

An almoner.

And all the masters employed in the education of the King's pages.

Twelve pages.

Chevalier d'honneur: the Comte de Saulx Tavarmes.

An equerry in ordinary: M. Petit de Vievigne.

Quarterly equerries:

Monsieur de Wallans.

Monsieur de Billy.

Monsieur le Chevalier de Vaussay de Beauregard.

Monsieur le Comte de Saint Angel.

Chapel

A grand almoner: the Bishop Duc de Laon.

A first almoner: the Bishop de Meaux.

Almoner in ordinary: the Abbé de Beaufoil de Saint Aulaire.

Confessor: the Abbé Poupast.

Four quarterly almoners.

An almoner in ordinary.
Four quarterly chaplains.
A chaplain in ordinary.
Chapel boys.
Four quarterly chapel boys.
A chapel boy in ordinary.
Two chapel summoners.

There were besides a great number of offices, especially for the table, such as esquire of the table, chief butler, head of the butlery officers, etc. But they had no opportunity of serving directly about the Queen.

The Queen had twelve footmen.

The Versailles almanac and old catalogues enumerate all the inferior offices.

PARTICULARS OF ETIQUETTE

The Queen's manner of living and the arrangement of her time

When the King slept in the Queen's apartment he always rose before her; the exact hour was communicated to the head *femme de chambre*, who entered, preceded by a servant of the bed-chamber bearing a taper; she crossed the room and unbolted the door which separated the Queen's apartment from that of the King. She there found the first *valet de chambre* for the quarter, and a servant of the chamber. They entered, opened the bed curtains on the King's side, and presented him slippers generally, as well as the dressing-gown, which he put on, of gold or silver stuff. The first *valet de chambre* took down a short sword which was always laid within the railing on the King's side. When the King slept with the Queen, this sword was brought upon the armchair appropriated to the King, and which was placed near the Queen's bed, within the gilt railing which surrounded the bed. The first *femme de chambre* conducted the King to the door, bolted it again, and leaving the Queen's chamber did not return until the hour appointed by her Majesty the evening before. At night the Queen went to bed before the King; the first *femme de chambre* remained seated at the foot of her bed until the arrival of his Majesty, in order, as in the morning, to see the King's attendants out and bolt the door after them. The Queen awoke habitually at eight o'clock, and breakfasted at nine, frequently in bed, and sometimes after she had risen, at a small table placed opposite her couch.

In order to describe the Queen's private service intelligibly, it must be recollected that *service* of every kind was *honour*, and had not any other denomination. *To do the honours of the service*, was to present the service to a person of superior rank, who happened to arrive at the moment it was about to be performed: thus supposing the Queen asked for a glass of water, the servant of the chamber handed to the first woman a silver gilt waiter, upon which were placed a covered goblet and a small decanter; but should the lady of honour come in, the first woman was obliged to present the waiter to her, and if Madame or the Comtesse d'Artois came in at the moment the waiter went again from the lady of honour into the hands of the Princess before it reached the Queen. It must be observed, however, that if a Princess of the blood instead of a Princess of the family entered, the service went directly from the first woman to the Princess of the blood, the lady of honour being excused from transferring to any but Princesses of the royal family. Nothing was presented directly to the Queen; her handkerchief or her gloves were placed upon a long salver of gold or silver gilt, which was placed as a piece of furniture of ceremony upon a side-table, and was called a *gantière*. The first woman presented to her in this manner all that she asked for unless the tire-woman, the lady of honour, or a Princess were present, and then the gradation pointed out in the instance of the glass of water was always observed.

Whether the Queen breakfasted in bed or up, those entitled to the *petites entrées* were equally admitted; this privilege belonged of right to her chief physician, chief surgeon, physician in ordinary, reader, closet secretary, the King's four first *valets de chambre* and their reversioners, and the King's chief physicians and surgeons. There were frequently from ten to twelve persons at this first *entrée*. The lady of honour or the superintendent, if present, placed the breakfast equipage upon the bed: the Princesse de Lamballe frequently performed that office.

As soon as the Queen rose the wardrobe woman was admitted to take away the pillows and prepare the bed to be made by some of the *valets de chambre*. She undrew the curtains, and the bed was not generally made until the Queen was gone to mass. Generally, excepting at Saint Cloud, where the Queen bathed in an apartment below her own, a slipper bath was rolled into her room, and her bathers brought everything that was necessary for the bath. The Queen bathed in a large gown of English flannel buttoned down to the bottom; its sleeves throughout, as well as the collar, were lined with linen. When she came out of the bath the first woman held up a cloth to conceal her entirely from the sight of her women, and then threw it over her shoulders. The bathers wrapped her in it and dried her completely, she then put on a long and wide open chemise, entirely trimmed with lace, and afterwards a white taffety bed-gown. The wardrobe woman warmed the bed; the slippers were of dimity, trimmed with lace. Thus dressed the Queen went to bed again, and the bathers and servants of the chamber took away the bathing apparatus. The Queen, replaced in bed, took a book or her tapestry work. On her bathing mornings she breakfasted in the bath. The tray was placed on the cover of the bath. These minute details are given here only to do justice to the Queen's scrupulous modesty. Her temperance was equally remarkable; she breakfasted on coffee or chocolate; at dinner ate nothing but white meat, drank water only, and supped on broth, a wing of a fowl, and small biscuits, which she soaked in a glass of water.

The public toilette took place at noon. The toilette table was drawn forward into the middle of the room. This piece of furniture was generally the richest and most ornamented of all in the apartment of the Princesses. The Queen used it in the same manner and place for undressing herself in the evening. She went to bed in corsets trimmed with ribbon, and sleeves trimmed with lace, and wore a large neck handkerchief. The Queen's combing cloth was presented by her first woman if she was alone at the commencement of the toilette; or, as well as the other articles, by the ladies of honour if they were come. At noon the women who had been in attendance four-and-twenty hours were relieved by two women in full dress; the first woman went also to dress herself. The *grandes entrées* were admitted during the toilette; sofas were placed in circles for the superintendent, the ladies of honour, and tire-women, and the governess of the children of France when she came there; the duties of the ladies of the bed-chamber having nothing to do with any kind of domestic or private functions, did not begin until the hour of going out to mass—they waited in the great closet, and entered when the toilette was over. The Princes of the blood, Captains of the Guards, and all great officers having the entry paid their court at the hour of the toilette. The Queen saluted by nodding her head or bending her body, or leaning upon her toilette table as if moving to rise; the last mode of salutation was for the Princes of the blood. The King's brothers also came very generally to pay their respects to her Majesty while her hair was being dressed. In the earlier years of the reign the first part of the dressing was performed in the bed-chamber and according to the laws of etiquette—that is to say, the lady of honour put on the chemise and poured out the water for the hands, the tire-woman put on the skirt of the gown or full dress, adjusted the handkerchief, and tied on the necklace. But when the young Queen became more seriously devoted to fashion, and the head-dress attained so extravagant a height that it became necessary to put on the chemise from below,—when, in short, she determined to have her milliner, Mademoiselle Bertin, with her whilst she was dressing, whom the ladies would have refused to admit to any share in the honour of attending on the Queen, the dressing in the bed-chamber was discontinued, and the Queen, leaving her toilette, withdrew into her closet to dress.

On returning into her chamber the Queen, standing about the middle of it, surrounded by the superintendent, the ladies of honour and tire-women, her ladies of the palace, the *chevalier d'honneur*, the chief equerry, her clergy ready to attend her to mass, the Princesses of the royal family who happened to come, accompanied by all their chief attendants and ladies, passed in order into the gallery as in going to mass. The Queen's signatures were generally given at the moment of entry into the chamber. The secretary for orders presented the pen. Presentations of colonels on taking leave were usually made at this time. Those of ladies, and such as had a right to the tabouret, or sitting in the royal presence, were made on Sunday evenings before card-playing began, on their coming in from paying their respects. Ambassadors were introduced to the Queen on Tuesday mornings, accompanied by the introducer of ambassadors on duty, and by M. de Sequeville, the secretary for the ambassadors. The introducer in waiting usually came to the Queen at her toilette to apprise her of the presentations of foreigners which would be made. The usher of the chamber, stationed at the entrance, opened the folding doors to none but the Princes and Princesses of the royal family, and announced them aloud. Quitting his post, he came forward to name to the lady of honour the persons who came to be presented, or who came to take leave; that lady again named them to the Queen at the moment they saluted her; if she and the tire-woman were absent, the first woman took the place and did that duty. The ladies of the bed-chamber, chosen solely as companions for the Queen, had no domestic duties to fulfil, however opinion might dignify such offices. The King's letter in appointing them, among other instructions of etiquette, ran thus: "Having chosen you to bear the Queen company." There were hardly any emoluments accruing from this place.

The Queen heard mass with the King in the tribune, facing the grand altar, and the choir, with the exception of the days of high ceremony, when their chairs were placed below upon velvet carpets fringed with gold. These days were marked by the name of *grand chapel days*.

The Queen named the collector beforehand, and informed her of it through her lady of honour, who was besides desired to send the purse to her. The collectors were almost always chosen from among those who had been recently presented. After returning from mass the Queen dined every Sunday with the King only, in public in the cabinet of the nobility, a room leading to her chamber. Titled ladies having the honours sat during the dinner upon folding-chairs placed on each side of the table. Ladies without titles stood round the table; the Captain of the Guards and the first gentleman of the chamber were behind the King's chair; behind that of the Queen were her first *maître d'hôtel*, her *chevalier d'honneur*, and the chief equerry. The Queen's *maître d'hôtel* was furnished with a large staff, six or seven feet in length, ornamented with golden fleurs-de-lis, and surmounted by fleurs-de-lis in the form of a crown. He entered the room with this badge of his office to announce that the Queen was served. The comptroller put into his hands the card of the dinner; in the absence of the *maître d'hôtel* he presented it to the Queen himself, otherwise he only did him the honours of the service. The *maître d'hôtel* did not leave his place, he merely gave the orders for serving up and removing; the comptroller and gentlemen serving placed the various dishes upon the table, receiving them from the inferior servants.

The Prince nearest to the Crown presented water to wash the King's hands at the moment he placed himself at table, and a Princess did the same service to the Queen.

The table service was formerly performed for the Queen by the lady of honour and four women in full dress; this part of the women's service was transferred to them on the suppression of the office of maids of honour. The Queen put an end to this etiquette in the first year of her reign. When the dinner was over the Queen returned without the King to her apartment with her women, and took off her hoop and train.

THE QUEEN'S PRIVY PURSE

Manner of Managing the Funds

The first women served by the month, and gave the accounts of the privy purse to the Queen herself at the end of every month; after having examined them, the Queen wrote at the bottom of the last page: "Found correct—*Marie Antoinette*." Each of the first women carried home her account thus audited, leaving in the office of their apartments in the Château the receipts for the pensions or other matters which she had paid during her month's service. In the same office was a statement of the pensions. It was taken away on the 10th of August, and probably mixed with a number of other things carried to the commune of Paris. The Assembly having decreed that charitable pensions should be continued, and not finding the statement of them, passed another decree, authorising the pensioners to demand certificates from the officers or sub-officers of the Queen's chambers; as there was no longer in France either superintendent or lady of honour, the first *femmes de chambre* were, after the abolition of royalty, authorised to give these certificates. The supply for the privy purse was handed over on the first of every month to the Queen. M. Randon de la Tour presented her this sum at noon, the hour of her toilette; it was always in gold, and contained in a white leather purse lined with taffety and embroidered with silver. The funds of the privy purse amounted to 300,000 livres; the monthly divisions of them were not equal—the January purse was the richest, those which corresponded in point of time with the fairs of Saint Germain and Saint Laurent were also richer than the others. This was an ancient etiquette, arising from a custom which was formerly in use for the Kings to present the Queens with money, to enable them to make purchases at the fairs. This sum of 300,000 livres was merely play money for the Queen, or for acts of beneficence, or any presents she might be desirous of making. Her toilette was furnished from other sources, even to her rouge and gloves. The Queen retained all the old pensioners of Maria Leczinska, the wife of Louis XV. She paid out of her 300,000 livres the amount of 80,000 livres annually in pensions or alms, and saved out of the rest. Every month the first woman put away two or three hundred *louis*, which had not been spent, in a strong chest in the Queen's inner closet. Out of these savings the Queen, in the course of several years, paid for a pair of earrings formed of pear-shaped diamonds of equal size, and a single diamond, which she bought of Bœhmer the jeweller in 1774. They were not completely paid for until 1780. Having seen that the young Queen took so much time to discharge out of her savings a debt she had contracted for an article that had tempted her, and which she did not like to make the public money pay for, Bœhmer ought never to have lent himself to the belief that eight or ten years afterwards she would, without the King's knowledge, have purchased an ornament at 1,500,000 livres. But the desire to dispose of so expensive an article as the famous necklace, and the hope of being paid in some way or other, induced him to believe that which he ought not to have thought even probable. The Queen had more than 110,000 livres in gold in her apartment at the Tuileries a few days before the 10th of August; deceived by an artful fellow, who called himself the friend of Pétion, and promised to interest him for the King in case of any attack upon the Tuileries, she preserved but 1,500 *louis* in gold, which were conveyed to the Assembly on the taking of the Tuileries. She had changed eighty and some odd thousands into assignats to make up a sum of 100,000 francs, which was to be remitted to the Mayor. It was agreed that Pétion should make a private signal on seeing the King on the 9th of August but he did not make it, and this circumstance, and still more his conduct on the disastrous 10th, produced a conviction that the so-called messenger was a mere thief.

The Queen's privy purse being thus prudently administered, and having always exceeded her wants, and as she had even made some investments of money, it is not difficult to give credit to an important truth—namely, that she never drew any extraordinary sum from the public treasury. She was, however, unjustly accused of having done so in all the provinces, and even in Paris, where people most distinguished for rank and education adopt and promulgate opinions unfavourable to the great with unaccountable levity.

The expenses of the Queen's household were controlled by the Secretary of State, to whom the department of the King's household belonged.

The first office was that of the secretariat for orders, in which were made out the brevets or titles of nomination of all the officers and ladies belonging to the establishment, and the original accounts known by the name of *menus* for the regulation of the expenses.

The general estimate included the supplies of bread, wine, meat, wood, wax, etc., and the divers accounts comprised under this general head formed a sort of imaginary estimate of expenditure; for instance, the bread, the wine, and the different dishes for the table were all specified, as well as the wood, and charcoal, and everything else that was necessary for consumption in the household. The nature of the articles might be, and was, varied, but the expenditure remained the same, unless it might be in the balance. By this means the expense of every article was so known and fixed before its consumption as not to allow of its being exceeded. Sometimes, however, articles were required, the expense of which had not been foreseen, as some novelty, or anything unusually rare or expensive. A separate account was kept of such things and the expense of them was defrayed out of the amounts saved.

The expenses of the chamber and of the stable department were provided for in the same manner by provisional estimates, which regulated the charges for liveries, equipages, and corn and hay for the horses.

For any unexpected expenses special accounts were made out, which were easily examined, as they consisted of very few articles.

These accounts or estimates fixed the emoluments of every one attached to the household or connected with its supplies.

The second office, that of comptroller-general, carried into execution the orders made out from these estimates and audited the execution of the whole of the service, and of the use of the funds assigned for the estimates, and of the balances when the expenses were not incurred.

This office was, in fact, the central bureau which decided and limited all the expenses, ordinary and extraordinary.

The expenses of the bed-chamber were under the regulation of the lady superintendent of the *dame d'honneur* and the comptroller-general of the household.

Those of the household comprehending the kitchen and offices were regulated by the first *maître d'hôtel*, the other *maîtres d'hôtel*, and the comptroller-general.

Those of the stables by the first equerry and the comptroller-general.

By these regulations the comptroller-general became especially responsible for all that occurred.

Measures of economy were deemed advisable; and it was thought necessary to deprive the grand officers of the part assigned them in the administration of the expenses. A new office was created in consequence under the name of commissariat-general, presided over by the comptroller-general, the minister of the King's household, and the different commissioners in the service of the King and Queen.

The Queen's household only retained this new form two years, the original officers demanding the restoration of their ancient rights at the end of that time.

The right which the grand officers had of making out expenses which they had the power of respectively influencing for their own interest or that of their dependents, sometimes for their old servants and always for their protégés, must certainly be regarded as an abuse. The chief officers had each a secretary paid by the Queen. These secretaries had no other employment than to receive the oaths which were taken before the chief officers. The secretary of the Queen's tire-woman had somewhat more to do, as that lady managed her own accounts, which she might almost be said to farm, having fixed prices for all the clothes of her Majesty.

The different duties were fulfilled by the officers in waiting, serving, some for three months together, some for six, and others in ordinary.

The Queen's Council was merely nominal. The lady superintendent and a chancellor were at its head. It sometimes met to receive accounts from the treasurer, but only as a matter of form.

The Queen had a chapel consisting of a grand, and first, and many other almoners; clerks of the chapel, chaplains, preachers, and *sommiers,* serving as above stated, some quarterly and others half-yearly.

The Queen had also several physicians attached to her household to attend on her own person, and likewise on those around her. These different establishments were paid from the funds of the household.

The lady superintendent and the lady of honour presided over the bed-chamber. There were attached to it twelve *dames du palais*; a *chevalier d'honneur*, gentlemen-in-waiting, and a train-bearer.

The establishment of the bed-chamber consisted of two first *femmes de chambre* and twelve others; ushers of the bed-chamber, of the closet, and of the antechamber; of valets, footmen, and other servants of an inferior description.

It is undeniable that so many persons, the greater part of whom were unknown, must have encumbered the service, rather than have been any honour to it. It may likewise be observed that the privilege of the officers to serve by three months at a time, leaving every individual at liberty to go into his province as soon as his quarter was expired, estranged him too much from the personage to whom he was attached, and rendered it easy for him or her to magnify their own importance. Officers in ordinary, consequently known, in sufficient number, would have rendered the duty more agreeable and more lucrative to those who might discharge it. Similar offices, which the nominal holders sell, are not increased without inconvenience; for it is evident that through this practice many a man holds a post which would never have been assigned to him if it had not been necessary to pay for it. Even when serving by commission all who approach the King ought to be sworn, nor should this oath be regarded as a mere ceremony. Those whose offices are honourable ought to take it before their royal master himself, and inferiors before their respective principals.

The stables are a department of the first importance, as well on account of the dignity as the expense connected with it.

The Queen's stables were governed by the first equerry, having as second an equerry *cavalcadour.* There were twelve pages. They did not receive any salary, but their board and maintenance and education, which was a military one, were all provided for. The outriders, coachmen, postilions, etc., were under the direction of the first equerry; they wore liveries, and their expenses, like those of the bed-chamber and tables, were regulated by the lists of direction for the Queen's household, as were also the keeping and replacing of the horses; by which means the whole expenditure, or at least the greater part of it, was known beforehand, which enabled the comptroller-general to manage with ease all the usual expenses, and gave him the means of meeting more readily any which might not have been foreseen.

Many supplies were purchased by tender at the lowest price offered; as, for instance, bread, wine, meat, and fish for the table, and in general every article purveyed.

It may finally be remarked that the registers and papers of the office of comptroller-general of the Queen's household were deposited among the archives of the prefecture of the department at Versailles.

RECORDS OF THE HOUSEHOLD OF LOUIS XVI AND MARIE ANTOINETTE

It may be interesting to supplement this account of Court offices and duties by some passages from the reminiscences of one who held office during the last years of the monarchy; the simplicity of his narrative seems to attest its veracity, and its somewhat gossiping minuteness serves to complete the picture of the times. The writer, Charles Alexandre François Felix, Comte d'Hézecques, Baron de Mailly, was born in 1774 at the Castle of Radinghem, in Artois. In his twelfth year he became a page of the King's chamber. In 1790 he was placed on the list of Court equerries, and on his retirement in the following year the King gave him a commission in the guards. At that time the Body Guard and the greater part of the nobility had emigrated, and d'Hézecques joined them at Coblentz and took part in the campaigns of 1792 and 1794. Many years of exile followed, till, in 1804, he re-entered the French army under the new flag; he commanded the Légion of the Somme in 1813 and 1814, and died in August 1835, leaving behind him the *Recollections of an Émigré*, in addition to the work from which the following extracts are taken.[4]

The Pages

The pages of the chamber were eight in number. Their service was entirely within the Château, and did not require height or strength; so it was undertaken at a very early age, and I have known some who began at nine years old. Two governors and a tutor had the task of superintending their education; and, thanks to their small number, this education was much superior to that given to the pages of the stable, which, I must say, left much to be desired.

Formerly the first gentlemen of the bed-chamber had the direction of the pages; each of them had six, who only served for one year. But in 1781 the number of pages was reduced to eight, and they were made permanent; and instead of giving them lodgings as before in the hotels of the first gentlemen to whom they were attached, a special lodging was assigned to them in the Rue de l'Orangerie. To be received as page it was necessary to prove at least 200 years of direct noble descent, and to have an allowance of 600 livres for minor expenses. Then the parents were delivered from any further care; clothing, food, masters, attendance in sickness, all were furnished with truly royal magnificence. One dress alone for a page of the chamber cost 1,500 livres, for it was of crimson velvet, with gold embroidery on all the seams. The hat was trimmed with a feather and a broad piece of point d'Espagne. They had, besides, an undress suit of scarlet cloth, with gold and silver lace. The service of the pages of the chamber consisted in being present at the grand *levée* of the King, going to mass with him, lighting him on returning from hunting, and attending his *coucher* to give him his slippers, when the servants of the chamber had removed his stockings. It was certainly quite unique to make two children sit up to hand slippers.

The economical spirit of Cardinal de Brienne did not overlook the pages. Forty pages of the private stable and two of the chase disappeared from Versailles. There was only the great stable left, and its fifty pages had to perform the whole service of the Court, even that of the pages of the chamber, who did not escape overthrow, though their number was so small, and we were all so young that we were transferred to the grand stable.

I should find it very hard to describe this noisy collection properly, and to characterise the kind of government that obtained among them. The authority of the elders over the new ones made it a kind of oligarchy; but the harshness of this authority, the profound submission required to be shown, made it approach to a despotism, while the licence that reigned among the members of this young society, and the slight respect they professed for the governor, gave it the appearance of a republic, if not of complete anarchy. So our education came to nothing, though there were numbers of masters and professors. It was a bad thing for any one who went there without a taste for self-instruction. He would leave a good dancer, a good fencer, a good rider, but with less morals and plenty of ignorance. A little compensation for these evils was to be found in an excellent temper, rendered docile by the severe education the juniors received from the seniors.

All the right side of the great stable was taken up with our lodgings; on the ground floor there was a very pretty chapel, a great hall for exercise, the offices, the kitchens, and the dining-room, with two billiard tables. This last room was vast and dark, its massive vault rested on four pillars, it was lighted by lamps, and must, by its appearance and still more by the noise that was made there, have resembled the cavern of Gil Blas. At least there was equally good cheer there. We were divided between four tables, and the King allowed the steward 80,000 francs a year for food, light, and the fire in three or four stoves. On the first floor in equal rank, in an enormous gallery, were ranged the fifty chambers where we slept, all painted yellow and varnished, and furnished uniformly. At the end of the gallery a great hall, well warmed, served for a study. The two under-governors, the preceptor, and the almoner had their rooms in the garrets, and the linen was kept there also. Our library was situated there, and was open for two hours a day for changing books and reading the public papers. There were also a collection of maps, objects for drawing from, and scientific instruments. The pages of the State stable wore the King's livery as their uniform, blue coats faced with crimson and white silk lace. But eighteen of them, chosen by the grand equerry, who had to superintend the supply of horses, had blue coats with gold lace, red waistcoats and breeches. Whether the pockets went across or upright marked the difference of the great and lesser stables. Two of them always went before the Princesses when they went out, with a third, one of those with the lace, and who was called a *surtout,* to bear the train of the dress; they rode as the escort when the Princesses went out in the carriage.

When the King went out shooting all the *surtouts* had to be at the meet. They took off their coats, and put on little vests of blue drill and leather gaiters, and each bearing a gun, they kept behind the Prince, who, after firing, took another gun while the empty one was passed from hand to hand to the armourer to load. Meanwhile, the first page had the game picked up, and kept an exact account in a little note-book; and as soon as the sport was over he went to the King's study to take orders for its distribution. This was a very pleasant post; besides the advantage of having a special work to do for the King, like a little minister, the first page got a good many birds for himself, as Louis XVI, every day that he went out, killed some four or five hundred head. We also received a dozen bottles of champagne on these occasions.

With the army, the pages became *aides-de-camp* to the *aides-de-camp* of the King. They also carried the King's armour, while it was still the fashion to wear a cuirass. Every page leaving the service after three or four years had the right to choose a sub-lieutenancy in any corps; and the leading pages of the King's chamber, of the stables, and of the Queen had a troop of cavalry and a sword.

At home the gradation of pages was by three degrees, the seniors having, after two years, absolute power over the fresh boys; those in the second year were a sort of hybrids, called *sémis,* who were not under orders, neither could give them, but if they behaved badly in the least thing to the seniors, order was given to the fresh boys to hold them under eight taps that delivered a large flow of water into a marble basin in the dining-room. The first year was passed in the novitiate of a fresh boy, and a very severe novitiate it was. Not one of the names used in a college was employed among us. The words passages, refectories, classes, were scrupulously exchanged for corridors, halls of study, etc; to mention the others would have been to endanger one's peace; and a fresh boy who called his comrade his "school-fellow", was called by that nickname all the time he was in the service. Many people were displeased at this severity of the seniors towards the fresh boys, and thought it cruel. In truth, it was sometimes carried to excess; but when exercised with moderation, as I saw it, the effect was very good. A page never entered a regiment without being well thought of, and a general favourite.

Mass was said in the chapel every day, and two Capuchins of the convent of Meudon had the duty of preaching and the direction of our consciences. Good heavens! what consciences! But though there was no great desire to confide the peccadilloes that had been perpetrated, there was a good deal more to hear the lectures one of them gave us,—Father Chrysologus, a celebrated astronomer, whose works are now published under his real name—M. de Gy. The mornings were employed in the riding-school, when all the pages of Versailles attended. It was the most famous in Europe, both for the beauty of the horses and the skill of the riding-masters. When I came, these horses were 240 in number, but they were afterwards reduced to 100. They were all very handsome, and were used on State occasions. Intractable by nature, not much used to the sun, excited by the noise, they often reduced their riders to desperation. For their common work the pages had a set of twenty or thirty light speedy horses. I should think that before any retrenchment took place the number of the King's horses must have amounted to 3,000. The Master of the Horse in France was Charles de Lorraine, with the French title of Prince de Lambesc. His family was not recognised as royal, and he was not allowed the title of Highness. The Prince de Lambesc became a general in the Austrian service; he was a good soldier, firm, even harsh, but not the least cruel, as the Revolutionists tried to make him out. He was one of the best riders in France. At five o'clock in the morning, even in winter, he was at the riding-school, having it lighted up, breaking or teaching horses, and giving lessons. After the office of constable was abolished, the Master of the Horse performed the duties. He then wore a dress of cloth of gold, and carried the King's sword in a scabbard of violet set with golden fleurs-de-lis.

The Queen's pages, twelve in number, were clothed in red with gold lace. Monsieur and the Comte d'Artois each had four pages of the chamber, and twelve of the stable, and their wives eight. Those of Monsieur and Madame were in red and gold. The pages of the chamber were dressed in embroidered velvet; when the colours were the same the difference was shown by the pattern of the lace. All these pages also had their governors and masters for mathematics, German, drawing, dancing, fencing, vaulting, athletics, and knowledge of horses, like us. A surgeon who lived in the Rue de Chenil had a contract to take in the pages of the grand stable when they were ill. As it was very comfortable there, they went into the infirmary on the slightest pretext. The King paid five francs a day for each page, and the prescriptions of our doctors came from the Court apothecary.

In the winter of 1790 a dispute arose between the King's and the Prince's pages. It was agreed to let the time of the carnival pass, not to interfere with the pleasures of that period, and that a meeting should take place on Ash Wednesday at the Porte Saint Antoine, under pretence of a game of prisoner's base on the road to Marly, when each should measure himself against his chosen antagonist. The meeting took place on the appointed day. Two or three had been wounded when M. de Lambesse, page to the Comtesse d'Artois, afterwards known by the name of Golden Branch in the Chouan war, was so dangerously run through the lungs by M. de Montlezun that there was nothing to be done but carry him back to Versailles, where he was bled seventeen times. The affair got wind, the governors met, and peace was restored.

The Body Guards

In 1786 the interior defence of the Court was composed of the Body Guards alone, with a company of a hundred Swiss, and a company of Guards of the Gate. I do not include the French and Swiss guards, as they might be considered a garrison, and their duty lay outside the palace. The Body Guards were about 1,300. They were relieved every quarter, and during their three months they spent in turn one week at the Château, one at the lodge for hunting, and the third at liberty. To be received into the Body Guards it was necessary to be of a good stature, and also to be of noble birth. But this latter condition was not quite so strictly required, for the nobles preferred the army to the Body Guards, as these were only privates in laced coats. The greater number of privates were furnished by the poorer nobles, especially from the southern provinces, but by no means the larger proportion of officers, for their posts were very much sought after.

The corps was dressed in blue, with red breeches and stockings, all laced with silver. It was a splendid corps, with its rich uniform and handsome men and horses; and when the King reviewed them every four years in the plain of the Trou d'Enfer, the sight was really incomparable.

At the Château the duty of the Body Guards was to stand sentry at the doors of the apartments, to turn out under arms when the Princes passed, to line the chapel during mass, and escort the dinners of the royal family. They had to know dukes and peers, for when they passed the sentry had to shoulder arms and stamp twice with the right heel. The guards were divided between four halls in the Château: the principal guard-room was at the top of the marble staircase,—the sentries on the Princes' apartments were posted thence; the second, which opened into the first, was the Queen's guard-room, the third the Dauphin's, and the fourth was on the ground floor to the right of the Marble Court, near the little staircase, by which the King came in from hunting.

One of the four companies that composed the Body Guards was called Scotch from the country where it was first raised; it had held this post of honour from the time of Charles VII, who had engaged some men of that nation in his service. They wore silver and white cross-belts, and their headquarters were at Beauvais. The others bore the names of their captains, and were—the Company of Villeroy, with green cross-belts, headquarters at Châlons-sur-Marne, Captains the Duc de Villeroy and the Duc de Guiche; the Company of Noailles, blue cross-belts, headquarters at Troyes, Captain the Prince de Poix; and lastly, the Company of Luxembourg, yellow cross-belts, head-quarters Amiens, commanded by the Prince de Luxembourg. The Scotch company was commanded by the Duc d'Ayen.

The duties of Captains of the Guards were among the best at Court. During their quarter they answered for the safety of the King's person, and after the attempt of Damiens to assassinate Louis XV the captain on duty had, as a matter of form, to apply to the Parliament for letters of pardon. After this had taken place a hedge of Swiss guards fenced the King's carriage when he entered it. The moment the King left his rooms he was always followed by a Captain of the Guards, who was bound never to lose sight of him, or allow himself to be separated from him except in a *défilé*, where custom required the equerry to go first, to give assistance in case of need. Several of these officers accompanied the King when he went to mass, and a sub-lieutenant commanded the picquet that followed the King's carriage.

I must say that the Body Guards were always very insubordinate to their chiefs. Their valour was sometimes forgotten in their murmurs and quarrels about the honours due to them. At the beginning of the Revolution they were the first to give a specimen of mutiny by going tumultuously to demand the restoration of a sergeant discharged for having presented a seditious memorial against the duties performed by the guards.

Eight Guards of the Scotch company had the title of Guards of the Sleeve, and two were on duty every day, sticking to the King's sleeve in public. Their orders were never for an instant to lose sight of the King's person; and it might be said that nothing but the lid of the coffin could come between, for they had to place him in it and lower the corpse at Saint Denis.

When Louis XI renewed the treaties, signed by his father Charles VII, with his "good gossips" the Swiss, he was desirous of keeping a hundred of them about his person. This was the beginning of the company of *Cent Suisses*, and they always were some of the handsomest men of the regiment of the Swiss guards. Faithful to their manners and customs on days of ceremony, they still wore the antique dress of the liberators of Switzerland; the large slashed breeches, the doublet, starched ruff, and plumed cap. This company was commanded by the brave Duc de Brissac, who was murdered at Versailles in the month of September 1792, among the prisoners from Orléans.

The Guards of the Gate really guarded the chief gate of the palace by day alone. They never opened it till the time appointed for the King's *levée*, generally half-past eleven. They had also to know who had the right of bringing their carriages into the court. This favour was known by the name of the Honours of the Louvre, and was confined to princes, marshals of France, and ambassadors. M. de Vergennes was captain of this company, and they were dressed like the Body Guards, except the lace, which was half gold and half silver. There were also two weak companies of *gendarmes* and of light horse; one in red and black, the other in red and white, with gold lace. The first was commanded by the Prince de Soubise, the other by the Duc de Aiguillon.

The Marquis de Sourches, grand provost of the hotel, commanded a company of guards, who performed the police duties. In addition to these measures of precaution the Swiss of the Château patrolled its many dark winding mazes; they were accompanied by spaniel dogs, trained to search all the corners, to see if any one was concealed in them. Every Sunday the regiment of French guards in garrison at Paris, and that of Swiss guards in barracks at Rueil and Courbevoie, sent a strong detachment to Versailles. They took charge of the external defence, and when the King went out they paraded in the Minister's Court.

Monsieur and the Comte d'Artois also, each of them, had two companies of Body Guards and one of Swiss for their rooms. The guards of Monsieur were in red, those of the Comte d'Artois in green. These guards never bore arms except in the apartments of their Princes.

Nothing less than the whole vigour of the old Maréchal de Biron could have maintained the exact discipline to which he reduced the regiment of French guards. His successor, the Duc de Châtelet, who was not without a certain spirit of order, left the regiment exposed to all the seductions that quarters like Paris could offer. And so this corps was the first to desert their King on the 14th of July. Those who were at Versailles held out a few days longer, but one morning they deserted their posts, and the regiment of Flanders was brought up to occupy them.

The Levée—The Chapel—Notre Dame—The Grand Couvert— Deputations—The Queen's Balls

Although the hall of the *Œil de Bœuf* was very large, there were days when it could hardly contain the crowd of courtiers who attended the King's *levée*. Some benches, and three or four pictures by Paul Veronese, were all the furniture. At last all were in attendance; half-past eleven struck. A few minutes later the King came out of his private apartments in morning dress and entered the room of ceremony. A servant appeared at the door and cried, "Wardrobe! gentlemen!" Then entered the Princes of the blood, the great officers of the Crown, and the gentlemen who had the privilege of the great *entrées,* among them any of the King's tutors in youth. When the King had nothing but his coat to put on they cried, "The Chamber!" Then all the officers of the chamber entered, the pages, their tutor, the equerries, chaplains, and all the courtiers admitted to the chamber; that is to say, the *Œil de Bœuf.* When the King was entirely dressed the folding-doors were flung open and all the rest of the officers admitted, with the strangers, visitors properly dressed, and, by custom, the humble author, shyly coming to offer a dedication. Then the King entered the railing around the bed, and, kneeling on a cushion, said a short prayer, with the clergy and chaplains around him; after which he received any petitions, and entered into the Council chamber, followed by those who had the right of entry. All other persons went into the gallery to await the hour of the King's going out on his way to mass. Louis XVI never had his hair dressed till he was entirely clothed. It was a curious custom, and, I think, must have been derived from the time when enormous wigs were worn. After his *levée* he went into a dressing-room, where his embroidered clothes were covered with a great gown, and the barber servant, who had prepared the hair on rising, finished the dressing, and added the powder.

Having been spectators of the King's *levée*, let us see what happened at his retiring. It was really his going to bed; but business or a little nap would often make the King late. The monarch arrived; the first gentleman of the chamber received his hat and sword and handed them to an under-official. The King commenced a conversation with the courtiers, that was longer or shorter according as he found it pleasant, and was often much too long for our sleepiness and weary legs. After the conversation was finished the King went within the *ruelle*, and knelt with the chaplain-in-waiting alone, who held a long taper-stand of silver gilt, with two tapers, while the Princes could only have one. The chaplain recited the prayer *Quaesumus omnipotens Deus*; and when the prayer was finished the taper-stand was handed to the first servant of the chamber, and he, at the King's orders, gave it to any gentleman he wished to distinguish. This honour was so much appreciated in France that many aspirants could not disguise their disgust if they did not obtain it. Maréchal de Broglie, the conqueror of Bergen, a blue ribbon and marshal of France, covered with glory at forty years old, seemed to feel the deprivation more than any one!

Before Louis XVI was absorbed by his troubles, bed-time was his time of relaxation and fun. He played tricks on the pages, teased Captain Laroche, and made them tickle an old officer, who was so sensitive that he used to run away for fear of it. When the King came home from hunting there was a ceremony for taking off his boots. It was the change of dress that the King made on such occasions, and the customs were much the same as at the *levée*. The King's wardrobe was in a little room looking on a small court behind the marble staircase. The King's coats, garments, and linen were kept there. Every day what was wanted for morning and evening toilette was brought up in great velvet wrappers.

After rising the King often received deputations of Parliament or of provincial estates. On one of these occasions I saw him give a copy of Mirabeau's work on the Court of Berlin to the Advocate-General Séguier, to give more solemn effect to the decree that ordered it to be burnt by the hands of the executioner. And then Prince Henry of Prussia, who was much maligned in the book, said to M. Séguier, "You have some dirt in your hand." "Yes, your Highness," replied the witty magistrate, "but it does not stain."

The chapel of Versailles was in a manner on two floors. The tribune was on the upper story, with a gallery on each side for the accommodation of persons on duty who could not find room in the tribune, as well as strangers. The tribune was very large; in front it was fenced with a marble balustrade, with a great hanging of crimson velvet fringed with gold thrown over it, and at each end was a gilded lantern enclosed with glass, which would hold one person, and was intended for the Princesses if they were ill or desired not to appear in public.

It was only on great feast days that the Court went down to the ground floor of the chapel by two winding stairs at each side of the tribune. A splendid carpet was laid on the floor; a desk and two armchairs were set for the King and Queen. The Princes had chairs and a footstool; all the officers and ladies placed themselves in the rear on stools and benches; lastly, the chaplains and Guards of the Sleeve were on each side of the desk. The King's band played masses and motets by the best composers. At the Christmas midnight mass there was the great pleasure of hearing the famous Bezozzi performing little airs on the *hautbois*, that sounded the more graceful in the quiet night. The King's band had twelve children attached to it, called band pages, who served as *falsettoes*. They were sons of servants of officers of the Court, and wore the livery of the great stable, with the difference that they could not wear silk stockings or silver buckles.

The Grand Almoner of France was the Cardinal de Montmorency Laval, Bishop of Metz, a proud and haughty prelate, whose name rather than his learning had raised him to the highest dignities of the State. He had succeeded Cardinal de Rohan, Bishop of Strasburg, after the unfortunate affair of the necklace, when the Queen's name had been used by rogues as a means of deceiving a great noble. The Cardinal de Rohan, who was called Prince Louis, was very well preserved when I saw him at the States-General, though he had become afflicted with many diseases in his exile at the Abbey of Chaise-Dieu, and a complaint in the eye, which obliged him to cover it with a piece of black silk. In the time of his grandeur he was the noblest and most magnificent lord at Court.

The Court went to Notre Dame in great state on Corpus Christi Day. The procession commenced after their arrival. A number of clergy, wearing magnificent ornaments and linen tunics of dazzling whiteness, went before the canopy, some singing the praises of God and Holy Canticles, others scattering perfume in the air from their censers at a signal from the master of the ceremonies. A cloud of incense rose to Heaven, and branches of flowers scattered by young Levites covered the path of the Host, borne under a superb canopy trimmed with feathers and brilliant fringes. The Host was followed by all the Court bearing wax tapers. This noble company marched between two ranks of guards and two files of pages bearing torches. After a station at an altar of rest, in a building constructed on purpose, at the entrance of the Rue Dauphine, the square was crossed between two edges formed of all the royal tapestries. On nearing the Court of the Ministers a military band announced the presence of two regiments of French and Swiss guards. As soon as the canopy appeared all these men of war bent the knee, and the colours were dipped. On Palm Sunday, also, the Court went out with the clergy, bearing long dried branches of palms. There was a gathering at the chapel door to listen to the thundering voice of a chaplain, the Abbé de Ganderatz, who made the arches quiver by singing the verse of the psalm *Attolite Portae*, as notice to open the doors. It is very rare to meet with so powerful a voice, it made the glass in the windows of the building shake.

The grand couvert only took place on days of ceremony, and was also in the Queen's rooms. None but the royal family were admitted, and the Princes of the blood were only admitted on the day of their marriage. The King and Queen had their *ships* or *cadenas* near them—that is, silver-gilt trays containing salt, pepper, napkins, and knives. It will be remembered that one day when Louis XIV was at his grand couvert, a packet of gold lace that had been stolen in the chapel was placed on the table before him. In my time a looking-glass maker who cleaned the looking-glasses of the gallery, took the lace off nearly forty window-curtains in broad day.

The King received any deputation from sovereign courts, from the clergy, or from his own kingdom in his bedroom, with his hat on, seated in the armchair. Indeed, very often he remained standing, and nearly all the deputations made their address on their knees. When it was an extraordinary deputation the fountains in the park were set playing, and the members were taken about in little carrioles, with two seats of crimson velvet and gold lace, drawn by the Swiss of the gardens, dressed in cassocks, a livery of the time of Louis XIV, giving them a most grotesque appearance.

M. de Dreux, Marquis de Brézé, was grand master of ceremonies. On State occasions he wore a cloak of the colour of his dress, and habitually carried a little baton covered with black velvet, with an ivory knob, as a mark of his office. He had to direct all the ceremonies, and keep exact and detailed accounts of them; and his registers were often consulted on unforeseen occasions, or disputes of precedence. The office of master of the ceremonies was created by Henri III in 1585.

The last of the balls was in 1787. The King gave them to the Queen every Wednesday, from the beginning of the year till Lent. The pages of the chamber had to do the honours, to lead the ladies to their places, offer them refreshments, and again take them to supper, or to their carriages. Strangers were always struck with the sight of these good little managers, most of them with the roses of childhood still on their faces, taking infinite pains, running, calling, hurrying the servants at the refreshment tables, leading out the ladies, without seeming surprised at their magnificence, or wearied with the weight of their splendid dresses.

There was an old theatre in the part of the Château to the right of the royal court, which had been abandoned as too small; the entertainments were held there. Several of the wooden pavilions kept at the Hôtel des Menus Plaisirs were added, that could be set up in a few minutes, ornamented in a few hours, and made movable palaces. The entrance led into a verdant thicket, with statues and rose-bushes, with an open temple at the end, and a billiard-table in it. On the right little alleys led to the rooms for dancing and for play; and one of the doors was filled with a great sheet of unsilvered plate-glass, so transparent that a Swiss had to be posted there to prevent any clumsy people coming through. This was in order that the billiard players might not lose sight of the dance, nor the warmth of this fine room. The ballroom was an oblong, reached by a few descending steps. There was a gallery all round, that allowed room to pass between the columns without interference with the dancing. Persons who had not been presented, and were permitted to enter the boxes, were allowed to look on from them, and the pages took care to have refreshments carried there. At the other end of the dancing-room was the refreshment table, and that terminated the view from the card-room. Enormous baskets of fruit and pastry stood between antique urns filled with liquors, whose colour was visible by the reflection of the light. Four marble shells held fountains that flowed all night, and produced a pleasant coolness in the dancing-room.

The dresses were simple and elegant. The gentlemen were in dress clothes, and danced with their plumed hats on their heads, a noble and graceful fashion that I never saw in use except at the Court of France. Several men wore black coats trimmed with jet, and these dresses were very brilliant from the reflection of the lustres in their trimming. A person must have been presented to have the *entrée* to these balls and to dance there. Any one on duty could be present, but could not dance nor sit down to table.

Supper was served at midnight in the old theatre. There were twelve places at each table, and people of the same set kept together. The King's and Queen's footmen waited. The most delicate and costly dishes were provided in plenty. The royal family often had their supper at the ball; the King never came there till after he had had his supper at nine o'clock in his own rooms. He stayed till one o'clock and went to bed after a game at tric-trac in a little room intended for that amusement. Though Louis XVI was so good-natured and simple, his rank and his virtues were a little oppressive. He retired early because he knew that the ball was much gayer and more lively when he was gone. The strictness of the etiquette diminished; the old young men, whose years were too many for mingling in these pleasures, would then take the liberty of enjoying a country dance, or a "Sir Roger". They could be distinguished by their bare heads, for they were not supposed to come for the sake of dancing, and were not dressed accordingly. The Queen, Madame Elizabeth, the Comte d'Artois, and the Duc de Bourbon, who had given up dancing, would do it once in a way for a wonder, and there never had been so much decorum at the Court and at the same time so much bright liveliness.

The Two Trianons—Fontainebleau—Marly—Versailles

The cost of Petit Trianon has been very much exaggerated. It had been built by Louis XV, and only embellishments introduced by a change of tastes could be set down to the subsequent reign. The house was a square detached block ornamented in the Corinthian style, and too small to afford more than the necessary lodging for a Queen of France. A dining-room, drawing-room, bedroom, and some dressing-rooms composed the first floor; the second only contained some small rooms for Madame Elizabeth and the ladies of the palace. The furniture was rather elegant than magnificent. The bedroom had muslin hangings, with embroidery and brilliant colours that in their way rivalled the most practised pencil. Some portraits of the children of Maria Theresa reminded the Queen of her family, amongst whom she might have found more happiness, if less splendour. But these pictures must have inspired serious reflections, for all the Princes and Princesses were represented as monks and nuns digging their own graves. The only luxury of the adjoining dressing-room consisted in two looking-glasses that rose out of the floor by a spring, and could darken the room by covering the windows. The famous table that was once in the Château de Choisy was fitted in the dining-room; by means of balance-weights and other mechanism it went down into the lower story to be laid with a fresh course.

One side of the block of Trianon looked over a garden laid out in the taste of Le Nôtre. Orange trees and statues alternated in niches of verdure, and adorned a grass plot with a theatre at the end; in front of the house was a lawn, with a rock at the end shaded by pines, cypresses, and larches, and a rustic bridge thrown over the stream. This wild prospect made that on the third side of the house seem more sweet, where the Temple of Love, containing a splendid statue of the god by Bouchardon, stood amid flowers and laurel groves. Near the mansion was a game of roundabout, in a great Chinese pavilion, in which the brightness of the sun's rays was reflected from gold and blue; these Chinese figures seemed to put the machine in motion, but it was really turned by persons concealed in a cellar.

At the end of the garden at Trianon, on the borders of the stream, were a number of cottages, rustic without, but elegant, and even exquisite, within. One of the huts was a dairy, and the cream, contained in China vases, placed on tables of white marble, was kept cool by the stream flowing through the room. Close by was the real farm, where the Queen had a splendid herd of Swiss cows, that grazed in the meadows around. In the midst of the little hamlet stood Marlborough's Tower, commanding the neighbourhood; the exterior stair, bordered with stocks and geraniums, seemed like a garden in the air.

This Trianon was called "le petit" to distinguish it from the Grand Trianon, standing very near and built by Louis X in Italian taste. It is composed of a ground floor alone, with balustrades and statues above it, forming two wings joined by a great peristyle of columns of red and green marble ... I only saw it occupied twice. The first time the body of the youngest daughter of Louis XVI[5] was placed there; the second time it served as the quarters of the Embassy of Tippoo Sahib. The gardens were large, but presented no noteworthy points except an amphitheatre of turf; with busts of the Roman Emperors, a copy of the Laocoon, and an ancient head of Minerva.

The Court only made one visit to Fontainebleau while I was at Versailles, and that was in October 1786. It only lasted till November 1 on account of the accident that befell M. de Tourzel, grand provost of the hotel, who was run away with while hunting with the King, and his head dashed against a pointed branch, that penetrated the skull. The wound was so severe that he could not be taken to the town, but was laid in the house of a gamekeeper until one of the great huts that were always conveyed after the King could be erected in the forest. He only survived for some days, and the visit was shortened by the general sorrow occasioned by his death, almost in the King's presence. The interest the King took in the family of M. de Tourzel was increased by this fatal accident, and no doubt it was an additional reason for the selection of Madame de Tourzel to succeed Madame de Polignac as governess to the children of France.

The visits to Fontainebleau took place in the autumn, to take advantage of the excellent opportunities for sport in the enormous forest, full of beautiful trees, and with rocks really remarkable, as they were found in a nearly flat country. These sequestered glades were a great resort of stags and boars, the former in herds of seventy or eighty. There was a great charm in the Forest of Fontainebleau towards the close of day; the great trees seemed to murmur their ancient recollections in the breeze; the gigantic masses of rock stood out in the twilight, and the stag passed by as quickly as lightning, emitting his hoarse and terrible cry.

The King's lodgings were in the circular part of the court called that of the Donjon. They were reached from that side, or by the Gallery of Francis I, connected with the chapel, and the grand flight of steps of the horse-shoe staircase in the court of the White Horse. I do not remember that these rooms contained anything curious; the furniture was very plain. But I have preserved a recollection of a little dressing-room of the Queen's, furnished in Oriental style and lit by lamps placed in a chamber separated from the room by a sheet of glass draped with taffety, the colour of which was often varied, giving a soft and pleasant light.

In the Gallery of the Stags, leading from the Oval Court to that of the Princes, and named from its view of the Wood of Stags, Queen Christina of Sweden ordered the murder of her grand equerry, the Marquis de Monaldeschi. I have seen a little stone in the gallery with a cross and sacred monogram engraved on it, which was placed on the spot where the unfortunate man received his death-blow. The Oval or Donjon Court was separated from the Court of the Fountains by a great portico surmounted by an open dome, under which Louis XIII was baptized. The anxiety of the people to behold this scion of a beloved King caused Henri IV to select this place rather than a church.

Marie Antoinette often went to Fontainebleau by water. She embarked at Choisy and ascended the Seine as far as Melun in a splendid yacht, commodious as a large house, with saloons, kitchens, and a quantity of trees in boxes making a sort of garden in it. The "voyages to Fontainebleau" were ultimately put a stop to for economical reasons.

Half-way from Saint Germain to Versailles was the little Château of Marly, at the bottom of a valley; in building it Louis XIV mocked at the laws of nature. Machines were invented to carry thither the largest trees, roots and all, so that they might be more speedily enjoyed. Work went on day and night; there was an endeavour to perform prodigies. It was necessary to descend a steep hill to reach the Château. At the top were two circular buildings and the stables. The main building of the Château was a square block with steps all round it. This pavilion was considered the palace of the God of Day, and twelve smaller ones placed round the lawn represented the signs of the zodiac. The frescoes on the walls were of allegorical subjects bearing on this idea. The gardens of Marly, "where the rain does not wet", in the words of a courtier of Louis XIV, were full of statues and fountains; at the end of the lawn a great balcony overlooked a horse-pond and the road to Saint Germain; there were the two fine marble horses made by Guillaume Couston, afterwards taken to Paris. Not far from Marly was the famous hydraulic machine invented by the Chevalier de Ville, and constructed by Rennequin Sualem. By a combination of wheels, pumps, and a multitude of pipes and aqueducts, it raised the water 500 feet, to the arcades of Marly, and fed the fountains in the town of Versailles, as well as the basins in the park—the wonder of strangers. For the time of its construction, in 1682, it was a wonderful work.

Louis XIII bought the site of a mill on an elevation, and built a small house there for a hunting-box. Louis XIV, fond of the arts, and undeterred by difficulties, selected the spot to make it the abode of Kings; the greater part was finished in less than seven years, and it was inhabited in 1687. The effects of this hasty construction were soon seen; in less than a century after its construction there were apprehensions that it would crumble away in many spots. The foundations had been laid upon made ground, and were not secure; the building was shored up in several places. I saw the beam that supported the alcove in the King's room falling into dust, and if it had not been observed the King might some night have found himself on the ground floor, in the presence of the Captain of his Guard. A bed was put in the large dressing-room for him, and he slept there for six months. The amount of expense incurred at Versailles was long made a pretext for the war declared against the ancient dynasty. Mirabeau asserts that Maréchal de Belle-Isle stopped in a fright when he had reckoned up to 1,200 millions. One of the principal faults to be found with the Château is that there is no entrance worthy of the edifice. A multitude of receding angles on the side to the court reduce the front to seven windows, and the only object of this arrangement was to preserve the little mansion of Louis XIII. The façade towards the garden is much superior, as the breadth is 600 yards. The real entrance to the apartments was by the splendid marble staircase; but it is at the side reached by three narrow arcades, and only leads to the King's antechambers, and the way into the gallery is only by a door in the middle, so that the King's rooms were reached without enjoying the beauty of the grand rooms. Those who had not the right to remain in the King's apartments passed at once into the gallery—the finest in Europe—where the pencil of Le Brun portrayed the victories of Louis XIV, and where an immense number of doors of looking-glass repeated in perspective the view from the windows overlooking the garden. In this gallery strangers who came from the farthest parts of France to see the King once in their lives stood to await the moment when, on Sunday, the whole royal family issued from the King's rooms to go to mass, and crossed the eight halls on their way. These halls were named, from the paintings on the ceiling, Diana, Mercury, Mars, etc., and as they were passages rather than rooms, only occupied permanently by the Swiss guards, they had no other ornaments but the pictures, lustres, and gilding. Turning to the right, the first hall was that of Apollo. There was a throne in it under a canopy of crimson damask, but it was never used. In this room there was a glass thermometer fixed in the window, and the King came several times a day to ascertain the temperature; a servant of the Château noted it in his book three times a day. There was a clock in the Hall of Mercury, formerly of much note; at every hour cocks crowed and flapped their wings, Louis XIV issued from a temple, and Fame, in a cloud, came and crowned him to the sound of a chime. A fine picture of the Queen by Madame Le Brun was placed for a time in the Hall of Mars; she had, with her surprising power of representing texture, portrayed the Queen in a dress of flame-coloured velvet, having her second son on her knees, and her eldest girl leaning on her shoulder, while the Dauphin pointed to his little sister asleep in her cradle. The figure of the youngest Princess was effaced after her death; and as her eldest brother soon followed her to the tomb the picture recalled painful remembrances, and was removed.

The Château of Versailles may be compared to an immense labyrinth, from the number of galleries, corridors, staircases, and rooms that it contains. A person needed to be very well used to it to find his way about, and many small towns had not so large a population.

The bedroom of Louis XIV was entered from the *Œil de Bœuf*, but in subsequent reigns it became the waiting-room. This great hall was the centre of the Château, and the end of the shabby little court called the Marble Court, with a great balcony over it. Above was placed the real *memento mori*, not, as in Persia, a slave to remind the sovereign of mortality, but a dial with the hand fixed at the hour of the death of the last monarch. Louis XV died on 11th May 1774, at three o'clock in the afternoon. I have found, by writing to Versailles, that the hand is in the same position as when I went away. Just opposite was the real sleeping-room of the King, with blue furniture and a bed ornamented with feathers, helmets, and gilding. Two magnificent golden candlesticks made by Père Germain were placed on a cabinet; between these two artistic marvels a single plaster figure attracted the looks of that kind father, Louis XVI—his daughter as an infant, praying; when accidentally broken he had it remodelled. In the middle of the great dressing-room was a small model of the Place Louis XV, and the famous clock of Passemant, seven feet high, which, besides showing the time, displayed the years, months, phases of the moon, and evolutions of the planets. The King always sat up till after midnight on New Year's Eve to see his clock make all its changes. A splendid pot of stocks, made of valuable china, which stood in one of the rooms, was broken by an unlucky visitor. The man was short-sighted, and not seeing the glass shade over the vase broke it with his forehead, and the splinters broke the flower into fragments. I mention this little event, for the poor man turned faint and gave his name and address very sorrowfully, fancying that the drawbridge of some fortress would be lowered for him. But Louis XVI sent to console and relieve him, though the accident cost more than a million crowns. In the King's private library he usually worked at a little bureau placed in the embrasure of the window. His amusement during his work was to look at the people crossing the courts; and visitors might convince themselves by the sight of the books in use lying on the floor and the numbers of papers strewed around, that Louis XVI did not spend his time in smith's work, in getting drunk, or in beating his servants, as his slanderers pretended.

Anecdotes of the King

When on his way to hunt, the King went out by a stair near the waiting-room of the servants of the Château. There was a guard-room at the bottom, at the entrance to which Louis XV was struck by Damiens, who had been hidden in a little passage leading to the Court of Stags. The assassins of our day directed their violence more against the Crown than the person of Louis XVI, or that might have been easily reached. Every evening, returning from supper with Madame, he would cross the courts or large dark galleries wrapped in a grey cloak, with an umbrella if it rained, and only accompanied by two servants bearing torches. In the little chambers round the Court of Stags the King had a whole set of geographical maps, plans in relief, models of ships, a little observatory, and the famous forge that public report would have it he was constantly using. I can assert that it looked very much neglected; and after mid-day the King was dressed in a manner that precluded such violent exercise. At any rate, his supposed talent was not always useless; for when a fire broke out in a set of apartments near the King's, and the door could not be beaten down, he came to the rescue with his tools and picked the lock soon enough for the fire to be extinguished, though not to save the life of the person in charge—an old woman, who had gone to sleep by the hearth. All these rooms were well lighted but badly warmed, for the King disliked heat. In summer, cloths were spread over the grand balcony of the *levée* room and watered with syringes, and the King would often push some one against them in joke to get a wetting, especially any one who seemed to care much for the extreme elegance of the large *frisure* then in vogue. His constitutional vigour made his proceedings rough, and what he only meant for a small joke would sometimes leave painful traces;[6] but he would have denied himself any amusement if he could have supposed it capable of giving the slightest pain, and during nearly six years at Court I never saw the King in the smallest instance act with intentional rudeness to the humblest of his servants.

His only passion was for hunting, and it was needful for his health. He used himself to select the meets, and kept notes of the stags hunted, of their age, and of the circumstances of their capture.[7] He also very often went out shooting, and although short-sighted shot very well, and often came back with his face blackened with powder. He was a bad rider and wanting in confidence. The Queen, on the other hand, rode on horseback with much elegance and boldness.

During the winter the various companies acting in Paris came to Versailles to wait on the Court. Tuesday was devoted to tragedy, Thursday to comedy, Friday to the comic opera. The grand opera was only performed five or six times each winter. Louis XVI preferred tragedy or comedy, and attended very constantly; knowing and appreciating all the great poets, and possessed of an excellent memory, the King there found himself in his element, while from his unmusical ear he was unable to enjoy the opera, and could not help yawning. I never heard any one sing so much out of tune as the poor King. In the Versailles theatre in 1788 I heard a joke that showed how far disrespect for the royal family had already advanced, they being present in a box taken for them. Passiello's opera called *King Theodore at Venice* was going on. In the scene where the King's servant, telling their host of his master's pecuniary embarrassment, several times repeats, "What shall we do?" a voice from the pit replied "Assemble the Notables!"—*Recollections of a Page*.

ROYAL ETIQUETTE

Madame Campan observes that before the Revolution there were customs and even words in use at Versailles with which few people were acquainted. The King's dinner was called *the King's meat*. Two of the Body Guard accompanied the attendants who carried the dinner; every one rose as they passed through the halls, saying, "There is the King's meat." All precautionary duties were distinguished by the words *in case*. Some chemises and handkerchiefs kept in readiness in a basket in the King's or Queen's apartments, in case their Majesties should wish to change their linen without sending to the wardrobe, constituted the packet *in case*. Their clothes, brought in great baskets, or cloths of green taffety were called the King's or Queen's *ready*. Thus the attendants would ask, "Is the King's *ready* come?" One of the guards might be heard to say, "I am *in case* in the forest of Saint Germain." In the evening they always brought the Queen a large bowl of broth, a cold roast fowl, one bottle of wine, one of orgeat, one of lemonade, and some other articles, which were called the *in case* for the night. An old medical gentleman, who had been physician in ordinary to Louis XIV, and was still living at the time of the marriage of Louis XV, told M. Campan's father an anecdote which seems too remarkable to have remained unknown; nevertheless he was a man of honour, incapable of inventing this story. His name was Lafosse. He said that Louis XIV was informed that the officers of his table evinced, in the most disdainful and offensive manner, the mortification they felt at being obliged to eat at the table of the comptroller of the kitchen along with Molière, *valet de chambre* to his Majesty, because Molière had performed on the stage; and that this celebrated author consequently declined appearing at that table. Louis XIV, determined to put an end to insults which ought never to have been offered to one of the greatest geniuses of the age, said to him one morning at the hour of his private *levée*, "They say you live very poorly here, Molière; and that the officers of my chamber do not find you good enough to eat with them. Perhaps you are hungry; for my part I awoke with a very good appetite this morning: sit down at this table. Serve up my *in case* for the night there." The King then cutting up his fowl, and ordering Molière to sit down, helped him to a wing, at the same time taking one for himself, and ordered the persons entitled to familiar entrance, that is to say, the most distinguished and favourite people at Court, to be admitted. "You see me," said the King to them, "engaged in entertaining Molière, whom my *valets de chambre* do not consider sufficiently good company for them." From that time Molière never had occasion to appear at the valets' table; the whole Court was forward enough to send him invitations.[8]

M. de Lafosse, used also to relate that a brigade-major of the Body Guard, being ordered to place the company in the little theatre at Versailles, very roughly turned out one of the King's comptrollers who had taken his seat on one of the benches, a place to which his newly acquired office entitled him. In vain he insisted on his quality and his right. The altercation was ended by the brigade-major in these words—"Gentlemen Body Guards; do your duty." In this case their duty was to take the party and turn him out at the door. This comptroller, who had paid 60 or 80,000 francs for his place, was a man of a good family, and had had the honour of serving his Majesty five-and-twenty years in one of his regiments; thus disgracefully driven out of the hall, he placed himself in the King's way in the great hall of the guards, and bowing to his Majesty requested him to vindicate the honour of an old soldier who had wished to end his days in his Prince's civil employment, now that age had obliged him to relinquish his military service. The King stopped, heard his story, and then ordered him to follow him. His Majesty attended the representation in a sort of amphitheatre, in which his armchair was placed; behind him was a row of stools for the Captain of the Guards, the first gentleman of the chamber, and other great officers. The brigade-major was entitled to one of these places; the King stopped opposite the seat which ought to have been occupied by that officer and said to the comptroller, "Take, sir, for this evening, the place near my person of him who has offended you, and let the expression of my displeasure at this unjust affront satisfy you instead of any other reparation."

During the latter years of the reign of Louis XIV he never went out but in a chair carried by porters, and he showed a great regard for a man of the name of D'Aigremont, one of those porters who always went in front and opened the door of the chair. The slightest preference shown by sovereigns, even to the meanest of their servants, never fails to excite observation.[9] The King had done something for this man's numerous family, and frequently talked to him. An Abbé belonging to the chapel thought proper to request D'Aigremont to present a memorial to the King, in which he requested his Majesty to grant him a benefice. Louis XIV did not approve of the liberty thus taken by his chairman, and said to him, in a very angry tone, "D'Aigremont, you have been made to do a very unbecoming act, and I am sure there must be *simony* in the case." "No, Sire, there is not the least *ceremony* in the case, I assure you," answered the poor man, in great consternation; "the Abbé only said he would give me a hundred *louis*."—"D'Aigremont," said the King, "I forgive you on account of your ignorance and candour. I will give you the hundred *louis* out of my privy purse; but I will discharge you the very next time you venture to present a memorial to me."

Louis XIV was very kind to those of his servants who were nearest his person; but the moment he assumed his royal deportment, those who were most accustomed to see him in his domestic character were as much intimidated as if they were appearing in his presence for the first time in their lives. Some of the members of his Majesty's civil household, then called *commensalité*, enjoying the title of equerry, and the privileges attached to officers of the King's household, had occasion to claim some prerogatives, the exercise of which the municipal body of Saint Germain, where they resided, disputed with them. Being assembled in considerable numbers in that town, they obtained the consent of the minister of the household to allow them to send a deputation to the King; and for that purpose chose from amongst them two of his Majesty's *valets de chambre* named Bazire and Soulaigre. The King's *levée* being over, the deputation of the inhabitants of the town of Saint Germain was called in. They entered with confidence; the King looked at them, and assumed his imposing attitude. Bazire, one of these *valets de chambre*, was about to speak, but Louis the Great was looking on him. He no longer saw the Prince he was accustomed to attend at home; he was intimidated, and could not find words; he recovered, however, and began as usual with the word *Sire*. But timidity again overpowered him, and finding himself unable to recollect the slightest particle of what he came to say, he repeated the word *Sire* several times over, and at length concluded by saying, "*Sire*, here is Soulaigre." Soulaigre, who was very angry with Bazire, and expected to acquit himself much better, then began to speak; but he also, after repeating *Sire* several times, found his embarrassment increase upon him, until his confusion equalled that of his colleague; he therefore ended with "*Sire*, here is Bazire." The King smiled, and answered,[10] "Gentlemen, I have been informed of the business upon which you have been deputed to wait on me, and I will take care that what is right shall be done. I am highly satisfied with the manner in which you have fulfilled your functions as deputies."

MESDAMES, THE AUNTS OF LOUIS XVI

The position of Mesdames at Court being obscure and unsatisfactory, they were seldom seen there. They spent the chief part of the year either at Bellevue, on that splendid height that commands the proud city and the charming country around it; or at the Hermitage, a little garden at the other end of Versailles, by the road leading to Marly.

Madame Adelaide and Madame Victoire were the only survivors of the four daughters of Louis XV who outlived their father. The third, Madame Sophie, had died two years before; and the other, Madame Louise, had quitted the world in one of those sudden resolutions that can only be inspired by great religious fervour, or by a quick and ardent spirit that will not be satisfied by smaller sacrifices—resolutions that always cause astonishment to men of the world, whatever be their cause.

It was in 1771 that Madame Louise, unmoved by her father's prayers and her sisters' tears, tore herself from the pleasures of the Court, to bury herself at thirty-four years of age in a cloister of Carmelites, and to forget the empty grandeurs of earth beneath a hair-cloth garment in one of the most austere religious orders. Scandal made many attempts to pursue her there, but found no response. And yet Madame Louise was blamed by several persons for having retired such a short distance from the Court, for seeing too much company, and still taking an active part in the affairs of the world and the interests of the State, while she practised the humblest labours like the lowest of the nuns. No doubt her self-denial would have seemed more complete at a greater distance from her family, and with vows of more absolute solitude; but her sacrifice seems large enough as it was, and without stopping to consider that perhaps the example of piety given by Madame Louise might have been of more use at Court than hid in a cloister, it must be said with truth that such a resolve must have required a great deal of courage. Madame Louise died in December 1787, and her death made so little sensation that, as I was unwell, I did not hear of it till some time afterwards. And it was no wonder, for the Princesses had not been slow to forget her, though they had visited her continually during the life of Louis XV.

The tempers of Mesdames were a little sharpened by the neglect they received at Court; so they were very hard to please in waiting upon them. The least unpunctuality received a sharp reproof. If I was not afraid of being thought spiteful, I could give some proofs of my own experience. I will only mention that I was sharply scolded one day by Madame Adelaide for putting my hands into a muff that she had given me to carry while she went upstairs. If the pictures of Louis XV that I have seen are good likenesses, this Princess resembled him exactly, and possessed his haughty glances. Madame Victoire was shorter and stouter.

Mesdames the Aunts only came to Paris in the winter, as they had been able to stay at Bellevue up to the 5th of October. Seeing that they were of very little use to their nephew, unable to enjoy his confidence, and fearing measures opposed to their religious opinions, they at last decided on going to Rome. Possibly in their solitude, standing in a position whence they could form a better judgment of the course of events, theirs was the surer presentiment of all the trouble that hung over their family; therefore, they separated themselves from it for life, but they could not prevail on Madame Elizabeth to leave her brother and accompany them … No doubt Mesdames did not find themselves happy at Rome. The news of the fall of the throne of their fathers and the sorrows of their family came to disturb the peace they might have enjoyed in the Eternal City. They could at least carry their tears and prayers for their guilty country to the foot of the altar, till the day when they were forced to quit the hospitable city that had received them, by conquests that the noble head of the Church could neither arrest nor foresee. So they left Rome to retire to Naples; and, after several changes of their place of refuge, Madame Adelaide had the sorrow of seeing her younger sister die at Trieste. Her own mournful existence was shortened by grief, and she soon died herself at Klagenfurth.— *Recollections of a Page*, by Comte d'Hézecques, pp. 79–82.

THE DIAMOND NECKLACE

"The Comtesse de Lamotte was born in Champagne, under a thatched roof and in indigent circumstances, though she has since proved her descent, on the side of the Comtes de Saint Rémi, from the royal House of Valois. D'Hozier, the genealogist, confirmed it by his certificate. She became the wife of M. de Lamotte, a gentleman and a private *gendarme*. Their united resources were very limited, and she presented herself before the Grand Almoner[11] to interest his generosity, and at the same time to implore his good offices with the King. The Comtesse de Lamotte, without possessing beauty, was gifted with all the graces of youth, and her countenance was intelligent and attractive. She expressed herself with fluency, and gave an air of truth to her appeals. The misfortunes of a descendant of the House of Valois excited a deep interest in the compassionate breast of the Cardinal de Rohan, who would have rejoiced in placing her on a level with her ancestors; but the finances of the King did not permit such bounty, and he could only supply the exigencies of the moment. The artful woman soon imagined that the heart of her benefactor was susceptible of yet stronger impressions; gratitude and fresh wants renewed her visits and her interviews. His Eminence advised her to address herself immediately to the Queen, presuming that that generous Princess would be struck by the contrast between her position and her birth, and would doubtless find some means of extricating her from so painful a situation. The Cardinal, avowing that he was himself unable to procure her an interview with the Queen, described to Madame de Lamotte the deep mortification he experienced in having incurred the displeasure of her Majesty; it created, he observed, a bitterness in his soul which poisoned his happiest moments. This confidence gave rise to a plan of imposture to which the annals of human credulity can furnish few parallels. The outline of the scheme was as follows:—Madame de Lamotte undertook to persuade the Cardinal that she had obtained a considerable degree of intimacy with the Queen; that, influenced by the excellent qualities she had discovered in the Grand Almoner, she had spoken of them so often and with so much enthusiasm to her Majesty, that she had by degrees succeeded in removing her prejudices, and Marie Antoinette had permitted the Cardinal to justify himself to her; and finally, had desired to have a correspondence with him, which should be kept secret till the auspicious moment should arrive for the open avowal of his complete restoration to her favour. The Comtesse de Lamotte was to be the vehicle of this correspondence, the result of which would be to place the Cardinal at the very summit of favour and influence.

"Madame de Lamotte, after having increased the hopes of the Cardinal with all the power of intrigue of which she was mistress, at length said to him, 'I am authorised by the Queen to demand of you, in writing, a justification for the faults that you are accused of.' This authorisation, invented by the Comtesse de Lamotte, and credited by the Cardinal, appeared to him the herald of an auspicious day; in a little time his written apology was confided to Madame de Lamotte. Some days afterwards she brought him an answer, written on a small sheet of gilt-edged paper, in which Marie Antoinette, whose handwriting was successfully imitated, was made to say, 'I have read your letter. I am rejoiced to find you not guilty. At present I am not able to grant you the audience you desire. When circumstances permit, you shall be informed of it. Be discreet.' These few words caused in the Cardinal a delirium of satisfaction which it would be difficult to describe. Madame de Lamotte from that moment was his tutelary angel, who smoothed for him the path to happiness, and from that period she might have obtained from him whatever she desired. Soon afterwards, encouraged by success, she fabricated a correspondence between the Queen and the Cardinal. The demands for money, which, under different pretexts, the Queen appeared to make on the Grand Almoner in these forged letters, produced Madame de Lamotte 120,000 livres; and yet nothing opened the eyes of this credulous and immoral man to the deceit practised on him …

"Meanwhile some speedy cures, effected in cases pronounced incurable in Switzerland and Strasburg, spread the name of Cagliostro far and wide, and raised his renown to that of a miraculous physician. His attention to the poor, and his contempt for the rich, excited the greatest enthusiasm. Those whom he chose to honour with his familiarity left his society in ecstasies at his transcendent qualities. The Cardinal de Rohan was at his residence at Saverne when the Comte de Cagliostro astonished Strasburg and all Switzerland with his conduct, and the extraordinary cures he had performed. Curious to behold so remarkable a personage, the Cardinal went to Strasburg. It was found necessary to use interest to be admitted. 'If M. le Cardinal is sick,' said he, 'let him come to me and I will cure him; if he be well, he has no business with me, nor have I with him.' This reply, far from giving offence to the Cardinal, increased his desire to be acquainted with the Count. At length, having gained admission to the sanctuary of this new Æsculapius, he saw, as he has since declared, on the countenance of this uncommunicative man, a dignity so imposing that he felt penetrated with religious awe. This interview, which was very short, excited more strongly than ever the wish for more intimate acquaintance. At length it was obtained, and the crafty empiric timed his advances so well that at length, without seeming to do it, he gained the entire confidence of the Cardinal, and the greatest ascendancy over him. 'Your soul,' said he one day to the Cardinal, 'is worthy of mine, and you deserve to be the confidant of all my secrets.' This declaration captivated the intellectual aspirations of a man who, at all times, had sought to discover the secrets of chemistry and botany.

"The Baron de Planta, whom the Cardinal had employed at the time of his embassy at Vienna, also became about this period his intimate confidant, and one of his most accredited agents with Cagliostro and Madame de Lamotte. I remember having heard that this Baron de Planta had frequent orgies at the palace of Strasburg, where it was said the tokay flowed in rivers, to render the repast agreeable to Cagliostro and his pretended wife. I thought it my duty to inform the Cardinal of the circumstance. His reply was, 'I know it; and I have even given him liberty to let it run to waste if he thinks proper.' ...

"One of the Queen's jewellers had in his possession a most superb diamond necklace, worth 1,800,000 livres. Madame de Lamotte knew that the Queen, who was much pleased with it, had not liked, under circumstances wherein the strictest economy became an indispensable duty, to propose to the King to buy it for her. Madame de Lamotte had had an opportunity of seeing this famous necklace, and Bœhmer, the jeweller whose property it was, did not conceal from her that he found it quite an encumbrance, that he had hoped in purchasing it to prevail on the Queen to buy it, but that her Majesty had refused; he added that he would make a handsome present to any one who might procure him a purchaser for it.

"Madame de Lamotte had already made trial of the credulity of his Eminence. She flattered herself that by continuing to deceive him she might be able to appropriate both the necklace and the promised present. She intended to persuade the Cardinal that the Queen had a great desire for this necklace; that, wishing to buy it unknown to the King, and to pay for it by instalments out of her savings, she proposed to give the Grand Almoner a particular proof of her goodwill by getting him to make the bargain in her name; that for this purpose he would receive an order, written and signed by her hand, which he should not give up until the payments should be completed: that he would arrange with the jeweller to give him receipts for the amount from one quarter to another, beginning from the first payment, which could not be made until the 30th of July 1785; that it would be essential not to mention the Queen's name in that transaction, which was to be carried on entirely in the name of the Cardinal; that the secret order, signed *Marie Antoinette de France*, would be quite authority enough; and that in giving it the Queen bestowed a signal mark of her confidence in his Eminence.

"Such was the romance composed by this mischievous woman. She offered the cup of Circe to this too credulous Cardinal, and persuaded him to drink of it. Her deceptions being hitherto so successful as to secure her from even the slightest suspicion, she boldly launched into her perilous career. The Cardinal was in Alsace. Madame de Lamotte despatched a courier through Baron de Planta with a gilt-edged billet, in which the Queen was made to say: 'The wished-for moment is not yet arrived, but I wish to hasten your return, on account of a secret negotiation which interests me personally, and which I am unwilling to confide to any one except yourself. The Comtesse de Lamotte will tell you from me the meaning of this enigma.' After reading this letter the Cardinal longed for wings. He arrived most unexpectedly in a fine frost in January. His return appeared as extraordinary to us as his departure had been precipitate. The Cardinal had no sooner learned the pretended solution of the enigma, than, delighted with the commission with which his sovereign had been pleased to honour him, he eagerly asked for the necessary order, in order that the necklace might be procured with as little loss of time as possible. The order was not long delayed; it was dated from Trianon, and signed *Marie Antoinette de France*. If the thickest web of deception had not blinded the eyes of the Cardinal, this signature alone, so clumsily imitated, might have shown him the snare which awaited him. The Queen never signed herself anything but *Marie Antoinette*; the words *de France* were added by the grossest ignorance. No remark, however, was made. Cagliostro, at that time recently arrived at Paris, was consulted. This Python mounted his tripod; the Egyptian invocations were made at night, illuminated by an immense number of wax tapers, in the Cardinal's own saloon. The oracle, under the inspiration of its familiar demon, pronounced 'that the negotiation was worthy of the Prince, that it would be crowned with success, that it would raise the goodness of the Queen to its height, and bring to light that happy day which would unfold the rare talents of the Cardinal for the benefit of France and of the human race'. I am writing facts, though it may be imagined that I am only relating fictions. The advice of Cagliostro dissipated all the doubts which might have been inspired, and it was decided that the Cardinal should acquit himself as promptly as possible of a commission which was regarded as equally honourable and flattering.

"Everything being thus arranged, the Cardinal treated with Bœhmer and Bassange for the necklace on the conditions proposed. He did not conceal from them that it was for the Queen, and he showed them the authority under which he acted, requiring it to be kept secret from all but the Queen. The jewellers must have believed all that the Grand Almoner told and showed them, as they accepted his note, and agreed on the 30th of January to deliver up the necklace to him on the 1st of February, being the Vigil of the Purification. The Countess had fixed on this day, when there was to be a grand fête at Versailles, as the epoch for which the Queen was anxious to have the superb ornament. The casket which contained this treasure was to be taken to Versailles that day, and carried to the house of Madame de Lamotte, whence the Queen was to be supposed to send for it. The Cardinal, to whom the time had been specified, came at dusk to the house of Madame de Lamotte, followed by a *valet de chambre*, who carried the casket. He sent him away when he got to the door, and entered alone the place where he was to be sacrificed to his credulity. It was an alcoved apartment, with a closet in it which had a glass door. The skilful actress puts her spectator into this closet, the room is dimly lighted, a door opens, a voice exclaims, 'From the Queen'. Madame de Lamotte advances with an air of respect, takes the casket and places it in the hands of the pretended messenger; thus the transfer of the necklace is made. The Cardinal, a mute and hidden witness of the transaction, imagined that he recognised this envoy. Madame de Lamotte told him that it was the Queen's confidential *valet de chambre* at Trianon. He wore the same garb, and had much the same air. Among her different modes of deception, Madame de Lamotte had succeeded in making it appear that she had paid several visits at Trianon to the Queen, who had lavished upon her marks of the most intimate familiarity. She often mentioned to the Cardinal the day on which she was to go, and the hour at which she was to return. His Eminence often watched her setting out and coming back again. One night, when she knew that he was aware of the time for her return, she got the principal agent in her schemes to walk some way back with her, and afterwards to appear as if returning to Trianon. The Cardinal, who was in disguise, joined her according to custom, and inquired who this person might be. She told him that it was the Queen's confidential *valet de chambre* at Trianon. This pretended *valet de chambre* was a man named De Villette, of Bar-sur-Aube, the friend of Madame de Lamotte, and the comrade of her husband. This woman had initiated him into her iniquitous practices. He concurred in them, and expected to have a share in the profits that might result. He it was who counterfeited the hand of the august Princess: the letters which Madame de Lamotte fabricated in the name of the Queen were written by him, as was also the order signed *Marie Antoinette de France* for the purchase of the necklace. The Cardinal having scrutinised the features of the man into whose hands the casket was delivered, and imagining that he recognised in them those of the pretended *valet de chambre* at Trianon who had accompanied Madame de Lamotte one evening on her way home, had no doubt of the necklace being safely conveyed to its place of destination.

"Thus did this intriguing woman attain her ends; and such ascendancy had she gained over the mind of the Cardinal that from the time of the necklace being given up, his Eminence incessantly pressed the jewellers to obtain an audience of the Queen, in order that they might make themselves easy respecting the purchase he had negotiated for her. This fact, the truth of which has been proved beyond the possibility of denial by the evidence of Bœhmer and Bassange in court, ought to remove every doubt as to the sincerity of the Cardinal, and his entire persuasion that he was only obeying the orders of the Queen. How shall I conceal in this place a fact which I would willingly omit, but which is too essentially connected with the consequences of this unfortunate affair to be passed over in silence. The jewellers, who had often access to the Queen on business, and were, moreover, pressed by the Cardinal to speak of it, took care not to leave her in ignorance of the negotiation and sale of the necklace. Notwithstanding the writing signed *Marie Antoinette de France* which had been shown to them; not withstanding the solvency of the Cardinal, who had given his note for it, it was important to their interest to assure themselves that this necklace was for her Majesty, and not to risk a thing of so much value on the least uncertainty. This fact is not admitted by Messieurs Bœhmer and Bassange in the *procès;* but they secretly acknowledged it to one who revealed it to me, only on condition that his name should in no way be compromised in the affair. The Cardinal in his defence appeared never to have had any doubt on the subject.[12] Bassange being at Bâle in 1797, and questioned by me on this matter, did not deny it, and formally confessed that his depositions, and those of his companion in this suit, had been regulated by the Baron de Breteuil; that they had not indeed indiscriminately followed everything that had been desired of them, but that they were obliged to be silent on what he was not willing that they should declare. After such an assurance, how can we attempt to justify the Queen from a connivance little honourable either to her principles or her rank?

"So shameless a manœuvre as that of Madame de Lamotte, in which the name of the Queen was introduced only to commit, with still more impunity and boldness, a fraud of such magnitude, ought to have shocked the delicacy and probity of this Princess. How was it that at this moment her indignation did not burst forth? If the Queen had only followed the first dictates of her wounded feelings she would surely have apprised the jewellers that they had been deceived, and that they must take their precautions accordingly. Even supposing that the Queen wished to be revenged on the Cardinal, and to ruin him, what had already passed, and what she had just heard, was more than sufficient to compel him to give up his place, to leave Court, and to retire to his diocese. The Queen would have done an act of justice, for which no one could have condemned her; the Grand Almoner would have been justly blamed for his credulity; the House of Rohan would have been grieved at his disgrace, but could not have opposed it; there would have been no shameful publicity, no criminal suit, no Bastille. Marie Antoinette, if left to her own inclinations, would surely have acted with this sincerity, but she suffered herself to be influenced by two men, who equally led her astray, though each from different motives."

The Abbé Georgel here flatters himself that he proves the Queen to have consulted the Abbé de Vermond, and the Baron de Breteuil (which is true), and that they suffered the Cardinal to fall more and more deeply into the snare, and continued him in his error to ruin him entirely, which is false, as is proved by the *Memoirs* of Madame Campan. She left Versailles on the 1st of August; on the 3rd, Bœhmer went to see her at her country house. It was not until the 6th or 7th that the Queen was informed with certainty of the matter, and on the 15th the Cardinal was arrested. Are any of the perfidious delays imagined by the Abbé Georgel to be found in this rapid progress of things? The reproach of dissimulation, after all, does not attach to the Queen, as Georgel only accuses the Abbé de Vermond and the Baron de Breteuil of these preconcerted tardinesses.

"The day fixed upon for the first payment of 100,000 crowns being the 30th of July, the Cardinal, whose presence was necessary for the payment, was summoned in the course of the month of June. He came with the eagerness of a man who believes himself on the point of obtaining his wishes. He was assured in a little billet that everything was arranged for the accomplishment of his desire and the fulfilment of the Queen's promises. It was adroitly added that measures were being taken for making up the first payment; that some unforeseen events had thrown obstacles in the way, but that it was hoped, nevertheless, that no delay would occur.

"The assemblies at Cagliostro's, in the meantime, were delightful: all was a joyful anticipation of the happy day when the Queen was to crown the good fortune of the Grand Almoner. Madame de Lamotte alone was in possession of a secret of a contrary nature. Sainte James, a proselyte of Cagliostro's, was admitted to those evening parties by the advice of this woman, for which she had her own reasons. She one day said to the Cardinal, 'I see the Queen is greatly perplexed about this hundred thousand crowns for the 30th of July. She does not write to you for fear of making you uneasy concerning it, but I have thought of a way for you to pay your court to her by setting her at ease. Write to Sainte James; a hundred thousand crowns will appear nothing to him when he is given to understand that it is to render the Queen a service. Profit by the enthusiasm which the attentions you and the Comte de Cagliostro lavish upon him have inspired. The Queen will not discountenance it: speak in her name. The success of this new negotiation can only add to the interest she already takes in you.' The Cardinal thanked Madame de Lamotte for her good advice. He then thought to secure the goodwill of Sainte James by relating to him, with an air of confidence, all that had passed regarding the purchase of the necklace. He showed him the order signed *Marie Antoinette de France*; he likewise confided to him the Queen's embarrassment, and assured him that an infallible way to merit her protection would be to take upon himself the making the first payment to the jeweller. Sainte James, like all upstarts, was more anxious for consequence than for money; he had wished to obtain the *cordon rouge* by some place or office, but he had not been able to succeed. The Cardinal promised it to him in the name of the Queen as a recompense for the service she asked of him. The financier replied that he looked upon himself as extremely fortunate to be able to give her Majesty proofs of his unbounded devotion; and that as soon as he should be honoured with her orders, she might make herself perfectly easy with respect to the 100,000 crowns for the first payment. The Grand Almoner informed Madame de Lamotte of the answer of Sainte James, and gave an account of it in the first letter which he sent the Queen through her hands. The forger who framed the answers was absent. M. de Lamotte had returned from London, and had sent for him to Bar-sur-Aube, where these skilful sharpers concerted together the precautions necessary in order to establish their fortunes out of the spoil of the necklace. The delay of the anxiously expected answer from the Queen tormented the Cardinal. He communicated his uneasiness to Madame de Lamotte; he could not conceive the motive for maintaining this silence as the time of payment approached. He was, moreover, afraid that Sainte James might suspect him of a design to impose upon him; he added, with infinite chagrin, that what he still less comprehended was the unabated coldness of the Queen towards him outwardly, in spite of the warm and lively interest expressed in her letters. This last observation was a daily complaint with the Cardinal after his return from Alsace. Till then Madame de Lamotte had always been able to calm his anxiety by different stratagems. The diabolical genius of this woman, fruitful in expedients, suggested a method of abusing still further the Cardinal's credulity, by which she hoped to make him exert himself to the utmost to complete the first payment for the necklace, either by himself or through M. de Sainte James. Meanwhile the forger De Villette returned from Bar-sur-Aube, and the long-expected answer from Marie Antoinette was immediately put into the hands of the Cardinal. The Queen, it was said in the letter, would not so long have delayed her reply had she not hoped to be able to dispense with the good offices of M. de Sainte James; that she would accept them for the first payment only, and promised a speedy reimbursement to him, adding that she should wish M. de Sainte James to furnish her with an early opportunity of showing her sense of his services. Some days elapsed before the Cardinal could communicate this answer to Sainte James. In the interval Madame de Lamotte, in concert with her husband and De Villette, had arranged everything for the performance of a farce, the plan and execution of which betrayed the most diabolical invention. She undertook to make the Cardinal believe that the Queen, not being able to give him the public proofs of her esteem which she could wish, would grant him an interview in the groves of Versailles, between eleven and twelve o'clock, and that she would then assure him of that restoration to her favour which she was not at liberty to write. These happy tidings were conveyed in a little gilt-edged note; it appointed the night and the hour for the meeting; never was an interview more eagerly anticipated.

"The Comtesse de Lamotte had remarked in the promenades of the Palais Royal at Paris a girl of a very fine figure, whose profile was extremely like the Queen's, and her she fixed on as principal actress in the grove. Her name was D'Oliva, and she had been made to believe that the part she undertook to perform was at the desire of the Queen, who had some plan of amusement in it.[13] The reward offered on this occasion was not refused by a creature who made a traffic of her charms. Mademoiselle d'Oliva accordingly proceeded to Versailles, conducted by M. de Lamotte in a hired carriage, the coachman belonging to which has been examined in evidence. She was led to inspect the scene of action to which she was to be secretly conveyed by M. de Lamotte; there she was made to rehearse the part she was expected to perform. She was given to understand that she would be accosted by a tall man in a blue riding-coat with a large hat turned down, who would approach and kiss her hand with the utmost respect; and that she was to say to him in a low tone of voice, 'I have but a moment to spare; I am satisfied with your conduct, and I shall speedily raise you to the pinnacle of favour;' that she was then to present him with a small box and a rose, and immediately afterwards, at the noise of persons who should approach, to observe, still in a low voice, 'Madame and Madame d'Artois are coming; we must separate.' The grove and the place of entrance agreed on had been also pointed out to the Cardinal, with the assurance that he might in that place pour out without constraint his sentiments of loyal devotion and explain his feelings in what most concerned his interests; and that, as a pledge of her good intentions towards him, the Queen would present him with a case containing her portrait and a rose. It was well known at Versailles that the Queen was in the habit of walking in the evening with Madame and the Comtesse d'Artois in the grove. The appointed night arrived; the Cardinal, dressed as agreed on, repaired to the terrace of the Château with the Baron de Planta; the Comtesse de Lamotte in a black domino was to come and let him know the precise time when the Queen was to enter the grove. The evening was sufficiently dark; the appointed hour glided away; Madame de Lamotte did not appear; the Cardinal became anxious; when the lady in the black domino came to meet him saying, 'I have just left the Queen—everything is unfavourable—she will not be able to give you so long an interview as she desired. Madame and the Comtesse d'Artois have proposed to walk with her. Hasten to the grove; she will leave her party, and, in spite of the short interval she may obtain, will give you unequivocal proofs of her protection and goodwill.' The Cardinal hastened to the appointed scene and Madame de Lamotte and the Baron de Planta retired to await his return. The scene was played as it had been arranged by Madame de Lamotte; the pretended Queen, in an evening *dishabille*, bore a striking resemblance in figure and dress to the personage she was to represent. The Cardinal in approaching her testified emotion and respect; the pretended Queen in a low voice pronounced the words that had been dictated to her, and presented the box. Meantime, as had been agreed, a noise as of persons approaching was made, and it was necessary to part somewhat abruptly. The Cardinal went to rejoin Madame de Lamotte and the Baron de Planta: he complained bitterly of the vexatious interruption which had shortened an interview so interesting and delightful for him. They then separated. The Cardinal appeared fully persuaded that he had spoken with the Queen, and had received the box from her hands. Madame de Lamotte congratulated herself on the success of her scheme. Mademoiselle d'Oliva, interested in keeping the part she had played secret, was conveyed back to Paris and well rewarded. M. de Lamotte and M. de Villette, who had counterfeited the voices and the approaching footsteps agreed on to abridge the interview, joined Madame de Lamotte, and every one rejoiced at the successful issue. The next day a little billet brought by the ordinary messenger expressed great regret at the obstacles which had prevented a longer conversation.

"Whatever the illusion might be that had so blinded the Cardinal, the unimpassioned reader will scarcely believe that a Prince endowed with so much intelligence and good sense could have entertained for more than a year not the slightest suspicion of the snare that was laid for him: and if it did enter his mind, why did he not put every method in force to throw a light on the behaviour of his conductress? The Queen still evincing complete estrangement towards the Cardinal, how could he possibly reconcile this mode of treatment with the sentiments contained in the little billets he received, wherein the greatest interest and kindness were expressed?

"The Cardinal acknowledges that, impelled by a boundless desire to be restored to the favour of the Queen, he rushed with impetuosity towards the object that promised to effect his purpose, without considering the nature of the path he was made to tread. However that might be, the adventure of the grove and the little billet next morning had given new energy to the zeal which entirely engrossed him for the interests and tranquillity of the Queen, whom he believed to be embarrassed respecting the first payment for the necklace. The return of the financier Sainte James hastened the *dénouement* of the intrigue, which was about to involve him in endless disgrace and vexation. The Cardinal having met with this financier at Cagliostro's, communicated to him the new orders which he imagined he had received."

It is needless to prolong this extract. The latter scenes and the catastrophe of this plot are well known. We ought, nevertheless, to mention the individual to whom the Cardinal at length owed the discovery of the means which had been put in practice to deceive him.

"A certain Abbé de Juncker, a sensible and well-informed man, came," says the Abbé Georgel, "to offer his services. I felt confidence in him because he seemed anxious for the honour and interest of the Cardinal. He it was who gave me the first clue by which the diabolical intrigue of Madame de Lamotte came to be unmasked. A friar of the order of Minims,[14] called Father Loth, had come to inform him that, urged by his conscience, and by gratitude to the Grand Almoner for services he had rendered him, he was anxious to make the most important disclosures; that, having lived on intimate terms with Madame de Lamotte, he could not longer be silent. This monk was *procureur* to the Minims of La Place Royale, which the house of Madame de Lamotte adjoined. This woman had found means to inspire him with pity in her moments of want and distress. He often relieved her, and his kindness at length induced her to communicate to him the particulars of her good fortune, which she attributed to the Queen and to the Cardinal. Being soon on terms of great intimacy, Father Loth saw at the house of Madame de Lamotte many things that excited his suspicions. A few words which her vanity and indiscretion let fall; the boast of a considerable present from the Court jewellers, on account of her expecting to procure them a purchaser for their valuable necklace; the display of some superb diamonds which she pretended to have had from Marie Antoinette; the communication of billets which she declared to be from the Queen to the Cardinal, and from the Cardinal to the Queen; the comparison which Father Loth had taken the trouble to make between the writing of these billets and other writings of M. de Villette, the friend of Madame de Lamotte, who was often shut up writing with her and her husband; the compliments which he had heard Madame de Lamotte pay a tall beautiful woman, named D'Oliva, respecting the success of some part she had played in the garden of Versailles; the perplexities which had spread confusion and alarm throughout the house of this intriguing woman in the early part of August; the declaration made in his presence that Bœhmer and Bassange would be the ruin of the Cardinal; the precipitate flight of De Villette, and of M. and Madame de Lamotte at that period—such were the details which Father Loth came to confide to me one evening between eleven and twelve, after disguising himself at the house of the Abbé Juncker, in order that he might not be suspected, should his judicial deposition be found necessary. The friar, wishing to have the title of preacher to the King in his Order, had requested to preach the sermon at Pentecost before his Majesty. The Grand Almoner had desired me to examine his discourse and his delivery. I was not satisfied with it, and gave it as my opinion that he should not preach; but I was not aware that Madame de Lamotte, who protected him, was desirous that this favour should be granted him, and that the Cardinal, yielding to the entreaties of this patroness, had procured Father Loth a well-written sermon, which he delivered with tolerable propriety.

"Amongst the particulars which I have just related, Father Loth, during the three hours' conversation I had with him, gave much important information respecting M. de Villette and some fragments of his writing, which he assured me greatly resembled that of the pretended billets from the Queen. He told me also that he had surprised Madame de Lamotte the evening before her departure burning those notes that she had told him were from the Queen. The friar, in speaking to me of Mademoiselle d'Oliva, recollected the time when she was taken by M. de Lamotte to Versailles in a hired carriage; at last he added, in such a manner as led me to suspect that he did not tell me all he knew, that he had strong reasons for believing that the Comtesse de Lamotte had imposed on the credulity of the Cardinal to obtain very considerable sums from him, and even to appropriate the necklace to herself. This important communication did not amount to certainty; but it was like the first blush of morn, which, dissipating the thick clouds of night, announces a fine day."—*Memoirs of the Abbé Georgel*, vol. ii.

We shall now add from another work details relative to the trial.

"The Cardinal was closely guarded in his apartments at Versailles. He was brought to his hotel in Paris in the afternoon, and remained there until the next day. The carriage was escorted by Body Guards, and M. d'Agoult, aide-major-general, had orders not to lose sight of the prisoner. In the evening the Marquis de Launay, Governor of the Bastille, came to lodge his Eminence in that same prison. The Cardinal wished to go thither on foot, under cover of the night; the favour was readily granted. On the following day, 17th August, he was sent in a carriage to his palace, to be present at the breaking of the seals, at which all the ministers assisted, except Maréchal de Ségur. M. de Rohan, looking on M. de Breteuil as his personal enemy, had required this formality; and the Baron de Breteuil had complied the more willingly as he had declared that his own sense of delicacy would not permit him to acquit himself of his ministerial duty in any other manner than publicly, and in the presence of respectable witnesses. Doubtless, no proof appeared of the secret crimes ascribed to the Cardinal, since no trace of it is to be found in the proceedings. The Cardinal had permission to see his friends in the hall of the Bastille. He was allowed to retain out of all his numerous retinue two *valets de chambre* and a secretary; this last favour showed him that he was to have the privilege of writing, at least for the purposes of his defence. He was treated in every other respect with much consideration, and his situation rendered as tolerable as it could be in such a fortress. The Abbé Georgel, Grand Vicar to the Grand Almoner, on whose papers seals were likewise put, testified as little uneasiness as the Cardinal. 'Authority must be respected,' said he, 'but we must nevertheless enlighten it.'[15]

"Madame de Lamotte, wishing to gratify at once her hatred and revenge, declared on her first examination that Comte de Cagliostro was the contriver of the fraud of the necklace; that he had persuaded the Cardinal to purchase it. She insinuated that it was taken to pieces by him and his wife, and that they alone reaped the profit of it. This declaration, supported by a thousand other falsehoods, which unfortunately, however absurd, wore an appearance of probability, caused the singular personage implicated to be sent to the Bastille, with the woman who resided with him. The latter remained there nearly eight months, and the pretended Count did not come out until after the suit was decided. It is certain that Cardinal de Rohan was credulous enough to place the greatest confidence in this charlatan, who had assured him that it was possible to make gold, and to transmute small diamonds into large precious stones; but he only cheated the Cardinal out of large sums, under pretence of revealing to him the secrets of the Rosicrucians and other mad men who have believed, or pretended to believe, the absurd fables of the philosopher's stone, the elixir of life, etc. Thus the Cardinal saw part of his money evaporate in the smoke of crucibles, and part find its way into the pockets of the sharper who passed himself off as a great alchemist. When this person was examined by the court touching the affair of the necklace, he made his appearance dressed in green embroidered with gold, and his locks, curled from the top of his head, fell in little tails down his shoulders, which completed his resemblance to a mountebank. 'Who are you? Whence came you?' he was asked. 'I am a noble traveller,' was his reply. At these words every countenance relaxed, and seeing this appearance of good humour, the accused entered boldly on his defence. He interlarded his jargon with Greek, Arabic, Latin, and Italian; his looks, his gestures, his vivacity, were as amusing as his speech. He withdrew very well pleased with having made his judges laugh.

"The Cardinal had sometimes permission to walk after dinner upon the platform of the towers of the Bastille, accompanied by an officer. He wore a brown greatcoat, with a round hat. The *parlement* issued a decree to arrest the Cardinal and the other parties. The fraud of the necklace was not the motive which determined this decree against the Cardinal de Rohan, but the forgery of the Queen's signature. It was concluded that, as soon as the true author of the forgery was discovered, all the rigour of the sentence would fall on him. On the 21st December this decree, more frightful to him in imagination than in reality, was made known to the Cardinal. The examinations were vigorously pursued. The commissioner, M. Dupuis de Marcé, a counsellor of Parliament, repaired for this purpose to the fortress of the Bastille. On one occasion he detained the Cardinal from nine in the morning until one o'clock, and then from four till midnight. On the appointed day Prince Louis de Rohan put on his State dress, his red calotte, red stockings, and all the insignia of his rank. The Governor of the Bastille came to lead him from his apartment, conducted him to the door of the Council chamber, left him with the magistrate and other official persons, and remained in attendance in the antechamber. When the judge wanted anything, he rang; the Marquis de Launay immediately presented himself, and if a glass of water was asked for, he carried it himself to the door, where the magistrate came to meet him. After the sitting the Governor took charge of his prisoner at the door of the Council chamber, and conducted him back to his apartment.

"It has been pretended that the all-powerful family of the Cardinal had so suborned the commissioner and the *greffier* that they altered the sense of the depositions and examinations, and when they were fearful of the Cardinal's involving himself in his replies, and saying something that would make against his cause, they suddenly broke up the sitting without even waiting for the conclusion of a sentence already begun. The following extract from the voluminous *Memoirs* of Madame de Lamotte supports this assertion:—'One day the Cardinal and I being confronted upon a delicate point, which neither of us had any intention to throw light upon, I said something not conformable to truth. "Ah, madame," cried the Cardinal, "how can you advance what you know to be false?" "As every one else does, sir; you know very well that neither you nor I have said a single word of truth to these gentlemen since they have begun to interrogate us." It was not in fact possible,' says this woman, whose testimony ought to be estimated at its proper value; 'our answers were prepared for us, as well as our questions, and we were obliged to say or reply this or that, or expect to be murdered in the Bastille.'

"The deposition of the Comtesse du Barry forms an interesting episode in this curious affair. She came into court on the evening of the 7th December, where she was received with all the honours due to persons of the first rank. The *greffier* went to hand her in, and one of the ushers carried the torch. Her deposition turned on the following circumstance. Madame de Lamotte called on her one day, after the death of Louis XV, to offer her services as a companion. When she declared her name and birth Madame du Barry regarded her as unfit for the situation; and, thanking her, assured her that she did not wish for society, and that, moreover, she was not such a great lady herself as to take one of Madame de Valois's elevated rank for her companion. The latter went again some days after, begging that Madame du Barry would recommend her to some persons who might lay one of her petitions before the King. In this petition she entreated an increase of her pension. She had signed the words *de France* after her name. The Comtesse du Barry could not help showing her surprise at the sight of the signature. Madame de Lamotte replied that as she was known to belong to the House of Valois she always signed herself *de France*. Madame du Barry smiled at her pretensions, and promised to get the petition recommended. So long as the Comtesse de Lamotte saw none of her accomplices arrested, she flattered herself that the Cardinal and Cagliostro would be the victims of her fraud; but Mademoiselle d'Oliva, the principal actress in the park scene, being taken at Brussels, where she had sought refuge, began to draw aside the veil with which the Countess had hitherto covered her intrigues.

"To crown her misfortunes, and ensure her the punishment she deserved, Rétaux de Villette suffered himself to be taken at Geneva. He was taken to the Bastille and confronted with the perfidious Lamotte, who was struck as by a thunderbolt at the unexpected sight. She was now convinced that she was lost, notwithstanding her natural effrontery. The prisoners who were detained in the Bastille on account of the necklace were transferred to the Conciergerie on the nights of the 29th and 30th of August 1786, by an officer of the court. The Cardinal was confined under the guard of the King's lieutenant of the Bastille, in the cabinet of the chief *greffier*. The justice of that day had the most profound respect for birth and titles.

"The examinations lasted from six in the morning until half-past four in the after-noon. When Madame de Lamotte appeared before the Grand Council assembled she was elegantly dressed, as she had been all the time she was in prison. This audacious woman, being sent for by the judges, often repeated *that she was going to confound a great rogue.* At the sight of the august Assembly her confidence somewhat abandoned her; above all, when the usher said to her in a severe tone, pointing out the stool for the accused, '*Madame, seat yourself there,*' she started back in affright, but on the order being given a second time, she took the ill-omened seat, and in less than two minutes she recovered herself, and her countenance was so composed that she appeared as if reclining in her own room upon the most elegant sofa. She replied with firmness to all the ques-tions of the First President. Being interrogated afterwards by the Abbé Sabathier, one of the ecclesiastical counsellors, whom she knew to be unfavourable to her, 'That is a very insidious question,' said she; 'I expected you would put it to me, and I shall now reply to it.' After extricating herself with sufficient address from many other questions, she made a long speech, with so much presence of mind and energy that she at least astonished her judges, if she could not succeed in convincing them. As soon as she had retired the First President ordered the stool to be removed, and sent to inform the Cardinal *that the stool having been taken out of the chamber, he might present himself before the court.* The Cardinal was habited in a long violet-coloured robe (which colour is mourning for cardinals); he wore his red calotte and stockings, and was decorated with his orders. His emotion was evident; he was extremely pale, and his knees bent under him; five or six voices, probably proceeding from members gained over to his side, observed that the Cardinal appeared to be ill, and that he ought to be allowed to sit, to which D'Aligre, the First President, replied, 'Monsieur le Cardinal can sit if he wish.' The illustrious accused profited by this permission, and seated himself at the end of the bench where the examiners sit when they attend the grand chamber. Having soon recovered himself, he replied extremely well to the questions of the First President; he afterwards, still remaining seated, spoke for about half an hour with emphasis and dignity, and repeated his protestations respecting the whole proceedings against him. His speech being finished, he bowed to the bench and the other magistrates. Every one returned his salute, and those on the bench even got up, which was a peculiar mark of distinction. Only the Cardinal and Cagliostro returned to the Bastille. M. de Rohan had in his coach the Governor and an officer of the ministerial prison. The Marquis de Launay gave the order to set off, and said "*à l'hôtel.*" instead of using the word *Bastille*. On the 31st, the day fixed for the final decision of this singular and famous trial—after more than a year of proceedings and delays—the judges met at a quarter before six in the morning. They were sixty-two in number, but were reduced to forty-nine by the retiring of the ecclesiastical counsellors, on account of its being a question which involved corporal punishment. Some time past nine in the evening the decision of the *parlement* was made known, as follows:—

"1st. The instrument which is the foundation of the suit, with the approvals and annexed signatures, are declared forgeries, and falsely attributed to the Queen.

"2nd. Lamotte, being in contumacy, is condemned to the galleys for life.[16]

"3rd. Madame de Lamotte to be whipped, branded on the two shoulders with the letter V, and shut up in the Hospital for life.

"4th. Rétaux de Villette banished from the kingdom for life.

"5th. Mademoiselle d'Oliva discharged.

"6th. Cagliostro acquitted.

"7th. The Cardinal acquitted of all suspicion. The injurious accusations against him, contained in the memorial of Madame de Lamotte, suppressed.

"8th. The Cardinal is allowed to cause the judgment of the court to be printed.

"The next day the court received an order for delay of execution. The Court of Versailles was much displeased with the sentence; it had hoped that the Cardinal would have been declared guilty, and the degrading sentence passed on the Comtesse de Lamotte appeared too severe; a writer has permitted himself to observe that the court had proceeded with so much severity against this female, a descendant from the House of Valois, in order to mortify to the utmost of their power the reigning branch of the Bourbons. The King was desirous to inspect all the writings belonging to the suit, but they only sent him copies of them.

"The *parlement,* after a few days' delay, was allowed to execute its sentence with respect to the Comtesse de Lamotte, who had remained at the Conciergerie. She was informed one morning that her presence was required at the palace. Surprised at this intelligence (for she had for some time been refused permission to speak to any one), she replied that she had passed a restless night, and desired to be left quiet. The gaoler said her counsel was waiting. 'I can see him, then, to-day?' she asked, and immediately rose, slipped on a loose robe, and followed. Being brought before her judges, the *greffier* pronounced her sentence; immediately astonishment, fear, rage, and despair pervaded her soul, and threw her into agitation difficult to describe. She had not strength to hear the whole of the matter read to her; she threw herself on the ground and uttered the most violent shrieks. It was with the greatest difficulty that she could be removed into the palace yard to undergo her sentence. It was scarcely six in the morning, and but few persons were present to witness its execution. No sooner did the Countess perceive the instruments of her punishment than she seized one of the executioners by the collar, bit his hands in such a manner as to take a piece out, and fell upon the ground in more violent convulsions than ever. It was necessary to tear off her clothes to imprint the hot iron upon her shoulders. Her cries and imprecations redoubled; at length they took her into a coach and conveyed her to l'Hôpital. After ten months' confinement[17] Madame de Lamotte found means to escape from l'Hôpital, either by having gained over some sister of the house, or through the connivance of the Government. This last opinion may be correct, if it be true that her flight was permitted on condition that M. de Lamotte should not publish in London his account of the trial, which it is said he threatened to do unless his wife should be restored to him."—*Anecdotes of the Reign of Louis XVI*, vol. i.

1. The Diary having obviously been intended as a basis for those records of the King's hunting parties mentioned by Soulavie (see p. 316), "nothing", of course, only meant "no hunting" or "no game".

2. The market women of Paris, who by ancient custom were admitted to take a prominent part in public rejoicings.

3. The servants were suspended by order of the head of the household for a fortnight, a month, or more. Dismission was more common than suspension; but resignations were signed by the parties themselves. It must not be forgotten that all the offices were trusts, and that the holders of them had been sworn before the Queen, the superintendent, the lady of honour, or the first gentleman usher.

4. *Recollections of a Page at the Court of Louis XVI*, by Felix, Comte d'Hézecques. Edited from the French by C.M. Yonge. (Hurst & Blackett, 1873.)

5. Madame Sophie.

6. In the *Œil de Bœuf* there was a shovel so heavy that it took a strong man to hold it out at arm's length. I have often seen the King perform this feat with a little page standing on the shovel as well.

7. See *ante*, pp. 411–6, "The King's Diary".

8. Louis XV also was desirous of encouraging literature; but he was only capable of affording it a cold and supercilious protection, unaccompanied by any demonstration of affability or kindness, and more humiliating than obliging.

In the *Memoirs* of Madame de Hausset, one of Madame de Pompadour's *femmes de chambre*, we meet with the following passage:—

The King, who admired all that was connected with the age of Louis XIV, recollecting that the Boileaus and Racines had been protected by him, and that part of the splendour of that reign was attributed to his own, was flattered with the idea that a Voltaire flourished in his own Court; but he feared that author and did not esteem him. He could not, however, help saying, 'I have treated him as well as Louis XIV behaved to Racine and Boileau; I gave him a place of gentleman in ordinary and a pension, as Louis XIV did to Racine. If he is presumptuous enough to aim at being a chamberlain, wearing a cross and supping with a King, it is not my fault. It is not the fashion in France; and as there are more wits and great lords here than in Prussia I should have occasion for an immense table to entertain them altogether.' He then counted on his fingers, 'Maupertuis, Fontenelle, La Motte, Voltaire, Piron, Destouches, Montesquieu, Cardinal Polignac.'— 'Your Majesty forgets,' said some one, 'D'Alembert and Clairault.' 'And Crébillon,' said he, 'and La Chaussée.' 'Crébillon, the son,' said another, 'who must be more agreeable than his father; and there is the Abbé Prevot, and the Abbé d'Olivet.' 'Very well,' said the King, 'all these people would have dined or supped with me for the last five-and-twenty years.'

9. People of the very first rank did not disdain to descend to the level of D'Aigremont. "Lauzun," says the Duchesse d'Orléans in her *Memoirs*, "sometimes affects stupidity in order to show people their own with impunity, for he is very malicious. In order to make Maréchal Tessé feel the impropriety of his familiarity with people of the common sort, he called out, in the drawing-room at Marly, 'Maréchal, give me a pinch of snuff; some of your best, such as you take in the morning with Monsieur d'Aigremont the chairman.'"—*Note by the Editor.*

10. In this pleasantry there is nothing bitter or harsh, as in most of those of Louis XV. Louis XIV never indulged in an expression capable of offending any one, and his repartees, which were almost always full of meaning, often show refined tact. Generally speaking, wit, either poignant and caustic or pleasant and lively, has not been wanting in the descendants of Henri IV. In the *Memoirs* of Madame de Hausset there is a striking observation on this subject:—

> M. Duclos was at Doctor Quesnay's haranguing with his usual warmth. I heard him say to two or three persons, 'The world is always unjust towards great men, ministers, and princes; nothing is more common than to deny them all claims to wit. A few days ago I surprised one of these gentlemen of the *infallible brigade* by telling him that there has been more wit in the House of Bourbon than in any other.' 'Did you prove that?' said some one with a sneer. 'Yes,' said Duclos, 'and I will prove it to you. I presume you will allow that the great Condé was no fool, and the Duchesse de Longueville is celebrated as one of the most brilliant of women. The Regent was unrivalled for wit of every kind. The Prince de Conti, who was elected King of Poland, was distinguished for this quality, and his verses are equal to those of La Fare and Saint Aulaire. The Duc de Bourgogne was learned and enlightened. The Duchess, Madame, daughter to Louis XIV, was an eminent wit, and made epigrams and couplets. The Duc de Maine was also an apt conversationalist; besides, I might add many members of the family now living.'

11. Cardinal de Rohan.

12. In the *Memoirs* of Madame Campan it is shown in how obscure, doubtful, and unintelligible a manner the jeweller Bœhmer explained himself the first time on the subject of the necklace, and what was the surprise, the indignation, and the wrath of the Queen when she was made to understand the odious nature of the intrigue in which her name was introduced. The secret disclosure was made, it is said, to a person who only revealed it under the assurance that his name should be neither cited nor compromised in the affair: this disclosure, received by an anonymous person, can scarcely be sufficient to overthrow the circumstantial details of Madame Campan. If the Queen only understands the former declarations of Bœhmer from

a tardy and unexpected communication, if her resentment bursts out immediately on her acquaintance with it, what becomes of the supposition made by the Abbé Georgel, of a plan conducted with coolness and deliberation, and for a considerable period, to lead the Cardinal deeper and deeper into the snare, to surprise him and to destroy him?—*Note by the Editor*.

13. Marie Nicole Leguay, called D'Oliva or Designy. See *Beugnot*, vol. i, p. 60, as to her resemblance to the Queen.

14. Minims, or Fratres Minimi, an order of religion instituted about the year 1440 (then called the Hermits of St Francis) by St Francis de Paulo. They were confirmed in 1473 by Sixtus IV, and by Julius II in 1507. The name Minims or Minimi ("the least or the smallest") was assumed as expressing the humility of the founder and his followers. They were called also "Bonshommes", it is said originally by Louis XI.

15. To show the spirit evinced by the clergy during the imprisonment of the Cardinal, we quote a passage from Jervis' *Gallican Church*, vol. ii, p. 379:—"The Abbé Georgel, Vicar-General to the Cardinal, in his quality of Grand Almoner, had occasion to publish a Lenten *mandement*. He began by comparing himself to Timothy, whom St Paul commissioned to supply his place in preaching the word of life to the disciples while the Apostle was detained in bonds at Rome for his faithfulness to the Christian cause."

16. He had escaped to England.

17. Madame Campan says "a few days", see p. 205.

[In the third series of *Notes and Queries*, vols vii, viii, and ix, will be found some remarks concerning the authenticity of the letters of Marie Antoinette, published after her death in the time of the Second Empire, which it may be useful to note here.]

POSTSCRIPT

As Madame Campan has several times stated in the foregoing pages that the money to foment sedition was furnished from English sources, the decree of the Convention of August 1793 may be quoted as illustrative of the *entente cordiale* alleged to exist between the insurrectionary Government and its friends across the Channel! The endeavours made by the English Government to save the unfortunate King are well known.

Art. i. The National Convention denounces the British Government to Europe and the English nation.

Art. ii. Every Frenchman that shall place his money in the English funds shall be declared a traitor to his country.

Art. iii. Every Frenchman who has money in the English funds or those of any other Power with whom France is at war shall be obliged to declare the same.

Art. iv. All foreigners, subjects of the Powers now at war with France, particularly the English, shall be arrested, and seals put upon their papers.

Art. v. The barriers of Paris shall be instantly shut.

Art. vi. All good citizens shall be required in the name of the country to search for the foreigners concerned in any plot denounced.

Art. vii. Three millions shall be at the disposal of the Minister at War to facilitate the march of the garrison of Mentz to La Vendée.

Art. viii. The Minister at War shall send to the army on the coast of Rochelle all the combustible materials necessary to set fire to the forests and underwood of La Vendée.

Art. ix. The women, the children, and old men shall be conducted to the interior parts of the country.

Art. x. The property of the rebels shall be confiscated for the benefit of the Republic.

Art. xi. A camp shall be formed without delay between Paris and the army.

Art. xii. All the family of the Capets shall be banished from the French territory, those excepted who are under the sword of the law, and the offspring of Louis Capet, who shall both remain in the Temple.

Art. xiii. Marie Antoinette shall be delivered over to the Revolutionary Tribunal, and shall be immediately conducted to the prison of the Conciergerie. Louise Elizabeth shall remain in the Temple till after the judgment of Marie Antoinette.

Art. xiv. All the tombs of the Kings which are at Saint Denis and in the departments shall be destroyed on August the 10th.

Art. xv. The present decree shall be despatched by extraordinary couriers to all the departments.